Springer Proceedings in Business and Economics

More information about this series at http://www.springer.com/series/11960

Nicholas Tsounis • Aspasia Vlachvei
Editors

Advances in Panel Data Analysis in Applied Economic Research

2017 International Conference on Applied Economics (ICOAE)

Springer

Editors
Nicholas Tsounis
Department of International Trade
Western Macedonia University
of Applied Sciences
Kastoria, Greece

Aspasia Vlachvei
Department of International Trade
Western Macedonia University
of Applied Sciences
Kastoria, Greece

ISSN 2198-7246 ISSN 2198-7254 (electronic)
Springer Proceedings in Business and Economics
ISBN 978-3-030-09929-9 ISBN 978-3-319-70055-7 (eBook)
https://doi.org/10.1007/978-3-319-70055-7

Printed on acid-free paper

This Springer imprint is published by the registered company Springer International Publishing AG part of Springer Nature.
The registered company address is: Gewerbestrasse 11, 6330 Cham, Switzerland

Preface

This year, the conference is co-organised by the School of Economics, Finance and Accounting of Coventry University and the Department of International Trade at Kastoria of the Western Macedonia University of Applied Sciences, Greece, after the kind invitation by Drs. Andrikopoulos and Serenis who are also co-chairs of the conference.

The aim of the conference is to bring together economists from different fields of applied economic research in order to share methods and ideas.

The topics covered include:

- Applied macroeconomics
- Applied international economics
- Applied microeconomics including industrial organisations
- Applied work on international trade theory including European integration
- Applied financial economics
- Applied agricultural economics
- Applied labour and demographic economics
- Applied health economics
- Applied education economics

All papers presented in ICOAE 2017 and published in the conference proceedings were peer reviewed by anonymous referees. In total, 81 works were submitted from 35 countries, while 61 papers were accepted for presentation and publication in the conference proceedings. The acceptance rate for ICOAE 2017 was 75%.

The full text articles will be published online by Springer in the series *Springer Proceedings in Business and Economics* under the title *Advances in Panel Data Analysis in Applied Economic Research: Proceedings of the 2017 International Conference on Applied Economics (ICOAE)*.

The organisers of ICOAE 2017 would like to thank:

- The Scientific Committee of the conference for their help and their important support for carrying out the tremendous work load organising and synchronising the peer-reviewing process of the submitted papers in a very specific short period of time

- The anonymous reviewers for accepting to referee the submitted conference papers and submitting their reviews on time for the finalisation of the conference programme
- Drs. Andrikopoulos and Serenis for proposing to host the conference at Coventry University and providing the required resources
- Ms. Nicola Boyle for arranging non-EU delegates to receive UK visa and liaising with the Techno Centre staff for the organisation of the conference
- The local organising committee and the volunteering students of Coventry University for their help for the success of the conference
- Mr. Gerassimos Bertsatos for running the reception desk of the conference

Kastoria, Greece Nicholas Tsounis
Kastoria, Greece Aspasia Vlachvei

Contents

Contributors

Damilola Ajayi Department of Economics, University of Lagos, Lagos, Nigeria

Muhammad Adli Amirullah International Islamic University Malaysia, Kuala Lumpur, Malaysia

Temidayo James Aransiola Institute of Economics, University of Campinas, Campinas, São Paulo, Brazil

Ivana Andrisková University of Zilina, Faculty of Operation and Economics of Transport and Communications, Department of Communications, Zilina, Slovak Republic

Vladimir Bakes University of Zilina, Faculty of Operation and Economics of Transport and Communications, Zilina, Slovak Republic

Rachna Banerjee Department of Business, Higher Colleges of Technology, Dubai, United Arab Emirates

Ewa Baranowska-Prokop Institute of International Management and Marketing, Warsaw School of Economics, Warsaw, Poland

Viera Bartošová University of Zilina, Faculty of Operation and Economics of Transport and Communications, Department of Economics, Zilina, Slovak Republic

Theranda Beqiri Faculty of Business, University "Haxhi Zeka", Pejë, Republic of Kosovo

Angela Besana IULM University, Milan, Italy

Alzbeta Bielikova University of Zilina, Faculty of Operation and Economics of Transport and Communications, Department of Economics, Zilina, Slovak Republic

A. Boudeghdegh University of Jijel "Faculty of Economics and Business", Jijel, Algeria

Martin Buno University of Zilina, Faculty of Operation and Economics of Transport and Communications, Department of Economics, Zilina, Slovak Republic

Chukiat Chaiboonsri Faculty of Economics, Chiang Mai University, Chiang Mai, Thailand

Prasert Chaitip Faculty of Economics, Chiang Mai University, Chiang Mai, Thailand

Darina Chlebikova University of Zilina, Faculty of Operation and Economics of Transport and Communications, Department of Economics, Zilina, Slovak Republic

Kanchana Chokethaworn Faculty of Economics, Chiang Mai University, Chiang Mai, Thailand

Tatiana Corejova University of Zilina, Faculty of Operation and Economics of Transport and Communications, Department of Communications, Zilina, Slovak Republic

Vilma Deltuvaitė Kaunas University of Technology, Kaunas, Lithuania

Chaido Dritsaki Department of Accounting and Finance, Western Macedonia University of Applied Sciences, Kozani, Greece

Nikolaos Dritsakis Department of Applied Informatics, University of Macedonia, Economics and Social Sciences, Thessaloniki, Greece

Pavol Durana University of Zilina, Faculty of Operation and Economics of Transport and Communications, Department of Economics, Zilina, Slovak Republic

Carlos Encinas-Ferrer Universidad del Valle de Atemajac Campus León, León, Gto, Mexico

Annamaria Esposito IULM University, Milan, Italy

K. Gaidi University of Borj.B.A "Faculty of Economics and Business", Bordj Bou Arreridj, Algeria

Zarinah Hamid International Islamic University Malaysia, Kuala Lumpur, Malaysia

Marcelo Justus Institute of Economics, University of Campinas, Campinas, São Paulo, Brazil

Adam Karbowski Department of Business Economics, Warsaw School of Economics, Warsaw, Poland

Mario Al Kassiri University of Zilina, Faculty of Operation and Economics of Transport and Communications, Department of Communications, Zilina, Slovak Republic

Mustafa Göktuğ Kaya KTO Karatay University, Konya, Turkey

Perihan Hazel Kaya Selçuk University, Faculty of Economics and Administrative Sciences, Department of Economics, Konya, Turkey

Huseyin Kaya Istanbul Medeniyet University, Istanbul, Turkey

Mohammed Khaled School of Economics and Finance, Victoria University of Wellington, Wellington, New Zealand

Eva Kicová University of Zilina, Faculty of Operation and Economics of Transport and Communication, Department of Economics, Zilina, Slovak Republic

Paraskevi Klazoglou Department of Applied Informatics, University of Macedonia, Economics and Social Sciences, Thessaloniki, Greece

Tomas Kliestik University of Zilina in Zilina, Faculty of Operation and Economics of Transport and Communications, Department of Economics, Zilina, Slovak Republic

Jana Kliestikova University of Zilina, Faculty of Operation and Economics of Transport and Communications, Department of Economics, Zilina, Slovak Republic

Anna Križanová University of Zilina, Faculty of Operation and Economics of Transport and Communication, Department of Economics, Zilina, Slovak Republic

Coenraad C. A. Labuschagne Department of Finance and Investment Management, University of Johannesburg, Johannesburg, South Africa

Chengchun Li Faculty of Business and Law, Coventry University, Coventry, UK

Elzbieta Majewska University of Bialystok, Bialystok, Poland

Sudipa Majumdar Business School, Middlesex University, Dubai, United Arab Emirates

Dominika Matusova University of Zilina, Faculty of Operation and Economics of Transport and Communications, Department of Economics, Zilina, Slovak Republic

Jaroslav Mazanec University of Zilina, Faculty of Operation and Economics of Transport and Communications, Department of Economics, Zilina, Slovak Republic

Lucia Michalkova University of Zilina, Faculty of Operation and Economics of Transport and Communications, Department of Economics, Zilina, Slovak Republic

Touitou Mohammed University of Algiers 3 "Faculty of Economics and Business", Dely Ibrahim, Algeria

Dominika Moravcikova University of Zilina, Faculty of Operation and Economics of Transport and Communications, Zilina, Slovak Republic

Katarina Moravcikova University of Zilina, Faculty of Operations and Economics of Transport and Communications, Zilina, Slovak Republic

Argiro Moudatsou University of Applied Sciences (TEI) of Crete, Crete, Greece,

Hellenic Open University, Patras, Greece

Michal Mursztyn Bialystok University of Technology, Bialystok, Poland

Margareta Nadanyiova University of Zilina, Faculty of Operation and Economics of Transport and Communications, Department of Economics, Zilina, Slovak Republic

Fatemeh Noorbakhsh Monetary and Banking Research Institute, Tehran, Iran

Ourania Notta Alexander Technological Educational Institute of Thessaloniki, Department of Agricultural Technology, (Agricultural Economics Program), Thessaloniki, Greece

Niel Oberholzer Department of Finance and Investment Management, University of Johannesburg, Johannesburg, South Africa

Olajumoke E. Oladipo Access Bank Plc, Lagos, Nigeria

Joanna Olbrys Bialystok University of Technology, Bialystok, Poland

Kingsley M. Oserei Nigerian Economic Summit Group (NESG), Lagos, Nigeria

Department of Economics University of Lagos, Lagos, Nigeria

Alpha Morgan Capital Managers Limited, Lagos, Nigeria

Martina Paliderova University of Zilina, Faculty of Operation and Enonomics of Transport and Communication, Department of Economics, Zilina, Slovak Republic

Sellamuthu Prabakaran School of Economics and Business Administration, Department of Accounting & Finance, Pontificia Universidad Javeriana Cali, Cali, Colombia

Jacek Prokop Department of Business Economics, Warsaw School of Economics, Warsaw, Poland

Aidar Puryaev Kazan Federal University, Kazan, Russia

Bruno G. Rüttimann Inspire AG/ETH Zürich, Zurich, Switzerland

M. Retia University of Media "Faculty of Economics and Business", Media, Algeria

Corlise L. Le Roux University of Johannesburg, Johannesburg, South Africa

Elżbieta Rychłowska-Musiał Poznań University of Economics and Business, Poznań, Poland

Anuphak Saosaovaphak Faculty of Economics, Chiang Mai University, Chiang Mai, Thailand

Karam Shaar School of Economics and Finance, Victoria University of Wellington, Wellington, New Zealand

Mahshid Shahchera Monetary and Banking Research Institute, Tehran, Iran

Tomasz Sikora Institute of International Management and Marketing, Warsaw School of Economics, Warsaw, Poland

Erika Spuchlakova University of Zilina, Faculty of Operation and Enonomics of Transport and Communication, Department of Economics, Zilina, Slovak Republic

Pavlos Stamatiou University of Macedonia, Thessaloniki, Greece

Zuzana Stofkova University of Zilina, Faculty of Operation and Economics of Transport and Communications, Department of Economics, Zilina, Slovak Republic

Waleerat Suphannachart Department of Agricultural and Resource Economics, Faculty of Economics, Kasetsart University, Bangkok, Thailand

Sailesh Tanna School of Economics, Finance and Accounting, Faculty of Business and Law, Coventry University, Coventry, UK

Godwin Enaholo Uddin School of Management and Social Sciences, Pan-Atlantic University, Lagos, Nigeria

Ladislav Vagner University of Zilina, Faculty of Operations and Economics of Transport and Communications, Department of Economics, Zilina, Slovak Republic

Katarina Valaskova University of Zilina, Faculty of Operation and Economics of Transport and Communications, Zilina, Slovak Republic

Marek Valica University of Zilina, Zilina, Slovak Republic

Pierre J. Venter Department of Finance and Investment Management, University of Johannesburg, Johannesburg, South Africa

Eddie Villegas-Zermeño Departamento de Ciencias Económico Administrativas, Universidad Iberoamericana León, León, Gto, Mexico

Aspasia Vlachvei Department of International Trade, Western Macedonia University of Applied Sciences, Kastoria, Greece

Satawat Wannapan Faculty of Economics, Chiang Mai University, Chiang Mai, Thailand

Silvia Zadnanova University of Zilina, Faculty of Operation and Economics of Transport and Communications, Department of Economics, Zilina, Slovak Republic

Katarina Zvarikova University of Zilina in Zilina, Faculty of Operation and Economics of Transport and Communications, Department of Economics, Zilina, Slovak Republic

Chapter 1
Spatial Analysis of Research-Productivity Nexus: A Case of Thai Rice Sector

Waleerat Suphannachart

Abstract Location matters for agricultural production and for farmers' decision on adopting new crop varieties. Similar outputs, inputs, and productivity tend to be observed in areas with close proximity suggesting the importance of neighbourhood influence. However, this spatial pattern has been ignored when estimating the agricultural research impact on productivity in which agricultural research has been recognised as a primary source of productivity change. This study aims to test the existence of any spatial pattern of research-productivity relation using subnational-level data for the case of Thai rice production. The estimation incorporates the spatial effects in the total factor productivity (TFP) determinant model using the provincial-level data which includes 76 provinces of Thailand during 2004–2012. The simple spatial econometric models, spatial lag and spatial error, are employed. The significance of the spatial dependence is confirmed using the spatial lag model suggesting the TFP in one province is significantly associated with the TFP in neighbouring provinces. The findings generally confirm the existence of neighbourhood influence, and so the spatial pattern should be taken into account when measuring the agricultural research impact on productivity using subnational-level data.

1.1 Introduction

Agricultural production and productivity are location-specific in which factors like soil conditions, physical infrastructure, and weather events play an important role. Location also matters for farmers' decision on choosing inputs and outputs as well as on adopting new crop varieties and other research-based technology. The adoption of agricultural research, recognised as a primary source of agricultural productivity

W. Suphannachart (✉)
Department of Agricultural and Resource Economics, Faculty of Economics, Kasetsart University, Bangkok, Thailand
e-mail: waleerat.sup@gmail.com

N. Tsounis, A. Vlachvei (eds.), *Advances in Panel Data Analysis in Applied Economic Research*, Springer Proceedings in Business and Economics,
https://doi.org/10.1007/978-3-319-70055-7_1

change in many countries, tends to be location-specific, and so neighbourhood influence is suspected to play a role in the research-productivity nexus. However, this spatial pattern has been ignored when estimating factors determining the agricultural productivity. In fact, there has never been any study undertaking the spatial analysis of research-productivity relationship in any developing countries. The key concern is that if the spatial dimension existed, then the previous investigation of agricultural research impact on productivity ignoring the role of spatial patterns could be biased (Anselin 1988).

This study is one of the first efforts bringing attention to spatial or geographic issues when investigating the agricultural research impact on productivity in developing countries. It aims to fill gap in the literature by incorporating spatial effects in the productivity determinant model using provincial-level data, covering 76 provinces of Thailand for the year of 2004, 2006, 2008, 2010, and 2012. The main objective is to test the existence of any spatial pattern of research-productivity relation for the case of Thai rice production. The rice sector of Thailand was chosen as a case study because rice is the dominant crop in Thai agriculture where regional difference in rice varieties and farming practices is well observed. Provinces in nearby areas often share similar inputs, types of rice varieties, and infrastructure (transportation and irrigation systems). It is possible that rice productivity in one province is related to nearby provinces and that site-specific factors could influence the determinants of rice productivity. Literature also shows that the benefits of R&D are spatially selective and tend to concentrate in certain areas (Capello and Lenzi 2015). Therefore, the spatial issue deserves serious attention and is attractive enough to conduct a spatial analysis.

The paper consists of six sections. This section provides an introduction and the motivation for the study. A literature review then briefly describes how previous studies conducted their analyses on the links between agricultural research and productivity, and studies applying spatial approaches are also highlighted. Section 1.3 specifies the models, estimation techniques, and testing strategies and begins with the standard OLS specifications in order to perform the diagnostic tests for the presence of spatial pattern followed by the spatial specifications. Section 1.4 describes the sources and definitions of data and variables used in the estimation models. The regression results are interpreted in the fifth section with emphasis on whether any spatial pattern exists and the implications for agricultural productivity. Finally, a conclusion is drawn.

1.2 Literature Review

Agricultural productivity and its link with agricultural research have long been studied, and a number of previous empirical studies confirm that agricultural research has a positive and significant impact on the productivity (Evenson 2001; APO 2001). Numerous studies associate productivity growth with technical change attributed to agricultural research (Ruttan 1987; Evenson and Pray 1991; Fan and Pardey 1997; Evenson 2001; Kelvin et al. 2005). Most studies have focused on the role of public research since research investment is primarily public sector activities and the influence of private research on productivity is mostly unknown. The majority of these studies employ both national- and subnational-level data using econometric models and techniques such as OLS, seemingly unrelated regression, error correction modelling, and panel data regression techniques. The overwhelming conclusion of this empirical research is that investment in public research and extension has been a primary source of agricultural productivity change in many countries (Evenson 2001). Similar conclusion also applies to the case of Thai agriculture in which recent studies found that agricultural research (public, private, and foreign research) together with infrastructure and climate factors plays a crucial role in stimulating the productivity growth (Suphannachart and Warr 2011, 2012; Suphannachart 2016). Suphannachart (2013), focusing on the rice sector, shows that the public investment in rice R&D and the adoption of high-yielding rice varieties have positive and significant impacts on the rice productivity. However, these previous studies do not take into account the role of spatial effects on the linkage between productivity and its determinants.

Spatial econometrics has been widely applied in a number of researches in economics in which location and neighbourhood influence play an important role (Anselin et al. 2004; Baylis et al. 2011; GeoDa Center 2016). Baylis et al. (2011), in particular, provide a review of empirical literature applying spatial econometric methods for panel data in agricultural economics with an emphasis on the effect of climate change on agriculture. The study also highlights an important role of location and application of spatial techniques in many research topics of agricultural economics, in which land is immobile, weather events affect farm decisions, policies are set by regional political boundaries, and information is often regionally explicit. There are also various examples of studies with applications of spatial models in finance and risk management, production and land economics, development economics, and environmental economics. Capello and Lenzi (2015) is one study that supports the existence of spatial dimension of knowledge-innovation nexus and shows that when the source of innovation is formal (R&D), the benefits are spatially selective and tend to concentrate in certain area. However, the application of spatial econometric methods in the analysis of productivity and technical change is still limited.

1.3 Methodology and Estimation Techniques

The productivity determinant model is constructed based on the production function framework in which TFP growth is identified as a shift in the production function representing technical change. The TFP is measured as that part of rice output growth not explained by growth of measured factor inputs using the Solow-type growth accounting method. Under this method, output growth can be decomposed into the growth rate of the efficiency level and the growth rate of primary factor inputs, weighted by their cost shares. The TFP measurement follows the same method employed in previous studies of Suphannachart and Warr (2011 and 2012). The potential determinants of rice TFP incorporate factors affecting mainly the technological change such as seed technology and expenditures on research and development, which is similar to the previous study of Suphannachart (2013). Specifically, the model includes rice TFP as the dependent variable and rice research budget, high-yielding rice varieties adoption, irrigation, rainfall, and weather conditions as explanatory variables. Extension from the previous studies is an incorporation of the spatial relation using provincial-level data.

As the objective of this study is to test the existence of a spatial pattern in the research-productivity nexus, three estimation methods are employed consecutively. The first estimation method applied to the TFP determinant model is pooled OLS. The second method is panel data techniques (fixed effects and random effects). The third method is spatial regression techniques (spatial lag and spatial error).

The estimation equation is as follows:

$$\mathbf{P} = \mathbf{X}\boldsymbol{\beta} + \alpha_i + t + \boldsymbol{\varepsilon} \tag{1.1}$$

where **P** is a vector of log of dependent variable (i.e. productivity or TFP index at provincial level); **X** is a matrix of log of explanatory variables including rice research budget (R), actual adoption of high-yielding or modern rice varieties (HYV), amount of rainfall (Rain), irrigated area (I), and weather-related and natural factors (W); $\boldsymbol{\alpha}_\mathbf{i}$ is provincial-specific fixed effect; and **t** is time dummies.

Equation (1.1) is first estimated by pooled OLS and lumping the fixed effect in the error term. Without considering the spatial effects, the pooled OLS is inconsistent when the omitted variable bias is a problem, but it is unbiased though inefficient otherwise. The model is then estimated using panel data techniques, fixed effect and random effect models. The Hausman test is used to determine whether fixed effects (FE) or random effects (RE) is more suitable. The null hypothesis under the Hausman test is that the coefficient of the FE model is the same as the coefficient of the RE model. If the null hypothesis is rejected, then the fixed effect is correlated with the explanatory variables. Hence, the omitted variable bias is a problem and the FE model is preferred. However, the interest of this study does not focus on the estimation results of the OLS specifications. The purpose here is to perform the diagnostic tests for the presence of spatial dependence in the error terms of OLS regressions. If there is a sign of spatial dependence in the OLS residuals, then OLS is inappropriate. The above equation is extended to incorporate the neighbourhood influence or spatial effects.

In the standard linear regression model, there are two types of spatial effects, spatial dependence and spatial heterogeneity, which can be incorporated in two ways (Anselin 1999). First, the spatial effect or spatial dependence is included as an additional regressor in the form of a spatial lagged dependent variable and so is called a spatial lag model. It is appropriate when the focus of interest is the assessment of the existence and strength of spatial interaction. Second, the spatial effect or spatial heterogeneity is incorporated in the error structure, called a spatial error model. This model is appropriate when the concern is to correct for the potential bias of spatial autocorrelation due to the use of spatial data that varied with location and are not homogeneous throughout the data set. It is typical to undertake the spatial analysis using both models since they are actually related. The spatial heterogeneity in the error structure can be considered an underlying reason behind the spatial lag model, although the spatial dependence can be observed more clearly. This study employs both spatial models.

In the spatial lag model, TFP in one province is assumed to be spatially interacted or dependent to TFP in neighbouring provinces. In other words, the model captures the neighbourhood spillover effects and hence takes the following form:

$$\mathbf{P} = \rho\mathbf{WP} + \mathbf{X}\boldsymbol{\beta} + \boldsymbol{\varepsilon} \tag{1.2}$$

where P and X are dependent and explanatory variables in the OLS specifications, $\boldsymbol{\rho}$ is spatial dependence parameter, and **W** is a $n\times n$ standardised spatial weight matrix (where n is the number of observations). In this study, W is 380 × 380 symmetric matrix as the data include 76 provinces for 5 years.

Spatial weight matrix, **W**, is taken to represent the pattern of potential spatial interaction or dependence. It reveals whether any pair of observations is neighbours. For example, if province i and province j are neighbours, then $w_{ij} = 1$ or zero otherwise. In this study, any pair of provinces is considered neighbours if they share common borders (contiguity basis).

For ease of interpretation, the spatial weight matrix is typically standardised so that every row of the matrix is summed to 1 (i.e. $\sum_j w_{ij} = 1$). That is, all neighbours of a province are given equal weight, and hence all provinces are equally influenced by their neighbours. It is also important to note that the elements of the weight matrix are non-stochastic and exogenous to the model.

In the spatial error model, the data collected at each province is assumed to be heterogeneous as every location has some degree of uniqueness relative to other locations. That is, the nature of spatial data can influence the spatial dependency, and hence the error term is spatially correlated. The model takes the following form:

$$\mathbf{P} = \mathbf{X}\boldsymbol{\beta} + \boldsymbol{\varepsilon};\quad \boldsymbol{\varepsilon} = \lambda\mathbf{W}\boldsymbol{\varepsilon} + \mathbf{u} \tag{1.3}$$

where P and X are dependent and explanatory variables in the OLS specifications, $\boldsymbol{\lambda}$ is spatial error parameter, and **u** is an error term that satisfies the classical assumptions of independent identical distribution (i.i.d) with constant variance σ^2. W is the spatial weight matrix.

For the estimation technique, the maximum likelihood estimation (MLE) is used. The reason for this is that in the spatial lag model, OLS is biased and inconsistent due to the endogeneity problem, whereas, in the spatial error model, OLS is unbiased but inefficient due to the spatial autocorrelation in the error term.

To test for the existence of a spatial pattern, two tests are conducted (Anselin 1988). A diagnostic test for the presence of spatial dependence in OLS residuals is conducted first using the Moran's I statistics (MI). The null hypothesis under this test is the absence of spatial dependence. If the null hypothesis is rejected, there is a sign of spatial pattern which it is necessary to investigate further using the spatial regression models. The second test is then conducted on the spatial models using the Lagrange multiplier (LM) test. This is the test for significances of spatial parameters. The null hypotheses are $\rho = 0$ under the spatial lag model and $\lambda = 0$ under the spatial error model. Under the null hypothesis, the test statistics have a chi-squared distribution with one degree of freedom. If the test statistics is greater than the critical value, the null hypothesis is rejected. The significances of spatial parameters confirm the existence of spatial effects or neighbourhood influence in the TFP determinant model.

1.4 Variables and Data Description

The estimation of TFP growth can be expressed as the residual part of output growth that cannot be explained by the combined growth of primary inputs. The primary conventional factor inputs used in this study include land, labour, and capital. Aggregate input is weighted average of growth of each input where weights are their varying cost shares.

The TFP determinant model employed in this study incorporates factors affecting mainly the technological change such as seed technology and expenditures on rice research. Other relevant economic and noneconomic factors are also included to explain the residual TFP such as infrastructure, rainfall, and natural factors. Specifically, agricultural research budget is used to represent a major source of technical change that raises productivity. An increase in rice research budget is expected to raise TFP. Only national public research is considered because rice research in Thailand has long been conducted by the public sector at national level and there are data limitations on other funding sources of research and extension. Seed technology is also included using the adoption of high-yielding rice varieties as it plays a crucial role in determining rice productivity (Evenson and Gollin 2003). The adoption is measured as shares of rice varieties planted areas. Amount of rainfall is included as water is a crucial factor for rice growing. Irrigation, measured as proportion of irrigated area, represents an infrastructure factor that can raise rice productivity. The natural factor, measured as a proportion of rice harvested to total rice planted area, is also included. It represents the weather shock such as drought, flooding, rice disease, and insect or pest epidemic. Good weather like less occurrence of drought or flooding or pest epidemic should raise TFP relative to the opposite. This natural factor proxy has commonly been used in earlier studies, for example, Setboonsarng and Evenson (1991), Pochanukul (1992), and Suphannachart and Warr (2012).

The output and input data are pooled cross section and time series at provincial level, covering 76 provinces of Thailand for the year of 2004, 2006, 2008, 2010, and 2012. Altogether, the data contain 380 repeated observations on the same individuals

(76 provinces) at different points in time (5 years). The data are mainly taken from the Office of Agricultural Economics, and some data series are drawn from Khunbanthao and Suphannachart (2016). All data are available at provincial level except research expenditure that is in national level. Definitions and sources of data used in this study are summarised in Table 1.1. All variables are transformed to logarithmic form, and summary statistics of variables used in the TFP determinant model are shown in Table 1.2.

1.5 Results and Discussion

This section reports the estimation results focusing on the main question of whether there exists any spatial pattern when estimating the relationship between TFP and its determinants, particularly technology factors (research budget and high-yielding rice varieties adoption). The results using the three-step estimation techniques explained earlier are shown in Table 1.3.

The TFP determinant model is first estimated by pooled OLS. The estimates of every coefficient from pooled OLS conform to prior expectations. However, it is more likely that the estimates are inconsistent since the unobserved fixed effect is expected to correlate with the explanatory variables. Accordingly, the coefficients cannot yet be interpreted from this estimation. The correlation between the unobserved heterogeneity and the explanatory variables is confirmed when the Hausman test suggests that the fixed effect (FE) model is suitable. This means the coefficients of FE are statistically different from those of the random effect (RE) model, and hence the omitted variable bias is an important problem. However, if there exists any spatial pattern or spatial interaction in the dependent variable, the FE estimates are also inconsistent.

Therefore, the diagnostic test for the presence of spatial dependence in OLS residuals is conducted on both the pooled OLS and FE estimations. Moran's I statistics is used to test the null hypothesis of the absence of spatial dependence. The null hypothesis is rejected at the 5% level of significance for the pooled OLS but failed to reject for the FE specification. Hence the presence of spatial dependence is confirmed only for the pooled OLS estimation. The pooled OLS estimation is inappropriate, and its estimates are only reported in Table 1.3 but not interpreted. The FE estimation is appropriate and its results are interpreted below. However, as the purpose of this study aims at testing the spatial relationship between research and productivity, the pooled OLS model which is proved exhibiting spatial patterns is extended to corporate spatial parameters. In this case spatial specifications are more appropriate, and the spatial lag and spatial error models, specified in Eqs. (1.2) and (1.3), respectively, are estimated by the maximum likelihood method.

To further test the significance of the spatial lag (ρ) and the spatial error (λ) parameters, the Lagrange multiplier test is conducted. The null hypotheses are $\rho=0$ and $\lambda=0$, and the test statistics follow chi-squared distribution with one degree of freedom. As shown in Table 1.3, only the p-value of spatial lag parameter is

Table 1.1 Summary of the data used in TFP measurement and TFP determinants

Variables	Definitions (units)	Sources
Output	Amount of total rice produced (ton)	Office of Agricultural Economics
Land	Planted area (rai)	Office of Agricultural Economics
Labour	Number of rice-farming household (household)	Office of Agricultural Economics and Department of Agricultural Extension
Capital	Stock of agricultural credit (million Baht) estimated using the perpetual inventory method (National Economic and Social Development Board, 2006)	Author's calculation based on the data from the Bank for Agriculture and Agricultural Cooperatives
Cost shares of land	Share of land rent in the total cost of rice production (Baht/rai)	Office of Agricultural Economics
Cost shares of labour	Share of labour cost in the total cost of rice production (Baht/rai)	Office of Agricultural Economics
Cost shares of capital	Share of capital cost in the total cost of rice production (Baht/rai)	Office of Agricultural Economics
Research expenditure	Rice research budget expenditure allocated to the Rice Department (or Department of Agriculture prior to March 2006) deflated by implicit GDP deflator using 1988 as base year (million Baht)	Bureau of the budget and National Economic and Social Development Board
High-yielding rice varieties adoption	Planted area of rice varieties that target output increasing as share of total planted area	Office of Agricultural Economics and Rice Department
Rainfall	Amount of regional rainfall (millimetre)	Office of Agricultural Economics
Irrigation	Accumulated irrigation area (rai), including small-, medium-, and large-scale irrigation projects	Office of Agricultural Economics
Natural factor	Rice harvested as share in total rice planted area	Office of Agricultural Economics

statistically significant; the null hypothesis is rejected at the 5% level of significance, and it is concluded that the spatial lag parameter is statistically significant. The significance of spatial lag parameter confirms that the neighbourhood influence is important. In particular, there exists spatial dependence between the rice productivity in neighbouring provinces. But there is no evidence that there exists spatial

Table 1.2 Summary statistics of variables in the TFP determinant model

Variables	Obs.	Mean	Standard deviation
Rice total factor productivity (P)	380	0.012	0.116
Rice research budget (R)	380	8.012	0.091
High-yielding rice varieties adoption (HYV)	380	−0.481	0.482
Irrigation (I)	380	5.574	0.821
Rainfall (Rain)	380	3.122	0.178
Weather and natural factor (W)	380	−0.038	0.314

Note: All variables are expressed in level terms and natural logs

Table 1.3 Estimation results of the TFP determinant model (Dependent variable is TFP: lnP)

	Pooled OLS	FE	Spatial lag	Spatial error
lnR	0.046 (0.058)	0.081[b](0.039)	0.046 (0.058)	0.044 (0.058)
lnHYV	0.038[a](0.011)	0.025[b](0.012)	0.038[a](0.011)	0.040[a](0.012)
lnI	0.048[a](0.007)	0.384[a](0.027)	0.048[a](0.008)	0.048[a](0.007)
lnRain	−0.102[a](0.034)	0.032 (0.038)	−0.101[a](0.035)	−0.095[a](0.035)
lnW	0.021(0.0169)	0.004 (0.012)	0.021 (0.017)	0.021 (0.017)
R-squared	0.23			
Moran's I statistics (p-value)	1.943[b](0.052)	−1.822 (1.932)		
Spatial lag parameter: ρ			0.009[b](0.101)	
Spatial error parameter: λ				0.120 (0.116)
Log likelihood			331.321	331.847
LM test of ρ: chi2(1)			0.013	
LM test of λ: chi2(1)				2.062
Observations	380	380	380	380

Notes: standard errors of estimated coefficients are in parenthesis, except Moran's I statistics that p-value is reported in parenthesis
[a]Means significant at 1%
[b]Means significant at 5%

heterogeneity across the spatial data as the spatial error parameter is not statistically significant.

In terms of the spatial dependence represented in the spatial lag model, it can be directly interpreted that the TFP in one province is significantly associated with the TFP in neighbouring provinces, given that the spatial relationship is specified by the weight matrix. It is typical to observe that if one province has a certain level of productivity, its neighbours are highly likely to have a similar level. Therefore, neighbourhood influence is significant. For example, a province located near a major research station or a dam tends to benefit from a discovery of new rice varieties and irrigation projects. This benefit may spill over to neighbouring provinces and may also affect rice productivity and its determinants. The rice TFP in a province located near research centres and dams and shares similar amount of rainfalls is thus associated with the TFP in nearby provinces.

Regarding the interpretation of the coefficient estimates, the FE and the spatial lag models which are shown to be appropriate confirm the significant relationship between the TFP and the technology factor represented by actual adoption of high-yielding rice varieties and the infrastructure factor represented by irrigation area. The magnitude of the technological impact is small and similar for both the FE and the spatial lag estimations. Specifically, a 1% increase in the proportion of planted area of rice varieties that target output increasing leads to 0.03% (under the FE) and 0.04% (under the spatial lag) increase in the TFP index (an output produced out of a unit of total inputs used), respectively. Despite the small magnitude of the research impact on productivity (measured in terms of the adoption of rice varieties developed by rice research stations), it conforms to economic intuition and supports the results of previous studies that agricultural and rice research can raise agricultural and rice productivity (Suphannachart and Warr 2011; Suphannachart 2013; Khunbanthao and Suphannachart 2016).

As for the magnitude of the irrigation coefficients, they are quite different between the FE and the spatial lag results. Under the FE model, a 1% increase in the irrigation area results in 0.38% increase in the TFP, while under the spatial lag model, the same level of change in the irrigation can only raise TFP by 0.05%. For rice research budget variable, it is shown to be positively significant only in the FE specification. This is probably due to the research budget data are only available at a national level, and so their location-specific impacts captured in the spatial lag model cannot be observed. Rainfalls are shown to have a negative and significant impact only in the spatial lag model which makes sense because the climatic factor is better observed in the location-specific model in which neighbouring provinces tend to share similar amount of rainfalls.

1.6 Conclusion

This study is one of the first efforts to conduct the spatial analysis of agricultural research impact on productivity at subnational level in developing countries. It attempts to find out whether there is any significant spatial pattern when estimating the TFP determinant model using provincial-level data for the case of Thai rice production. The data cover 76 provinces of Thailand during the year 2004, 2006, 2008, 2010, and 2012. The analysis begins with the standard OLS specifications in order to test for the presence of spatial structure in the error terms. The estimation then proceeds to simple spatial econometric models as the empirical results confirm the presence of spatial structure in the error components. The significance of the spatial dependence is confirmed using the spatial lag model suggesting that the TFP in one province is significantly associated with the TFP in neighbouring provinces.

However, there is no statistical evidence that there exists spatial heterogeneity across the spatial data as represented in the spatial error model.

The estimation results of both the OLS and spatial regression found the agricultural research (measured as high-yielding rice varieties adoption) impact on productivity (measured as rice TFP) to be statistically significant though small in magnitude. This is consistent with prior economic intuition and the results of previous studies. In overall, the spatial estimation results confirm that the rice TFP in Thailand tends to concentrate in particular areas where neighbourhood influence plays an important role. Therefore, when estimating the determinants of rice TFP for the case of Thailand or any other case where regional differentials are evident, the productivity level in one area tends to be related to the productivity in neighbouring areas, and this pattern should be incorporated in the estimation model. The significance of spatial correlation among provinces also implies that productivity-enhancing policy shall be developed targeting groups of provinces in close proximity or larger regional bases, rather than focusing on various small areas.

References

Anselin, L. (1988). *Spatial econometrics: Methods and models*. Boston: Kluwer Academic.

Anselin, L. (1999). *Spatial econometrics. Center School of Social Sciences*. Bruton: University of Texas at Dallas.

Anselin, L., Bongiovanni, R., & Lowenberg-DeBoer, J. (2004). A spatial econometric approach to the economics of site-specific nitrogen management in corn production. *American Economic Journal of Agricultural Economics, 86*, 675–687.

APO. (2001). *Measuring total factor productivity: Survey report*. Tokyo: Asian Productivity Organization.

Baylis, R., Paulson, D., & Piras, G. (2011). Spatial approaches to panel data in agricultural economics: A climate change application. *Journal of Agricultural and Applied Economics, 43*(3), 325–338.

Capello, R., & Lenzi, C. (2015). The knowledge-innovation Nexus: Its spatially differentiated returns to innovation. *Growth and Change, 46*(3), 379–399.

Evenson, R. (2001). Economic impacts of agricultural research and extension. In B. Gardner & G. Rausser (Eds.), *Handbook of agricultural economics* (1st ed., pp. 573–628). Amsterdam: Elsevier.

Evenson, R., & Gollin, D. (2003). *Crop variety improvement and its effect on productivity*. Cambridge: CABI Publishing.

Evenson, R., & Pray, C. (1991). *Research and productivity in Asian agriculture*. Ithaca: Cornell University Press.

Fan, S., & Pardey, P. (1997). Research, productivity, and output growth in chinese agriculture. *Journal of Development Economics, 53*(1), 115–137.

GeoDa Center. (2016). Research. The Center for Spatial Data Science, The University of Chicago. Available via http://spatial.uchicago.edu/research2. Accessed 19 Nov 2016.

Kelvin, B., Alastair, B., & Iain, F. (2005). Measuring the impact of R&D on productivity from a econometric time series perspective. *Journal of Productivity Analysis, 24*(1), 49–72.

Khunbanthao, K., & Suphannachart, W. (2016). Analysis of total factor productivity of rice in Thailand. *5th National Conference on Agricultural economics, resource economics, food economics and agribusiness*, Bangkok, Thailand, 15 July 2016.

Pochanukul, P. (1992). *An economic study of public research contributions in Thai crop production: A time and spatial analysis*. Dissertation, Kyoto University.
Ruttan, V. (1987). *Agricultural research policy and development*. Rome: Food and Agriculture Organization of the United Nations.
Setboonsarng, S., & Evenson, R. (1991). Technology, infrastructure, output supply, and factor demand in Thai agriculture. In R. Evenson & C. Pray (Eds.), *Research and productivity in Asian Agriculture*. Ithaca: Cornell University Press.
Suphannachart, W. (2013). Total factor productivity of main and second rice production in Thailand. *Applied Economics Journal, 20*(1), 1–22.
Suphannachart, W. (2016). Returns to major agricultural R&D sources in Thailand. *American Journal of Economics, 6*(1), 22–26.
Suphannachart, W., & Warr, P. (2011). Research and productivity in Thai agriculture. *The Australian Journal of Agricultural and Resource Economics, 55*(1), 35–52.
Suphannachart, W., & Warr, P. (2012). Total factor productivity in Thai agriculture: Measurement and determinants. In K. O. Fuglie, S. L. Wang, & V. E. Ball (Eds.), *Productivity growth in agriculture: An international perspective*. Oxfordshire: CAB International.

Chapter 2
Application of Thermodynamics Entropy Concept in Financial Markets

Sellamuthu Prabakaran

Abstract Entropy is a mathematically defined quantity that is generally used for characterizing the probability of outcomes in a system that is undergoing a process. It was originally introduced in thermodynamics by Rudolf Clausius (Philos Mag J Sci 40:122–127, 1870) to measure the ratio of transferred heat through a reversible process in an isolated system. In statistical mechanics the interpretation of entropy is the measure of uncertainty about the system that remains after observing its macroscopic properties (pressure, temperature, or volume). In this work, we attempt that the concept of entropy in thermodynamics be applied to financial markets. The main goal of this study is fourfold: (1) First we begin our approach through the concept of financial economics entropy. (2) Next we introduce the concept of entropy in economic systems. (3) Here we are exploring the interpretation of entropy in finance. (4) Then we extend the concept of entropy used in finance with standard economic utility theory by using of entropy and its maximization. (5) Finally, we construct the model of variance equilibrium under an entropy (financial) risk measure. And this paper ends with conclusion.

Keywords Financial markets · Entropy · Shannon entropy · Risk measure and thermodynamics

2.1 Introduction

The application of entropy in this perspective was introduced by Ludwig Boltzmann (Boltzmann and Hasenöhrl 2012). He defined the configuration entropy as the diversity of specific ways in which the components of the system may be arranged. He found a strong relationship between the thermodynamic and the statistical

S. Prabakaran (✉)
School of Economics and Business Administration, Department of Accounting & Finance, Pontificia Universidad Javeriana Cali, Cali, Colombia
e-mail: jopraba@gmail.com

N. Tsounis, A. Vlachvei (eds.), *Advances in Panel Data Analysis in Applied Economic Research*, Springer Proceedings in Business and Economics,
https://doi.org/10.1007/978-3-319-70055-7_2

aspects of entropy: the formulae for thermodynamic entropy and configuration entropy only differ in the so-called Boltzmann constant. There is an important application of entropy in information theory as well, and this is often called Shannon (1948) entropy. The information provider system operates as a stochastic cybernetic system, in which the message can be considered as a random variable. The entropy quantifies the expected value of the information in a message or, in other words, the amount of information that is missing before the message is received. The more unpredictable (uncertain) the message that is provided by the system, the greater the expected value of the information contained in the message. Consequently, greater uncertainty in the messages of the system means higher entropy. Because the entropy equals the amount of expected information in a message, it measures the maximum compression ratio that can be applied without losing information.

In financial applications, Philippatos and Wilson (1972) find that entropy is more general and has some advantages over standard deviation; in their paper they compare the behaviors of standard deviation and entropy in portfolio management. Kirchner and Zunckel (2011) argue that in financial economics entropy is a better tool for capturing the reduction of risk by diversification; however, in their study they suppose that the assets are Gaussian. Dionisio et al. (2006) argue that entropy observes the effect of diversification and is a more general measure of uncertainty than variance, since it uses more information about the probability distribution. The mutual information and the conditional entropy perform well when compared with the systematic risk and the specific risk estimated through the linear equilibrium model. Regarding the predictability of stock market returns, Maasoumi and Racine (2002) point out that entropy has several desirable properties and is capable of efficiently capturing nonlinear dependencies in return time series. Nawrocki and Harding (1986) propose applying state-value weighted entropy as a measure of investment risk; however, they are dealing with the discrete case.

2.2 Concept of Entropy in Economics Systems

Thermodynamics is a statistical theory for large atomic systems under constraints of energy. An economy is a large system of economic agents and goods under the constraints of capital. Both systems may be handled by the Lagrange principle, the law of statistics for large systems under constraints. Thermodynamics is a statistical theory for large systems, which is actually based on two corresponding concepts: one approach is based on the first and second laws of thermodynamics and leads to "macrophysics" of motors, refrigerators, and heat pumps and the other is the free energy concept that leads to "microphysics" of atomic interactions in physics, chemistry, metallurgy, or meteorology.

According to the second law of thermodynamics

$$\delta W = dY - TdlnP \tag{2.1}$$

Work (W) reduces entropy ($ln\ P$). In economics work reduces the entropy of capital distribution: business collects capital from customers by selling goods. This may be repeated by economic Carnot cycles and leads to economic growth. Equation (2.1) leads "macroeconomic" to production of industrial goods and monetary cycles. Work in thermodynamics and production in economics are the same. Industrial workers often become too expensive and are replaced by robots, computers, and machines. These machines follow the second law of thermodynamics and often work with a higher efficiency than people.

According to free energy concept that is based on Lagrange principle of statistics

$$L = TInP - Y \rightarrow \quad \max \tag{2.2}$$

Probability (P) is maximized under the constraint (Y), and T is the Lagrange parameter. In thermodynamics L is the free energy, Y is the energy of atomic bonds, and T is the mean kinetic energy or temperature. This concept may be translated to socioeconomic systems with constraints and leads to "microeconomics." Economy is a market with traders under the constraint of prices. Society is a system of social agents under the constraints of social bonds. Statistical laws like Eq. (2.2) are never concerned with the type of object, but only with the number of objects. For this reason it will be necessary to discuss new meanings for the functions L, T, P, and Y in social and economic systems. In atomic systems all thermal properties of materials (solids, liquids, or gases) may be derived from the Lagrange principle, and it is the object of this paper to investigate whether this concept is also valid in other systems like economics, social science, and politics.

To draw a cycle or a closed integral requires at least two dimensions, x and y. The closed line integral has the general form:

$$\oint a(x, y)\, dx + b(x, y)\, dy \tag{2.3}$$

The two-dimensional differential forms

$$df = a(x, y)\, dx + b(x, y)\, dy \tag{2.4}$$

are the total differential forms, and the function f exists and is given by the limits of integral, if

$$\partial \frac{a(x, y)}{\partial y} = \frac{\partial^2 f}{\partial y \partial x} = \frac{\partial^2 f}{\partial x \partial y} = \frac{\partial b(x, y)}{\partial x} \tag{2.5}$$

Since $df(x, y)$ depends on the limits of the integral, only the closed integral is zero.

And another two-dimensional differential forms

$$\delta\omega = a(x, y)\, dx + b(x, y)\, dy \tag{2.6}$$

are nontotal differential forms, and the function ω depends on the path of integration, if

$$\frac{\partial a(x, y)}{\partial y} \neq \frac{\partial b(x, y)}{\partial x} \tag{2.7}$$

Since the integral depends on the path of integration, the closed integral is generally not zero:

$$\oint \delta w \neq 0 \tag{2.8}$$

A two-dimensional nontotal differential form (2.6) can be transformed into a total differential form *df* by an integrating factor 1/*y*. The closed integral will be zero:

$$\oint \frac{\delta w}{y} = \oint df = 0 \tag{2.9}$$

According to the first law of thermodynamics that states that heat *dQ* is a nontotal differential, the closed integral is not zero, and the value of *Q* depends on the path of integration:

$$\oint \delta Q \neq 0 \tag{2.10}$$

The same is true in economics. Investing money in Japan, Europe, or the USA will lead to different profits in each case. The profit may also be negative, as losses are included. Profit δQ is a nontotal differential; the value of profit depends on the way of investment. Accordingly, Eq. (2.10) may be called the first law of economics.

The integrating factor 1/*y* leads to a total differential form *df* of a new function *f*. In thermodynamics the integrating factor 1/*T* leads to the new function *S*:

$$dS = \frac{\delta Q}{T} \tag{2.11}$$

which is called entropy. The closed integral of entropy is zero. The closed integral of heat may now be written in terms of entropy:

$$\oint \delta Q = \oint TdS \neq 0 \tag{2.12}$$

The closed line integral Eq. (2.12) leads to profit:

$$\Delta Q = \oint TdS = \oint ydx \neq 0 \tag{2.13}$$

In thermodynamics entropy is closely connected to the probability (*P*) of energy distribution in a system like a gas:

$$S = InP \tag{2.14}$$

$$P = \frac{N!}{(N_1!N_2!\ldots N_k!)\,/K^N} \tag{2.15}$$

In economic systems the entropy is closely connected to the capital distribution in an economic system like a market.

2.3 Interpretation of Entropy in Finance

Entropy is a well-defined quantity in physics that is associated with unused energy (e.g., thermal radiation). It can also be defined as a quantitative representation of "disorder" (or measure of uncertainty). In this context, entropy is viewed as a relationship between macroscopic and microscopic quantities that describes the dispersion of energy. In finance, this relationship can be viewed as to how the number of states (or regimes) in a market translates themselves into a probability distribution of the aggregate market sentiment.

In particular, the concept of entropy (in many different existing formulations) has been extensively used in finance to quantify the diversity and regularity of movements in price across a variety of markets (i.e., stock, currency, future, and commodity).

The main objective of this part is to highlight the interpretation of entropy in the study of financial markets. Focus is emphasized on the application of Shannon entropy measures on the extensive financial markets.

One well-known entropy is the Shannon information measures applied to a probability density function. In 1948 C.E. Shannon proposed a measure of uncertainty, subsequently termed Shannon entropy, to mathematically quantify the degree of "lost information" in phone line signals. The measure was introduced in his famous work *A Mathematical Theory of Communication* (Shannon 2001), based on papers by Nyquist (1924, 1928) and Hartley (1928), and served as a cornerstone in the formulation of information theory – the first coherent mathematical theory of communication. Shannon's grand contribution lies in proving that entropy could be generalized for any series where probabilities exist, a significant progress from previous works by Clausius and Boltzmann valid only for thermodynamic systems.

Shannon formally defined entropy as the average amount of "information, choice, and uncertainty" encoded in patterns drawn from a signal or message. Other interpretations refer to entropy as a measure of disorder and unpredictability in a system. Generalization of Shannon entropy to any series with a well-defined probability distribution was early recognized and widely exploited, particularly in finance. Applications involve financial forecasting (Molgedey and Ebeling 2000; Zapart 2009), market efficiency (Yang et al. 2008; Mensi et al. 2012; Zhang 1999), and foreign exchange rates (Petroni and Serva 2003). A classical formulation of Shannon entropy is described as follows.

In physics, the thermodynamic entropy of a macrostate (defined by specifying pressure, volume, energy, etc.) is essentially the logarithm of the number of microstates (quantum states) consistent with it, i.e., the number of ways the macrostate can be realized.

Likewise, the economy entropy S to which we refer is a function:

$$S(X, Y, Z \dots) = \log W(X, Y, Z \dots)$$

of whatever macroeconomic variables $(X, Y, Z \ldots)$ our theory recognizes. Here W is the multiplicity factor of the macroeconomic state (number of different microeconomic ways in which it can be realized).

Let X be a discrete random variable of finite range $x_i, \ldots x_n$ and p_i the probability of X assuming the value x_i. The probabilities obey $p_i \geq 0 (i = 1, \ldots, n)$ and $\sum_{i=1}^{n} p_i = 1$. Shannon entropy is then defined with an arbitrary base (i.e., 2, e, 10) as

$$S(X) = -\sum_{i=1}^{n} p_i \log p_i \tag{2.16}$$

where S denotes the entropy. Entropy reaches a minimum $S = 0$ when X is constant and characterized by a fully localized probability distribution $p(x_0) = 1$ and $p(x) = 0$ for all $x \neq x_0$. In contrast, entropy is maximum $S = \log n$ for uniform distributions, where all instances x_i are equally probable. Shannon entropy can also be defined for a continuous random variable Z as follows. Let $f(z)$ be the probability density function (pdf) of Z, where $f(z) \geq 0$ and $\int f(z) = 1$. The entropy is then defined as

$$S(Z) = -\int f(Z) \log f(z) dz \tag{2.17}$$

and follows similar rules to the discrete case. The choice of base for the logarithm is arbitrary and only serves as a scaling factor for entropy. Conventionally log base 2 is used, in which case entropy defines the minimum number of bits required to store a message without loss of information – also known as a measure of compressibility.

The Shannon entropy (Shannon 1948b) of a probability measure on a finite set X is given by

$$S_n(P) = -\sum_{i=1}^{n} p_i \ln p_i \tag{2.18}$$

where $\sum_{i=1}^{n} p_i = 1, p_i \geq 0$ and $0 In 0 = 0$.

When dealing with continuous probability distributions, a density function is evaluated at all values of the argument. Given a continuous probability distribution with a density function $f(x)$, we can define its entropy as

$$H = -\int_{-\infty}^{+\infty} f(x) Inf(x) dx \tag{2.19}$$

where $\int_{-\infty}^{+\infty} f(x) dx = 1$ and $f(x) \geq 0$.

2.4 Entropy and Maximization

In standard economic utility theory, consumers, faced with a limited income or budget which they can spend, are imagined to choose a particular consumption bundle from a range of possible bundles of goods, services, and opportunities at particular prices, such that their perceived utility Y is maximized over time in some manner. Utility decisions of consumers encompass risk (Neumann 1947), social factors, and value. A time element is involved, both in relation to the point at which purchases can be initiated and the period over which benefits are spread. As consumers proceed through life, each has a developing process that governs their decision-making concerning the opportunities that present themselves, with the nearer term being more knowable than the longer term.

In thermodynamics, entropy is a property that measures the amount of energy in a physical system that cannot be used to do work. In statistical mechanics it is defined as a measure of the probability that a system would be in such a state, which is usually referred to as the "disorder" or "randomness" present in a system. Given that systems are not in general reversible, then, following whatever means that are applied to return a system to its starting point, the net change in cycle entropy is commonly stated as

$$\oint \frac{dQ}{T} \geq 0 \tag{2.20}$$

As per the second law of thermodynamics, it is impossible to construct a system which will operate in a cycle, extract heat from a reservoir, and do an equivalent amount of work on the surroundings. Entropy tends to rise. It is a measure of dispersed value. And for a reversible process, the first law of thermodynamics states that

$$dQ - PdV = dU \tag{2.21}$$

and for closed reversible thermodynamics system, there exists a property **S**, such that a change in its value between two states is equal to

$$S_2 - S_1 = \int_1^2 \left(\frac{dQ}{T}\right)_{rev} \tag{2.22}$$

or in differential form:

$$dS = \left(\frac{dQ}{T}\right)_{rev} \quad or \quad dQ = TdS_{rev} \tag{2.23}$$

The property **S** is called the entropy of the system, and the value **dS** is the incremental change in entropy. The suffix "rev" is added as a reminder that the relation holds only for a reversible process.

Now, by combining Eq. (2.21) for the first law and (2.23) for the second law and inserting the term for the incremental work done $dW = PdV$, we could also construct an entropy function for an economic system:

$$TdS = dU + PdV \tag{2.24}$$

and in unit stock terms ($N = 1$), we can write

$$TdS = du + Pdv \tag{2.25}$$

Equations (2.24) and (2.25) set out the general relations between the properties and, when integrated, give the change in entropy occurring between two equilibrium states for a reversible process. It should be noted that entropy change in economic terms is associated with changes in flow of economic value.

In order to represent the potential work value occasioned by the impact of a motive force/utility value initiating increased or decreased activity flow rates of capital stock, labor, and resources and converted into a changed product flow rate, resort can be made to two thermodynamic properties known as the Helmholtz free energy function **F** [German physicist Hermann von Helmholtz 1821–1894] and the Gibb free energy function **X** [American physicist Josiah Willard Gibb 1839–1903]. These functions are common concepts in the thermodynamic analysis of chemical and gas reactions, particularly for closed systems, though there is no reason why they should not be used also for flows of inputs and output per unit of time, in which case we are considering free energy per unit of time. They express the total amount of exergy (available energy) which can be used up or passed on during a reaction to equilibrium. In thermodynamic terms they, respectively, have the formulae:

$$dF = -(PdV + SdT) \quad \text{and} \quad dX = (VdP - SdT) \tag{2.26}$$

where **P** is pressure, **V** is volume, **T** is temperature, and **S** is entropy. In economic terms the free energy might better be described as free value, being the amount of additional or reduced useful value available per unit of time that can be used up during a reaction between inputs such as labor, capital stock, and resources, potentially to produce additional or reduced output product flow. Equation (2.26) could therefore represent also an economic equivalent, relating free value to price/cost **P**, volume flow **V**, entropy **S**, and the index of trading value **T**.

The choice of which function to use is a matter of preference. The Helmholtz function works in terms of partial volumes, whereas the Gibb function works in terms of partial pressures [economic equivalent price]. The choice made here is the Helmholtz function **F** though whichever function is used, the result in economic terms is essentially the same.

Continuing with the Helmholtz function, the assumption is made that immediately before the actual point of increased/decreased conversion rate of inputs into outputs, no change in the index of trading value **T** of either inputs or outputs has occurred:

$$PV = PvN = NkT \quad \text{or} \quad Pv = kT = \text{Constant} \tag{2.27}$$

Thus value flow rate Pv per unit of stock, equal to price **P** multiplied by specific volume rate **v**, is assumed to be constant for both inputs and outputs, irrespective of the number of units in the stock. The productive content **k** is of course constant. This equates to the iso-trading process met, and the factor **v** for a unit of stock has some similarities to the chemical concept of an "activity coefficient" applying to the total concentration of stock **N** available, to equal the effective net input or output in the reaction.

Thus $V = vN$ and the factor v was equal to

$$v = \left(\frac{1}{\xi t_1}\right) \tag{2.28}$$

where ξ was the ratio of the natural lifetime t_L of a unit in a stock, compared to the standard transaction time t_1 (usually a year). This differs from stock to stock.

Returning to our development, because we have assumed **dT** = **0**, then for either input or output flows at the system boundary, Eq. (2.26) can be reduced to

$$dF = -PdV \tag{2.29}$$

which is the negative of the incremental work done **dW** that we encountered, and hence, for a spontaneous reaction to take place to produce additional output flow, consumption (reduction) of free value F occurs, that is, **dF** is negative. By substituting in **PV** = **NkT**, we have

$$dF = -NkT\left(\frac{dV}{V}\right) \tag{2.30}$$

It will be noted that this expression is similar in construction to the iso-trading process, and it will state as

$$dS = Nk\left(\frac{dV}{V}\right) \tag{2.31}$$

Thus a change in free value equates to an opposite change in entropy, adjusted by the index of trading value **T**:

$$dF = -TdS \tag{2.32}$$

By integrating Eq. (2.30), the free value **F** inclusive of that for the equilibrium flow volume level of the active output flow and for each of the inactive potential input flows can be stated as

$$F = F_{*} - NkT\ln(V) \tag{2.33}$$

2.5 Construction of Entropy-Based Risk Measure

Most of academic papers recognize that entropy could be a good measure of risk; however, it seems to be difficult to use this measure. Our main motivation is to show that an entropy-based risk measure is, on the one hand, more precise and, on the other hand, no more complicated to use than variance equilibrium models.

Entropy functions can be divided into two main types, discrete and differential entropy functions.

Let X^* be a discrete random variable. The possible outcomes of this variable are denoted by $o_1, o_2, \ldots, o_n$, and the corresponding probabilities by $p_i = \Pr(X^* = o_i)$, $p_i \geq 0$ and $\sum_{i=1}^{n} p_i = 1$. The generalized discrete entropy function (Renyi 1961) for the variable X^* is defined as

$$H_\alpha\left(X^*\right) = \frac{1}{1-\alpha}\log\left(\sum_{i=1}^{n} p_i^\alpha\right) \tag{2.34}$$

where α is the order of entropy, $\alpha \geq 0$ and $\alpha \neq 1$, and the base of the logarithm is 2. The order of entropy expresses the weight taken into account in each outcome; if the order of entropy is lower, the more likely outcomes are underweighted, and vice versa. The most widely used orders are $\alpha = 1$ and $\alpha = 2$.

$\alpha = 1$ is a special case of generalized entropy. However the substitution of $\alpha = 1$ into (2.34) results in a division by zero. It can be shown, using l'Hopital's rule for the limit of $\alpha = 1$, that H_α converges to the Shannon entropy:

$$H_1\left(X^*\right) = -\sum_{i=1}^{n} p_i \log\left(p_i\right) \tag{2.35}$$

The case of $\alpha = 2$ is called collision entropy, and similarly to the literature we refer to this special case as "Renyi entropy" further in the paper:

$$H_2\left(X^*\right) = -\log\left(\sum_{i=1}^{n} p_i^2\right) \tag{2.36}$$

$H_\alpha(X)$ is a nonincreasing function in a, and both entropy measures are greater than zero provided that there is a finite number of possible outcomes:

$$0 < H_2\left(X^*\right) \leq H_1\left(X^*\right) \tag{2.37}$$

Now, let X be a continuous random variable taking values from R with a probability density function $f(x)$. Analogously to (2.1), the continuous entropy is defined as

$$H_\alpha(X) = \frac{1}{1-\alpha} \ln \int f(x)^\alpha dx \tag{2.38}$$

One can see that the bases of the logarithms in (2.34) and (2.38) are different. Although the entropy depends on the base, it can be shown that the value of the entropy changes only by a constant coefficient for different bases. We use the natural logarithm for all differential entropy functions. The formulas for the special cases ($\alpha = 1$ and $\alpha = 2$) are the following:

$$H_1(X) = -\int f(x) \ln f(x) dx \tag{2.39}$$

$$H_2(X) = -\ln \int f(x)^2 dx \tag{2.40}$$

An important difference between discrete and continuous entropy is that while discrete entropy takes only nonnegative values, continuous entropy can also take negative values:

$$H_\alpha(X) \in R \tag{2.41}$$

For the estimation of differential entropy, the probability density function of the return values needs to be estimated. Let $x_1, x_2, \ldots, x_n$ be the observations of the continuous random variable X and $H_{\alpha,n}(X)$ the sample-based estimation of $H_\alpha(X)$. The plug-in estimations of entropy are calculated on the basis of the density function estimation. The probability density function $f(x)$ is estimated by $f_n(x)$, the integral estimate of entropy, in the following way:

$$H_{\alpha,n}(X) = \frac{1}{1-\alpha} \ln \int_{A_n} f_n(x)^\alpha dx, \tag{2.42}$$

where A_n is the range of integration, which may exclude small and tail values of $f_n(x)$. We propose to select $A_n = (\min(x), \max(x))$.

One of the simplest methods of density estimation is the histogram-based density estimation. Let $b_n = (\max(x), \min(x))$ be the range of sample values; partition the range into k bins of equal width and denote the cutting points by t_j.

The width of a bin is constant: $h = \frac{b_n}{k} = t_{j+1} - t_j$.

The density function is estimated by using the following formula:

$$f_n(x) = \frac{v_j}{nh} \tag{2.43}$$

if $x(t_j, t_{j+1})$, where v_j is the number of data points falling in the jth bin.

Based on the properties of the histogram, a simpler nonplug-in estimation formula can be deduced for Shannon and Renyi entropy using (2.39), (2.40), (2.41), and (2.42):

$$H_{1,n}(X) = \frac{1}{n}\sum_{j=1}^{k} v_j \ln\left(\frac{v_j}{nh}\right) \tag{2.44}$$

$$H_{2,n}(X) = -\ln\sum_{j=1}^{k} h\left(\frac{v_j}{nh}\right)^2 \tag{2.45}$$

The parameter of this method is the number of equal width bins (k). However, there are several methods for choosing this parameter (e.g., the square root choice, Scott's normal reference rule (Scott 1979), or the Freedman-Diaconis rule (Freedman and Diaconis 1981)).

The kernel-based density estimation is another commonly used method. It applies the following formula:

$$f_n(x) = \frac{1}{nh}\sum_{i=1}^{n} K\left(\frac{x - x_i}{h}\right) \tag{2.46}$$

where $K(x)$ is the kernel function and h is the bandwidth parameter. We propose using the indicator-based Epanechnikov kernel function:

$$K(z) = \frac{3}{4}\left(1 - z^2\right) I_{\{|Z|\leq 1\}}, \tag{2.47}$$

where I is the indicator function.

Hardle (2004) shows that the choice of the kernel function is only of secondary importance, so the focus is rather on the right choice of bandwidth (h). One of the most widely used simple formulas for the estimation of h is Silverman's rule of thumb (Silverman 1986):

$$\widehat{h}_{rot} = 1.06 \ \min \left\{ \sqrt{\frac{1}{n-1}\sum_{i=1}^{1}(x_i - \overline{x})^2}, \frac{IQR(x)}{1.34} \right\} n^{-\frac{1}{5}} \tag{2.48}$$

where $IQR(x)$ is the interquartile range of x. As the formula assumes a normal distribution for X, it gives an approximation for optimal bandwidth; despite this, Silverman's rule of thumb can be used for a good initial value for more sophisticated optimization methods (Turlach 1993).

For sample spacing estimation, let $x_{n,1} \leq x_{n,2} \ldots \leq x_{n,n}$ be the corresponding order of $x_{1,}x_2 \ldots, x_n$, assuming that this is a sample of i.i.d. real-valued random variables. $x_{n,i+m} - x_{n,i}$ is called a spacing of order $m(1 \leq i < i + m < n)$. The simple sample spacing density estimate is the following (Beirlant et al. 1997):

$$f_n(x) = \frac{m}{n} \frac{1}{x_{n,im} - x_{n,(i-1)m}}, \tag{2.49}$$

if $x[x_{n,(i-1)m}, x_{n,im}]$

Renyi (1961) introduced another variation of the sample spacing density estimation, called the Correa estimator:

$$f_n(x) = \frac{1}{n} \frac{\sum_{j=i-m/2}^{i+m/2} (x_j - \overline{x}_i)(j - i)}{\sum_{j=i-m/2}^{i+m/2} (x_j - \overline{x}_i)^2} \tag{2.50}$$

$$\text{If } i : x \in [x_{n,i}x_{n,i+1}]\, ; \overline{x}_i = \frac{1}{m+1} \sum_{j=i-m/2}^{i+m/2} x_j, \quad \text{and} \quad 1 \leq j \leq n. \tag{2.51}$$

The parameter for sample spacing methods is the fixed order m. For practical reasons (e.g., different sizes of samples) we suggest using m_n, which depends on the size of the sample and is calculated by the following formula:

$$m_n = \frac{n}{k} \tag{2.52}$$

where k is the number of bins and the braces indicate the ceiling function.

Beirlant et al. (1997) overview several additional entropy estimation methods, such as resubstitution, splitting data, and cross-validation; however, our paper focuses on the applications that are used most often.

Now we will estimate the risk and let the following be a given set of data:

$$D : \{S, R, R_M, R_F\} \tag{2.53}$$

The elements are the set of securities $S : \{S_1, S_2, \ldots S_l\}$, with the corresponding observations being $R : \{R_1, R_2, \ldots R_l\}$, where $R_i = (r_{il}, r_{i2}, \ldots, r_{in})$. The observation for the market return is $R_M = (r_{M1}, r_{M2}, \ldots, r_{Mn})$, and the observation for the risk-free return is $R_F = (r_{F1}, r_{F2}, \ldots, r_{Fn})$ where l is the number of securities and n is the number of samples. Let us recall that the main goal of this paper is to apply entropy as a novel risk measure. In order to handle the risk measure uniformly, we introduce k as a unified property for securities. Let $k(S_i)$ be the risk estimate for the security i.

In the economic literature the most widely used risk measures are the standard deviation and the CAPM beta. Let us denote these by k_α and k_β, respectively. The estimation of these risk measures for the security i is the following:

$$\widehat{k_\beta}\left(S_i\right) = \beta_i = \frac{\operatorname{cov}\left(R_i - R_F, R_M - R_F\right)}{\sigma^2\left(R_M - R_F\right)}, \tag{2.54}$$

where β is the CAPM beta, cov (β) is the covariance of the arguments, and s is the standard deviation.

Our hypothesis is that uncertainty about the observation values can be interpreted as a risk of the security, and for this reason we apply entropy as a risk measure. Because the differential entropy function can also take negative values, for better interpretability, we apply the exponential function to the entropy, and we define the entropy-based risk measure by the following formula:

$$\widehat{k_H}\left(S_i\right) = e^{Hn(R_i - R_F)} \tag{2.55}$$

One can see that k_H takes values from the nonnegative real numbers, $k_H \in [0, +\infty]$

2.6 Conclusion

Entropy is a measure of randomness. Much like the concept of infinity, entropy is used to help model and represent the degree of uncertainty of a random variable. It is used by financial analysts and market technicians to determine the chances of a specific type of behavior by a security or market.

Although the word entropy was originally used in thermodynamics, its concepts and relevant principles have been applied to the field of finance for a long period of time. Entropy has its unique advantages in measuring risk and describing distributions. As a result, the applications of entropy in finance are important. This paper reviewed representative work on how the entropy as a novel risk measure combines the advantages of the CAPM's risk parameter (beta) and the standard deviation. It captures risk without using any information about the market, and it is capable of measuring the risk reduction effect of diversification. The explanatory power for the expected return within the sample is better than the beta, especially in the long run covering bullish and bearish periods; the predictive power for the expected return is higher than for standard deviation. Here first we instigated our approach through the relation between the finance and physics. Then we introduced the concept of entropy in economic systems, and we extended the concept of entropy used in finance. Also here you can understand the maximization of entropy in the standard economic utility theory. Finally, we constructed the model of variance equilibrium under an entropy (financial) risk measure. And this paper ended with conclusion.

References

Aoki, M. (2002). *Modeling aggregate behavior and fluctuations in economics: Stochastic views of interacting agents*. Cambridge: Cambridge University Press.

Beaudreau, B. (1998). *Energy and organization: Growth and distribution reexamined*. Westport, CT: Greenwood Press.

Beirlant, J., Dudewicz, E. J., Györfi, L., & Van der Meulen, E. C. (1997). Nonparametric entropy estimation: An overview. *International Journal of Mathematical and Statistical Sciences, 6*, 17–40.

Biddle, J. (2001). *Economics broadly considered: Essays in honor of Warren J. Samuels*. New York: Routledge.

Blake, D. (2000). *Financial market analysis*. Chichester: Wiley.

Board, J. (2002). *Transparency and fragmentation: Financial market regulation in a dynamic environment*. New York: Palgrave.

Boltzmann, L., & Hasenöhrl, F. (2012). Weitere Studien über das Wärmegleichgewicht unter Gas-moleku¨ len Wissenschaftliche Abhandlungen. Cambridge University Press. doi:https://doi.org/10.1017/CBO9781139381420.023.

Çengel, Y. A., & Boles, M. A. (2011). *"6–7." Thermodynamics: An engineering approach* (7th ed., p. 299). New York: McGraw-Hill. Print.

Claesens, S. (2006). *A reader in international corporate finance* (Vol. 2). Washington, DC: World Bank.

Clausius, R. (1870). XVI. On a mechanical theorem applicable to heat. *The London, Edinburgh, and Dublin Philosophical Magazine and Journal of Science, 40*, 122–127. https://doi.org/10.1080/14786447008640370.

Cleveland, C. (2006). Dictionary of Energy, Amsterdam: Elsevier. Wissler, J. (2006). Achieving balance. *Air and Space Power Journal, 23*(4), 25–35.

Das, D. (2003). *International finance: Contemporary issues*. New York: Routledge.

Dincer, I. (2007). *Exergy: Energy, environment, and sustainable development*. Boston: Elsevier.

Dionisio, A., Menezes, R., & Mendes, D. A. (2006). An econophysics approach to analyse uncertainty in financial markets: An application to the Portuguese stock market. *The European Physical Journal B, 50*, 161–164. https://doi.org/10.1140/epjb/e2006-00113-2.

El-Sayed, M. (2003). *The thermoeconomics of energy conversions*. Oxford: Pergamon.

Feynman, R. P., Leighton, R. B., & Sands, M. (1963). *The Feynman lectures on physics*. Addison-Wesley Publishing Company.

Freedman, D., & Diaconis, P. (1981). On the histogram as a density estimator: L2 theory. *Probability Theory and Related Fields, 57*, 453–476. https://doi.org/10.1007/BF01025868.

Giordano, N. (2009). *College physics: Reasoning and relationships* (p. 510). Cengage Learning. 0-534-42471-6.

Halliday, D., & Resnick, R. (1978). *Physics* (3rd ed.). John Wiley & Sons.

Hansen, A. (1953). *A guide to Keynes*. New York: McGraw Hill.

Härdle, W. (2004). Nonparametric and semiparametric models. Springer. doi:https://doi.org/10.1007/978-3-642-17146-8.

Hartley, R. V. L. (1928). Transmission of information. *Bell System Technical Journal, Blackwell Publishing Ltd, 7*(3), 535–563.

Kirchner, U., & Zunckel, C. (2011). Measuring Portfolio diversification. arXiv preprint arXiv:11024722.

Kittel, C., & Kroemer, H. (1980). *Thermal physics* (2nd ed.). W. H. Freeman Company.

Kostic, M. (2011). *"Revisiting The Second Law of Energy Degradation and Entropy Generation: From Sadi Carnot's Ingenious Reasoning to Holistic Generalization"*. AIP Conf. Proc. American Institute of Physics.

Maasoumi, E., & Racine, J. (2002). Entropy and predictability of stock market returns. *Journal of Econometrics, 107*, 291–312. doi:10.1.1.27.1423.

Malkiel, B. G. (2007). *Random walk down wall street: The time-tested strategy for successful investing*. Mishawaka, IN: Better World Books.
Mensi, W., et al. (2012). Crude oil market efficiency: An empirical investigation via the shannon entropy. *International Economics, 129*, 119–137.
Molgedey, L., & Ebeling, W. (2000). Local order, entropy and predictability of financial time series. *The European Physical Journal B-Condensed Matter and Complex Systems, 15*(4), 733–737.
Nawrocki, D. N., & Harding, W. H. (1986). State-value weighted entropy as a measure of investment risk. *Applied Economics, 18*, 411–419. https://doi.org/10.1080/00036848600000038.
von Neumann, J. (1947). Theory of games and economic behavior, Princeton University Press, Second Printing.
Nyquist, H. (1924). Certain factors affecting telegraph speed. *Bell System Technical Journal, Blackwell Publishing Ltd, 3*(2), 324–346.
Nyquist, H. (1928). Certain topics in telegraph transmission theory. *Transactions of the American Institute of Electrical Engineers, 47*(2), 617–644.
Petroni, F., & Serva, M. (2003). Spot foreign exchange market and time series. *The European Physical Journal B - Condensed Matter and Complex Systems, 34*(4), 495–500.
Philippatos, G. C., & Wilson, C. J. (1972). Entropy, market risk, and the selection of efficient portfolios. *Applied Economics, 4*, 209–220. https://doi.org/10.1080/00036847200000017.
Renyi, A. (1961). *On measures of entropy and information. Fourth Berkeley symposium on Mathematical statistics and probability* (pp. 547–561). Berkeley, CA: University of California Press.
Scott, D. W. (1979). On optimal and data-based histograms. *Biometrika, 66*, 605–610. https://doi.org/10.1093/biomet/66.3.605.
Shannon, C. E. (1948). A mathematical theory of communication. *Bell System Technical Journal, 27*, 379–423. https://doi.org/10.1002/j.1538-7305.1948.tb00917.x.
Shannon, C. E. (2001). A mathematical theory of communication. *SIGMOBILE Mob. Comput. Commun. Rev., ACM, New York, NY, USA, 5*(1), 3–55.
Silverman, B. W. (1986). Density estimation for statistics and data analysis. CRC press. Monographs on Statistics and Applied Probability, p. 26. doi:https://doi.org/10.1007/978-1-4899-3324-9.
Turlach, B. A. (1993). Bandwidth selection in kernel density estimation: A review: Universite´ catholique de Louvain. doi: 10.1.1.44.6770.
Yang, J. S., Kwak, W., & Kaizoji, T. (2008). Increasing market efficiency in the stock markets. *The European Physical Journal B, 61*(2), 241–246.
Zapart, C. A. (2009). On entropy, financial markets and minority games. *Physica A: Statistical Mechanics and its Applications, 388*(7), 1157–1172.
Zhang, Y.-C. (1999). Toward a theory of marginally efficient markets. *Physica A: Statistical Mechanics and its Applications, 269*(1), 30–44.

Chapter 3
Economic and Business Cycle of India: Evidence from ICT Sector

Chukiat Chaiboonsri, Satawat Wannapan, and Anuphak Saosaovaphak

Abstract This paper aims to study the relationship between Indian ICT industries and GDP by applying Bayesian inference. Five yearly predominant indexes collected during 2000–2015, including Indian GDP, fixed phone usages, mobile phone distributions, Internet servers, and broadband suppliers, are analyzed by employing the Markov-switching model (MS model) and Bayesian vector autoregressive (BVAR) models. In addition, the Bayesian regression model is used to investigate the ICT multiplier related to Indian economic growth. The empirical results indicate that IT sectors are becoming the major role of Indian economic expansion in the forthcoming future, compared with telecommunication sectors. Moreover, the result of the ICT multiplier confirms that high technological industrial zones should be systematically enhanced continuously, in particular, research and development in cyberspace.

Keywords Information and Communication Technology (ICT) · Bayesian inference · Markov-switching model (MS model) · Bayesian vector autoregressive (BVAR) model

3.1 Introduction

Information and Communication Technology (ICT) can be broadly considered concerning two sectors, which are information technology and communication. Specifically in India, the growth of both sectors has been highly significant in the last two decades. Obviously, the data from the United Nations specialized agency for information and communication technologies (ITU) represented that smartphone-density trends in India were rapidly growing during 2007–2014, which is more than

C. Chaiboonsri (✉) · S. Wannapan · A. Saosaovaphak
Faculty of Economics, Chiang Mai University, Chiang Mai, Thailand
e-mail: chukiat1973@gmail.com; lionz1988@gmail.com

N. Tsounis, A. Vlachvei (eds.), *Advances in Panel Data Analysis in Applied Economic Research*, Springer Proceedings in Business and Economics,
https://doi.org/10.1007/978-3-319-70055-7_3

a double increment from 233.6 to 581.1 billion units. Simultaneously, Indian secure Internet servers were enormously enlarged, which is more than a triple improvement from 1462 Internet providers to 8944 servers. As a result, it is undeniable that ICT industries in India are the world's economic spotlight.

ICT industries based on the information from the industry association for the IT-BPM sector in India (NASSCOM) are promoted to be the highest relative share in the nation's GDP and private sector employers and predicted to be the source that generates the biggest amount of revenue for India (USD 75 billion). Interestingly, understanding the characteristics and statistical properties of business cycles is significantly essential for forming the basis for the construction, validations of theoretical business cycle models, and recommendations for ICT industrial policies (Siriphirunphong et al. 2015). Consequently, this leads the authors to intensively specify in the business cycle of Indian ICT industries as well as statistically clarify it.

Following the previous statement, the principles of this research are divided into two sections. First, the investigation of the characteristics of ICT cycle in India's economy is analyzed by using the Markov-switching model to classify the periods of economic boom and recession. Also, Bayesian vector autoregression (BVAR) is employed to express the adjusted tendency of ICT industries when economic shocks have impacted. Second, the macroeconomic indexes of ICT industries in India are estimated by applying the Bayesian regression model for seeking an economic multiplier. Ultimately, the results of research will be significantly useful for Indian ICT policy contemplations.

3.2 Literature Review

Markov-switching analysis and Bayesian inferences have become a powerful statistical model that many researchers apply for analyzing in different types of research areas. In other words, Zhu et al. (2014) constructed the Bayesian vector autoregressive (BVAR) forecast model to express and forecast coal usage in China. Moreover, Mallick and Sousa (2009) used the BVAR model to seek evidence on the monetary policy transmission in the BRICS countries. Furthermore, Moreira et al. (2013) employed the BVAR analysis and Markov-switching method (MS models) to verify empirical connections between expected and effective short-term interest rates in Brazil. As seen in the literature, there is no evidence that the BVAR and MS models have been employed in investigating the business cycle in India, especially studying the IT industrial sector.

3.3 Theoretical Concept and Methodology

3.3.1 Business Cycle Features

Taking consideration into the real business cycle theory, shocks in economic activities are the main cause that varies productivity in IT industries. Basically, in the theory, the market is always cleared by adjusting prices (Siriphirunphong et al. 2015). Some real business cycle theories emphasize changes in the technologies of different sectors rather than focusing economy-wide changes in technology (Long and Plosser 1983; Mankiw 1989). Thus, in actual economies, the essential concept is the measure of various economic activities and trends (Long and Plosser 1983).

3.3.2 Bayesian Statistics

Specifying the Bayesian inference, "the prior," an identical solution, is given for w as least squares, and maximum likelihood estimation will also display in overfitting. To solve the complex model, we specified earlier a "prior distribution" which explains our "belief level" over values that w might take before the weight penalty is regularized. The prior equation is expressed in Eq. (3.1):

$$p(w|\alpha) = \prod_{m=1}^{M} \left({}^{\alpha}/_{2\pi} \right)^{\frac{1}{2}} \exp\left[-\frac{\alpha}{2} w_m^2 \right] \tag{3.1}$$

After setting the prior, we gave the error measure and computed a single-point estimate of WLS for the weight. The likelihood and the prior are specified. Thus, we calculated the "posterior distribution" over w via Bayes' rule:

$$p\left(w|t, \alpha, \sigma^2\right) = \frac{\text{likelihood} \times \text{prior}}{\text{normalised factor}} = \frac{p\left(t|w, \sigma^2\right) p\left(w|\alpha\right)}{p\left(t|\alpha, \sigma^2\right)} \tag{3.2}$$

In academic research, Bayesian statistics considers hypotheses regarding multiple parameters by adapting Bayes factor comparisons. Let M_i be the model devised in the term of the null hypothesis and M_j be the model of the alternative hypothesis. The posterior odds ratio of M_i and M_j is shown in Eq. (3.3):

$$\frac{pr\left(M_i|y\right)}{pr\left(M_{j1}|y\right)} = \frac{pr\left(y|M_i\right)}{pr\left(y|M_{j1}\right)} \times \frac{\pi\left(M_i\right)}{\pi\left(M_j\right)}. \tag{3.3}$$

The Bayes factor is summarized by the statistical model proposed by Jeffrey (1961). The interpretation in half-units on Jeffrey's scales is simply explained as:

Bayesian factor (BF)	Evidence against M
BF < 1/10	Strong evidence for M_j
1/10 < BF < 1/3	Moderate evidence for M_j
1/3 < BF < 1	Weak evidence for M_j
1 < BF < 3	Weak evidence for M_i
3 < BF < 10	Moderate evidence for M_i
10 < BF	Strong evidence for M_i.

3.3.3 The ADF Unit Root Test Based on Bayesian Inference

The ADF test analyzes the null hypothesis that a time-series index is stationary against the alternative (nonstationary data), assuming that dynamics in data have the autoregressive moving average model (ARMA) (Said and Dickey 1984). The ADF test is based on estimating the regression test, which is expressed by Eq. (3.4):

$$\Delta y_t = c + \alpha' D_t + \phi y_{t-1} + \sum_{j=1}^{p} \gamma_j \Delta y_{t-j} + \varepsilon_t. \tag{3.4}$$

The prior density of ϕ is factorized and shown in Eq. (3.5):

$$p(\phi) = p(\varphi)\, p\left(a^* | \varphi\right) \tag{3.5}$$

The marginal likelihood for φ is

$$l(\varphi|D)\, \alpha \int l(\phi|D)\, \varphi\left(a^* | \varphi\right) da^*. \tag{3.6}$$

3.4 The Markov-Switching Bayesian Model

Applying from Hamilton (1989) who employed a Markov-switching autoregressive model to study the quarterly data of US GNP, the Markov-switching version of Bayesian vector autoregressive model is conducted for breaking down normality assumptions in time-series forecasting. The structural equation of Markov-switching Bayesian VAR (MS-BVAR) is defined as

$$\sum_{i=0}^{p} y_{t-i} A_i(s_t) = d(s_t) + \varepsilon_t(s_t) \quad , \quad t = 1, 2, \ldots, T \tag{3.7}$$

According to Eq. (3.7), $S_t = j$ is an h-dimensional vector state of the process, and j is the term of integer labels for the state, with an $h \times h$ Markov transition matrix. The matrix is given the probability of transitioning from the state S_{t-i} to S_t, which can be mathematically expressed as $\Pr(S_t = k | S_{t-i} = j)$. For setting the prior in MS-BVAR, the parameters A_i and d are determined by beliefs, the random walk prior in the Sims and Zha model (Sims and Zha 1998; Brandt et al. 2011). Consequently, the forecasts from a Markov-switching VAR model like Eq. (3.7) are the weighted combination of the forecasts for each state or phase (Brandt et al. 2011).

3.5 The Bayesian Vector Autoregressive Model

The vector autoregressive version of Bayesian inference (BVAR) is applied from the original VAR model, which is broadly defined as Eq. (3.8) (Moreira et al. 2013):

$$\begin{aligned} \Delta Y_t &= A' x_t + u_t \\ \Delta Y &= (I_M \otimes x)\,\alpha + u \end{aligned} \tag{3.8}$$

Given that α = vector (A), $u \sim N(0, \Theta \otimes I_T)$, and estimating the OLS of A, we now achieve

$$\widehat{A}' = \left[\sum\nolimits_{t=1}^{T} \Delta Y_t x_t'\right]\left[\sum\nolimits_{t=1}^{T} x_t x_t'\right]^{-1} \tag{3.9}$$

Employing Bayesian inference, Litterman and Minnesota priors (Koop and Korobilis 2009; Moreira et al. 2013) and Sims-Zha priors (Sims and Zha 1998) are suggested to be the estimated prior. Thus, $\otimes$ is conducted to make an estimation process and expressed as

$$\alpha \sim \mathrm{N}\,(\alpha_{\mathrm{nM}}, V_{nM}) \tag{3.10}$$

Considering the accuracy of forecasting prior, the most suitable prior is chosen by verifying the term of residuals, applying the forecast precision of root mean square errors (RMSE). The RMSE formulation is expressed in the Eq. (3.11):

$$\mathrm{RMSE} = \left(\frac{\sum_{n=1}^{N} \left(Y - \widehat{Y}\right)^2}{N}\right) \tag{3.11}$$

3.6 The Regression Version of Bayesian Inference for Economic Multipliers

The multiplier effect refers to an economic idea which was formulated in the nineteenth century, but not formalized till the conceptual development of John Maynard Keynes in the 1930s (Rusu 2011). For empirically expressing ICT industries in India, the multiplier can be illustrated by using a simple regression equation as

$$Y = IT_a + \beta\left(ICT_f\right) + \delta\left(ICT_m\right) + \varphi\left(ICT_i\right) + \gamma\left(ICT_b\right) + \varepsilon \tag{3.12}$$

Note that:

$Y =$ Indian yearly gross domestic product
$ICT_a =$ yearly constant terms of ICT industrial investment
$ICT_f =$ yearly data of fixed phone usages
$ICT_m =$ yearly data of mobile phone usages
$ICT_i =$ yearly data of internet servers
$ICT_b =$ yearly data of broadband providers
$\varepsilon =$ error terms
$\beta, \delta, \varphi, \gamma =$ parameters

In this paper, the impact of ICT multipliers in economy applied from Archer (1982) relies on the Keynesian multiplier as

$$\text{Multiplier} = \frac{1}{1 - \beta - \delta - \varphi - \gamma} \tag{3.13}$$

Applying Bayesian inference, posterior probability ratios of parameters are explained as (Diniz et al. 2011; Wannapan and Chaiboonsri 2016)

$$\beta = \frac{l[(\beta=1),|D]}{\int_0^1 l[(\beta)|D)](\beta)[(\beta)d(\beta)]}, \quad \delta = \frac{l[(\delta=1),|D]}{\int_0^1 l[(\delta)|D)](\delta)[(\delta)d(\delta)]}$$
$$\varphi = \frac{l[(\varphi=1),|D]}{\int_0^1 l[(\varphi)|D)](\varphi)[(\varphi)d(\varphi)]}, \quad \gamma = \frac{l[(\gamma=1),|D]}{\int_0^1 l[(\gamma)|D)](\gamma)[(\gamma)d(\gamma)]}.$$

3.7 Empirical Results

Before statistical estimations are evaluated, all of the time-series data should be checked first by unit root testing. As seen in Table 3.1, the ADF test-based Bayesian inference represented that every index is stationary and ready to be statistically

Table 3.1 The ADF unit root test based on Bayesian inference in yearly data of Indian IT industries and economy during 2001–2015

Variables	Bayesian factor model	Hypothesis	Numbers of MCMC regress iterations	Bayesian factor ratios	Interpretation of the Bayesian factor	Result
GDP_{India}	Model 1	H_0 (M_i): Ncnstationary data	2600	0.021	Strong evidence for M_j	*I(0)*
	Model 2	H_1 (M_j): Stationary data	6300	48		
Fixed phones	Model 1	H_0 (M_i): Nonstationary data	4900	1.38	Weak evidence for M_i	*I(0)*
	Model 2	H_1 (M_j): Stationary data	4900	0.726		
Mobile phones	Model 1	H_0 (M_i): Nonstationary data	19,000	0.001	Strong evidence for M_j	*I(0)*
	Model 2	H_1 (M_j): Stationary data	25,000	84.5		
Internet servers	Model 1	H_0 (M_i): Nonstationary data	62,000	0.041	Strong evidence for M_j	*I(0)*
	Model 2	H_1 (M_j): Stationary data	38,000	24.6		
Broadband providers	Model 1	H_0 (M_i): Nonstationary data	19,000	0.034	Strong evidence for M_j	*I(0)*
	Model 2	H_1 (M_j): Stationary data	62,000	29.1		

Source: From computing

Table 3.2 MS-BVAR model: GDP_{India} = f(fixed phones, mobile phones, Internet users, and broadband providers)

Sector	State	Switching parameter	Duration
Telecommunication sectors	Boom periods	6.912646	7 times
(Fixed phones and mobile phones)	Recession periods	7.087354	7 times
IT sectors	Boom periods	6.815122	7 times
(Internet servers and broadband providers)	Recession periods	7.184878	7 times

Source: From elaborate computing

Table 3.3 Forecasting prior selection for the BVAR model

Sector	State	Prior	RMSE	Selected paper
Telecommunication sector	Boom	Litterman/Minnesota	0.0320	Litterman/Minnesota
		Sims-Zha (Normal-Wishart)	0.3241	
		Sims-Zha (Normal-Flat)	0.1651	
	Recession	Litterman/Minnesota	0.1624	Sims-Zha (Flat-Wishart)
		Sims-Zha (Normal-Wishart)	0.8891	
		Sims-Zha (Normal-Flat)	0.0092	
IT sector	Boom	Litterman/Minnesota	6.5875	Sims-Zha (Normal-Wishart)
		Sims-Zha (Normal-Wishart)	5.4710	
		Sims-Zha (Normal-Flat)	6.5292	
	Recession	Litterman/Minnesota	3.0648	Sims-Zha (Normal-Wishart)
		Sims-Zha (Normal-Wishart)	1.8350	
		Sims-Zha (Normal-Flat)	2.3837	

Source: From elaborate computing

estimated. The second procession of Markov-switching models was employed to seek the periods of boom and recession states in Indian ICT industrial data relating to Indian GDP. The empirical results in this section showed both telecommunication and IT sectors have 7 years in higher response regimes and 7 years in lower response regimes (see the findings in Table 3.2).

In order to verify the prior for Bayesian statistics, the most suitable prior set in each state was chosen by the root mean square error calculation (RMSE), which provided the lowest number between three types of Bayesian priors such as Litterman/Minnesota, Sims-Zha (Normal-Wishart), and Sims-Zha (Flat-Wishart). As seen in the details of Table 3.3, the Litterman and Minnesota prior was selected to be the prior for BVAR estimation in boom periods of telecommunication data. On the other hand, the Flat-Wishart Sims and Zha prior was chosen to forecast the recession situations in the telecommunication sector. Considering IT data, the Normal-Wishart Sims and Zha prior was selected to estimate both boom and recession periods.

Taking into consideration for BVAR estimations, these methods yield dynamic and probabilistic connections which are described by the impulse-response function between the Indian economy and ICT industries. The first evidence estimated from BVAR focused on the booming periods in IT sectors (Internet servers and broadband providers). The result stated that shocks affecting Indian cyber industries had a negative impact on Indian GDP and broadband suppliers in the next 15 years (see the detail in Picture 3.1). Secondly, the forecasting indication in the recession phases of the IT sector is shown in Picture 3.2. It is obvious that the shocks in recession periods from the Internet suppliers inevitably menaced Indian GDP and broadband suppliers, and it seems that economic reformation cannot easily occur during the next 15 years.

Speaking to the third evidence, the dynamic forecasting result of the booming periods in Indian telecommunication such as fixed phone and mobile phone usage is presented in Picture 3.3. The result indicates that disturbances caused by the suppliers of fixed and mobile phones negatively impacted the Indian economy over 5 years, and this would be recovered from the shocks in the next 10 years. Lastly, focusing on the recession time of the Indian telecoms, the impulse-response function is shown in Picture 3.4. The result states that shocks from fixed and mobile phone suppliers had a damaging impact on Indian GDP during the recession period, and it obviously seems this negative situation would not be reformed.

Ultimately, the final section is ICT multipliers based on Bayesian inference. As seen in Table 3.4 below, four parameters estimated by the Bayesian regression model were employed in the Keynesian multiplier theorem. The empirical result shows that the ICT multiplier equals 8.4731. This solution implies one investment unit increasing in Indian ICT production caused Indian GDP to increase by 8.4731 US dollars.

3.8 Conclusion

This paper successfully verified the relationship between Indian ICT industries and GDP by applying Bayesian inference. According to the empirical results, it is evident that ICT and economic data has two regimes in the Indian economic cycle system: booming and recession periods. Specifically considering profitable and downturn periods of IT sectors, the result clearly confirms that shocks which occurred from Internet suppliers have a critically negative impact on broadband productions as well as Indian GDP, and it seems to be sure that neglect of problem solutions can cause the Indian economic system to collapse in at least the next 5 years. As a result, it is undeniable that Indian IT sectors, especially Internet sources, are being prepared to be the essential key for Indian economic growth. Inevitably, high technological industrial zones should be systematically enhanced continuously.

Focusing on the evidence of telecommunication sectors, the result shows that shocks from both fixed phone usage and mobile phone products shortly affected

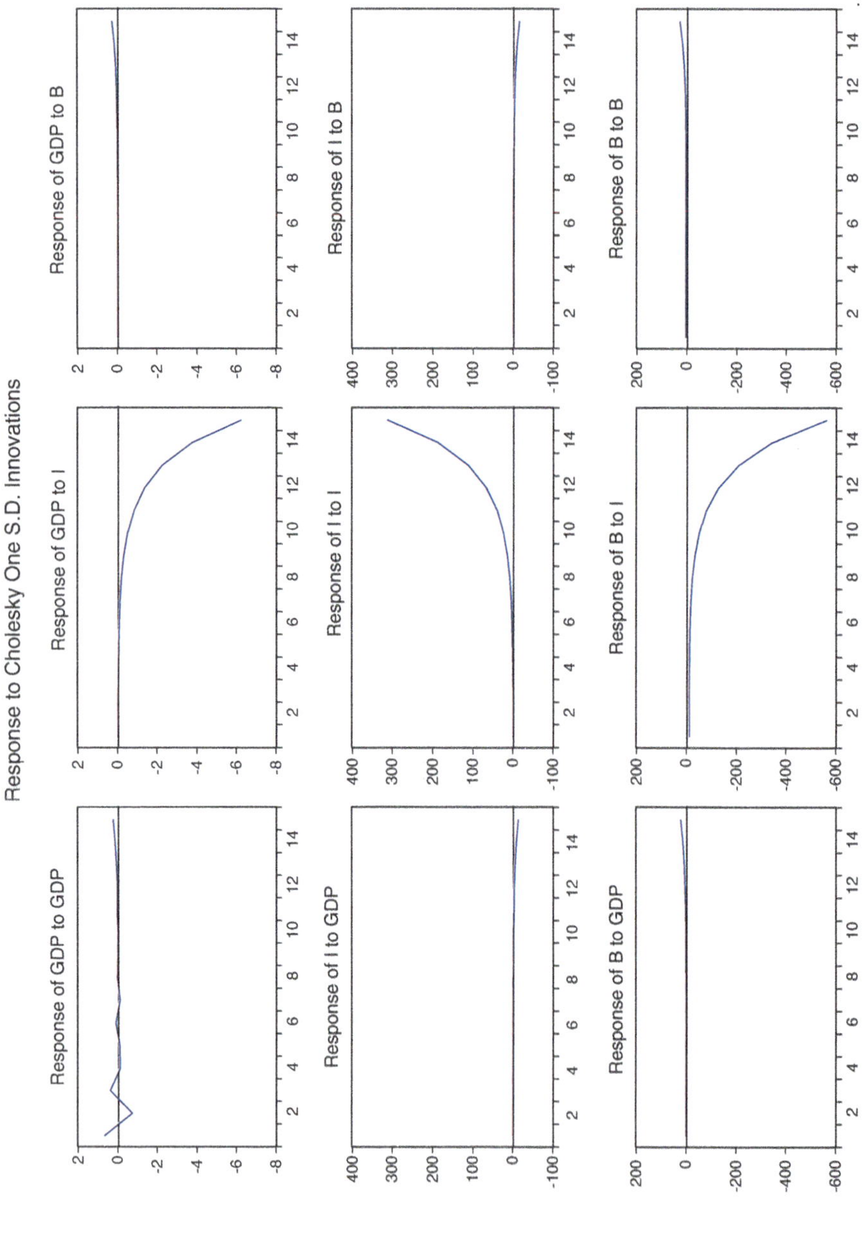

Picture 3.1 Impulse-response function from BVAR: the boom period of IT sector

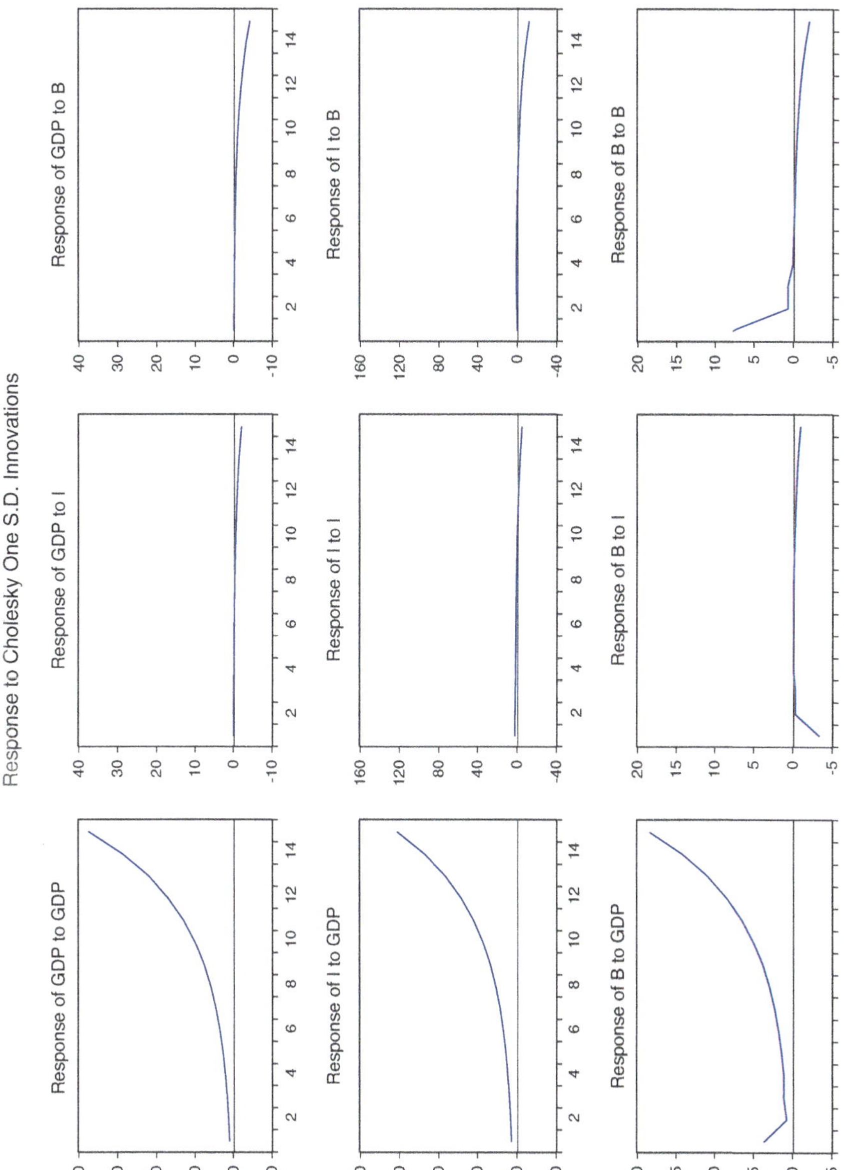

Picture 3.2 Impulse-response function from BVAR: the recession period of IT sector

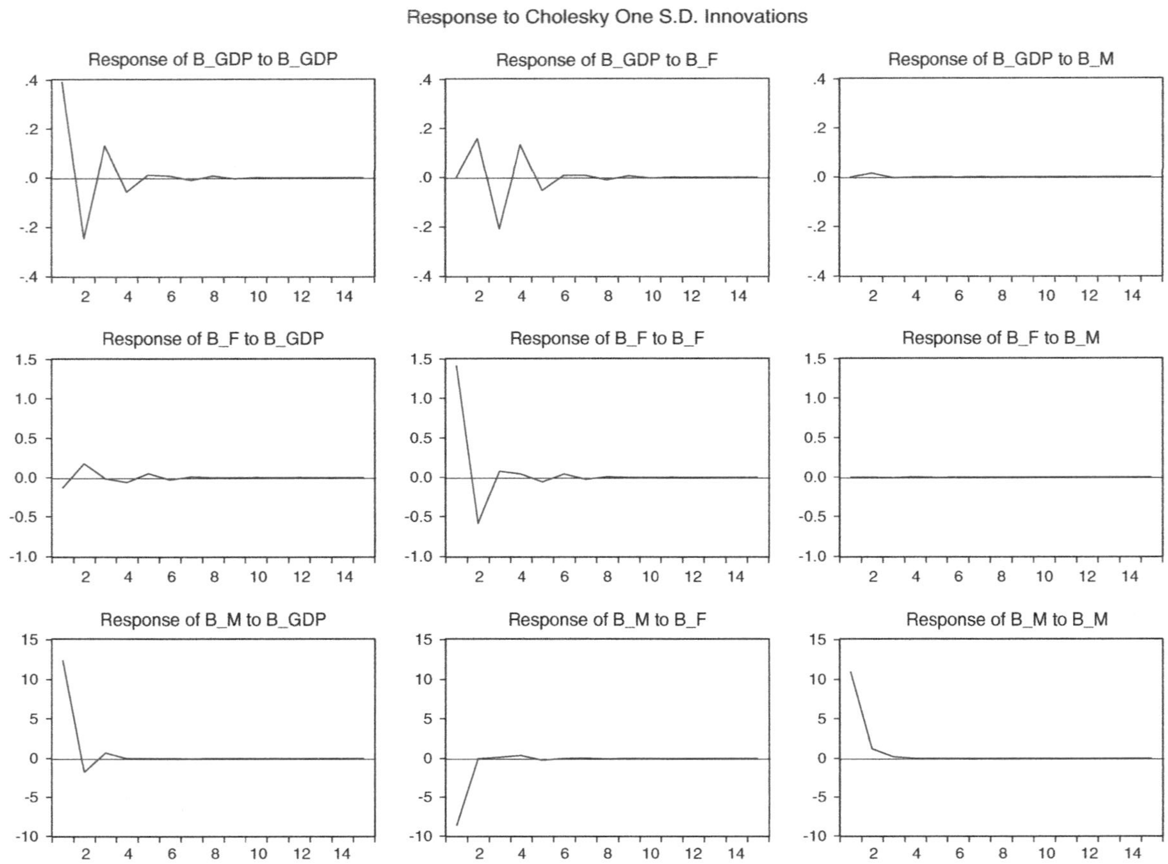

Picture 3.3 Impulse-response function from BVAR: the boom period of telecommunication sector

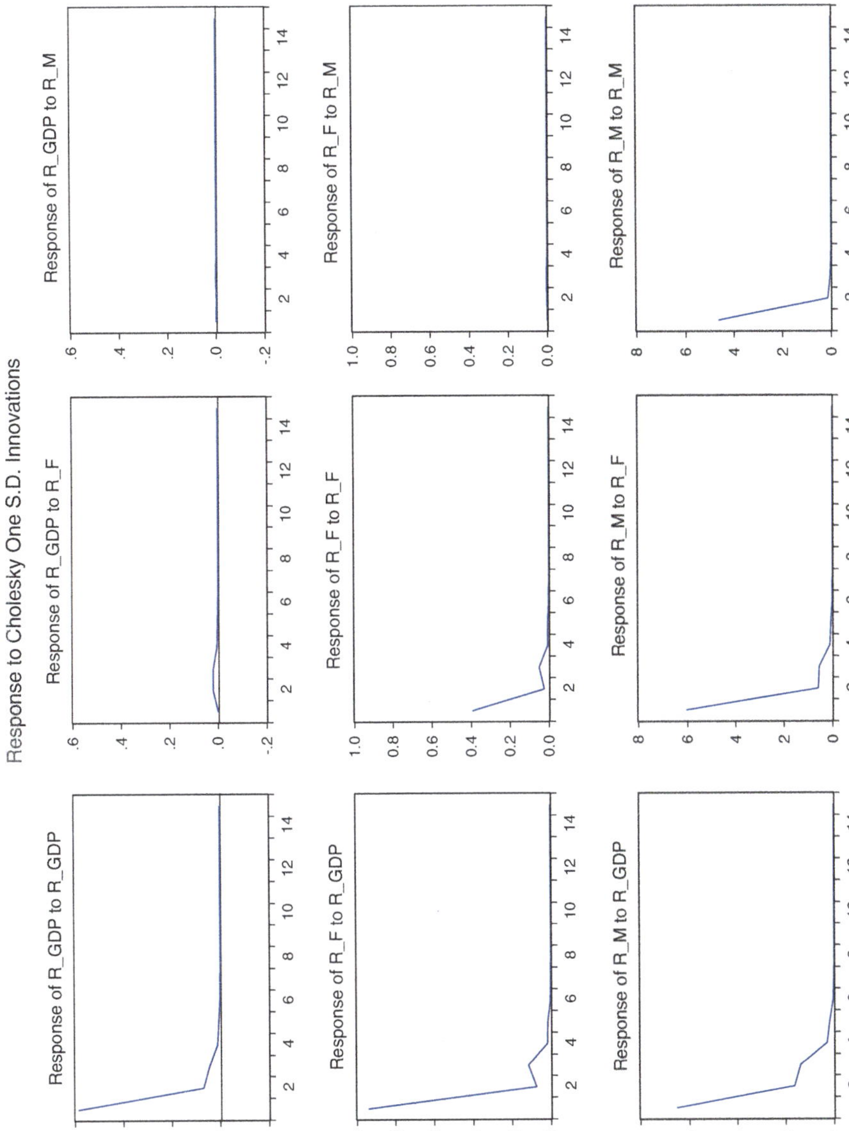

Picture 3.4 Impulse-response function from BVAR: the recession period of telecommunication sector

Table 3.4 The estimated multiplier of Indian IT industries

Variables	Index	Estimated values of parameters
Fixed phone usages	β	−0.1495
Mobile phone usages	δ	0.0079
Internet servers	φ	0.0135
Broadband providers	γ	0.0099
Numbers of data iterations	400	
Log-likelihood	−28.405	
Observations	15	
IT multiplier	*8.4731*	

Source: From computing

Indian GDP in booming and recession situations. This implies that Indian telecom industries are being slowly substituted by IT sectors. Consequently, it is appropriate to suggest policy makers to focus intently on research and development in IT industries rather than relying on the enormous amount of fixed and mobile phone usage. Moreover, the ICT multiplier calculated by the Bayesian regression model supported that Indian IT sectors are becoming the considerable key that vastly drives the Indian economy in the upcoming future.

Acknowledgment The authors would like to sincerely acknowledge the National Research Council of Thailand (NRCT) for the 2016 India research grant, the Indian Council of Social Science Research (ICSSR) for supporting accommodations and transportation costs, and Mr. Jason Petrea for the linguistic checking.

References

Archer, B. (1982). The value of multipliers and their policy implications. *Tourism Management, 3*(4), 236–241.

Brandt, P. T., Freeman, J. R., & Schrodt, P. A. (2011). Real time, time series forecasting of inter- and intra-state political conflict. *Conflict Management and Peace Science, 28*(1), 41–64.

Diniz, M., Pereira, C. A. B., & Stern, J. M. (2011). Unit roots: Bayesian significance test. *Communications in Statistics – Theory and Methods, 40*(23), 4200–4213.

Hamilton, J. (1989). A new approach to the economic analysis of nonstationary time series and business cycle. *Econometrica, 57*(2), 357–384.

Jeffreys, H. (1961). *Theory of probability* (3rd ed.). New York: Oxford University Press.

Koop, G., & Korobilis, D. (2009). Bayesian multivariate time series methods for empirical macroeconomics. MPRA paper no. 20125, University Library of Munich.

Long, J. R., & Plosser, I. C. (1983). Real business cycles. *Journal of Political Economy, 91*, 39–69.

Mallick, S. K., & Sousa, R. M. (2009). Monetary policy and economic activity in the BRICS. Working paper 27/2009, NIPE. Available: http://www.nipe.eeg.uminho.pt/Uploads/WP_2009/NIPE%20WP_27_2009.pdf, http://www.nipe.eeg.uminho.pt/Uploads/WP_2009/NIPE%20WP_27_2009.pdf

Mankiw, N. G. (1989). Real business cycles: A new Keynesian perspective. *Journal of Economic Perspectives, 3*(3), 79–90.

Moreira, R. R., Chaiboonsri, C., & Chaitip, P. (2013). Relationships between effective and expected interest rates as a transmission mechanism for monetary policy: Evidence on the Brazilian economy using MS-models and a Bayesian VAR. *Procedia Economics and Finance, 5*, 563–570.

Rusu, S. (2011). Tourism multiplier effect. *Journal of Economics and Business Research, 1*, 70–76.

Said, S. E., & Dickey, D. (1984). Testing for unit roots in autoregressive moving-average models with unknown order. *Biometrika, 71*, 599–607.

Sims, C. A., & Zha, T. A. (1998). Bayesian methods for dynamic multivariate models. *International Economic Review, 39*(4), 949–968.

Siriphirunphong, D., Chaiboonsri, C., & Saosaovapak, A. (2015). Thai business cycle from macroeconomic model using BVAR and MS-BVAR methods. *International Journal of Social Sciences, 1*(1), 452–466.

Wannapan, S., & Chaiboonsri, C. (2016). Sustainable international tourism demands of Thailand: Evidence from Chinese tourists. Proceedings paper at Actual Economy International Conference, October 2016, Bangkok, Thailand.

Zhu, Q., Zhang, Z., Li, R., Lai, K. K., Wang, S., & Chai, J. (2014). *Structural analysis and total coal demand forecast in China* (pp. 1–20). Discrete Dynamics in Nature and Society. Available: https://doi.org/10.1155/2014/612064.

Chapter 4
Patents and R&D Cartels

Adam Karbowski and Jacek Prokop

Abstract The objective of this paper is to compare the impact of R&D competition and R&D cooperation under patent protection and under no patent protection on enterprise innovation and performance. For simplicity we focus on the case of duopoly. In particular, the impact of R&D competition and R&D cooperation on enterprise research investments, output, market price, company profits, consumer surplus, and total social welfare was investigated. The analysis revealed that when competition is Cournot, for any level of research spillovers, the R&D investments under patent protection are smaller than in the case of no patent protection. When firms create a research cartel, then, for any level of spillovers, the R&D investments will be higher than those under patent protection with Cournot competition. However, they will be higher than the R&D investments when Cournot competition takes place in the case of no patent protection only for relatively high levels of spillovers. When the level of spillovers is relatively low, the R&D investments in the case of Cournot competition with no patents are higher than in the case of research cartel formed by the duopolists.

4.1 Introduction

Kamien et al. (1992) distinguished four different patterns of R&D that may arise in the industry, i.e., (1) R&D competition, (2) R&D cartelization, (3) RJV (research joint venture) competition, and (4) RJV cartelization. R&D competition occurs when companies decide upon their R&D investments unilaterally, so as to maximize individual economic profits. R&D cartelization means that firms coordinate their R&D investments but at the same time maintain competition in the production stage, so as to maximize the sum of their economic profits. RJV competition occurs in

A. Karbowski (✉) · J. Prokop
Department of Business Economics, Warsaw School of Economics, Warsaw, Poland
e-mail: adam.karbowski@sgh.waw.pl; jacek.prokop@sgh.waw.pl

N. Tsounis, A. Vlachvei (eds.), *Advances in Panel Data Analysis in Applied Economic Research*, Springer Proceedings in Business and Economics,
https://doi.org/10.1007/978-3-319-70055-7_4

turn when companies act as in the R&D competition pattern, but the results of R&D activity are fully shared. Last but not least, RJV cartelization translates into forming an RJV in which companies share their knowledge, fully disclose their information, and coordinate their R&D investments, so as to maximize the sum of the overall economic profits (for more details, please see Kamien et al. 1992).

According to Amir et al. (2011), R&D cartels can be perceived as an alternative to noncooperative R&D. The incentives to form an R&D cartel are, according to the abovementioned authors, particularly strong when knowledge spillover rates in the industry are either close to 0% or close to 100%. For mid-level values of technological spillovers, the firms' incentives to create an R&D cartel in the industry are very weak (and completely nonexistent when the knowledge spillover rate in the industry is exactly 50%; cf. Amir et al. 2011). When high-level technological spillovers are a case, forming an R&D cartel in the industry is believed to be an efficient way of internalizing the large knowledge externalities occurring in the market (see, e.g., Bernstein and Nadiri 1988; Kamien et al. 1992; Amir et al. 2011).

Poyago-Theotoky (1999) in a nontournament model and De Fraja (1993) in a tournament model (firms are engaged in a patent race) note that firms can in fact deliberately choose R&D disclosure rates and, to a high extent, determine the level of technological spillovers in the industry. Another thing is the firms' ability to appropriate the disclosed knowledge, e.g., in the form of patents. But nowadays business firms can strategically use technological knowledge generated in the industry, e.g., via different forms of patent licensing or cross-licensing (Haruna 2004).

From the policy-maker's viewpoint, the interesting question is however which form of enterprise R&D – (i) R&D cartel or (ii) R&D competition incentivized by a patent protection – can bring about more innovation. The first form of R&D is oriented at seeking interfirm cooperation at the R&D stage, often leaving benefits from patent protection aside, whereas the second form is targeted at strictly competitive race for a patent that constitutes a reward in the form of a monopoly (see also Karbowski and Prokop 2013). The abovementioned "R&D cartels or patents" dilemma will be succinctly addressed in the following article.

The paper itself is organized as follows. In the next section, the case of a noncooperative duopoly is analyzed, i.e., there is no cartel neither at the R&D stage nor in the final product market. Separately, the analysis is run for (a) no patent protection and (b) patent protection case. In Sect. 4.3, we consider the conduct and performance of companies that formed an R&D cartel and coordinated their R&D expenditures but at the same time maintained competition in the production stage, so as to maximize the sum of their economic profits. Based on the comparison of the above two cases, the conclusions regarding the incentives for the companies to innovate are given in the last section.

4.2 Cournot Competition

Consider an industry composed of two firms, denoted 1 and 2. Firms manufacture q_1 and q_2 units of a homogeneous product, respectively. The market demand for the product is given as a linear price function:

$$p = a - q_1 - q_2 \tag{4.1}$$

where p denotes the market price, q_i is the volume produced by firm i, while a is the demand intercept. Initially, the cost functions of each firm are given by a linear function:

$$\frac{q_i}{c} \tag{4.2}$$

where c is a given parameter of an initial efficiency of firm i.

Since the entry barriers to the industry are assumed to be high, there is no issue of new entry to this industry.

The firms engage in a two-stage game. In the first stage, both companies simultaneously and independently decide about their levels of R&D investments, x_i. The costs of investments are given as a quadratic function:

$$\gamma \frac{x_i^2}{2} \tag{4.3}$$

where γ ($\gamma > 0$) is a constant parameter.

In the second stage, the companies compete in the final product market according to the Cournot model, i.e., they set their production quantities simultaneously and independently. The outcome depends on whether there is patent protection or not.

First, let us consider the case of no patent protection. When firm i invests in R&D, its cost of manufacturing is given by the following function:

$$C_i\left(q_i, x_i, x_j\right) = \frac{q_i}{c + x_i + \beta x_j} \tag{4.4}$$

where x_i denotes the amount of R&D investments made by the company i and x_j denotes the amount of R&D investments made by the competitor. Parameter β ($0 \leq \beta \leq 1$) determines the size of R&D externalities, i.e., the benefits for a given company obtained as a result of research undertaken by the competitor (Geroski 1995; Griliches 1995). Higher level of β means that the R&D investments made by one company allow the competitor to reduce the manufacturing costs by a greater amount for free. The lack of patent protection means that there will be no possibility to exclude the rival from the benefits of R&D investment.

In the case of no patent protection, the profit of firm i in the second stage of the game for a given amount of R&D investments, x_1 and x_2, is given by

$$\pi_i = \left(a - q_i - q_j\right) q_i - \frac{q_i}{c + x_i + \beta x_j} - \gamma \frac{x_i^2}{2} \tag{4.5}$$

The first-order conditions for profit maximization, $\frac{\partial \pi_i}{\partial q_i} = 0$, generate the optimal output level of each firm:

$$q_i = \frac{1}{3}\left(a + \frac{1}{c + \beta x_i + x_j} - \frac{2}{c + x_i + \beta x_j}\right) \tag{4.6}$$

The outputs q_i $(i = 1, 2)$ given by (4.6) constitute the Cournot-Nash equilibrium for given levels of R&D investments, x_1 and x_2.

After substituting (4.6) into (4.5), we obtain the profits of each firm, π_1 and π_2, as the function of research investments, x_1 and x_2.

In the first stage of the game, when firms simultaneously decide about their R&D spendings, the Nash equilibrium strategies are obtained as a solution to the following set of two equations with two unknowns, x_1 and x_2: $\frac{\partial \pi_i}{\partial x_i} = 0$ $(i = 1, 2)$. Under certain conditions satisfied by the parameters a, c, γ and β, the above system has exactly one solution. Let's denote it by x_1^* and x_2^*. Substituting x_1^* and x_2^* for x_1 and x_2 in (4.5), we obtain the equilibrium profits of the firm and denote them by π_1^* and π_2^*. Now, we can also calculate the equilibrium levels of output, q_1^*, and q_2^*. Since the equilibrium is symmetric, we have $x_1^* = x_2^*$, $q_1^* = q_2^*$, and $\pi_1^* = \pi_2^*$.

For the analysis of social efficiency, we also consider consumer surplus and total welfare. The consumer surplus, *CS*, is obtained as the area of a triangle under the demand curve and above the market price. The total welfare, *TW*, is calculated as the sum of consumer surplus and the profits of both firms.

Due to a relatively vague algebraic form of the above solutions, we will use a simplified numerical analysis in order to show possibilities of certain outcomes. For the purpose of this paper, we will restrict our considerations to the case when three parameters of the model are $a = 100$, $c = 1$, and $\gamma = 5$. The results of the calculations for various levels of parameter β are given in Table 4.1.

Using Table 4.1, let us consider the impact of parameter β, i.e., the size of R&D externalities, on the equilibrium conduct of firms. When the external benefits for a given company resulting from the research undertaken by the rival are relatively small (parameter β is low), the R&D investments of each firm are relatively high, and they decline with the growing scale of spillovers. The supply of the final product achieves its maximum for the parameter $\beta = 0.5$, which results in the lowest level of the market price and the highest consumer surplus.

The profits of each firm are growing together with the greater extent of technological spillovers. Thus, when there is no patent protection, both competing firms are interested in the largest extent of technological spillovers.

Table 4.1 Cournot equilibrium under no patent protection for $a = 100$, $c = 1$, $\gamma = 5$, and $\beta \in [0, 1]$

β	x_i^*	q_i^*	p	π_i^*	CS^*	TW^*
0.0	1.46132	33.1979	33.6042	1096.76	2204.20	4397.73
0.1	1.35544	33.1995	33.6010	1097.61	2204.42	4399.65
0.2	1.26125	33.2007	33.5986	1098.31	2204.58	4401.20
0.3	1.17638	33.2015	33.5969	1098.88	2204.69	4402.45
0.4	1.09904	33.2020	33.5959	1099.36	2204.75	4403.46
0.5	1.02784	33.2022	33.5956	1099.74	2204.77	4404.26
0.6	0.96166	33.2020	33.5959	1100.06	2204.75	4404.88
0.7	0.89958	33.2015	33.5969	1100.32	2204.69	4405.32
0.8	0.84083	33.2007	33.5986	1100.52	2204.58	4405.62
0.9	0.78473	33.1995	33.6010	1100.67	2204.42	4405.75
1.0	0.73068	33.1979	33.6042	1100.77	2204.20	4405.73

The total welfare is increasing with the level of technological spillover β growing from 0 to 0.9, but when β gets very close to 1.0, there is a slight decline in the total welfare.

Next, we consider the case of patent protection. When firm i obtains the patent, it reduces its manufacturing cost according to (4.4). However, when firm j $(j \neq i)$ obtains the patent, firm i is not allowed to use the new technology, and its manufacturing cost is characterized by the initial cost function given by (4.2). Assuming that both firms undertake R&D investments, each of them obtains the patent with probability half.

When patent protection is in place, the expected profit of firm i at the second stage of the game is

$$\pi_i^e = pq_i - \gamma \frac{x_i^2}{2} - \left(\frac{1}{c + x_i + \beta x_j} + \frac{1}{c} \right) \frac{q_i}{2} \tag{4.7}$$

For given levels of R&D investments, the optimal production volume of firm i in this case amounts to

$$q_i = \frac{1}{6} \left(2a - \frac{1}{c} + \frac{1}{c + \beta x_i + x_j} - \frac{2}{c + x_i + \beta x_j} \right) \tag{4.8}$$

After substituting (4.8) into (4.7), we obtain the equilibrium expected profit of firm i as the functions of R&D investments, x_1 and x_2:

$$\pi_i^e (x_1, x_2) \tag{4.9}$$

Table 4.2 Cournot equilibrium under patent protection for $a = 100$, $c = 1$, $\gamma = 5$, and $\beta \in [0, 1]$

β	$\hat{x}_i$	$\hat{q}_i$	$\hat{p}$	$\hat{\pi}_i^e$	$\widehat{CS}$	$\widehat{TW}$
0.0	1.04985	33.0854	33.8293	1091.89	2189.28	4373.05
0.1	0.97535	33.0863	33.8275	1092.32	2189.40	4374.05
0.2	0.90864	33.0869	33.8261	1092.68	2189.49	4374.85
0.3	0.84819	33.0874	33.8252	1092.98	2189.55	4375.51
0.4	0.79280	33.0877	33.8247	1093.22	2189.59	4376.03
0.5	0.74156	33.0878	33.8245	1093.43	2189.60	4376.45
0.6	0.69370	33.0877	33.8247	1093.59	2189.59	4376.77
0.7	0.64861	33.0874	33.8252	1093.72	2189.55	4377.00
0.8	0.60576	33.0869	33.8261	1093.83	2189.49	4377.15
0.9	0.56468	33.0863	33.8275	1093.90	2189.40	4377.21
1.0	0.52493	33.0854	33.8293	1093.95	2189.28	4377.19

The Nash equilibrium strategies at the first stage of the game are found as a solution to the following system of two equations with two unknowns x_1 and x_2: $\frac{\partial \pi_i^e}{\partial x_i} = 0$ $(i = 1, 2)$. Under certain restrictions on the value of parameters a, c, β, and γ, the above system has exactly one solution; denote it by $\hat{x}_1$ and $\hat{x}_2$. Substituting $\hat{x}_1$ and $\hat{x}_2$ for x_1 and x_2 in (4.8), we obtain the equilibrium outputs of firms; denote them by $\hat{q}_1$ and $\hat{q}_2$. Now, we can also calculate the equilibrium expected profits of the firms and denote them by $\hat{\pi}_1^e$ and $\hat{\pi}_2^e$. Observe that the equilibrium is symmetric; thus $\hat{x}_1 = \hat{x}_2$, $\hat{q}_1 = \hat{q}_2$, and $\hat{\pi}_1^e = \hat{\pi}_2^e$.

Table 4.2 shows the Cournot equilibrium under patent protection for various levels of parameter β.

From Table 4.2, it follows that under patent protection, the changes of the technological spillovers measured by β have similar impact on the Cournot equilibrium as in the case of no patent protection. However, comparing Tables 4.1 and 4.2, it can be concluded that for every level of spillovers, the research investments of firms are lower in the case of patent protection than in the case of no patents $\left(\hat{x}_i < x_i^*\right)$. Thus, the tournament effect discussed by Chowdhury (2005) is confirmed, i.e., the existence of patent protection reduces the R&D spendings. Interestingly enough, the consumer surplus $\left(\widehat{CS}\right)$ and the total welfare $\left(\widehat{TW}\right)$ are also lower in the case of patent protection.

Now, we move on to analyze the cooperation of firms in the R&D stage and competition in the final product market.

4.3 R&D Cartel

For the sake of comparison, we now consider a model in which the companies have formed a cartel at the R&D stage but compete according to the Cournot model in the final product market. We assume that the demand function as well as the cost functions of the firms are the same as in the previous section. When firm creates an R&D cartel, the existence of patent protection plays no role as long as the cooperation is not discontinued.[1]

At the second stage of the game, the companies choose the production levels q_1 and q_2 simultaneously and independently to maximize their individual profits given by (4.5), for the fixed amounts of R&D investments, x_1 and x_2.

At the Cournot-Nash equilibrium, the optimal production level of each firm is calculated according to (4.6). After substituting (4.6) into (4.5), we obtain the profits of each firm, π_1 and π_2, as the function of research investments, x_1 and x_2.

In the first stage of the game, the companies choose the R&D investments, x_1 and x_2, to maximize their joint profit, $\pi(x_1, x_2) = \pi_1 + \pi_2$. When the firms cooperate within an R&D cartel, the equilibrium arises when the research investments of each of the companies are the solution to

$$\frac{\partial \pi}{\partial x_i} = 0 \quad \text{for } i = 1, 2 \; <?pag? > \tag{4.10}$$

denoted it by $\widetilde{x}_i$. Since the equilibrium is symmetric, we have $\widetilde{x}_1 = \widetilde{x}_2$. The production level of each of the firms is obtained by substituting $\widetilde{x}_i$ for x_i in (4.6); denote the equilibrium quantity by $\widetilde{q}_i$; again $\widetilde{q}_1 = \widetilde{q}_2$. The equilibrium price of the final product offered by the companies is calculated by substituting $\widetilde{q}_i$ for q_1 and q_2 in (4.1); denote that price by $\widetilde{p}$.

Finally, the profit of each of the firms in the situation of R&D cooperation and Cournot competition in the final product market is obtained by substituting $\widetilde{x}_i$ for x_1 and x_2 and by substituting $\widetilde{q}_i$ for q_1 and q_2 in (4.5); denote the equilibrium profit of firm i by $\widetilde{\pi}_i$; since the equilibrium is symmetric, we have $\widetilde{\pi}_1 = \widetilde{\pi}_2$.

For the sake of a comparison with the results obtained in the previous section, we will limit our numerical analysis to the case when the parameters are $a = 100$, $c = 1$, and $\gamma = 5$. The results of the calculations for various levels of parameter β have been presented in the Table 4.3.

Using Table 4.3, let us consider the equilibrium behavior of firms, for various levels of the parameter β, i.e., the size of technological spillovers. In the case of cooperation in the R&D stage, together with the increase in the scale of R&D externalities, there is also a decline in research investments aimed at the reduction of production costs. At the same time, we observe an increase in the supply of final products offered by each of the firms. That results in price reductions of the manufactured products when the amount of spillovers increases. Finally, the profits of each firm operating in an R&D cartel increase monotonically together with the growing extent of research externalities.

By comparing Tables 4.2 and 4.3, we observe that when firms cooperate in the research activities, the level of R&D investments is higher than in the case of competitive outcome under patent protection ($\widetilde{x}_i > \hat{x}_i$). Thus, similar to the

[1]A cartel disruption may lead to patent disputes and lawsuits. We do not consider such possibilities in this paper.

conclusions of Che and Yang (2009), the existence of a research cartel generates higher incentives to innovate than in the case of full competition under patent protection.

The equilibrium levels of product manufacturing are higher in the case of R&D cartel rather than when the firms fully compete under patent protection. Since the consumer surplus is directly linked to the output levels, it is greater in the case of R&D cooperation rather than in the noncooperative situation under patent protection $\left(\widetilde{CS} > \widehat{CS}\right)$. Also, profits earned by the companies are clearly higher when the R&D cartel is formed. Thus, the cooperation of firms in the research stage results in an increased social welfare in comparison to the noncooperative case under patent protection $\left(\widetilde{TW} > \widehat{TW}\right)$.

By comparing Tables 4.1 and 4.3, we observe that when firms cooperate in research and development, the level of R&D expenditures is higher than in the case of competitive outcome with no patents, but only for relatively high values of technological spillovers in the industry ($\beta \geq 0.5$). This result is in line with the previous literature that treats R&D cooperation as an efficient way of internalizing the large knowledge externalities occurring in the market (see, e.g., Bernstein and Nadiri, 1988; Kamien et al., 1992; Amir et al., 2011; Karbowski, 2016). The equilibrium levels of product manufacturing are higher in the case of R&D cartel rather than when the firms fully compete under no patent protection, but again for $\beta \geq 0.5$. For this range of technological spillover values, the equilibrium price is higher under competition with no patents than under R&D cartel, but company profits are significantly lower. What is also interesting, for a relatively high level of knowledge spillovers (threshold at 0.5), is that the values of consumer surplus and total welfare are higher under R&D cartel than under R&D competition with no patents.

Table 4.3 Equilibrium in the model of R&D cooperation and final product competition

β	$\widetilde{x}_i$	$\widetilde{q}_i$	$\widetilde{p}$	$\widetilde{\pi}_i$	$\widetilde{CS}$	$\widetilde{TW}$
0.0	1.05119	33.1708	33.6583	1097.54	2200.61	4395.69
0.1	1.04896	33.1786	33.6429	1098.07	2201.64	4397.77
0.2	1.04505	33.1855	33.6291	1098.54	2202.55	4399.64
0.3	1.04000	33.1916	33.6168	1098.98	2203.37	4401.32
0.4	1.03418	33.1972	33.6057	1099.38	2204.10	4402.86
0.5	1.02784	33.2022	33.5956	1099.74	2204.77	4404.26
0.6	1.02117	33.2068	33.5864	1100.08	2205.38	4405.55
0.7	1.01429	33.2110	33.5780	1100.40	2205.94	4406.73
0.8	1.00730	33.2148	33.5703	1100.69	2206.45	4407.83
0.9	1.00027	33.2184	33.5632	1100.96	2206.93	4408.85
1.0	0.99326	33.2217	33.5566	1101.22	2207.37	4409.80

4.4 Concluding Remarks

In this paper, we analyzed the impact of, first, R&D competition (i) with and (ii) without patents and, second, R&D cooperation in the form of R&D cartel on enterprise innovation and performance. In particular, the impact of R&D competition and R&D cooperation on enterprise research investments, output, market price, company profits, consumer surplus, and total social welfare was investigated. The analysis revealed that when competition is Cournot, for any level of research spillovers, the R&D investments under patent protection are smaller than in the case of no patent protection. When firms create a research cartel, then, for any level of spillovers, the R&D investments will be higher than those under patent protection with Cournot competition. However, they will be higher than the R&D investments when Cournot competition takes place in the case of no patent protection only for higher levels of spillovers ($\beta \geq 0.5$). When the level of spillovers is relatively low ($\beta \leq 0.4$), the R&D investments in the case of Cournot competition with no patents are higher than in the case of research cartel formed by the duopolists.

The above results are in line with the previous knowledge on the topic. Claude d'Aspremont and Alexis Jacquemin (1988) stated that when companies behave strategically, R&D cooperation leads to more R&D than R&D competition when knowledge spillovers are large but less R&D when technological spillovers are relatively small. This is also a case in our study. What is more, our research shows that R&D cooperation between firms promotes enterprise innovation to a higher extent than R&D competition incentivized by patents. This may constitute one more argument against patents (see, e.g., Boldrin and Levine 2013; Karbowski and Prokop 2013).

References

Amir, R., Garcia, F., Halmenschlager, C., & Pais, J. (2011). R&D as a prisoner's dilemma and R&D-avoiding Cartels. *The Manchester School, 79*, 81–99.

Bernstein, J., & Nadiri, I. (1988). Interindustry R&D spillovers, rates of return, and production in high-tech industries. *American Economic Review, 78*, 429–434.

Boldrin, M., & Levine, D. (2013). The case against patents. *Journal of Economic Perspectives, 27*, 3–22.

Che, X., & Yang, Y. (2009). Patent protection with cooperative R&D option. Working paper.

Chowdhury, P. R. (2005). Patents and R&D: The tournament effect. *Economics Letters, 89*, 120–126.

d'Aspremont, C., & Jacquemin, A. (1988). Cooperative and noncooperative R&D in Duopoly with spillovers. *American Economic Review, 78*, 1133–1137.

De Fraja, G. (1993). Strategic spillovers in patent races. *International Journal of Industrial Organization, 11*, 139–146.

Geroski, P. (1995). Do spillovers undermine the incentive to innovate? In S. Dowrick (Ed.), *Economic approaches to innovation*. Aldershot: Edward Elgar.

Griliches, Z. (1995). R&D and productivity: Econometric results and productivity issues. In P. Stoneman (Ed.), *Handbook of the economics of innovation and technological change*. Oxford: Basil Blackwell.

Haruna, S. (2004). Disclosure policy, and competition and cartelization in R&D: Cournot and Bertrand competition. Working paper.

Kamien, M. I., Muller, E., & Zang, I. (1992). Research joint ventures and R&D Cartels. *The American Economic Review, 82*, 1293–1306.

Karbowski, A. (2016). The elasticity-based approach to enterprise innovation. *International Journal of Management and Economics, 49*, 58–78.

Karbowski, A., & Prokop, J. (2013). Controversy over the economic justifications for patent protection. *Procedia – Economics and Finance, 5*, 393–402.

Poyago-Theotoky, J. (1999). A note on endogenous spillovers in a non-tournament R&D Duopoly. *Review of Industrial Organization, 15*, 253–262.

Chapter 5
A Mean-Variance Analysis of the Global Minimum Variance Portfolio Constructed Using the CARBS Indices

Coenraad C. A. Labuschagne, Niel Oberholzer, and Pierre J. Venter

Abstract The purpose of this paper is to construct a global minimum variance portfolio (GMVP) using the log returns of the CARBS (Canada, Australia, Russia, Brazil, South Africa) indices. The weights obtained indicate that most of the portfolio should be invested in Canadian equity. The returns series of the CARBS and the GMVP seem to be consistent with the stylized facts of financial time series. Further empirical analysis shows that the CAPM relationship holds for Canada, South Africa, and the GMVP. The systematic risk (β) of the GMVP is the lowest, and the Russian equity index is the highest. However the R^2 of all the models indicate that the CAPM relationship is not a good fit for all the variables and can therefore not be considered a reliable measure of risk.

5.1 Introduction

This paper derives an expression for the portfolio weights of a GMVP that consists of the CARBS equity indices. The method is based on constant means, variances, and covariances determined using historical data. The risk of the individual assets and the portfolio is then measured using classical methods; this gives an opportunity to compare the measured risk of the individual assets and the portfolio. And in later chapters, compare the measured risk using classical methods to the risk obtained using volatility models.

Conventional wisdom among finance researchers and practitioners is that it is necessary to diversify. Diversification is necessary to reduce the level of idiosyncratic risk. However, another important aspect to consider is how to determine the weight of each asset in a diversified portfolio. Furthermore, by minimizing risk, it is

C. C. A. Labuschagne (✉) · N. Oberholzer · P. J. Venter
Department of Finance and Investment Management, University of Johannesburg, Johannesburg, South Africa
e-mail: ccalabuschagne@uj.ac.za; nielo@uj.ac.za; pventer@uj.ac.za

N. Tsounis, A. Vlachvei (eds.), *Advances in Panel Data Analysis in Applied Economic Research*, Springer Proceedings in Business and Economics,
https://doi.org/10.1007/978-3-319-70055-7_5

possible that the return might be insignificant. Therefore, a GMVP is constructed in this chapter. By viewing each asset simultaneously in mean-variance space, it will in some cases be clear which asset is more attractive than another.

In mean-variance space, it is that an asset with a greater return, but less risk, is more attractive than an asset with a lower return and the same level of risk or greater. This is referred to as mean-variance dominance (Bailey 2005). Therefore, the validity of the capital asset pricing model (CAPM) relationship is tested in this chapter. This gives an indication of the level of systematic risk and the expected return. The method used gives an indication of the goodness of fit of the model; this determines the applicability.

In this paper, the relevant literature on mean-variance analysis will be discussed, and the dataset of the CARBS indices will be analyzed. Using the data, a GMVP will be constructed. In addition, the risk-return trade-off of the CARBS indices and the GMVP will be illustrated; finally the CAPM relationship will be estimated for the CARBS indices and the GMVP. The empirical analysis of this chapter makes extensive use of the `PerformanceAnalytics` package (Carl et al. 2008) of the `R` statistical programming language.

5.2 Literature Review

Several existing papers make use of matrix algebra techniques to construct a GMVP, or a target return portfolio that minimizes risk. Watson and Seetharam (2014) estimated a GMVP which included the equity indices of the BRICS (Brazil, Russia, India, China, and South Africa). The purpose of the analysis was to determine which indices are the most significant. The findings suggest that more than half of the GMVP should be invested in South African equity. Moreover, Brazilian and Russian equity are insignificant when constructing a GMVP for the BRICS equity indices.

Cardoso (2015) constructed efficient portfolios using 15 equity shares on the S&P500 index; both the maximum likelihood and robust methods were used. In order to test the performance of the methods, Cardoso (2015) performed two Monte Carlo simulations, one assuming a normal distribution and another with contaminated non-normal samples. The results show that when a normal distribution is assumed, the maximum likelihood method outperforms the robust method. However, the robust method proved to be more efficient when non-normal samples were used.

Li et al. (2003) investigated the benefit of diversification subject to portfolio weight restrictions, more specifically constraints on short-selling. The portfolio was constructed by minimizing the variance, subject to two constraints: the portfolio weights must sum to one and weights cannot be negative. Using a dataset that consists the dollar denominated equity indices of seven developed countries, and eight emerging countries, the results indicate that short-sale constraint reduce, but do not eliminate the benefit of diversification.

There have also been many studies that have tested the validity of the CAPM relationship. Iqbal and Brooks (2007) tested the linearity of the CAPM relationship of the Karachi equity index and found that the relationship between risk and return is generally not linear, which is inconsistent with the relationship predicted by the CAPM.

In a similar, more recent study, Ali and Ali (2010) tested the applicability of the CAPM relationship for the Dhaka (Bangladesh) equity index. In terms of methodology, the Fama and MacBeth approach was used. The findings finally showed that the systematic risk coefficient is not sufficient to explain the risks for returns. Hence it is necessary to consider other factors in addition to the risk premium of the market portfolio.

5.3 Portfolio Theory: Matrix Algebra

The objective of this section is to derive an expression for the weighting of each asset included in a GMVP, when five assets are included in the portfolio. The following derivation follows Zivot (2011) closely. Let R_i[1] denote the return on asset i and σ_{ij} the covariance between rates of return R_i and R_j (for $i, j = 1, 2, .., 5$). Furthermore, assume that R_i is identically and independently (normally) distributed, with constant mean and variance. More specifically,

$$R_i \sim \mathcal{N}\left(\mu_i, \sigma_i^2\right)$$
$$\text{cov}\left(R_i, R_j\right) = \sigma_{ij}.$$

A portfolio can be defined as a vector of asset holdings with weighting, $\omega_1, \omega_2, \ldots, \omega_5$. Bailey (2005) explains that the expected rate of return (μ_p) and variance of the rate of return (σ_p^2) of a portfolio that contains five risky assets take the form

$$\mu_p = \sum_{i=1}^{5} \omega_i \mu_i, \text{and} \tag{5.1}$$

$$\sigma_p^2 = \sum_{i=1}^{5} \sum_{j=1}^{5} \omega_i \omega_j \sigma_{ij}. \tag{5.2}$$

To find an expression for the weighting of each asset included in a GMVP, the following problem needs to be evaluated:

The problem is given by

$$\min_{\sum_{i=1}^{5} \omega_i = 1} \left\{ \sum_{i=1}^{5} \sum_{j=1}^{5} \omega_i \omega_j \sigma_{ij} \right\}.$$

[1] $R_{i,t} = \ln\left(\frac{S_{i,t+1}}{S_{i,t}}\right)$ where $S_{i,t}$ is the value of asset i at time t and $t \in \mathbb{N}$.

This implies that we need to minimize the variance of the portfolio, subject to the constraint that the sum of the portfolio weightings should be equal to one.

The method of Lagrange multipliers is used to solve the problem above. The method of Lagrange multipliers is best explained by the following theorem from Wrede and Spiegel (2010)

Theorem 1 *A method for obtaining the relative maximum or minimum values of a function $F(x, y, z)$ subject to the constraint $\phi(x, y, z) = 0$ consists of the formation of the auxiliary function*

$$L(x, y, z, \lambda) = F(x, y, z) + \lambda\phi(x, y, z)$$

subject to the conditions

$$\frac{\partial L}{\partial x} = 0, \qquad \frac{\partial L}{\partial y} = 0, \qquad \frac{\partial L}{\partial z} = 0, \qquad \frac{\partial L}{\partial \lambda} = 0,$$

which are required conditions for a relative maximum or minimum.

The Lagrangian for minimization problem 5.3 is given by

$$L(\omega_1, \omega_2, \omega_3, \omega_4, \omega_5, \lambda) = \sum_{i=1}^{5}\sum_{j=1}^{5} \omega_i\omega_j\sigma_{ij} + \lambda\left(\sum_{i=1}^{5} \omega_i - 1\right).$$

The first order conditions are given by

$$\frac{\partial L}{\partial \omega_i} = \sum_{j=1}^{5} \omega_j\sigma_{ij} = 0, \text{for } i = 1, 2, \ldots, 5,$$

$$\frac{\partial L}{\partial \lambda} = \sum_{i=1}^{5} \omega_i - 1 = 0$$

The first order conditions give rise to the following system of linear equations

$$\begin{bmatrix} 2\sigma_1^2 & 2\sigma_{12} & 2\sigma_{13} & 2\sigma_{14} & 2\sigma_{15} & 1 \\ 2\sigma_{12} & 2\sigma_2^2 & 2\sigma_{23} & 2\sigma_{24} & 2\sigma_{25} & 1 \\ 2\sigma_{13} & 2\sigma_{23} & 2\sigma_3^2 & 2\sigma_{34} & 2\sigma_{35} & 1 \\ 2\sigma_{14} & 2\sigma_{24} & 2\sigma_{34} & 2\sigma_4^2 & 2\sigma_{45} & 1 \\ 2\sigma_{15} & 2\sigma_{25} & 2\sigma_{35} & 2\sigma_{45} & 2\sigma_5^2 & 1 \\ 1 & 1 & 1 & 1 & 1 & 0 \end{bmatrix} \begin{bmatrix} \omega_1 \\ \omega_2 \\ \omega_3 \\ \omega_4 \\ \omega_5 \\ \lambda \end{bmatrix} = \begin{bmatrix} 0 \\ 0 \\ 0 \\ 0 \\ 0 \\ 1 \end{bmatrix}.$$

For any system of linear equations $Ax = b$, the solution is equal to $x = A^{-1}b$. Solving the above system of linear equations will provide the necessary portfolio weights $(\omega_1, \ldots, \omega_5)$ to construct a GMVP.

Table 5.1 Indices used in this study

Country	Index
Canada	S&P/TSX 60
Australia	A&P/ASX All Australian 50
Russia	IRTS
Brazil	IBRX
South Africa	FTSE/JSE Top 40
USA	Dow Jones Composite

5.4 The Dataset

The purpose of this section is to illustrate the statistical properties of the dataset used in this study. In order to avoid loss of information, daily data from 11 January 2010 to 31 December 2015 was used for the purpose of most of the empirical analysis that follow.[2] Missing data points were interpolated using a cubic spline. Data from 2010 was used to exclude the Global Financial Crisis (GFC) period which is considered a structural break in the data. When financial time series data is considered, Embrechts et al. (2005) outline the following stylized facts:

1. Return series show little autocorrelation.
2. Squared returns show evidence of significant autocorrelation.
3. The conditional expectation of returns is close to zero.
4. Volatility seems to fluctuate over time.
5. Return series show signs of leptokurtosis or fat tails.
6. Return series exhibit evidence of volatility clustering.

The following indices are used in this study: The Dow Jones will be used as a benchmark in the empirical analysis (Table 5.1).

5.4.1 Graphical Analysis

From the above, it is evident that the index values of all the indices are trended, except Russia, which seems to be mean reverting. Furthermore, the log returns of the indices all seem to be mean reverting and also tend to exhibit signs of volatility clustering. Brooks (2014) explains that volatility clustering is the tendency for volatility to occur in bunches; hence periods of high volatility are usually followed by periods of high volatility, and low volatility is expected to follow low volatility. This will be investigated in more detail in later chapters. The line graphs above are consistent with facts 4 and 6 listed above (Fig. 5.1).

[2]The data was obtained from the Thomson Reuters Eikon databank.

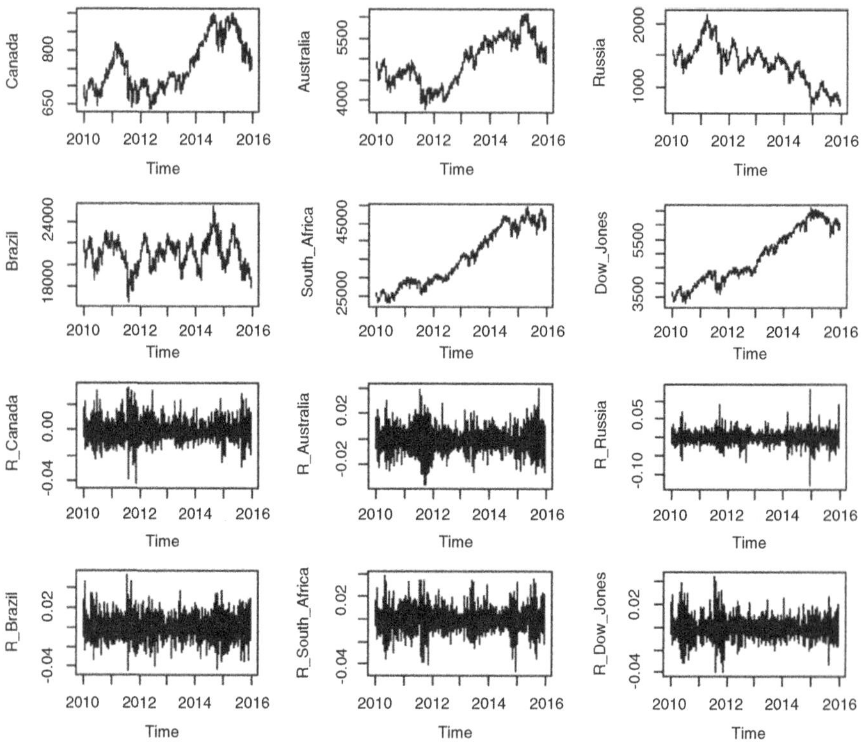

Fig. 5.1 Line graphs of the CARBS indices

Figure 5.2 illustrates the histograms of the log returns of the indices; the normal density (in red) is also included for comparison purposes. The log return series do not seem normally distributed. The log return series are more highly peaked at the mean and show signs of fat tails; this is referred to as leptokurtosis. In addition, the mean of the log return series seems to be approximately equal to zero in each case. The histograms provide evidence of facts 3 and 5 mentioned above.

Tsay (2005) explains that the ACF is the correlation of a variable and lagged values of itself. Figure 5.3 shows that the log returns do not exhibit signs of high autocorrelation. When there is autocorrelation, it seems to die out immediately. However, when the squared returns are considered (Fig. 5.3), there is evidence of significant autocorrelation. This is consistent with the stylized facts of financial time series.

Another important aspect to consider in this section is the statistical properties of the GMVP. By making use of the data of the CARBS indices, a GMVP is constructed by using the method outlined in Sect. 5.3. The weights obtained are given by the table below (Table 5.2):

The portfolio weights above show that most of the GMVP should be invested in Canadian equity, which is close to half of the portfolio. Similar to the findings

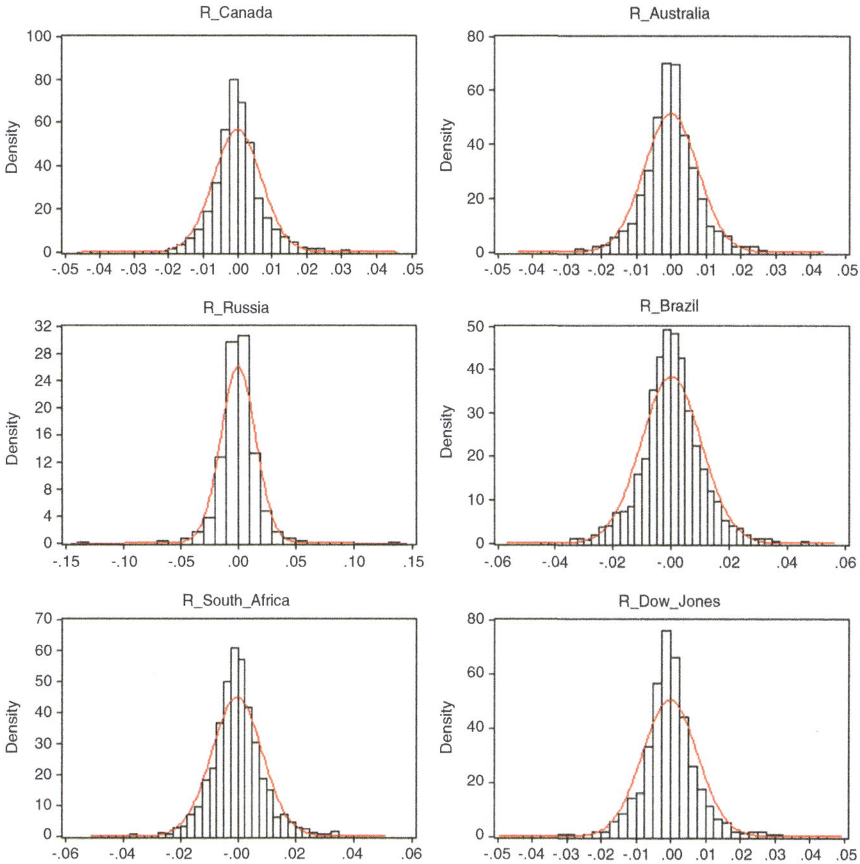

Fig. 5.2 Histograms of the log returns

by Watson and Seetharam (2014), a small amount of the portfolio is invested in Brazilian equity. A negative amount (sell short) should be invested in Russian equity. Finally, a small positive amount should be invested in South African equity (Fig. 5.4).

As mentioned, the return of the portfolio is given by Eq. 5.1. The line graph below illustrates the returns of the GMVP: It is evident that the log returns of the portfolio also show signs of volatility clustering. Furthermore, the time series seems to be mean reverting; the mean is approximately equal to zero. The histogram also indicates that the mean of the distribution is close to zero. In addition, the histogram shows signs of leptokurtosis which is consistent with the stylized facts of financial time series (Fig. 5.5).

Finally, Fig. 5.6 shows that there does not seem to be significant autocorrelation when the log returns are considered. However, the squared log returns show signs of profound autocorrelation. It is important to note that visual methods are subjective and not always reliable. Therefore, the descriptive statistics are considered in the following subsection.

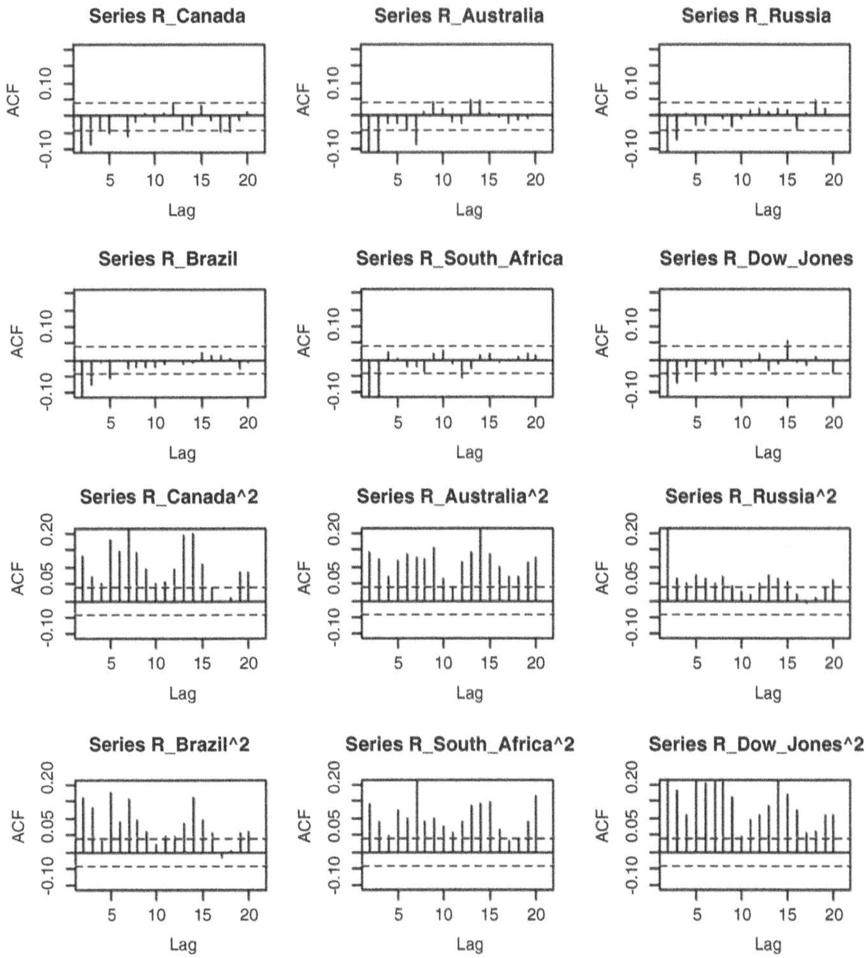

Fig. 5.3 Autocorrelation function (ACF) graphs

Table 5.2 GMVP weights

Country	Weight
Canada	0.4760
Australia	0.3899
Russia	−0.0851
Brazil	0.0485
South Africa	0.1707

5.4.2 Descriptive Statistics

The descriptive statistics in the table above confirm our expectations (Table 5.3). The mean is approximately equal to zero for each index. The Jarque-Bera probability

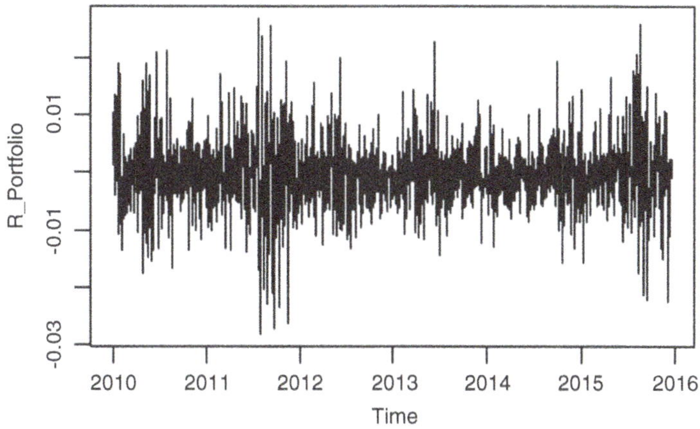

Fig. 5.4 Log returns of the GMVP

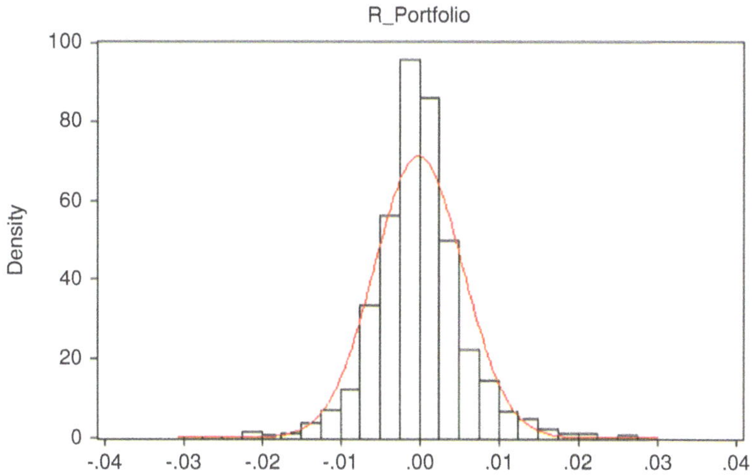

Fig. 5.5 Histogram of the log returns of the GMVP

shows that all the return series are not normally distributed. The skewness and kurtosis show that the return series are slightly positively skewed and all show signs of leptokurtosis (kurtosis > 3).

It is evident that the standard deviation of the GMVP is less than the individual assets (CARBS indices); this is consistent with expectations. The standard deviation of the GMVP is also slightly less than the standard deviation of the Dow Jones index. Moreover, based on the standard deviation, the Russian equity index is the most volatile.

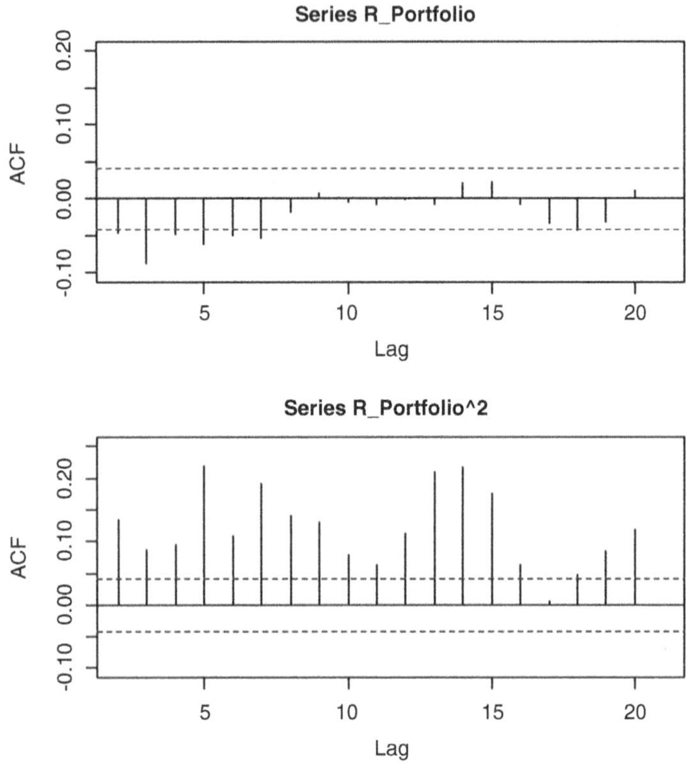

Fig. 5.6 Autocorrelation function (ACF) graphs of the GMVP

Table 5.3 Descriptive statistics of the log returns

	R_Can	R_Aus	R_Rus	R_Bra	R_SA	R_DJ	R_GMVP
Mean	0	0	0.0004	0.0001	−0.0003	−0.0002	−0.0001
Median	−0.0003	−0.0001	0.0002	0	−0.0006	−0.0004	−0.0003
Maximum	0.0334	0.0401	0.1325	0.052	0.0384	0.0448	0.0267
Minimum	−0.0424	−0.0361	−0.1325	−0.0445	−0.0468	−0.0402	−0.0279
Std. Dev.	0.0070	0.0078	0.0154	0.0104	0.0089	0.0079	0.0056
Skewness	0.2039	0.1241	0.2105	0.056	0.1452	0.3683	0.1640
Kurtosis	6.2056	5.1704	10.9406	4.7523	5.3709	7.1022	6.0977
Jarque-Bera	948	433	5743	280	518	1577	881
Probability	0	0	0	0	0	0	0
Sum	−0.0865	−0.0698	0.8089	0.2213	−0.5777	−0.4921	−0.2251

5.5 Empirical Results

In this section, the risk vs return trade-off of the different indices included in this study will be analyzed. This will provide an indication of whether it would be more beneficial to invest in individual portfolios rather than the GMVP. Furthermore, the systematic risk of the different indices will be estimated in the CAPM framework. The Dow Jones index will be used as a benchmark.

For the purpose of this empirical analysis, monthly return data was used. According to Bodie et al. (2013), it is common to assume that treasury bills are risk-free. Because treasury bills are relatively short-term investments, hence their prices are usually insensitive to changes in interest rates. Monthly data for the US Treasury bill rate was obtained from the IMF International Financial Statistics databank.

5.5.1 Mean-Variance Approach

Figure 5.7 above illustrates the risk-return trade-off of the CARBS indices and the GMVP; the dotted lines give an indication of the Sharpe ratio which is given by

$$\frac{R_i - R_f}{\sigma_i}.$$

Consider the following definition of mean-variance dominance from Bailey (2005).

Portfolio A mean-variance dominates portfolio B if either of the following conditions are satisfied.

1. $R_A \geq R_B$ and $\sigma_A < \sigma_B$
2. $R_A > R_B$ and $\sigma_A \leq \sigma_B$.

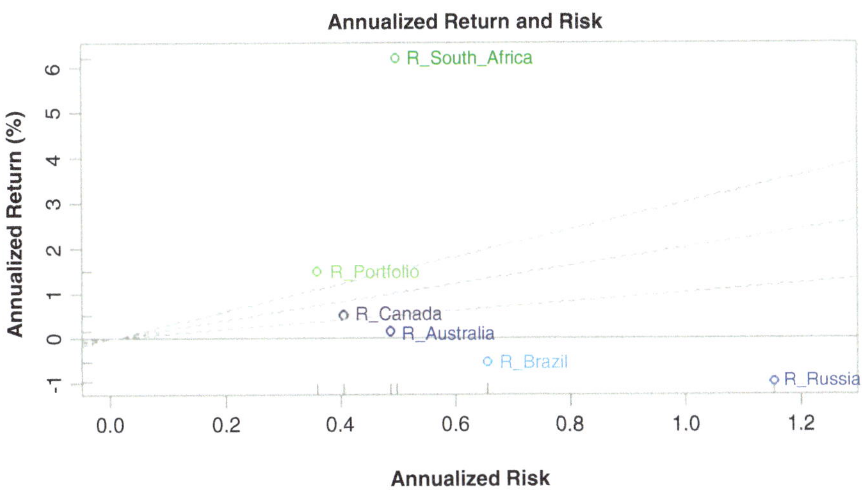

Fig. 5.7 Risk vs return scatter diagram

Hence, it is clear that the GMVP contains the least risk, and mean-variance dominates the individual assets, the indices of Canada, Australia, Russia, and Brazil. However, none of the two conditions above are met when the GMVP is compared to the South African index. This is considered a shortcoming of the mean-variance approach; it is unclear which portfolio is dominated by the other.

5.5.2 Risk Measurement in the CAPM Framework

As shown above, the mean-variance model can only be used in certain cases. The mean-variance model does not give an indication of the expected return of the asset. Bodie et al. (2013) explain that the CAPM provides a prediction of the relationship between the expected return of an asset and its risk. Therefore, the model provides a reliable estimate of the rate of return, which is invaluable when evaluating possible investments.

Bailey (2005) outlines the assumptions of the CAPM as follows:

- Asset markets are in equilibrium,
- investors are rational in the sense that they behave according to mean-variance portfolio criterion, and
- investors have the same beliefs, which implies that all investors use the same probability distributions when it comes to asset returns.

The CAPM model is specified as follows,

$$R_i - R_f = \beta_i \left(R_M - R_f\right) \text{ for } i = 1, \ldots, n. \tag{5.3}$$

where R_i is the return on asset i, R_f is the risk-free rate, R_M is the rate of return on the market portfolio, n is the number of assets, and β is an estimate of the systematic risk. Clearly, the β_i of the market portfolio is equal to one.

Using a similar approach to Zivot (2013), the CAPM relationship is tested by adding an intercept to Eq. 5.3. The following model is estimated

$$R_i - R_f = \alpha_i + \beta_i \left(R_M - R_f\right) \text{ for } i = 1, \ldots, n.$$

where α_i is the excess return on asset i. For the purpose of the empirical analysis, R_f is set equal to the US Treasury bill rate, and R_M is set equal to the monthly return on the Dow Jones index. The following results were obtained: The CAPM parameters are consistent with the findings of the mean-variance model. The GMVP does have the lowest systematic risk. The variance of Brazil was the highest when implementing the mean-variance model, and when estimating the CAPM model, it has the highest value of β. Furthermore, the CAPM relationship holds for Canada, South Africa, and the GMVP. The intercept (α) is statistically significant when Australia, Russia, and Brazil are considered (Table 5.4).

Table 5.4 CAPM parameters

	Canada	Australia	Russia	Brazil	SA	GMVP
α	−0.0035	−0.0054*	−0.0195**	−0.0084*	0.0019	−0.0009
β	0.6435***	0.7667***	1.2707***	0.7712***	0.7687***	0.5522***
R^2	0.4762	0.4705	0.2306	0.2605	0.4488	0.4439

*(**) [***]: Statistically significant at a 10(5)[1] % level

Asteriou and Hall (2015) explain that the R^2 of a simple regression model indicates the amount of variation in the dependent variable that is explained by variation in the independent variable. The R^2 of the estimated regression models is relatively low in each case. The models explain roughly 40% of the variation in the dependent variables and can therefore not be considered an accurate measurement of risk.

The CAPM does give an indication of the systematic risk of an asset and gives an idea of a relationship between the risk and return of an asset. However, neither the mean-variance model nor the CAPM give an indication of how the risk of an asset varies over time. This notion, and different ways of modeling time-varying volatility, is discussed in the next chapter.

5.6 Conclusion

In this paper, using a similar approach to Zivot (2011), an expression for the weights of a GMVP is derived for the CARBS indices. The weights are computed using the historical means, variances, and covariances of the indices. The GFC can be considered a structural break in the data and is therefore excluded from the dataset. The weights obtained indicate that most of the portfolio should be invested in Canadian equity. Furthermore, a small negative amount should be invested in Russian equity and a small positive amount be invested Brazilian equity; this is consistent with the findings by Watson and Seetharam (2014). Finally, a positive amount should be invested in South African equity.

In addition to the GMVP weights, the statistical properties of the CARBS indices and the GMVP are explored. The statistical properties of the indices and the GMVP seem to be consistent with the stylized facts of financial time series, as outlined by Embrechts et al. (2005). The return series seem to exhibit signs of volatility clustering. However, this is investigated using a formal test in the next chapter. Another important aspect of the historical return series data is that it is not normally distributed; there are signs of leptokurtosis. This presents a challenge when it comes to the quantitative measurement of risk.

Classical methods were used to measure risk of the CARBS indices and the GMVP. The risk vs return scatter plot and risk measurement in the CAPM framework were considered. The risk vs return scatter diagram indicates that the

GMVP mean-variance dominates all the indices, except South Africa. The GMVP is the least risky according to the risk vs return scatter diagram, which is consistent with expectations. Furthermore, the Russian equity index is the most risky. In addition, the CAPM relationship holds for Canada, South Africa, and the GMVP. The systematic risk (β) of the GMVP is the lowest, and the Russian equity index is the highest. However the R^2 of all the models indicate that the CAPM relationship is not a good fit for all the variables and can therefore not be considered a reliable measure of risk.

Another important aspect to consider is the strong assumptions made by the mean-variance and CAPM frameworks. It is unreasonable to assume that investors have the same beliefs, which makes the model less realistic. In addition, a constant volatility is assumed; in reality volatility is very volatile as shown by Figs. 5.1 and 5.4. Therefore, different time-varying volatility models are considered in the next chapter in order to determine the best fitting model for the CARBS indices and the GMVP.

References

Ali, M. H., & Ali, R. (2010). Test of CAPM in emerging stock markets: A study on Dhaka stock exchange. In *Symposium of USM Fellowship Holders 2009* (p. 618).

Asteriou, D., & Hall, S. G. (2015). *Applied econometrics*. Basingstoke: Palgrave Macmillan.

Bailey, R. E. (2005). *The economics of financial markets*. New York: Cambridge University Press.

Bodie, Z., Drew, M., Basu, A. K., Kane, A., & Marcus, A. (2013). *Principles of investments*. North Ryde: McGraw-Hill Education (Australia).

Brooks, C. (2014). *Introductory econometrics for finance*. Cambridge: Cambridge University Press.

Carl, P., Peterson, B. G., Boudt, K., & Zivot, E. (2008). *PerformanceAnalytics: Econometric tools for performance and risk analysis*. R package version 0.9, 7.

Cardoso, J. N. M. (2015). *Robust mean variance*. Doctoral dissertation, Instituto Superior de Economia e Gestao.

Embrechts, P., Frey, R., & McNeil, A. (2005). *Quantitative risk management* (Princeton series in finance, vol. 10). Princeton: Princeton University Press.

Iqbal, J., & Brooks, R. (2007). A test of CAPM on the Karachi stock exchange. *International Journal of Business, 12*(4), 429.

Li, K., Sarkar, A., & Wang, Z. (2003). Diversification benefits of emerging markets subject to portfolio constraints. *Journal of Empirical Finance, 10*(1), 57–80.

Tsay, R. S. (2005). *Analysis of financial time series*. Hoboken: Wiley.

Watson, J., & Seetharam, Y. (2014). Building a Portfolio with BRICS: The case of the international diversifier. *Investment Risk and Performance Feature Articles, 2014*(1), 1–4.

Wrede, R. C., & Spiegel, M. R. (2010). *Advanced calculus*. New York: McGraw-Hill.

Zivot, E. (2011). Portfolio theory with matrix algebra. In *Introduction to computational finance and financial econometrics, Econ 424*. Seattle: University of Washington.

Zivot, E. (2013). Capital asset pricing model. Econ 424/Amath 462 University of Washington lecture notes.

Chapter 6
Univariate and Multivariate GARCH Models Applied to the CARBS Indices

Coenraad C. A. Labuschagne, Niel Oberholzer, and Pierre J. Venter

Abstract The purpose of this paper is to estimate the calibrated parameters of different univariate and multivariate generalised autoregressive conditional heteroskedasticity (GARCH) family models. It is unrealistic to assume that volatility of financial returns is constant. In the empirical analysis, the symmetric GARCH and asymmetric GJR-GARCH and EGARCH models were estimated for the CARBS (Canada, Australia, Russia, Brazil, and South Africa) indices and a global minimum variance portfolio (GMVP); the best fitting model was determined using the AIC and BIC. The asymmetric terms of the GJR-GARCH and EGARCH models indicate signs of the leverage effect. The information criterion suggests that the EGARCH model is the best fitting model for the CARBS indices and the GMVP.

6.1 Introduction

Classical methods used to measure risk assume that volatility is constant over time. However, the stylised facts of financial time series indicate that volatility fluctuates over time and that return series show evidence of volatility clustering. Therefore, in order to measure risk using a more realistic approach, it is necessary to use time-varying volatility models.

When it comes to the topic of time-varying volatility models in finance, most financial modelling researchers agree that the GARCH model is the most widely used and accepted model. Many different GARCH model specifications have been introduced in recent years. In this study, the focus is on the standard GARCH model and the asymmetric Glosten-Jagannathan-Runkle GARCH (GJR-GARCH) and exponential GARCH (EGARCH) univariate models. This will give an indication of the degree of asymmetry and whether positive and negative shocks have the

C. C. A. Labuschagne (✉) · N. Oberholzer · P. J. Venter
Department of Finance and Investment Management, University of Johannesburg, Johannesburg, South Africa
e-mail: ccalabuschagne@uj.ac.za; nielo@uj.ac.za; pventer@uj.ac.za

N. Tsounis, A. Vlachvei (eds.), *Advances in Panel Data Analysis in Applied Economic Research*, Springer Proceedings in Business and Economics,
https://doi.org/10.1007/978-3-319-70055-7_6

same effect on volatility. Furthermore, the dynamic conditional correlation GARCH (DCC-GARCH) and the generalised orthogonal GARCH (GO-GARCH) model will be considered in the multivariate GARCH framework.

In order to approximate reliable risk measures using volatility models, it is necessary to use volatility models that are a good fit. The univariate GARCH models are compared using information criterion in this paper, which is based on the study by Oberholzer and Venter (2015). Furthermore, news impact curves (univariate) and surfaces (multivariate) are approximated. This gives an indication of how the conditional variance or covariance changes after a positive or negative shock. This gives an indication of the degree of asymmetry predicted by the model.

The empirical analysis in this paper relies heavily on the `rugarch` (Ghalanos 2014) and `rmgarch` (Ghalanos 2012) packages of the `R` programming language. The remainder of this paper is structured as follows: the relevant recent literature is discussed, the different univariate and multivariate GARCH models used in this thesis are specified, the empirical results are reported and interpreted, and finally the problem and results are summarised.

6.2 Literature Review

Literature focussing on the application of GARCH used to model volatility dates back to 1986 (Bollerslev 1986). Furthermore, the use of univariate symmetric and asymmetric GARCH models is also well-documented. Ahmad and Ping (2014) made use of the standard GARCH, GARCH in mean, threshold GARCH, and exponential GARCH (EGARCH) to model volatility of the volatility of Malaysian gold prices; the Akaike (AIC) and Schwarz (SIC) information criteria were used to determine the best fitting model. The EGARCH model was found to be the best model. In addition, the asymmetric GARCH models indicate that positive shocks lead to a greater rise in volatility when compared to negative shocks.

In a similar study, Oberholzer and Venter (2015) used the standard GARCH, GJR-GARCH, and EGARCH to determine the best fitting model for the five indices of the Johannesburg Stock Exchange (JSE) before, during, and after the global financial crisis (GFC) of 2008. Using a similar approach to Ahmad and Ping (2014), the AIC and SIC were used to determine the best fitting GARCH model. The GJR-GARCH model was found to be the best fitting model for the JSE in general. Moreover, the results showed signs of the leverage effect, which according to Black (1976) occurs when negative shocks give rise to a greater volatility when compared to positive shocks.

The use of multivariate GARCH to model conditional covariance and correlation among return series is also well-documented. By making use of the asymmetric BEKK multivariate GARCH model, Wen et al. (2014) investigated the volatility spillover effect among stock prices of Chinese fossil fuel and energy companies. The findings indicate that negative news about energy and fossil fuel leads to greater volatility in their counter assets. In addition, there is evidence of significant volatility spillovers and asymmetry, which has potential implications for financial risk management and asset allocation.

In a recent study, Basher and Sadorsky (2016) used dynamic conditional correlation (DCC) GARCH, asymmetric DCC-GARCH, and generalised orthogonal (GO) GARCH to estimate optimal cross hedging ratios between emerging market share prices, bond prices, gold prices, and oil prices. Basher and Sadorsky (2016) add to the literature by comparing the hedge ratios obtained by using different model specifications and use a one step ahead forecast for the next period hedge, which is usually assumed to be equal to the current hedge. Their results suggest that the asymmetric DCC model is superior when hedging share prices using bonds, gold, and oil.

6.3 Univatiate GARCH Models

In this section, the different univariate GARCH models will be defined and specified. The models discussed in this section will be implemented in order to determine the best fitting univariate GARCH model for the CARBS indices and the GMVP. Zivot and Wang (2007) explain that univariate GARCH models are concerned with the modelling of the conditional variance of a univariate time series.

6.3.1 Standard GARCH Model

According to Duncan and Liu (2009), a typical GARCH(1,1) model is specified as follows:

$$R_t = \mu + \varepsilon_t, \qquad \varepsilon_t|\Omega_{t-1} \sim \mathcal{N}(0, \sigma_t^2)$$

$$\sigma_t^2 = \gamma + \upsilon\varepsilon_{t-1}^2 + \delta\sigma_{t-1}^2.$$

Returns are modelled as being dependent on their (zero) mean observation. The error term ϵ_t is assumed to be conditioned on past information (Ω_{t-1}) and normally distributed with an expected value of zero and conditional variance σ_t^2.

Because variance can never be negative and cannot be greater than one, it is necessary to impose the following coefficient restrictions:

$$\gamma \geq 0,$$

$$0 \leq \upsilon, \delta < 1, \text{and}$$

$$\upsilon + \delta \leq 1.$$

In addition to coefficient restrictions, Wennesström (2014) explains that another shortcoming of the standard GARCH model is that it does not capture the effect of asymmetries. Hence, the model assumes that positive and negative news will lead to the same rise in volatility.

6.3.2 GJR-GARCH Model

Intuitively, one would expect a greater rise in volatility after a negative shock; this is referred to as the leverage effect (Brooks 2014). Therefore, the GJR-GARCH model accounts for negative shocks by including an indicator function, which takes a value of one when the shock is negative and zero otherwise. According to Asteriou and Hall (2015), the specification of the GJR-GARCH(1,1) model takes the following form:

$$\sigma_t^2 = \gamma + \upsilon\varepsilon_{t-1}^2 + \delta\sigma_{t-1}^2 + \eta 1_{\{\varepsilon_t<0\}}\varepsilon_{t-1}^2,$$

where $1_{\{\epsilon_t<0\}}$ is the indicator function.

Asteriou and Hall (2015) further explain that good news has an impact equal to υ, while the bad news impact is captured by $\upsilon + \eta$. Clearly, if η is statistically equal to zero, the news impact is symmetric. As mentioned previously, variance cannot take on a negative value or values greater than one. Therefore Brooks (2014) shows that the following coefficient restrictions are necessary:

$$\gamma > 0,$$
$$\upsilon > 0,$$
$$\delta \geq 0, \text{and}$$
$$\upsilon + \eta \geq 0.$$

Although the GJR-GARCH model does capture asymmetric news effects, it does require coefficient restrictions which can be considered a drawback as far as volatility models are concerned.

6.3.3 The Exponential GARCH (EGARCH) Model

To overcome the problem of coefficient restrictions, a possible solution of a different functional form is utilised (i.e. the natural log function). Consider the following model specification of an EGARCH(1,1) process from (Francq and Zakoian 2011):

$$\ln \sigma_t^2 = \gamma + \upsilon \left| \frac{\epsilon_{t-1}}{\sqrt{\sigma_{t-1}^2}} \right| + \delta \ln \sigma_{t-1}^2 + \eta \frac{\epsilon_{t-1}}{\sqrt{\sigma_{t-1}^2}}$$

In order to solve for σ_t^2, it is necessary to exponentiate the above equation. The exponential function does not take on negative values; this implies that the non-negativity constraints can be dropped. The EGARCH model does capture the effect of asymmetric news, if $\eta < 0$, then it is evidence of a leverage effect.

6.3.4 *Information Criterion*

In order to compare the goodness of fit of the univariate GARCH models, the AIC and Bayesian (BIC) information criterion are used. According to Asteriou and Hall (2015), the AIC and BIC are defined as follows:

$$AIC = \left(\frac{RSS}{k}\right) \exp\left\{\frac{2m}{k}\right\}$$

$$BIC = \left(\frac{RSS}{k}\right) \exp\left\{\frac{m}{k}\right\},$$

where *RSS* denotes the residual sum of squares, m is the number of explanatory variables, and k is the sample size. In addition, the model that produces the lowest level of AIC or BIC is the best fitting model. These values are usually logged by most statistical software packages.

6.4 Multivariate GARCH Models

The univariate GARCH models considered are used to model the conditional variance. However, these models do not consider how the conditional covariance varies over time. Therefore, multivariate GARCH models are used to model the conditional covariance matrix in this study. According to Alexander (2008) in a multivariate GARCH framework, each return series has a conditional variance (the diagonal of the covariance matrix) modelled by a univariate GARCH model, and each pair of return series has a conditional covariance modelled by a similar equation. Both the generalised orthogonal GARCH (GO-GARCH) and the dynamic conditional correlation GARCH (DCC-GARCH) models are considered below.

6.4.1 GO-GARCH

Alexander (2001) explains that when using the orthogonal GARCH model, an $(n \times n)$ covariance matrix (Σ_t) can be estimated using m univariate GARCH models, where $m < n$. For this procedure, uncorrelated components are transformed in order to obtain observed data. Van Weide (in Jondeau et al. 2007) extended this idea; the generalised orthogonal GARCH model includes an invertible matrix which forms a link between innovations.

The model specification that follows is based on the work by Broda (2009). Consider the following:

$$\bar{R}_t = \bar{\mu}_t + \bar{\epsilon}_t$$

where $\bar{R}_t$ is the return vector of n assets, $\bar{\mu}_t$ is a vector of constant (zero) mean returns, and $\bar{\epsilon}_t$ is a vector of disturbances. The disturbances are modelled by a linear combination of n factors $\bar{f}_t$, in matrix form:

$$\bar{\epsilon}_t = M\bar{f}_t.$$

It is assumed that each factor follows a GARCH(1,1) process, i.e. $\bar{f}_t \sim \mathcal{N}(\bar{0}, \bar{H}_t)$, where

$$\bar{H}_t = \Gamma + \sum_{k=1}^{d} \upsilon_k e_k e_k' \bar{H}_{t-1} e_k e_k' + \sum_{k=1}^{d} \delta_k e_k e_k' \bar{f}_{t-1} \bar{f}_{t-1}' e_k e_k',$$

$\Gamma = \sum_{k=1}^{d} (1 - \upsilon_k - \delta_k)\, e_k e_k'$, and e_k is a $d \times 1$ vector with the kth element equal to one and zeros elsewhere. The unconditional covariance is given by $\Sigma = MM'$, and the conditional covariance of the return vector becomes

$$\Sigma_t = M\Gamma M' + \sum_{k=1}^{d} \upsilon_k \nu_k \zeta_k' \Sigma_{t-1} \zeta_k \nu_k' + \sum_{k=1}^{d} \delta_k \nu_k \zeta_k' \epsilon_{t-1} \epsilon_{t-1}' \zeta_k \nu_k'. \tag{6.1}$$

where $\nu_k = Me_k$ and $\zeta_k = (M^{-1})' e_k$. In order to simplify the computation, the matrix M can be factorised as follows, using a polar decomposition:

$$M = \Sigma^{\frac{1}{2}} U,$$

where U is an orthogonal matrix and $\Sigma^{\frac{1}{2}}$ is the square root matrix of the unconditional covariance matrix. Therefore, it is necessary to estimate the matrix U and then the matrix M in order to estimate the conditional covariance matrix given by Eq. 6.1.

6.4.2 DCC-GARCH

The DCC-GARCH model provides an effective method for modelling volatility dynamics of time series that have time-dependent conditional correlations (Gregoriou 2009). Hence, the DCC-GARCH model is an extension of the constant conditional correlation GARCH (CCC-GARCH) model which includes a dynamic for the conditional correlation. The assumption of constant conditional correlation can be considered arbitrary, as argued by Francq and Zakoian (2011).

In order to specify the DCC-GARCH model, it is assumed that the vector of disturbances is normally distributed $\bar{\epsilon}_t \sim \mathcal{N}(0, \Sigma_t)$. The DCC-GARCH model by Engle (2002) is specified by

$$\Sigma_t = D_t P_t D_t, \tag{6.2}$$

where D_t is a diagonal matrix with the conditional variances of the individual assets along the diagonal and P_t is the time-dependent correlation matrix. Gregoriou (2009) elaborates and shows that by manipulating Eq. 6.2, the time-dependent correlation matrix is given by

$$P_t = D_t^{-1} \Sigma_t D_t^{-1},$$

which is in turn equal to

$$P_t = diag\left(q_{11,t}^{-1/2} \ldots q_{nn,t}\right) Q_t diag\left(q_{11,t}^{-1/2} \ldots q_{nn,t}\right).$$

The matrix Q_t is positive definite and given by

$$Q_t = (1 - \bar{\upsilon} - \bar{\delta})\tilde{Q} + \bar{\upsilon}\tilde{\epsilon}_{t-1}\tilde{\epsilon}'_{t-1} + \bar{\delta}Q_{t-1},$$

where $\tilde{\epsilon}_t$ are the standardised residuals and $\tilde{Q}$ is the unconditional variance matrix. Therefore, it is necessary to estimate the two vectors, $\bar{\upsilon}$ and $\bar{\delta}$.

6.5 Graphical Analysis

Using a similar approach to Narsoo (2016), the squared returns are used as a proxy for volatility. The squared returns are plotted below. The y-axis limits are the same for each plot; this presents an opportunity to compare the volatility of the different indices. It seems as though the returns on the Russian index is the most volatile. Moreover, the GMVP seems to be the least volatile. This is consistent with our expectations. However, the graphical analysis does not give an indication of how volatility reacts to positive and negative news (Fig. 6.1).

6.6 Empirical Results

The purpose of this section is to report and interpret the calibrated parameters of the different univariate and multivariate GARCH models outlined in previous sections. By making use of a similar approach to Oberholzer and Venter (2015), the AIC and BIC information criterion will be used to determine which GARCH model is the best fit for the indices included in this study and for the GMVP.

6.6.1 Univariate GARCH Models

In order to estimate the optimal parameters of the different GARCH models in this study, it is necessary to establish the presence of autoregressive conditional heteroskedasticity (ARCH) effects. This is done by performing the ARCH Lagrange Multiplier (ARCH LM) test. This is shown in the table below. Both the F-statistic and the Obs*R^2 show evidence of the presence of ARCH effects at a 1% level. Hence, there is volatility clustering, and it is possible to estimate the optimal parameters of different GARCH family models (Table 6.1).

The table below illustrates the optimal parameters of the GARCH(1,1) model for the CARBS indices and the GMVP (Table 6.2):

It is evident from the table that the coefficients do not violate any of the constraints, which implies that the models are admissible. Furthermore, according to Koop (2006), if the sum of υ and δ is close to one, it suggests that shocks to the index (positive or negative) will be persistent. This is the case for all the CARBS indices and the GMVP. The optimal parameters of the GJR-GARCH(1,1) model are shown in the table below (Table 6.3).

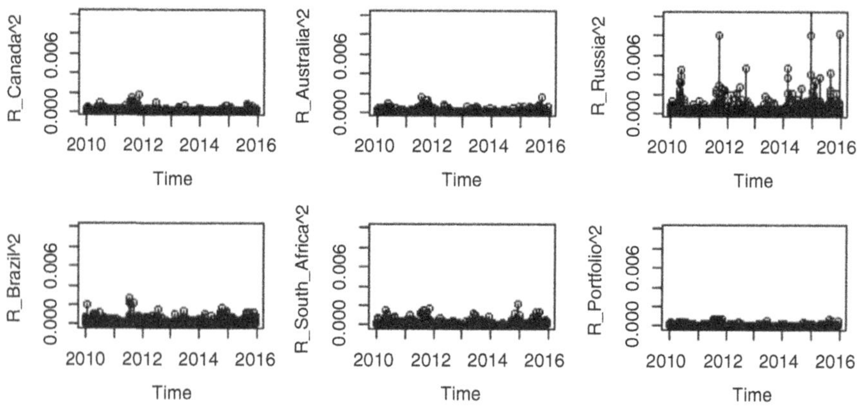

Fig. 6.1 Volatility of the CARBS indices and the GMVP

From the above, it is clear that the volatility of the CARBS indices and the GMVP shows a certain degree of asymmetry. The asymmetry terms of all the return series are statistically significant at a one percent level. Moreover, the estimated parameters do not violate any of the constraints discussed in the previous section. In addition, the AIC and BIC indicate that the asymmetric GJR-GARCH model is a better fit when compared to the symmetric GARCH model. The optimal parameters and information criterion of the EGARCH model are illustrated by the table below (Table 6.4).

As stated, if the asymmetry term of the EGARCH model is statistically significant and less than zero, it implies the existence of the leverage effect. This is the case for all the return series used in this study. This suggests that negative news will lead to a greater rise in volatility, when compared to the rise in volatility after a positive shock. Finally, the information criterion shows that the EGARCH model is the best fit for all the variables included in this study.

The analysis shows that asymmetric GARCH models perform better when explaining the time-varying volatility of the return series. News impact curves can be defined as a graphical representation of the degree of asymmetry of volatility to positive and negative shocks (Brooks 2014). Hence, the news impact curve plots the value of the conditional variance (σ_t^2) that would arise from various values of lagged shocks (ϵ_{t-1}). The news impact curves of the univariate models estimated are plotted below (Fig. 6.2).

As expected, the news impact curves derived from the estimated GARCH(1,1) parameters are symmetric. There is some degree of asymmetry when the GJR-GARCH and EGARCH news impact curves are considered. When the value of

Table 6.1 ARCH LM test

	F-statistic	Obs*R^2
Canada	59.6887***	58.1492***
Australia	129.6562***	122.4807***
Russia	869.9389***	622.1316***
Brazil	58.4749***	56.9977***
South Africa	72.2573***	70.0003***
GMVP	161.7760***	150.7241***

*(**) [***]: Statistically significant at a 10(5)[1] % level

Table 6.2 GARCH(1,1) optimal parameters

	Canada	Australia	Russia	Brazil	SA	GMVP
γ	$1.0E-06$	$1.0E-06$**	$6.0E-06$	4.0E-06***	$2.0E-06$**	0
υ	0.0748	0.0685***	0.1122***	0.0622***	0.1200	0.0583
δ	0.9087***	0.9150***	0.8686***	0.9034***	0.8593***	0.929***
AIC	−7.2544	−7.0382	−5.7269	−6.3749	−6.7718	−7.7090
BIC	−7.2440	−7.0278	−5.7165	−6.3644	−6.7614	−7.6986

*(**) [***]: Statistically significant at a 10(5)[1] % level

Table 6.3 GJR-GARCH(1,1) optimal parameters

	Canada	Australia	Russia	Brazil	SA	GMVP
γ	1.00E-06	1.00E-06	4.00E-06	3.00E-06***	2.00E-06**	0
υ	0	0.0006	0.0439***	0	0.0079***	0
δ	0.9267***	0.9261***	0.9031***	0.9284***	0.8835***	0.9248***
η	0.1084***	0.1068***	0.0748***	0.0947***	0.1681***	0.1122***
AIC	−7.2807	−7.0661	−5.7383	−6.4002	−6.8033	−7.7562
BIC	−7.2676	−7.0531	−5.7253	−6.3871	−6.7903	−7.7432

*(**) [***]: Statistically significant at a 10(5)[1] % level

Table 6.4 EGARCH(1,1) optimal parameters

	Canada	Australia	Russia	Brazil	SA	GMVP
γ	−0.1903***	−0.2707***	−0.2599***	−0.2408***	−0.2650***	−0.2303***
υ	−0.1177***	−0.0966***	−0.0702***	−0.0834***	−0.1210***	−0.1163***
δ	0.9810***	0.9723***	0.9686***	0.9735***	0.9720***	0.9782***
η	−0.0582***	−0.1081***	−0.1852***	−0.0792***	−0.1351***	−0.0475***
AIC	**−7.3024**	**−7.0783**	**−5.7482**	**−6.4020**	**−6.8124**	**−7.7748**
BIC	**−7.2893**	**−7.0653**	**−5.7352**	**−6.3890**	**−6.7993**	**−7.7618**

*(**) [***]: Statistically significant at a 10(5)[1] % level

a lagged shock is negative, it is clear that the value conditional variance, as modelled by the GJR-GARCH and EGARCH models, increases at a faster rate when compared to the conditional variance modelled by the GARCH model. Furthermore, when the value of a lagged shock is positive, the conditional variance increases at a slower rate when modelled by the GJR-GARCH and EGARCH models.

6.6.2 Multivariate GARCH Models

In this section, the coefficients and estimated matrices of both the GO-GARCH and DCC-GARCH models are reported. The data used to estimate the models includes the five indices of the CARBS countries. The GMVP is not included in this analysis. Given the covariance matrix of the five indices used to construct the GMVP, it is easy to estimate the variance of the GMVP. In addition to the coefficients and estimated matrices, the news impact surfaces of the estimated models are considered.

When the GO-GARCH model is applied to the data, the following matrices are obtained:

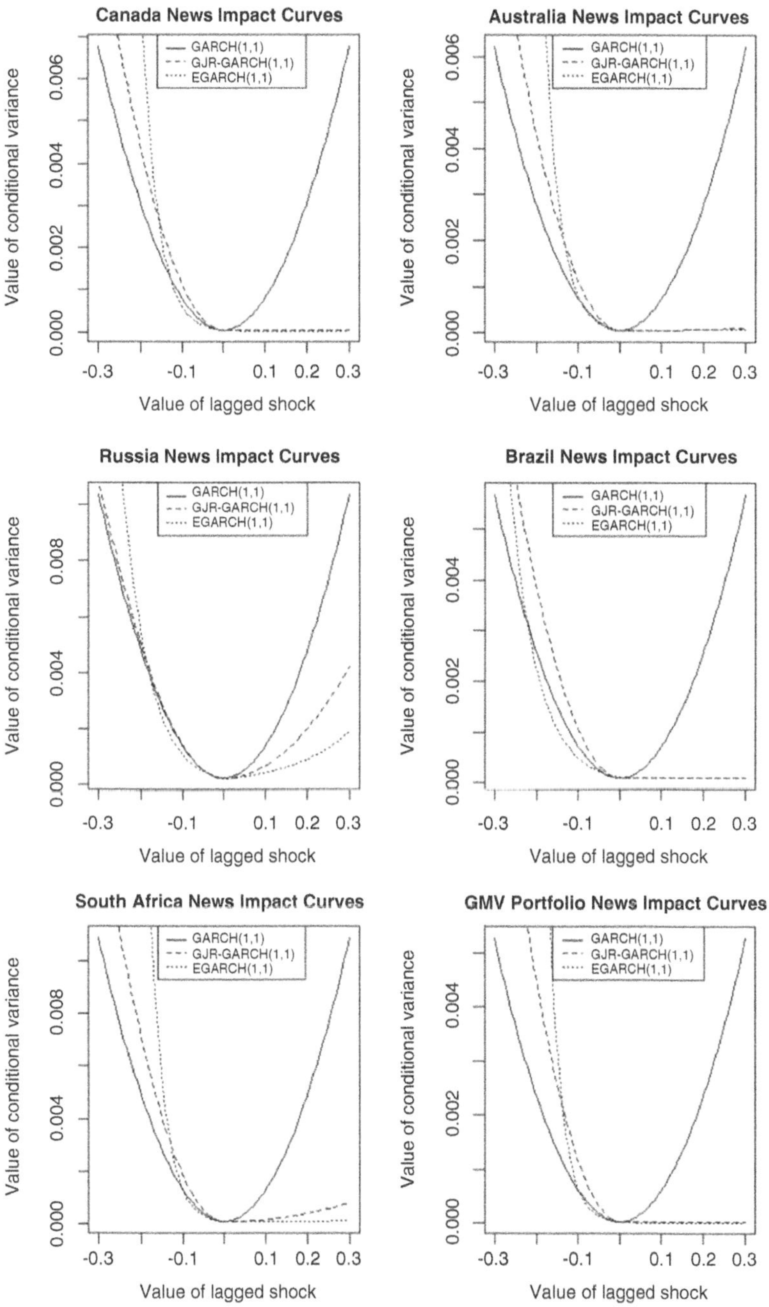

Fig. 6.2 News impact curves derived from univariate GARCH models

Table 6.5 DCC-GARCH(1,1) optimal parameters

	Canada	Australia	Russia	Brazil	South Africa
υ	0.0748	0.0685	0.1122***	0.0622***	0.1200
δ	0.9087	0.9150***	0.8686***	0.9034***	0.8593*

*(**) [***]: Statistically significant at a 10(5)[1] % level

Table 6.6 DCC-GARCH(1,1) optimal parameters

	Canada	Australia	Russia	Brazil	South Africa
υ	0.0748	0.0685	0.1122***	0.0622***	0.1200
δ	0.9087	0.9150***	0.8686***	0.9034***	0.8593*

*(**) [***]: Statistically significant at a 10(5)[1] % level

$$U = \begin{bmatrix} -0.6337 & 0.6751 & -0.3560 & -0.0996 & 0.0798 \\ 0.6051 & 0.5814 & -0.1140 & 0.5303 & 0.0408 \\ -0.0393 & -0.3900 & -0.6140 & 0.2931 & 0.6197 \\ 0.1416 & 0.2238 & 0.4490 & -0.3698 & 0.7692 \\ 0.4591 & 0.0632 & -0.5320 & -0.6973 & -0.1278 \end{bmatrix}$$

$$M = \begin{bmatrix} 0.0067 & -0.0004 & -0.0010 & -0.0016 & -0.0005 \\ 0.0019 & -0.0006 & 0.0033 & 0 & -0.0067 \\ 0.0061 & -0.0135 & 0.0040 & -0.0002 & -0.0008 \\ 0.0076 & -0.0013 & 0.0006 & 0.0070 & 0.0002 \\ 0.0049 & -0.0014 & 0.0071 & -0.0008 & 0.0014 \end{bmatrix}.$$

Moreover, when the DCC-GARCH model is applied to the CARBS index data, the following parameters are obtained (Table 6.5):
The above coefficients are statistically significant when used to model the conditional covariance of the CARBS indices. However, this does not show how the conditional covariance changes after a shock to a specific index.

Caporin and McAleer (2011) explain that a news impact surface is a multivariate extension of the news impact curve (Table 6.6). Hence, it shows how the conditional covariance reacts after a shock to a specific index. The news impact surfaces of the conditional covariance between Canada and Australia, when modelled by GO-GARCH and DCC-GARCH models, are plotted below:

It is important to note that shock[f1] and shock[f2] in Fig. 6.3 denote specific shocks to Canada and Australia in the GO-GARCH framework, respectively. It is evident that when the conditional covariance is modelled by a GO-GARCH model, the conditional covariance is close to zero when shocks to Canada are approximately equal to zero and increases as shocks to Canada approach −4 and also increases as shocks to Canada increase to 4.

Similarly, shock[z_1] and shock[z_2] in Fig. 6.3 denote specific shocks to Canada and Australia in the DCC-GARCH framework. It seems as though the conditional covariance in figure increases as shocks to the two indices are of the

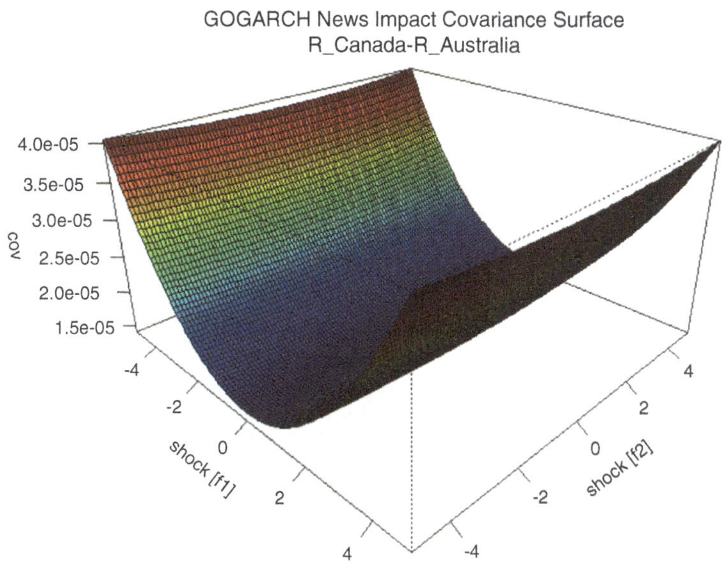

Fig. 6.3 Multivariate GARCH model news impact surfaces

same sign and decreases when shocks are of opposite signs when modelled using the DCC-GARCH model. Put differently, the conditional covariance is negative when the magnitude of a shock to Canada is 5 and the magnitude of a shock to Australia is −5. The conditional covariance is significantly positive when both shocks have a magnitude equal to 5 or −5.

The above models show how the optimal parameters when a GARCH process is used to model conditional variance or the conditional covariance matrix. However, the use of the estimated models to measure risk is not considered in this study.

6.7 Conclusion

The purpose of this paper is to estimate the calibrated parameters of different univariate and multivariate GARCH family models. It is unrealistic to assume that volatility of financial returns is constant. Therefore, it is necessary to estimate the parameters of time-varying volatility models. The ARCH LM test showed that evidence of volatility clustering and therefore the GARCH family models could be estimated.

Using a similar approach to Oberholzer and Venter (2015), the symmetric GARCH and asymmetric GJR-GARCH and EGARCH models were estimated for the CARBS indices and the GMVP; the best fitting model was determined using the AIC and BIC. The asymmetric terms of the GJR-GARCH and EGARCH models indicate signs of the leverage effect, which suggests that negative news leads to a greater rise in volatility when compared to the rise in volatility after a positive shock.

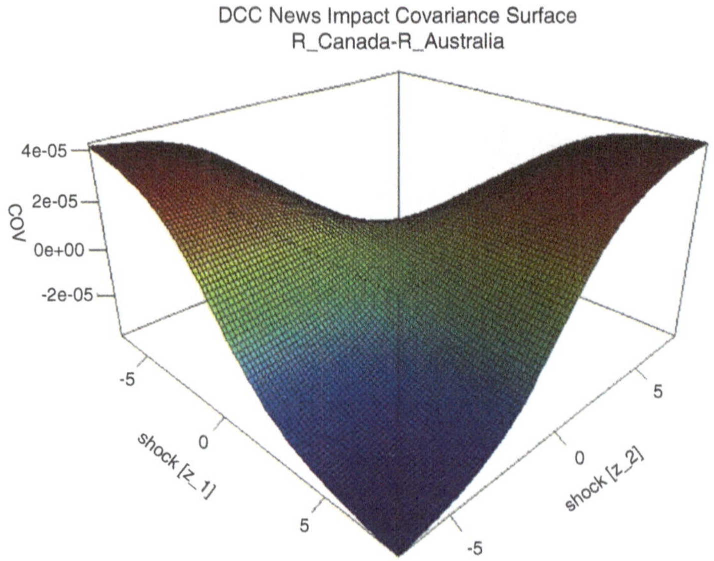

In addition, the AIC and BIC indicate that the EGARCH model is the best fitting model for all the indices and the GMVP.

The news impact curves derived from the GARCH family models show the degree of asymmetry, which shows that there is a greater rise in volatility after a negative shock. In terms of multivariate GARCH models, the optimal parameters of the GO-GARCH and the DCC-GARCH models were used to approximate a news impact surface. When the GO-GARCH model is used to model the conditional covariance matrix, the covariance seems to increase if the magnitude of the shock to a specific index increases. However, when the DCC-GARCH model is used, the covariance increases when the shocks are of the same sign and magnitude.

References

Ahmad, M. H., & Ping, P. Y. (2014). Modelling Malaysian gold using symmetric and asymmetric GARCH models. *Applied Mathematical Sciences, 8*(17), 817-822.

Alexander, C. (2001). Orthogonal GARCH. *Mastering risk* (Vol. 2, pp. 21–38). Harlow: Financial Times Prentice Hall.

Alexander, C. (2008). *Market risk analysis: Practical financial econometrics* (Vol. II). Hoboken: Wiley.

Asteriou, D., & Hall, S. G. (2015). *Applied econometrics*. Basingstoke: Palgrave Macmillan.

Basher, S. A., & Sadorsky, P. (2016). Hedging emerging market stock prices with oil, gold, VIX, and bonds: A comparison between DCC, ADCC and GO-GARCH. *Energy Economics, 54*, 235–247.

Black, F. (1976). Studies of stock price volatility changes. *Proceedings of the Business and Economics Section of the American Statistical Association* (pp. 177–181).

Bollerslev, T. (1986). Generalized autoregressive conditional heteroskedasticity. *Journal of Econometrics, 31*(3), 307–327.
Broda, S. A., & Paolella, M. S. (2009). Chicago: A fast and accurate method for portfolio risk calculation. *Journal of Financial Econometrics, 7*(4), 412–436.
Brooks, C. (2014). *Introductory econometrics for finance*. Cambridge: Cambridge University Press.
Caporin, M., & McAleer, M. (2011). Thresholds, news impact surfaces and dynamic asymmetric multivariate GARCH. *Statistica Neerlandica, 65*(2), 125–163.
Duncan, A. S., & Liu, G. (2009). Modelling South African currency crises as structural changes in the volatility of the rand. *South African Journal of Economics, 77*(3), 363–379.
Engle, R. (2002). Dynamic conditional correlation: A simple class of multivariate generalized autoregressive conditional heteroskedasticity models. *Journal of Business & Economic Statistics, 20*(3), 339–350.
Francq, C., & Zakoian, J. M. (2011). *GARCH models: Structure, statistical inference and financial applications*. Somerset: Wiley.
Ghalanos, A. (2012). *rmgarch: Multivariate GARCH models*. R package version 0.98.
Ghalanos, A. (2014). *rugarch: Univariate GARCH models*. R package version 1.3-3.
Gregoriou, G. N. (2009). *Stock market volatility*. Boca Raton: CRC Press.
Jondeau, E., Poon, S. H., & Rockinger, M. (2007). *Financial modeling under non-Gaussian distributions*. London: Springer Science & Business Media.
Koop, G. (2006). *Analysis of financial data*. Oxford: Wiley.
Narsoo, J. (2016). Evaluation of GARCH-type models in volatility and Value-At-Risk forecasting: Evidences from USD/MUR exchange rates. *University of Mauritius Research Journal, 22*, 1–17.
Oberholzer, N., & Venter, P. J. (2015). Univariate GARCH models applied to the JSE/FTSE stock indices. *Procedia Economics and Finance, 24*, 491–500.
Wen, X., Guo, Y., Wei, Y., & Huang, D. (2014). How do the stock prices of new energy and fossil fuel companies correlate? Evidence from China. *Energy Economics, 41*, 63–75.
Wennesträm, A. (2014). Volatility forecasting performance: Evaluation of GARCH type volatility models on nordic equity indices.
Zivot, E., & Wang, J. (2007). *Modeling financial time series with S-Plus* (Vol. 191). New York: Springer Science & Business Media.

Chapter 7
Value-At-Risk Forecasting of the CARBS Indices

Coenraad C. A. Labuschagne, Niel Oberholzer, and Pierre J. Venter

Abstract The purpose of this paper is to use calibrated univariate GARCH family models to forecast volatility and value at risk (VaR) of the CARBS indices and a global minimum variance portfolio (GMVP) constructed using the CARBS equity indices. The reliability of the different volatility forecasts is tested using the mean absolute error (MAE) and the mean squared error (MSE). The rolling forecast of VaR is tested using a back-testing procedure. The results indicate that the use of a rolling forecast from a GARCH model when estimating VaR for the CARBS indices and the GMVP is not a reliable method.

7.1 Introduction

An empirical analysis that gives an indication of the best fitting univariate GARCH model does not give indication of how the models can be used to measure risk. Furthermore, the Akaike and Schwartz information criterion (AIC and SIC) show which model is the best fit. However, this does not provide a forward-looking estimate of the dependent variable. Therefore, the forecasting ability of three univariate GARCH models is tested in this study.

The optimal parameters of the GARCH models show how volatility reacts after a shock to the index, how significant previous volatility is when modelling current period volatility, and the effect of positive and negative news. It is important to consider how the volatility models can be used in financial risk management and how risk measures can be obtained from the estimated models.

Forecasting from a GARCH model provides an estimate of future volatility. This does not give provide an estimate of possible losses in the future. Hence, using a similar approach to Narsoo (2016), univariate GARCH family models are

C. C. A. Labuschagne (✉) · N. Oberholzer · P. J. Venter
Department of Finance and Investment Management, University of Johannesburg, Johannesburg, South Africa
e-mail: ccalabuschagne@uj.ac.za; nielo@uj.ac.za; pventer@uj.ac.za

N. Tsounis, A. Vlachvei (eds.), *Advances in Panel Data Analysis in Applied Economic Research*, Springer Proceedings in Business and Economics,
https://doi.org/10.1007/978-3-319-70055-7_7

estimated and used to obtain an out-of-sample forecast of volatility; the reliability of the different forecasts are tested using the mean absolute error (MAE) and the mean squared error (MSE). Finally, the univariate GARCH models are then used to construct a rolling forecast of VaR; this is tested using a back-testing procedure.

The empirical results in this paper are obtained by making use of the `rugarch` `R` package by Ghalanos (2014). The remainder of this paper is structured as follows: In the next section, the relevant and recent literature is discussed, this is followed by a more formal definition and derivation of VaR and a GARCH model forecast, the empirical results are reported and interpreted, and finally the main results and concluding remarks are summarised.

7.2 Literature Review

Many studies have evaluated the forecasting performance of GARCH family models. Alberg et al. (2008) estimated various GARCH type models to forecast the conditional variance of the Tel Aviv Equity Exchange. The AIC indicates that the asymmetric models are a better fit when compared to the symmetric GARCH model. Finally, the forecast performance statistics show that the EGARCH skewed student-*t* model produces the most reliable forecast.

In a recent study, Braione and Scholtes (2016) tested the VaR forecasting ability of univariate and multivariate GARCH models using different distributional assumptions: the distributional assumptions of three symmetric and three skewed distributional assumptions. The accuracy of each model was tested using a back-testing procedure. The results showed that the skewed distributions with heavy tails outperform the other distributions. Therefore, it is important to model skewness and kurtosis.

Jimenez-Martin et al. (2009) estimated GARCH, GJR, and EGARCH models, with Gaussian, student-*t*, and generalised normal distribution errors to forecast VaR before, during, and after the Global Financial Crisis (GFC) of 2008. Furthermore, different VaR forecasting models were also combined. The models were compared based on a back-testing procedure. Jimenez-Martin et al. (2009) finally conclude that taking the supremum of the different forecasts is the most robust and reliable method before, during, and after the GFC.

Similarly, Narsoo (2016) employed three different GARCH models, the standard GARCH, EGARCH, and integrated GARCH models, to forecast volatility and VaR for the US Dollar/Mauritian Rupee (USD/MUR) exchange rate. In addition, different error distributions were considered for each GARCH family model. The EGARCH model with a student-*t* error distribution is the best fitting model when modelling volatility of the USD/MUR exchange rate. The standard GARCH model with a fat-tailed error distribution is the best performing model when forecasting volatility and VaR of the USD/MUR exchange rate.

7.3 Methodology

7.3.1 Value-At-Risk (VaR)

The purpose of this section is to discuss the concept of VaR more formally. Particular attention will be given to the derivation of VaR for a portfolio. The following definition from Hull (2012) explains the concept:

When using VaR as a risk measure, the following statement is of interest:

We are X percent certain that we will not lose more than VaR_X in time T,

where X is the confidence level ($X \in (0, 1)$) and T is the time horizon.

The following derivation of VaR for a portfolio of equity shares follows Embrechts et al. (2005) closely. Consider a portfolio of stocks at time t (Π_t), which consists of ψ_i units of each stock i. Hence, the weighing at time t of each stock i is given by

$$\omega_{i,t} = \frac{\psi_i S_{i,t}}{\Pi_t}. \tag{7.1}$$

Define the loss factor $Z_{i,t} = \ln(S_{i,t})$. The value of the portfolio at time t in terms of $Z_{i,t} = \ln(S_{i,t})$ is

$$\Pi_t = \sum_{i=1}^{n} \psi_i \exp\{Z_{i,t}\}.$$

Moreover, the gain of the portfolio (G_t) is defined as difference between the portfolio at time $t + 1$ and time t,

$$\begin{aligned} G_t &= \Pi_{t+1} - \Pi_t \\ &= \sum_{i=1}^{n} \psi_i S_{i,t}(\exp\{R_{i,t}\} - 1) \end{aligned}$$

where $R_{i,t}$ denotes the log return at time t. The linearised gain (G_t^{Δ}) is in turn given by

$$G_t^{\Delta} = \sum_{i=1}^{n} \psi_i S_{i,t} R_{i,t} \tag{7.2}$$

Finally, by making use of Eq. 7.1 it is possible to write Eq. 7.2 as

$$G_t^{\Delta} = \Pi_t \sum_{i=1}^{n} \omega_{i,t} R_{i,t}.$$

In vector notation, the linearised gain is given by $G_t^{\Delta} = \Pi_t \bar{\omega}_t' \bar{R}_t$, where $\bar{\omega}_t'$ is an $(n \times 1)$ vector of portfolio weights and $\bar{R}_t$ is a $(1 \times n)$ vector of log returns which is assumed to follow a distribution with mean vector $\bar{\mu}_t$ and covariance matrix Σ. When the rules regarding the mean and variance of a linear combination of a random vector are applied, the following is obtained:

$$\mathbb{E}[G_t^{\Delta}] = \Pi_t \bar{\omega}_t' \bar{\mu}_t = \mu, \text{ and}$$

$$\mathbb{V}ar[G_t^{\Delta}] = \Pi_t^2 \bar{\omega}_t' \Sigma \bar{\omega}_t = \sigma^2$$

If it is assumed that the gain distribution follows a normal distribution, with mean μ and variance σ^2, VaR can be calculated using the variance-covariance and can be computed as follows:

$$\text{VaR}_X = -\mu - \sigma \phi^{-1}(X)$$

where X is the confidence interval and ϕ^{-1} is the inverse of the standard normal distribution function. The above assumes that the volatility is constant and based on the historical information.

The accuracy of VaR is usually tested using a back-testing procedure. The back-testing parameter takes a value of 1 when the actual loss is greater than VaR (there is an exception) and zero otherwise. The back-testing parameter is defined by the following indicator function:

$$BT_t = 1_{\{\text{VaR} > R_t\}}.$$

The percentage of exceptions is equal to the sum of BT_t, for t is equal to 0 until the end of the period, divided the number of periods used to back-test. An important factor to consider is the accuracy of a forecast of volatility, which can be seen as a forward-looking approach which can ultimately be used to compute VaR.

7.3.2 Forecasting from a GARCH Model

To illustrate the concept, the use of forecasting volatility from a GARCH(1,1) model is derived below. A similar approach is used when forecasting from a GJR-GARCH(1,1) and EGARCH(1,1) model; therefore the derivation of the forecast from these models is excluded from this section.

The derivation that follows is based on the work by Hull (2009). The GARCH(1,1) model takes the following specification:

$$\sigma_t^2 = \gamma + \upsilon \varepsilon_{t-1}^2 + \delta \sigma_{t-1}^2, \tag{7.3}$$

where $\gamma = (1-\upsilon-\delta)\kappa_L$ and κ_L is the long run average variance rate. Equation 7.3.2 can be manipulated to obtain

$$\sigma_t^2 - \kappa_L = \upsilon(\varepsilon_{t-1}^2 - \kappa_L) + \delta(\sigma_{t-1}^2 - \kappa_L).$$

Furthermore, the volatility in period $t + \tau$ is

$$\sigma_{t+\tau}^2 - \kappa_L = \upsilon(\varepsilon_{t+\tau-1}^2 - \kappa_L) + \delta(\sigma_{t+\tau-1}^2 - \kappa_L)$$

However, because this information is unknown at time t, it is necessary to take the expectation. In addition, the expected value of $\epsilon_{t+\tau-1}^2$ is $\sigma_{t+\tau-1}^2$. Hence,

$$\mathbb{E}[\sigma_{t+\tau}^2 - \kappa_L] = (\upsilon + \delta)\mathbb{E}[\sigma_{t+\tau-1}^2 - \kappa_L],$$

where $\mathbb{E}$ denotes the expectation. If the above equation is used repeatedly, the following is an expression for the forecast of volatility, τ periods in future:

$$\mathbb{E}[\sigma_{t+\tau}^2] = \kappa_L + (\upsilon + \delta)^\tau(\sigma_{t+\tau-1}^2 - \kappa_L).$$

This implies that it is possible to forecast future volatility using historical information. The accuracy of this idea is tested when applied to financial risk management in the next section.

7.3.3 *Forecast Performance Measures*

In this study, the MAE and MSE are used to determine the forecasting performance of each model used to forecast volatility. Brooks (2014) explains that the MAE and MSE are obtained by comparing the actual values to an in-sample forecast. More specifically, the MAE and MSE consider

$$\text{MAE} = \left|\sigma_{t+\tau}^2 - \mathbb{E}\left[\sigma_{t+\tau}^2\right]\right|, \text{and}$$
$$\text{MSE} = \left(\sigma_{t+\tau}^2 - \mathbb{E}\left[\sigma_{t+\tau}^2\right]\right)^2$$

respectively. This provides an estimate of the reliability of the forecasting model. Clearly, the model that minimises the MAE and MSE is the most reliable forecasting model.

7.4 Empirical Results

The empirical results section is split into two components: one tests the out-of-sample forecasting ability of the three GARCH family models and the other tests the VaR forecasting ability of the GARCH family models.

7.4.1 *Forecasting Volatility*

In the tables below, the forecast performance measures of the GARCH(1,1), GJR-GARCH(1,1), and EGARCH(1,1) models are reported. In order to test the out-of-sample forecasting ability of the three GARCH family models included in this study, a 90-day out-of-sample forecast for volatility was performed. The best performing model for each respective index is the model that minimises the mean squared error (MSE) or the mean absolute error (MAE). The minimum MSE and MAE for each index is shown in bold (Tables 7.1, 7.2, and 7.3).

It is evident that the EGARCH(1,1) model produces the best performance measures for most of the indices included in this study and the GMVP. The results show that the MAE and MSE are consistent, however not for the case of Australia. The GARCH(1,1) model minimises the MSE of the Australian index, but the GJR-GARCH(1,1) minimises the MAE (Figs. 7.1 and 7.2).

The forecast graphs of the best performing GARCH models according to the MAE are plotted below. The graphs show that the out-of-sample forecast for the volatility of the indices is close to the mean in each case. The unconditional standard deviation bands also seem fairly small for each out-of-sample forecast.

Table 7.1 GARCH(1,1) forecast performance measures

	Canada	Australia	Russia	Brazil	South Africa	GMVP
MSE	6.47E-05	**6.97E-05**	3.57E-04	1.32E-04	8.10E-05	3.55E-05
MAE	6.12E-03	6.42E-03	1.42E-02	8.32E-03	6.97E-03	4.42E-03

Table 7.2 GJR-GARCH(1,1) forecast performance measures

	Canada	Australia	Russia	Brazil	South Africa	GMVP
MSE	6.46E-05	6.98E-05	**3.56E-04**	1.32E-04	8.09E-05	3.55E-05
MAE	6.11E-03	**6.41E-03**	**1.42E-02**	8.29E-03	6.97E-03	4.40E-03

Table 7.3 EGARCH(1,1) forecast performance measures

	Canada	Australia	Russia	Brazil	South Africa	GMVP
MSE	**6.46E-05**	6.99E-05	3.56E-04	**1.32E-04**	**8.08E-05**	**3.54E-05**
MAE	**6.10E-03**	6.41E-03	1.42E-02	**8.29E-03**	**6.97E-03**	**4.40E-03**

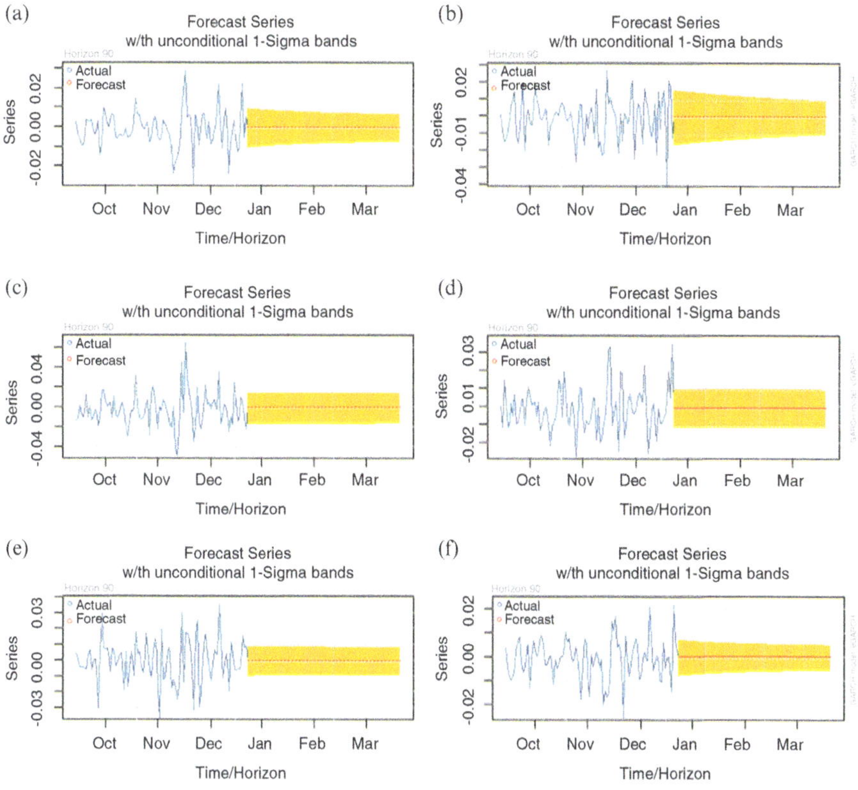

Fig. 7.1 Volatility forecast: best performing GARCH models. (**a**) Canada: EGARCH(1,1). (**b**) Australia: GJR-GARCH(1,1). (**c**) Russia: GJR-GARCH(1,1). (**d**) Brazil: EGARCH(1,1). (**e**) South Africa: EGARCH(1,1). (**f**) GMVP: EGARCH(1,1)

7.4.2 Forecasting VaR

The out-of-sample forecast does provide an estimate of future volatility based on historical information. However, this does not provide an estimate of what the maximum loss is with a certain level of confidence. Therefore, the same GARCH family models were used to obtain a forecast of 99% one day VaR. The performance of each model is assessed using a back-test when using the last 1000 observations of the CARBS indices and the GMVP. A rolling forecast of volatility is used to estimate VaR.

The percentage of exceptions of each model for the CARBS indices and the GMVP is reported; the lowest percentage of exceptions for each index and the GMVP is shown in bold. From the above, it is evident that the GARCH family models used in this study under-forecast VaR. The expected percentage of exceptions is 1%, the back-test of each model yields a greater percentage of exceptions.

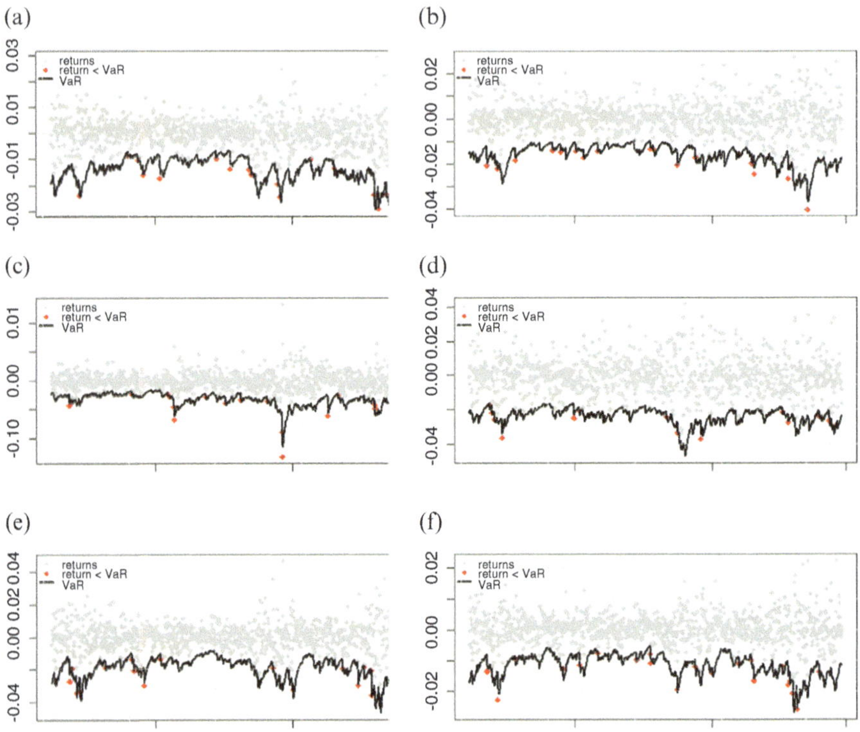

Fig. 7.2 Back-testing: GARCH rolling forecast. (**a**) Canada: EGARCH(1,1). (**b**) Australia: GARCH(1,1). (**c**) Russia: EGARCH(1,1). (**d**) Brazil: GARCH(1,1). (**e**) South Africa: EGARCH(1,1). (**f**) GMVP: EGARCH(1,1)

Table 7.4 GARCH rolling forecast: percentage of exceptions

	Canada	Australia	Russia	Brazil	South Africa	GMVP
GARCH	2.10%	**1.70%**	2.00%	**1.50%**	1.90%	2.60%
GJR-GARCH	2.20%	1.90%	1.90%	1.90%	1.90%	2.30%
EGARCH	**1.80%**	1.90%	**1.80%**	1.90%	**1.70%**	**2.10%**

However, the EGARCH model produces the lowest percentage of exceptions for four out of six variables. The GARCH(1,1) model produces the lowest percentage of exceptions for Australia and Brazil (Table 7.4).

A graphical representation of the back-testing procedure is shown by the figure below. The y-axis denotes the daily log returns, and the x-axis denotes time. The back-testing procedure of the models that produces the lowest percentage of exceptions is included in the figure. The back-testing graph shows that the rolling forecast VaR estimate for Russia is the highest, and the estimate for the GMVP is the lowest. In addition, it is evident that a rolling forecast VaR from a GARCH model is not a reliable method when estimating VaR. Therefore, a different approach is required.

7.5 Conclusion

In this study, three univariate GARCH models were estimated and used to forecast volatility and VaR. Volatility is a measure of the degree of uncertainty in financial markets, and VaR summarises the risk of a financial position in a single number. VaR gives an indication of the maximum loss with a certain level of confidence (Hull 2009).

Many studies in the literature have focused on the forecasting performance of different volatility models. The empirical analysis of this paper is based on the recent work by Narsoo (2016). The empirical analysis consists of two parts. Firstly, the out-of-sample forecasting ability of the different univariate GARCH models was considered. This was tested using the MAE and MSE, which is the absolute and squared difference, respectively, between an in-sample forecast based on the model and the actual value. Secondly, a rolling forecast from the different GARCH models is used to estimate daily value at risk. This process is tested using a back-testing procedure.

Both forecast performance statistics of the out-of-sample forecast suggest that the EGARCH model produces the most reliable forecast for Cabada, Brazil, South Africa, and the GMVP. Moreover, the MAE and MSE show that the asymmetric GJR-GARCH model produces the most reliable forecast for Russia. Finally, the MSE indicates that the symmetric GARCH model produces the most accurate forecast of volatility for Australia; this is inconsistent with the model suggested by the MAE, which is the asymmetric GJR-GARCH model.

When estimating 99% VaR, the expected number of exceptions when back-testing is 1%. The EGARCH model produces the lowest percentage of exceptions for most of the variables. However, VaR is underestimated in each case when a rolling forecast is used. This implies that the use of a rolling forecast from a GARCH model when estimating VaR for the CARBS indices and the GMVP is not a reliable method. Therefore, a different approach is necessary.

References

Alberg, D., Shalit, H., & Yosef, R. (2008). Estimating stock market volatility using asymmetric GARCH models. *Applied Financial Economics, 18*(15), 1201–1208.

Braione, M., & Scholtes, N.K. (2016). Forecasting value-at-risk under different distributional assumptions. *Econometrics, 4*(1), 3.

Brooks, C. (2014). *Introductory econometrics for finance*. Cambridge: Cambridge University Press.

Embrechts, P., Frey, R., & McNeil, A. (2005). *Quantitative risk management* (Princeton Series in Finance, Vol. 10). Princeton: Princeton University Press.
Ghalanos, A. (2014). Rugarch: Univariate GARCH models, R package version 1.3-3.
Hull, J. (2009). *Options, futures and other derivatives* (7th ed.). Boston: Pearson Education.
Hull, J. (2012). *Risk management and financial institutions* (3rd ed.). New York: Wiley.
JimenezMartin, J.A., McAleer, M., & PrezAmaral, T. (2009). The ten commandments for managing value at risk under the Basel II Accord. *Journal of Economic Surveys, 23*(5), 850–855.
Narsoo, J. (2016). Evaluation of GARCH-Type models in volatility and value-at-risk forecasting: evidences from USD/MUR exchange rates. *University of Mauritius Research Journal, 22*, 1–7.

Chapter 8
A Vector Error Correction Model (VECM) of FTSE/JSE SA Listed Property Index and FTSE/JSE SA Capped Property Index

Coenraad C. A. Labuschagne, Niel Oberholzer, and Pierre J. Venter

Abstract In this paper, the efficient market hypothesis (EMH) will be investigated from an empirical and theoretical basis. The closing $(Close_t)$, intraday high $(High_t)$, intraday low (Low_t) and opening $(Open_t)$ values of the FTSE/JSE SA Listed Property Index (FTJ253) and the FTSE/JSE Capped Property Index (FTJ254)will explore the impact on returns resulting from a one standard deviation shock. The examination of the interrelationship between the closing $(Close_t)$, intraday high $(High_t)$, intraday low (Low_t) and opening $(Open_t)$ values of the FTSE/JSE SA Listed Property Index (FTJ253) and the FTSE/JSE Capped Property Index (FTJ254) was conducted by making use of the Johansen cointegration test, a vector error correction model (VECM) and an impulse response function. The results of these tests provided an indication of the short- and long-run dynamics of all the variables included and the reaction of the variables to a one standard deviation shock. The results obtain indicate that there is an opportunity for arbitrage when the price deviates from the long-run equilibrium until a new equilibrium is reached.

8.1 Introduction

Market efficiency is a fundamental concept to investments. Efficiency refers to the formation of an asset price that comprises all the available price information. The defining of efficacy in markets or efficient markets is problematic in itself. Fama (1965a) defines an efficient market as a market that at every price at every point in time reflects all the available information and where the asset price represents intrinsic value. Fama (1965b) describes an efficient market as a large numbers of competing rational profit maximising individuals trying to foretell future asset

C. C. A. Labuschagne (✉) · N. Oberholzer · P. J. Venter
Department of Finance and Investment Management, University of Johannesburg, Johannesburg, South Africa
e-mail: ccalabuschagne@uj.ac.za; nielo@uj.ac.za; pventer@uj.ac.za

N. Tsounis, A. Vlachvei (eds.), *Advances in Panel Data Analysis in Applied Economic Research*, Springer Proceedings in Business and Economics,
https://doi.org/10.1007/978-3-319-70055-7_8

values on almost freely available information. Fama et al. pronounce an efficient market as a market that reacts and adjusts quickly to new information. Fama (1970) states that a market price that is fully reflective of all available information is called efficient.

The market efficiency hypothesis is described as the market efficiency hypotheses is describeds as asset prices that fully reflect all available information. It is clear that an efficient market, as described by Fama, is one that is rational that provides accurate asset price that is based on the available information, in other words, a market that is free from arbitrage or abnormal excess returns. The efficient market hypothesis is based on three elementary assumptions: (1) all investors are rational and they value assets on their fundamental value reflecting all available information, (2) investors may be irrational; however, their investment activity is unrelated and uncorrelated without any negative effect on the underlying asset price; and (3) if activities are irrational and correlated, the action of arbitrageurs will result in profits. However, these actions will restore the asset price to its fundamental value via the buy and sell activities of arbitrageurs and rational investors (Campbell and Shiller 1988).

However, Black (1986) states that investor's value assets based on the noise rather than fundamental information imply that investors act irrational. De Long et al. (1990) are of the opinion that irrational investors affect the asset price to such an extent that arbitrageurs are unwilling to take a position in order to obtain a profit. According to De Long et al. (1990), this introduces an extra risk, namely, noise trader risk into the market. Implying that arbitrageurs will refrain from trading as they fear the continuous irrational investment conduct of investors. In other words, arbitrageurs will not buy undervalued asset as they fear they will have to liquidate their position resulting in an unexpected loss. Therefore, in theory, a market is efficient when trading on or when price formation, from available information does not result in abnormal profit (Roberts 1959; Fama 1970).

In assessing the effectiveness of markets, it is of critical importance to consider the types of available informational datasets and the corresponding level of efficiencies achieved with each of these informational datasets: (1) Historical or past prices as characterised by the weak-form efficiency, (2) public available information represented by the semi-strong efficiency and (3) private information as considered by the strong-form efficiency.

When considering the efficiency of markets, it is of importance to consider the implications of randomness of price movements. As deviations from an assets true value is random, it implies that there is an equal chance that an asset may be overvalued or undervalued at any specific time in point. It also implies that these deviations of prices are uncorrelated with no observable variability. In considering the randomness of an asset price deviation from intrinsic value, it would imply that no investor or group of investors will be able to, on a constant basis, outperform the market using any investment strategy (Damodaran 2012).

There are currently four property indices listed on the Johannesburg Stock Exchange. In this paper, the closing ($Close_t$), intraday high ($High_t$), intraday low (Low_t) and opening ($Open_t$) values of the FTSE/JSE SA Listed Property Index

(FTJ253) and the FTSE/JSE Capped Property Index (FTJ254) comprise the top 20 most liquid companies, by full market cap, in the real estate investment and services sector and the real estate investment trusts sector, with a primary listing on the JSE. However, the FTSE/JSE Capped Property Index (FTJ254) capped at 15% at each quarterly review.

These two indices will be analysed for the presence of information that will allow the investor to make an abnormal return. A vector error correction (VEC) proses will be applied to investigate the return generation process and represent the short- and long-run dynamics of the variables included. The study will try and explain the relationship both static and dynamic in the two selected time series datasets for the FTJ253 and FTJ254. The investigation will be done by making use of Johansen cointegration test, a vector error correction model (VECM) (Engle and Granger 1987), and finally impulse response was used.

The remainder of the paper is structured as follows; part 2 discusses the data. In part 3 will be a brief explanation of the methodology used and in part 4 will cover the results and interpretation of the findings. Part 5 discusses the conclusion of the study. When appropriate, the EViews nations and table headings were retained.

8.2 Data Specification and Methodology

In this study, the daily opening, closing, intraday high and intraday lowest prices of the FTSE/JSE SA Listed Property Index (FTJ253) and the FTSE/JSE Capped Property Index (FTJ254) will be used. The study period is from 4 January 2010 until 31 December 2014. All the datasets were obtained from Thomson Reuters Eikon. In order to determine the short- and long-run dynamics of the variables included in this study, a Johansen cointegration test was performed in order to determine whether a long-run relationship exists among these variables; thereafter, a vector error correction model was employed, and finally impulse response was used to show how the variables respond after a shock has occurred to a given variable. With regard to model specification, according to Koop (2006), the VAR and VECM models should be specified as follows:

$$Close_t = \alpha_1 + \sum_{i=1}^{p} \beta_{1i} Close_{t-i} + \sum_{i=1}^{p} \delta_{1i} High_{t-i} + \sum_{i=1}^{p} \kappa_{1i} Low_{t-i} + \sum_{i=1}^{p} \gamma_{1i} Open_{t-i} + u_{1t}$$
$$High_t = \alpha_2 + \sum_{i=1}^{p} \beta_{2i} Close_{t-i} + \sum_{i=1}^{p} \delta_{2i} High_{t-i} + \sum_{i=1}^{p} \kappa_{2i} Low_{t-i} + \sum_{i=1}^{p} \gamma_{2i} Open_{t-i} + u_{2t}$$
$$Low_t = \alpha_3 + \sum_{i=1}^{p} \beta_{3i} Close_{t-i} + \sum_{i=1}^{p} \delta_{3i} High_{t-i} + \sum_{i=1}^{p} \kappa_{3i} Low_{t-i} + \sum_{i=1}^{p} \gamma_{3i} Open_{t-i} + u_{3t}$$
$$Open_t = \alpha_4 + \sum_{i=1}^{p} \beta_{4i} Close_{t-i} + \sum_{i=1}^{p} \delta_{4i} High_{t-i} + \sum_{i=1}^{p} \kappa_{4i} Low_{t-i} + \sum_{i=1}^{p} \gamma_{4i} Open_{t-i} + u_{4t}$$

$$
\begin{aligned}
\Delta Close_t &= \omega_1 u_{1(t-1)} + \alpha_1 + \sum_{i=1}^{p} \beta_{1i}\Delta Close_{t-i} + \sum_{i=1}^{p} \delta_{1i}\Delta High_{t-i} \\
&\quad + \sum_{i=1}^{p} \kappa_{1i}\Delta Low_{t-i} + \sum_{i=1}^{p} \gamma_{1i}\Delta Open_{t-i} + \xi_{1t} \\
\Delta High_t &= \omega_2 u_{2(t-1)} + \alpha_2 + \sum_{i=1}^{p} \beta_{2i}\Delta Close_{t-i} + \sum_{i=1}^{p} \delta_{2i}\Delta High_{t-i} \\
&\quad + \sum_{i=1}^{p} \kappa_{2i}\Delta Low_{t-i} + \sum_{i=1}^{p} \gamma_{2i}\Delta Open_{t-i} + \xi_{2t} \\
\Delta Low_t &= \omega_3 u_{3(t-1)} + \alpha_3 + \sum_{i=1}^{p} \beta_{3i}\Delta Close_{t-i} + \sum_{i=1}^{p} \delta_{3i}\Delta High_{t-i} \\
&\quad + \sum_{i=1}^{p} \kappa_{3i}\Delta Low_{t-i} + \sum_{i=1}^{p} \gamma_{3i}\Delta Open_{t-i} + \xi_{3t} \\
\Delta Open_t &= \omega_4 u_{4(t-1)} + \alpha_4 + \sum_{i=1}^{p} \beta_{4i}\Delta Close_{t-i} + \sum_{i=1}^{p} \delta_{4i}\Delta High_{t-i} \\
&\quad + \sum_{i=1}^{p} \kappa_{4i}\Delta Low_{t-i} + \sum_{i=1}^{p} \gamma_{4i}\Delta Open_{t-i} + \xi_{4t}
\end{aligned}
$$

8.3 Results

The results will be explained in two sections. Firstly, all the results for the FTJ53 will be discussed followed by the result of the FTJ254. The comparison of the two sets of results will be conducted in the conclusion section of the paper.

8.3.1 FTSE/JSE SA Listed Property Index (FTJ253)

In Fig. 8.1, the index level of the open, intraday high, intraday low and close of the FTJ253 can be seen. It is clear that from the start of the study period, the indices have been upward trending with a large decrease in prices in the second quarter of 2013. This was due to an increase in yields resulting from an increase in rental inflation.

Figure 8.2 below shows that the log returns of the FTJ253 seem to be mean reverting. The mean of each return series is close to zero. There also seems to be an increase in volatility during the second quarter of 2013.

We observe that the return series are not normally distributed and the histograms exhibit signs of leptokurtosis. The mean of each variable seems to be close to zero as indicated in Fig. 8.3 below. The observations are in line with the stylized facts of financial time series, as explained by McNeil et al. (2005).

The descriptive statistics in Table 8.1 confirm our expectation of leptokurtic distributions; in addition, the Jarque-Bera probability in each case is less than five percent, and therefore we can reject the null hypothesis of normality. Furthermore, Table 8.1 indicates that the return series are negatively skewed.

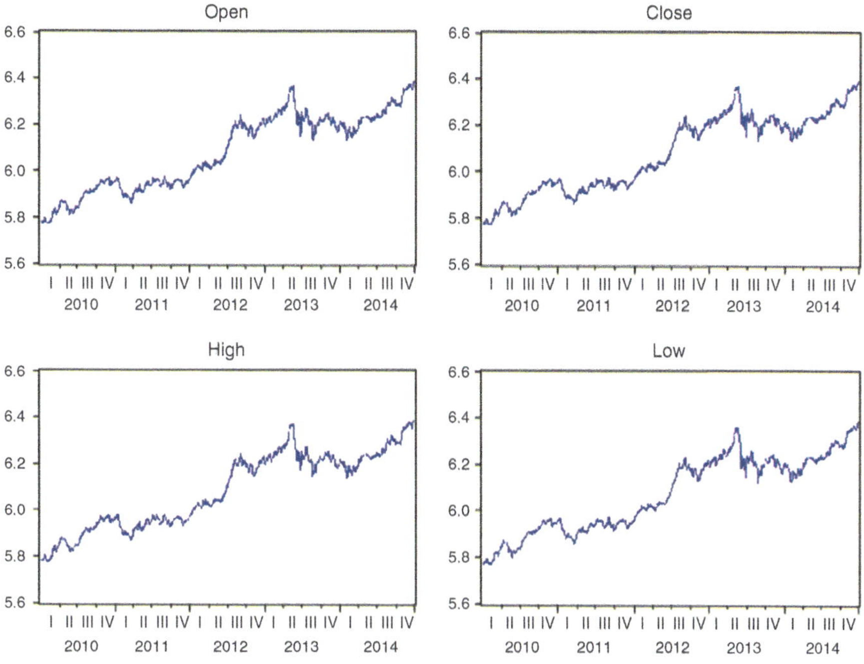

Fig. 8.1 Line graphs of the FTSE/JSE SA Listed Property Index (FTJ253)

The augmented Dickey-Fuller unit root test and the Phillips-Perron test in Table 8.2 show that the variables are not stationary at level; however, the log returns are stationary. This implies that the logged series are integrated of order one.

In Table 8.3, the sequential modified LR test statistic, final prediction error and Akaike information criterion suggest that the optimal lag length is nine lags.

The AR roots graph (Fig. 8.4) shows that all the roots lie within the unit circle. Hence, we can conclude that the VAR model is stable when estimated using nine lags.

The cointegration test suggests that when three cointegrating equations are the hypothesised number of cointegrating equations, we do not reject the null hypothesis. Therefore, we conclude that three (of a possible three) long-run relationships exist among the variables included. The results can be observed in Tables 8.4 and 8.5.

When one considers the error correction coefficients of the three long-run relationships, it is evident that the error correction coefficient of the opening price is statistically significant; however, the coefficient is positive; this implies that the variable is nonresponsive and will take very long time to return to equilibrium after a deviation. The error correction coefficients of the closing, high and lowest prices are significant and of the correct sign; this means that a deviation from the long-run relationship will be corrected. The error correction process is rapid when closing

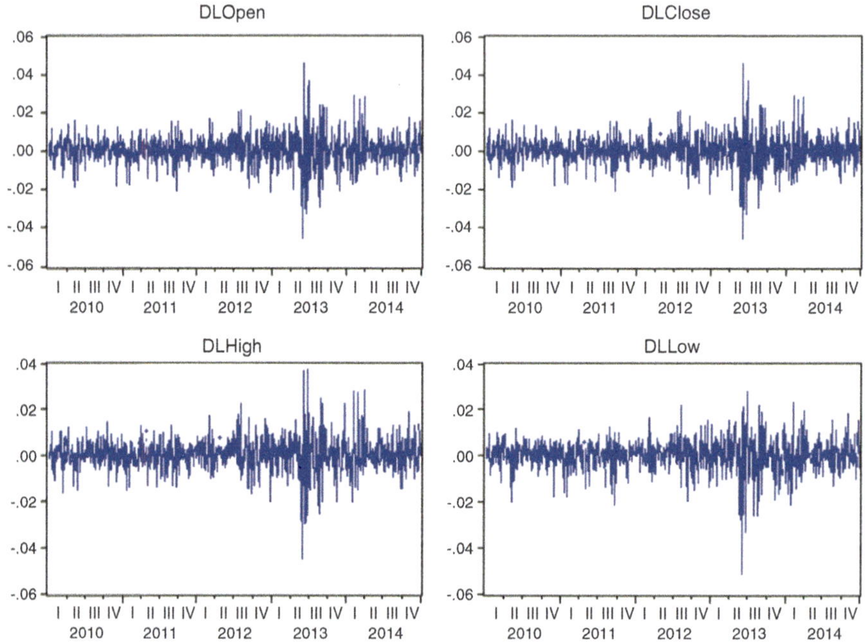

Fig. 8.2 Log returns of the FTSE/JSE SA Listed Property Index (FTJ253)

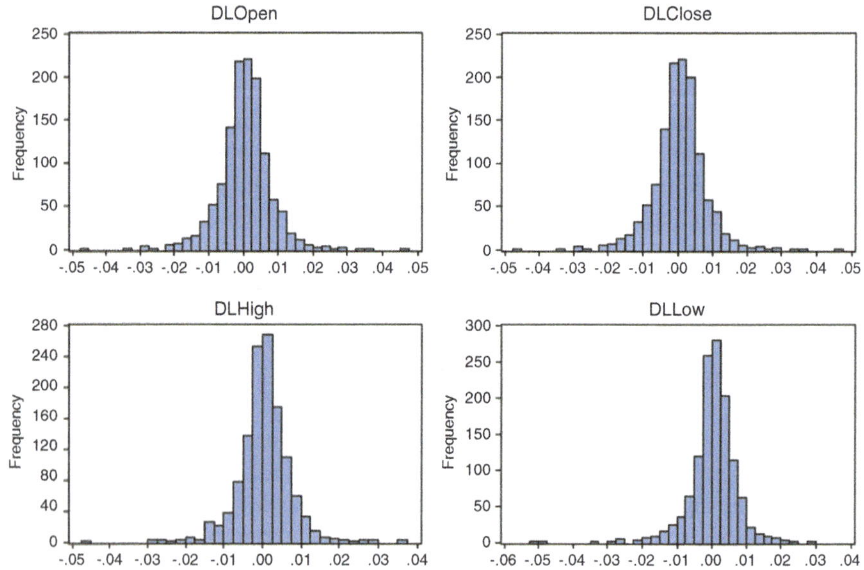

Fig. 8.3 Histogram of the log returns of the FTSE/JSE SA Listed Property Index (FTJ253)

Table 8.1 Descriptive statistics SA Listed Property Index (FTJ253)

	OPEN	CLOSE	HIGH	LOW
Mean	0.0005	0.0005	0.0005	0.0005
Median	0.0007	0.0007	0.0005	0.0007
Maximum	0.0465	0.0465	0.0372	0.0281
Minimum	−0.0452	−0.0452	−0.0452	−0.0516
Std. Dev.	0.0073	0.0074	0.0066	0.0064
Skewness	−0.0911	−0.0949	−0.1008	−1.2224
Kurtosis	7.65	7.6202	8.9924	11.382
Jarque-Bera	1124.305	1110.094	1866.392	3957.893
Probability	0	0	0	0
Sum	0.6153	0.6108	0.6158	0.6127
Sum Sq. Dev.	0.0672	0.0674	0.0543	0.0516
Observations	1246	1246	1246	1246

Source: Researchers' analysis

Table 8.2 Unit root test FTJ253

Variable	ADF	PP
Open	−0.8723	−0.8085
Close	−0.8937	−0.8702
High	−0.8956	−0.8055
Low	−0.9957	−0.8311
D(Open)	−30.2213***	−30.2689***
D(Close)	−19.5353***	−30.2698***
D(High)	−27.0048***	−27.0337***
D(Low)	24.3469***	−23.7835***

Source: Researchers' analysis
*(**) [***]: Statistically significant at a 10(5)[1]% level

and highest prices are considered but slow when highest prices are considered. The error correction coefficients of the highest and lowest prices are significant and of the correct sign; the variables will adjust back to the long-run relationship by a magnitude equal to the error correction coefficient daily (Table 8.6).

Figure 8.5 indicates the impulse responses of the FTJ253 to the introduction of a one standard deviation shock to the close, intraday high, intraday low and closing values. If a shock is introduced to all variables individually, the closing price response is an increase at first before reaching a new equilibrium after 15 days or lag periods. The reaction of each individual variable to each variables individual shock is very similar except for the opening price. The initial response of the opening price to the introduction of a shock to each individual variable is very little. For the first 5 lag periods (days). In each instance, the opening price reacts with an upward move around lag period 5 reaching a high around lag period of 8 to 10 before levelling off to a new equilibrium around lag period 15.

Table 8.3 Lag length criteria FTJ253

Lag	LogL	LR	FPE	AIC	SC	HQ
0	15691.66	NA	1.13E-16	−25.364	−25.3475	−25.3578
1	24021.38	16592.11	1.65E-22	−38.8058	−38.72300*	−38.7747
2	24057.24	71.20199	1.60E-22	−38.8379	−38.6889	−38.78186*
3	24077.59	40.26732	1.58E-22	−38.8449	−38.6297	−38.764
4	24093.03	30.45303	1.59E-22	−38.844	−38.5626	−38.7382
5	24106.24	25.961	1.59E-22	−38.8395	−38.4918	−38.7087
6	24130.77	48.06931	1.57E-22	−38.8533	−38.4394	−38.6976
7	24155.62	48.53774	1.55E-22	−38.8676	−38.3874	−38.687
8	24180.61	48.6429	1.53E-22	−38.8821	−38.3357	−38.6766
9	24197.06	31.92286*	1.53e-22*	−38.88288*	−38.2702	−38.6525
10	24210.05	25.12696	1.53E-22	−38.878	−38.1992	−38.6227

Source: Researchers' analysis

LR sequential modified LR test statistic (each test at 5% level), *FPE* Final prediction error, *AIC* Akaike information criterion, *SC* Schwarz information criterion, *HQ* Hannan-Quinn information criterion

*Indicates lag order selected by the criterion

Fig. 8.4 AR roots graph FTJ253

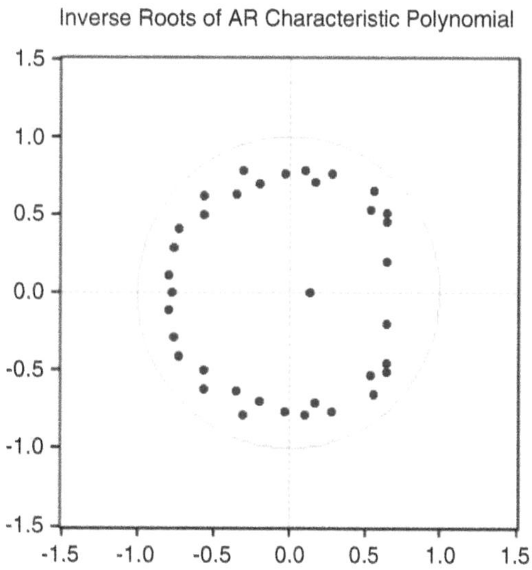

8.3.2 *FTSE/JSE SA Capped Property Index (FTJ254)*

The line graphs below in Fig. 8.6, of the opening, closing, intraday high and intraday lowest prices of the FTJ254 exhibit an upward trend. There also seems to be a slight decrease in the level of the index during the second quarter of 2013.

Table 8.4 Unrestricted cointegration rank test (Trace) FTJ253

Hypothesized No. of CE(s)	Eigenvalue	Trace statistic	Critical value	Prob.
None*	0.104761	287.0159	47.85613	0.0001
At most 1*	0.069652	150.124	29.79707	0.0001
At most 2*	0.047571	60.81625	15.49471	0
At most 3	0.000425	0.52546	3.841466	0.4685

Source: Researchers' analysis

Table 8.5 Unrestricted cointegration rank test (maximum eigenvalue) FTJ253

Hypothesized No. of CE(s)	Eigenvalue	Max-Eigen statistic	Critical value	Prob.
None*	0.104761	136.8919	27.58434	0
At most 1*	0.069652	89.30772	21.13162	0
At most 2*	0.047571	60.29079	14.2646	0
At most 3	0.000425	0.52546	3.841466	0.4685

Source: Researchers' analysis

The log returns of the opening, closing, highest and lowest prices of the FTJ254 index seem to exhibit signs of volatility clustering, as indicated in Fig. 8.6 below. As to be expected, the log returns of the intraday high and intraday low prices seem to be the most volatile. Furthermore, the histograms show that the returns do not look normally distributed and show signs of leptokurtosis (Fig. 8.7).

The ADF and PP unit root tests show that the variables are nonstationary at level; however, the variables are stationary at first difference. Therefore, we conclude that the logged price indices are integrated of order one.

The FTJ254 is slightly positively skewed, as apposed to the slightly negatively skewed FTJ253. The descriptive statistics results for the FTJ254 can be seen in Table 8.7 below (Table 8.8).

The lag length criteria of the estimated VAR model can be seen in Table 8.9. The final prediction error and Akaike information criterion suggest that eight lags should be used; this is one less than the optimal lag length of the VAR model estimated for FTJ253. The stability test and the cointegration test are performed using eight lags.

Tables 8.10 and 8.11 show that if we assume a linear deterministic trend in the data, the trace statistic and the maximum eigenvalue, there are three cointegrating relationships among the variables included.

When one considers the long-run relationship of the variables included, it is evident that the loading coefficients are negative and close to one; this is an evidence of future spot parity. In addition, the error correction coefficients of the closing price and intraday low are statistically significant and of the correct sing in the first cointegration equation. Both variables will adjust rapidly after a deviation from the long- run relationship. In the second cointegrating equation, the closing price, intraday high and intraday low are statistically significant and of the correct sign; the variables will adjust by a magnitude equal to the error correction coefficient daily

Table 8.6 Vector error correction model FTJ253

Standard errors in ( ) & t-statistics in [ ]				
Cointegrating Eq:	CointEq1	CointEq2	CointEq3	
CLOSE(−1)	1	0	0	
HIGH(−1)	0	1	0	
LOW(−1)	0	0	1	
OPEN(−1)	−1.00005	−1.0018	−0.99403	
	−3.90E-05	−0.00114	−0.00136	
	[−25423.5]	[−876.326]	[−730.578]	
C	−0.0002	0.005838	−0.03164	
Error Correction:	D(CLOSE)	D(HIGH)	D(LOW)	D(OPEN)
CointEq1	−3.86014	−0.34781	−2.81503	0.991302
	−2.65804	−1.66617	−1.74035	−0.08628
	[−1.45225]	[−0.20875]	[−1.61750]	[11.4891]
CointEq2	−0.48235	−0.7303	−0.42994	0.0032
	−0.17534	−0.10991	−0.1148	−0.00569
	[−2.75093]	[−6.64458]	[−3.74501]	[0.56217]
CointEq3	−0.14242	−0.20922	−0.52639	0.002996
	−0.14388	−0.09019	−0.09421	−0.00467
	[−0.98982]	[−2.31971]	[−5.58758]	[0.64149]
C	−0.00158	−0.00013	−0.00144	0.000489
	−0.00133	−0.00083	−0.00087	−4.30E-05
	[−1.18870]	[−0.16162]	[−1.65694]	[11.3599]
R-squared	0.121764	0.572368	0.509245	0.999074
Adj. R-squared	0.09315	0.558435	0.493255	0.999044
Sum sq. resids	0.058986	0.023177	0.025287	6.22E-05
S.E. equation	0.00702	0.0044	0.004596	0.000228
F-statistic	4.255371	41.08041	31.84869	33105.98
Log likelihood	4399.409	4977.168	4923.282	8639.505
Akaike AIC	−7.04836	−7.98249	−7.89536	−13.9038
Schwarz SC	−6.88278	−7.81691	−7.72979	−13.7382
Mean dependent	0.000478	0.000485	0.000487	0.000493
S.D. dependent	0.007372	0.006622	0.006457	0.007368
Determinant resid covariance (dof adj.)	1.34E-22			
Determinant resid covariance	1.18E-22			
Log likelihood	24209.79			
Akaike information criterion	−38.8647			
Schwarz criterion	−38.1527			

Source: Researchers' analysis

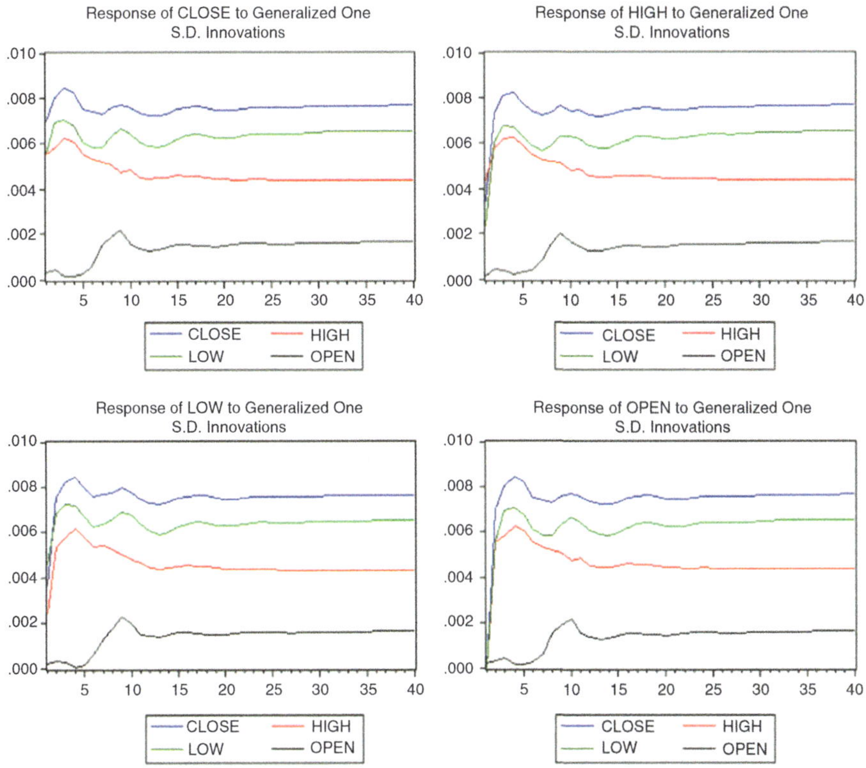

Fig. 8.5 Impulse response of FTJ253

after a deviation from the long-run relationship. Finally, the intraday high and low are statistically significant in the third cointegrating equation (Table 8.12).

Figure 8.8 indicates the individual response of a one-period standard deviation shock to each individual variable for the FTJ254. The response to the introduction of shock to the index values is similar to those of the FTJ253. It seems that in all for cases the market reaches new equilibrium after 15 lag periods (days).

8.4 Conclusion

The purpose of this paper was to explore the market efficacy of the FTSE/JSE SA Listed Property Index (FTJ253) and the FTSE/JSE Capped Property Index (FTJ254) to the introduction of a one standard deviation shock. The one standard deviation shock introduced the closing ($Close_t$), intraday high ($High_t$), intraday low (Lowt) and opening ($Open_t$) values for the daily values for the period 4 January 2010 until

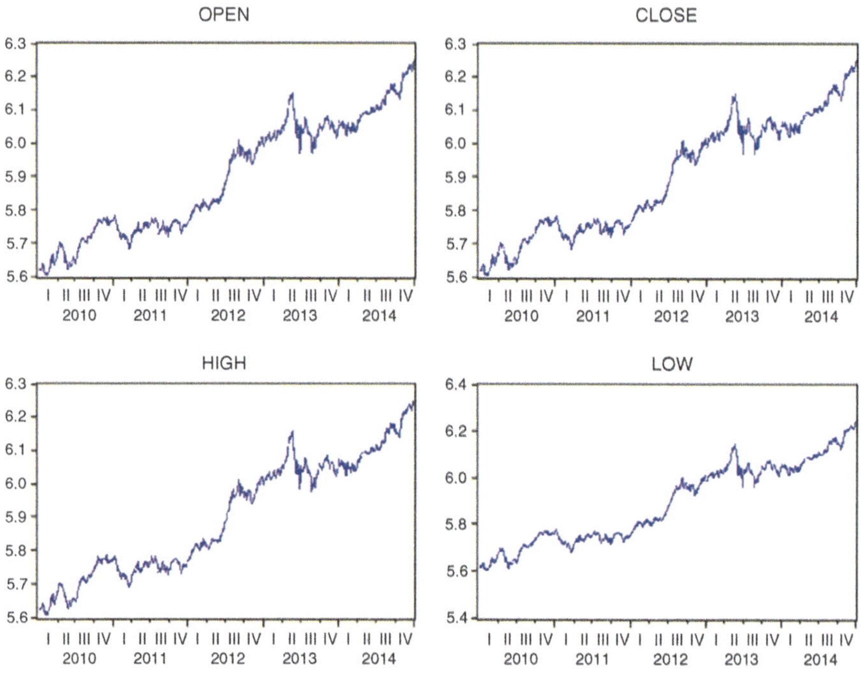

Fig. 8.6 Line graphs of the FTSE/JSE SA Capped Property Index (FTJ254)

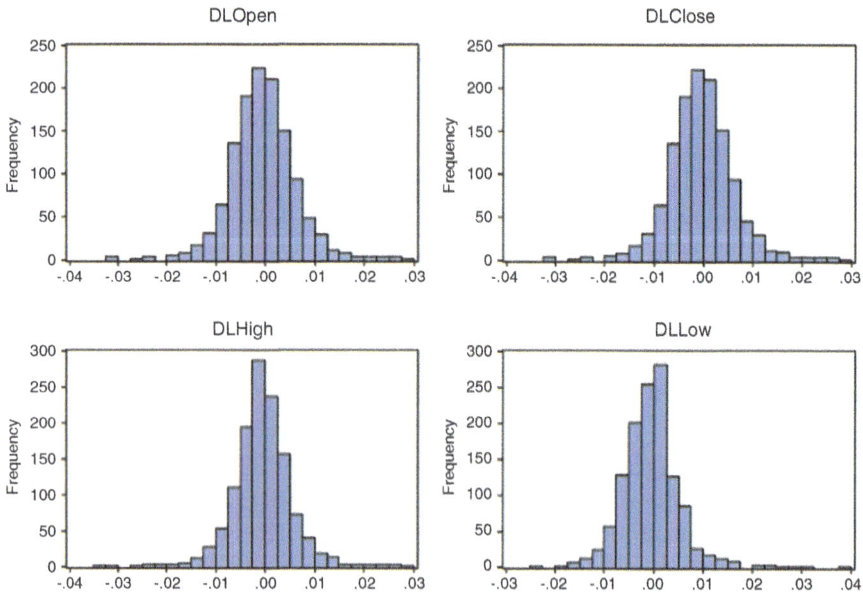

Fig. 8.7 Log returns of the FTSE/JSE SA Capped Property Index (FTJ254)

Table 8.7 Unit root test FTJ254

Variable	ADF	PP
Open	−0.063	−0.1492
Close	−0.0684	−0.1838
High	−0.281	−0.1331
Low	−0.2702	−0.1576
D(Open)	−20.0804***	−30.5064***
D(Close)	−20.1441***	−30.5502***
D(High)	−27.2292***	−27.2292***
D(Low)	−21.7472***	−24.6395***

Source: Researchers' analysis
*(**) [***]: Statistically significant at a 10(5)[1]% level

Table 8.8 Descriptive statistics FTJ254

	DLOPEN	DLCLOSE	DLHIGH	DLLOW
Mean	−0.00051	−0.0005	−0.0005	−0.0005
Median	−0.00074	−0.00071	−0.00063	−0.00055
Maximum	0.028928	0.028928	0.027553	0.037855
Minimum	−0.03158	−0.03158	−0.03335	−0.02498
Std. Dev.	0.006517	0.006527	0.005845	0.005658
Skewness	0.11894	0.127422	0.064193	0.869502
Kurtosis	5.773846	5.774902	6.799788	7.585408
Jarque-Bera	402.3961	403.1343	750.4488	1248.601
Probability	0	0	0	0
Sum	−0.62938	−0.6238	−0.62823	−0.62547
Sum Sq. Dev.	0.052884	0.053038	0.042531	0.03985
Observations	1246	1246	1246	1246

Source: Researchers' analysis

31 December 2014. The results obtained for both the indices are very similar except for the distribution of the FTJ254 that is slightly positively skewed vs. the FTJ253 that is negatively skewed.

It is clear from the results obtained that arbitrage opportunity is present when the one standard deviation shock is introduced to each individual variable. The results indicate that after 15 lag periods (15 days), the market values of the two indices reach a new equilibrium. One aspect of the variables included in this study that was not explored any further is the volatility of the property indices on the JSE. Therefore, further research might include a volatility model that accounts for volatility clustering shown in Figs. 8.2 and 8.9.

Table 8.9 Lag length criteria FTJ254

Lag	LogL	LR	FPE	AIC	SC	HQ
0	15961.37	NA	5.94E-17	−26.0104	−25.9937	−26.0041
1	24205.63	16421.32	8.90E-23	−39.4224	−39.3391*	−39.3910*
2	24235.76	59.81042	8.69E-23	−39.4454	−39.2954	−39.3890
3	24251.76	31.67215	8.69E-23	−39.4454	−39.2288	−39.3639
4	24271.35	38.63187	8.64E-23	−39.4513	−39.1679	−39.3447
5	24280.96	18.88971	8.73E-23	−39.4408	−39.0909	−39.3092
6	24298.98	35.3082	8.70E-23	−39.4441	−39.0275	−39.2874
7	24326.91	54.54307	8.54E-23	−39.4636	−38.9803	−39.2817
8	24345.48	36.13411	8.50e-23*	−39.4678*	−38.9178	−39.2608
9	24354.65	17.79696	8.60E-23	−39.4567	−38.8400	−39.2246
10	24365.65	21.26716	8.67E-23	−39.4485	−38.7652	−39.1914
11	24374.82	17.66519	8.76E-23	−39.4374	−38.6874	−39.1552
12	24385.06	19.65633	8.85E-23	−39.4280	−38.6113	−39.1207
13	24398.31	25.34798	8.89E-23	−39.4235	−38.5402	−39.0911
14	24413.42	28.82524	8.90E-23	−39.4220	−38.4721	−39.0646
15	24420.74	13.92084	9.03E-23	−39.4079	−38.3913	−39.0254
16	24448.59	52.73121*	8.86E-23	−39.4272	−38.3439	−39.0196

Source: Researchers' analysis

LR sequential modified LR test statistic (each test at 5% level), *FPE* Final prediction error, *AIC* Akaike information criterion, *SC* Schwarz information criterion, *HQ* Hannan-Quinn information criterion

*Indicates lag order selected by the criterion

Table 8.10 Unrestricted cointegration rank test (Trace) FTJ254

Hypothesized No. of CE(s)	Eigenvalue	Trace statistic	Critical value	Prob.**
None*	0.12095	344.9973	47.85613	0.0001
At most 1*	0.093934	185.4025	29.79707	0.0001
At most 2*	0.049794	63.28194	15.49471	0
At most 3	4.02E-05	0.0498	3.841466	0.8234

Source: Researchers' analysis

Table 8.11 Unrestricted cointegration rank test (maximum eigenvalue) FTJ254

Hypothesized No. of CE(s)	Eigenvalue	Trace statistic	Critical value	Prob.**
None*	0.12095	159.5948	27.58434	0.0001
At most 1*	0.093934	122.1206	21.13162	0.0001
At most 2*	0.049794	63.23214	14.2646	0
At most 3	4.02E-05	0.0498	3.841466	0.8234

Source: Researchers' analysis

Table 8.12 Vector error correction model FTJ254

Standard errors in ( ) & t-statistics in [ ]				
Cointegrating Eq:	CointEq1	CointEq2	CointEq3	
CLOSE(−1)	1	0	0	
HIGH(−1)	0	1	0	
LOW(−1)	0	0	1	
OPEN(−1)	−1.00004	−1.0007	−0.99656	
	−3.90E-05	−0.0009	−0.00105	
	[−25950.8]	[−1107.91]	[−945.766]	
C	−0.00028	−0.00069	−0.01601	
Error Correction:	D(CLOSE)	D(HIGH)	D(LOW)	D(OPEN)
CointEq1	−5.2508	−2.14882	−2.85458	0.997668
	−2.12903	−1.35323	−1.36859	−0.08156
	[−2.46629]	[−1.58793]	[−2.08579]	[12.2317]
CointEq2	−0.40982	−0.79014	−0.47831	0.003972
	−0.17427	−0.11076	−0.11202	−0.00668
	[−2.35170]	[−7.13349]	[−4.26983]	[0.59498]
CointEq3	−0.10275	−0.24832	−0.57626	0.003426
	−0.14598	−0.09279	−0.09384	−0.00559
	[−0.70389]	[−2.67629]	[−6.14094]	[0.61262]
C	−0.00229	−0.00107	−0.00152	0.000506
	−0.00109	−0.00069	−0.0007	−4.20E-05
	[−2.09533]	[−1.53217]	[−2.16626]	[12.0896]
R-squared	0.104717	0.549725	0.508178	0.998682
Adj. R-squared	0.078648	0.536614	0.493857	0.998644
Sum sq. resids	0.047383	0.019143	0.01958	6.95E-05
S.E. equation	0.006279	0.003991	0.004036	0.000241
F-statistic	4.016902	41.92801	35.48498	26027.44
Log likelihood	4539.038	5100.067	5086.095	8577.43
Akaike AIC	−7.2747	−8.18105	−8.15847	−13.7988
Schwarz SC	−7.12578	−8.03212	−8.00955	−13.6498
Mean dependent	0.000501	0.000505	0.000502	0.000507
S.D. dependent	0.006541	0.005862	0.005673	0.006532
Determinant resid covariance (dof adj.)	7.45E-23			
Determinant resid covariance	6.62E-23			
Log likelihood	24585.25			
Akaike information criterion	−39.4657			
Schwarz criterion	−38.8203			

Source: Researchers' analysis

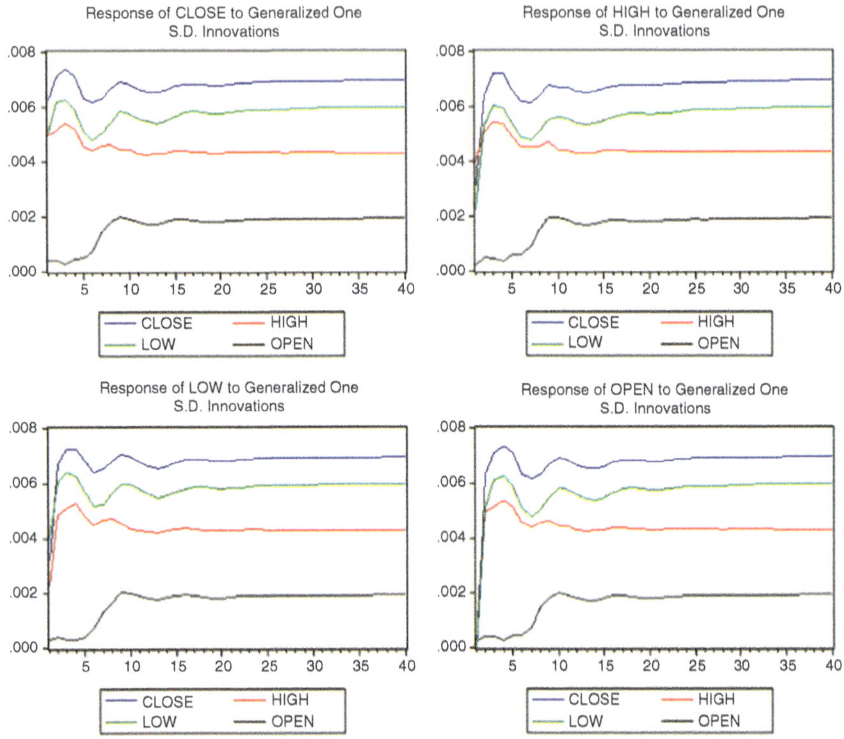

Fig. 8.8 Impulse response of FTJ254

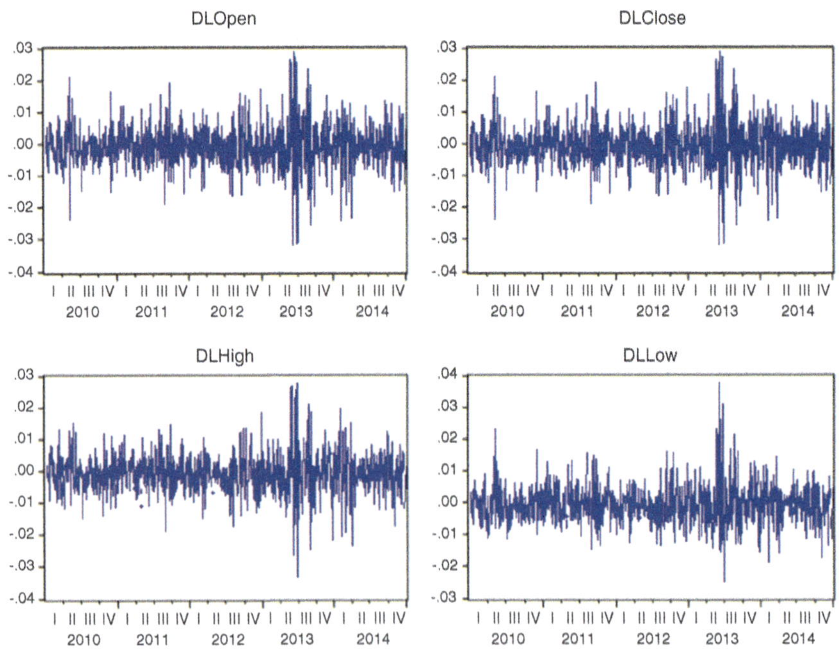

Fig. 8.9 Lag length criteria FTJ254

References

Black, F. (1986). Noise. *The Journal of Finance, 41*(3), 528–543.

Campbell, J. Y. & Shiller, R. J. (1988). Stock prices, earnings, and expected dividends. *The Journal of Finance, 43*(3), 661–676.

Damodaran, A. (2012). *Investment valuation: Tools and techniques for determining the value of any asset*. Hoboken: Wiley.

De Long, J. B., Shleifer, A., Summers, L. H., & Waldmann, R. J. (1990). Noise trader risk in financial markets. *Journal of Political Economy, 98*(4), 703–738.

Engle, R. F. (2003). Risk and volatility: Econometric models and financial practice. Nobel Lecture. https://www.nobelprize.org/nobel_prizes/economic-sciences/laureates/2003/engle-lecture.html.

Engle, R. F., & Granger, C. W. (1987). Co-integration and error correction: Representation, estimation, and testing. *Econometrica: Journal of the Econometric Society, 55*, 251–276.

Fama, E. F. (1965a). The behavior of stock-market prices. *The Journal of Business, 38*(1), 34–105.

Fama, E. F. (1965b). Portfolio analysis in a stable Paretian market. *Management Science, 11*(3), 404–419.

Fama, E. F. (1970). *The Journal of Finance, 25*(2), 383–417.

Koop, G. M. (2006). *Analysis of financial data*. Chichester: Wiley.

McNeil, A., Frey, R., & Embrechts, P. (2005). *Quantitative risk management* (Princeton series in finance, Vol. 10(4)). Princeton: Princeton University Press.

Roberts, H. V. (1959). Stock-market "patterns" and financial analysis: Methodological suggestions. *The Journal of Finance, 14*(1), 1–10.

Chapter 9
Liquidity Proxies Based on Intraday Data: The Case of the Polish Order-Driven Stock Market

Joanna Olbrys and Michal Mursztyn

Abstract The objective of this paper is to estimate selected liquidity measures based on high-frequency intraday data and to examine their magnitude on the Warsaw Stock Exchange (WSE). We construct and analyze a panel of data which consists of daily proxies of five liquidity estimates for 53 WSE-traded companies divided into three size groups. Although the WSE is classified as an order-driven market with an electronic order book, the raw data set does not identify trade direction. Therefore, the trade classification Lee and Ready (J Finance 46(2):733–746, 1991) algorithm is employed to infer trade sides and to distinguish between so-called buyer- and seller-initiated trades. Moreover, the paper provides a robustness analysis of the obtained results with respect to the whole sample and three adjacent subsamples each of equal size: the precrisis, global financial crisis (GFC), and postcrisis periods. The constructed panel of data would be utilized in further investigation concerning commonality in liquidity on the Polish stock market.

Keywords Intraday data · Liquidity · Trade classification algorithm · Order-driven market · Global financial crisis

9.1 Introduction

The role of liquidity in empirical finance and market microstructure has grown over the last years influencing conclusions in asset pricing, corporate finance, and market efficiency. In his seminal work, Kyle (1985) argues that market liquidity is a slippery and elusive concept, in part because it encompasses a number of transactional properties of markets. For example, the inconsistent evidence of commonality in liquidity on various stock markets in the world might be attributed to the differences in market designs. It is important to distinguish between order-

J. Olbrys (✉) · M. Mursztyn
Bialystok University of Technology, Bialystok, Poland
e-mail: j.olbrys@pb.edu.pl; m.mursztyn@student.pb.edu.pl

N. Tsounis, A. Vlachvei (eds.), *Advances in Panel Data Analysis in Applied Economic Research*, Springer Proceedings in Business and Economics,
https://doi.org/10.1007/978-3-319-70055-7_9

driven and quote-driven market structures because market structure determines how orders are transformed into trades and how this transformation affects liquidity. In an order-driven market, no designated market maker has an obligation to provide liquidity to the market. Traders and investors submit a limit order book to buy and sell shares, e.g., Harris (2003). Unfortunately, although the Warsaw Stock Exchange (WSE) is classified as an order-driven market with an electronic order book, the information of the best bid and ask price is not publicly available, e.g., Olbryś and Mursztyn (2015) and Nowak (2017).

It is important to note that direct measurement of liquidity, bid/ask spreads, other trading costs, etc. is difficult and even impossible as intraday trading data are not available free of charge in the case of most emerging stock markets. The lack of access to intraday trading data for emerging markets in general is a fact that is both widely known and amply commented in the literature, e.g., Lesmond (2005), Bekaert et al. (2007), and Olbryś (2014).

Measuring liquidity/illiquidity on the WSE is a crucial subject as Nowak and Olbryś (2016) documented cross-time and cross-security patterns in non-trading among the WSE-listed stocks. The empirical results reveal that a large number of the companies exhibit substantial non-trading problem, which means the lack of transactions over a particular period when the WSE is open for trading. Therefore, investors should recognize whether they have to take illiquidity risk into consideration in their financial decisions.

The goal of this paper is to estimate selected liquidity/illiquidity proxies derived from intraday data and to examine their magnitude on the WSE. We construct and analyze the panel of data which consists of daily estimations of five liquidity measures for 53 WSE-traded companies divided into three size groups. The high-frequency intraday data "rounded to the nearest second" covers the period from January 3, 2005, to June 30, 2015. As the raw data set does not identify a trade direction on the WSE, the trade classification Lee and Ready (1991) algorithm is employed to infer trade sides and to distinguish between so-called buyer- and seller-initiated trades (Olbryś and Mursztyn 2015). Moreover, the paper provides a robustness analysis of the obtained results with respect to the whole sample and three adjacent subsamples each of equal size: precrisis, crisis, and postcrisis periods. The global financial crisis (GFC) on the WSE is formally set based on the papers (Olbrys and Majewska 2014, 2015), in which the Pagan and Sossounov (2003) method for formal statistical identification of market states was employed.

To the best of the author's knowledge, the presented empirical results on the WSE are novel and have not been reported in the literature thus far. The constructed panel of data could be used in further investigation concerning commonality in liquidity on the WSE. It is worth to note that empirical market microstructure research has recently shifted its focus from the examination of liquidity of individual securities toward analyses of the common determinants and components of liquidity.

The remainder of the study is organized as follows. Section 9.2 describes the methodological background concerning the measurement of liquidity using intraday data. Section 9.3 presents a brief analysis of the obtained data panel and discusses the empirical results on the WSE. The last section summarizes the main findings with the conclusion.

Nomenclature	
WSE	Warsaw Stock Exchange
GFC	The 2007–2009 global financial crisis
LR	The Lee and Ready (1991) trade side classification algorithm
%RS	Percentage relative spread
%ES	Percentage effective spread
%RealS	Percentage realized spread
%PI	Percentage price impact
%OR	Percentage order ratio

9.2 Measuring Liquidity/Illiquidity Using Intraday Data

There is a growing body of empirical literature concerning direct measurement of liquidity based on intraday transaction data. Specifically, there has been quite extensive research on various versions of a bid/ask spread. The related literature indicates that different versions of a bid/ask spread are proper measures for stock illiquidity because they approximate the cost of immediate execution of a trade. In this research, percentage relative spread, percentage effective spread, and percentage realized spread are employed. It is worth to note that sometimes the same spread measure has different names. For example, relative spread is sometimes referred to as inside bid/ask spread, e.g., Levin and Wright (1999) and Acker et al. (2002), or as proportional (quoted) spread, e.g., Corwin (1999), Chordia et al. (2000, 2001), Chung and Van Ness (2001), Korajczyk and Sadka (2008), and Hameed et al. (2010). As for effective spread, the nomenclature is not unambiguous either. For example, in his seminal work Roll (1984) introduces the estimator of effective bid/ask spread in an efficient market, but he does not utilize intraday transaction data. Moreover, there are at least two basic versions of an effective spread derived from intraday data. One of them is calculated using a quote midpoint in the denominator, e.g., Corwin (1999), Finucane (2000), and Theissen (2001), while the second is computed using a transaction price, e.g., Chordia et al. (2000), Peterson and Sirri (2003), and Chakrabarty et al. (2007).

The literature is far too vast to give a complete citation list. Therefore, Table 9.1 presents a brief literature review concerning various versions of liquidity/illiquidity proxies based on the bid/ask spread concept. It is worth to note that both relative and effective spreads have been explored quite extensively, but relatively little empirical research has been conducted using realized spread. Realized spread is a temporary component of effective spread, which is defined as the amount earned by a dealer or other supplier of immediacy, e.g., Huang and Stoll (1996) and Theissen (2001). Realized spread is sometimes referred to as a price reversal component since a dealer takes profits only if price reverses.

Moreover, a price impact estimate is employed in our study. According to the literature, a proxy of price impact measures the sensitivity of a stock's price to trades (Stoll 2000, p. 1495), and most of researchers derive price impact from intraday

Table 9.1 Summarized literature review: selected papers including various empirical applications of relative spread, effective spread, and realized spread

The authors	Relative spread	Effective spread	Realized spread
Lee, Mucklow, and Ready (1993)	–	+	–
Lin, Sanger, and Booth (1995)	+	+	–
Huang and Stoll (1996)	–	+	+
Kluger and Stephan (1997)	+	–	–
Corwin (1999)	+	+	–
Levin and Wright (1999)	+	–	–
Brockman and Chung (2000)	+	–	–
Elyasiani, Hauser, and Lauterbach (2000)	+	–	–
Van Ness, Van Ness, and Pruitt (2000)	+	+	–
Chordia, Roll, and Subrahmanyam (2000)	+	+	–
Finucane (2000)	–	+	–
Stoll (2000)	–	+	–
Theissen (2001)	+	+	+
Chordia, Roll, and Subrahmanyam (2001)	+	+	–
Chung and Van Ness (2001)	+	–	–
Acker, Stalker, and Tonks (2002)	+	–	–
Piwowar and Wei (2003)	+	+	–
Peterson and Sirri (2003)	+	+	–
von Wyss (2004)	+	+	+
Chakrabarty, Li, Nguyen, and Van Ness (2007)	–	+	–
Korajczyk and Sadka (2008)	+	+	–
Pukthuanthong-Le and Visaltanachoti (2009)	+	–	–
Goyenko, Holden, and Trzcinka (2009)	+	+	+
Hameed, Kang, and Viswanathan (2010)	+	–	–
Olbrys and Mursztyn (2017)	+	–	–
Olbryś (2017)	+	–	–

transaction data, e.g., Chakrabarty et al. (2007), von Wyss (2004), and Coppejans et al. (2004). Kyle (1985) provides a theoretical model for such a measure based on the adverse information conveyed by a trade. Price impact could be defined as the increase (decrease) in the quote midpoint over a time interval beginning at the time of the buyer- (seller-) initiated trade. This is the permanent price change of a given transaction, or equivalently, the permanent component of effective spread, e.g., Goyenko et al. (2009, p. 156).

Furthermore, order ratio as an order imbalance indicator is utilized in this research. Order imbalance has important influence on stock liquidity, considerably even more important than volume. Therefore, order imbalance indicators could be employed among other liquidity and trading activity measures to estimate liquidity. The literature proposes various proxies of order imbalance, e.g., Chan, Fong (2000), Ranaldo (2001), Chordia et al. (2002, 2005), von Wyss (2004), Korajczyk and

Sadka (2008), Pukthuanthong-Le and Visaltanachoti (2009), Nowak (2017), Olbrys and Mursztyn (2017), and Olbryś (2017). In this study, percentage order ratio is employed.

9.2.1 Selected Spread Proxies Derived from Intraday Data

In this research, we utilize the high-frequency data "rounded to the nearest second." The data set contains the opening, high, low, and closing (OHLC) prices and volume for a security over one unit of time. In measuring spread proxies, high, low, and closing prices are needed.

The midpoint price P_t^{mid} at time t is calculated as the arithmetic mean of the best ask price $P_t(a)$ and the best bid price $P_t(b)$ at time t. Considering that the bid and ask prices are not made public on the WSE, the midpoint price at time t is rounded by the arithmetic mean of the lowest price P_t^L and the highest price P_t^H at time t, which approximate the best ask price and the best bid price, respectively (Olbryś and Mursztyn 2015, p. 43):

$$P_t^{\text{mid}} = \frac{P_t^H + P_t^L}{2} \tag{9.1}$$

The transaction price P_t at time t is approximated by the closing price.

Percentage Relative Spread The percentage relative spread value is given by Eq. (9.2):

$$\%RS_t = \frac{100 \cdot \left(P_t^H - P_t^L\right)}{P_t^{\text{mid}}} \tag{9.2}$$

where P_t^H, P_t^L are the highest and lowest prices at time t, respectively, while the midpoint price P_t^{mid} at time t is given by Eq. (9.1). Percentage relative spread is in fact a measure of illiquidity. A wide percentage relative spread value denotes low liquidity. Conversely, a narrow percentage relative spread value denotes high liquidity. The %RS at time t is equal to zero when $P_t^H = P_t^L$. Daily percentage relative spread value is calculated as a volume-weighted average of percentage relative spreads computed over all trades within a day.

Percentage Effective Spread The percentage effective spread value is obtained by relating the transaction price to the midpoint of the bid and ask quote and it is given by Eq. (9.3):

$$\%ES_t = \frac{200 \cdot \left|P_t - P_t^{\text{mid}}\right|}{P_t^{\text{mid}}} \tag{9.3}$$

where the midpoint price P_t^{mid} at time t is given by Eq. (9.1), while the transaction price P_t at time t is approximated by the closing price. Similarly to percentage relative spread, percentage effective spread is an illiquidity measure. A wide percentage effective spread value denotes low liquidity. Conversely, a narrow percentage effective spread value denotes high liquidity. The %ES at time t is equal to zero when $P_t = P_t^{\text{mid}}$. Daily percentage effective spread value is calculated as a volume-weighted average of percentage effective spreads computed over all trades within a day.

9.2.2 *Trade Side Classification Algorithm*

To calculate several liquidity/illiquidity measures using intraday data, it is essential to recognize the side initiating the transaction and to distinguish between so-called buyer- and seller-initiated trades. The WSE is classified as an order-driven market with an electronic order book, but information of the best bid and ask price is not publicly available. In fact, even the nonproprietary financial databases that provide information on trades and quotes do not identify the trade direction. As a consequence, the researchers rely on indirect trade classification rules to infer trade sides. There are some trade classification procedures described in the literature, but the Lee and Ready (1991) algorithm (LR) remains the most frequently used (Chakrabarty et al. 2012, p. 468). The LR algorithm proceeds in three steps (Theissen 2001, p. 148):

1. Transactions that occur at prices higher (lower) than the quote midpoint are classified as buyer-initiated (seller-initiated) trades.
2. Transactions that occur at a price that equals the quote midpoint but is higher (lower) than the previous transaction price are classified as being buyer-initiated (seller-initiated).
3. Transactions that occur at a price that equals both the quote midpoint and the previous transaction price but is higher (lower) than the last different transaction price are classified as buyer-initiated (seller-initiated) trades.

In this paper, the LR procedure is employed as Olbryś and Mursztyn (2015) indicated that this algorithm performs quite well on the WSE, the empirical results turn out to be robust to the choice of the sample and do not depend on a firm size.

9.2.3 *Some Liquidity Proxies Supported by the Trade Side Classification Algorithm*

As mentioned in the previous section, to compute some liquidity estimates using intraday data, it is essential to distinguish between the buyer- and seller-initiated trades. In this research, three alternative estimates of liquidity, supported by the trade side classification algorithm, are employed: (1) percentage realized spread, (2) percentage price impact, and (3) percentage order ratio as an order imbalance indicator. Both the realized spread and price impact proxies are treated as effective spread components, and they are calculated over a time interval beginning at the moment of the buyer- or seller-initiated transaction. For example, Goyenko et al. (2009, p. 156) employ a 5-min interval, and the subscript $t + 5$ means the trade 5-min after the trade t. Chakrabarty et al. (2007, p. 3820) use the subscript $t + 10$ which means the trade 10-min after the trade t. Theissen (2001, p. 159) proposes more general approach and the subscript $t + \tau$. In this study, the subscript $t + 5$ means the fifth trade after the trade t, as Nowak and Olbryś (2016) documented that a large number of the WSE-listed companies exhibit substantial non-trading problem, i.e., the lack of transactions over a particular period when the WSE is open for trading.

Percentage Realized Spread The percentage realized spread value, which is a temporary component of the effective spread, is given by Eq. (9.4):

$$\%\text{Real } S_t = \begin{cases} 200 \cdot \ln \frac{P_t}{P_{t+5}}, \text{ when the trade } t \text{ is classified as a buyer-initiated} \\ 200 \cdot \ln \frac{P_{t+5}}{P_t}, \text{ when the trade } t \text{ is classified as a seller-initiated} \end{cases} \tag{9.4}$$

where the transaction price P_t at time t is approximated by the closing price. The price P_{t+5} is the closing price of the fifth trade after the trade t. The %RealS at time t is equal to zero when $P_t = P_{t+5}$. The post-trade revenues earned by the dealer (or other supplier of liquidity) are estimated on the basis of actual post-trade prices. Daily percentage realized spread value is calculated as a volume-weighted average of percentage realized spreads computed over all trades within a day. Moreover, daily percentage realized spread value is defined as equal to zero when all transactions within a day are unclassified.

Percentage Price Impact The proxy of price impact focuses on the change in a quote midpoint after a signed trade, and it is given by Eq. (9.5):

$$\%PI_t = \begin{cases} 200 \cdot \ln \frac{P_{t+5}^{\text{mid}}}{P_t^{\text{mid}}}, \text{ when the trade } t \text{ is classified as a buyer-initiated} \\ 200 \cdot \ln \frac{P_t^{\text{mid}}}{P_{t+5}^{\text{mid}}}, \text{ when the trade } t \text{ is classified as a seller-initiated} \end{cases} \tag{9.5}$$

where the midpoint price P_t^{mid} at time t is given by Eq. (9.1), while P_{t+5}^{mid} is the quote midpoint of the fifth trade after the trade t. Price impact could be defined as the increase (decrease) in the midpoint over a five-trade interval beginning at the time of buyer- (seller-) initiated transaction. The %PI at time t is equal to zero when $P_t^{\text{mid}} = P_{t+5}^{\text{mid}}$. Daily proxy of percentage price impact value is calculated as a volume-weighted average of percentage price impact estimates computed over all trades within a day. Moreover, daily percentage price impact value is defined as equal to zero when all transactions within a day are unclassified.

Percentage Order Ratio The percentage order ratio as daily order imbalance indicator is given by the following Eq. (9.6):

$$\%\mathrm{OR} = 100 \cdot \frac{\left|\sum_{i=1}^{m} \mathrm{VBuy}_i - \sum_{j=1}^{k} \mathrm{VSell}_j\right|}{\sum_{n=1}^{N} V_n} \tag{9.6}$$

where the sums $\sum_{i=1}^{m} \mathrm{VBuy}_i$, $\sum_{j=1}^{k} \mathrm{VSell}_j$, $\sum_{n=1}^{N} V_n$ denote daily cumulated trading volume related to transactions classified as buyer- or seller-initiated trades, and daily cumulated trading volume for all transactions, respectively. The OR indicator captures imbalance in the market since it rises as the difference in the numerator becomes large. According to the literature, a high order ratio value denotes low liquidity. Conversely, a small order ratio value denotes high liquidity. The OR indicator is equal to zero when the numerator is equal to zero. It happens when daily cumulated trading volumes related to transactions classified as buyer- or seller-initiated trades are equal. Moreover, the daily order ratio value is defined as equal to zero in two cases: (1) when all transactions within a day are unclassified, or (2) when total daily trading volume in the denominator is equal to zero.

9.3 Data Description and Empirical Results on the WSE

As mentioned in previous section, we utilize the database containing the high-frequency data "rounded to the nearest second" (available at www.bossa.pl) for 53 WSE-traded stock divided into three size groups, in the period from January 3, 2005 to June 30, 2015. When forming the database, we included only those securities which existed on the WSE for the whole sample period since December 31, 2004, and were not suspended. All companies entered into the database (147) were sorted according to their market capitalization at the end of each year. Next, the stocks were divided into three size groups based on the breakpoints for the bottom 30% (small companies), middle 40% (medium companies), and top 30% (big companies) (Fama and French 1993). The companies that remained in the same group during the period investigated were selected. Finally, the 53 WSE-listed companies were gathered into separate groups, specifically: 27 firms into the BIG group, 18 firms into the MEDIUM group, and 8 firms into the SMALL group (Nowak and Olbryś 2016).

We construct and analyze the panel of data which consists of daily proxies of five liquidity/illiquidity estimates presented in Sect. 9.2. As the intraday data set is large, special programs in the C++ programming language have been implemented to reduce the time required for calculations.

To verify the robustness of the obtained empirical results, the research is provided over the whole sample (2626 trading days) and three adjacent subsamples each of equal size (436 trading days): (1) the precrisis period September 6, 2005, to May 31, 2007; (2) the crisis period June 1, 2007, to February 27, 2009; and (3) the postcrisis period March 2, 2009, to November 19, 2010 (Olbrys and Mursztyn 2015; 2017). The global financial crisis on the WSE is formally set based on the papers (Olbryś and Majewska 2014; 2015), in which the Pagan and Sossounov (2003) method for formal statistical identification of market states was employed.

9.3.1 Summarized Results of Liquidity Estimates

Tables 9.2, 9.3, and 9.4 present summarized results of the average daily values of five liquidity proxies described in Sect. 9.2, for each WSE-traded company entering the size group (i.e., BIG, MEDIUM, or SMALL, respectively). These results are worth of a comment. In general, the values of all liquidity estimates rather do not depend on a firm size and turn out to be robust to the choice of the period. Moreover, we observe the lower values of illiquidity proxies (i.e., %RS, %ES, %OR) for the most liquid big companies with the largest market capitalization (namely, KGH, OPL, PEO, PKN, PKO), regardless of the subsample choice.

Moreover, one can observe in Tables 9.2, 9.3, and 9.4 that average daily estimations of realized spread (%RealS) are positive for almost all stocks from three size groups, except for isolated cases. These findings are rather consistent with the literature because the existence of a bid/ask spread has several consequences in time series properties, and one of them is the bid/ask bounce, e.g., Roll (1984) and Tsay (2010). According to definition (4), realized spread is in fact a percentage logarithmic rate of return. As a price reversal component of a bid/ask spread the realized spread is usually positive since an investor realizes earnings only if price reverses. A small positive realized spread value informs about higher liquidity, while a high positive realized spread value denotes lower liquidity. Furthermore, the evidence is that average daily estimations of price impact (%PI) are negative in most cases, which is a probable consequence of the fact that both the realized spread and price impact proxies are treated as the effective bid/ask spread components complementing each other, e.g., Glosten (1987) and Huang and Stoll (1996, 1997).

Tables 9.2, 9.3, and 9.4 are based on (1) the whole sample period P_1 (3.01.2005 to 30.06.2015), (2) the precrisis period P_2 (6.09.2005 to 31.05.2007), (3) the global financial crisis period P_3 (1.06.2007 to 27.02.2009), and the postcrisis period P_4 (2.03.2009 to 19.11.2010). Ticker symbols are in alphabetical order according to the company's full name.

Table 9.2 The BIG group – the average daily values of five liquidity proxies: %RS (2), %ES (3), %RealS (4), %PI (5), and %OR (6)

	%RS				%ES				%RealS				%PI				%OR			
BIG	P_1	P_2	P_3	P_4	P_1	P_2	P_3	P_4	P_1	P_2	P_3	P_4	P_1	P_2	P_3	P_4	P_1	P_2	P_3	P_4
BHW	0.04	0.04	0.04	0.04	0.04	0.04	0.04	0.04	0.09	0.14	0.11	0.11	−0.06	−0.11	−0.07	−0.07	38.4	46.9	47.0	49.2
BPH	0.10	0.02	0.06	0.10	0.10	0.02	0.06	0.10	0.14	0.07	0.16	0.20	−0.07	−0.05	−0.11	−0.11	40.1	32.9	40.7	40.0
BNP	0.09	0.15	0.20	0.02	0.09	0.15	0.20	0.02	0.03	0.01	0.06	−0.001	−0.01	0.03	−0.02	0.001	31.0	26.7	38.3	16.0
BOS	0.11	0.12	0.08	0.14	0.11	0.12	0.08	0.13	0.04	0.01	0.007	0.06	−0.01	−0.001	−0.01	−0.03	34.2	30.9	27.9	34.7
BDX	0.08	0.10	0.07	0.06	0.07	0.10	0.07	0.06	0.11	0.03	0.15	0.10	−0.06	0.04	−0.09	−0.05	42.8	52.8	47.1	44.7
BZW	0.04	0.03	0.03	0.03	0.04	0.03	0.03	0.03	0.07	0.09	0.08	0.07	−0.04	−0.06	−0.05	−0.04	30.7	31.9	24.7	26.4
DBC	0.10	0.09	0.08	0.12	0.10	0.09	0.08	0.12	0.09	0.12	0.07	0.12	−0.04	−0.05	−0.03	−0.07	43.6	41.3	49.0	41.3
ECH	0.08	0.09	0.07	0.10	0.08	0.09	0.07	0.09	0.16	0.10	0.17	0.22	−0.10	−0.04	−0.10	−0.14	44.6	47.5	39.6	43.2
GTN	0.06	0.04	0.04	0.03	0.05	0.04	0.04	0.03	0.11	0.15	0.08	0.07	−0.06	−0.11	−0.04	−0.04	27.4	25.9	29.1	25.2
GTC	0.05	0.05	0.04	0.03	0.05	0.05	0.03	0.03	0.09	0.11	0.05	0.08	−0.05	−0.07	−0.02	−0.05	30.1	33.1	24.8	26.0
ING	0.06	0.06	0.09	0.06	0.06	0.06	0.09	0.05	0.10	0.13	0.09	0.09	−0.05	−0.08	−0.03	−0.04	48.0	57.6	53.2	43.4
KTY	0.07	0.04	0.07	0.08	0.07	0.04	0.06	0.08	0.13	0.22	0.13	0.09	−0.08	−0.18	−0.09	−0.04	46.0	44.2	50.6	48.9
KGH	0.02	0.02	0.03	0.03	0.02	0.02	0.03	0.03	0.02	0.02	0.03	0.03	0.000	0.000	−0.01	−0.007	17.0	16.7	18.9	18.5
LPP	0.08	0.09	0.11	0.09	0.08	0.09	0.10	0.09	0.09	0.05	0.19	0.12	−0.05	−0.01	−0.12	−0.08	45.8	53.0	48.8	51.7

MBK	0.03	0.04	0.03	0.04	0.03	0.04	0.03	0.04	0.07	0.13	0.06	0.08	−0.04	−0.10	−0.03	−0.04	29.3	39.6	28.0	24.2
MIL	0.05	0.07	0.05	0.06	0.05	0.07	0.04	0.05	0.11	0.15	0.13	0.10	−0.07	−0.09	−0.09	−0.05	35.2	38.0	39.0	29.8
MOL	0.07	0.07	0.08	0.09	0.07	0.07	0.07	0.09	0.07	0.17	0.14	0.04	−0.04	−0.11	−0.11	−0.02	46.6	43.6	49.2	49.5
NET	0.05	0.03	0.07	0.06	0.05	0.03	0.07	0.05	0.12	0.15	0.13	0.13	−0.08	−0.11	−0.07	−0.08	36.5	29.2	42.3	39.4
OPL	0.02	0.01	0.02	0.02	0.02	0.01	0.02	0.02	0.04	0.04	0.04	0.04	−0.02	−0.03	−0.02	−0.04	21.4	19.6	20.1	21.7
ORB	0.08	0.05	0.05	0.10	0.08	0.05	0.05	0.10	0.13	0.17	0.10	0.17	−0.08	−0.12	−0.07	−0.10	49.8	45.2	48.9	51.2
PEO	0.02	0.02	0.02	0.02	0.02	0.02	0.02	0.02	0.03	0.03	0.04	0.04	−0.008	−0.02	−0.02	−0.02	21.1	24.2	21.0	21.1
PKN	0.02	0.01	0.02	0.02	0.02	0.01	0.02	0.02	0.02	0.02	0.03	0.02	0.001	−0.004	−0.01	−0.004	18.8	18.9	19.5	20.3
PKO	0.02	0.01	0.02	0.02	0.02	0.01	0.02	0.02	0.03	0.04	0.03	0.03	−0.01	−0.03	−0.14	−0.08	19.5	23.3	20.5	19.7
STP	0.14	0.12	0.14	0.12	0.13	0.12	0.13	0.12	0.14	0.16	0.22	0.16	−0.07	−0.08	−0.10	−0.31	44.7	43.0	47.5	45.8
SNS	0.07	0.11	0.08	0.07	0.06	0.11	0.07	0.06	0.12	0.12	0.20	0.20	−0.07	−0.03	−0.13	−0.14	31.7	40.9	37.8	34.4
TVN	0.04	0.03	0.03	0.04	0.04	0.03	0.03	0.03	0.08	0.09	0.08	0.08	−0.05	−0.06	−0.06	−0.05	27.2	28.4	25.2	26.1
ZWC	0.14	0.12	0.22	0.17	0.13	0.12	0.22	0.16	0.03	0.03	0.04	0.03	−0.01	−0.01	0.003	0.001	38.8	41.1	41.6	42.3
Mean	*0.06*	*0.06*	*0.07*	*0.07*	*0.06*	*0.06*	*0.07*	*0.06*	*0.08*	*0.09*	*0.10*	*0.10*	*−0.05*	*−0.06*	*−0.06*	*−0.07*	*34.8*	*36.2*	*36.3*	*34.6*

Table 9.3 The MEDIUM group – the average daily values of five liquidity proxies: %RS (2), %ES (3), %RealS (4), %PI (5), and %OR (6)

	%RS				%ES				%RealS				%PI				%OR			
MEDIUM	P_1	P_2	P_3	P_4	P_1	P_2	P_3	P_4	P_1	P_2	P_3	P_4	P_1	P_2	P_3	P_4	P_1	P_2	P_3	P_4
ALM	0.17	0.16	0.14	0.18	0.17	0.16	0.14	0.17	0.22	0.26	0.20	0.23	−0.13	−0.14	−0.12	−0.09	42.9	38.7	46.6	36.8
AMC	0.12	0.15	0.15	0.15	0.12	0.15	0.15	0.14	0.17	0.21	0.25	0.17	−0.08	−0.09	−0.14	−0.06	37.3	37.3	40.0	27.0
ATG	0.17	0.16	0.16	0.15	0.17	0.16	0.16	0.15	0.12	0.03	−0.003	0.04	−0.04	0.02	0.04	0.01	43.7	42.8	47.3	50.3
ATM	0.13	0.15	0.14	0.14	0.13	0.15	0.14	0.14	0.16	0.19	0.25	0.16	−0.10	−0.10	−0.16	−0.09	44.3	45.2	43.3	42.2
CNG	0.12	0.10	0.12	0.12	0.12	0.10	0.12	0.11	0.14	0.17	0.08	0.18	−0.08	−0.11	0.004	−0.11	44.4	37.3	49.9	46.8
COL	0.16	0.15	0.18	0.13	0.15	0.15	0.18	0.12	0.17	0.04	0.20	0.19	−0.07	0.02	−0.08	−0.08	37.2	47.0	40.1	24.8
IND	0.12	0.15	0.11	0.17	0.12	0.15	0.11	0.17	0.09	0.10	0.08	0.20	−0.05	−0.04	−0.06	−0.14	43.7	45.1	46.4	46.2
IPL	0.13	0.15	0.14	0.13	0.13	0.15	0.14	0.13	0.11	0.17	0.08	0.10	−0.04	−0.06	−0.02	−0.03	44.7	37.9	42.0	41.6
LTX	0.13	0.15	0.13	0.16	0.13	0.15	0.13	0.15	0.15	0.17	0.18	0.19	−0.06	−0.03	−0.06	−0.08	33.7	28.5	28.4	33.0
MCI	0.13	0.13	0.13	0.14	0.12	0.13	0.12	0.12	0.16	0.20	0.15	0.12	−0.05	−0.08	−0.03	−0.01	24.9	24.4	24.7	17.4
MNI	0.17	0.14	0.15	0.11	0.16	0.14	0.14	0.10	0.21	0.23	0.20	0.15	−0.09	−0.10	−0.09	−0.06	34.1	26.8	27.8	40.8
PEK	0.14	0.14	0.12	0.16	0.14	0.14	0.12	0.16	0.14	0.23	0.22	0.07	−0.08	−0.14	−0.16	−0.03	43.4	40.7	45.8	47.5
PUE	0.18	0.19	0.22	0.20	0.18	0.19	0.22	0.20	0.05	0.02	0.06	0.08	−0.01	0.02	−0.02	−0.03	41.5	42.1	38.6	42.6
SKA	0.11	0.14	0.10	0.10	0.11	0.14	0.10	0.10	0.02	0.04	0.08	−0.02	0.000	−0.01	−0.07	−0.04	43.9	43.6	43.3	45.6
STF	0.13	0.12	0.16	0.15	0.13	0.12	0.16	0.15	0.13	0.18	0.19	0.17	−0.06	−0.08	−0.07	−0.09	40.9	28.1	39.4	42.2
STX	0.13	0.11	0.14	0.09	0.12	0.11	0.12	0.07	0.19	0.17	0.15	0.18	−0.10	−0.06	−0.03	−0.11	30.5	24.0	18.4	28.2
TIM	0.16	0.14	0.14	0.15	0.16	0.14	0.14	0.15	0.11	0.20	0.15	0.06	−0.05	−0.10	−0.09	−0.01	43.4	38.4	46.2	47.5
VST	0.15	0.11	0.11	0.16	0.13	0.11	0.11	0.14	0.20	0.07	0.20	0.19	−0.09	−0.01	−0.12	−0.07	36.1	47.9	49.9	23.4
Mean	*0.14*	*0.14*	*0.14*	*0.14*	*0.14*	*0.14*	*0.14*	*0.14*	*0.14*	*0.15*	*0.16*	*0.14*	*−0.06*	*−0.06*	*−0.07*	*−0.06*	*39.5*	*37.5*	*39.9*	*38.0*

Table 9.4 The SMALL group – the average daily values of five liquidity proxies: %RS (2), %ES (3), %RealS (4), %PI (5), and %OR (6)

	%RS				%ES				%RealS				%PI				%OR			
SMALL	P_1	P_2	P_3	P_4	P_1	P_2	P_3	P_4	P_1	P_2	P_3	P_4	P_1	P_2	P_3	P_4	P_1	P_2	P_3	P_4
APL	0.17	0.25	0.33	0.25	0.17	0.25	0.33	0.25	0.17	0.31	0.27	0.29	−0.07	−0.11	−0.10	−0.14	29.0	31.4	32.5	29.8
BDL	0.16	0.19	0.21	0.15	0.15	0.19	0.20	0.13	0.25	0.22	0.29	0.24	−0.15	−0.06	−0.12	−0.14	29.2	25.9	24.6	29.5
EFK	0.23	0.28	0.21	0.16	0.23	0.28	0.20	0.16	0.14	0.32	0.21	0.005	−0.07	−0.12	−0.13	0.02	42.3	35.9	42.4	47.9
ENP	0.24	0.29	0.31	0.25	0.24	0.29	0.30	0.24	0.24	0.46	0.28	0.29	−0.13	−0.23	−0.12	−0.17	37.8	29.8	31.5	37.5
KMP	0.21	0.32	0.23	0.24	0.20	0.32	0.23	0.24	0.25	0.38	0.33	0.40	−0.14	−0.13	−0.19	−0.25	33.2	32.7	34.5	35.5
MZA	0.19	0.28	0.24	0.17	0.19	0.28	0.24	0.17	0.20	0.41	0.27	0.11	−0.12	−0.21	−0.15	−0.05	35.9	32.8	39.0	33.1
PLA	0.20	0.19	0.24	0.22	0.20	0.19	0.24	0.21	0.15	0.26	0.20	0.24	−0.06	−0.11	−0.04	−0.14	35.8	31.5	32.1	34.8
SME	0.25	0.34	0.20	0.29	0.25	0.34	0.20	0.29	0.15	0.45	0.04	0.12	−0.06	−0.22	0.03	−0.06	41.5	37.6	39.1	43.2
Mean	*0.21*	*0.27*	*0.25*	*0.22*	*0.20*	*0.27*	*0.24*	*0.21*	*0.20*	*0.35*	*0.24*	*0.21*	*−0.10*	*−0.17*	*−0.09*	*−0.13*	*35.6*	*32.2*	*34.5*	*36.4*

9.4 Conclusion

The aim of this paper was to compute and to analyze the following liquidity proxies derived from intraday data on the WSE: (1) percentage relative spread, (2) percentage effective spread, (3) percentage realized spread, (4) percentage price impact, and (5) percentage order ratio. A panel of data consisted of daily estimates of five liquidity measures for 53 WSE-listed companies divided into three size groups was constructed. As the information about trade side is essential for estimation of some liquidity measures, the Lee and Ready (1991) algorithm was employed to infer trade sides and to distinguish between the buyer- and seller-initiated trades. Moreover, the paper provided a robustness analysis of empirical findings with respect to the whole sample and three adjacent subsamples each of equal size: precrisis, crisis, and postcrisis periods. The results revealed that values of all liquidity estimates rather do not depend on a firm size and turn out to be robust to the choice of the period.

The constructed panel of data would be utilized in further investigation concerning commonality in liquidity on the WSE. It is important to note that empirical market microstructure research has recently shifted its focus from the examination of liquidity of individual securities toward analyses of the common determinants and components of liquidity. Beginning with Chordia et al. (2000), the identification of the common determinants of liquidity, or commonality in liquidity, emerged as a new and fast growing strand of the literature on liquidity.

Acknowledgments This study was supported by the grant "Comparative research on commonality in liquidity on the Central and Eastern European stock markets" from the National Science Center, Poland, No. 2016/21/B/HS4/02004.

References

Acker, D., Stalker, M., & Tonks, I. (2002). Daily closing inside spreads and trading volumes around earnings announcements. *Journal of Business Finance & Accounting, 29*(9/10), 1149–1179.

Bekaert, G., Harvey, C. R., & Lundblad, C. (2007). Liquidity and expected returns: Lessons from emerging markets. *Review of Financial Studies, 20*(6), 1783–1831.

Brockman, P., & Chung, D. Y. (2000). An empirical investigation of trading on asymmetric information and heterogeneous prior beliefs. *Journal of Emp Finance, 7*, 417–454.

Chakrabarty, B., Li, B., Nguyen, V., & Van Ness, R. A. (2007). Trade classification algorithms for electronic communications network trades. *Journal of Banking & Finance, 31*, 3806–3821.

Chakrabarty, B., Moulton, P. C., & Shkilko, A. (2012). Short sale, long sale, and the Lee-Ready trade classification algorithm revisited. *Journal of Financial Markets, 15*(4), 467–491.

Chan, K., & Fong, W.-M. (2000). Trade size, order imbalance, and the volatility-volume relation. *Journal of Financial Economics, 57*, 247–273.

Chordia, T., Roll, R., & Subrahmanyam, A. (2000). Commonality in liquidity. *Journal of Financial Economics, 56*, 3–28.

Chordia, T., Roll, R., & Subrahmanyam, A. (2001). Market liquidity and trading activity. *The Journal of Finance, 56*(2), 501–530.

Chordia, T., Roll, R., & Subrahmanyam, A. (2002). Order imbalance, liquidity, and market returns. *Journal of Financial Economics, 65*, 111–130.
Chordia, T., Sarkar, A., & Subrahmanyam, A. (2005). An empirical analysis of stock and bond market liquidity. *Review of Financial Studies, 18*(1), 85–129.
Chung, K. H., & Van Ness, R. A. (2001). Order handling rules, tick size, and the intraday pattern of bid-ask spreads for Nasdaq stocks. *Journal of Financial Markets, 4*, 143–161.
Coppejans, M., Domowitz, I., & Madhavan A. (2004). Resiliency in an automated auction. Working Paper.
Corwin, S. A. (1999). Differences in trading behavior cross NYSE specialist firms. *Journal of Finance, 54*(2), 721–745.
Elyasiani, E., Hauser, S., & Lauterbach, B. (2000). Market response to liquidity improvements: Evidence from exchange listings. *Financial Review, 41*, 1–14.
Fama, E. F., & French, K. R. (1993). Common risk factors in the returns on stocks and bonds. *Journal of Financial Economics, 33*(1), 3–56.
Finucane, T. J. (2000). A direct test of methods for inferring trade direction from intra-day data. *Journal of Financial and Quantitative Analysis, 35*(4), 553–576.
Glosten, L. R. (1987). Components of the bid-ask spread and the statistical properties of transaction prices. *The Journal of Finance, 42*(4), 1293–1307.
Goyenko, R. Y., Holden, C. W., & Trzcinka, C. A. (2009). Do liquidity measures measure liquidity? *Journal of Financial Economics, 92*, 153–181.
Hameed, A., Kang, W., & Viswanathan, S. (2010). Stock market decline and liquidity. *The Journal of Finance, 65*(1), 257–293.
Harris, L. (2003). *Trading and exchanges: Market microstructure for practitioners*. Oxford University Press, New York.
Huang, R. D., & Stoll, H. R. (1996). Dealer versus auction markets: A paired comparison of execution costs on NASDAQ and the NYSE. *Journal of Financial Economics, 41*, 313–357.
Huang, R. D., & Stoll, H. R. (1997). The components of the bid-ask spread: A general approach. *Review of Financial Studies, 10*(4), 995–1034.
Kluger, B. D., & Stephan, J. (1997). Alternative liquidity measures and stock returns. *Review of Quantitative Finance and Accounting, 8*, 19–36.
Korajczyk, R., & Sadka, R. (2008). Pricing the commonality across alternative measures of liquidity. *Journal of Financial Economics, 87*(1), 45–72.
Kyle, A. S. (1985). Continuous auctions and insider trading. *Econometrica, 53*(6), 1315–1336.
Lee, C. M. C., & Ready, M. J. (1991). Inferring trade direction from intraday data. *The Journal of Finance, 46*(2), 733–746.
Lee, C. M. C., Mucklow, B., & Ready, M. J. (1993). Spreads, depths, and the impact of earnings information: An intraday analysis. *Review of Financial Studies, 6*(2), 345–374.
Lesmond, D. A. (2005). Liquidity of emerging markets. *Journal of Financial Economics, 77*(2), 411–452.
Levin, E. J., & Wright, R. E. (1999). Explaining the intra-day variation in the bid-ask spread in competitive dealership markets – A research note. *Journal of Financial Markets, 2*(2), 179–191.
Lin, J.-C., Sanger, G. C., & Booth, G. G. (1995). Trade size and components of the bid-ask spread. *Review of Financial Studies, 8*(4), 1153–1183.
Nowak, S. (2017). Order imbalance indicators in asset pricing: Evidence from the Warsaw Stock Exchange. In K. Jajuga, L. Orlowski, & K. Staehr (Eds.), *Contemporary trends and challenges in finance. Springer proceedings in business and economics* (pp. 91–102). Cham: Springer.
Nowak, S., & Olbryś, J. (2016). Direct evidence of non-trading on the Warsaw Stock Exchange. *Research Papers of Wroclaw University of Economics, 428*, 184–194.
Olbryś, J. (2014). Is illiquidity risk priced? The case of the Polish medium-size emerging stock market. *Bank & Credit, 45*(6), 513–536.
Olbryś, J. (2017). Interaction between market depth and market tightness on the Warsaw Stock Exchange: A preliminary study. In K. Jajuga, L. Orlowski, & K. Staehr (Eds.), *Contemporary trends and challenges in finance. Springer proceedings in business and economics* (pp. 103–111). Cham: Springer.

Olbrys, J., & Majewska, E. (2014). Direct identification of crisis periods on the CEE stock markets: The influence of the 2007 U.S. subprime crisis. *Proceedings of the Economics & Finance, 14*, 461–470.

Olbryś, J., & Majewska, E. (2015). Bear market periods during the 2007-2009 financial crisis: Direct evidence from the Visegrad countries. *Acta Oecon, 65*(4), 547–565.

Olbryś, J., & Mursztyn, M. (2015). Comparison of selected trade classification algorithms on the Warsaw Stock Exchange. *Advanced Computer Science Research, 12*, 37–52.

Olbrys, J., & Mursztyn, M. (2017). Dimensions of market liquidity: The case of the Polish stock market. In N. Tsounis & A. Vlachvei (Eds.), *Advances in applied economic research. Springer proceedings in business and economics* (pp. 151–166). Cham: Springer.

Pagan, A. R., & Sossounov, K. A. (2003). A simple framework for analysing bull and bear markets. *Journal of Applied Econometrics, 18*(1), 23–46.

Peterson, M., & Sirri, E. (2003). Evaluation of the biases in execution costs estimation using trades and quotes data. *Journal of Financial Markets, 6*(3), 259–280.

Piwowar, M. S., & Wei, L. (2003). The sensitivity of effective spread estimates to trade-quote matching algorithms. *Electronic Markets, 16*(2), 112–129.

Pukthuanthong-Le, K., & Visaltanachoti, N. (2009). Commonality in liquidity: Evidence from the Stock Exchange of Thailand. *Pacif-Basin Finance Journal, 17*(1), 80–99.

Ranaldo, A. (2001). Intraday market liquidity on the Swiss Stock Exchange. *Swiss Soc Financ Mark Res, 15*(3), 309–327.

Roll, R. (1984). A simple implicit measure of the effective bid-ask spread in an efficient market. *The Journal of Finance, 39*(4), 1127–1140.

Stoll, H. S. (2000). Friction. *The Journal of Finance, 55*(4), 1479–1514.

Theissen, E. (2001). A test of the accuracy of the Lee/Ready trade classification algorithm. *Journal of International Financial Markets Institutions and Money, 11*, 147–165.

Tsay, R. S. (2010). *Analysis of financial time series*. New York: Wiley.

Van Ness, B. F., Van Ness, R. A., & Pruitt, S. W. (2000). The impact of the reduction in tick increments in major U.S. markets on spreads, depth, and volatility. *Review of Quantitative Finance and Accounting, 15*, 153–167.

von Wyss, R. (2004). Measuring and predicting liquidity in the stock market. Dissertation Nr. 2899, University of St. Gallen.

Chapter 10
Measuring Dynamics of Financial Integration on the Euro Area Stock Markets, 2000–2016

Elzbieta Majewska and Joanna Olbrys

Abstract The goal of this paper is to measure the dynamics of financial integration between the euro area stock markets over the long time period 2000–2016. The panel of data consists of monthly logarithmic returns of 19 major euro area stock market indexes. The evolution of the integration process is analyzed using a dynamic principal component approach. The index of integration, which measures the proportion of total variation in individual stock index logarithmic returns explained by the first principal component, serves as a measure of integration. The empirical results reveal that the dynamics of integration across the whole group of markets increased significantly after January 2008, during the global financial crisis (GFC). An inverted U-shaped pattern in the index of integration has been found in this period. The GFC and the subsequent euro area crises were formally detected based on the statistical procedure for an identification of down markets. Moreover, the estimation results of the index of integration turn out to be robust to the choice of a rolling window length.

Keywords Euro area stock markets · Dynamic principal component analysis · Index of integration · Global financial crisis

10.1 Introduction

The literature has shown that the level of financial integration across markets varies over time. The evidence is that capital markets are becoming increasingly integrated. The extent of international financial integration has important practical implications,

---

E. Majewska (✉)
University of Bialystok, Bialystok, Poland
e-mail: e.majewska@uwb.edu.pl

J. Olbrys
Bialystok University of Technology, Bialystok, Poland
e-mail: j.olbrys@pb.edu.pl

N. Tsounis, A. Vlachvei (eds.), *Advances in Panel Data Analysis in Applied Economic Research*, Springer Proceedings in Business and Economics,
https://doi.org/10.1007/978-3-319-70055-7_10

especially in the context of portfolio choice and diversification. It also has crucial implications for economic theory and policy debates. Although integrated financial markets have easier access to foreign capital, they are more vulnerable to various global events, for example financial crises. Nowadays, there is a growing body of empirical literature concerning integration effects on the European Economic and Monetary Union (EMU) stock markets, e.g., Büttner and Hayo (2011), Hardouvelis et al. (2006), Kleimeier and Sander (2006), Connor and Suurlaht (2013), and the references therein. Therefore, an important problem is verifying to what extent the results obtained during research depend on the choice of the period investigated, especially taking the pre-, post-, and crisis periods into consideration. The causes and consequences of the 2007–2009 global financial crisis (GFC) have been strictly connected with international financial integration between markets. On the one side, the crisis transmission through financial and banking channels has been very rapid and substantial. Pisani-Ferry and Sapir (2010) stress that the European banks were particularly vulnerable given the high degree of internationalization in their activities, both within the euro area and outside. On the other side, the degree of financial integration between the European financial markets increased substantially during such a critical event as the GFC.

As the international market integration varies over time, the dynamics of this process merits deeper research. Therefore, the main goal of this paper is to recognize the dynamics of financial integration processes across the euro area stock markets over the last 17 years. The panel of data consists of monthly logarithmic returns of 19 major euro area stock market indexes.

The dynamic principal component analysis is applied to investigate the evolution of the integration process in a group of markets. The index of integration (Volosovych 2011), which measures the proportion of total variation in individual stock index logarithmic returns explained by the first principal component, serves as a robust measure of integration. We explore the dynamics of financial integration processes across the groups of the euro area markets in the context of the influence of the GFC. The long time sample period begins in January 2000, ends in December 2016, and includes the 2007 US subprime crisis period. The GFC period and the subsequent euro area crises on the euro area stock markets are formally detected based on the Pagan and Sossounov (2003) method for statistical identification of market states. Majewska and Olbrys (2017) employ the Pagan and Sossounov methodology to identify crises on the 19 euro area stock markets, but the empirical results are generated in shorter period from January 2004 to December 2015. We recognize that the dynamics of the financial integration process between the euro area stock markets increased significantly after January 2008. An inverted U-shaped pattern in the index of integration has been found in this period. Moreover, the estimation results of the index of integration turn out to be robust to the choice of a rolling window length.

To the best of the authors' knowledge, no such research has been undertaken for the euro area stock markets thus far.

The remainder of this study is organized as follows. Section 2 presents a brief literature review concerning financial integration in the euro area. Section 3 specifies the methodological background of the dynamic principal component approach and the index of integration. Section 4 presents data description and empirical results on the indexes in the euro area stock markets. Section 5 recalls the main findings and presents the conclusions.

10.2 Measuring Financial Integration: A Brief Literature Review

There is no unanimity in the literature regarding the definition of integration. Bekaert et al. (2005) point out that integration can be regional or global. Beine et al. (2010) distinguish between trade and financial integration. Hardouvelis et al. (2006) assert that when stock markets are partially integrated, both global and local risk factors are priced. Bekaert and Harvey (1995) assume that markets are completely integrated if assets with the same risk have identical expected returns irrespective of the market. Risk refers to exposure to some common world factor. If a market is segmented from the rest of the world (which means the opposite of integration), its covariance with a common world factor may have little or no ability to explain its expected return. Intuitively, a quantitative measure of financial integration might be the proportion of an individual stock market return that can be explained by global factors. Pukthuanthong and Roll (2009) stress that although the degree of integration may seem intuitively apparent to many, quantitative measures of integration have not often agreed with the intuition.

The majority of researchers indicate that financial markets in the world exhibit time-varying integration. Bekaert et al. (2002) recognize the problem of dating the integration of equity markets in the context of liberalization. Obstfeld and Taylor (2003) present a stylized view of capital mobility in modern history, 1860–2000. A figure of global capital market integration reveals the overall U-shaped trend line. Moreover, Donadelli and Paradiso (2014) indicate that markets do not necessarily follow identical dynamics and therefore one can observe three different financial integration patterns: (1) increasing trend, (2) J-shaped trend, or (3) U-shaped trend. Billio et al. (2016) compare and rank the financial integration patterns that are generated by applying different empirical methodologies for three different country groups in different time periods. They observe that integration has been increasing in the past decades.

It has been reported in the literature that growing international integration and globalization could lead to a progressive increase in cross-market correlations, especially in periods of high volatility (Longin and Solnik 1995). Moreover, Longin and Solnik (2001) find that international stock market correlations increase in bear markets, but not in bull markets. There are many studies analyzing the evolution of stock market integration over time using various methods based on correlations. For example, Büttner and Hayo (2011) analyze the determinants of stock market integration among the EU member states and they try to extract dynamic conditional correlations between the European markets. The empirical results reveal that in general the impact of the European political integration on financial market integration is stronger than the evidence for the influence of macroeconomic factors. Kearney and Poti (2006) investigate the correlation trends and dynamics in the equity markets of the euro area and they find significant persistence in all conditional correlation estimates. Connor and Suurlaht (2013) find that European markets show a significant positive trend toward higher inter-market correlations over the 1992–2010 time period.

The evaluation of integration has been often carried out by applying tests interpreted as integration tests in the group of stock markets. Integration has been evaluated by employing the equality tests of correlation matrices computed over nonoverlapping subsamples: the precrisis and crisis periods, e.g., Longin and Solnik (1995), Chesnay and Jondeau (2001), Goetzmann et al. (2005), Brière et al. (2012), and Olbryś and Majewska (2015, 2017). The null hypothesis states that there is no integration effect during crisis. To address this issue, different test statistics have been proposed in the literature, for example, the Jennrich (1970) or the Larntz and Perlman (1985) tests. However, the robustness analysis reveals that the empirical results of integration effects are not homogeneous and they are linked both to the integration test and data frequency (Olbryś and Majewska 2015).

The approach of measuring financial integration using correlations is often considered as questionable. Among others, Pukthuanthong and Roll (2009) point out that cross-country correlations as the most widely used measures of integration, are flawed. The authors stress that the correlation across markets is a poor measure because even perfectly integrated markets can exhibit weak correlation. This occurs whenever there are multiple global sources of return volatility and individual stock markets do not share the same sensitivities to all of them. Moreover, Carrieri et al. (2007) provide evidence on the impropriety of directly using stock market correlations of market-wide index returns as a measure of market integration. The authors stress that such approach is problematic because it does not control for economic fundamentals within each country. Volosovych (2011, 2013) emphasizes that various interpretational and statistical issues make correlation coefficient an inadequate measure of integration. Firstly, the choice of the reference market might be problematic over a relatively long time period. Secondly, the sample correlation is not a robust statistic in the presence of outliers or a heavy-tailed distribution. Thirdly, conclusions drawn from correlations may be biased by the conditional heteroskedasticity of market returns. Forbes and Rigobon (2002) argue that correlation coefficients are conditional on market volatility. Furthermore, if the financial markets are affected by a global shock in a similar fashion, the cross-market correlations might be high even without significant integration. To avoid these problems, Volosovych (2011) proposes a methodology extending the classic principal component analysis (PCA) to capture the dynamics of financial integration processes.

10.3 Dynamic Principal Component Analysis

The classical principal component analysis (PCA) has been employed in several studies by itself or to complement other techniques of measuring financial integration. For example, Nellis (1982) utilize PCA to investigate to what extent international financial integration has been enhanced as a result of the move to a floating exchange rate regime by the major industrialized countries in the early 1970s. Gagnon and Unferth (1995) use panel data techniques to estimate a common component to the ex post real interest rates of nine countries with liberal capital markets over 16 years. Mauro et al. (2002) analyze yield spreads on sovereign bonds issued by emerging markets and they use a variety of statistical techniques including PCA. The authors point out that there is a growing consensus in the literature, that global economic integration reached a peak in the late nineteenth and early twentieth century, collapsed with the world wars and the intervening great depression, and gradually increased again after the collapse of the Bretton Woods system to attain levels similar to pre-1914. Bordo and Murshid (2006) apply PCA among other methods to compare the patterns in the transmission of shocks and currency crises during two periods of globalization: (1) the pre-WWI classical gold standard era, 1880–1914, and (2) the post-Bretton Woods era, 1975–2001. Their results suggest that financial market shocks were more globalized before 1914 compared to the present. Pukthuanthong and Roll (2009) investigate the issue concerning a global market integration and they employ the classic PCA to estimate a set of global factors with principal components.

10.3.1 Classical Principal Component Analysis (PCA)

This subsection presents a brief methodological background of the classical principal component approach. PCA is a nonparametric empirical methodology used to reduce dimensionality of data and describe common features of a set of economic variables. The main idea of this procedure is to reduce the dimensionality of a data set consisting of a large number of interrelated variables, while retaining as much as possible of the variation present in the data. This is achieved by transforming to a new set of variables, the principal components, which are uncorrelated, and which are ordered so that the first few retain most of the variation present in all of the original variables.

Suppose that $\mathbf{x}$ is a vector of p random variables, and that the variances of these variables and the structure of the covariances or correlations between them are of interest. The $\boldsymbol{\Sigma}$ is a covariance (or correlation) matrix of elements of vector $\mathbf{x}$. The first step of PCA is to look for a linear function $\boldsymbol{\alpha}_1^T\mathbf{x}$ of elements of a vector $\mathbf{x}$ (the first principal component) having maximum variance and given by Eq. (10.1):

$$\boldsymbol{\alpha}_1^T \mathbf{x} = \alpha_{11}x_1 + \alpha_{12}x_2 + \cdots + \alpha_{1p}x_p = \sum_{j=1}^{p} \alpha_{1j}x_j, \tag{10.1}$$

where $\boldsymbol{\alpha}_1$ is a vector of p constants $\alpha_{11}, \alpha_{12}, \ldots, \alpha_{1p}$. The next step is to look for a linear function $\boldsymbol{\alpha}_2^T \mathbf{x}$ (the second principal component), uncorrelated with $\boldsymbol{\alpha}_1^T \mathbf{x}$ and having maximum variance, and so on. The k-th derived variable is the k-th principal component and it is given by Eq. (10.2):

$$z_k = \boldsymbol{\alpha}_k^T \mathbf{x}, \quad k = 1, 2, \ldots, p, \tag{10.2}$$

where $\boldsymbol{\alpha}_k$ is an eigenvector of $\boldsymbol{\Sigma}$ corresponding to its k-th largest eigenvalue λ_k. Furthermore, if $\boldsymbol{\alpha}_k$ is chosen to have unit length, that is $\boldsymbol{\alpha}_k^T \boldsymbol{\alpha}_k = 1$, then $\mathrm{var}(z_k) = \lambda_k$ (Jolliffe 2002, pp. 2–4).

As for the notation (which is sometimes confusing), it is preferable to reserve the term "principal component" for the derived new variable z_k and refer to $\boldsymbol{\alpha}_k$ as the vector of coefficients or loadings for the k-th principal component.

PCA is scale dependent. The principal components of a covariance matrix and those of a correlation matrix are different. In applied research, PCA of a covariance matrix is useful only if the variables are expressed in commensurable units.

10.3.2 Dynamic Principal Component Approach: The Index of Integration

In general, the goal of PCA is to capture most of the observed variability in the data in a lower-dimensional object and, thereby, filter out noise. Volosovych (2011, 2013) stresses that very often a single component summarizes most of the variation of the original data. The author argues that the first principal component has a natural interpretation when PCA is applied to a comparable (such as price, return) series across markets. The proportion of total variation in individual returns explained by the first principal component serves as an index of integration. The main idea of a dynamic principal component approach is to estimate the index of integration over the long time period via rolling windows, which enables us to reveal important patterns and trends in financial integration processes.

Donadelli and Paradiso (2014) employ the index of integration as a robust measure of the financial integration process in one global emerging region and three emerging subregions (Asia, Eastern Europe, Latin America). They divide the whole sample period into three specific subperiods. The first period includes pre-2003 observations and is influenced by relevant international crises (that is the Asian and Russian crises). The second period includes 2003–2007 observations and is not contaminated by crises. The third period encompasses post-2007 data and it includes the GFC. The authors use the percentage of variance in equity excess returns explained by the first principal component. To get a dynamic integration index, they perform PCA in a rolling window framework.

10.4 Data Description and Empirical Results on the Euro Area Stock Markets

The panel of data consists of monthly logarithmic returns of 19 euro area stock market indexes (Table 10.1). There are 204 monthly observations for each series for the period beginning January 2000 and ending December 2016.

10.4.1 Preliminary Statistics

Table 10.1 includes information about the year of the country's accession to the eurozone.

Subsequent Table 10.2 presents brief information about the euro area stock market indexes employed in the research, in order of decreasing value of market capitalization at the end of 2015. Moreover, it reports summarized statistics for monthly logarithmic returns for the indexes, as well as statistics testing for normality.

Results in Table 10.2 are worth a comment. The measure for skewness shows that the return series are skewed, except for the SBITOP (Slovenia), MSE (Malta), CSE GENERAL (Cyprus), OMXT (Estonia), and OMXR (Latvia) series. The measure for excess kurtosis shows that almost all series are highly leptokurtic with respect to the normal distribution, except for the IBEX 35 (Spain), FTSE MIB (Italy), ATHEX (Greece), and MSE (Malta) series. The Doornik and Hansen (2008) test rejects normality for almost all return series at the 5% level of significance, except for the MSE (Malta) index.

Table 10.1 The euro area country's accession to the eurozone

Year	Country
1999	Austria, Belgium, Finland, France, Germany, Ireland, Italy, Luxembourg, Netherlands, Portugal, and Spain
2001	Greece
2007	Slovenia
2008	Cyprus, Malta
2009	Slovakia
2011	Estonia
2014	Latvia
2015	Lithuania

Table 10.2 Summarized statistics for monthly logarithmic returns for the euro area stock market indexes used in the study

Country	Index	Market Cap. EUR billion Dec 2015	Mean	Standard deviation	Skewness	Excess kurtosis	Doornik-Hansen test
France	CAC 40	1911.23	−0.001	0.052	−0.621 [0.000]	0.796 [0.022]	12.135 [0.002]
Germany	DAX	1781.59	0.003	0.063	−0.926 [0.000]	2.886 [0.000]	26.257 [0.000]
Spain	IBEX 35	720.44	−0.001	0.059	−0.367 [0.034]	0.667 [0.054]	6.168 [0.046]
Netherlands	AEX	666.82	−0.001	0.057	−1.093 [0.000]	2.749 [0.000]	30,574 [0.000]
Italy	FTSE MIB	573.60	−0.004	0.062	−0.372 [0.032]	0.638 [0.065]	6.027 [0.049]
Belgium	BEL 20	379.40	0.001	0.049	−1.390 [0.000]	4.085 [0.000]	46.100 [0.000]
Finland	OMXH	187.00	−0.003	0.073	−0.478 [0.006]	2.853 [0.000]	37.227 [0.000]
Ireland	ISEQ	117.15	0.001	0.059	−0.945 [0.000]	1.797 [0.000]	25.418 [0.000]
Austria	ATX	87.93	0.004	0.062	−1.412 [0.000]	5.102 [0.000]	43.262 [0.000]
Portugal	PSI 20	43.34	−0.005	0.057	−0.570 [0.001]	1.398 [0.000]	13.407 [0.001]
Luxembourg	LuxX	43.13	0.001	0.067	−1.336 [0.000]	4.470 [0.000]	40.204 [0.000]
Greece	ATHEX	37.55	−0.010	0.090	−0.483 [0.005]	0.643 [0.063]	7.862 [0.020]
Slovenia	SBITOP	5.52	0.004	0.054	−0.334 [0.054]	1.669 [0.000]	18.601 [0.000]
Slovakia	SAX	4.26	0.007	0.054	0.800 [0.000]	5.278 [0.000]	70.164 [0.000]
Malta	MSE	4.03	0.001	0.042	0.301 [0.082]	0.544 [0.115]	4.722 [0.094]
Lithuania	OMXV	3.38	0.008	0.069	−0.483 [0.005]	7.517 [0.000]	154.727 [0.000]
Cyprus	CSE GENERAL	2.46	−0.024	0.122	−0.284 [0.100]	1.629 [0.000]	18.548 [0.000]
Estonia	OMXT	1.88	0.010	0.072	−0.033 [0.849]	6.522 [0.000]	145.209 [0.000]
Latvia	OMXR	1.27	0.009	0.067	−0.103 [0.551]	4.877 [0.000]	98.364 [0.000]

Source: National stock exchange websites and the authors' calculation

Notes: The table is based on all sample observations during the period from January 2000 to December 2016. The test statistic for skewness and excess kurtosis is the conventional t-statistic. The Doornik and Hansen test (2008) has a χ^2 distribution if the null hypothesis of normality is true. Numbers in brackets are p-values

10.4.2 *Formal Identification of Crisis Periods on the Euro Area Stock Markets*

According to the literature, there is no unanimity among researchers in determining the phases of the 2007–2009 GFC on the European stock markets. On the other side, researchers are rather unanimous in observing crisis periods in the eurozone, and they describe the same events connected with the European crises during the period beginning from the late 2009; see, e.g., Majewska and Olbrys (2017) and the references therein. Therefore, it is instructive to formally detect crisis periods on the euro area stock markets. A direct identification of crisis periods is possible based on statistical procedures for dividing market states into up and down markets. Pagan and Sossounov (2003) developed an algorithm that seems to be successful in locating bull and bear market periods in time. Majewska and Olbrys (2017) employed the Pagan and Sossounov (2003) methodology to identify crises on the 19 euro area stock markets, but the empirical results were generated in different (shorter) period from January 2004 to December 2015.

Figure 10.1 presents overall information about the euro area down markets in the whole sample period January 2000 – December 2016. The dates stipulate the beginning of the GFC. The empirical results indicate February 2009 as the end of the GFC for almost all countries investigated, except for Slovenia, Lithuania, Malta, Estonia, and Latvia, for which March 2009 was obtained as the end of the GFC.

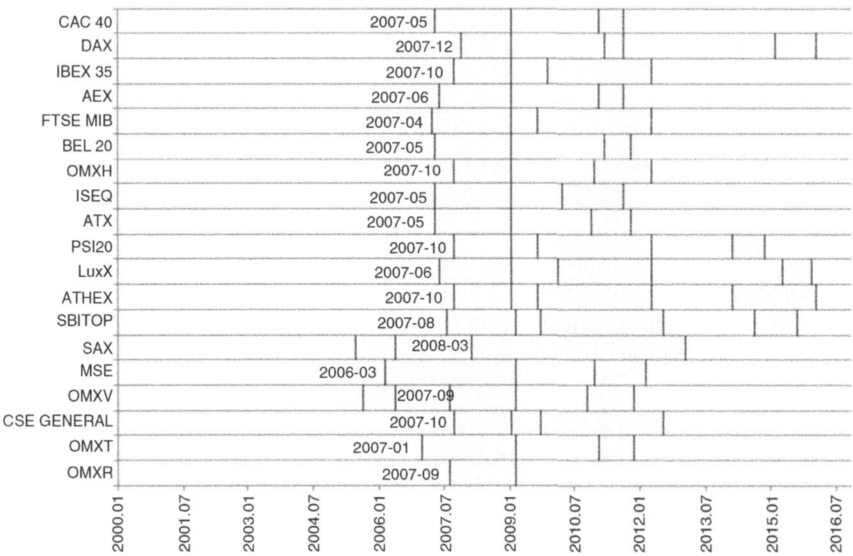

Fig. 10.1 Overall information about the euro area down markets in the whole sample period from January 2000 to December 2016 (the euro area stock market indexes in the order analogous to that in Table 10.2). The dates stipulate the beginning of the GFC

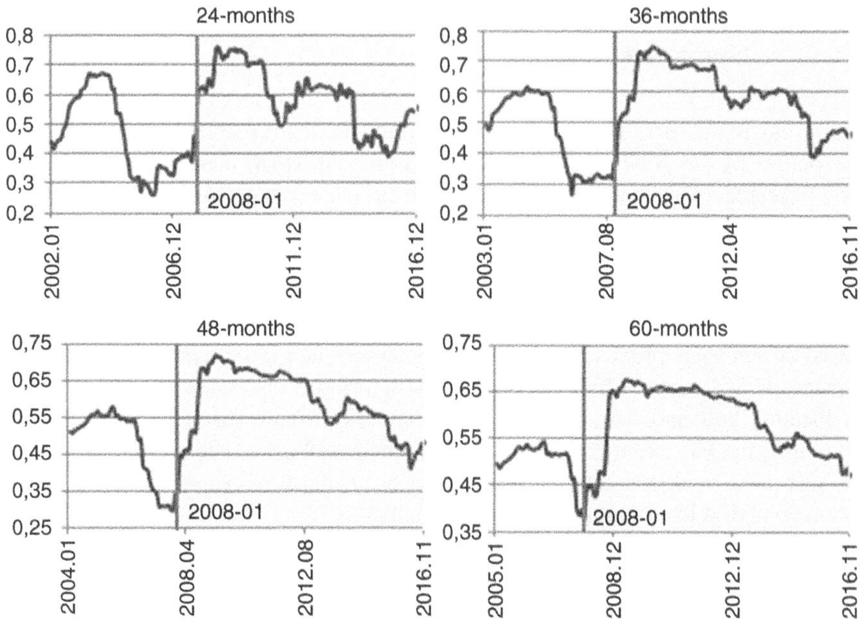

Fig. 10.2 The dynamics of the integration index in the group of investigated markets. The light gray areas stand for the period beginning January 2008. The index of integration is estimated using four different rolling windows of 24, 36, 48, and 60 months

10.4.3 Empirical Evidence from the Index of Financial Integration

To investigate the evolution of financial integration processes across the euro area markets, we utilize the dynamic principal component approach and calculate the index of integration. This index measures the proportion of total variation in individual stock index monthly logarithmic returns explained by the first principal component given by Eq. (10.1). To test the robustness of empirical results, the first principal component is estimated using various rolling windows of 24, 36, 48, and 60 months (Fig. 10.2).

Figure 10.2 presents the dynamics of the financial integration process across the group of the euro area stock markets in the whole sample period January 2000–December 2016. One can observe that the most noticeable rise in the level of integration occurred after January 2008, during the GFC. The light gray areas stand for the period beginning January 2008. Moreover, the integration index exhibits an inverted U-shaped trend in this period. This pattern is consistent with the literature and it reveals three specific phases. The first phase is characterized by a substantial increase in the degree of integration between international equity markets after a crucial event. The second one relies on the relatively high cross-country integration observed in the period following the event. The third phase indicates a subsequent decrease in the level of integration over a long time after the event.

Furthermore, the empirical results in Fig. 10.2 reveal that the level of integration in the group of the euro area markets was rather high and persistent not only during the GFC but also in a relatively long post-GFC period. A probable explanation of this phenomenon could be the ongoing European crisis, which has become evident in 2010. According to the literature, the researchers are rather unanimous that the ongoing European crisis is a sequence of interactions between sovereign debt problems and banking problems. Among others, Shambaugh (2012) indicates that the euro area has faced three interlocking crises recently. The crises have been interlinked in several ways. Firstly, there has been a banking crisis, i.e., banks have been undercapitalized and have faced liquidity problems. Secondly, there has been a sovereign debt crisis, i.e., a number of countries have faced rising bond yields and challenges funding themselves. Thirdly, there has been a macroeconomic crisis, i.e., economic growth has been slow in the eurozone overall and unequally distributed across countries. Similarly, Lane (2012) stresses that the sovereign debt crisis has been deeply intertwined with the banking crisis and macroeconomic imbalances in the euro area. Also Constâncio (2014) points out that the European crisis has been as much a banking crisis as a sovereign debt crisis. Moro (2014) emphasizes that the European Great Crisis has begun with Greece, but suddenly it has spread over some other countries of the eurozone like Portugal, Ireland, Italy, and Spain. As a consequence, Europe since 2010 has faced a severe economic and financial crisis.

As mentioned, testing the robustness of empirical results of the index of integration is performed by using four different rolling windows of 24, 36, 48, and 60 months. It is important to note, that the main findings reported in Fig. 10.2 turn out to be robust to the choice of a rolling window length.

10.5 Conclusion

The purpose of this paper was to investigate the dynamics of financial integration processes across the euro area stock markets over the long time sample period 2000–2016. The evolution of the integration process was explored using the dynamic principal component approach. The empirical results confirmed that the dynamics of integration processes is time-varying. A visible inverted U-shaped pattern in the index of integration has been found during the period beginning January 2008, during the global financial crisis.

It is important to note that a high level of financial integration among the euro area stock markets could be a considerable impediment to international portfolio diversification, especially during crises. Although the number of the eurozone countries has varied over time and it has risen from 11 in 1999 to 19 in 2015, only relatively small markets (i.e., Slovenia, Cyprus, Malta, Slovakia, Estonia, Latvia, and Lithuania) have joined the group after 2001 (see Table 10.1). Essentially, international portfolio diversification concerns bigger European stock markets.

This study might be viewed as a contribution to the debate regarding integration processes in Europe. We are aware of the fact that our analysis cannot provide definitive conclusions concerning the dynamics of financial integration across the euro area countries. Therefore, a possible direction for further investigation could be to study the dynamics of integration processes in an alternative way, for example, using different measure of integration.

Furthermore, the empirical results revealed that the level of integration in the group of the euro area markets was rather high and persistent not only during the GFC but also in a relatively long post-GFC period. Although this evidence is in general in accordance with theoreticians' and practitioners' intuition, this is an important finding which requires further quantitative investigation. A probable explanation of this phenomenon could be the ongoing European crisis, which has become evident in 2010. The GFC has affected the European markets in general, but the euro area, along with most of the world, has emerged from recession in 2009. Next, the eurozone has suffered from the subsequent financial crises since late 2009. As Mishkin (2011) stressed, the GFC started in 2007 in one small part of the financial system, but led to worldwide economic conflagration by late 2008 and early 2009. This revealed that the global financial system is far more interconnected than was previously recognized.

Acknowledgments The contribution of the second named author was supported by the grant from the National Science Center, Poland, No. 2016/21/B/HS4/02004.

References

Beine, M., Cosma, A., & Vermeulen, R. (2010). The dark side of global integration: Increasing tail dependence. *Journal of Banking & Finance, 34*, 184–192.

Bekaert, G., & Harvey, C. R. (1995). Time-varying market integration. *The Journal of Finance, 1*(2), 403–444.

Bekaert, G., Harvey, C. R., & Lumsdaine, R. L. (2002). Dating the integration of world equity markets. *Journal of Financial Economics, 65*, 203–247.

Bekaert, G., Harvey, C. R., & Ng, A. (2005). Market integration and contagion. *Journal of Business, 78*(1), 39–69.

Billio, M., Donadelli, M., Paradiso, A., & Riedel. (2016). Which market integration measure? SAFE Working Paper No. 159.

Bordo, M. D., & Murshid, A. P. (2006). Globalization and changing patterns in the international transmission in financial markets. *Journal of International Money and Finance, 25*, 655–674.

Briere, M., Chapelle, A., & Szafarz, A. (2012). No contagion, only globalization and flight to quality. *Journal of International Money and Finance, 31*(6), 1729–1744.

Büttner, D., & Hayo, B. (2011). Determinants of European stock market integration. *Economic Systems, 35*, 574–585.

Carrieri, F., Errunza, V., & Hogan, K. (2007). Characterizing world market integration through time. *Journal of Financial and Quantitative Analysis, 42*(4), 915–940.

Chesnay, F., & Jondeau, E. (2001). Does correlation between stock returns really increase during turbulent periods? *Economic Notes, 30*(1), 53–80.

Connor, G., & Suurlaht, A. (2013). Dynamic stock market covariances in the Eurozone. *Journal of International Money and Finance, 37*, 353–370.

Constâncio, V. (2014). The European crisis and the role of the financial system. *Journal of Macroeconomics, 39*, 250–259.

Donadelli, M., & Paradiso, A. (2014). Is there heterogeneity in financial integration dynamics? Evidence from country and industry emerging market equity indexes. *Journal of International Financial Markets Institutions and Money, 32*, 184–218.

Doornik, J. A., & Hansen, H. (2008). An omnibus test for univariate and multivariate normality. *Oxford Bulletin of Economics and Statistics, 70*(Supplement1), 927–939.

Forbes, K. J., & Rigobon, R. (2002). No contagion, only interdependence: Measuring stock market comovements. *The Journal of Finance, 57*(5), 2223–2261.

Gagnon, J. E., & Unferth, M. D. (1995). Is there a world interest rate? *Journal of International Money and Finance, 14*, 846–855.

Goetzmann, W. N., Li, L., & Rouwenhorst, K. G. (2005). Long–term global market correlations. *Journal of Business, 78*(1), 1–38.

Hardouvelis, G. A., Malliaropulos, D., & Priestley, R. (2006). EMU and European stock market integration. *Journal of Business, 79*(1), 365–392.

Jennrich, R. I. (1970). An asymptotic chi-square test for the equality of two correlation matrices. *Journal of American Statistical Association, 65*(330), 904–912.

Jolliffe, I. T. (2002). *Principal component analysis, Springer series in statistics* (2nd ed.). New York: Springer.

Kearney, C., & Poti, V. (2006). Correlation dynamics in European equity markets. *Research in International Business and Finance, 20*, 305–321.

Kleimeier, S., & Sander, H. (2006). Regional versus global integration of euro-zone retail banking markets: Understanding the recent evidence from price-based integration measures. *The Quarterly Review of Economics and Finance, 46*, 353–368.

Lane, P. R. (2012). The European sovereign debt crisis. *The Journal of Economic Perspectives, 26*(3), 49–68.

Larntz, K., & Perlman, M. D. (1985). *A simple test for the equality of correlation matrices*. Technical Report No. 63, Department of Statistics, University of Washington.

Longin, F., & Solnik, B. (1995). Is the correlation in international equity returns constant: 1960-1990? *Journal of International Money and Finance, 14*(1), 3–26.

Longin, F., & Solnik, B. (2001). Extreme correlation of international equity markets. *The Journal of Finance, 56*(2), 649–676.

Majewska, E., & Olbrys, J. (2017). Formal identification of crises on the euro area stock markets, 2004–2015. In N. Tsounis & A. Vlachvei (Eds.), *Advances in applied economic research – Proceedings of the 2016 International Conference on Applied Economics (ICOAE)*. Springer Proceedings in Business and Economics, 167–180.

Mauro, P., Sussman, N., & Yafeh, Y. (2002). Emerging market spreads: Then versus now. *Quarterly Journal of Economics, 117*, 695–733.

Mishkin, F. S. (2011). Over the cliff: From the subprime to the Global financial crisis. *The Journal of Economic Perspectives, 25*(1), 49–70.

Moro, B. (2014). Lessons from the European economic and financial great crisis: A survey. *European Journal of Political Economy, 34*, S9–S24.

Nellis, J. G. (1982). A principal components analysis of international financial integration under fixed and floating exchange rate regimes. *Applied Economics, 14*, 339–354.

Obstfeld, M., & Taylor, A. T. (2003). Globalization and capital markets. In M. Bordo, A. T. Taylor, & J. G. Williamson (Eds.), *Globalization in historical perspective*. Chicago: University of Chicago Press.

Olbryś, J., & Majewska, E. (2015). Testing integration effects between the CEE and U.S. stock markets during the 2007–2009 Global financial crisis. *Folia Oeconomica Stetinensia, 14*(1), 101–113.

Olbryś, J., & Majewska, E. (2017). Increasing cross-market correlations during the 2007–2009 financial crisis: Contagion or integration effects? *Argumenta Oeconomica, 39*(2), (in press).

Pagan, A. R., & Sossounov, K. A. (2003). A simple framework for analyzing bull and bear markets. *Journal of Applied Econometrics, 18*(1), 23–46.

Pisani-Ferry, J., & Sapir, A. (2010). Banking crisis management in the EU: An early assessment. *Economic Policy, 62*, 341–373.

Pukthuanthong, K., & Roll, R. (2009). Global market integration: An alternative measure and its application. *Journal of Financial Economics, 94*, 214–232.

Shambaugh, J. C. (2012). The euro's three crises. *Brookings Papers on Economic Activity, 44*(1), 157–231.

Volosovych, V. (2011). Measuring financial market integration over the long run: Is there a U-shape?*Journal of International Money and Finance, 30*, 1535–1561.

Volosovych, V. (2013). Learning about financial market integration from principal components analysis. *CESifo Economic Studies, 59*(2), 360–391.

Chapter 11
The Effect of Inflation-Targeting Policy on Economic Growth in AEC Countries

Chukiat Chaiboonsri, Prasert Chaitip, and Kanchana Chokethaworn

Abstract Bayesian econometrics is very useful for subjective probability judgments of risk insecurity. This examination was inspired by the key issue for the investigation of inflation-targeting policy in Asian Economic Community (AEC) countries under the concept of the inflation-targeting framework of effective inflation policy for the economic growth of each of the AEC countries. Further, it was aimed at analyzing time series data of the annual inflation target rate and the gross domestic product growth rate from 1960 to 2015. Three key distinctive stages of analysis reveal enhancement prospects in the panel model. The estimation result provided by the Bayes factor approach can be used as guidance on how information on comparative monetary policy is under the control of price stability. The appropriate relationship is best employed across important inflation-targeting policy, setting the monetary policy to stimulate long-term economic growth in Thailand, Singapore, Malaysia, and Indonesia respectively, but not in the Philippines economy.

11.1 Introduction

The inflation-targeting framework set as a percentage range is a form of monetary policy in which a central bank has an explicit annual inflation rate target for the medium term. This sets a goal for inflation that is announced to the public and is an important tool of monetary policy. The assumption is that the best contribution of monetary policy is to support the long-term growth of the economy and to maintain price stability by affecting consumer spending. Annual inflation targeting and the conditions of the utilization of data at a minimum cost should be the primary objective applied to historical gross domestic product (GDP) growth rates in achieving economic stability.

C. Chaiboonsri (✉) · P. Chaitip · K. Chokethaworn
Faculty of Economics, Chiang Mai University, Chiang Mai, Thailand
e-mail: chukiat1973@gmail.com; pchaiti@hotmail.com

N. Tsounis, A. Vlachvei (eds.), *Advances in Panel Data Analysis in Applied Economic Research*, Springer Proceedings in Business and Economics,
https://doi.org/10.1007/978-3-319-70055-7_11

11.2 The Objective of the Research

This research is aimed at assessing the effect of inflation-targeting policy, where the central bank sets a specific goal inflation rate to affect the economic growth of each Asian Economic Community (AEC) country. In this research, it is also attempted to find out the relationship between the potential of the inflation-targeting framework to introduce a formal inflation rate target and economic growth in AEC countries.

11.3 The Scope of the Research

The macro variables of each AEC country were analyzed to estimate the tested inflation-targeting and the challenged GDP growth rate using the Bayesian panel data approach. The AEC countries considered in this study included Thailand, Singapore, Malaysia, Philippines, and Indonesia. Further, to analyze the time series data of the annual inflation target rate and GDP growth rate the years 1960 to 2015 were covered.

11.4 The Conceptual Framework and Research Methodology

11.4.1 The Impact on Economic Growth of the Policy of Inflation Targeting

In terms of inflation targeting, it was certain that the central bank would publicly announce the monetary policy of setting the target inflation rate for the medium term of the economy (Fisher 1922). The assumption was to define that whenever a central bank made such an announcement, the economy reflected the long-term growth. For this reason, the advantage of this policy is maintaining the price stability of the economy for the long term (Gill Hammond 2012). In addition, the simple inflation-targeting model was used to estimate the established functioning relationship between inflation and economic growth in AEC countries, which could be written as a mathematical model (Eq. 11.1), as follows (for more detail, see Laurrabaquio 2014).

$$\tilde{y} = r_0 - \phi(\pi_t - \bar{\pi})_{it} + u_{it} \tag{11.1}$$

where

$\tilde{y}_{it}$ = Economic production, i = the country, t = time
r_0 = Constant terms

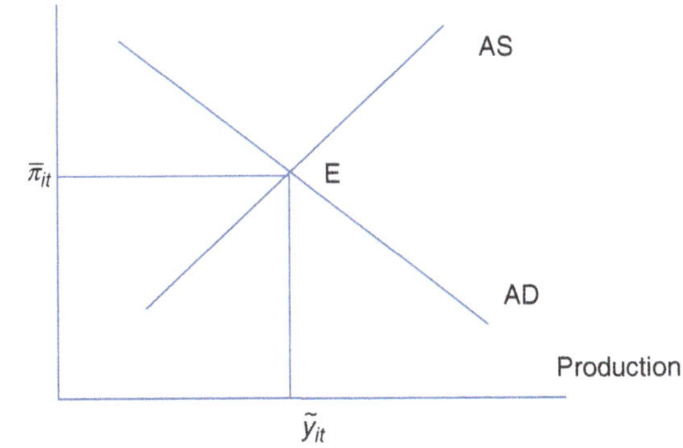

Fig. 11.1 Aggregate demand (AD) and aggregate supply (AS) affected by the inflation-targeting policy for long-term economic growth

ϕ = The parameter would be estimated for evaluation of the relationship between economic products and the inflation-targeting rate
$(\pi_t - \bar{\pi})_{it}$ = The variation of inflation rates
u_{it} = Error terms.

However, the inflation-targeting model of this investigation was constructed from Eq. (11.1) to create a new model in Eq. (11.2) by estimating Bayesian panel data analysis (for more detail, see Eq. 11.2).

$$\tilde{y} = c_0 - \phi(\bar{\pi}_{it}) + u_{it}, \tag{11.2}$$

where i = 1,. . .,5, t = 1960,. . .,2015, and
$\tilde{y}_{it}$ = GDP growth rate for country i
i = 1: (Thailand), 2: (Singapore), 3(Malaysia), 4(Philippines), and 5(Indonesia)

In addition, the theoretical framework of this examination is shown more noticeably by Fig. 11.1.

In Fig. 11.1, point E represents the long-term. growth rate of the economy and $\bar{\pi}_{it}$ characterizes the target inflation rate publicly announced in AEC countries. However, in 2013, each AEC country faced inflation concerns and was looking for a stimulating monetary package that would result in a return to a more satisfactory rate of growth. Each of the AEC countries Thailand, Singapore, Malaysia, Philippines, and Indonesia has an annual inflation-targeting policy that is difficult to shift politically, and the government resisted a total change in terms of inflation rates Therefore, growth policy in the AEC countries has to take into account price unpredictability and the inadequacy of monetary policy price stability. Thus, in this investigation, it is attempted to look for ways to solve this problem by using inflation rates effectively to stimulate economic growth in the AEC countries. As a result, Bayesian panel data analysis measured the effect of inflation-targeting policy that was scheduled to be implemented on economic growth.

11.4.2 Nonparametric Regression Model

In the monetary activity of AEC countries, as ordinarily understood, the regression model estimates the relationship among the variables across the observed data presented in simple linear form. Thus, some problems occur through the observed data with a designated nonlinear relationship between the variables (Li and Racine 2007). Therefore, nonparametric regression estimates patterns of relationships among the variables across the observed data. The process of a nonlinear relationship creates previous patterns of relationships among the variables used for Bayesian panel data analysis. Nonparametric regression analysis maintains closed information relationships to define some conventional beliefs. In addition, nonparametric regression models carried out for estimation in this examination consist of the local linear kernel regression approach, the local polynomial kernel regression approach, and the Nadaraya–Watson kernel regression approach. Equation (11.3) explains local linear kernel fit regression in the panel data model to evaluate the relationship between the inflation rate and the GDP growth rate in AEC countries. The form of the relationship typically used to present raw data displays the trends and patterns of the relationship.

$$y_{it} = m(x_{it}) + u_{it},\ \ \mu + v_{it},\ \ i = 1, \ldots, 5,\ \ t = 1960\ to\ 2015 \tag{11.3}$$

Consider Eq. (11.3), denoting the GDP growth rate of the AEC countries Thailand, Singapore, Malaysia, Philippines, and Indonesia. In addition, $m(x_{it})$ represents the unknown function of x_{it} as the inflation rate of those countries, which is predetermined y_{it}. Once again, x_{it} represents the inflation rates of each AEC country. Furthermore, all processes for the calculation of the unknown function $m(x_{it})$ are completed by using the calculations from Eqs. (11.4) to (11.6), as follows (see Gupta et al. 2008):

$$\min_{\alpha(x_0),\beta(x_0)} \sum_{i=1}^{N} \sum_{t=1}^{n} K_{h\lambda}(x_0, x_{it})(y_{it}(x_{it}) - \lambda(x_0) - \beta(x_0)x_{it})^2 \tag{11.4}$$

$$\hat{y}(x_0) = \lambda(x_0) + \beta(x_0)x_0 \tag{11.5}$$

$$\hat{y} = (1, x_0) + (B^T w(x_0)B)^{-1} B^T w(x_0)y \tag{11.6}$$

where

$y_{it} = (y_{1t}(x_{1t}, \ldots, y_{it}(x_{it})))^T$
$w(x_0) = diag(K_{h\lambda}(x_0, x_{it}))_{NxN}$
$B^T = \begin{pmatrix} 1 & 1 & \ldots & 0 \\ x_{1t} & x_{2t} & \ldots & x_{nt} \end{pmatrix}$
$K_{h\lambda} D(\frac{\|x_{it} - x_0\|}{h_\lambda(x_0)})$, where (kernel radius), D (distance between the x_{it} and x_0).

In addition, from Eq. (11.3) the estimation conducted to evaluate this relationship involved the local polynomial kernel regression approach to panel data (Eq. (11.7) to (11.11)). In the case of p = 1, the local polynomial kernel regression approach to panel data could be calculated from the equations as follows (see Gupta et al. 2008):

$$\min_{\alpha(x_0),\beta(x_0),j=1,\ldots,d} \sum_{i=1}^{N}\sum_{t=1}^{n} K_{h\lambda}(x_0, x_{it})(y_{it}(x_{it}) - \alpha(x_0) - \sum_{j=1}^{d} \beta(x_0)x_0^j) \tag{11.7}$$

$$\hat{y}(x_0) = \alpha(x_0) + \sum_{j=1}^{d} \beta(x_0)x_0^j \tag{11.8}$$

Further, if $p > 1$, then the local polynomial kernel regression approach to panel data would be able to be calculated from the equations below:

$$\hat{\beta}(x_0) = arg\min_{\beta} \sum_{i=1}^{N}\sum_{t=1}^{n} K_{h\lambda}(x_0, x_{it})(y_{it}(x_{it}) - b(x_{it})^T\beta(x_0))^2 \tag{11.9}$$

$$b(x_{it}) = (1, x_{1t}, x_{2t}, \ldots, x_{1t}^2, x_2^2, \ldots x_{1t}x_{2t}) \tag{11.10}$$

$$\hat{y}(x_{it}) = b(x_0)^T\hat{\beta}(x_0) \tag{11.11}$$

The last approach employed to describe the relationship between the inflation-targeting rate and the GDP growth rate among the countries of the AEC is the Nadaraya–Watson kernel regression approach. This regression approach to panel data can be written in mathematical form by starting from Eq. (11.12) as follows:

$$E(y_{it}|x_{it}) = m(x_{it}) \tag{11.12}$$

$$y_{it} = m(x_{it}) + \varepsilon_{it}, E(\varepsilon_{it}) = 0, Var(y_{it}|x_{it}) = \sigma^2 \tag{11.13}$$

$$\hat{m}_{h(x_0)} = \left(\sum_{i=1}^{N} k(\frac{x_{it} - x_0}{h})y_{it}/k(\frac{x_{it} - x_0}{h})\right) \tag{11.14}$$

Suppose that Eq. (11.12) is the expectation value of two independent variables in an unknown form of the function that was computed by the Nadaraya–Watson estimator (Eq. (11.14)). Equation (11.13) was used to describe the relationship unknown form between two independent variables (GDP growth rate and inflation rate in the AEC countries).

11.4.3 Bayesian Approach Based on Panel Data

Bayesian econometrics is very useful for subjective probability judgments of risk insecurity, whereas the statistical analysis depends on the probability level in several situations, especially subjective probability. In terms of time series subjective modeling for panel data analysis, the efficiency of the econometric approach should produce more better assessments, selecting the best model for estimation. Thus, Bayesian econometrics was adapted to the process of estimation for panel time series data. It is important to choose three appropriate types of econometrics model, leading to better reliability and efficiency, which are employed to measure the relationship between the time series data of the annual inflation target rate and the GDP growth rate of AEC countries for the period 1960 to 2015, presented as the following (Eqs. (11.15), (11.16), and (11.17)):

Pooled model : –

$$y_{it} = \alpha + \beta x_{it} + \varepsilon_{it} \tag{11.15}$$

Random effect model : –

$$y_{it} = \alpha + \beta x_{it} + \varepsilon_{it}, \varepsilon_{it} = \alpha_i + \lambda_t + v_{it} \tag{11.16}$$

Fixed effect model : –

$$y_{it} = \sum_{j=1}^{N} \alpha_j d_{it}^j + \beta x_{it} + u_{it}, \qquad u_{it}\ iid(0, \sigma_u^2) \tag{11.17}$$

Suppose that y_{it} is represented by the GDP growth rate of each AEC country and as the inflation rate of those AEC countries. Overall, three types of panel model are used for estimation by choosing the Bayesian approach applied to this computation. The usual approach to selecting a technique that increases efficiency can be broken down into three distinctive stages. The process starts by testing for the regression model to accomplish a rigorous study of the computation. The first stage is to select the priors for these parameters as follows:

$\beta\ N(\mu_\beta, V_\beta)$, for all parameters in three types of panel model
$\sigma^2 - IG(a.b)$, for all errors in three types of panel model

Three distinctive key stages of analysis reveal enhancement prospects in the panel document-based model. In the next stage, this process elucidates the panel analysis and narrows the panel scope of the study further for construction of the likelihood function form employing Bayes' theorem (see Koop et al. 2007) to estimate the panel regression model (see Eq. (11.18)).

$$p(\beta, \sigma^2|y)\alpha L(\beta, \sigma^2)exp\left(-\frac{1}{2}(\beta - \mu_\beta)' V_\beta^{-1}(\beta - \mu_\beta)\right)(\sigma_2)^{-[a+1]}exp\left(-\frac{1}{b\sigma^2}\right) \tag{11.18}$$

The last stage of the Bayesian approach to estimation of the panel regression model needs to fill in the different characteristics for success using the simulation method Markov chain Monte Carlo (MCMC),[1] whereas all the last parameters (β) and sigma squared (σ^2) were obtained whenever MCMC converted to the stable process. The successful completion summary of the exact posterior distribution of each stage is critical of both coefficients and sigma squared in the panel regression model (see Eq. (11.19)).

$$\beta|\sigma^2, \quad y\, N(D_\beta, d_\beta, D_\beta) \tag{11.19}$$

where

$$D_\beta = (x^{'}x/\sigma^2 + V_\beta^{-1})^{-1}$$
$$d_\beta = x^{'}y/\sigma^2 + V_\beta^{-1}\mu_\beta$$

Furthermore, sigma squared (σ^2) in the likelihood function under the Bayes' theorem (see Eq. (11.20)) for this panel regression model was found completely using the MCMC simulation method (see Eq. (11.21) and (11.22)).

$$p(\sigma^2|\beta, y) \propto p(\beta, \sigma^2|y) \tag{11.20}$$

$$\alpha(\sigma^2)^{-[n/2]+a+1} exp\left(-\frac{1}{\sigma^2}[b^{-1} + \frac{1}{2}(y - x\beta)^{'}(y - x\beta)]\right) \tag{11.21}$$

$$\sigma^2|\beta, y\, IG\left(\frac{n}{2} + a, \; [b^{-1} + \frac{1}{2}(y - x\beta)^{'}(y - x\beta)]^{-1}\right) \tag{11.22}$$

Consider the model comparison approach based on Bayes' theorem for the selection of the appropriate panel regression model as the Bayes factor approach. Thus, Jeffreys' guidelines[2] would be used to conduct the testing of these models. The Bayes factor approach was shown in the following process:

$$\begin{aligned} R_{12} &= p(M_1|y)/p(M_2|y) \\ &= (p_1/p_2)[(\int f_1(y|\theta_1, M_1)\pi_1(\theta|M_1)d\theta_1)/(\int f_2(y|\theta_2, M_2)\pi_2(\theta|M_2)d\theta_2)] \\ &= (p_1/p_2)[(m_1(y)/(m_2(y)))] \end{aligned}$$

Testing of the panel model would be started to define it as a pooled model and to define M_1 as a fixed effect model. The result was that the value of $\log_{10}(R_{12})$ was as shown in Table 11.1.

[1]MCMC is a general purpose technique for sampling from complex probabilistic models, source: *http : //vcla.stat.ucla.edu/old/MCMC/MCMC$_t$utorial/Lect1$_M$CMC$_I$ntro.pdf*.

[2]The Theory of Probability (3 ed.). Oxford. p. 432.

Table 11.1 Summary of Jeffreys' guideline for model comparison

Items	Jeffreys' recommendations were modified by the authors
$\log_{10}(R_{12})>2$	Decisive support for a pooled model
$3/2<\log_{10}(R_{12})<2$	Very strong evidence for a pooled model
$1<\log_{10}(R_{12})<3/2$	Strong evidence for a pooled model
$1/2<\log_{10}(R_{12})$	Substantial evidence for a pooled model
$0<\log_{10}(R_{12})<1/2$	Weak evidence for a pooled model

Source: Modified from Jeffreys (1991) by the authors

11.5 Data Description

Notably, for each AEC country, Table 11.2 presents the descriptive statistics of the GDP growth rate (for more detail, see appendix A). In addition, Table 11.3 offers the descriptive statistics of the inflation rate. The inflation rate plays an important role in the economic growth process, especially in the economies of developing countries (Fattahia et al. 2016). However, it could not be concluded that the inflation target rate plays an important role in economic growth in a positive or negative way (Pollin and Zhu 2005). In addition, in most developing countries, it is still believed that the stability of price control that occurs with the use of inflation-targeting policy is involved in the re-creation of the central role in economic development (Pollin and Zhu 2005). Furthermore, this policy goal of maintaining the stability of price control is achieved when a central bank attempts to direct the optimal rate, resulting in economic growth for AEC countries.

According to Table 11.2, the Indonesian economy still displays the maximum GDP growth rate, whereas the inflation rate of Indonesia is higher than that of other AEC countries (see Table 11.3). In addition, good practice for controlling the price inflation of individual countries is to maintain it within a specific range of 3–5% (Pollin and Zhu 2005). In Singapore and Malaysia, a target range for the inflation rate was specified (see Table 11.3).

The forecast for economic growth by 2020 in these AEC countries is within a specific range of 3.5–6.5%, which is a reasonable rate of sustainable growth. Table 11.2 displays the average economic growth of AEC countries under which the benchmark for economic growth may be raised higher than the average GDP growth rate forecast. Nevertheless, the results of the testing of the two statistics using the Jarque–Bera test and the panel unit root test suggested that the time series data analysis, especially the Bayesian regression approach to panel data, would be the overall result regarding the efficiency of measuring the relationship between the inflation rate and economic growth in AEC countries.

The Jarque–Bera fitting test for normality[3] does not confirm that both the GDP growth rate and the inflation rate of each AEC country are not normally distributed.

[3]H0: the data are normally distributed; Ha: the data are not normally distributed.

Table 11.2 Summary of the statistics for gross domestic product (GDP) growth rates in Asian Economic Community (AEC) countries as yearly data of the study (during the period 1960 to 2015)

	Thailand GDP (%)	Singapore GDP (%)	Malaysia GDP (%)	Philippines GDP (%)	Indonesia GDP (%)
Mean	9.905471	12.00275	10.08122	7.834827	57.66904
Median	10.44449	12.39773	10.34108	9.791093	19.70963
Maximum	32.53561	41.23379	51.94505	36.67869	1232.334
Minimum	−24.30716	−14.43269	−27.83609	−39.37183	5.861841
Standard deviation	9.654905	10.14807	12.13022	11.59526	166.8692
Skewness	−1.061197	0.119322	−0.008606	−1.286608	6.428122
Kurtosis	5.609200	3.724846	5.524576	7.126699	45.49656
Jarque–Bera	26.39579	1.358824	14.87215	55.18587	4599.561
Probability	0.000002	0.506915	0.000590	0.000000	0.000000
Panel unit root test Levin, Lin & Chu (p value)	−10.6833 (0.000)	−10.6833 (0.000)	−10.6833 (0.000)	−10.6833 (0.000)	−10.6833 (0.000)
Status	Stationary	Stationary	Stationary	Stationary	Stationary
Observations	56	56	56	56	56

Source: World Bank

Table 11.3 Summary of statistics for inflation rates in AEC countries as yearly data of the study (during the period 1960 to 2015)

	Thailand GDP (%)	Singapore GDP (%)	Malaysia GDP (%)	Philippines GDP (%)	Indonesia GDP (%)
Mean	4.425295	2.637722	3.063150	9.010722	47.54148
Median	3.768179	1.743551	2.703538	6.616582	9.732185
Maximum	24.31356	22.36842	17.32898	50.33898	1136.254
Minimum	−0.895021	−1.841893	−0.409015	1.148138	3.720024
Standard deviation	4.686133	4.115872	2.957814	8.432798	156.6333
Skewness	2.218695	3.327647	2.400166	2.748232	6.243698
Kurtosis	9.118134	15.40797	11.57681	12.58762	43.35804
Jarque–Bera	133.2847	462.5849	225.4114	284.9784	4164.315
Probability	0.000000	0.000000	0.000000	0.000000	0.000000
Panel unit root test Levin, Lin & Chu (p value)	−10.4075 (0.000)	−10.4075 (0.000)	−10.4075 (0.000)	−10.4075 (0.000)	−10.4075 (0.000)
Status	Stationary	Stationary	Stationary	Stationary	Stationary
Observations	56	56	56	56	56

Source: World Bank

Thus, the results of the regression approach obtained statistical inefficiency from a simple stationary time series because the estimation did not suggest a normal distribution (H0: the data are normally distributed). Hence, a general approach to Bayesian data analysis was conducted, as an alternative adopted Bayesian regression approach would be advantageous for a panel data modeling-enabled solution of a complex non-normal distribution problem with a large number as a solution because of an emphasis on the power of interval estimation instead of hypothesis testing.

11.6 Empirical Results of the Research

For the Bayesian approach, the prior would be identified from subjective justification of a passive belief in some additional information on an unknown quantity. One had know only the probability of the contained information before he/she accepted the interval estimation. Therefore, the proposed procedure of Bayesian data analysis is used. From the measurement risk related to the subjective probability mentioned, the nonparametric regression was conducted by identifying the prior predictive distribution for the Bayesian regression approach to estimate the relationship between the GDP growth rate and the inflation rate of each AEC country during the period 1960–2015.

From three nonparametric regressions; namely, the local linear kernel regression approach, the local polynomial kernel regression approach, and the Nadaraya–Watson kernel regression approach, as suggested, the positive relationship between the GDP growth rate and the inflation rate during specific time periods were reported (for more detail, see Appendix B). Nevertheless, the information cannot practicably be identified by the anticipated prior predictive approach in the event of a crisis occurring in AEC countries, because inverse relationships between the GDP growth rate and the existing inflation rate as in higher dimensional data were obtained using three nonparametric regression estimations (see Appendix B).

According to Tables 11.4 and 11.5, AEC policy of inflation-targeting decided that the monetary policy should focus on what can be achieved by supporting long-term growth. Hence, lower inflation rates have fostered economic growth that the monetary policy focuses increases by 1%, change in inflation rate on average, GDP growth rate will increase by more than 1% for AEC long-term growth rate. Regarding Table 11.6, it shows the effect of inflation-targeting policy on true long-term growth change in AEC countries. As the largest economy, Indonesia was supported by successfully employing this inflation-targeting policy. Consequently, the monetary policy can support by having a lasting impact on long-term growth,

Table 11.4 Presentation of the Bayesian approach results estimated using pooled ordinary least squares regression analysis

Items	Pooled model				
Posterior quantiles	2.50%	25%	50%	75%	97.50%
Constants	3.546	4.541	5.059	5.585	6.594
Inflation	1.037	1.052	1.059	1.066	1.081
σ^2	146.583	162.78	172.345	182.778	204.248

Source: Authors' calculations

Table 11.5 Bayesian approach results estimated using a random effects model

Items	Random effects model				
Posterior quantiles	2.50%	25%	50%	75%	97.50%
Constants	3.62622	4.60379	5.1217	5.6381	6.6449
Inflation	1.03278	1.04706	1.05476	1.05476	1.0769
Random	−0.01627	0.03772	0.06687	0.0957	0.1514
σ^2	145.4339	161.6009	171.0307	0.0957	0.1514

Source: Authors' calculations

providing greater insight in terms of what the true growth has been and the true change in AEC countries.

The Thai economy, which is the second largest AEC country, is no longer suitable for using inflation-targeting policy to stimulate economic growth. However, the Thai economy had a good response employing only inflation-targeting policy during the period 1991–2015. In addition, in Malaysia, which is the third largest economy among the AEC countries regarding inflation-targeting policy during 1991–2015, and in Singapore, which is the fourth, economic growth was stimulated for more than an annual average of 2.5%. In contrast, the Philippines inflation-targeting policy indicates a sense of the negative impact of changes in which the monetary policy under control of price stability does not successfully foster long-term economic growth.

The Bayes factor approach shown in Table 11.7 was confirmed to describe the appropriate relationship between the GDP growth rate and the inflation rate of all AEC countries as the appropriate pooled model. Because $\log_{10}(R_{12}) = 6.13 > 2$ demonstrates strong evidence that the pooled model is the best guideline for good practices in modeling that have been delivered to explain the relationship between two macro variables. The estimation result provided by the Bayes factor approach can be used as guidance on how information on comparative monetary policy under the control of price stability can be used to stimulate long-term economic growth. The appropriate relationship can be best employed across important inflation-targeting policy, setting the monetary policy to stimulate long-term AEC economic growth, except for the Philippines economy.

11.7 Conclusion and Policy Recommendation

This chapter provides a methodology that explores how statistical models can be used for preparation for setting lower inflation-targeting rates, fostering economic growth. The findings suggest that if monetary policy increases on average inflation rate by 1%, GDP growth rate will increase by more than 1% in the long-term, in AEC countries. The estimation result promoted the implementation of the best Bayes factor practice by setting the monetary policy to stimulate long-term economic growth in AEC countries. Inflation-targeting policy can be used as

Table 11.6 Results of the estimation were obtained from the Bayesian approach to the fixed effects model

Items	Fixed effects model				
Posterior quantiles (Yearly)	2.50% (1960–1970)	25% (1971–1980)	50% (1981–1990)	75% (1991–2000)	97.50% (2001–2015)
Inflation rate of Indonesia	1.0385	1.05262	1.05984	1.067	1.081
Inflation rate of Thailand	−3.4882	−1.26565	−0.09841	1.077	3.325
Inflation rate of Singapore	−0.5063	1.80728	2.99451	4.165	6.419
Inflation rate of Malaysia	−2.2288	−0.01288	1.15242	2.331	4.57
Inflation rate of the Philippines	−8.9598	−6.67859	−5.51995	−4.286	−2.061
σ^2	136.5259	152.0681	160.9032	170.555	191.123

Source: Authors' calculations

Table 11.7 Guideline results of the comparison using the Bayes factor approach to the appropriate model

Item	Jeffreys' recommendations were modified by the authors
$\log_{10}(R_{12}) = 6.13 > 2$	Decisive support for the pooled model

Source: Modified from Jeffreys (1991)

guidance on how information on comparative monetary policy under control of the price stability can be used for achieving high rates of growth. The adopted inflation-targeting model in the monetary policy appeared, as a result, to apply to key long-term economic growth in AEC countries, except for the Philippines economy. If each AEC country had the lessons of experience for implementation of the best Bayes factor practice, to set lower inflation-targeting rates for economic growth, each country would continue to set inflation-targeting rates. However, the economic growth already announced produces possible inflation, once a lower inflation-targeting rate has appeared, as a result. To allow each member country to be guided by the present sense of inflation-targeting rates and the indications for the comparative monetary policy to that effect is to crucially control the price stability for the long-term growth rate. The result of this price stability course would be a rise in the long-term growth rate to the desired level. Thus, there is constant oscillation of the long-term growth rate, although the fluctuations become larger as each AEC country becomes more experienced.

Appendix A

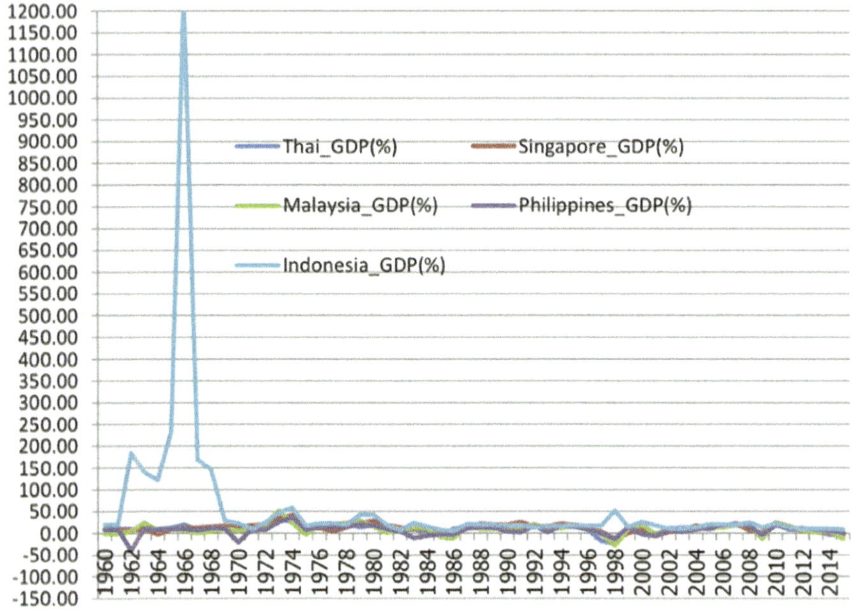

Fig. 11.2 Time series of the gross domestic product (GDP) growth rate for each country in Asian Economic Community (AEC) countries during the period of 1960–2015 as yearly data. Source: Authors' calculations with data extracted from the UN statistical office

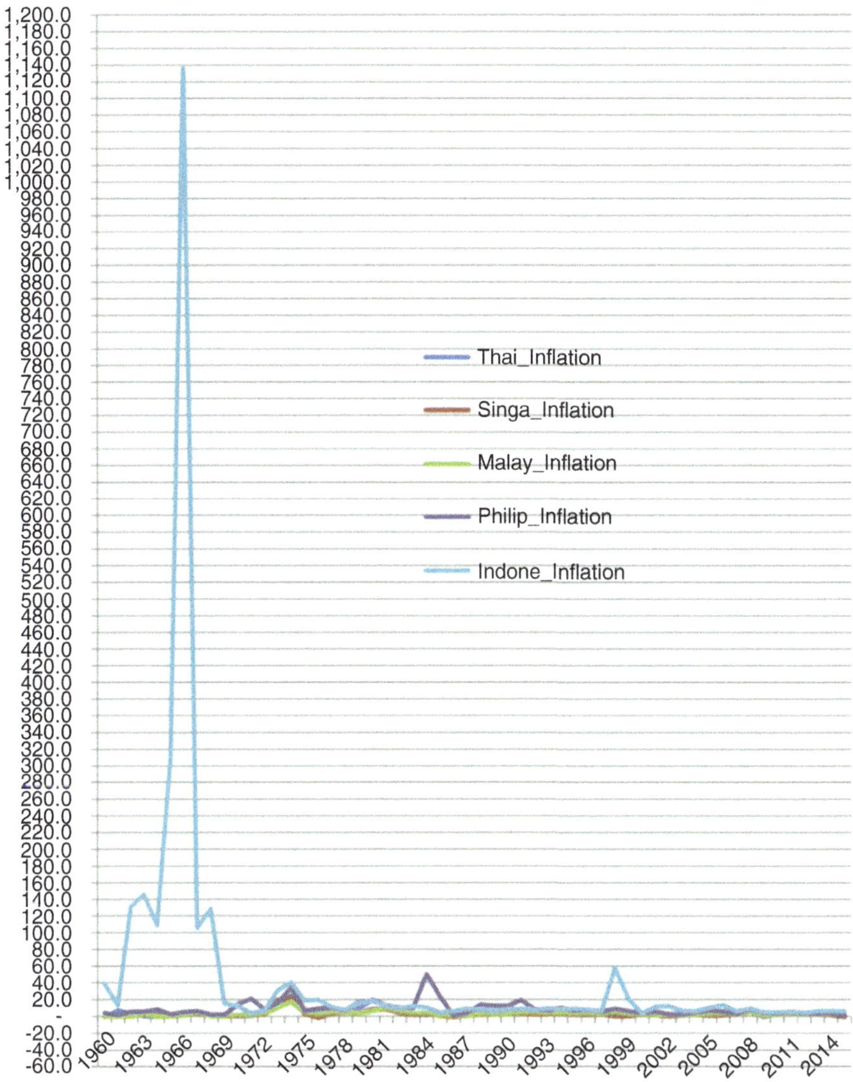

Fig. 11.3 Time series of the inflation rate for each AEC country during the period 1960–2015 as yearly data. Source: Authors' calculations with data extracted from the UN statistical office

Appendix B

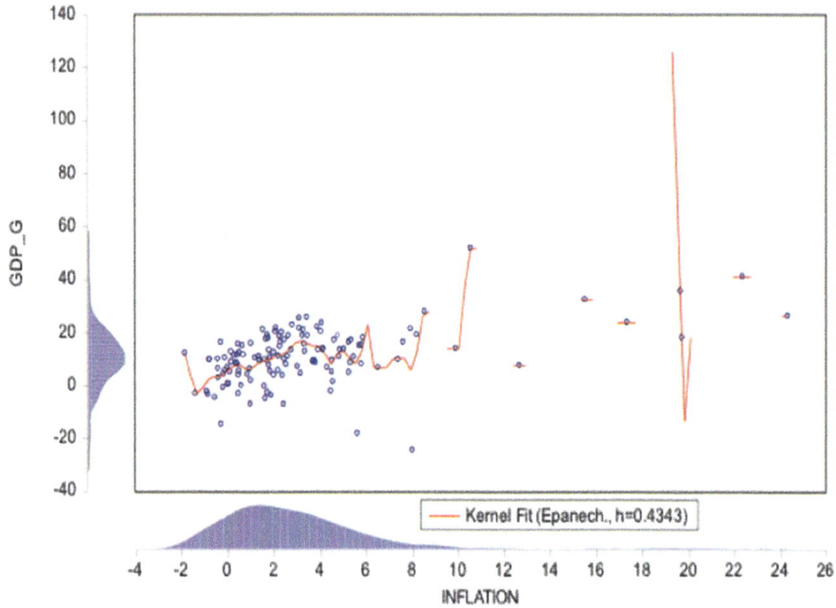

Fig. 11.4 Result of estimation by local linear kernel regression for the GDP growth rate and inflation rate of AEC countries during the period 1960–2015 as yearly data. Source: Authors' calculations with data extracted from the UN statistical office

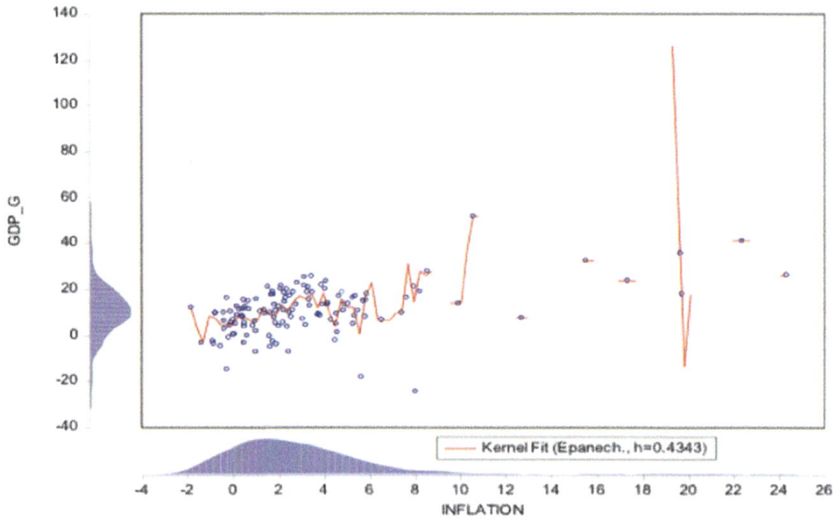

Fig. 11.5 Result of estimation by the local polynomial kernel regression for the GDP growth rate and inflation rate of AEC countries during the period 1960–2015 as yearly data. Source: Authors' calculations with data extracted from the UN statistical office

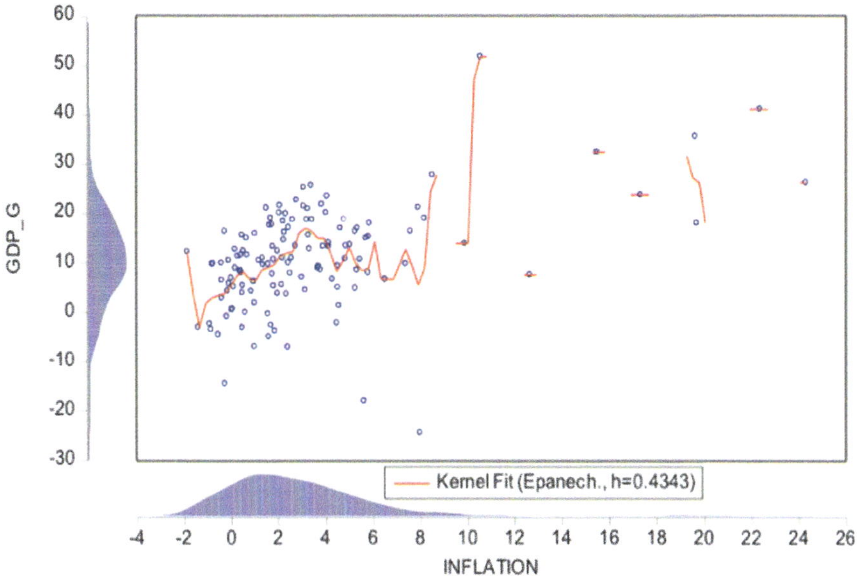

Fig. 11.6 Result of estimation by the Nadaraya–Watson kernel regression for the GDP growth rate and inflation rate of AEC countries during the period 1960–2015 as yearly data. Source: Authors' calculations with data extracted from the UN statistical office

References

Fattahia, S., Tiatorajb, A., & Nima, N. (2016) International academic institute for science and technology. *International Academic Journal of Economics, 3*(6), 46–61.

Fisher, I. (1922). In C. Hugh (Ed.) *Dollar stabilization* (12th ed.). London/New York.

Gupta, M., Garcia, E., & Chin, E. (2008). *Adaptive local linear regression with application to printer color management*. Retrieved from: http://www.mayagupta.org/publications/GuptaGarciaChinTIP2008.pdf.

Hammond, G. (2012). *State of the art of inflation targeting*. (PDF). Bank of England – Centre for Central Banking Studies. 17, 18–44.

Koop, G., Poirier, D. J., & Tobias, J. L. (2007). *Bayesian econometric methods*. New York: Cambridge University Press. 100013-2473.

Laurrabaquio, O. P. (2014). The non-linear relationship between inflation and economic growth in Mexico. *Problemas del Desarrollo, 45*(177).

Li, Q., & Racine, J. S. (2007). *Nonparametric econometrics: Theory and practice*. Princeton: Princeton University Press. ISBN-0691121613.

Pollin, R. & andZhu, A. (2005). *Inflation and economic growth: A cross-country non-linear analysis*. Working Paper Series. University of Massachusetts, Amherst.

Chapter 12
Economics, Marketing and Performances of US Classical Music: *Journeyin' Together to de Promise Land*

Angela Besana and Annamaria Esposito

Abstract Since the beginning of the latest financial and real crisis in 2008, US symphony orchestras and opera houses have revealed adaptation to the turmoil of scarce resources and a very keen competition (Jeannotte and Duxbury J Arts Manag Law Soc 45(2):84–99, 2015; Turbide et al. Int J Arts Manag 10(2):4–13, 2008).

Adaptation has had multiple implications: implementation of websites and social media as innovative tools for audience exploration and development (Pierotti et al. Eur Sci J 10(34):1–22, 2014; Ravanas Int J Arts Manag 10(2):68–78, 2008); revenue diversification and performance measurement (Hong J Arts Manag Law Soc 44(3):181–201, 2014; Besana J Arts Manag Law Soc 42(2):79–89, 2012); community engagement together with testing of new segments like tourists (Kemp and Poole J Arts Manag Law Soc 46(2):53–62, 2016. Guachalla Eur J Tour Res 6(1):83–87, 2012; Woosnam et al. J Hosp Mark Manag 18:500–511, 2009; Poon and Lai Urban Stud 45(11): 2273–2289, 2008).

Marketing, and especially social media marketing, has had a crucial new role and enhanced "interactive online world in which participants with different interests, resources and power co-create value" (Kornum and Mülbacher J Bus Res. 66(9):1460–1464, 2013). Marketing and fundraising have extracted both willingness to pay and willingness to donate from audiences, while audiences have been spending more time than ever using social media, and the US classical music has been striving to use social media and to reach, engage, catch and hold the millions of consumers who use it daily, tourists included (Parsons A (2011) Social media from a corporate perspective: a content analysis of official Facebook pages. Allied Academies International Conference: proceedings of the

Angela Besana wrote paragraphs 1 and 3. Annamaria Esposito wrote paragraph 2. They wrote together paragraph 4.

A. Besana (✉) · A. Esposito
IULM University, Milan, Italy
e-mail: angela.besana@iulm.it

N. Tsounis, A. Vlachvei (eds.), *Advances in Panel Data Analysis in Applied Economic Research*, Springer Proceedings in Business and Economics,
https://doi.org/10.1007/978-3-319-70055-7_12

Academy of Marketing Studies. 16(2):11–15). Marketing has called for e-commerce of audiences; fundraising has called for s-commerce of philanthropists.

After analysing the new marketing scenario and pointing out social media marketing strategies of the US classical music, this paper investigates 100 symphony orchestras and 100 opera houses according to their revenues, expenses and gains (or losses) in 2015. Thanks to cluster analysis, three groups will emerge with different performances and prevailing fundraising.

12.1 US Classical Music: Not Only a Matter of *Claps*

US symphony orchestras and opera houses are today facing a very competitive arena and hard times of scarce resources. Multiple strategies have been developed so that they are able to diversify and maximize revenues (Pompe and Tamburri 2016; Jeannotte and Duxbury 2015; Besana 2012; Turbide et al. 2008). Flexible pricing stimulates engagement of several and multifaceted audiences: from local communities in big and small cities to tourists, who represent the very next frontier for their marketing (Guachalla 2012; Woosnam et al. 2009; Poon and Lai 2008). Flexible pricing is supported by segmentation, which is granted by new explorative tools like websites and social media. It's a matter of new data research, collections and development so that they adapt and innovate marketing and fundraising (Turbide and Laurin 2009; Ravanas 2008; Rushton 2008; Turrini 2006; Smith 2007). Performances will follow, and they will be evident in revenues and gains (Kemp and Poole 2016; Hong 2014; Anderson 2009).

Marketing and fundraising have been leading strategies for more than four decades, and fundraising has fostered and nurtured revenues much more than marketing (Song and Yi 2011; Yi 2010; Boerner et al. 2011; Ravanas 2007; Bussell and Forbes 2006; Borgonovi 2006; Bennett 2005; Johnson and Garbarino 2001). Friends' schemes have included different categories with focus on contents, prices, subscription fees and benefits. Multiple schemes have continually been developed, monitored and changed. As a matter of fact, marketing and fundraising have been facing a trade-off since when boundaries among segments were crossed with confusion of benefits and last-minute sales. Nevertheless, supported by relationship marketing of social media, strategic conflicts have been coped with, while marketing and fundraising have been fully developed on parallel paths, providing the US classical music with more than 80% of total revenues.

Next to marketing and fundraising, the US classical music has not eluded investments, sales of assets and other revenue sources, these strategies generating investment income and other revenues for 10% of total revenues.

With focus on revenue diversification, marketing officers and fundraisers of the US classical music have started with their *social media era*. If information and promotion stream thanks to multiple channels, audiences are immediately reached with persuasive messages and multiple display formats; the customer's experience is not more a commercial transaction but a relationship (Pierotti et al. 2014).

Multichannel consumers experience what is more than a sale (Nadeem et al. 2015; Verhoef et al. 2015; Xu et al. 2014; Zhang et al. 2010; Neslin and Shakar 2009, Radbourne et al. 2009). The relationship is continually nurtured and enhanced thanks to Facebook, Twitter and other meeting places (Stelzner 2015; Parsons 2011). The opportunity to build an e-community around the consumer is immediately caught: the opera board, the orchestra social media manager, the maestro and musicians and any other stakeholders in a virtual network; they are all ready to grasp attention and match with customers' needs. It is not more a matter of e-commerce but also s-commerce, social commerce where classical music organizations are implementing a wide range of strategies to engage consumers and philanthropists (Buratti et al. 2016; Ceruti et al. 2015; Huang and Benyoucef 2013; Zhou et al. 2013; Liang and Turban 2011).

If attention is a scarce resource, effective marketing and fundraising can stimulate attention. Attention, sense and sensibility for philanthropy of different audiences can be impacted by advertising and any offline and online marketing. A little research has been deserved to these intangible features of demand, above all, assuming attention as a given. The high competition in e-markets has emphasized the importance of attention and engaging social media for at least one decade. The rising cost of this resource is stimulating managers to think about how to catch and exploit it (Teixeira 2014; Lewicki 2016; Rigby 2011; Corbitt et al. 2003).

The paper is an analysis of performances of 200 biggest symphony orchestras and opera houses according to the latest available accounted revenues (2015).

The next paragraph will focus on marketing and fundraising of US classical music in times of e- and s-commerce. The third paragraph will refer to cluster analysis of 100 symphony orchestras and 100 opera houses, so that significant clusters can be separated according to the latest available accounting data of revenues, costs and gains (or losses) in 2015.

12.2 Marketing for E-Commerce and Fundraising for S-Commerce: A New 'Stage' for the US Classical Music

Marketing scenario has changed considerably over the last decade. Technology, the Internet and the WEB 2.0 have really reshaped the way consumers and organizations interact and communicate (Kornum and Mülbacher 2013). Digital communication raises new opportunities and challenges both for organizations and consumers. For-profit and not-for-profit organizations and cultural and creative organizations, they are all profiting by the digital society, and they stimulate their targets and audiences with increasing efforts.

On the one hand, thanks to social media and social networks, consumers have access to large amount of information about organizations, brands and products. On the other hand, companies strive to manage marketing communications via social media to create customer and brand value. Social media, as Internet-based application Web 2.0, allows the creation and exchange of user-generated content (Kaplan and Haenlein 2010) that are leading a transformation in the management of relationships with customers (Moretti and Tuan 2014; Kietzmann et al. 2011).

Companies in order to grasp the attention of consumers and boost online B2C sales are investing in social media marketing. Social media marketing strategies are designed to offer customer new experiences and to enhance customer participation and engagement (Brodie et al. 2011; Huang and Benyoucef 2013; Ceruti et al. 2015). This is true for not-for-profit and cultural organizations, too. Especially, when experiences can be enhanced with music, videos, downloads, recordings, virtual participation to rehearsals and primas, very next to the stage, offline and online.

Social media marketing strategies allows companies to *hear* and *talk with* prospects and customers, to develop and deepen the relationship between companies and customers. Marketers are aware that social media marketing can bring companies near customers and, in doing so, generate knowledge that helps to increase revenues, decrease costs and improve efficiency. Consequently, companies can achieve a greater economic value (Michaelidou et al. 2011; Huang and Benyoucef 2013).

As can be understood, social media marketing implies a new way to manage the relationships with customers, and, according to Moretti and Tuan (2014), it can be considered as an evolution of relationship marketing concept and practice (Vivek et al. 2012). In s-commerce, customers, audiences and philanthropists have to be engaged more and more via social and interactive ways in order to build trust that is a crucial factor in the success of s-commerce companies. Trust leads to relationship commitment that is really important in the social media environment, where normally online communities generate conversations and relationships, which are no longer under company control (Mangold and Faulds 2009; Moon et al. 2014). In addition, these conversations and interactions between customers, sellers and other stakeholders can affect company marketing decisions (Pastore 2009; Sashi 2012), making customers to become coproducers and cocreators of the value of the firm, and finally pro-sumers. Trustworthy e-commerce relations can evolve in friendships, and marketing can be complimentary with fundraising, in order to exploit both willingness to pay and the willingness to donate.

To successfully exploit the potential of social media, companies need to facilitate collaborative experiences and dialogue, to become part of the conversation and design experiences that deliver tangible value in return for customers' time, attention, endorsement and data (Baird and Parasnis 2011). Furthermore, they need to integrate the experience with other customer-facing initiatives. Maestros, orchestras and singers' engagement become essential in order to personalize relationships and cultivate customers' tastes, emotions and advocacy.

Social media marketing managers must strengthen social commerce campaigns with time-sensitive offers or discounts that motivate customers to act (Naadem 2012) and incentives for people to share content with friends to capitalize on the viral benefits a community platform offers. Regarding social media platforms, Facebook and Twitter are the top choices. But as marketers gain experience, their marketing efforts seem to expand across all major social platforms such as LinkedIn,

Google+, YouTube, Pinterest and Instagram. Social media are useful to facilitate prospect and customer transition from the social platform to the company website and vice versa, and they participate in all stages before and after product or service purchase.

Concluding, in the above-depicted scenario, marketers have great opportunities to boost online business integrating social networks and e-commerce platforms.

On the one hand, social media marketing conveys also promotional messages, transforming social media in effective and powerful advertising channels, able to engage, motivate and convince users to seek and share information about company products or services, including those relating to their online purchases.

On the other hand, social media marketing is able to solve one of the most important problems which are connected to e-commerce research phase, when user tends to get lost and bored and often does not finalize the purchase. E-commerce must be an environment, where everything user needs can be found easily.

Social media could be the solution transforming e-commerce in *social commerce*. Prospect and customers can use the social media platforms on which they spend most of the time to go through all the steps before and after the purchase without ever getting out of there.

Considering the two most important platforms and a B2B approach, it could be useful to consider how companies can take advantage from them to implement s-commerce.

Facebook is not the best platform to improve sales, but it could be considered the best platform for increasing awareness of corporate brand identity. The most interesting feature of Facebook is the targeting capability. In fact, the platform collects many personal details, posted by users onto the platform, useful to target prospect. Furthermore, it is a tool to keep people engaged between purchases. Recently Facebook has been provided with a *buy button* to make it easy to transact directly within the social media experience.

In fact, unlike the traditional button generally used to carry traffic from social media to company website, companies can sponsor a post with a picture of a product or a video or a soundtrack and offer the user concerned the opportunity to make the purchase without leaving Facebook, guaranteeing respect for privacy and security of credit card data or against the current one used for the payment. Facebook requires no commission on the transition, but only the cost of the ad, which is the same as any other sponsored post. This function is very useful, because the possibility of profiling the target audience through Facebook ads is very high and allows companies to advertise the right product to the right audience.

The same happened for Twitter that allows companies to build relationships with influencers and to communicate with customers. The buy button, in this case, brings the user to the seller e-commerce site.

In 2014, Twitter has signed an agreement with the e-dealer Amazon USA and UK. The new feature lets Twitter users add items to their Amazon carts by including a hashtag within a tweet. After the user connects their Twitter account to Amazon, they can extend their Amazon shopping experience by tweeting a reply to Amazon product links they see on Twitter including the hashtag #AmazonCart—or #AmazonBasket in the UK—to add the product to their shopping basket.

The feature not only extends the retail reach of Amazon beyond its own website, reducing purchase friction, but co-opts Twitter users into product marketing activity, since they are publishing tweets indicating which items they are buying from Amazon.

As it is not only a matter of e- and s-commerce for the US classical music, buttons like 'buy now' or 'give now' proliferate together with music, videos, interviews, atmosphere and the experience of 'virtual touching' divas or, at least, writing to them. What was far for classical music audiences yesterday, it is today 'off the stage', and relationship marketing can dominate both the commercial and social experiences.

As above depicted, the relationship between social media and classical music is close and full of interesting and engaging ideas, opportunities and promising scenarios.

12.3 Performances of US Classical Music in 2015: A Cluster Analysis

First of all, we investigated accounting data of revenues and expenses of biggest USA 100 symphony orchestras and 100 opera houses, listed for the highest total income at www.guidestar.org in 2015 (990 Forms).

As reported in the 990 Form Glossary, revenues of a US not-for-profit organization include *direct public support*, contributions, gifts, grants and bequests received directly from the public (it refers to amounts received from individuals, trusts, corporations, estates, foundations and public charities or raised by an outside professional fundraiser), and *government contributions or grants*, payments from the government to a nonprofit organization to further the organization's public programmes. Direct public support, government contributions and grants are summed so that the whole *contributions* are estimated.

The other main revenue category is *program service revenues*: fees and other monies received by an organization for services rendered.

If contributions and program service revenues are more than 80% of the sample, ancillary revenues are derived from *membership*, members' and affiliates' fees that are not contributions; *interest on savings and temporary cash investments*, the amount of interest income from savings and temporary cash; *dividends and interests from securities*, the income from equities and securities; the *rental income* (net of costs) received from investment property and *other investment income*; revenues of *fundraising (special) events* (net of costs); revenues from *sales of assets*, items owned by the organization and *sales of inventory*; and *other revenues*, revenues not previously counted.

The revenue diversification was here investigated for main categories: contributions with the target of the willingness to donate, program service revenue with the target of willingness to pay, investment income and other revenue.

Expense categories include *program service expense* related to marketing and production of the core business; *fundraising expense* and *management and general expense*, a miscellaneous cost that is not related to the previous accounting lines.

Next to them, *personnel expense* was here investigated to appreciate what is the best evidence of the creative content of the US classical music, the creative labour intensity of orchestras, singers, dancers, maestros, fundraisers and marketing officers, too.

Next to revenue and expense categories, the *(net) gain or loss of the year* as the difference (positive or negative) between revenues and costs was also here considered.

All these data for 158 (out of listed 200 organizations) available 990 2015's Forms were filed in Excel and indexed to total revenues and total expenses. Ratios were then k-means clustered to separate significant groups.

Cluster analysis is often applied in biology and other natural sciences to segment populations (species) into significant groups (subspecies), according to specific features or selected variables. In microeconomics and industrial organizations, cluster analysis is very useful in order to classify industries, districts, networks, strategic groups and any other aggregate that reveal significant and differentiated patterns.

Cluster analysis has matured both in applied economics and marketing, for it is a leading tool in order to segment audiences, stakeholders and competitors.

Having clustered above-mentioned ratios with JMP statistical software, we obtained three clusters, whose performances (k-means) are presented in Table 12.1. Composition of clusters is presented in Table 12.2. Extraordinary performances of seven outliers will be not here commented.

Table 12.1 2015's performances of clusters of US classical music (k-means)

Clusters, number of organizations	Contributions/ total revenues	Program service revenue/total rev.	Investment income/total rev.	Other rev./total rev.
Cluster 1, 68	56.34	36.43	2.08	5.13
Cluster 2, 52	64.56	23.82	10.38	1.22
Cluster 3, 31	54.95	39.86	0.78	4.39
Clusters	Program service expense/total expenses	Management and general expense/total exp.	Fundraising expense/total expenses	
Cluster 1	74.78	17.45	7.75	
Cluster 2	80.03	12.74	7.22	
Cluster 3	74.83	23.95	1.20	
Clusters	Personnel expense/total expenses	Gain or loss/total revenues		
Cluster 1	49.38	0.16		
Cluster 2	45.52	14.43		
Cluster 3	34.48	1.33		

Table 12.2 Composition of clusters

Clusters	US symphony orchestras and opera houses
Cluster 1	BERKELEY SYMPHONY ORCHESTRA – BERKELEY, BOSTON YOUTH SYMPHONY ORCHESTRA INC – BOSTON, BUFFALO PHILHARMONIC ORCHESTRA SOCIETY INC – BUFFALO, CAPE ANN SYMPHONY ORCHESTRA INC – GLOUCESTER, CHARLOTTE SYMPHONY ORCHESTRA INC - PORT CHARLOTTE, …, FAIRFAX SYMPHONY ORCHESTRA – FAIRFAX, …, LONG BEACH SYMPHONY ASSOCIATION - LONG BEACH, LONGWOOD SYMPHONY ORCHESTRA INC – BROOKLINE, LUBBOCK SYMPHONY ORCHESTRA INC – LUBBOCK, LYRIC OPERA SAN DIEGO - SAN DIEGO, MEMPHIS ORCHESTRAL SOCIETY INC – MEMPHIS, METROPOLITAN OPERA ASSOCIATION INC - NEW YORK, …, PORTLAND MAINE SYMPHONY ORCHESTRA – PORTLAND, PORTLAND OPERA ASSOCIATION – PORTLAND, …, SAINT LOUIS SYMPHONY ORCHESTRA - SAINT LOUIS, SEATTLE YOUTH SYMPHONY ORCHESTRAS – SEATTLE, …, THE ATLANTA OPERA INC – ATLANTA, THE HENDERSONVILLE SYMPHONY ORCHESTRA INC - HENDERSONVILLE, THE LOUSIANA PHILHARMONIC ORCHESTRA - NEW ORLEANS, THE OPERA COMPANY OF NORTH CAROLINA – RALEIGH, …
Cluster 2	… ARIZONA OPERA COMPANY – PHOENIX … BOSTON LYRIC OPERA COMPANY – BOSTON … CHICAGO OPERA THEATRE – CHICAGO, CHICAGO SINFONIETTA – CHICAGO, CHICAGO SYMPHONY ORCHESTRA – CHICAGO …, CINCINNATI SYMPHONY ORCHESTRA – CINCINNATY, HAWAII OPERA THEATRE – HONOLULU … KANSAS CITY SYMPHONY - KANSAS CITY, KENTUCKY OPERA ASSOCIATION – LOUISVILLE, LOS ANGELES OPERA COMPANY - LOS ANGELES, LYRIC OPERA OF CHICAGO – CHICAGO …, PITTSBURGH OPERA INC – PITTSBURGH, SACRAMENTO PHILHARMONIC ORCHESTRA ASSOCIATION INC – SACRAMENTO, SAN DIEGO SYMPHONY ORCHESTRA ASSOCIATION - SAN DIEGO, SAN FRANCISCO OPERA ASSOCIATION - SAN FRANCISCO, SANTA BARBARA SYMPHONY ORCHESTRA ASSOCIATION - SANTA BARBARA, …
Cluster 3	ALBANY SYMPHONY ORCHESTRA INC – ALBANY, AMERICAN SYMPHONY ORCHESTRA - NEW YORK, BALTIMORE OPERA COMPANY INC – BALTIMORE, …, MODESTO SYMPHONY ORCHESTRA ASSOCIATION – MODESTO, MUSIC CENTER OF SOUTH CENTRAL MI - BATTLE CREEK, NEW ORLEANS OPERA ASSOCIATION - NEW ORLEANS, …, ROCKFORD SYMPHONY ORCHESTRAS INC – ROCKFORD, SAN ANTONIO OPERA - SANT ANTONIO, SHREVEPORT OPERA – SHREVEPORT, …, THE CARNEGIE HALL CORPORATION - NEW YORK, …

Source: Elaboration with JMP Statistics Software

Table 12.2 shows average performances. Revenue diversification is present with different intensity in all clusters, for which contributions are prevailing.

The highest contributions match with a fundraising expense of more than 7% for clusters 1 and 2. When program service expense is the highest one of the sample (39.86%), the lowest fundraising expense counts for 1.20% (cluster 3). The personnel expense is more than 40% in clusters 1 and 2, while it is 35% in the cluster 3, where the hospitality of touring orchestras and performances is constantly planned next to an own production.

The highest contributions match with the highest investment income, the highest program service expense and the highest gain in cluster 2. Revenue diversification is, therefore, significant for symphony orchestras and opera houses, which profit by the highest gain.

The most crowded cluster 1 includes Metropolitan Opera, whose engagement of several audiences is experience-full thanks to multimedia performances, dining, brunches, membership for at least five categories (national member, supporting member, donor, sponsor, patron), single tickets, rush ones, groups for students, professionals, friends, under 40 and travellers. With this multiple marketing and fundraising, Met is particularly concerned with local community and communities, national, local and international friends and tourists (travellers). Most of orchestras and opera houses in this cluster use more than three social media: from marketing to fundraising, customers can evolve in friends, when these organizations launch and promote fundraising campaigns and call for memberships through social media. The engagement of web- and media users can be significant with videos, photos, interviews of maestro and stars (opera singers and musicians). The engagement can involve volunteering for the whole season or spot events (fundraising events, too).

With the highest contributions, cluster 2 includes Cincinnati Symphony, whose fundraising comprises individual giving with different funds and the endowment, corporate and foundations support, volunteering students and the multicultural awareness council for the greater Cincinnati area. This stakeholder refers to communities and their empowerment. Next to Cincinnati Symphony, in this cluster Kansas City Symphony can be found. Fundraising of Kansas City Symphony embraces individual giving and family foundations, sponsors and volunteering. This symphony supplies audiences with multiple services: ticket returns and above all, 'plan your experience' with hotels, restaurants and parking. Tourists are well served, as they can bundle their holiday contents at multiple links of the symphony website. Fundraising can be enhanced thanks to social media, which enable s-commerce of multiple and strong relationships. Next to individuals, officers of foundations and sponsoring companies crowd social media with storytelling, monitoring and benchmarking of their fund-giving and sponsorships to orchestras and opera houses.

With the highest program service revenue, cluster 3 includes the Carnegie Hall, whose concert hall reveals the best occupancy with flexible pricing, focus on education, community and any kind of tourists in New York. Social media have a pivotal role in community (students) engagement. Flexible pricing and subscriptions are launched, advertised and monitored together with appealing videos, backstages, online rehearsals and e-stores for everything, from merchandising to dinners with musicians.

12.4 Conclusion

With three clusters of different size and membership, cluster analysis of the here investigated sample reveals the prevailing fundraising, with websites and social media supporting relations, both s-commerce and e-commerce of fees, subscriptions and flexible pricing.

The US classical music is innovating and diversifying businesses and strategies. Marketing and fundraising are continually evolving, with multiple pricing and friends' schemes.

Offline and online marketing and fundraising are determinant strategies to shape relationships, helping managers to rethink who are crucial customers, audiences and cultural travellers, what are their needs and how the organization should address them.

The objective of this new way of selling and buying is not only to change the way to buy one to one, between sellers and buyers, but also to allow a real social and sociable purchase. S-commerce brings together members of a community and facilitates communication between members giving them the possibility to talk about purchases and products but also to make proposals on what products to sell. Through this specific exchange of information between supply and demand, the classic paradigm, according to which must be companies to offer customers their own products, is reversed. A new era, rich of potentialities, is beginning. Audiences are participating to this reshaping of relations.

As far as limitation as concerned, the short-term period of the analysis must be considered. Furthermore, some questions remain unanswered, thus leaving room for thought on forthcoming research. First, the research should be extended to the next years' performances in order to verify if economic results can consolidate thanks to offline and online strategies. Second, further investigations are needed, to detect, if they exist, attracting factors (such as mission, stars' or divas' leading roles, dimensions, geographic area, heritages other than classical music, etc.). Third, revenue diversification refers to investment income and other revenues whose percentages should be detected in order to profile art organizations according to their propensity for investments and investors' relationship marketing, too. Another role for social media could be examined and supported for this kind of relationship.

(Recalling Serena in 'Porgy and Bess') *The journey to the promise land* of increasing performances has just started. Social media can support marketing and fundraising efforts. New segments, like musical tourists, are ready to be empowered and engaged in these experiences with their divas and not-divas.

References

Anderson, C. (2009). *The longer long tail: How endless choice is creating unlimited demand*. New York: Ramdom House Business.

Baird, C. H., & Parasnis, G. (2011). From social media to social customer relation management. *Strategy & Leadership, 39*(5), 30–37.

Bennett, R. (2005). Factors encouraging competitive Miopia in the performing arts sector: An empirical investigation. *The Service Industries Journal, 25*(3), 391–401.

Besana, A. (2012). Alternative resources: Revenue diversification in the Not-for-Profit USA Symphony Orchestra. *The Journal of Arts Management, Law and Society, 42*(2), 79–89.

Boerner, S., Moser, V., & Jobst, J. (2011). Evaluating cultural industries: investigating visitors' satisfaction in theatres. *The Service Industries Journal, 31*(6), 877–895.

Borgonovi, F. (2006). Do public grants to American theatres crowd-out private donations? *Public Choice, 126*, 429–451.

Brodie, R. J., Hollebeek, L. D., Juric, B., & Illic, A. (2011). Customer engagement: Conceptual domain, fundamental propositions and implications for research. *Journal of Service Research, 14*(3), 252–271.

Buratti, N., Lanzara, R., & Simoni, M. (2016). Technological innovation and marketing. A multi-perspective analysis. *Mercati e Competitività, 1*, 19–44.

Bussell, H., & Forbes, D. (2006). "Friends" schemes in arts marketing. *International Journal of Arts Management, 8*(2), 39–49.

Ceruti, F., Mazzucchelli, A., & Di Gregorio, A. (2015). E-commerce or s-commmerce? A managerial perspective on online customers engagement. Proceedings of 2015 SIM (Società Italiana di Marketing) Conference, Turin, 2015.

Corbitt, B. J., Thanasankit, T., & Yi, H. (2003). Trust and e-commerce: A study of consumer perceptions. *Electronic Commerce Research and Applications, 2*(3), 203–215.

Guachalla, A. (2012). The role of cultural flagships in the perception and experience for tourism and culture. Case study: The Royal Opera House in Covent Garden. *European Journal of Tourism Research, 6*(1), 83–87.

Hong, J. (2014). Data envelopment analysis in the strategic management of Youth Orchestras. *The Journal of Arts Management, Law and Society, 44*(3), 181–201.

Huang, Z., & Benyoucef, M. (2013). From e-commerce to social commerce. A close look at design features. *Electronic Commerce Research and Applications, 12*(4), 246–259.

Jeannotte, M. S., & Duxbury, N. (2015). Advancing knowledge through grassroots experiments: connecting culture and sustainability. *The Journal of Arts Management, Law and Society, 45*(2), 84–99.

Johnson, M. S., & Garbarino, E. (2001). Customers of performing arts organizations: Are subscribers different from non-subscribers? *International Journal of Nonprofit and Voluntary Sector Marketing, 6*(1), 61–72.

Kaplan, A. M., & Haenlein, M. (2010). Users of the world, unite! The challenges and opportunities of social media. *Business Horizons, 53*(1), 59–68.

Kemp, E., & Poole, S. M. (2016). Arts audiences: Establishing a gateway to audience development and engagement. *The Journal of Arts Management, Law and Society, 46*(2), 53–62.

Kietzmann, J. H., Hermkens, K., Mccarthy, I. P., & Silvestre, B. S. (2011). Social media? get serious! understanding the functional building blocks of Social Media. *Business Horizons, 54*(3), 241–251.

Kornum, N., & Mülbacher, H. (2013). Multi-stakeholder virtual dialogue: introduction to the special issue. *Journal of Business Research, 66*(9), 1460–1464.

Lewicki, M. (2016). E-Shop offer as a tool creating value for customer. In M. H. Bilgin, H. Danis, E. Demir, & U. Can (Eds.), *Business challenges in changing economics landscape, Eurasian Studies in Business and Economics 2/2* (pp. 221–230). Cham: Springer International Publishing.

Liang, T. P., & Turban, E. (2011). Introduction to the special issue social commerce: A research framework for social commerce. *International Journal of Electronic Commerce, 16*(2), 5–14.

Mangold, G. W., & Faulds, D. J. (2009). Social media: The new hybrid element of the promotion mix. *Business Horizons, 52*, 357–365.

Michaelidou, N., Siamagka, N. T., & Christodoulides, G. (2011). Usage, barriers and measurement of social media marketing: AB exploratory investigation of small and medium B2B brands. *Industrial Marketing Management, 40*(1), 1153–1159.

Moon, S., Park, Y., & Kim, Y. (2014). The impact of text product reviews on sales. *European Journal of Marketing, 48*(11/12), 2176–2197.

Moretti, A., & Tuan, A. (2014). Social media marketing and relationship marketing: revolution or evolution? A first step analysis. *Sinergie, 93*, 115–137.

Nadeem, W. (2012). Social customer relationship management (SCRM): How connecting social analytics to business analytics enhances customer care and loyalty? *International Journal of Business and Social Science, 3*(21), 88–102.

Nadeem, W., Andreini, D., Salo, J., & Laukkanen, T. (2015). Engaging consumers online through websites and social media: a gender study of Italian Generation Y clothing consumers. *International Journal of Information Management, 35*(4), 432–442.

Neslin, S. A., & Shakar, V. (2009). Key issues in multichannel customer management: Current knowledge and future directions. *Journal of Interactive Marketing, 23*, 70–81.

Parsons, A. (2011). Social Media from a corporate perspective: A content analysis of official Facebook pages. *Allied academies international conference: Proceedings of the academy of marketing studies, 16*(2):11–15.

Pastore, A. (2009). Market driven management nell'economia digitale. *Mercati e competitività, 1*, 5–11.

Pierotti, M., Risaliti, G., & Cestari, G. (2014). Managing IC in an Opera House: the case of La Scala. *European Scientific Journal, 10*(34), 1–22.

Pompe, J., & Tamburi, L. (2016). Fiddling in a Vortex: Have American orchestras squandered their supremacy on the American cultural scene? *The Journal of Arts Management, Law and Society, 46*(2), 63–72.

Poon, J. P. H., & Lai, C. A. (2008). Why are non-profit performing arts Organisations successful in mid-sized US Cities? *Urban Studies, 45*(11), 2273–2289.

Radbourne, J., Johanson, K., Glow, H., & White, T. (2009). The audience experience: Measuring quality in the performing arts. *International Journal of Arts Management, 11*(3), 16–29.

Ravanas, P. (2007). A quiet revolution: The Metropolitan Opera Reinvents Client Relations Management. *International Journal of Arts Management, 9*(3), 79–87.

Ravanas, P. (2008). Hitting a high note: The Chicago Symphony Orchestra reverses a decade of decline with new programs, new services and new prices. *International Journal of Arts Management, 10*(2), 68–78.

Rigby, D. (2011). The Future of shopping. *Harvard Business Review, 89*(12), 64–75.

Rushton, M. (2008). Who pays? Who benefits? Who decides? *Journal of Cultural Economics, 32*, 293–300.

Sashi, C. M. (2012). Customer engagement, buyer-seller relationship and social media. *Management Decision, 50*(2), 253–272.

Smith, T. (2007). The impact of government funding on private contribution to nonprofit performing arts organizations. *Annals of Public and Cooperative Economics, 78*(1), 137–160.

Song, S., & Yi, D. T. (2011). The fundraising efficiency in US non-profit art organizations: An application of a Bayesian estimation approach using the stochastic frontier production model. *Journal of Production Analysis, 35*, 171–180.

Stelzner, M. A. (2015). *How marketers are using social media to grow their businesses*. Social Media Marketing Industry Report, Social Media Examiner.

Teixeira, T. S. (2014). *The rising cost of consumer attention: Why you should care, and what you can do about it*. Working Paper 14-055, Harvard Business School http://www.hbs.edu/faculty/Publication%20Files/14-055_2ef21e7e-7529-4864-b0f0-c64e4169e17f.pdf

Turbide, J., & Laurin, C. (2009). Performance measurement in the arts sector: The case of the performing arts. *International Journal of Arts Management, 11*(2), 56–70.

Turbide, J., Laurin, C., Lapierre, L., & Morissette, R. (2008). Financial crises in the arts sector: Is governance the illness or the cure? *International Journal of Arts Management, 10*(2), 4–13.

Turrini, A. (2006). Measuring audience addiction to the arts. *International Journal of Arts Management, 8*(3), 43–53.

Verhoef, P. C., Kanna, P. K., & Inman, J. J. (2015). From multi-channel retailing to Omni-channel retailing: Introduction to the special issue of multi-channel retailing. *Journal of Retailing, 91*(2), 174–181.

Vivek, S. D., Beatty, S. E., & Morgan, R. M. (2012). Consumer engagement: Exploring customer relationships beyond purchase. *Journal of Marketing Theory and Practice, 20*(2), 122–146.

Woosnam, K. M., McElroy, K. E., & Van Winkle, C. M. (2009). The role of personal values in determining tourist motivations: An application to the Winnipeg Fringe Theatre Festival, a cultural special event. *Journal of Hospitality Marketing and Management, 18*, 500–511.

Xu, J., Forman, C., Kim, J. B., & Van Ittersum, K. (2014). News media channels: Complements or substitutes? evidence from mobile phone usage. *Journal of Marketing, 78*(4), 97–112.

Yi, D. T. (2010). Determinants of fundraising efficiency of nonprofit organizations: Evidence from US public charitable organizations. *Managerial and Decision Economics, 31*, 465–475.

Zhang, J., Farris, P. W., Irvin, J. W., Kushwaha, T., Steenburgh, T. J., & Weitz, B. A. (2010). Crafting integrated multichannel retailing strategies. *Journal of Interactive Marketing, 24*(2), 168–180.

Zhou, L., Zhang, P., & Zimmermann, H. D. (2013). Social commerce research: an integrated view. *Electronic Commerce Research and Applications, 12*(2), 61–68.

Chapter 13
An Investigation into the Notion of "Efficiency"

Aidar Puryaev

Abstract In this work we make the research concerning the subject of defining the essence of the concepts "efficiency" and "efficiency of investment project." We present and summarize the achieved result on the problem of evaluating the efficiency of investment projects before the carrying special survey. The research technique is the analysis of existing definitions, techniques, criteria, and parameters of the effectiveness evaluation (literary review). We analyzed a number of the most quoted sources from the Scopus database, and articles have been recently published and indexed in Scopus. Based on the analysis, we reveal the essence of the concept "efficiency," being defined in the articles. As a result, the signs and definition of the "efficiency" concept are refined. Also the work helps to observe the tendency in the process of evaluating of investment projects efficiency which is realized in solving of an optimization problem simultaneously taking into consideration noneconomic and economic parameters. It is established that the criterion "energy efficiency," as a special case of an economic criterion, is more relevant and used in the evaluation of investment projects.

Keywords Efficiency · Efficiency of investment project · Assessment efficiency · Energy efficiency

13.1 Introduction

What does exactly "effective" or "ineffective" mean? What are the efficiency evaluation criteria for economists and investors nowadays? Which of them can be developed in the future? This article briefly summarizes the existing knowledge on this issue. We have made an attempt to outline trends in the issue study of efficiency evaluating in a global economy. The global economy of the twenty-first

A. Puryaev (✉)
Kazan Federal University, Kazan, Russia
e-mail: aidarp@mail.ru

N. Tsounis, A. Vlachvei (eds.), *Advances in Panel Data Analysis in Applied Economic Research*, Springer Proceedings in Business and Economics,
https://doi.org/10.1007/978-3-319-70055-7_13

century is fundamentally based on different kinds of problems: political, social, environmental, climatic, military threats, threats of terrorist organizations, and problems of population emigration in the conditions of instability in the Middle East and North Africa. At the heart of investment decision-making, especially at the level of global problems, noneconomic parameters and evaluation indicators play an important and sometimes the main role: resource security, scientific and technical security, information security, environmental and social responsibility, the performance quality of project functions, the implementation speed of projects, etc.

Therefore, today we can talk about increasing of research trends relevant in evaluating effectiveness of economic entities (enterprises). It is necessary to identify new signs in the definition of the concepts "efficiency and effectiveness of the investment project."

Earlier, we have conducted a study on the evaluation of investment projects effectiveness, in which critical importance has been paid to the notion of "efficiency" and "efficiency of the investment project" (Puryaev 2011, 2009).

The following entities of the "efficiency" category are established as follows:

1. Efficiency as a ratio of costs and the corresponding results (Novozhilov 1972; Cagolov et al. 1970; Starik 1983; Strumilin 1958; Chistov 2005)
2. Efficiency as an approximation measure to the optimal state of the economic system (Pareto efficiency 2017; Definition of "efficiency" n.d.)
3. Efficiency as a characteristic of the economic system state or as a characteristic of the quality of management (Gizatullin 2003)
4. Efficiency as a quality of movement and using of limited resources (Sidorov 2001)
5. Efficiency as a complex category of conformity to the interests of project participants (Kosov et al. 2000; Gibson et al. 2000; Zavlin et al. 1995)

We offer a new interpretation of the "efficiency" concept as a characteristic of compromise compliance with the conditions and restrictions (including value) of the person making the decision (decision-maker) and (or) the supervisory authority. On the basis of this understanding, a fundamentally new concept and methodology for assessing the investment projects effectiveness was proposed, which name was "Compramultifactor" (Puryaev 2011, 2009).

In this work we propose to take under analysis foreign sources for finding notions of "efficiency" and "efficiency of the investment project." Initially, it is necessary to distinguish clearly between two concepts – "effectiveness" and "effect" – so that in the process of analyzing and clarifying the definition of these categories, we may rely on concreteness, clarity, and objectivity. In the value of the classical concept of effectiveness evaluation, the term "effect" is understood as the excess of the object result over its costs, measured in absolute monetary units. The object is understood as the object of activity itself as a system (enterprise, association of enterprises, consortium, i.e., any economic entity possessing productive forces) and the process of activity as a system (investment project, program of actions, a set of measures aimed at growth, development, i.e., any quantitative and qualitative change of this system). The category of "effect" can only be expressed by an absolute indicator reflecting the extensive factor of change in the system (object). Efficiency is a relative category that reflects the intensive factor of the system change. Efficiency is expressed in the classical value concept as the ratio of absolute indicators (results and costs).

The actual is the problem of the correlation between the economic efficiency theory and the actual process of investment decision-making (Pimenov 2005). Since, it is established:

- The axiomatic of the theory of investments effectiveness evaluation does not reflect the real level of complexity of entrepreneurial activity.
- Existing methodological approaches and technology for obtaining the result are closed to the investor (or to the decision-maker).
- The financial profile of the project in real high uncertainty conditions is only a tool for the language description of the project, but not for the evaluation of effectiveness.

There is an urgent need to study the essence of the categories "efficiency" and "efficiency of the investment project" in order to develop in the future the new criteria for their evaluation that are necessary and appropriate to modern realities.

13.2 Method of Research Problems

The task of the research is to clarify the essence of the notions of "efficiency" and "efficiency of the investment project" in the current conditions of activity based on a comparative analysis of various interpretations and understandings of these definitions and various approaches to assessing the performance of economic entities on indexed sources in the Scopus database, to refine the features of these concepts, and to identify trends in the development theory and methodology for evaluating the investment projects effectiveness.

The research method is the analysis of existing definitions, methods, criteria, and parameters of the effectiveness evaluation (literary review).

13.3 Research

When we search in the Scopus database for the term "efficiency," then in March 2017, the program issued more than 1,839,800 articles (publications) that mention the concept of "efficiency." The analysis of the first ten most cited works showed that the term "efficiency" is referred to the following entities, which are presented in Table 13.1.

Table 13.1 The concept "efficiency" of the most quoted articles indexed in Scopus

№	The essence of the "efficiency" concept	Subject area	Source (publication)	Citation index (year of publication)
1.	Efficiency is a characteristic that reflects the minimization of the total length of the branch at each OTU clustering step, starting with a star-shaped tree; a characteristic of the rapid obtaining of the branches length and the topology of a regular undivided tree	Agricultural and Biological Sciences: Ecology, Evolution, Behavior, and Systematics	Scopus (Saitou and Nei 1987)	35,978 (1987)
2.	Efficiency is a characteristic that reflects the availability and usability of Molecular Evolutionary Genetics Analysis version 5 (MEGA5) software on Mac OS X and Linux desktops	Agricultural and Biological Sciences: Ecology, Evolution, Behavior, and Systematics	Scopus (Tamura et al. 2011)	24,043(2011)
3.	Efficiency is a characteristic that reflects the accuracy of the projector augmented-wave (PAW) method	Physics and Astronomy: Condensed Matter Physics	Scopus (Kresse and Joubert 1999)	22,182 (1999)
4.	Efficiency is a characteristic that reflects the accuracy and speed of performing quantum-mechanical calculations using pseudo potentials and a plane-wave basic set	Mathematics: Computational Mathematics	Scopus (Kresse and Furthmüller 1996)	19,584 (1996)
5.	Efficiency is a characteristic that reflects the quantum efficiency, i.e., a quantity which is equal to the ratio of the number of photons, the absorption of which by the sample caused the formation of quasiparticles, to the total number of absorbed photons	Biochemistry, Genetics, and Molecular Biology: Biochemistry	Scopus (Grynkiewicz et al. 1985)	16,952 (1985)

6.	Efficiency is a characteristic that reflects accuracy of quantification assessment of nucleic acids and receiving of reliable result while using an adequate mathematical model for data analysis	Biochemistry, Genetics, and Molecular Biology: Genetics	Scopus (Pfaffl 2001)	14,676 (2001)
7.	Efficiency is a characteristic that reflects the conversion of incident photons into electric current (more than 80%)	Medicine	Scopus (O'Regan and Grätzel 1991)	12,291 (1991)
8.	Efficiency is a characteristic that reflects the quantum efficiency, i.e., a quantity equal to the ratio of the number of photons, the absorption of which by the sample caused the formation of quasiparticles, to the total number of absorbed photons	Physics and Astronomy: Physics and Astronomy (miscellaneous)	Scopus (Tang and Vanslyke 1987)	10,522 (1987)
9.	Efficiency is a characteristic that reflects the speed and parallelism of solving the molecular dynamics problem by using three new algorithms for supercomputers	Physics and Astronomy: Physics and Astronomy (miscellaneous)	Scopus (Plimpton 1995)	10,041 (1995)
10.	Efficiency is a characteristic that reflects the evaluation of nonprofit organizations activity participating in public programs, obtained by the method of linear programming	Mathematics: Modeling and Simulation	Scopus (Charnes et al. 1978)	10,027 (1978)

The next step is to review the latest publications. Analysis of the first ten works have been recently published and indexed in Scopus showed that the term "efficiency" is understood as the following, presented in Table 13.2.

To determine the essence of the "efficiency of investment project" concept, we also analyzed the first ten works that have been recently published and indexed in Scopus. The results of the analysis are presented in Table 13.3.

The search for the most cited works on the term "efficiency of investment project" leads to the same list of authors and their works. This situation indicates that the topic of evaluating the investment projects effectiveness is treated as a solved problem or a problem that does not require special scientific attention. Officially developed and accepted methodological recommendations for evaluating the investment projects effectiveness are based only on the cost concept of "cash flow" (Kosov et al. 2000). At the same time, under the term of "efficiency of investment project" in the analyzed works (Table 13.3) are meant various components that cannot be directly related to the cost parameters: ecological, social component, uncertainty and risk, and various parameters of the physical essence used in solving the multicriteria optimization problem.

After having study the works in which the term "efficiency" is mentioned, we can see a diverse picture of understanding this term. It depends on the field of research, the subject of research. If generalized, then more often the term "efficiency" is understood as the term "optimality," and efficiency criteria are understood to be strictly defined as specific optimization criteria. Therefore, the issue of efficiency evaluation as such and the investment projects effectiveness requires additional careful study in the development of evaluation criteria and parameters.

13.4 Results

What do we have as a result of studying the material described above? If the abovementioned definitions of the concept of "efficiency" (Tables 13.1 and 13.2) are denoted by a keyword from each definition and display the frequency of occurrence of this entity in works, the following distribution indicated in Table 13.4 will be obtained.

It can be concluded that "effective" is the optimal one, i.e., the best, minimum or maximum by any criterion. This essence is directly reflected in 9 cases out of 23. There is a tendency in recent works that the term "effective" means energy saving, which in fact refers to minimizing energy use, i.e., optimization (two cases). There are nine cases of attributing a more accurate, faster, and accelerating process to an effective process, which also applies to the process of optimization (finding an extremum). Availability and reliability as indicators of efficiency are presented in two cases. An effective process is also referred to as normalizing process (reduction to the norm) – one case. There is no single case that reflects the notion of "efficiency" as a category of economic or valuable.

In the abovementioned definitions of the "efficiency of investment project" concept (Table 13.3), the following important components of this concept can

Table 13.2 The concept "efficiency" of the articles indexed in Scopus and issued recently

№	The essence of the "efficiency" concept	Subject area	Source (publication)	Year of publication (citation index)
1.	Efficiency is a characteristic that reflects the ability of sunlight absorption by a surface and conversion into an electric current	Materials Science	Scopus (Yan et al. 2017)	2017(0)
2.	Efficiency is a characteristic that reflects the use of energy for fixed and adaptive wireless data transmission mode with consideration of circuit power	Computer Science: Computer Networks and Communications	Scopus (Cai et al. 2017)	2017(0)
3.	Efficiency is a characteristic that reflects the power conversion of solar cells based on N-TiO2 with a doping content of N 1% in electric current	Materials Science	Scopus (Zhang et al. 2017a)	2017(0)
4.	Efficiency is a characteristic that reflects the time of encoding and compressing video images	Engineering: Electrical and Electronic Engineering	Scopus (BenHajyoussef et al. 2017)	2017(0)
5.	Efficiency is a characteristic reflecting the photocatalytic property of composite materials	Materials Science	Scopus (Xu et al. 2017)	2017(0)
6.	Efficiency is a characteristic that reflects the effects of primary prevention of smoking and secondary interventions to reduce smoking in systolic blood pressure (SBP) and hypertension	Medicine: Health Policy	Scopus (Platt et al. 2017)	2017(0)
7.	Efficiency is a characteristic that reflects the accuracy of the robot's milling operation and the robot's assessment of performing the task with the desired precision	Mathematics	Scopus (Klimchik et al. 2017)	2017(0)
8.	Efficiency is a characteristic that reflects the use of energy (energy efficiency) in the transmission of waves in two-hop relay-aided cellular networks	Computer Science: Computer Networks and Communications	Scopus (Chen and Zhao 2017)	2017(0)
9.	Efficiency is a characteristic that reflects the transformation of solar energy into electric current	Materials Science	Scopus (Zhang et al. 2017b)	2017(0)
10.	Efficiency is a characteristic that reflects bandwidth allocation scheme of mobile system based on the Petri network	Computer Science	Scopus (Guo and Si 2017)	2017(0)

Table 13.3 The concept "efficiency of the investment project" of articles indexed in Scopus

№	The essence of the "efficiency of investment project" concept	Subject area	Source (publication)	Year of publication (citation index)
1.	The effectiveness of the investment project is a characteristic that reflects the economic, environmental, and technological feasibility of investing funds	Engineering: Industrial and Manufacturing Engineering	Scopus (Makara et al. 2016)	2016(2)
2.	The effectiveness of the investment project is a characteristic that reflects the economic and energy-saving feasibility of investing funds	Engineering	Scopus (Kvon et al. 2016)	2016(0)
3.	The effectiveness of the investment project is a characteristic that reflects the economic, social, and budgetary components when evaluating the project effectiveness	Arts and Humanities	Scopus (Kudryavtseva and Kuporov 2015)	2015(0)
4.	The effectiveness of the investment project is a characteristic reflecting the solution of multicriteria Boolean Markowitz's investment problem with the criteria of extreme optimism (MAXMAX) of the investment portfolio return	Mathematics	Scopus (Emelichev and Karelkina 2015)	2015(0)
5.	The effectiveness of the investment project is a characteristic that reflects the economic feasibility of investing funds, estimated by the "cash flow" technique	Arts and Humanities	Scopus (Khasanova et al. 2015)	2015(0)

6.	The effectiveness of an investment project is a characteristic that reflects the solution of a multicriteria problem by the method of optimization and reduction into one criterion that is built with the terms of decision theory	Mathematics: Applied Mathematics	Scopus (Zenkovich and Drevs 2015)	2015(0)
7.	The effectiveness of the investment project is a characteristic that reflects the economic feasibility of investing funds, estimated by the "cash flow" technique. At the same time, it is expected to pay considerable attention to the uncertainty and risk parameter	Engineering: Industrial and Manufacturing Engineering	Scopus (Szymszal et al. 2014)	2014(0)
8.	The efficiency of the investment project is a characteristic that reflects the economic, environmental, and energy-saving feasibility of investing funds, estimated by the "cash flow" technique	Materials Science: Surfaces, Coatings and Films	Scopus (Belousov et al. 2014)	2014(0)
9.	The effectiveness of the investment project is a characteristic that reflects the economic feasibility of investing funds, estimated by the "cash flow" technique. Special attention is paid to the development of the method of calculation of risks based on improvement of the method of expert evaluations	Biochemistry, Genetics, and Molecular Biology	Scopus (Abdibekov et al. 2014)	2014(0)
10.	The effectiveness of the investment project is a characteristic that reflects the economic feasibility of investing funds, estimated by the "cash flow" technique	Economics, Econometrics and Finance: Economics and Econometrics	Scopus (Tsushko 2014)	2014(0)

Table 13.4 Distribution of essence of the concept "efficiency"

The keyword of the identified entity	Ten most cited works	Ten recent works
Optimum (maximum forming, maximum bandwidth, minimum size, etc.)	5	4
Accurate	3	1
Fast	3	1
Reliable	1	0
Available	1	0
Energy saving	0	2
Normalizing	0	1
Accelerating	0	1
Total	*13*	*10*

be singled out: economic, ecological, technological, social, budgetary, and energy saving. And also under the term of "efficiency of investment project" is meant the solution of a multicriteria task, reducible to one criterion. Economic feasibility of evaluation is found in nine cases out of ten. The issue of evaluating the investment project effectiveness is not solved without an assessment of economic feasibility, because any investment project is accompanied by investment. But at the same time, there is a tendency of taking into account other components simultaneously. So, the tendency of considering noneconomic parameters is revealed when evaluating the investment projects effectiveness by solving an optimization problem using various mathematical methods.

13.5 Conclusion

In conclusion, let us draw conclusions on the research conducted and fix judgments and deductions:

1. Efficiency is a characteristic that reflects the extremum (minimum, maximum) according to a certain criterion. The concept of "efficiency" and the concept of "optimality" are synonymous. There is not a single case of the observed studies (out of 40 cases), where efficiency would be defined as an economic category.
2. The economic component of the "efficiency of investment project" concept is essential for the implementation of the project, as the project is accompanied by investments. But economic parameters in the current activity conditions are no longer system forming in assessing efficiency. The actual in project becomes evaluation parameters related to security, image, ecological, social, and energy components. The tendency to take into account noneconomic parameters is revealed when assessing the investment projects effectiveness by the method of solving the optimization problem according to a strictly defined criterion.

3. In recent works, the criterion of efficiency is often the indicator of "energy efficiency," which determines the energy-saving problem as topical and requiring special attention. This criterion is a particular case of an economic criterion.

References

Abdibekov, S. U., Bedelbayeva, A. E., Akhmetova, Z. S., Burnasheva, V. R., & Syzdykbayeva, N. B. (2014). Analysis and improvement of methods of management by investment risks. *Life Science Journal, 11*(1), 158–162.

Belousov, M. V., Sirotkin, S. A., & Rakipov, D. F. (2014). Technical and economic peculiarities of magnesium production in Russia. *Tsvetnye Metally, 6*(1), 68–76.

BenHajyoussef, A., Ezzedine, T., & Bouallègue, A. (2017). Gradient-based pre-processing for intra prediction in high efficiency video coding. *Eurasip Journal on Image and Video Processing, 2017*(1), 9. https://doi.org/10.1186/s13640-016-0159-9

Cagolov, N. A., Rumjancev, A. M., & Hachaturov, T. S. (1970). *The course of political economy. T. 2: Socializm*. Moscow: Jekonomika.

Cai, C., Qiu, R., Jiang, X.-Q., & Xu, W. (2017). Adaptive wireless transmission strategy for maximizing energy efficiency. *EURASIP Journal on Wireless Communications and Networking, 2017*(1), 20. https://doi.org/10.1186/s13638-017-0807-5

Charnes, A., Cooper, W. W., & Rhodes, E. (1978). Measuring the efficiency of decision making units. *European Journal of Operational Research, 2*(6), 429. https://doi.org/10.1016/0377-2217(78)90138-8

Chen, H., & Zhao, F. (2017). A hybrid half-duplex/full-duplex transmission scheme in relay-aided cellular networks. *EURASIP Journal on Wireless Communications and Networking, 2017*, 1. https://doi.org/10.1186/s13638-016-0795-x

Chistov, L. M. (2005). *The theory of efficient management of socio-economic systems*. SPb.: Asterion.

Definition of "efficiency". Collins Dictionary. (n.d.). Retrieved March 4, 2017, from https://www.collinsdictionary.com/dictionary/english/efficiency

Emelichev, V., & Karelkina, O. (2015). Stability radius bounds in multicriteria markowitz portfolio problem with venturesome investor criteria. Buletinul Academiei de Stiinte a Republicii Moldova. *Matematica, 77*(1), 83–94.

Gibson, D. L., Ivancevich, D. M., & Donnelli, D. H. (2000). *Organizations: Behavior, structure, processes* (8th ed.). Moscow: INFRA-M. Retrieved from http://znanium.com/go.php?id=417454

Gizatullin, H. N. (2003). On the problem of the creation of enterprise management systems in transition economies. In *Proceedings of the all-Russian symposium on economic theory* (pp. 31–44). Ekaterinburg: Institute of Economics of UB RAS.

Grynkiewicz, G., Poenie, M., & Tsien, R. Y. (1985). A new generation of Ca2+ indicators with greatly improved fluorescence properties. *Journal of Biological Chemistry, 260*(6), 3440.

Guo, S.-Y., & Si, Q. (2017). Embedded protocols based on the crowd petri networks and opportunistic bandwidth allocation. *EURASIP Journal on Embedded Systems, 2017*(1), 17. https://doi.org/10.1186/s13639-016-0068-0

Khasanova, A. S., Kvon, G. M., Yakupova, N. M., Khamidullin, F. F., & Samysheva, E. Y. (2015). Assessment of efficiency of capital investment project implementation of resource-saving technology for the real sector of the economy in Tatarstan Republic. *Mediterranean Journal of Social Sciences, 6*(2), S3. https://doi.org/10.5901/mjss.2015.v6n2s3p155

Klimchik, A., Ambiehl, A., Garnier, S., Furet, B., & Pashkevich, A. (2017). Efficiency evaluation of robots in machining applications using industrial performance measure. *Robotics and Computer-Integrated Manufacturing, 48*, 12. https://doi.org/10.1016/j.rcim.2016.12.005

Kosov, V. V., Livshic, V. N., & Shahnazarova, A. G. (2000). *Metodicheskie rekomendacii po ocenke jeffektivnosti investicionnyh proektov [methodical recommendations according to efficiency of investment projects]* (2nd ed.). Moscow: Jekonomika.

Kresse, G., & Furthmüller, J. (1996). Efficiency of ab-initio total energy calculations for metals and semiconductors using a plane-wave basis set. *Computational Materials Science, 6*(1), 15. https://doi.org/10.1016/0927-0256(96)00008-0

Kresse, G., & Joubert, D. (1999). From ultrasoft pseudopotentials to the projector augmented-wave method. *Physical Review B: Condensed Matter and Materials Physics, 59*(3), 1758–1775.

Kudryavtseva, T. J., & Kuporov, J. J. (2015). Evaluation of social and economic efficiency of investments in public utility services. *Asian Social Science, 11*(19), 151–158. https://doi.org/10.5539/ass.v11n19p151

Kvon, G. M., Khamidullin, F. F., Samysheva, E. Y., Vaks, V. B., & Mararov, N. V. (2016). Methods of evaluating the efficiency of energy saving projects with taking risks into account. *International Journal of Environmental and Science Education, 11*(15), 7441.

Makara, A., Smol, M., Kulczycka, J., & Kowalski, Z. (2016). Technological, environmental and economic assessment of sodium tripolyphosphate production – A case study. *Journal of Cleaner Production, 133*, 243. https://doi.org/10.1016/j.jclepro.2016.05.096

Novozhilov, V. V. (1972). *Measurement problems the costs and results in optimal planning*. Moscow: Nauka.

O'Regan, B., & Grätzel, M. (1991). A low-cost, high-efficiency solar cell based on dye-sensitized colloidal TiO_2 films. *Nature, 353*(6346), 737.

Pareto efficiency. (2017). Retrieved March 4, 2017, from https://en.wikipedia.org/wiki/Pareto_efficiency

Pfaffl, M. W. (2001). A new mathematical model for relative quantification in real-time RT-PCR. *Nucleic Acids Research, 29*(9), e45.

Pimenov, S. V. (2005). Problems of application of the theory of economic efficiency in the actual process of making investment decisions. *Vestnik INZhJeKONa. «Jekonomika» [Bulletin of ENGECON. "Economics"], 4*(9), 25–30.

Platt, J. M., Keyes, K. M., & Galea, S. (2017). Efficiency or equity? Simulating the impact of high-risk and population intervention strategies for the prevention of disease. *SSM – Population Health, 3*, 1. https://doi.org/10.1016/j.ssmph.2016.11.002

Plimpton, S. (1995). Fast parallel algorithms for short-range molecular dynamics. *Journal of Computational Physics, 117*(1), 1. https://doi.org/10.1006/jcph.1995.1039

Puryaev, A. S. (2009). *Theory and methodology compromise efficiency assessment of investment projects in mechanical engineering*. Autoabstract of Doctoral Dissertation, 39. Retrieved from http://www.scopus.com/inward/record.url?eid=2-s2.0-84897642131&partnerID=tZOtx3y1

Puryaev, A. S. (2011). *Compromise efficiency assessment of investment projects. Research and development*. Saarbrücken: LAP LAMBERT Academic Publishing. Retrieved from http://www.scopus.com/inward/record.url?eid=2-s2.0-84897659371&partnerID=tZOtx3y1

Saitou, N., & Nei, M. (1987). The neighbor-joining method: A new method for reconstructing phylogenetic trees. *Molecular Biology and Evolution, 4*(4), 406.

Sidorov, I. I. (2001). *Logisticheskaja koncepcija upravlenija predprijatiem [Logistic concept of enterprise management]*. SPb.: «Znanie».

Starik, D. J. (1983). *Economic efficiency of the equipment*. Moscow: Mashinostroenie.

Strumilin, S. G. (1958). *About economic efficiency of the new equipment*. Moscow: AN SSSR, VSNTO.

Szymszal, J., Lis, T., Gajdzik, B., & Klis, J. (2014). Analysis of the possibility of using dynamic methods for assessment of investment projects in the domestic foundry industry. *Archives of Foundry Engineering, 14*(3), 103. https://doi.org/10.2478/afe-2014-0071

Tamura, K., Peterson, D., Peterson, N., Stecher, G., Nei, M., & Kumar, S. (2011). MEGA5: Molecular evolutionary genetics analysis using maximum likelihood, evolutionary distance, and maximum parsimony methods. *Molecular Biology and Evolution, 28*(10), 2731. https://doi.org/10.1093/molbev/msr121.

Tang, C. W., & Vanslyke, S. A. (1987). Organic electroluminescent diodes. *Applied Physics Letters, 51*(12), 913. https://doi.org/10.1063/1.98799

Tsushko, V. V. (2014). The influence of property rights protection on foreign direct investment inflow. *Actual Problems of Economics, 156*(6), 539–543.

Xu, J., Wang, Z., Li, W., Zhang, X., He, D., & Xiao, X. (2017). Ag nanoparticles located on three-dimensional pine tree-like hierarchical TiO_2 nanotube Array films as high-efficiency Plasmonic Photocatalysts. *Nanoscale Research Letters, 12*(1), 54. https://doi.org/10.1186/s11671-017-1834-1

Yan, X., Zhang, C., Wang, J., Zhang, X., & Ren, X. (2017). A high-efficiency Si nanowire Array/Perovskite hybrid solar cell. *Nanoscale Research Letters, 12*(1), 14. https://doi.org/10.1186/s11671-016-1785-y

Zavlin, P. N., Vasil'ev, A. V., & Knol', A. I. (1995). *Ocenka jekonomicheskoj jeffektivnosti investicionnyh proektov (sovremennye podhody) [Estimation of economic efficiency of investment projects (modern approaches)]*. SPb: Nauka.

Zenkovich, M. V., & Drevs, Y. G. (2015). An application of simulation for foundry plants investment projects estimation of efficiency. *International Journal of Mathematical Models and Methods in Applied Sciences, 9*(1), 99–104.

Zhang, Z.-L., Li, J.-F., Wang, X.-L., Qin, J.-Q., Shi, W.-J., Liu, Y.-F., Gao HP Mao, Y.-L. (2017a). Enhancement of Perovskite solar cells efficiency using N-doped TiO_2 Nanorod arrays as electron transfer layer. *Nanoscale Research Letters, 12*(1), 43. https://doi.org/10.1186/s11671-016-1811-0

Zhang, Z. L., Men, B. Q., Liu, Y. F., Gao, H. P., & Mao, Y. L. (2017b). Effects of precursor solution composition on the performance and I-V hysteresis of perovskite solar cells based on $CH_3NH_3PbI_{3-x}Cl_x$. *Nanoscale Research Letters, 12*(1), 84. https://doi.org/10.1186/s11671-017-1872-8

Chapter 14
An Analysis of ICT Sectors and Economic Growth: Evidence from ASEAN Countries

Satawat Wannapan and Chukiat Chaiboonsri

Abstract This paper proposes to investigate the causal relationship between ICT segments and economic expansionary rates in ASEAN countries. Methodologically, the panel time-series data observed during 2006 to 2015 is employed to estimate the panel Granger causality test. According to the technical problem of lag selection for the panel causality analysis, the computationally statistical approach called Newton's optimization method is originally applied to verify the suitable lag selection. The empirical results found that ICTs are not the major factor that causally motivates economic growth in ASEAN. To address the issue, equitable educational systems and advanced infrastructural developments are the primary policies that should be corporately implemented.

14.1 Introduction

ICT technology is very crucial for economic and societal convergence in AEC. This ICT development directly relates to the improvement of human resource skills, the invention of knowledge, and innovation in industrial sectors. Because ASEAN countries have been appointed as the new emerging market, this is reasonable for strength building toward the ASEAN community and moving forward to become the world center of ICT (TOT Academy 2016). Moreover, in the current moment, ICT in AEC countries, which is also defined as digital economy, generates approximately 150 billion in revenue per year. Connectivity and online services are

S. Wannapan (✉)
Faculty of Economics, Chiang Mai University, Chiang Mai, Thailand
e-mail: lionz1988@gmail.com

C. Chaiboonsri
Faculty of Economics, Chiang Mai University, Chiang Mai, Thailand
e-mail: chukiat1973@gmail.com

N. Tsounis, A. Vlachvei (eds.), *Advances in Panel Data Analysis in Applied Economic Research*, Springer Proceedings in Business and Economics,
https://doi.org/10.1007/978-3-319-70055-7_14

the major components. In particular, the revenue generated by online services such as technologies and content rights has been growing rapidly. Interestingly, online services and products have created close to five times the value of connectivity (ATKearney 2016). Hence, this would undoubtedly guarantee that ASEAN can be a global digital leader in the upcoming future.

The evidence of ICT development in AEC led the authors to question whether ICTs contribute to economic growth in each country among the AEC (Heeks 2011). To answer the question, the panel Granger causality test was employed to statistically solve and clarify a determiner between the improvement of ICT sectors and economic growth. Consequently, the remainder of this paper is organized as follows: Sect. 14.1 is the investigation of the causality relation between ICT factors and economic growth; Sect. 14.2 applies the statistical optimizing estimation, namely, Newton's method, for improving the accuracy of lag selection in the panel Granger causality test. Ultimately, the empirical results will be manipulated for policy remarks regarding ICT development in AEC.

14.2 The Objective and Scope of Research

The purpose of this study is to clarify the causal relationship between ASEAN ICT variables, including Internet servers, broadband suppliers, fixed phone usage, and mobile phone subscriptions, and each country's economic growth. The yearly time-series data was observed from eight AEC member countries, including Thailand, Singapore, Malaysia, the Philippines, Indonesia, Laos, Cambodia, and Myanmar. All of the observed data is expounded as panel data during 2006 to 2015.

14.3 Literature

The causal relationships between the two variables of economic growth and information and communication technology (ICT) have been investigated broadly in economic literature. Focusing on the panel Granger causality test, the journal papers of Pradhan et al. (2015) and Yousefi (2015) who studied the panel causality between ICT variables and the rates of economic growth in developed and developing countries represent that ICT expenditures appear to cause economic expansion. Also, in the Middle East area, Haghshenas et al. (2013) studied the causal relation of ICT affecting economic growth in Iran, and the results of this paper empirically stated that ICT is an economic contributor. However, in the Asia-Pacific area, Khalili et al. (2013), who explored the panel data regarding ICT contribution related to aggregate output growths of Asia-Pacific countries, stated that there is no causality relationship between ICT and TFP growth in the short run. Moreover, in other economic branches, the panel causality test has been commonly applied, such as in financial economics by Lin and Ali (2009) and Won and Hsiao (2008), international trade economics by Hossain (2012), and in tourism economics by Lien (2016) and Caglayan and Sak (2014).

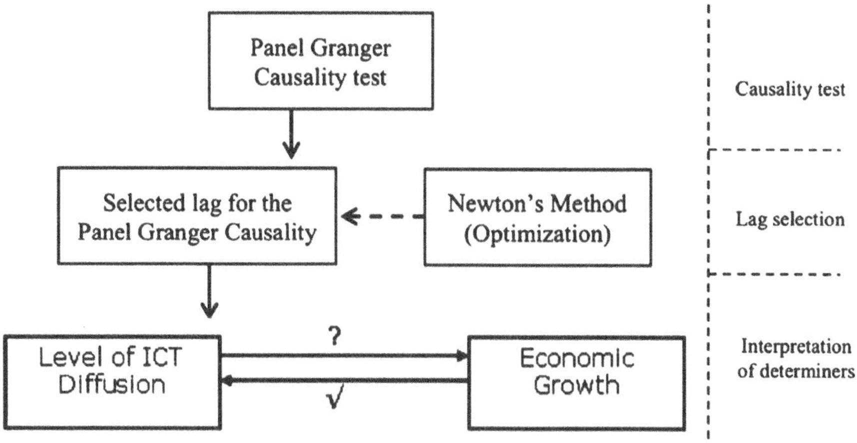

Fig. 14.1 The conceptual framework of research

Considering specifically in ASEAN countries, from the literature, it seems that there are two major issues in this paper that the authors enthusiastically looked for to fulfill the empirical solutions. Firstly, although ICT has been academically mentioned and enormously used to publish research papers in the last few years, the panel Granger causality test is not broadly applied to econometric research. Secondly, the lag selection for estimating the causal relationship between the panel dependent and panel explanatory variables was picked by personal choice. Hence, it is reasonable that applying a computationally statistical method can solve this issue effectively (Fig. 14.1).

14.4 The Conceptual Framework and Methodology of Research

14.4.1 Research Methodology

14.4.1.1 The Data Stationary Testing

In this paper, the panel unit root test is based on combining the observed significant levels from the individual tests. Such a strategy based on Fisher (1932)-type tests is noticeably employed by Choi (2001) and Maddala and Wu (1999). Basically, let us consider a heterogeneous model (Eq. 14.1):

$$\Delta y_{i,t} = \alpha_i + \rho_i y_{i,t-1} + \sum_{z=1}^{p_i} \beta_{i,z} \Delta y_{i,t-z} + \varepsilon_{i,t} \tag{14.1}$$

The null hypothesis is explained as $H_0 : \rho_i = 0$ for all $i = 1, \ldots, N$, and the alternative hypothesis is $H_0 : \rho_i < 0$ for $i = 1, \ldots, N$ and $\rho_i = 0$ for $i = N_1+1 \ldots N$ with $0 \leq N_1 \leq N$. If the pure time-series unit root test statistics such as ADF (Pesaran 2003) and Elliott-Rothenberg-Stock (Elliott et al. 1996) are continuous, the corresponding p-values, denoted p_1, are random variables and uniformly distributed on [0, 1]. Thus, under the crucial assumption of cross-sectional independence, this statistical testing can be defined as:

$$P_{MW} = -2 \sum_{i=1}^{N} \log(p_i) \tag{14.2}$$

The model has a chi-square distribution with $2N$ degrees of freedom, when T tends to infinity and N is fixed. As mentioned by Banerjee (1999) and Hurlin and Mignon (2007), the obvious simplicity of this test and its robustness to statistic choice, lag length, and sample size make it extremely attractive. For large N samples, the statistical panel unit root testing proposed by Choi (2001) is similarly standardized and expressed as:

$$Z_{MW} = \frac{\sqrt{N}[N^{-1}P_{MW} - E(-2\log(p_i))]}{\sqrt{Var[-2\log(p_i)]}} = -\frac{\sum_{i=1}^{N} \log(p_i + N)}{\sqrt{N}} \tag{14.3}$$

p_i is associated p-values, which is based on the asymptotic theory (Barbieri 2006). Under the cross-sectional independence assumption, the Lindeberg-Levy theorem is sufficient to show that it converges to a standard normal distribution under the unit root hypothesis (Hurlin and Mignon 2007).

14.4.1.2 The Panel Granger Causality Test

As in the discussion by Won and Hsiao (2008), a panel data analysis has been broadly used for information concerning cross-sectional and time-series analyses. This statistical panel approach can be efficiently applied to econometrical researches. Technically, panel models can take heterogeneity of each cross-sectional unit explicitly into account by allowing for individual-specific effects (Davidson and MacKinnon 2004; Won and Hsiao 2008) and provide more degree of freedom, more variability, and less collinear dependences among variables. Suitably, the panel exploration is better to study the relationship of macroeconomic factors, especially financial sectors, tourism economics, and even ICT economics.

In this paper, the panel data analysis is assumed first of all to be the fixed effects model (FEM), which expresses that the slope coefficients are constant for all cross-sectional units and the intercept varies over individual cross-sectional units but does not vary over time (Won and Hsiao 2008). Econometrically, the data is estimated by regression models, and the application of the panel FEM equation is defined as follows:

$$y_{it} = \alpha_i + x_{it}\beta + u_{it}, \quad u_{it} N\left(0, \sigma_u^2\right) \tag{14.4}$$

where y_{it} can be one of endogenous variables, i is the ith cross-sectional unit, and t is the time of observation. The intercept, α_i, takes into account the heterogeneity influenced from unobserved variables which may differ across the cross-sectional units. The x_{it} is a row vector of all lag endogenous variables. The β is a column vector of the common slope coefficients for the group of economies.

Applying from Haghshenas et al. (2013), to test for Granger causality between outputs and ICT sectors in ASEAN countries, two bivariate models are specified. Corresponding to the stationary time-series data of GDP and ICT (including Internet servers, INT_{t-i}; broadband suppliers, BND_{t-i}; fixed phone usages, FIX_{t-i}; and mobile phone subscriptions, $MOBILE_{t-i}$), the Granger causality equations are described as follows:

$$GDP_{it} = \sum_{i=1}^{n} \beta_{it} GDP_{i-1} + \sum_{i=1}^{n} \beta_{it} INT_{i-1} + \sum_{i=1}^{n} \beta_{it} BND_{i-1} + \sum_{i=1}^{n} \beta_{it} FIX_{i-1} + \sum_{i=1}^{n} \beta_{it} MOBILE_{i-1} \tag{14.5}$$

$$INT_{it} = \sum_{i=1}^{n} \beta_{it} INT_{i-1} + \sum_{i=1}^{n} \beta_{it} GDP_{i-1} + \sum_{i=1}^{n} \beta_{it} BND_{i-1} + \sum_{i=1}^{n} \beta_{it} FIX_{i-1} + \sum_{i=1}^{n} \beta_{it} MOBILE_{i-1} \tag{14.6}$$

$$BND_{it} = \sum_{i=1}^{n} \beta_{it} BND_{i-1} + \sum_{i=1}^{n} \beta_{it} INT_{i-1} + \sum_{i=1}^{n} \beta_{it} GDP_{i-1} + \sum_{i=1}^{n} \beta_{it} FIX_{i-1} + \sum_{i=1}^{n} \beta_{it} MOBILE_{i-1} \tag{14.7}$$

$$FIX_{it} = + \sum_{i=1}^{n} \beta_{it} FIX_{i-1} + \sum_{i=1}^{n} \beta_{it} INT_{i-1} + \sum_{i=1}^{n} \beta_{it} BND_{i-1} + \sum_{i=1}^{n} \beta_{it} GDP_{i-1} + \sum_{i=1}^{n} \beta_{it} MOBILE_{i-1} \tag{14.8}$$

$$MOBILE_{it} = \sum_{i=1}^{n} \beta_{it} MOBILE_{i-1} + \sum_{i=1}^{n} \beta_{it} FIX_{i-1} + \sum_{i=1}^{n} \beta_{it} INT_{i-1} + \sum_{i=1}^{n} \beta_{it} BND_{i-1} + \sum_{i=1}^{n} \beta_{it} GDP_{i-1} \tag{14.9}$$

14.4.1.3 The Lag Selection in Panel Data Using Newton's Optimization Approach

As reviewed in the literatures, the problem that can be noticed in the panel Granger analysis is the lag selection, which is chosen by personal perspectives. To mathematically solve the issue, a computationally operational method, namely, *Newton's method*, is employed to investigate the optimization for choosing the suitable lag. Typically, the basic idea of Newton's method is used as a basis on linearization. Given $R_1 \to R$ is a differential function, thus, we are trying to solve the equation as:

$$F(X) = 0 \tag{14.10}$$

Technically, the initial point x_0 is made to be the starting points and assembled the linear approximation of $F(x)$ in the neighbor of $x_0 : F(x_0 + h) \approx F(x_0)h$ and resolved the consequent linear formation $F(x_0) + F'(x_0)h = 0$. As a result, the recurrent method is expressed as follows (Polyak 2007):

$$x_{k+1} = x_k - F'(x_k)^{-1}F(x_k), \quad k = 0, 1, \ldots \tag{14.11}$$

The above equation is the method invented by Newton in 1669. More precisely, this linear equation is dealt with a polynomial. Moreover, the progress in improvement of the method is related to such famous mathematicians such as Fourier who proved the quadratic method convergences in the neighborhood of a root in 1818 as well as Cauchy who provided the multidimensional extension and used the method to prove the existence of a root of an equation in 1829 (Polyak 2007). In this paper, the authors employ the values of F-statistics, which are estimated from the panel Granger causality test, to be the data set for lag optimization.

Theoretically, the quadratic convergence in Newton's method is based on two fundamentals.

Theorem 1 *The main convergence result is defined as continuously differentiable on the data set:* $B = [x : |x - x_0| \leq r]$, *which is the visible linear operation model* $(F'(x_0))$, *where* $x \in B$, *expressed as* $|F'(x_0)^{-1}F(x_0)| \leq \eta$ *and* $|F'(x_0)^{-1}F(x_0)| \leq K$. *Consequently, the process in the Eq.* 14.11 *is well clarified, and it will converge to* $x*$ *with a quadratic rate as follows (Polyak 2007):*

$$|x_k - x^*| \leq \left(\eta/h2^k\right)(2h)^{2k} \tag{14.12}$$

Theorem 2 *Suppose F is defined and twice continuously differentiable on the balls* $B = [x : |x - x_0| \leq r]$. *Differentially, the linear function* $F'(x)$ *is invertible on B and* $|F'(x)^{-1}| \leq \beta$, $|F'| \leq K$, $|F(x_0)| \leq \eta$, *where* $x \in \beta$. *Now, we can achieve linear parameters as follows:*

$$h = K\beta^2\eta < 2, \quad r \geq \beta\eta \sum_{n=0}^{\infty} \left(\frac{(h)}{2}\right)^{2^n - 1} \tag{14.13}$$

Thus, the solution of $x^* \in \beta$ and the quadratic rate of convergence to x^* can be defined as:

$$|x_k - x^*| \leq \frac{\beta\eta(h/2)^{2^k - 1}}{1 - (h/2)^{2^k}} \tag{14.14}$$

14.5 Empirical Results

14.5.1 Descriptive Panel Data

Generally, all variables used in this study are modified to be the rates of expansion and are represented as descriptive statistical indexes, including average values, standard errors, and max-min values (as seen in Table 14.1). Technically, first of all, the panel stationarity testing models such as Fisher chi-square and Choi z-stat are employed to verify that the observed time-series data is not invalid and ensure they can be econometrically estimated. Obviously, all observed data has been significantly reported to be stationary data (as seen in Table 14.1).

14.5.2 The Lag Selection in Panel Granger Causality Test

The results of the optimization method applied from the computational experiment by Denoeux (2016) state that there are different lag levels chosen among AEC countries (see details in Table 14.2). Considering all AEC countries (eight countries), the third lag (3), which is the only one where the optimum point closed up the overview value (0.563), is selected. This implies that the previous 3 years of the observed data were added into the panel Granger causality model. For exploration in each country, the empirical results show that choosing the previous year (the first lag, (1)) to slot into the panel causal estimation is suitable for the seven countries, including Thailand, Singapore, Malaysia, the Philippines, Indonesia, Laos, and Myanmar. Except for Cambodia, adding the previous 2 years of the panel data (the second lag, (2)) is appropriate to determine the panel causality analysis.

Table 14.1 Presentation of the descriptive data of ICT factors in AEC and the panel stationary testing

Details	GDP	INT	BND	FIX	MOBILE
Mean	4.61	39.39	74.20	13.83	27.16
Standard error	3.14	61.60	201.08	73.15	45.57
Max	13.22	300.00	1530.04	562.08	324.88
Min	−4.16	−75.00	−89.82	−28.99	−21.55
	Panel unit root test				
Fisher chi-square	0.0004***	0.0000***	0.0002***	0.0000***	0.0000***
Choi z-stat	0.0003***	0.0000***	0.0026***	0.0000***	0.0000***

GDP the growth rates of panel gross domestic products, *INT* the growth rates of panel Internet servers in AEC countries, *BND* the growth rates of panel broadband supplies in AEC countries, *FIXED* the growth rates of fixed phone usages in AEC countries, *MOBILE* the growth rates of mobile phone subscriptions in AEC countries

*** 99 percent significant level

*** 95 percent significant level

Table 14.2 Showing the comparisons of optimized values by using Newton's method

Country	Optimized overview value	Optimized value for lag (1)	Optimized value for lag (2)	Optimized value for lag (3)	Lag selection
All AEC	0.563	0.672	0.521	0.534	(3)
Thailand	0.573	0.306*	0.975	–	(1)
Singapore	0.606	0.409*	0.913	–	(1)
Malaysia	0.415	0.256*	0.706	–	(1)
Philippines	0.389	0.294*	0.508	–	(1)
Indonesia	0.448	0.294*	0.690	–	(1)
Laos	0.792	0.625*	0.922	–	(1)
Cambodia	0.415	0.339	0.514*	–	(2)
Myanmar	0.688	0.578*	0.862	–	(1)

Noted: * stands for the optimizing value that is close to the optimized overview value

14.5.3 The Panel Granger Causality Test

Considering in Table 14.3, the results of pairwise Granger causal analysis are separately reported on two sections: (1) the causal relationship between the rates of economic expansion and growth rates of ICTs in ASEAN and (2) the causality test between IT segments and telecoms. Interestingly, when we focus only on all AEC countries, ICT is not the determiner that causally drives economic growth. However, there are some internally causal connections between IT sectors and telecoms. Consequently, this can be implied that ICT sectors are still not the major factor which stimulates economic enlargements in ASEAN.

According to the panel causality test in each country (see more details in Table 14.3), the empirical result shows four countries such as Malaysia, the Philippines, Cambodia, and Myanmar having the causal determiner between ICTs and economic growth. In Malaysia, three major ICT sectors, for instance, broadband suppliers, fixed phone usages, and mobile phone subscriptions, are the key factors that causally drive Malaysian economy. On the other hand, fixed phone systems in the Philippines and Cambodia are dependent on economic expansion. Lastly, mobile phone using rates are causally relied on economic growth in Myanmar.

Interestingly, in Thailand, there is only an internal causal relationship between rates of Internet servers, growth rates of fixed phone usages, and increasing rates of mobile phone subscriptions. Similarly, ICTs are not the major factor that causally stimulates the economic growth in Singapore, Indonesia, and Laos (see more details in Table 14.3).

Table 14.3 Presentation the estimated outcomes of panel granger causality testing in AEC countries

Granger causality test (null hypothesis)	All AEC countries (p-value)	TH	SG	MY	PH	IND	LA	KH	MM
Economic growth/ICT									
INT ->GDP	0.86	0.942	0.559	0.534	0.816	0.735	0.664	0.791	0.117
GDP ->INT	0.11	0.405	0.712	0.949	0.633	0.808	0.293	0.173	0.505
BND ->GDP	0.57	0.923	0.894	0.817	0.799	0.308	0.299	0.934	0.337
GDP ->BND	0.76	0.562	0.811	*0.040	0.251	0.816	0.248	0.210	0.281
FIXED ->GDP	0.75	0.649	0.257	*0.082	0.956	0.943	0.632	0.846	0.893
GDP ->FIXED	0.43	0.149	0.115	0.904	0.075	0.795	0.405	*0.013	0.226
MOBILE ->GDP	0.46	0.816	0.535	**0.019	0.354	0.818	0.856	0.607	0.756
GDP ->MOBILE	0.70	0.642	0.893	0.966	0.908	0.374	0.552	0.655	0.056
Causal relationships between IT sectors and telecoms									
BND ->INT	0.84	0.932	0.499	0.357	0.803	0.858	0.268	**0.040	0.354
INT ->BND	0.97	0.624	0.336	0.687	0.535	0.742	0.074	0.610	0.403
FIXED ->INT	0.46	0.604	0.252	0.919	0.928	0.655	0.545	0.840	0.525
INT ->FIXED	**0.00	0.549	0.406	0.114	0.343	0.753	0.580	0.786	0.490
MOBILE ->INT	***0.00	0.869	0.896	0.793	0.837	0.722	0.521	0.789	0.925
INT ->MOBILE	0.45	0.674	0.948	0.927	0.493	0.728	0.760	0.358	0.876
FIXED ->BND	0.86	0.273	0.460	0.954	*0.080	0.549	0.938	0.169	0.406
BND ->FIXED	0.99	0.099	0.408	0.317	0.998	**0.005	0.544	0.883	0.087
MOBILE ->BND	0.92	**0.030	0.933	0.930	0.994	0.200	0.801	0.609	0.984
BND ->MOBILE	0.91	0.596	*0.028	*0.016	0.680	*0.034	0.213	0.490	0.403
MOBILE ->FIXED	0.71	**0.011	0.878	0.112	0.116	0.129	0.523	0.646	0.848
FIXED ->MOBILE	0.20	0.961	0.735	0.867	0.749	0.465	0.254	*0.026	0.674
Lag selection	3	1	1	1	1	1	2	1	1
Observations	56	9	9	9	9	9	8	9	9

Noted: ->: the null hypothesis stated that it is not a causal determiner

TH Thailand, *SG* Singapore, *MY* Malaysia, *PH* Philippines, *IND* Indonesia, *LA* Laos, *KH* Cambodia, *MM* Myanmar

*** 99 percent significant level

** 95 percent significant level

* 90 percent significant level

14.6 Conclusion and Policy Recommendations

This paper successfully explored the panel causal relationship between ICT data and economic growth in ASEAN countries. The panel Granger causality test was econometrically used to investigate two types of causal relations: (1) ICTs Granger-cause economic expansions; (2) IT sectors (Internet servers and broadband providers) Granger-cause telecoms (fixed phone usage and mobile phone subscriptions) internally. As we can see, the remarkable point is the lag selection by personal ordered selection. To address this issue, the optimization approach named Newton's method was originally applied to verify the suitable lag for the panel causality analysis. Obviously, this computationally statistical approach can be the critical improvement that allows the authors to choose the precise lag efficiently.

Taking into consideration the results of the panel Granger causality test, empirically, ICTs are not the causal determiner driving economic growth when we focus on the overall ASEAN countries (eight countries). However, there is an internal causal relationship between IT sectors and telecoms. Accordingly, this indicates that ICTs are still not the major factor which stimulates economic enlargements in ASEAN, even though they are being intensively mentioned in the current moment. To concentrate on problem solutions, ensuring equitable educational systems in ICTs and the development of high-technology infrastructures should be accomplished among ASEAN countries.

Furthermore, specifically considering each country, there are many different causal results that can be explained as follows.

14.6.1 ICTs and Economy in Thailand

It is evident that ICT sectors are not the causal determiner that motivates the expansion of Thailand's economy. Using ICTs, the problems of equity in education are accounted to be the great obstruction, especially shortage of specialist teachers in remote areas and the insufficiency of advanced institutions and industrial zones with all required facilities (UNESCO 2013). As a solution, ICT industries have to be the leaders of development in major regions. ICTs can be used as a tool to raise the quality of Thai society. Therefore, increasing the capability of advanced-technology researchers in ICTs must be of first priority (Mongkhonvanit 2014).

14.6.2 ICTs and Economy in Singapore

Singapore has intensively relied on foreign workers, since it has a particularly acute shortage of skilled labor in cybersecurity, especially at the middle and senior levels (Azahar 2016). The empirical result confirms ICT sectors are not an economic stimulator. Moreover, there is only an internal causal connection between telecommunication sectors. To overcome this issue, strengthening the integration of ICTs into the learning process and transforming the learning experiences through ICTs should be the priority policy.

14.6.3 ICTs and Economy in Malaysia

It is reasonable that the establishment of the IT industrial zone named Cyberjaya can drive Malaysian economy (Kuppusamy and Shanmugam 2007). Evidently, the panel Granger causality result affirms that ICTs are the crucial economic stimulator. Moreover, because high-technology industrial infrastructures and the educational blueprint during 2013 to 2025 are already initiated, it seems that Malaysia can have a high possibility to fulfill the aspiration of becoming an intelligent nation (Ministry of Education Malaysia 2001).

14.6.4 ICTs and Economy in the Philippines

As the discussion on the paper of Alampay (2006), the result stated that most of the Filipinos preferred a landline phone over a cell phone primarily since the latter is more expensive to maintain than the former. Also, telephone lines are the main infrastructure particularly in urban areas. This is confirmed by the empirical Granger estimation. Rates of fixed phone usages are causally determined by GDP of the Philippines. To deal with this issue, the expansion of accessible ICT infrastructures, for instance, phone networks or broadband and mobile Internet connections, must be feasibly provided.

14.6.5 ICTs and Economy in Indonesia

Because the lack of research and development (R&D) in high technologies in Indonesia is ignored, this issue becomes the huge obstruction that causes this country to difficultly improve its ICT sectors (Tabor 2015). The result of this paper also assures that ICTs are not the causal determiner driving Indonesian economic growth. To address this problem, first of all, developing ICT networks and using ICTs as an essential part of learning are the crucial priority policies that should be implemented.

14.6.6 ICTs and Economy in Laos

The infeasible allocation of ICTs in Laos is the main problematic topic. ICTs are strictly accessible in the urban area, especially in Vientiane, the capital city. In addition, most of the local software vendors are considered to be small and work independently with minimum collaboration (Lao ICT Commerce Association 2013). Moreover, the outcome estimated from panel causality test states that ICTs are not the key that motivates expansionary rates of economy. As a solution, it seems that the backward improvement in poverty, standardization, and localization should be a concern and implemented.

14.6.7 ICTs and Economy in Cambodia and Myanmar

Both Cambodia and Myanmar are defined as a new emerging market of ASEAN. However, in Cambodia, there is a paradox. Although the number of mobile phone subscriptions is enormous (Adler 2014), the estimated result shows that mobile phone selling is not the causal economic determiner. Moreover, fixed phone usages are causally determined by GDP. Consequently, the main problem is an infrastructural development for telecommunications. In Myanmar, the contradiction is although most of the ICT sectors are based on telecom lines, the result represents that economic growth causally determines the rates of mobile phone subscriptions. Accordingly, the major problem is an infrastructural improvement for network systems. To address these issues, increasing phone networks and providing broadband and mobile Internet connections can be suitable suggestions for these two countries.

References

Adler, D. (2014). The status of ICT in Cambodia. Retrieved from http://discover.isif.asia/2014/08/the-status-of-ict-in-cambodia/.

Alampay, E. (2006). Analysing socio-demographic differences in the access and use of ICTs in the Philippines using the capability approach. *EJISDC, 27*(5), 1–39.

ATKearney. (2016). The ASEAN digital revolution. Axiata Advancing Asia. Available at: https://www.atkearney.com/documents/10192/7567195/ASEAN+Digital+Revolution.pdf/86c51659-c7fb-4bc5-b6e1-22be3d801ad2.

Azahar, W. (2016). Study: Lack of focus on developing soft skills of employees in Singapore. Retrieved from http://www.humanresourcesonline.net/study-lack-focus-developing-soft-skills-employees-singapore/.

Banerjee, A. (1999). Panel data unit root and cointegration: An overview. *Oxford Bulletin of Economics and Statistics, 61*, 607–629. Special Issue.

Barbieri, L. (2006). Panel unit root tests: A review. Serie Rossa: Economia – Quaderno N. 43. Università Cattolica del Sacro Cuore. Piacenza.

Caglayan, E., & Sak, N. (2014). Relationship between tourism and economic growth: A panel granger causality approach. *Asian Economic and Financial Review, 2*(5), 591–602.

Choi, I. (2001). Unit root tests for panel data. *Journal of International Money and Finance, 20*, 249–272.
Davidson, R., & MacKinnon, J. G. (2004). *Econometrics theory and methods*. New York: Oxford University Press.
Denoeux, T. (2016). Computational statistics: Computer projects. Retrieved from https://www.hds.utc.fr/~tdenoeux/dokuwiki.
Elliott, G., Rothenberg, T., & Stock, J. (1996). Efficient tests for an autoregressive unit root. *Econometrica, 64*, 813–836.
Fisher, R. A. (1932). *Statistical methods for research workers*. Oliver and Boyd: Edinburgh.
Haghshenas, M., Kasimin, H., & Berma, M. (2013). Information and communication technology (ICT) and economic growth in Iran: Causality analysis. *Jurnal Ekonomi Malaysiaxi, 47*(2), 55–68.
Heeks, R. (2011). ICT and economic growth: Evidence from Kenya. ICT4D Statistics. Available at: https://ict4dblog.wordpress.com/2011/06/26/ict-and-economic-growth-evidence-from-kenya/.
Hossain, S. (2012). Multivariate granger causality between economic growth, electricity consumption, exports and remittance for the panel of three SAARC countries. *Global Journal of Management and Business research, 12*(4), 41–54.
Hurlin, C., & Mignon, V. (2007). Second generation panel unit root tests. HAL Id: halshs-00159842. Available at: https://halshs.archives-ouvertes.fr/halshs-00159842.
Khalili, F., Lau, W. Y., & Cheong, K. C. (2013). The ICT contribution-real GDP Nexus revisited: Empirical evidence from Asia-Pacific countries. *Journal of Business Management and Applied Economics, 11*(5), 1–14.
Kuppusamy, M., & Shanmugam, B. (2007). Islamic countries economic growth and ICT development: The Malaysia case. *Journal of Economic Cooperration, 28*(1), 99–114.
Lao ICT Commerce Association. (2013). Research for ASEAN free trade agreement impact to Lao ICT industry. Japan International Cooperation Agency, Vientiane, Lao.
Lien, N. P. (2016). Relationship among institutional quality, Tax revenue and economic growth at province level: Evidence from Vietnam. *Asian Economic and Social Society, 6*(9), 228–239.
Lin, E. S., & Ali, H. E. (2009). Military spending and inequality: Panel granger causality test. MRRA paper No. 40159. Available at https://mpra.ub.uni-muenchen.de/40159/.
Maddala, G. S., & Wu, S. (1999). A comparative study of unit root tests with panel data and a new simple test. *Oxford Bulletin of Economics and Statistics, 61*, 631–652. Special Issue.
Ministry of Education Malaysia. (2001). *Education in Malaysia: A journey to excellence*. Kuala Lumpur: Ministry of Education.
Mongkhonvanit, P. (2014). Information technology preparation to enter ASEAN community. *International Journal of the Computer, the Internet and Management, 22*(2), 1–6.
Pesaran, H. M. (2003). A simple panel unit root test in the presence of cross section dependence, Mimeo, University of Southern California.
Polyak, B. T. (2007). Newton's method and its use in optimization. *European Journal of Operational Research, 181*, 1086–1096.
Pradhan, R. P., Arvin, M. B., & Norman, N. R. (2015). The dynamics of information and communications technologies infrastructure, economic growth, and financial development: Evidence from Asian countries. *Technology in Society, 42*, 135–149.
Tabor, S. R. (2015). Constraints to Indonesia's economic growth. Paper No. 10. Asia Development Bank, Manila, Philippines.
TOT Academy. (2016). ASEAN ICT skills upgrading and development: Final report. In workshop at TOT Academy between 24th to 27th November 2014. Available at: http://mict.go.th/assets/portals.
UNESCO. (2013). ICT in education policy, infrastructure and ODA status in selected ASEAN countries. Asia and Pacific Regional Bureau for Education, UNESCO Bangkok.
Won, Y., & Hsiao, F. S. T. (2008). Panel causality analysis on FDI: Exports – economic growth Nexus in first and second generation ANIEs. *The Journal of the Korea Exconomy, 9*(2), 237–236.
Yousefi, A. (2015). A panel granger causality test of investment in ICT capital and economic growth: Evidence from developed and developing countries. *Economics World, 3*(5), 109–127.

Chapter 15
FDI Spillover Effects in China's Manufacturing Sector: New Evidence From Forward and Backward Linkages

Chengchun Li and Sailesh Tanna

Abstract This paper assesses the spillover effects of inward foreign direct investment (FDI) on firm-level productivity growth in China's manufacturing sector over the period 2006–2009. We use a detailed industrial classification of data to characterise both intra-industry and interindustry linkages, in contrast to most previous studies for developing countries. Our findings suggest that there is a negative short-term effect and a positive long-run effect from FDI at both linkage levels. Among the interindustry linkages, in line with previous studies, the backward linkage is an important channel for domestic firms to obtain technology spillovers in the long run. However, our results also indicate that forward linkages are equally important, as we find a strongly positive impact of this linkage on productivity growth of domestic manufacturing firms in China.

Keywords Foreign direct investment · Technology spillovers · Productivity growth

15.1 Introduction

It has been widely recognised that the accrued economic benefits from FDI stem mainly from the embedded technology or knowledge spillover effects associated with such flows rather than having to 'reinvent the wheel' (Lorentzen and Barnes 2004). In assessing the benefits in terms of the significance of FDI on economic

---

C. Li
Faculty of Business and Law, Coventry University, Coventry, UK
e-mail: lic24@uni.coventry.ac.uk

S. Tanna (✉)
School of Economics, Finance and Accounting, Faculty of Business and Law, Coventry University, Coventry, UK
e-mail: s.tanna@coventry.ac.uk

N. Tsounis, A. Vlachvei (eds.), *Advances in Panel Data Analysis in Applied Economic Research*, Springer Proceedings in Business and Economics,
https://doi.org/10.1007/978-3-319-70055-7_15

growth, most of the early empirical studies have relied on using country-level FDI data. However, Moran (2011) points out that the stage of studying the impact of inward FDI in developing countries has become ‘second generation’ which is distinguished by more careful, thorough, and sophisticated research using disaggregated data, while ‘first-generation’ studies that are directly testing the linkage between FDI and economic growth using aggregated data seem to be unreliable. Taking this argument further, Moran (2011) suggests that FDI inflows to different economic sectors or to different industries can have different effects on economic growth (or productivity growth of firms), pointing to the need for industry-level studies to gauge the spillover effects from inward FDI. Most of ‘second-generation’ FDI spillover studies test the nexus between industry-level FDI and firm-level productivity. Among these, a famous study by Javorcik (2004) measures the extent of spillover effects associated with the presence of foreign capital using an input-output table of a host country. This kind of research represents a firm-level case study for an individual country but yielding industry-level spillover effects.

With regard to the evidence for China, which has been a major beneficiary of FDI over the past few decades, a number of micro-level empirical studies have emerged assessing the importance of spillover effects associated with inward FDI in specific industries. Liu (2008), for example, investigates whether FDI spillovers exist in China’s manufacturing sector by using firm-level data over the period 1995–1999. Using Javorcik’s (2004) framework, his findings suggest that FDI does not always exert a positive effect on firm productivity growth, being associated with the industrial linkage and time effect. Other related studies for China have investigated spillover effects of FDI but focussed on the importance of causal factors rather than industrial linkages. For example, Abraham et al. (2010) examine the FDI spillover effects using 15,000 Chinese manufacturing firms over the period 2002–2004 and argue that special economic zones matter for spillover effects. Agarwal et al. (2013) also use firm-level data from 2001 to 2005 and provide evidence that credit constraints negatively affect the spillover effects in China. Jeon et al. (2013), using firm-level data from China’s manufacturing sector over the period 1988–2008, find that FDI negatively impacts on local firms within the same industry, and the negative effect is even stronger particularly in low-tech industries.

This paper contributes to the empirical literature by investigating FDI spillover effects via industrial linkages as a source of firm-level productivity gains in China’s manufacturing sector. Specifically, following the approach of Liu (2008), we reassess the relationship between FDI and productivity growth with recent data and a detailed data classification. In order to assess the importance of both horizontal and vertical linkages for investigation of FDI spillovers, we utilise a 135×135 sectoral input-output matrix which provides a more detailed classification compared to most of the previous studies for developing countries. The reason for choosing China is that it has been one of the developing countries with the fastest economic growth over the past decade, and its successful experience has been attributed to the beneficial effect from FDI spillovers (Zou 2009). Additionally, the availability of a detailed input-output classification for China’s manufacturing sector makes it appropriate to focus on this country – whereas most other developing countries have a two-digit industrial classification which is generally not sufficient for detailed examination of spillover effects. More specifically, we investigate the importance of linkages in the transmission of FDI spillover effects using a huge sample of large and medium-size firms which operated in the Chinese manufacturing sector over the period 2006–2009.

Our results indicate that spillover effects from inward FDI are negative in the short term but positive in the long run, at both the intra-industry and interindustry levels. Furthermore, consistent with Liu (2008), horizontal (intra-industry) linkages do not always have a positive effect on the productivity of firms, while spillover effects via backward (interindustry) linkages are significant. However, we find that forward linkages are also an importance source of productivity gains to be accrued from FDI.

The rest of the paper is organised as follows. Section 2 provides the literature review. Section 3 discusses the empirical analysis. Section 4 concludes.

15.2 Literature Review

Among the early studies examining FDI spillover effects, Scott-Kennel (2004) demonstrates that spillovers occur through both direct and collaborative linkages. Direct linkages are generated via transactions between affiliates and domestic firms, including backward linkage (sourcing input from domestic suppliers), forward linkage (supplying domestic firms through selling products or services) and horizontal linkage via interfirm transfer of resources and assistance (e.g. market information, product specifications and technical equipment). Collaborative linkages occur during the alliance activities between affiliates and indigenous firms, involving management contracts, development agreements, and technology sharing. In the long run, these linkages are expected to bring technological benefits and generate virtuous firm-level upgrading and, in the process, drive economic growth. Using questionnaire data for New Zealand, Scott-Kennel (2004) provides supportive evidence that affiliates of multinational enterprises (MNEs), via parent companies, contribute unique capabilities to local firms, as a consequence of the spillover effect. The findings also show that more transfer of various types of capabilities from parent firms to affiliates yields greater likelihood that complementary capabilities can be transferred to domestic firms via affiliates; collaborative linkages create more effect on transfer of new technologies, R&D, distribution systems, economies of scale, and inputs to New Zealand.

Bell and Marin (2004) investigate numerous aspects of technological and economic behaviour of 1533 Argentine firms in the 1990s to provide a more comprehensive view of FDI-related spillovers and linkages. They suggest that spillovers occur via a much more complicated and locally centred knowledge diffusion and production system rather via a single way pipeline to local firms. This view is confirmed by Ford et al. (2008) who mention that by watching and participating in foreign firms' activities, domestic firms enhance growth not only by the learning-by-doing approach but also via emerging new technologies; and also some original innovations generated by affiliates make great contribution to productivity growth of local firms, implying that the competition effect due to the FDI inflows is another possible way to increase the productivity growth of domestic firms. Bell and Marin (2004) use the expenditures on R&D, training, and the recruitment of high-skilled employees to measure the spillovers. They find bidirectional spillovers between affiliates and local firms; their empirical results also demonstrate that local firms benefit more from domestic technological advantages than from FDI driven technologies in Argentina.

Sinani and Meyer (2004) examine the spillovers from FDI with three alternative proxies, namely, ratio of foreign firms' employment, foreign share of equity and industry sales. They use panel data of Estonian firms during 1994–1999 and find that all the measures of the spillovers are significantly positively correlated to the sales growth of domestic firms. However, Sinani and Meyer (2004) also highlight the adverse effects from FDI for domestic firms. As MNEs with advanced technologies enjoy lower marginal cost and take market share from local firms, domestic firms may decrease their productivity especially in the short run. As Sinani and Meyer's work consider both the positive and negative effects associated with FDI spillovers, it started to shape the framework for assessing the benefits and costs in more recent studies.

Javorcik (2004) uses a framework which allows for assessment of horizontal, backward, and forward linkages as well as the competition effects. Using firm-level data for Lithuania covering the period 1996–2000, Javorcik (2004) finds that mere backward linkages can bring positive spillovers to domestic firms. She explains that MNEs have incentives to protect the new technologies and prevent leakage (which would improve the performance of their domestic competitors). However, the local suppliers could benefit – since spillovers are more likely to be vertical rather than horizontal. Mortimore and Vergara (2004) confirm the above argument through their case study of FDI in Costa Rica, the country which has largely benefitted from FDI, although MNEs stick on information protection. For example, Intel restricts the global expansion to avoid leaking its principal technology to competitors; however, the local related businesses (especially, software) in Costa Rica contribute to economic growth remarkably. Javorcik and Spatareanu (2008) apply a similar framework as Javorcik (2004) but consider the influence of ownership structure. Examining the relationship between FDI inflows and TFP growth at firm-level for Romania during 1998–2003, they find a positive vertical spillover effect only for firms with shared domestic and foreign ownership.

Building upon the framework put forward by Javorcik (2004), Liu (2008) examines FDI spillover effects on manufacturing firms in China from 1995 to 1999, distinguishing between short-run and long-run effects, alongside intra-industry and interindustry linkages. His results indicate that FDI has a negative impact in the short run and a positive impact in the long run on domestic firms' productivity, which operates through the vertical linkage, and domestic firms need around 11 years to recover from initial losses. He also discovers that only backward linkage has a robustly significant long-run effect on domestic firms' productivity growth and domestic firms have to overtake the negative short-run effect between 2 and 8 years (depending on which of the different estimations are used).

Recent studies, however, have pointed out some limitations in Javorcik's work which employs a two-digit standard industrial classification (SIC). For instance, Alfaro and Charlton (2009) warn that there are misclassifications about horizontal and vertical FDI linkages with two-digit classification, as many foreign affiliates are regarded the same as their parent firms ('horizontal'). By disaggregating to the four-digit level, the majority of the MNE subsidiaries are regarded as suppliers ('vertical') to their parents by producing highly specialised inputs. For example, General Motors Corporation has 42 'vertical' and 68 'horizontal' affiliates under the four-digit classification. The foreign 'vertical' affiliates manufacture intermediate inputs rather than 'raw materials' or 'low-tech' products for the parent productions. Alfaro and Charlton (2009) show there is more vertical FDI in four-digit classifications than in two-digit ones, implying that there are underestimations of spillover effects in many studies which use the latter classification. In line with Alfaro and Charlton (2009), Fons-Rosen et al. (2013) confirm that positive spillover effects can be found in a more disaggregated classification scheme. They spilt the aggregate spillovers into knowledge spillovers and the competition effect. Knowledge spillovers capture foreign presence in the same two-digit sector but exclude output produced by foreign affiliates in the same four-digit sector. The competition effect captures the foreign presence in the same four-digit sector and output in the same four-digit sector, meaning that foreign affiliates directly compete with domestic firms at the four-digit level.

Apart from the above studies which employ Javorcik's (2004) framework, there are other studies using different measurement techniques for investigating spillovers and linkages. For example, Lin et al. (2011) examine spillover effects on the FDI-productivity nexus at provincial level over the period 1997–2006 and discover that higher levels of human capital associated with provincial FDI has a positive effect on productivity but a higher level of technology gap associated with FDI exhibits a negative effect on productivity. Ni et al. (2015) study the FDI spillover effect in Vietnam using firm-level panel data over the period 2002–2011. They encounter that the association between the origin of FDI and linkages matters. Asian FDI can exert a positive effect on a domestic firm's TFP growth through backward linkages, while European and North American FDI cannot. However, FDI inflows from Asia or Europe all have a negative impact on horizontal links. Additionally, they find empirical evidence that a firm's size and location also can influence spillover effects. Liu et al. (2016) empirically examine the relationship between inward FDI and total factor productivity growth in the Chinese electronics industry using the data for 1328 firms from 2003 to 2008. They find that inward FDI does bring technological transfer and thus increases TFP growth, just as investing in human capital and R&D, and implementing proper labour regulatory policies can increase TFP growth.

15.3 Empirical Analysis

15.3.1 Total Factor Productivity Estimation

Testing the impact of aggregated FDI spillovers at country level on economic growth may yield ambiguous results (Moran 2011). A better way to such conduct empirical estimation of spillover effects is using firm-level data, as suggested by Javorcik (2004) and Liu (2008). The first step in this process is to calculate firm-level total factor productivity (TFP). While the origins of TFP analysis can be traced back to Solow (1956), most TFP studies in recent years have tended to use firm-level data (to estimate TFP at the individual establishment level). Specifically, in TFP studies, a Cobb-Douglas production function is used with output measured as deflated revenues or value added, and TFP is obtained as a residual after accounting for the inputs in the estimation of firm productivity (Olley and Pakes 1996; Van Beveren 2012).

Traditionally, OLS estimation has been applied to calculate the TFP. However, as productivity is likely to be correlated with inputs, the estimation of firm-level TFP by OLS suffers from the usual problem of simultaneity or endogeneity bias. Although the problem might be overcome by using fixed effects, instrumental variables, or generalised method of moments (GMM), these estimations generally have poor performances in the case of production functions (Van Beveren 2012). Hence, following Javorcik (2004) and Liu (2008), we estimate firm-level productivity using the Olley and Pakes (OP) method, which addresses the endogeneity issues properly.

15.3.2 Spillover Estimation

The spillover effects of FDI (associated with the presence of MNEs or their affiliates) can be distinguished into horizontal, backward, and forward linkages. While horizontal linkage characterises within industry spillover effects, backward and forward linkages represent across industry spillover effects. Of the latter two, backward linkage effects can occur when domestic firms supply inputs for MNEs and forward linkage effects can similarly arise when MNEs supply outputs to domestic firms. Javorcik (2004) quantifies these linkages and a model for capturing their effects on TFP, which we adopt in this study.

Horizontal linkage, Horizontal_{jt}, capturing the effect from foreign presence within industry j in year t, is measured as:

$$\text{Horizontal}_{jt} = \frac{\sum_{i,\ i\in j} (\text{Foreign share}_{it} \times Y_{it})}{\sum_{i,\ i\in j} Y_{it}} \tag{15.1}$$

where $\text{Foreign share}_{it}$ is defined as the percentage of foreign ownership of firm i[1] in year t; Y_{it} denotes the revenue (or sales) of firm i in year t.

[1]The firms are only foreign owned with a minimum of 25% foreign capital to total assets.

Backward linkage, Backward_{jt}, which captures the potential spillover effects between MNEs and domestic suppliers, is measured as:

$$\text{Backward}_{jt} = \sum\nolimits_{k,\ k \neq j} \left(\text{Horizontal}_{kt} \times \rho_{jkt}\right) \tag{15.2}$$

where ρ_{jkt} stands for the proportion of the outputs from industry j supplied to another industry k, obtained from the input-output matrix of year t.

Forward linkage, Forward_{jt}, captures the potential spillover effects of MNEs on domestic firms, which is measured as:

$$\text{Forward}_{jt} = \sum\nolimits_{l,\ l \neq j} \left(\text{Horizontal}_{lt} \times \rho_{jlt}\right) \tag{15.3}$$

where ρ_{jlt} is the proportion of the intermediate goods used by industry j from another industry k, obtained from the input-output matrix of year t.

Treating the natural logarithm of TFP as a dependent variable and the horizontal, backward, and forward linkages as the main independent variables representing the determinants of TFP, Javorcik (2004) specifies a regression model to estimate the impact of FDI spillovers on TFP in linear form as follows:

$$tfp_{it} = \beta_0 + \beta_1 \text{Horizontal}_{jt} + \beta_2 \text{Backward}_{jt} + \beta_3 \text{Forward}_{jt} + \beta_4 Z_{it} + \epsilon_{it} \tag{15.4}$$

where Z_{it} are a set of control variables, which in our case includes industry-level competition as well as regional, time, and industrial dummies.

Liu (2008) extends the above model by incorporating interaction terms in (15.4) to distinguish between the short-term *level* effect of FDI spillovers from the longer-term *rate* effects. The rate effect of FDI, expected to be positive, will offset a negative level effect he found in the situation of China. Following Liu (2008), we use the TFP model by adding to the above model interaction terms with time trend t to capture the net effect of the spillovers as follows:

$$\begin{aligned} tfp_{it} = {} & \beta_0 + \beta_1 \text{Horizontal}_{jt} + \beta_2 \text{Backward}_{jt} + \beta_3 \text{Forward}_{jt} + \beta_4 Z_{it} + \beta_5 \\ & \left(\text{Horizontal}_{jt} \times t\right) + \beta_6 \left(\text{Backward}_{jt} \times t\right) + \beta_7 \left(\text{Forward}_{jt} \times t\right) + \beta_7 t + \epsilon_{it} \end{aligned} \tag{15.5}$$

15.3.3 Data

Firm-level data for Chinese manufacturing firms is collected from the Oriana database developed by Bureau Van Dijk (BvD). This commercial database incorporates the data for the income statements and balance sheets as well as the relative information (such as legal status and ownership information) for most of the larger- and medium-sized companies in Asia. Typically, the selected data from the database

Table 15.1 Variables for calculating TFP

Variable	Data from the Oriana database
Output, $\boldsymbol{Y}_{it}$	Sales
Capital, $\boldsymbol{K}_{it}$	Fixed assets
Material, $\boldsymbol{M}_{it}$	Costs of goods sold
Labour, $\boldsymbol{L}_{it}$	Number of employees

only includes firm-level accounting data and ownership information for mainland China (excluding Hong Kong and Macao).

The specific data for Chinese manufacturing firms included in the sample comprise values for output, capital input, material input, labour input, as well as information relating to the SIC code, location, and status (such as foreign ownership). As for the four main variables used in calculating TFP, the relevant information is shown in Table 15.1.

The OP method requires an investment variable as a proxy, which is calculated using the data for fixed assets for each firm. Moreover, the data for output and material input are deflated by provincial producers' price indices of industrial product; capital input and investment are deflated by provincial price indices of investment in fixed assets.[2] The price indices are all obtained from China Statistical Yearbook.

Following Li (2017), some cleaning procedures had to be applied to the original data, which are (i) the sample was restricted to large- and medium-size manufacturing firms in manufacturing firms in China; (ii) the SIC code for each firm was reclassified to three-digit level based on Chinese classification standards; (iii) the location of each firm was reclassified from 'city', 'town', 'village', 'county', or 'street' to 'province' (in order to create provincial-level location dummies); (iv) firms that had more than 25% foreign capital were categorised as 'foreign owned', following the identification criterion of the National Bureau of Statistics of China; (v) outliers were removed from the sample. After applying the above filtering procedures, the final sample consisted of 239,643 firms covering 81 industries in the manufacturing sector over the period of 2006–2009 with 679,199 firm-year observations. Appendix I lists the 81 industries with their three-digit Chinese SIC code.

Turing to the details of constructing the linkage variables, it is important to choose an input-output matrix which contains a detailed industrial classification. Alfaro and Charlton (2009) and Fons-Rosen et al. (2013) emphasise the main advantage of using a four-digit classification compared to using a two-digit one – firms within a same two-digit sector may compete for each other; however decomposing by four-digit classification, they may actually have 'supplier-customer' relationship rather than direct competition – thus a more detailed classification can lead to more precise estimation. As noted earlier, this is the main drawback of Liu (2008) who only uses the two-digit input-output matrix for classification. The National Bureau

[2]The price index of investment in fixed assets is not available for Tibet. Therefore, the average national level is used for deflating the data of the firms located in Tibet.

of Statistics of China provides two types of input-output matrix for the year 2007, namely, 42 × 42 sectors and 135 × 135 sectors. This study uses the latter[3] and assumes that the input-output linkage does not change during 2006–2009. Using different input-output matrix for every year is more ideal, but such information is only made available every 5 years – this is also a limitation according to Liu (2008) and Javorcik (2004).

As for the proportions ρ_{jkt} in Eq. (15.2) – the proportions of the outputs from industry j supplied to industry k for calculating backward linkages – these are determined by including product supplier information for intermediate products consumption only (i.e. not for final consumption and exports).[4] Also, the inputs supplied within the sector are excluded, because the horizontal linkage variable already captures this effect. For calculating the forward linkage (in terms of ρ_{jlt}), the proportion is also exclusive of the inputs purchased within the same sector.

In addition, Javorcik (2004) emphasises that exports should be excluded for calculating the forward linkage – using total output minuses the volume of exports for an individual firm. However, the Oriana database does not provide sufficient data on exports. Therefore, assuming that all the firms within the same sectors have the same proportion of exports from their total output, using the industry-level exports could be an alternative.[5]

To account for the effect of competition, the Herfindahl-Hirschman index (HHI) is used for calculating industry-level concentration. The index is defined as the sum of the square of the market shares (based on the sales) of each firm within the same industry within a same year.

Table 15.2 provides the summary statistics for the data used in this study, indicating that most of the observations are within reasonable limits (i.e. no outliers).

15.3.4 Results and Discussion

15.3.4.1 Total Factor Productivity Estimation: Factor Shares

Table 15.3 shows the estimated results of TFP estimation based on the Cobb-Douglas production function, using OLS and OP methods. As explained earlier OLS estimation suffers from the endogeneity problem. Therefore, the coefficients of labour and material are expected to be overestimated, while the coefficient on capital is expected to be underestimated. For the OP method, the coefficients of labour and

---

[3]The 135 sectors input-output matrix cannot be strictly treated as a three-digit level classification. However, it provides at least a better classification than the 42 sectors which is two-digit level classification.

[4]However, imported intermediation products should be excluded from the calculation but the input-output matrix which excludes such imports does not exist.

[5]We consider both situations, namely, inclusive of exports and exclusive of exports, and the results are found to be fairly robust.

Table 15.2 Summary statistics

Variable	Mean	Std. dev.	Min	Max	Obs.
Output (y, thousand CNY)	164382.8	1,239,610	1	3E + 08	679,199
Capital (c, thousand CNY)	45900.56	497895.9	1	1.3E + 08	679,199
Labour (l)	333.2316	2241.222	1	566,391	679,199
Materials (m, thousand CNY)	141313.5	1,093,590	1	2.7E + 08	679,199
Investment (i, thousand CNY)	17464.79	191187.5	0.0034	34,000,000	268,732
ln(y)	17.8004	1.2369	6.7533	26.38975	679,145
ln(c)	15.9687	1.6008	6.8188	25.62051	679,146
ln(l)	12.0002	1.0310	6.9078	20.1548	679,199
ln(m)	17.6313	1.2500	6.7533	26.2844	679,145
ln(i)	14.5788	2.0210	1.2367	24.2501	268,732
Horizontal	0.0515	0.0528	0	0.6751	679,199
Backward	0.0298	0.0318	0	0.2163	679,199
Forward	0.0193	0.0135	0	0.1009	679,199
HHI	0.0115	0.0244	0.0007	0.1936	679,199

Table 15.3 Total factor productivity estimation

	Olley-Pakes	OLS
Capital	0.0161934***	0.026636***
	(0.0046105)	(0.0002411)
Labour	0.006557***	0.0070611***
	(0.0017705)	(0.0007429)
Material	0.9480313***	0.9543233***
	(0.0008265)	(0.0004103)
N	268732	679145

Note: ***p value < 0.01, denoting statistical significance at the 1 per cent level. Dependent variable is Output. Standard errors calculated by using 200 bootstrap replications are shown below the coefficient estimates. All estimations are conducted with maximum number of observations

material are lower than those estimated by OLS. However, the coefficient on capital is also lower and not line with theory. This situation is also observed in Van Beveren (2012), Javorcik (2004), and Abraham et al. (2010). In fact, the results are very similar to the results of estimated production function in the study of Abraham et al. (2010) who used the same database and also showed that the estimated coefficient on capital by using OP is somewhat lower than the OLS results. However, since OLS ignores the endogeneity problem, it underestimates the TFP. Table 15.4 provides the estimated summary values of TFP and shows that the mean of the TFP estimated by the OP method (0.7481) is higher than that obtained by using OLS (which is close to zero). Henceforth, the use of OLS is discarded in further estimation below.

Table 15.4 Total factor productivity estimation: Summary

ln(tfp)	Obs.	Mean	Std. dev.	Min	Max
Olley-Pakes	679,145	0.7481	0.1930	−7.2243	8.3898
OLS	679,145	−3.06e-12	0.1917	−8.0018	7.7403

Table 15.5 Estimation of Spillover effects of FDI on TFP

	1	2	3	4
Horizontal	−0.0022	−0.0059	−0.0571***	−0.0580***
	(0.0191)	(0.0215)	(0.0206)	(0.0206)
Forward	0.25184***	0.2968***	−0.5572***	−0.5868***
	(0.0919)	(0.1002)	(0.0931)	(0.0932)
Backward	−0.5225***	−0.5227***	−0.2640***	−0.2641***
	(0.0602)	(0.0737)	(0.0687)	(0.0687)
HHI	0.0168*	0.0352***	−0.0627***	−0.0636***
	(0.0089)	(0.0112)	(0.0108)	(0.0108)
Constant	0.7455***	0.7091***	0.7367***	0.7177***
	(0.0022)	(0.0036)	(0.0031)	(0.0035)
Firm dummy	YES			
Year dummy	YES	YES		
Industry dummy		YES	YES	YES
Place dummy		YES		YES
N	679145	679145	679145	679145

Note: ***p-value < 0.01, * p value < 0.1; indicating statistical significance at 1 per cent and 10 per cent level, respectively. The dependent variable is ln (tfp) obtained using the Olley-Pakes (OP) method. Robust standard errors clustered by firm are shown below the coefficient estimates.

15.3.4.2 Spillover Effects of FDI on TFP

The data for the linkage variables (horizontal, backward, and forward linkages) are computed using Eqs. (15.1), (15.2), (15.3), and, after computing the TFP estimates using the OP method, the results of estimation of FDI spillover effects on TFP are obtained both without and with interaction effects using the regression models (15.4) and (15.5), respectively. The results without the interaction effects are shown in Table 15.5, and the corresponding results with interaction effects are shown in Table 15.6. In all regressions, the control variable included is the HHI index to account for differences in industry-level competition. However, in Table 15.5, the results are also presented variously with added control variables including firm, time, industry, and location dummies.

Table 15.5 presents the results of the FDI spillover effects using the OP method to calculate TFP, showing the estimates of horizontal (intra-industry) and vertical (interindustry) FDI inflows. In column 1, which controls additionally for firm-specific and time dummies, horizontal linkage does not appear to have a significant impact on TFP, which is in line with previous literature (e.g. Javorcik 2004; Zou 2009). The forward linkage variable has a positive and significant effect on firm

Table 15.6 Interaction model estimations for spillover effect

	1	2	3	4	5	6
Horizontal	−0.0399**				−0.0014	0.0085
	(0.0200)				(0.0219)	(0.0222)
Horizontal×time	0.0345***				0.0113**	0.0070
	(0.0040)				(0.0051)	(0.0054)
Forward		−0.3020***			−0.2216**	
		(0.0738)			(0.0902)	
Forward×time		0.1611***			0.1064***	
		(0.0204)			(0.0239)	
Forward (excluding exports)			−0.2222***			−0.1606**
			(0.0651)			(0.0802)
Forward (excluding exports)×time			0.1257***			0.0951***
			(0.0151)			(0.0184)
Backward				−0.1690***	−0.0759	−0.0992
				(0.0482)	(0.0599)	(0.0602)
Backward*time				0.0660***	0.0566***	0.0582***
				(0.0074)	(0.0078)	(0.0078)
Time	−0.0072***	−0.0078***	−0.0077***	−0.0073***	−0.0092***	−0.0092***
	(0.0003)	(0.0003)	(0.0003)	(0.0003)	(0.0004)	(0.0004)
HHI	−0.0218**	−0.0243***	−0.0238***	−0.0295***	−0.0205**	−0.0201**
	(0.0086)	(0.0086)	(0.0086)	(0.0086)	(0.0087)	(0.0087)
Constant	0.7580***	0.7605***	0.7600***	0.7609***	0.7615***	0.7613***
	(0.0010)	(0.0011)	(0.0012)	(0.0014)	(0.0016)	(0.0016)
N	679145	679145	679145	679145	679145	679145

Note: ***p value < 0.01; ** p value < 0.05, * p value < 0.1. Dependent variable is productivity which is obtained by using Olley-Pakes method. Robust standard errors clustered by firm show below the coefficient estimates productivity at the 1% level. This result indicates that, on average, a 1% increase of FDI inflows (forward linkage) can improve domestic firm-level productivity by about 0.25%. However, contrary to expectation, backward linkage has a negative influence on productivity. Column 2 shows similar results as column 1, after controlling for time, industrial, and location-specific factors. In columns 3 and 4, after excluding the time-specific effect, both the horizontal and forward linkages turn out to have negative impacts on productivity. In column 3, the effect of intra-industry spillover is also negative, suggesting that a 1% average increase in FDI leads to a 0.057% decrease of TFP; in contrast, the loss of productivity due to forward spillover effect tends to be relatively high, a 1% increase of FDI in upstream industries causing a 0.557% drop of productivity on average.

A possible reason for the negative backward linkage effect is that, in China, the government policy for promoting FDI inflows gives MNEs many privileges (Zou 2009). For example, after MNEs enter into the local Chinese market, they will have a 2-year tax exemption period; and then they will have a further 3-year period to pay only half the amount of the corporate tax; and if MNEs invest in the western or middle provinces of China, these enterprises will have another 3-year period to pay half the corporate tax. Because of these super privileges, the backward spillover effect where domestic firms supply inputs for MNEs might be negatively impacted. To illustrate by way of two examples, first, some low-tech foreign firms can enter the Chinese market without a relatively high competitive advantage, which can lead to barely little positive spillover effect, and, second, the high-tech MNEs may face a less competitive environment so they do not have to bring advanced technology from home country or engage in product innovation immediately. This implies that domestic firms might have to take a few years to overcome the disadvantages due to the privilege policy for MNEs. Therefore, we need to use the interaction model to examine this effect.

In Table 15.6, the results are presented with interaction effects associated with each linkage variable, entered individually (in the first four columns) and then jointly. Accounting for linkage effects interacting with time captures the longer-term (rate) effect of spillovers. As expected, in most cases, the negative short-term (level) effect of each linkage variable (horizontal, backward, and forward) is offset by the positive longer-term (rate) effect. For example, the results in column 1 suggests that horizontal FDI has a negative level impact on firm productivity, whereas the interaction term *horizontal* × *time* is positive and statistically significant (at 1% level), meaning that, FDI has a positive rate effect on productivity which can offset the negative level effect over time. Similarly, in column 2, forward spillover has a negative level effect which is offset by a positive rate effect on productivity. The forward variable here is constructed by including intermediate goods for exports which theoretically should not be taken into account (Javorcik 2004). The results in column 3, where the forward variable excludes the intermediate goods for exports,[6]

[6]Data limitations (insufficient annual export records at firm level) do not permit removal of the export outflows precisely. The only way to remove the outflows of export is to assume that each

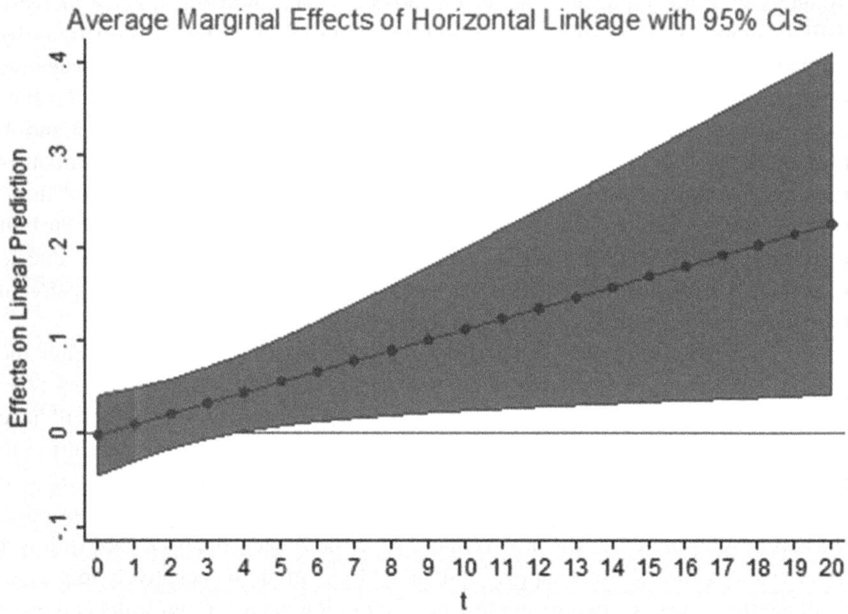

Fig. 15.1 Horizontal spillover effect (column 5 in Table 15.6)

are similar, the coefficients on *forward* and *forward*×*time* being marginally smaller compared to the corresponding forward variable including exports in column 2. In column 4, the backward linkage effect is quite similar to the horizontal and forward linkage. In column 5, the effects of all the linkage variables as well as their interaction terms are included together, showing consistent results. *Horizontal*×*time* is significant at 5% level, again indicating that the positive rate impact of horizontal FDI spillover offsets the negative level effect – and it takes around up to 3.5 years, observed from Fig. 15.1.[7] Among the vertical linkages, both forward and backward linkages also have a statistically significant effect at the 1% level. Figures 15.2 and 15.3 correspondingly show that it takes from half to 4 years for domestic firms

firm in the same industry has an exactly same behaviour towards exports, allowing for the use of the industrial average proportion.

[7]At this point, it is appropriate to point out that it is not correct to simply divide the coefficient on the interaction term, for example, *horizontal*time* by the coefficient of horizontal variable to obtain the length of time it takes for the positive rate effect to overcome the negative level effect. As emphasised by Brambor et al. (2006), it is important to calculate the corresponding standard errors for obtaining the correct marginal effect of the spillover variables. Accordingly, from here on, Figs. 15.1, 15.2, and 15.3 are used to illustrate the marginal effects with 95% confidence intervals, to gauge the time period it takes for the net positive effect to emerge from the results.

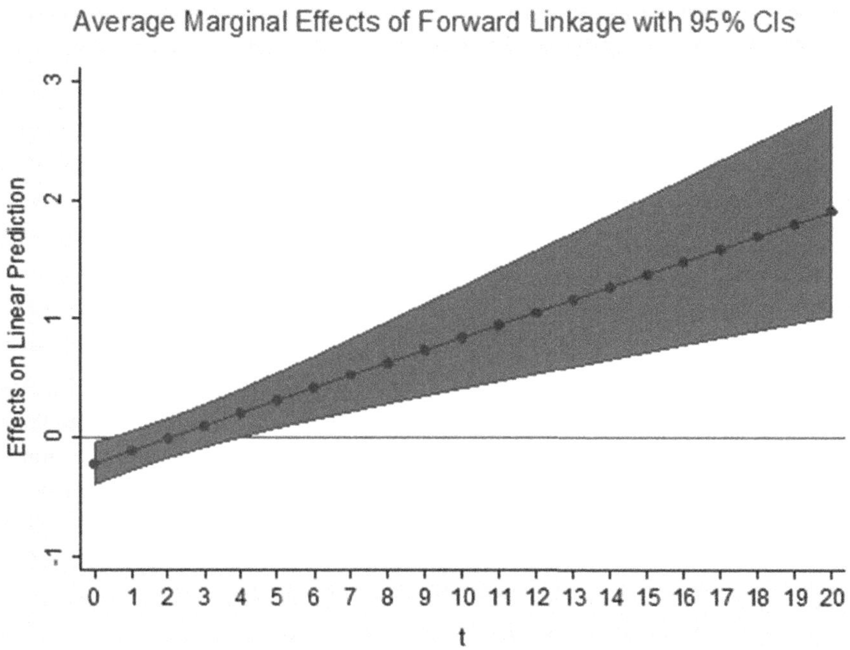

Fig. 15.2 Forward spillover effect (column 5 in Table 15.6)

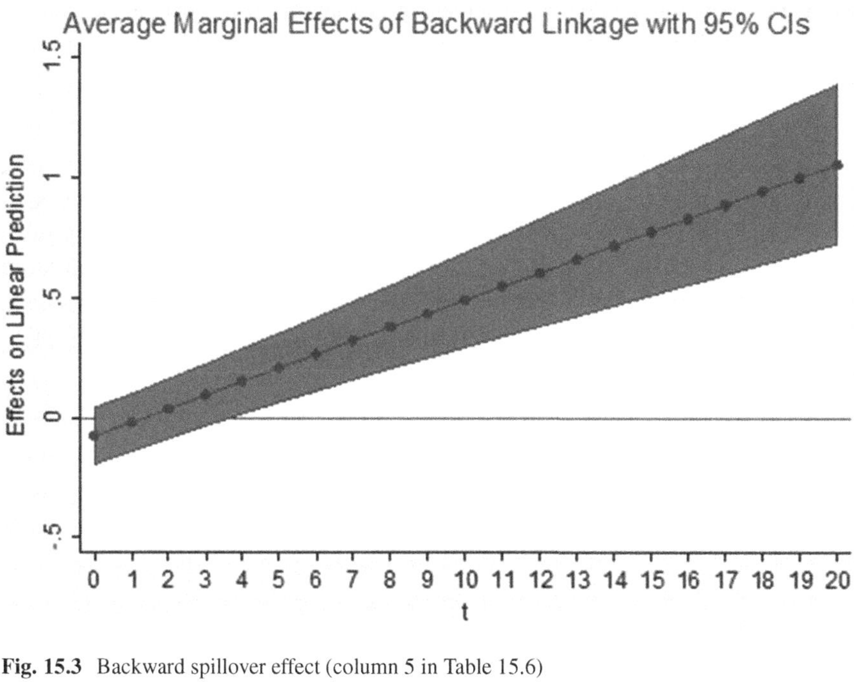

Fig. 15.3 Backward spillover effect (column 5 in Table 15.6)

in China to realise the positive benefits from forward and backward spillovers, respectively. In column 6, the results are similar with the forward variable excluding export volumes. In all the columns, the HHI variable is always negatively associated with TFP, indicating that a higher level of competition among firms in China can, in fact, improve productivity. This result is consistent with the argument that MNEs bring competition which may influence the local firms' incentives for catching-up in terms of productivity.

15.4 Conclusion

This study conducts a micro-level analysis for China's manufacturing industry to investigate FDI spillover effects on firm-level productivity. In contrast to previous studies for China, we employ a three-digit industrial classification using an input-output matrix to appropriately account for the apparent misclassification of firms that may appear as competing with each other in a two-digit classification, whereas in the three-digit classification, they may actually have a 'supplier-customer' relationship rather than direct competition. This represents an advance on previous work by Liu (2008) in addition to using a much larger sample of industrial firms and more recent data.

The empirical results demonstrate that there is a negative short-term effect and a positive long-run effect from FDI at both the intra-industry and interindustry levels. However, the findings suggest that horizontal linkage does not always have a positive effect on productivity, which is in line with Liu (2008). Also consistent with most previous studies, backward linkage is the most important way for domestic firms to obtain technology spillovers from MNEs. In China, manufacturing firms can benefit from FDI in downstream industries after 3.5 years.

However, by using a more disaggregated industrial classification than in previous studies, our findings also suggest that forward spillover effects from the presence of MNEs cannot be neglected since these effects are strongly significant with a positive impact on productivity. This empirical finding stands in contrast to Liu (2008), in which the forward linkage does not bring benefits for domestic firms no matter how long it takes. According to our results, firms in upstream industries could take up to 4 years to realise the positive spillover effects from FDI.

Appendix I

Three-digit Chinese SIC code	Industries
131	Grain grinding industry
132	Feed processing industry
133	Vegetable oil processing industry
134	Sugar industry
135	Slaughtering and meat processing industry
136	Fishery processing industry
137/139	Other food processing
143	Convenience food manufacturing
144	Liquid milk and milk products manufacturing
146	Condiments, fermentation products manufacturing
141/142/145/149	Other food manufacturing
151/152	Alcohol and wine manufacturing
153/154	Soft drinks and tea processing industry
161/162/169	Tobacco industry
171	Cotton, chemical fibre textile and dyeing industry
172	Weaving and dyeing fine processing industry
173/174	Linen textile, silk spinning and fine processing industry
175	Textile goods manufacturing
176	Knitwear and woven products manufacturing
181/182/183	Garment, shoes and hats manufacturing
191/192/193/194	Leather, fur, and feathers manufacturing
201/202/203/204	Wood processing and wood, bamboo, cane, palm and grass products
211/212/213/214/219	Furniture manufacturing
221/222/223	Papermaking and paper products industry
231/232/233	Duplicating industry of printing and recording medium
241/242/243/244/245	Cultural educational and sports goods manufacturing
251/253	Oil and nuclear fuel processing industry
252	Petroleum processing and coking
261	Basic chemical raw materials manufacturing
262	Fertilizer manufacturing
263	Pesticide manufacturing
264	Coatings, printing ink, paint and similar products manufacturing
265	Synthetic materials manufacturing
266	Special chemical products manufacturing

(continued)

Three-digit Chinese SIC code	Industries
267	Daily-use chemical products manufacturing industry
271/272/273/274/275/276/277	Pharmaceutical industry
281/282	Chemical fibre manufacturing
291/292/293/294/295/296/299	Rubber products industry
301/302/303/304/305/306/307/308/309	Plastic product industry
311	Cement, lime and gypsum manufacturing
312	Cement and gypsum products manufacturing
313	Brick, stone and other building materials manufacturing
314	Glass and glass products manufacturing
315	Ceramic products manufacturing
316	Refractory products manufacturing
319	Graphite and other non-metallic mineral products manufacturing
321	Iron-making industry
322	Steel manufacturing
323	Steel rolling processing industry
324	Ferroalloy smelting industry
331/332/333/334	Smelting non-ferrous metal and alloy manufacturing
335	Non-ferrous metal rolling processing
341/342/343/344/345/346/347/348/349	Metal products manufacturing
351	Boiler and prime mover manufacturing
352	Metal processing machinery manufacturing
353	Lifting transportation equipment manufacturing industry
354	Pumps, valves, compressors and similar machinery manufacturing
355/356/357/358/359	Other common equipment manufacturing
361	Mining, metallurgy, building special equipment manufacturing
362	Chemical, wood, non-metal processing special equipment manufacturing
367	Agriculture, forestry and fishing special-purpose machinery manufacturing
363/364/365/366/368/369	Other special equipment manufacturing
371	Railway transportation equipment manufacturing industry
372	Automobile manufacturing
375	Ships and floating device manufacturing
373/374/376/379	Other transportation equipment manufacturing industry
391	Electric manufacturing

(continued)

Three-digit Chinese SIC code	Industries
392	Transmission, distribution and control equipment manufacturing
393	Wire, cable, fibre optic cable and electrical equipment manufacturing
395/396	Household electricity and the electric appliance manufacturing industry
394/397/399	Other electrical machinery and equipment manufacturing
401	Communication equipment manufacturing industry
402/403	Radar and radio equipment manufacturing
404	Electronic computer manufacturing
405/406	Electronic components manufacturing
407	Home audio and video equipment manufacturing
409	Other electronic equipment manufacturing industry
411/412/413/414/419	Instrument manufacturing
415	Culture and office machinery manufacturing
421/422/423/424/429	Craftwork and other manufacturing
431/432	Waste processing industry

References

Abraham, F., Konings, J., & Slootmaekers, V. (2010). FDI spillovers in the Chinese manufacturing sector. *The Economics of Transition, 18*(1), 143–182.

Agarwal, N., Milner, C., & Riaño, A. (2013). *Credit constraints and FDI Spillovers in China*. SSRN Working Paper. Available at SSRN: https://ssrn.com/abstract=1966037.

Alfaro, L., & Charlton, A. (2009). Intra-industry foreign direct investment. *The American Economic Review, 99*(5), 2096–2119.

Bell, M., & Marin, A. (2004). Where do foreign direct investment-related technology spillovers come from in emerging economies? An exploration in Argentina in the 1990s. *The European Journal of Development Research, 16*(3), 653–686.

Brambor, T., Clark, W. R., & Golder, M. (2006). Understanding interaction models: Improving empirical analyses. *Political Analysis, 14*, 63–82.

Fons-Rosen, C., Kalemli-Ozcan, S., Sørensen, B. E., Villegas-Sanchez, C., & Volosovych, V. (2013). 'Quantifying Productivity Gains from Foreign Investment'. NBER Working Paper 18920.

Ford, T. C., Rork, J. C., & Elmslie, B. T. (2008). Foreign direct investment, economic growth, and the human capital threshold: Evidence from US states. *Review of International Economics, 16*(1), 96–113.

Javorcik, B. S. (2004). Does foreign direct investment increase the productivity of domestic firms? In search of spillovers through backward linkages. *The American Economic Review, 94*(3), 605–627.

Javorcik, B. S., & Spatareanu, M. (2008). To share or not to share: Does local participation matter for spillovers from foreign direct investment? *Journal of Development Economics, 85*(1), 194–217.

Jeon, Y., Park, B. I., & Ghauri, P. N. (2013). Foreign direct investment spillover effects in China: Are they different across industries with different technological levels? *China Economic Review, 26*, 105–117.

Li, C. (2017). *The impact of foreign direct investment on civil conflict, economic growth, and productivity in less developed countries: Evidence from country-level and firm-level analysis*. Unpublished PhD thesis: Coventry University.

Lin, C., Lee, C., & Yang, C. (2011). Does foreign direct investment really enhance China's regional productivity? *The Journal of International Trade and Economic Development, 20*(6), 741–768.

Liu, Z. (2008). Foreign direct investment and technology spillovers: Theory and evidence. *Journal of Development Economics, 85*(1), 176–193.

Liu, W. S., Agbola, F. W., & Dzator, J. A. (2016). The impact of FDI spillover effects on Total factor productivity in the Chinese electronic industry: A panel data analysis. *Journal of the Asia Pacific Economy, 21*(2), 217–234.

Lorentzen, J., & Barnes, J. (2004). Learning, upgrading, and innovation in the south African automotive industry. *The European Journal of Development Research, 16*(3), 465–498.

Moran, T. (2011). *Foreign direct investment and development: Launching a second generation of policy research: Avoiding the mistakes of the first, reevaluating policies for developed and developing countries*. New York: Columbia University Press.

Mortimore, M., & Vergara, S. (2004). Targeting winners: Can foreign direct investment policy help developing countries industrialise? *The European Journal of Development Research, 16*(3), 499–530.

Ni, B., Spatareanu, M., Manole, V., Otsuki, T., & Yamada, H. (2015). *How will the origin of FDI affect domestic firms' TFP? – Evidence from Vietnam*. Osaka University Working Paper. Available from http://s3.amazonaws.com/academia.edu.documents/40066563/How_Will_the_Origin_of_FDI_revise_20151020.pdf?AWSAccessKeyId=AKIAIWOWYYGZ2Y53UL3A&Expires=1485957708&Signature=7HN%2BohVUxdvRpxlk7%2FqqHrUxQY0%3D&response-content-disposition=inline%3B%20filename%3DHow_Will_the_Origin_of_FDI_Affect_Domest.pdf.

Olley, S., & Pakes, A. (1996). The dynamics of productivity in the Telecomunications equipment industry. *Econometrica, 64*, 1263–1297.

Scott-Kennel, J. (2004). Foreign direct investment: A catalyst for local firm development? *The European Journal of Development Research, 16*(3), 624–652.

Sinani, E., & Meyer, K. E. (2004). Spillovers of technology Transfer from FDI: The case of Estonia. *Journal of Comparative Economics, 32*(3), 445–466.

Solow, R. M. (1956). A contribution to the theory of economic growth. *The Quarterly Journal of Economics, 70*(1), 65–94.

Van Beveren, I. (2012). Total factor productivity estimation: A practical review. *Journal of Economic Surveys, 26*(1), 98–128.

Zou, B. (2009). *A study on FDI Techonology spillover channels and TFP growth of China's manufacturing sector* (1st ed.). Nanjing: Southeast University Press.

Chapter 16
Environmental Kuznets Curve and Turkey: An ARDL Approach

Mustafa Göktuğ Kaya and Perihan Hazel Kaya

Abstract In this study, we analyze the validity of environmental Kuznets curve hypothesis in Turkey. Using autoregressive distributed lag (ARDL) approach, the relationship between CO_2 emissions per capita, gross domestic product per capita, energy consumption, and financial development has been investigated during 1975–2012. In this direction, after empirical literature is firstly dealt with, model and dataset have been determined and analysis has been realized.

ARDL model results show that according to the long-term coefficients which obtained for quadratic model, EKC hypothesis is not valid for Turkey economy, and besides energy consumption and financial development affect CO_2 emissions positively in the long term. In this framework, in order to reduce the CO_2 emissions, Turkey should give more importance to renewable energy.

Keywords Environmental Kuznets curve · CO_2 emissions · Economic growth · Financial development · Energy consumption · Turkey · ARDL approach

16.1 Introduction

In the recent years, one of the most important problems threatening humankind is global climatic change. The studies carried out carbon dioxide (CO_2) emission as one of the most causes of climatic change. Therefore, the most effective way in

M. G. Kaya (✉)
KTO Karatay University, Konya, Turkey
e-mail: mustafa.kaya@karatay.edu.tr

P. H. Kaya
Selçuk University, Faculty of Economics and Administrative Sciences, Department of Economics, Konya, Turkey
e-mail: perihaner@selcuk.edu.tr

N. Tsounis, A. Vlachvei (eds.), *Advances in Panel Data Analysis in Applied Economic Research*, Springer Proceedings in Business and Economics,
https://doi.org/10.1007/978-3-319-70055-7_16

struggling with climatic change and environmental deterioration is to reduce CO_2 emission. The most important attempts performed by the international community on this issue are the Kyoto Protocol and United Nations Framework Convention on Climate Change. According to the Kyoto Protocol, developed countries have entered into substantial obligations in terms of reducing greenhouse gas (GHG) emissions.

Kuznets (1955) stated the inverted U-shaped relationship between income and income inequalities, and then his view has been reinterpreted in environmental economic literature since the 1990s under the name of environmental Kuznets curve (EKC). However, the developed countries have been claiming that they are reducing the rate of GHG emission gradually after a certain threshold on the level of income as environmental Kuznets curve (EKC) hypothesis proves. EKC asserts that initially economic growth will lead to environmental degradation, but eventually as income level increases, this degradation will decrease and a clean environment will take in prosperous countries (Akbostancı et al. 2009:861). Hence, the final result of EKC approach is that economic growth does not form a problem in terms of environment, on the contrary, that economic growth positively affects environment.

Turkey became a participant to the Kyoto Protocol on 26 August 2009. To comply with the Kyoto Protocol, Turkey should achieve to reduce CO_2 emissions. However Turkey's contributions to CO_2 emissions are quite low. In Turkey, per capita greenhouse gas emission is 5.9 ton. This rate is one-third of OECD average and one-half of EU average. The contribution of Turkey to global warming is in the rate of 0.04% in the last 150 years. In 1990, while greenhouse emission is 187 million ton as equivalent of CO_2, this value rose to 401.9 million ton in 2010 and 467.6 million ton in 2014 (TUIK 2016). Turkey, in order to reduce greenhouse emission, has carried out important studies in the areas of renewable energy resources. Nowadays, Turkey, which produces 20% of its energy from the renewable energy, targets on rising this rate to 30% in 2023.

The period of analysis is from 1975 to 2012. One of the most important factors affecting CO_2 emission is also financial development. Because financial development causes negative pressures on environment by reducing the financial costs, financial development increases the investments, production, energy consumption, and carbon emission (Abbasi and Riaz 2016). Therefore, while presenting EKC hypothesis in the study, the variable "financial development" has been added to the variables of CO_2 emission per capita, economic growth, and energy consumption. In this direction, after empirical literature is firstly dealt with, model and dataset have been determined and analysis has been realized.

16.2 Literature Review

The relationship between environmental degradation and economic growth has gained increasing research attention in recent years to contribute to the development of emission reduction strategies. The inverted U-shaped relationship between economic growth and environmental degradation has been known as the environmental Kuznets curve (EKC).

The EKC hypothesis states that the environmental degradation level increases as a country develops but begins to decrease when the rising income passes beyond a turning point; in other words, the environmental quality gets worse first and then improves with the economic growth (Odhiambo 2012:37).

Tamazian et al. (2009) investigate the impact of economic and financial development on environmental pollution for BRIC countries by panel regression analysis. The results show that economic and financial developments are negatively linked with environmental pollution and the EKC hypothesis is valid for BRIC countries. Jalil and Feridun (2011) deal with the effect of economic growth, energy consumption, and financial development on carbon emissions in China. According to the results, financial development decreases carbon emissions in the long run. Using ARDL bound test approach to co-integration and VECM causality method, Shahbaz et al. (2013) examine the relationship between energy consumption, economic growth, financial development, international trade, and carbon emissions in Indonesia. The study indicates that energy consumption and economic growth contribute to carbon emissions and also that financial development and trade openness decrease carbon emissions. Charfeddine and Khediri (2016) investigate the impact of economic development, energy consumption, financial development, and trade openness on environmental pollution for the United Arab Emirates. Gregory-Hansen and Hatemi-J test and VECM causality tests indicate that there exists unidirectional causality from financial development to carbon emissions. Otherwise, energy consumption and trade openness decrease carbon emissions in the long run, and EKC hypothesis is valid for the United Arab Emirates.

Some part of the studies related to EKC hypothesis on Turkish economy is summarized in the following (Table 16.1).

Koçak (2014), using the data of the period 1960–2010, analyzed the relationship between carbon dioxide emission, energy consumption, and income for Turkish economy by establishing a cubic model. According to ARDL bound test, a conclusion was resulted, which supports EKC hypothesis, in the long term. In addition, in the long term, energy consumption increases CO_2 emission.

Kılıç and Akalın (2016) analyzed environmental Kuznets curve for Turkish economy by means of ARDL bound test, using cubic and quadratic models. Among the variables of model, CO_2 emission, economic growth, and openness take place. According to the results of analysis made for quadratic model, there is a relationship in the shape of inversed U between per capita income and environmental pollution. This result supports that EKC hypothesis is valid for Turkey in the period of 1960–2011. The results of cubic model show that there is an N-shaped relationship between income and environment.

Table 16.1 Summary of selected studies on the EKC hypothesis in Turkey

Study	Periods	Variables	Methods	Long-run results	EKC hypothesis
Atıcı and Kurt (2007)	1968–2000	CO_2, Y, X, M	OLS method	X contributes to CO_2 Y decreases CO_2	Yes
Başar and Temerlunk (2007)	1950–2000	CO_2, Y, Y^2, Y^3	OLS method, KPSS unit root	Y contributes to CO_2	No
Halıcıoğlu (2009)	1960–2005	CO_2, Y, Y^2, EC, FT	ADF, PP unit root, ARDL model, Granger causality	EC, CO_2, Y^2, FT → Y CO_2 ↔ EC CO_2 ↔ Y	Not investigated
Ozturk and Acaravci (2010)	1968–2005	CO_2, Y, Y^2, EC, UNM	ARDL model, Granger causality	CO_2 decreases Y, EC attributes Y	No
Ozturk and Acaravci (2013)	1960–2007	CO_2, Y, Y^2, EC, FD, OP	ARDL model, VECM causality	EC and OP contribute to CO_2 FD → CO_2	Yes
Koçak (2014)	1960–2010	CO_2, EC, Y, Y^2, Y^3	Zivot-Andrews test, ARDL method	EC contributes to CO_2	No
Özcan (2015)	1971–2008	CO_2, EC, Y, Y^2	Panel unit root, ECM panel, FMOLS	Y and EC → CO_2	Yes
Lebe (2016)	1960–2010	CO_2, Y, Y^2, EC, FD, OP	VECM causality, ARDL model	EC, FD, and OP contribute to CO_2 FD → CO_2	Yes
Kılıç and Akalın (2016)	1960–2011	CO_2, Y, Y^2, Y^3	ADF, PP unit root, ARDL model	Y and Y^3 affect CO_2; positively Y^2 affects CO_2 negatively	Yes/no
Erdoğan et al. (2015)	1975–2010	CO_2, Y, Y^2, Y^3	ADF unit root, ARDL model, Granger causality	Y → CO_2	No
Bölük and Mert (2015)	1961–2010	CO_2, Y, EPR	ADF, KPSS unit root, ARDL model	EPR contributes to CO_2	Yes
Dam et al. (2013)	1960–2010	CO_2, EC, Y, Y^2, Y^3	ADF, PP unit root, DOLS method	EC contributes to CO_2	No

Notes: Y, Y^2, Y^3,CO_2, EC, OP, FD, X, M, FT, and EPR indicate the GDP per capita, square of GDP per capita, cube of GDP per capita, carbon emissions, energy consumption, trade openness, financial development, export, import, foreign trade, and electricity from renewable sources per capita, respectively. → and ↔ denote unidirectional causality and bi-directional causality, respectively

16.3 Data and Methodology

In this study, using the data of Turkish economy for the period of 1975–2012, the effects of EKC hypothesis and financial developments on CO_2 emission were analyzed. Dependent variable is the natural logarithm of carbon emissions (metric tons per capita), which is a measure of environmental deterioration. Descriptive variables are real GDP per capita, energy consumption, and domestic credits/GDP as indicator of financial development. All data were obtained from the World Bank. Table 16.2 shows descriptive statistics.

In order to test EKC hypothesis and analyze the effect of financial development on emission, the following equation was established:

$$CO_{2it} = \lambda_i dt + \alpha_{1i} Y\mathrm{it} + \alpha_{2i} Y_{it}^2 + \alpha_{3i}\mathrm{DM}_i t + \alpha_{4i}\mathrm{EC} + £_{it} \tag{16.1}$$

where CO_{2it} is the CO_2 emission per capita, Y is the natural logarithm of gross domestic product per capita, Y^2 is the natural logarithm of gross domestic product per capita squared, DM is the domestic credit to GDP ratio, EC is the natural logarithm of energy consumption, and $\varepsilon_{\mathrm{it}}$ is the error term.

In quadratic model, in the case that α_1 is positive and α_2 is negative, inversed U-shaped EKC relationship is obtained between income and environmental deterioration. Therefore, in the study, taking into consideration the coefficients of α_1 and α_2, the estimation is carried.

16.3.1 ARDL Co-integration Model

The most encountered and used co-integration tests in the literature are the Eagle and Granger (1987) method, based on error term, and Johansen (1988) and Johansen and Jesulius (1990) method, based on system approach. For this co-integration method to be able to apply, it is necessary for the variables to be integrated at the same degree. This state is one of the important problems for co-integration tests. But, Pesaran et al. (1996) developed ARDL approach enabling to test the relationship between integrated variables at different degrees. The most important advantage of this approach is that regardless of the variables being $I(0)$ or $I(1)$, both short-term

Table 16.2 Descriptive statistics

Variable	Mean	Std. dev.	Min.	Max.	OBS
Carbon Emissions	0.8896	0.6392	0.4529	1.2495	38
Income per capita	14.4678	3.0481	3.7284	7.5394	38
Income per capita squared	72.1241	14.6091	24.1563	110.6573	38
Domestic credit to GDP ratio	1.7463	1.1264	0.6264	10.1572	38
Energy consumption	9.2384	0.2761	4.8246	6.1573	38

and long-term relationships can be tested between them. However, ARDL bound test approach is more effective compared to the other co-integration approaches and gives better results for small samples. Due to these advantages, in the study, in the examination of co-integration relationship, the method of ARDL bound test will be applied. For ARDL bound test, first of all, unrestricted error correction model (UECM) is defined. The model of the study is as follows:

$$\begin{aligned}\Delta \ln CO_{2t} = \alpha_0 + \sum_{i=1}^{m} \alpha_{1i}\, \Delta \ln CO_{2t-i} + \sum_{i=0}^{m} \alpha_{2i} \Delta \ln\, Y_{t-i} + \sum_{i=0}^{m} \alpha_{3i} \Delta \ln Y_{t-i}^{2} \\ + \sum_{i=0}^{m} \alpha_{4i} \Delta \ln DM_{t-i} + \sum_{i=0}^{m} \alpha_{5i} \Delta \ln EC_{t-i} + \alpha_6 \ln CO_{2t-1} + \alpha_7 \ln Y_{t-1} \\ + \alpha_8 \ln Y_{t-1} + \alpha_9 \ln DM_{t-1} + \alpha_{10} \ln EC_{t-1} + £_t\end{aligned} \quad (16.2)$$

where Δ denotes the first difference of the variables. In the above model, it is necessary to find lagging length, expressed as *m*. In the determination of lagging length, information criteria such as AIC (Akaike information criterion) and SIC (Schwarz information criterion) are utilized. Then, in the research of the presence of co-integration relationship, applying F test (Wald test), the significance of first period laggings of the dependent and independent variables is tested. The hypothesis expressing whether or not there is co-integration relationship between the variables and the hypothesis expressing whether or not there is a co-integration relationship between the variables are as follows:

$$H_0 : \alpha_7 = \alpha 8 = \alpha 9 = \alpha 10 = 0 \quad (16.3)$$

$$H_1 : \alpha_7 \# \alpha_8 \# \alpha_9 \# \alpha_{10} \# 0 \quad (16.4)$$

H_0 hypothesis expresses that there is no co-integration relationship between variables, while H_1 hypothesis expresses that there is co-integration relationship between the variables.

In this stage, if it is proved that there is a long-term relationship between the variables, in the next stage, long- and short-term ARDL models are estimated. In order to determine the long-term relationship between the variables, ARDL model adjusted in accordance with EKC hypothesis is as follows:

$$\begin{aligned}\ln CO_{2t} = \alpha_0 + \sum_{i=1}^{m} \alpha_{1i} \ln CO_{2t-i} + \sum_{i=0}^{m} \alpha_{2i} \ln Y_{t-i} + \sum_{i=0}^{m} \alpha_{3i} \ln Y_{t-i}^{2} \\ + \sum_{i=0}^{m} \alpha_{4i} \ln DM_{t-i} + \sum_{i=0}^{m} \alpha_{5i} \ln EC_{t-i} + £_t\end{aligned} \quad (16.5)$$

In order to research the short-term relationship between the variables, error correction model, based on ARDL approach, is established:

$$\Delta\ln CO_{2t} = \alpha_0 + \alpha_1 ECM_{t-1} + \sum_{i=0}^{m} \alpha_{2i}\Delta\ln CO_{2t-i} + \sum_{i=0}^{m} \alpha_{3i}\Delta\ln Y_{t-i} + \sum_{i=0}^{m} \alpha_{4i}\Delta\ln Y_{t-i}^2 + \sum_{i=0}^{m} \alpha_{5i}\Delta\ln DM_{t-i} + \sum_{i=0}^{m} \alpha_{6i}\Delta\ln EC_{t-i} + \pounds_t \quad (16.6)$$

The coefficient of ECM (α_1) taking place in the model concerned shows how much of short-term unbalance will be eliminated in the long term. The coefficient of error term should be negative and statistically significant.

16.4 Estimation Results

Before passing to co-integration analysis, ADF (Augmented Dickey–Fuller), developed by Dickey-Fuller (1981), and PP, developed by Phillips and Peron (1988), unit root tests were applied to understand at what degree the series were integrated. H_0 hypothesis expresses that there is a unit root, i.e., series are not stationary, while alternative H_1 hypothesis expresses that there is no unit root, i.e., series are stationary (Table 16.3).

When the table is examined, except for energy consumption and financial development, since absolute values of ADF and PP statistics of all variables are less than those of critical table values, series are not stationary at their level values. Therefore, the first differences of the series that are not stationary at the level were taken, and it was seen that they became stationary. In other words, while EC and DM series are $I(0)$, the series of Y, Y^2, and CO_2 are $I(1)$. Hence, as a requirement of ARDL approach, it can be said that the variables, which will take place in the model, are $I(0)$ and $I(1)$ and, in addition, any variable is not $I(2)$.

In order to be able to carry out co-integration analysis with ARDL approach, first of all, it is necessary to identify the suitable lagging number. According to AIC and SC information criteria, the most suitable lagging length was identified as 2. Considering the suitable lagging length, it is decided to whether or not there is a co-integration relationship between the variables in the long period as a result of comparing critical boundary values in F statistics and Pesaran et al. (2001). In

Table 16.3 Augmented Dickey–Fuller and Phillips–Perron unit root tests

	ADF (constant and trend)		PP (constant and trend)	
Variable	Level	First difference	Level	First difference
$\ln CO_2$	−2.24	−5.76	−2.67	−5.59
$\ln Y$	−1.78	−5.36	−2.44	−5.94
$\ln Y^2$	−2.25	−6.42	−2.32	−6.17
lnDM	−4.72	–	−4.63	–
lnEC	−5.66	–	−5.28	–

*Critical values for ADF and PP are −4.15 for 1%, −3.50 for 5%, and −3.18 for 10%

Table 16.4 Co-integration test results

Model	m	k	F statistic	t statistic	$I(0)$ Lower limit	$I(1)$ Upper limit
ARDL (1,1,1,0)	2	4	4.35	0.002	$F = 3.23$ $t = -3.78$	$F = 4.31$ $t = -3.78$

Note: m max. expresses lagging number and k the number of independent variables taking place in the model. At the significance level of 5%, F statistics critical boundary values were drawn from Pesaran (2001:300) and t statistics boundary values from (2001:303)

Table 16.5 Estimation of long-term ARDL (1,1,1,0) model

Dependent variable ln CO_2			
Variables	Coefficient	t statistic	Prob.
ln CO_2 (−1)	0.314	1468	0.124
ln$Y$	0.445	2163	0.021
lnY^2	0.216	1846	0.011
lnDM	0.382	1988	0.002
lnEC	0.687	4321	0.001
C	−1707	−6243	0.000
$R^2 = 0.9287$ Adj. R^2	Adj. $R^2 = 0.9769$	F statistic = 1864.1	
AIC = −4.76	SC = −4.42	DW = 2.24	
Descriptive statistics			
Breusch-Godfrey LM test	1.46(0.42)	Jarque-Bera	2.14(0.35)
White test	4.13(0.28)	Ramsey Reset	2009(0.06)

*Breusch-Godfrey is the test used for successive dependency; Ramsey Reset, for model establishing error in regression; Jarque-Bera, for normality; and White test, for testing the varying variance. The values in parentheses are probability values belonging to diagnostic tests

Table 16.4, the results of F statistics related to testing co-integration relationship take place.

As shown in the table, it is seen that F statistics calculated is bigger than upper critical values at the significance level of 5%. Hence, it can be said that there is a long-term relationship between the variables.

After identifying long-term relationship between the variables, in the second stage, in order to analyze long-term relationship between the variables, ARD model should be estimated. In this estimation, maximum lagging length was found as 2. In the case that CO_2 emission is a dependable variable, long-term coefficient results of ARDL (1,1,1,0) model are given in Table 16.5.

When diagnostic test results of the model are evaluated, it can be said that there is no autocorrelation according to the results of the Breusch-Godfrey LM test, that there is no varying variance according to White test, that error terms are normally distributed according to Jarque-Bera, and that model is correctly established according to the results of Ramsey Reset.

However, in order to identify whether or not there is a structural fragility regarding the variables, CUSUM and CUSUM-Q tests were carried out. Using this test, calculated by the squares of successive residuals, the residuals of model are

Table 16.6 CUSUM and CUSUM-Q test results

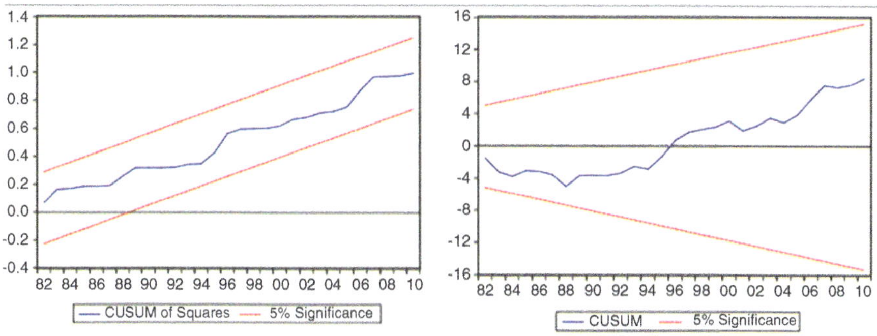

Table 16.7 Long-term ARDL (1,1,1,0) model coefficients

Dependent variable ln CO_2		
Independent variables	Coefficient	*t* statistic
ln*Y*	−0,767	−0,184
ln*Y*^{2}	0,185	0,176
lnDM	0,439	2271
lnEC	0,762	3614
C	−18,467	−2381

*Statistical significance at the level of 5%

plotted in a certain confidence interval and confidence limits are identified. It is concluded that there is no structural change in confidence limits (Table 16.6).

When the results of both CUSUM and CUSUM-Q tests are examined, any structural fragility is not met in the variables taking place in the model in the period of 1975–2012.

After co-integration is identified in the variables, estimation is made by the most suitable ARDL model; and there is no structural fragility by CUSUM and CUSUM-Q; in the next stage, the coefficients of long-term relationships are estimated and evaluations are made. The results of long-term coefficients take place in the following table.

According to the results of Table 16.7, it is seen that the coefficients belonging to the variables of economic growth and square of economic growth are statistically insignificant in the long term. Therefore, in Turkey, in the period of 1975–2012, a result supporting the relationship of environmental Kuznets curve was not reached. However, it is seen that financial development and energy consumption affect CO_2 emission per capita positively.

After the coefficients of long-term relationship between the variables are estimated, finally, short-term coefficients are estimated. For studying short-term relationship between the variables, the estimation results of error correction model, established based on ARDL approach, are as follows:

According to the results of Table 16.8, the signs of the relevant variables are in the way that will support long-term results. In addition, the coefficient of the term error correction (ECM*t*−1) is statistically significant and a negative sign. According to this, 47% of short-term deviations are corrected in the next period.

Table 16.8 ARDL (1,1,1,0) error correction estimation results

Dependent variable ln CO_2		
Independent variables	Coefficient	*t* statistic
ln$Y$	−2986	−1164
lnY^2	0,625	1089
lnDM	0,224	2157
lnEC	1216	9823
C	−8243	−5394
lnECM$_{t-1}$	−0,473	−6826

*Statistical significance at the level of 5%

16.5 Conclusion

The relationship between economic growth and environmental deterioration is one of the most important subjects discussed in the recent years. In relation to this subject, the approach of environmental Kuznets curve puts forward that growth will not finally have negative effect on environment and that in time, growth will affect environment in the positive direction.

In this scope, the aim of this study is to test EKC hypothesis for Turkish economy. In the framework of this aim, the relationship between the variables of CO_2 emission, economic growth, energy consumption, and financial development was examined by means of ARDL bound test.

According to the results of co-integration analysis, there was a long-term relationship between the variables. As a result of ARDL bound test, it can be said that in both short and long term, EKC hypothesis is not valid for the period of 1975–2012 in Turkey. In the period dealt with, while economic growth affects the level of CO_2 emission in negative direction, energy consumption and financial development affect it in positive direction. In the short term, the coefficient of the term error correction was estimated as 47%, and it was identified that deviations in the short term were corrected in the long term.

From this aspect, the study shows similarity to the studies of Başar and Temurlenk (2007), Akbostancı et al. (2009), Öztürk and Acaravcı (2010), Koçak (2014), and Erdoğan et al. (2015), which are about Turkey. Among the reasons for the studies of EKC hypothesis tested for Turkey, the distinctness of the period selected and econometric methods applied and distinctness in the selection of dependent and independent variables can be shown.

It emerged that energy consumption, among the variables in the study, positively affects CO_2 emission. Hence, this state shows that in the period dealt with, energy consumption in Turkey has an effect increasing CO_2 emission. When the data of the World Bank that are related to this subject are examined, it is seen that the share of fossil energy resources in total energy consumption of Turkey is 89% in 2012. This state creates problem in terms of both environment and foreign dependencies in energy for Turkey.

It was identified that financial development, added to the study as control variable, has a positive and significant effect on CO_2 emission level in short and long period. Although that the coefficient of financial development is estimated as positive shows that the developments in the financial sector are mostly focused on increasing the number of firms in the sector, it also shows that the developments in the financial markets are not at the level to enable environmental friendly technologies to be adapted to the sector through the firms.

Today, when considered that more than 60% of total CO_2 emission at the global level is originated from the use of fossil fuel, it is necessary for policy makers to give weight environmental policies and legal arrangements. In Turkey, in terms of environmental problems resulted from CO_2 emission, on the one hand, and economic growth, on the other hand, energy policies have a critical importance. Therefore, energy policies in Turkey should be developed in favor of renewable energy and stable growth policies should be applied, which will reduce environmental pollution to the minimum level. In this direction, in the area of renewable energy, firms can be encouraged with the various subventions, tax reductions, and lending facilities. If these kinds of policies can be implemented, on the one hand, while the fossil resources decrease, on the other hand, the decrease of our foreign dependency in energy will be largely provided.

References

Abbasi, F., & Riaz, K. (2016). CO2 emissions and financial development in an emerging economy: An augmented VAR approach. *Energy Policy, 90*, 102–114.

Akbostancı, E., Türüt-Aşık, S., & Tunç, İ. (2009). The relationship between income and environment in Turkey: Is there an environmental Kuznets curve? *Energy Policy, 37*, 861–867.

Atıcı, C., & Kurt, F. (2007). Türkiye'nin Dış Ticareti ve Çevre Kirliliği: Çevresel Kuznets Eğrisi Yaklaşımı. *Tarım Ekonomisi Dergisi, 13*(2), 61–69.

Başar, S., & Temurlenk, M. S. (2007). Çevreye Uyarlanmış Kuznet Eğrisi: Türkiye Üzerine Bir Uygulama. *İktisadi ve İdari Bilimler Dergisi, 21*, 1–12.

Bölük, G., & Mert, M. (2015). The renewable energy, growth and environmental Kuznets curve in Turkey: An ARDL approach. *Renewable and Sustainable Energy Reviews, 52*, 587–595.

Charfeddine, L., & Khediri, K. B. (2016). Financial development and environmental quality in UAE: Cointegration with structural breaks. *Renewable and Sustainable Energy Reviews, 55*, 1322–1335.

Dam, M. M., Karakaya, E., & Bulut Ş. (2013). Çevresel Kuznet Eğrisi ve Türkiye:Ampirik Bir Analiz. *Dumlupınar Üniversitesi Sosyal Bilimler Dergisi*, 85–96.

Dickey, D. A., & Fuller, W. A. (1981). Likelihood ratio statistics for autoregressive time series with a unit root. *Econometrica: Journal of the Econometric Society, 49*(4), 1057–1072.

Erdoğan, İ., Türköz, K., & Görüş, M. (2015). Çevresel Kuznets Eğrisi Hipotezinin Türkiye Ekonomisi için Geçerliliği. *Dumlupınar Üniversitesi Sosyal Bilimler Dergisi, 44*, 113–123.

Engle, R. F., & Granger, C. W. (1987). Co-integration and error correction: Representation, estimation, and testing. *Econometrica: Journal of the Econometric Society, 55*(2), 251–276.

Halicioglu, F. (2009). An econometric study of CO2 emissions, energy consumption, income and foreign trade in Turkey. *Energy Policy, 37*(3), 1156–1164.

Jalil, A., & Feridun, M. (2011). The impact of growth, energy and financial development on the environment in China: A cointegration analysis. *Energy Economics, 33*, 284–291.

Johansen, S. (1988). Statistical analysis of cointegration vectors. *Journal of Economic Dynamics and Control, 12*(2), 231–254.

Johansen, S., & Juselius, K. (1990). Maximum likelihood estimation and inference on cointegration— With applications to the dand for money. *Oxford Bulletin of Economics and Statistics, 52*(2), 169–210.

Kılıç, R., & Akalın, G. (2016). Türkiye'de Çevre ve Ekonomik Büyüme Arasındaki İlişki: ARDL Sınır Testi Yaklaşımı. *Anadolu Üniversitesi Sosyal Bilimler Dergisi, 16*, 49–60.

Koçak, E. (2014). Türkiye'de Çevresel Kuznet Eğrisi Hipotezinin Geçerliliği:ARDL Sınır Testi Yaklaşımı. *İşletme ve İktisat Çalışmaları Dergisi, 2*, 62–73.

Kuznets, S. (1955). Economic growth and income inequality. *The American Economic Review, 45*(1), 1–28.

Lebe, F. (2016). Çevresel Kuznets Eğrisi Hipotezi: Türkiye İçin Eşbütünleşme ve Nedensellik Analizi. *Doğuş Üniversitesi Dergisi, 17*, 177–194.

MacKinnon, J. G. (1996). Critical Values for Cointegration Tests, Queen's Economics Department Working Paper No. 1227.

Odhiambo, N. (2012). Economic growth and carbon emissions in South Africa: An emprical investigation. *The Journal of Applied Business Research, 28*, 37–46.

Özcan, B. (2015). ÇKE Hipotezi Yükselen Piyasa Ekonomileri İçin Geçerli mi? Panel veri analizi. *Doğuş Üniversitesi Dergisi, 16*(1), 1–14.

Özturk, I., & Acaravci, A. (2010). CO2 emissions, energy consumption and economic growth in Turkey. *Renewable and Sustainable Energy Reviews, 14*(9), 3220–3225.

Öztürk, I., & Acaravci, A. (2013). The long-run and causal analysis of energy, growth, openness and financial development on carbon emissions in Turkey. *Energy Economics, 36*, 262–267.

Pesaran, M. H., & Shin, Y. (1996). An autoregressive distributed lag model in Gapproachtoco integration analysis. In S. Strom (Ed.), *Econometrics and economic theory in the 20th century*. Cambridge: Cambridge University Press.

Pesaran, M. H., Shin, Y., & Smith, R. J. (2001). Bounds testing approaches to the analysis of level relationships. *Journal of Applied Econometrics, 16*(3), 289–326.

Phillips, P. C., & Perron, P. (1988). Testing for a unit root in time series regression. *Biometrika, 75*(2), 335–346.

Shahbaz, M., Adnan Hye, Q. M., Tiwari, A. K., & Leitão, N. C. (2013). Economic growth, energy consumption, financial development, international trade and CO2 emissions in Indonesia. *Renewable and Sustainable Energy Reviews, 25*, 109–121.

Tamazian, A., Chousa, J. P., & Vadlamannati, K. C. (2009). Does higher economic and financial development lead to environmental degradation: Evidence from BRIC countries. *Energy Policy, 37*, 246–253.

Turkish Statistical Institute (2016). www.tuik.gov.tr

Chapter 17
Selected Aspects of Managerial Success Perception: The Case of Polish Born Globals

Tomasz Sikora and Ewa Baranowska-Prokop

Abstract The main goal of this paper is to analyze the influence of three groups of factors on managerial success perception in Polish small- and medium-sized international new ventures (Born Globals). We considered the following explanatory variables: (1) international entrepreneurial orientation, (2) the perceived level of excellence in the use of marketing mix tools, and (3) sector-specific determinants (i.e., industry type). Financial situation and the success relative to competitors have been considered as the measures of success perception. The results indicate that the substantial majority of interviewed managers of Polish Born Globals considered their firms to be successful. The first hypothesis concerning the positive relationship of international entrepreneurial orientation and the perception of success was confirmed in the case of internationally experienced and capable top management but disconfirmed as far as orientation on domestic market or international markets was concerned. The second hypothesis related to marketing mix tools was confirmed with the exception of innovativeness: innovative firms evaluated their success in less favorable terms compared to the innovative ones. The third hypothesis was confirmed in the sense that there were significant differences between industries concerning the success perceptions and their considering improved explanation of success based on the first two groups of variables.

17.1 Introduction

A large group of researchers shows interest in the relatively new phenomenon of SMEs operating on global markets right from the start of their activities.

T. Sikora (✉) · E. Baranowska-Prokop
Institute of International Management and Marketing, Warsaw School of Economics, Warsaw, Poland
e-mail: tsikora@sgh.waw.pl; ebarano@sgh.waw.pl

N. Tsounis, A. Vlachvei (eds.), *Advances in Panel Data Analysis in Applied Economic Research*, Springer Proceedings in Business and Economics,
https://doi.org/10.1007/978-3-319-70055-7_17

Early internationalization is stimulated by a number of internal and external factors, well described in the literature. The problem is related to differences in classification, terminology, and definitions.

In our research, we applied the widely cited definition of Born Globals (BG) by Rennie (1993). It describes enterprises satisfying the following criteria:

SMSs receiving at least 25% of their income from foreign markets within the first 3 years of their existence.

The founder has a global vision of target markets.

There is a strong managerial urge for internationalization with the use of modern technologies.

Quantitative analyses of Born Globals from developed countries are numerous, but firms from developing countries and emerging markets are still under-researched (Poland may be considered as a representative of emerging markets). Authors researching BGs expressed opinion that successful and rapid internationalization of BGs should be first of all attributed to the strong international entrepreneurial orientation of the founder and managers: Fletcher (2000), McDougall et al. (2003), Knight and Cavusgil (2004), etc. This observation inspired us to formulate the following hypothesis:

H1. In the case of Polish BGs, there is a positive relationship between international entrepreneurial orientation and the managerial success perception.

Another important factor influencing the success of BGs is efficiency in the use of marketing tools. A number of authors, e.g., Altshuler and Tarnovskaya (2010), Luostarinen and Gabrielsson (2006), Danik and Kowalik (2015), and Gabrielsson (2005), proved that marketing orientation of the firm and skillful use of marketing instruments were essential in BG's successful performance. Thus, our subsequent hypothesis goes as follows:

H2. In the case of Polish BGs, there is a positive relationship between the excellence in the use of marketing mix tools and the managerial success perception.

In the opinion of many researchers, rapid internationalization of BGs is strongly related to the sector/branch of their activity. Sleuwaegen and Onkelinx (2010) and Cannone and Ughetto (2015) indicated that BGs operating in high-tech sector are performing much better than those in traditional sectors. Although enterprises in our sample belong to "traditional" industries, we also test whether the type of industry contributes to the explanation of the success perception. It has been formulated as the next hypothesis:

H3. In the case of Polish BGs, the success perception of enterprises depends on the branch of industry in which they operate.

The research on Polish BGs started at the end of 1990s, but publications of empirical findings appeared much later. Cieślik (2010) was the first to indicate that during the transformation period, nearly 75% of Polish exporters started selling abroad during the first 3 years since the beginning of their business activities. This observation led him to conclusion that the phenomenon of early internationalization was widely spread among Polish exporters. The further research on this subject and its results have been published by Gorynia (2007), Przybylska (2010), Duliniec (2013), Danik and Kowalik (2013), Kowalik and Baranowska-Prokop (2013), and Baranowska-Prokop and Sikora (2014). They concentrate on general characteristics of Polish BGs, choice of entry mode, determinants of their formation, barriers to expand, etc. The growing importance and scale of BGs operations encouraged us to further analysis of this phenomenon.

17.2 Research Method

The sample of 233 Polish small- and medium-sized INVs was drawn out of the population of 19,594 Polish firms with 10–249 employees and belonging to the industrial processing sector of the Polish Classification of Activity (PKD) in September to October 2014 by an external market research agency. The response rate was 82.2%. The interviewed persons (questionnaire and CATI technique) were companies' owners, top managers, or managers responsible for the firms' relations with international partners. Collected data were statistically analyzed (SPSS).

In order to test hypothesis H1, the international orientation (international markets vs domestic market) and capabilities of firms' top managers have been assessed with the use of 3-item 5-point semantic-differential scale adapted from the scale of international entrepreneurial orientation elaborated by Knight and Cavusgil (2004).

When testing hypothesis H2, we considered the marketing mix tools known as 4P – the most commonly accepted concepts in marketing management. For industrial firms producing goods of mass consumption, it takes a form of four marketing instruments: product (and brand) management strategy, pricing strategy, distribution (place) strategy, and promotion strategy.

Questions concerning marketing management and all aspects of four marketing mix tools have been included in the questionnaire (2–5 questions per marketing mix tool). The measures have been based on 5-point Likert scales, 5-point semantic-differential scales, a binary scale (for introducing innovations), and a 10-point scale (one of the scales for evaluating product quality).

The hypothesis H3 captures the impact of industry type on the success perception. Industries have been taken into account with binary scales.

The perception of the success by managers has been measured by two statements (on 5-point Likert scales: the lack of success corresponded to values of 1 and 2 on the scales; the success corresponded to values 4 and 5).

17.3 Research Results

Tables 17.1 and 17.2 present the distribution of answers to both statements concerning the perception of success by managers.

Table 17.1 Considering the financial indices (e.g., profitability) for our firm, it can be concluded that our company has been successful

		Frequency	Percent	Valid percent	Cumulative percent
Valid	Definitely not	3	1.3	1.3	1.3
	Rather not	12	5.2	5.2	6.5
	Midpoint	37	15.9	16.0	22.5
	Rather yes	103	44.2	44.6	67.1
	Definitely yes	76	32.6	32.9	100.0
	Total	231	99.1	100.0	
Missing		2	0.9		
Total		233	100.0		

Source: Own calculations

Table 17.2 Considering the situation on the (domestic and foreign) markets, where our firm operates, it can be concluded that our company has been successful in comparison to its competitors

		Frequency	Percent	Valid percent	Cumulative percent
Valid	Definitely not	5	2.1	2.2	2.2
	Rather not	4	1.7	1.7	3.9
	Midpoint	49	21.0	21.4	25.3
	Rather yes	101	43.3	44.1	69.4
	Definitely yes	70	30.0	30.6	100.0
	Total	229	98.3	100.0	
Missing		4	1.7		
Total		233	100.0		

Source: Own calculations

The distribution of answers in the Tables 17.1 and 17.2 indicates that substantial majority of respondents declared that their firms (or the firms employing them) were successful. This creates problems, because the results of regression models apply mainly to successful or "in-between" companies. The correlation between both measures of success, although significant, was quite weak: 0.29 (Pearson), 0.23 (Spearman), and 0.205 (Kendall).

Since managers evaluated the excellence of the marketing mix tools in a similar way, i.e., the answers were skewed to the positive evaluations, this led to the situation of weak correlations and problems with multicollinearity when the regression analysis was applied with all variables. Therefore, the use of the stepwise selection procedure has been adopted.

The use of the stepwise regression is also justified by moderate correlations between different measures of the same explanatory variables. For international orientation (3 items), correlation coefficients ranged between 0.083 and 0.653, at best, and for the characteristics of the marketing mix tools, the two measures of the price strategy, for example, their values, were between 0.469 (Kendall) and 0.539 (Spearman).

Table 17.3 First measure of success: multiple regression model for marketing and management variables

Coefficients[a]					
	Unstandardized coefficients		Standardized coefficients		
Model	B	Std. error	Beta	*t*	Sig.
(constant)	2.483	0.479		5.190	0.000
We compete on the foreign markets primarily through low prices [1:5]	0.119	0.045	0.175	2.627	0.009
Quality of our basic export product compared to competitors [much lower 1/much higher 10]	0.119	0.052	0.150	2.304	0.022
In our company, we consider foreign markets as priority [1] – (...) Polish market as priority [5]	0.104	0.050	0.139	2.091	0.038

Source: Own calculations

[a]Dependent variable: Considering the financial indices (e.g., profitability) for our firm, it can be concluded that our company has been successful [1:5]; *R-square* = 0.059, adjusted *R-square* = 0.046; (without two outliers)

The results of the linear regression model (stepwise selection) for the first measure of success in the first BGs sample are presented in Table 17.3. The first two models (Tables 17.3 and 17.4) have been elaborated without taking into account industrial branches in which firms operated.

Results indicate that there are two ways of successful competition on the market: positive relationships may be seen for both low prices and high quality (H2 confirmed). The correlation between both ways of competing is very weakly negative: −0.101 (Kendall) and −0.124 (Spearman). This indicates that some companies managed to conciliate low prices with high quality (thanks to low labor costs and undervalued domestic currency: the Polish Zloty depreciated from 1€ $\approx$ 3,2 PLZ in August 2008 to the level around 4 PLZ in the following years). Surprisingly, firms declaring emphasis on the Polish market evaluated their success in more positive terms, thus disconfirming H1.

The results of the linear regression model for the second measure of success are presented in Table 17.4 (a "relaxed" signification level of 0.1 has been adopted for all models due to the small size of the sample).

Two out of three items expressing international orientation have been selected into the regression model as uncorrelated with other variables, but they verify the first hypothesis in the contradictory manner: the better the evaluation of managers' competences, the greater the success (the coefficient is negative because high competences are evaluated at the "lower" end of the scale), but looking for new opportunities more often abroad leads to less favorable evaluations of the success

Table 17.4 Second measure of success: multiple regression model for marketing and management variables

Coefficients[a]					
	Unstandardized coefficients		Standardized coefficients		
Model	B	Std. error	Beta	*t*	Sig.
(constant)	2.797	0.447		6.258	0.000
Our firm is superior in terms of marketing planning in comparison to its competitors [1:5]	0.144	0.057	0.174	2.530	0.012
The management is experienced in running business in international markets [1] – the management has no experience in running business in international market [5]	−0.126	0.063	−0.139	−2.010	0.046
In our company, we look for new market opportunities more often abroad rather than domestically [1] – (...) more often domestically rather than abroad [5]	0.107	0.056	0.133	1.926	0.056
We compete on the foreign markets primarily through high quality [1:5]	0.168	0.089	0.132	1.900	0.059
Introducing innovations [0:1]	−0.239	0.131	−0.126	−1.824	0.070
In our firm, the most important issues are cost savings and continuous cost reduction [1] – (...) cost savings and continuous cost reduction are not the most important [5]	0.081	0.045	0.125	1.792	0.075

Source: Own calculations
[a]Dependent variable: Considering the situation on the (domestic and foreign) markets, where our firm operates, it can be concluded that our company has been successful in comparison to its competitors [1:5]; *R-square* = 0.116, adjusted *R-square* = 0.087 (all observations)

(similarly to the situation in the first model). Excellence in marketing planning and the product strategy based on high quality led to more favorable evaluation of the success, confirming H2, but it should also be noted that non-innovative firms evaluated their success better than the non-innovative ones (if one considers

Table 17.5 First measure of success: multiple regression model for marketing and management variables and industries

Coefficients[a]					
	Unstandardized coefficients		Standardized coefficients		
Model	B	Std. error	Beta	*t*	Sig.
(Constant)	2.381	0.458		5.198	0.000
Quality of our basic export product compared to competitors [much lower 1:much higher 10]	0.140	0.049	0.179	2.824	0.005
We compete on the foreign markets primarily through low prices [1:5]	0.129	0.044	0.193	2.952	0.003
In our company we consider foreign markets as priority [1] – (...) Polish market as priority [5]	0.117	0.048	0.158	2.440	0.015
Production of articles from wood. Timber and cork (excluding furniture)	−0.608	0.222	−0.173	−2.735	0.007
Metal production	−0.357	0.161	−0.143	−2.221	0.027
Production of goods from mineral nonmetallic raw materials	−0.664	0.319	−0.132	−2.083	0.038
Production of electric tools and appliances	−0.824	0.419	−0.124	−1.967	0.050

Source: Own calculations
[a]Dependent variable: Considering the financial indices (e.g., profitability) for our firm, it can be concluded that our company has been successful [1:5]; *R-square* = 0.133, adjusted *R-square* = 0.105 (without two outliers)

that innovative product strategy is superior to a non-innovative one, this finding disconfirms H2). The issue of cost-reduction importance in management was supposed to correlate negatively with high-quality product strategy and positively with low price strategy, but it was not the case, because some companies succeeded in applying the two strategies simultaneously. Thus, not putting emphasis on continuous cost reductions appeared as a positive correlate of success independently of the type of marketing strategy.

The explanatory power of the two models is weak. Taking into account the industry type improves somewhat explanatory power of the regression models. The results of the linear regression model for the first measure of success are presented in Table 17.5.

Table 17.6 Second measure of success: multiple regression model for marketing and management variables and industries

Coefficients[a]					
	Unstandardized coefficients		Standardized coefficients		
Model	B	Std. error	Beta	*t*	Sig.
(Constant)	3.772	.295		12,779	.000
Our firm is superior in terms of marketing planning in comparison to its competitors [1:5]	.148	.055	.183	2684	.008
Production of goods from rubber and synthetic materials	−.564	.212	−.182	−2657	.009
In our firm, the most important issues are cost savings and continuous cost reduction [1] – (...) cost savings and continuous cost reduction are not the most important [5]	.102	.043	.159	2334	.021
Metal production	−.340	.174	−.135	−1957	.052
Introducing innovations [0:1]	−.234	.126	−.126	−1851	.066
Our basic export product is sold under our brand [0:1]	.222	.119	.128	1861	.064
The prices of our basic export product are the lowest on the market [1] – the prices of our basic export product are the highest on the market [5]	−.119	.068	−.118	−1740	.083

Source: Own calculations

[a]Dependent variable: Considering the situation on the (domestic and foreign) markets, where our firm operates, it can be concluded that our company has been successful in comparison to its competitors [1:5]; *R-square* = 0.148, adjusted *R-square* = 0.116 (without one outlier)

The results of the linear regression model for the second measure of success are presented in Table 17.6.

The fact that values of all coefficients for industries are below zero indicates that only branches with the least favorable evaluations of the companies' success have been selected to the model and is another evidence of the skewness in the data.

The "rerunning" of the stepwise regression procedure for the second measure of success with industries led, partially, to selection of different variables representing management orientation and marketing mix compared to the model in Table 17.4.

However, the results are coherent in the way that marketing strategies based on high quality (and branded products) and low prices led to the success on the market. None of the international orientation items appears as an uncorrelated explanatory variable for the second measure of success.

Although international orientation of the management team and the excellence in use of the marketing mix variables explained the success perception by managers in the case of Polish small- and medium-sized BGs, the explanatory power of the regression models was weak. Adding industrial branches improved the situation (confirming H3), but still the percentage of explained variance was around 10%. Such results may be due to the composition of the sample: the percentage of non-successful firms was only between 3.9 and 6.5% depending on the success measures.

We should consider that during the non-crisis time of economic activity profitable and successful enterprises are a substantial majority. Taking also into account that respondents from non-successful firms may have lower propensity to participate in a survey (although we do not have evidence that this has happened in our study), it is not surprising that share of successful firms in the sample is so much higher than the share of the non-successful ones.

However, this situation shows the limits of the procedure of the random sampling. Although considered as the best solution for statistical inference and generalization purposes, it should be completed by additional sampling aimed at selecting unsuccessful enterprises (in this case).

17.4 Conclusion

The first hypothesis has been confirmed in the aspect that the level of experience of the top management in international markets was positively correlated with the perceived success. However, when domestic or international orientation was considered, the relationship was contrary to this hypothesis. Although all firms were exporters, those more strongly interested in selling on the domestic market evaluated their success in more favorable terms.

As far as the second hypothesis is concerned, marketing mix tools showed significant and mostly positive relationships with the success perceptions with one exception: non-innovative firms evaluated their success better than the innovative ones. This may be due to psychological factors (higher expectations of success by managers from innovative companies) or to the market-related factors: the costs of both innovations elaboration and their introduction on the market may be burdensome for small- and medium-sized enterprises compared to those which apply strategies based on imitation.

The third hypothesis has been confirmed: evaluation of success by managers was significantly different among analyzed industrial branches and taking them into account improved the success explanation.

The variables used in this research covered international orientation and marketing. Considering also economic environment on both domestic and export markets, financial management, accounting, etc. may lead to improved explanation of firms' success in future research.

References

Altshuler, L., & Tarnovskaya, V. V. (2010). Branding capability of technology born globals. *Journal of Brand Management, 18*(3), 212–227.

Baranowska-Prokop, E., & Sikora, T. (2014). Relationship between competitive strategies and the success perception of Polish born globals. *International Journal of Management and Economics, 43*, 94–113.

Cannone, G., & Ughetto, E. (2015). Internationalization flows of high-tech start-ups: A gravity model. *European Business Review, 27*(1), 60–79.

Cieślik J. (2010). Internacjonalizacja polskich przedsiębiorstw. Aktualne tendencje – implikacje dla polityki gospodarczej. Nauka dla Praktyki i Polityki Gospodarczej 1.

Danik, L., & Kowalik, I. (2013). The studies on born global companies – A review of research methods. *Journal of Economics & Management, 13*, 9–26.

Danik, L., & Kowalik, I. (2015). Success factors and development barriers perceived by the Polish born global companies. Empirical study results. *Journal of East European Management Studies, 20*(3), 360–390.

Duliniec, E. (2013). Ujęcia teoretyczne wczesnej i szybkiej internacjonalizacji przedsiębiorstw. *Gospodarka Narodowa, 1–2*, 31–51.

Fletcher, D. (2000). Learning to think global and act local: Experiences from the small business sector. *Education+Training, 42*(4/5), 211–219.

Gabrielsson, M. (2005). Branding strategies of born globals. *Journal of International Entrepreneurship, 3*(3), 199–222.

Gorynia M (2007) Strategie zagranicznej ekspansji przedsiębiorstw. PWE, Warszawa.

Knight, G., & Cavusgil, S. T. (2004). Innovation, organizational capabilities and born global firm. *Journal of International Business Studies, 35*(2), 15–35.

Kowalik, I., & Baranowska-Prokop, E. (2013). Determinanty powstawania i motywy ekspansji polskich przedsiębiorstw wcześnie umiędzynarodowionych. *Gospodarka Narodowa, 4*, 41–64.

Luostarinen, R., & Gabrielsson, M. (2006). Globalization and global marketing strategies of born globals in SMOPECs. *Thunderbird International Business Review, 48*(6), 773–801.

McDougall, P. P., Oviatt, B. M., & Shrader, R. C. (2003). A comparison of international and domestic new ventures. *Journal of International Entrepreneurship, 1*(1), 59–82.

Przybylska, K. (2010). Born Global – nowa generacja małych polskich przedsiębiorstw. *Gospodarka Narodowa, 7-8*, 63–83.

Rennie, M. W. (1993). Global competitiveness: Born global. *McKinsey Quarterly, 4*, 45–52.

Sleuwaegen, L., & Onkelinx, J. (2010). Internationalization strategy and performance of small and medium size enterprises. *NBB Working Paper, 197*, 1–45.

Chapter 18
CSR Communication on Social Networks

Anna Križanová, Dominika Moravcikova, and Katarina Moravcikova

Abstract Marketing communication is one of the most important tools through which a company communicates with its customers. This instrument has been significantly influenced by globalization, leading to business innovations in the communication process. A number of studies on social responsibility indicate the growing importance of the Internet as part of an integrated communications strategy for corporate social responsibility (CSR). This chapter provides an overview of CSR communication with stakeholders through social networks and the possibilities of using online platforms for the promotion of CSR activities. It also includes a marketing survey on the issue of online tools, showing that social networks are useful for CSR communications with stakeholders. The survey was conducted between October and December 2016 with a sample of 391 customers and 434 companies. The methods used in this chapter include deduction, induction, analysis, and marketing research based on documentation, marketing and CSR communications, and journal articles.

Keywords CSR communication · Social networks · CSR communication on social networks · Marketing survey

18.1 Introduction

The term "socially responsible" is a new concept to many businesses. However, an important part of a holistic marketing campaign is internal marketing based on the principles of ethics and social responsibility. To achieve a higher level of social responsibility, corporate social responsibility (CSR) should be considered in

A. Križanová · D. Moravcikova (✉) · K. Moravcikova
University of Zilina, Faculty of Operations and Economics of Transport and Communications, Zilina, Slovak Republic
e-mail: anna.krizanova@fpedas.uniza.sk; dominika.moravcikova@fpedas.uniza.sk; katarina.moravcikova@fpedas.uniza.sk

N. Tsounis, A. Vlachvei (eds.), *Advances in Panel Data Analysis in Applied Economic Research*, Springer Proceedings in Business and Economics,
https://doi.org/10.1007/978-3-319-70055-7_18

a business's internal factors (e.g., growing expectations and customer needs, goals and ambitions of employees) and external factors (e.g., strict legislation, government pressure, investor interest in social criteria). When implementing the concept of CSR in business activities, regular disclosures should be provided in promotions oriented to customers, investors, employees, and other stakeholders (Musova 2016). Published information about CSR activities should be clear, regular, and truthful.

Companies also should make an extra effort to inform the general public about their efforts toward CSR. To do this, they may need to find new ways to communicate with their stakeholders—not only through the use of brochures, leaflets, magazines, and annual reports, but also through corporate websites and social networks (primarily geared toward the younger generations). The digitization of marketing communication allows businesses with CSR to communicate faster and more effectively with internal and external stakeholders, providing them with timely information and the opportunity for feedback. Various social networks (e.g., Facebook, LinkedIn, YouTube, Google+) may be used as part of the digital platform of marketing communication (Fitzpatrick 2013). Among other things, the development of mobile applications has contributed to the promotion and communication of CSR activities when a company uses so-called augmented reality.

This chapter focuses on a marketing survey conducted about CSR communication on social networks. Specifically, it examines the intensity of use of specific social networks among the population of the Slovak Republic and the purposes for which social networks are used within the concept of CSR.

18.2 CSR Communication

The modern history of corporate social responsibility began to develop in the 1950s, when the idea of CSR fully penetrated the literature for managers. Howard R. Bowen, who wrote the book *Social Responsibilities of the Businessman* in 1953, is considered to be the first theorist on the concept.

Rapid development and the considerably broad scope of this concept have resulted in very high terminological consistency. Currently, there is no globally accepted definition of CSR (Kuldova 2012). H. R. Bowen (2013) defined corporate social responsibility as a commitment of entrepreneurs to establish policies, make decisions, and conduct activities in a manner that meets the objectives and values of our society. According to Kotler and Lee (2005), corporate social responsibility is a commitment to improve the welfare of society through voluntary corporate actions and the contributions of corporate resources.

Corporate social responsibility leads to a broader view of a business and is based on three pillars (i.e., the triple-bottom line): economic, social, and environmental. The economic pillar of CSR is primarily devoted to corporate transparency through good relationships with stakeholders, which has an impact on the economic activity of the enterprise. In this area, investors, owners, customers, suppliers, business partners, and the parties responsible for the company are significant. The social pillar can be divided into two areas: internal and external. The internal area is also called the social enterprise policy, whereas the external area is primarily devoted to philanthropy, altruism, and cooperation with the local community. The social policy and its instruments must establish a partnership between a company and its employees; the company is envisaged as a co-adventurer, providing opportunities for employees to use their active skills, expand their abilities, and achieve the satisfaction of reaching business goals. The external social sphere is focused on philanthropy and cooperation with the local community. Philanthropy is a set of activities and actions that lead to the conscious support of other persons (e.g., individuals, groups, organizations). Issues in the environmental pillar have been attracting increasing attention lately. Corporate management should be aware that a company's environmental responsibilities must be applied within the company itself, as well as in the outside world. Their activities affect the outside world in a variety of ways, including the landscape, noise, resource use, emissions, waste, and traffic flows (Morsing and Schultz 2006).

Communication on CSR initiatives and enforcement is crucial for successful businesses. This type of communication provides information for stakeholders who are interested in buying products from the company, who are considering investing in the company, and who want to support business activities in their community. The aim is to communicate CSR progress in a meaningful way that will have a positive impact on the company and the stakeholders. Through CSR communication, the company may receive additional benefits, such as higher levels of customer satisfaction and loyalty, an improved reputation, brand and product recognition, more motivated and productive workers, improved relationships with the community and public authorities, and better access to finance.

CSR communication strategies should follow these three steps:

1. The company identifies the individuals and groups that should receive communications with a CSR focus. Then, the communication targets for each group of stakeholders can be defined. Possible target groups for CSR communications are employees, customers, local communities, the media, associations, consumers, suppliers, investors, business partners, the general public, trade unions, public authorities, nongovernmental organizations, and so on.
2. The company must decide what it will communicate to the target group of the market in which operates (customers, investors, business partners, suppliers). The company should aim to integrate CSR initiatives into the business and to highlight performance goals. For example, the communications may describe the initiatives related to supporting local suppliers, product quality and safety, fair purchasing, reducing the use of water and energy, sustainable packaging, emission reduction, environmental production, working conditions, and human rights (Corejova and Rostasova 2014). If the target group is the community in which the company operates (e.g., local community, local media, potential employees, nongovernmental organizations), the communications should describe the company's efforts related to health, safety conditions, and investments in the local economy. If the target group is labor business (e.g., employees, trade unions), the communications should focus on describing CSR initiatives related to safety, the

balance between work and personal life, diversity in the workplace, education and professional development, and corporate culture (Tokarcikova et al. 2015).

3. Finally, the company should determine how it will interact with the target groups, how to transmit its message, and what will be the most effective tool for communication. The most effective media and communication channels for communicating CSR vary depending on the audience and communication objectives. The options may include awareness campaigns with brochures on CSR initiatives, advertising, and speeches. The choice of approach is critical to ensure that the message and its medium are in line with the target group and objectives.

A company may use a variety of tools for its CSR communications. CSR initiatives and activities can be communicated to external stakeholders using such tools as a CSR report, advertising, websites, social networking, information packages, brochures, newsletters, mailing lists, point-of-sale materials, training vendors, media, and events (Majerova 2015).

18.3 Social Networks

Companies are now placing greater emphasis on transparency and corporate governance for a number of reasons, including increased responsibility, a shift in social values, and the integrity of global business activities (Corejova and Weick 2009). Thus, a company that is characterized by efficiency and transparency of corporate governance has a higher return on investment. Other benefits may include an improved reputation, attractiveness of the enterprise, greater public trust, the creation of basic internal values within the company, a firm foundation and development of an efficient enterprise culture, and the creation of an internal corporate environment with duplex communication.

Developments in communications and information technology have affected not only marketing communication itself, but also the tools in the marketing mix. Modern communication channels offer the possibility for an individualized customer approach. For example, social media has led to changes from one-way to two-way communication between a business and its customers (Majerova and Zvarikova 2014). Providing information on the CSR activities of a company through the Internet via social networks rather than physical messages also positively reduces a company's financial and environmental impacts.

Internet development has progressed each year with more speed and more versions (i.e., Web 1.0, Web 2.0, and Web 3.0). The most evolutionary version is Web 2.0, which caused radical changes for CSR, with a transition from the classical conception of CSR 1.0 (corporate social responsibility) to an integrated approach as CSR 2.0 (sustainability and responsibility in business) (Cervinschi and Butucea 2010). The transformation of the Internet through social networking is a suitable metaphor for the changes that the concept of CSR is currently undergoing (Visser 2012). Table 18.1 shows the formation of strong relationships, two-way

Table 18.1 Web 2.0 and the concept of CSR 2.0

WEB 2.0	CSR 2.0
Defined password, "collective intelligence", "cooperation network"	Defining passwords, "global goals", and "innovative partnerships"
Tools include social media	Tools include transparency in providing information on the "new wave" of social entrepreneurship
A new philosophy or way of understanding the world by differentials	Changes in the attitude of the individual to the diverse and unique from the shared

Source Visser 2012. CSR 2.0: Reinventing Corporate Social Responsibility for the 21st Century. Available at http://www.managementexchange.com/hack/csr-20-reinventing-corporatesocial-responsibility-21st-century. Accessed 3 March 2017

communication, innovation, and other characteristics in Web 2.0 and the concept of CSR 2.0.

According to various experts, there are four main trends in online news and CSR communications:

- Easy access to information on CSR and flexibility of online content
- Reporting on progress and performance updates related to CSR
- Effective use of the multimedia features in social networking
- Easy-to-use feedback from CSR communication tools (Kumar 2014).

Currently, many companies issue CSR reports as a version of the traditional printed report that is shared on the company's website and social media profiles. For example, the BASF website allows a user to access its report on corporate social responsibility in multiple formats (e.g., PDF, Excel) or view an online version that uses innovative interactive graphical tools. Multimedia content of videos, podcasts, presentations, animations, and other innovative formats provide the user with a better understanding of the complex issues of CSR communication. Businesses promote their activities of an economic, social, and environmental nature not only through annual CSR reports, but also by promotion on their websites or social networks (Facebook, Twitter, YouTube, Google+, LinkedIn, etc.). Information on the company's social and corporate responsibility is extremely important for cementing relationships between internal and external stakeholders.

The socially responsible dissemination of information via social networking affects the way that a company can communicate with many customers, personally or professionally (Moxley 2014). Communication channels formed by digital platforms have a positive impact on a business, providing an opportunity to influence the planning of current and future business activities. According to a global statistical database (Nielsen 2016), social networks have millions of active users each month (Facebook: 1.15 million, Google+: 359 million, Twitter: 215 million, Instagram: 150 million). This constitutes a business opportunity to create a promotional platform and develop communication channels.

18.3.1 Types of Social Networks and Their Use

The complex virtual social organism of the Internet is now becoming a great clone of traditional social structures. One of the typical products of this development is the social network. Despite that there is no single universal definition of this concept, social networks can be seen as a set of relationships associated with different positions, statuses, and particularly social roles, or as a metaphorical expression of the social structure (i.e., a description of a number of social units together with the social relationships that exist between them). In other words, a social network is a structure of nodes that represent either individuals, groups, or organizations. These nodes are connected by mutual bonds. This bond is not necessarily friendship or partnership: it can also be based on shared ideas, hobbies, sexual relations, or hatred. It follows that the social network (community) is a connected group of people who interact with each other. In real life, the social network can be, for example, members of a school class, computer ring, sports club, an aggregation of gardeners, or a street gang. In the strict sense, it is characterized as a social networking service on the Internet, allowing registered users to create personal or public profiles, communicate with each other, share information (or photos and videos), and more (Visser 2012).

It is incorrect to associate the concept of social networking only with Facebook. Social networks vary in terms of the functions they offer to their user base. Based on the purpose of their use, social networks can be classified as follows:

- Profile-focused: Organized around user profiles (e.g., Facebook, MySpace)
- Content-based: At the heart is content, with the user profile having a secondary role (e.g., YouTube video sharing)
- Virtual-based: An online virtual world where an individual's communication is represented by an avatar (e.g., Second Life)
- Microblogging networks: The aim is to publish short messages to other users (e.g., Twitter)
- "White-label": A network aimed at creating its own versions of social networking as a mini-community (e.g., PeopleAggregator) (Majerova and Zvarikova 2013).

The following sections describe the most commonly used social networks in the Slovak Republic.

18.3.1.1 Facebook

Facebook is the most popular and most visited social networking site in nearly every country. Facebook users can create profiles, add friends, browse the profiles of other users of Facebook, write different statuses, and share content with others (e.g., photographs, videos, interests). Facebook users can organize themselves into various interest groups to express their views, play simple games, and use applications. Facebook also allows users to maintain contact with friends by sending private messages(Majerova and Zvarikova 2013). Facebook has become very popular not only for individuals but also for businesses. Companies are creating sites, maintaining contact with their customers, taking orders for their goods, and using Facebook as a marketing tool.

18.3.1.2 YouTube

In most countries, YouTube is the second most-visited social network (although it is the most-visited in Japan). YouTube is used primarily to share and watch videos. Users can create profiles, add favorite videos, and make video comments. YouTube also recommends videos based on a user's viewing history (Svec et al. 2015). YouTube is the largest video social network today. It is possible to find a massive number of videos on various topics, whether professional, entertainment, musical, or otherwise. Many companies also use YouTube to distribute promotional videos.

18.3.1.3 LinkedIn

LinkedIn is different from other social networking sites because its primary purpose is not to provide entertainment. Rather, a user on LinkedIn shares technical information and details about his or her professional life. LinkedIn users also create profiles, which provide a lot of information about their work experience, skills, education, and the like (Velsic 2012). LinkedIn is used to maintain and establish relationships with colleagues and classmates or between employees and employers. LinkedIn users can also access potential employers and may receive invitations for job interviews from employment agencies looking for workers for their clients (Mura and Sleziak 2015).

18.3.1.4 Twitter

Twitter is said to be an SMS Internet gateway, with postings limited to 140 characters. Videos and photos may also be attached to these text messages, but only by reference. On Twitter, users also establish profiles, follow other users, and monitor others' short statuses. Twitter is a useful tool for obtaining the latest information or tips on a variety of attractions.

18.3.1.5 Instagram

Instagram is public photo blog to which users post messages from their mobile phone. Instagram was once the domain of the iPhone. However, after its purchase by Facebook, it also became part of Android and Windows phones. Via the Instagram app on a mobile phone or tablet, the user pulls up a photo or short video, edits it using one of the available visual filters, and then uploads it to his or her profile. Because it is easy to use and has photo editing capabilities, Instagram has gained favor with tens of millions of people around the world, including musicians, actors, and other pop culture personalities.

18.3.1.6 Google+

Google+ is similar to Facebook, but it does not work on the same principles. Instead of adding known friends on Google+, a user is added to the circles that define a particular group of people (e.g., family, close friends, acquaintances). The aim of Google+ is to be in touch with almost everyone, no matter how well you know them. The sharing of content can then be set according to the group who you wish to view it—specifically the choice of only one circle or a number of them (Majerova 2015).

Google+ is built on the very broad user base of Google. If an individual has a Gmail or YouTube account, then he or she automatically has a Google + profile and everything in it is centralized. If the user has a smartphone with an Android operating system and is using Instant backup, then all photos and videos are automatically backed up right to his or her Google+ account, with the ability to share them with the user's circles. Just as on Facebook, a user can add photos, videos, events, news, fan groups, and celebrities alike. Nevertheless, Google+ does not enjoy the great popularity of its competitor Facebook, possibly because of the apparent lack of transparency, fragmentation of the social network, and lack of active users.

Despite the great diversity and virtually unlimited regional availability of social networks in the Slovak Republic, the dominant social network is Facebook. As shown in Chart 18.1, Facebook is used by 49% of the Slovak population older than 14 years and 70% of Internet users overall. Second place belongs to Slovakian

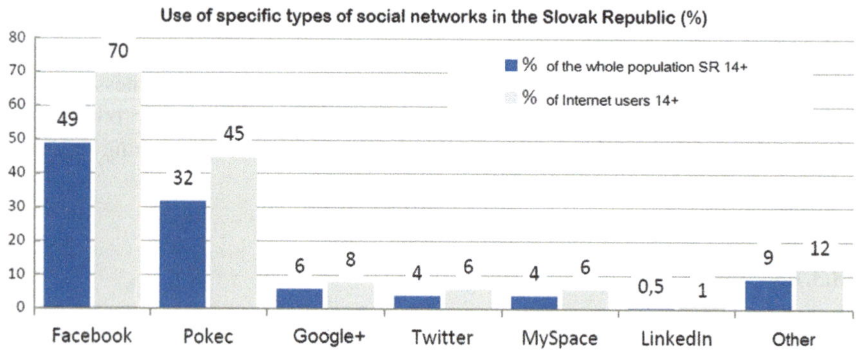

Chart 18.1 Use of specific types of social networks in the Slovak Republic (Source: Own research)

Network Chat (an Azet company), which is used by approximately one-third of the population and 45% of Internet users. Other social networks rank much lower, with a relatively large gap after the leading two sites. For example, Google+ is used by only 6% of the population, Twitter by 4%, MySpace by 4%, and LinkedIn by 0.5% of the population. Approximately 10% of respondents used other types of networks or social media, such as Badoo, YouTube, and Instagram. This survey was conducted by the Department of Economics at the University of Zilina between March and April 2016 with a sample of 286 Slovakian customer. The survey was realized electronically thrugh which e-mail and social network Facebook.

18.4 CSR Communications on Social Networks in Slovakia

The easiest way to provide information on CSR initiatives is to publish it on corporate websites or social networks. This is an economical way to provide the latest information on CSR issues, including successes and areas for improvement. The involvement of current and potential customers, employees, and business partners in CSR initiatives and performance through social networking is not only cheap but also effective. Social networking sites such as Facebook, Twitter, and Instagram enable an instant connection with a business's so-called followers by sharing materials relating to CSR; feedback can also be received more quickly and cheaply than through any other media. A lengthy extensive report may be of interest to some people, but a short online summary of the CSR performance of a company can provide the information required by most customers.

The Department of Economics, University of Zilina conducted a marketing survey aimed at consumers and businesses in Slovakia between October and December 2016. The survey titled "Perceptions of CSR and its communication on the part of customers" included 391 respondents and the survey titled "Perceptions of CSR and its communication on the part of enterprises" involved 434 respondents.

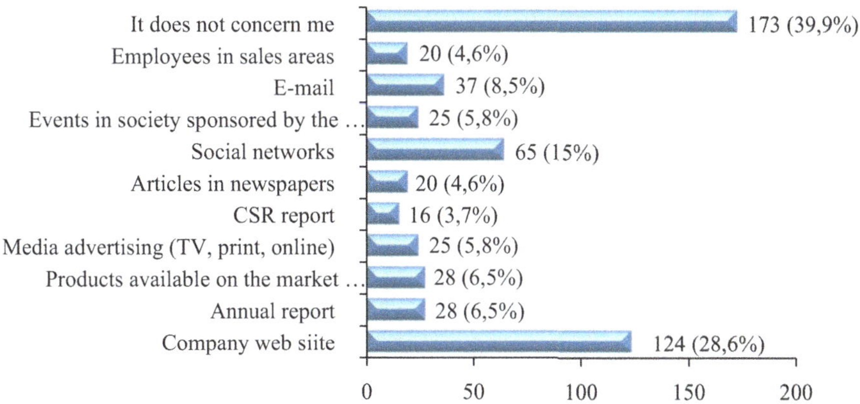

Chart 18.2 Preferred CSR communication channels for Slovakian businesses (Source: Own research)

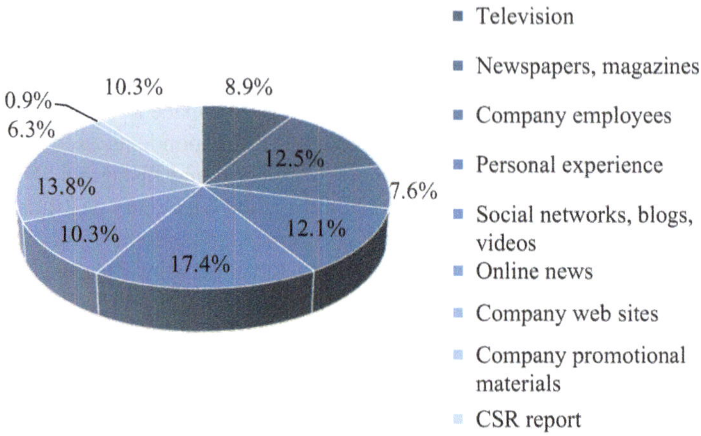

Chart 18.3 CSR communication tools through which Slovak businesses communicate with their customers

We found that companies provided information about their CSR initiatives mainly through corporate websites (18.7%) and social networks (14.7%) (Chart 18.2). Businesses that were considering expansion or change of instruments particularly preferred to provide information on CSR activities through a website (28.6%) or social networks (15%), followed by email (8.5%) and company-sponsored enterprises (5.8%). These results indicate that social networks play an important role in communication about CSR initiatives and projects with customers.

The survey also indicated how customers prefer to obtain information about CSR from companies. Most customers obtain information about a company's CSR activities from social networks (17.4%), followed by corporate websites (13.8%) and personal experience (12.1%) (Chart 18.3). As a tool for CSR communication, social networks are preferred by customers younger than 40 years. Older age groups preferred newspapers, magazines, and television (Table 18.2).

For receiving information about CSR activities and the projects a company, customers mostly preferred an Internet portal (33%), the actual product and its packaging (29.9%), and social networks, namely Facebook (17%) (Chart 18.4). Thus, social networks are very important communication tools because customers can directly acquire CSR information from the tool.

18.5 Conclusion

Communications about CSR are very important in today's world. Businesses are increasingly accountable to consumers and society, who support their CSR efforts. However, it is necessary for a business to choose the appropriate tools to provide information about CSR activities and projects. Enterprises in Slovakia primarily

Table 18.2 Preferred communication tools by age

Tool	Age				Total
	≤29 years	30–39 years	40–49 years	50–59 years	
CSR report	0	2	0	0	2
Newspapers, magazines	14	4	6	4	28
Company web sites	19	9	1	2	31
Not interested in this information	17	3	2	1	23
Online news	17	4	0	2	23
Personal experience	12	8	4	3	27
Company promotional materials	9	2	3	0	14
Social networks, blogs, videos	21	13	2	3	39
Television	8	4	7	1	20
Company employees	8	4	5	0	17
Total	125	53	30	16	224

Source: Own research

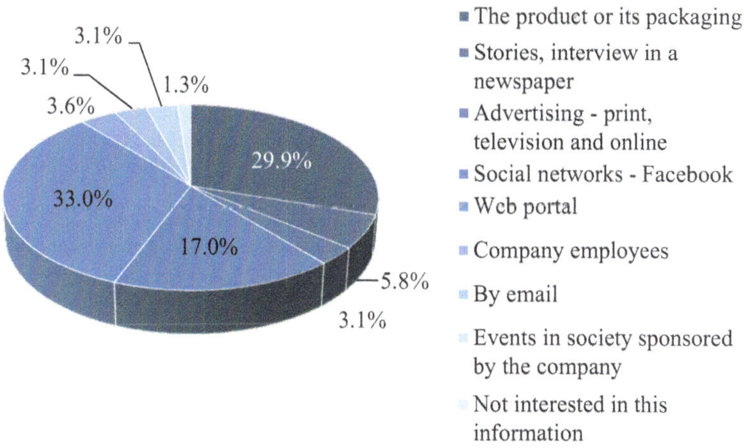

Chart 18.4 Preferred CSR communication tools by Slovakian customers

use websites and social networks to inform external stakeholders about CSR activities. Businesses that want to change or expand CSR communications tools should investigate their website and social network options. Social networks rank among the three most preferred tools from which customers would like to receive CSR information. Thus, in the context of CSR communications, businesses should continue to focus on or expand their use of specific social networks, such as Facebook, to provide information to their customers in the future.

Acknowledgements This chapter was supported by a scientific grant from Vega (n. 1/0024/15).

References

Bowen, H. R. (2013). *Social responsibilities of the businessman*. New York: Harper.

Cervinschi, C. L., & Butucea, D. (2010). Integration of web technologies in software applications. Is web 2.0 a solution? In: Database Systems Journal, vol 1. http://www.dbjournal.ro/archive/2/5_Cervinschi_Butucea.pdf. Accessed 15 Feb 2017.

Corejova, T., & Rostasova, M. (2014, June). Ethical aspects of online advertising in the Slovak Republic. In: *VII. World congress on communication and arts* (pp. 215–224) Salvador.

Čorejová, T., & Weick, L. (2009, October). B2B Market Research in the context of regional disparities. In: *3rd Central European Conference in Regional Science*, (p. 160–167) Kosice.

Fitzpatrick, W.-J. (2013). The Ages and Stages of CSR. http://www.honeycomb-co.com/the-ages-and-stages-of-csr/. Accessed 02 March 2017.

Kotler, P., & Lee, N. (2005). *Corporate social responsibility*. USA: Wiley.

Kuldova, L. (2012). *Společenská odpovědnost firem: etické podnikání a sociální odpovědnost v praxi*. Kanina: OPS.

Kumar, A. (2014). Digital influence – Social media as an enabler of CSR communication https://www.linkedin.com/today/post/article/20140806074728-243816305-digital-influence-social-media-as-an-enabler-of-csr-communication. Accessed 08 March 2017.

Majerova, J. (2015, October). E-marketing as a promising part of the concept of CSR and its specific features of pricing policy in a global context. In: *15th International scientific conference on globalization and its socio-economic consequences* (pp. 393–399) EDIS: Žilinská univerzita, Rajecke Teplice, Slovakia.

Majerova, J., & Zvarikova, K. (2013, November). Social networks and their place in the process of brand building and management. In: Cyril, S.S & Methodius *International scientific Conference on Marketing Identity, University* (pp. 71–88) Smolenice, Marketing Identity .

Majerova, J., & Zvaríkova, K. (2014, October). New trends In marketing communication of car brands – results of a survey of consumer's perception in Slovak Republic. In: *18th International Conference on Transport Means, Kaunas. Transport Means – Proceedings of the International Conference Kaunas University* (pp. 145–148). Lithuana.

Morsing, M., & Schultz, M. (2006). Corporate social responsibility communication: Stakeholder information, response and involvement strategies. *Business Ethics: A European Review, 15*. Blackwell Publishing, 323–338.

Moxley, A. (2014). Corporate Social Responsibility for the Digital Age http://www.huffingtonpost.co.uk/adrian-moxley/corporate-social-responsibility_b_4567034. Accessed 16 March 2017.

Mura, L., & Sleziak, J., (2015). Innovation and entrepreneurship network. In: *5thCERS Central European Conference in Regional Science* (p. 643–651).

Mussova, Z. (2016). Spoločenská zodpovednosť v marektingových aktivitách podnikov. In: *Ekonomicko-manažérske spectrum* (6):12–23.

Nielsen, A. C. (2016). Global Faces and Networking Places: Nielsen Report on Social Networking's New Global Fotoprint. http://www.gt.nielsen.com/content/dam/corporate/us/en/reportsdownloads/Global%20Faces%20and%20Networked%20PlacesA%20Nielsen%20Report%20on%20Social%20Networkings%20New%20Global%20Footprint.pdf. Accessed 15 March 2017.

Svec M, Olsovská A, Mura L (2015, November). Protection of an "Average Consumer" in the Digital Society – European Context. In: *International Scientific Conference on Marketing Identity* (pp. 273–282). Marketing Identity.

Tokarcikova, E., Bartošová, V. & Durisova, M. (2015, November) .Corporate social responsibility of public administrations employees. In: *Innovation Vision 2020: from regional development sustainability to global economic growth, Marketing Identity* (pp. 1437–1445).

Velsic, M. (2012). Sociálne siete na Slovensku. http://www.ivo.sk/6749/sk/studie/socialne-siete-na-slovensku. Accessed 16 March 2017.

Visser, W. (2012). CSR 2.0: Reinventing Corporate Social Responsibility for the 21st Century. http://www.managementexchange.com/hack/csr-20-reinventingcorporate-social-responsibility-21st-century. Accessed 7 March 2017.

Chapter 19
Tax Bonus Versus Tax Allowance in Slovak and Czech Republic

Martina Paliderova and Alzbeta Bielikova

Abstract This article analyses the impact of tax bonus in Slovakia and tax allowance in Czech Republic on a taxpayer. It outlines the circumstances that are essential to be entitled for tax bonus/allowance. Using illustrative examples, an impact of tax bonus on a taxpayer in Slovak Republic (SR) is analysed in comparison with an impact of tax allowance on a taxpayer in Czech Republic (CR).

19.1 Tax Bonus in Slovak Republic

Since 2004 the tax system of Slovak Republic has got a new component – child tax bonus. Since that year, the tax exemption per dependent child, which is deducted from the tax base of the physical entities' income, has not been applied. In contrast, tax bonus is applied directly to the calculated tax of a taxpayer so that the income tax is deducted by the tax bonus. Tax bonus is defined as the tax benefit measure that a taxpayer is entitled to in case a common household is shared with a child maintained by the taxpayer. Since 2017 taxpayers have to fulfil the following conditions to be entitled to tax bonus:

1. They must declare taxable income from dependent activity or enterprise income, or other self-employment income, of value at least sixfold to the minimal income that is 2610 €.
2. Self-employed persons claim tax bonus once a year in the tax return form filled in the next calendar year by March 31. Taxable income under § 6 of Income Tax Act shall be equal to not less than six times the minimum wage, and the self-employed person shall book a tax base on such income. The entitlement to tax

M. Paliderova (✉) · A. Bielikova
University of Zilina, Faculty of Operation and Enonomics of Transport and Communication, Department of Economics, Zilina, Slovak Republic
e-mail: martina.paliderova@fpedas.uniza.sk; alzbeta.bielikova@fpedas.uniza.sk

N. Tsounis, A. Vlachvei (eds.), *Advances in Panel Data Analysis in Applied Economic Research*, Springer Proceedings in Business and Economics,
https://doi.org/10.1007/978-3-319-70055-7_19

bonus lapses in case a self-employed person booked a tax loss, even if his/her taxable income is equal to not less than six times the minimum wage.
3. A taxpayer is entitled to tax bonus with respect to each maintained child sharing a common household with the taxpayer. If more taxable parties share common household, only one of them is entitled to tax bonus. If the criteria for tax bonus entitlement are satisfied by more taxable parties and unless they agree otherwise, tax bonus shall be claimed under § 33 Section 4 in the following order: mother, father and other beneficiaries (Paliderová 2015).
4. If a taxpayer maintains his/her child only during one or more calendar months in the taxable period, the taxpayer may deduct income tax or tax advances for the amount equal to tax bonus for each calendar month in which eligibility for tax bonus were met (Harumová 2006).
5. A taxpayer is eligible for tax bonus in the calendar month in which:
   - The child was born if a copy of birth certificate is provided.
   - Systematic studies of the child for the future profession began and if confirmation of school attendance is provided.
   - The child was adopted or accepted for a foster care under decision of the competent authority (Schultzová 2011).
6. Tax bonus may be claimed up to the amount of the tax calculated for the relevant taxable period pursuant to the Income Tax Act. If the amount of the tax calculated for the relevant taxable period is lower than the tax bonus claimed by the taxpayer, the taxpayer filing the tax return shall ask the tax administration having jurisdiction to pay the difference between the tax bonus and the tax calculated for the relevant taxable period, while as regards the refund of the difference, the tax administration shall proceed as if there were a tax overpayment.
7. Since 2009, a taxpayer with a limited tax liability is also eligible for tax bonus on the assumption that difference of income on territory of Slovak Republic to his total income during the given period of taxation reaches at least 90% (Bieliková 2010).
8. Tax bonus eligibility shall be always judged at the beginning of relevant calendar month (Paliderová 2015).

Tax bonus in SR was not being changed from 2014. From 2015, tax bonus was being adjusted, always at the beginning of the year, by the coefficient that is equal to the living wage increment on the date of July 1 of the prior year. The aftermost living wage increment was on July 1, 2013, since that tax bonus has not been changed.

19.1.1 Tax Bonus in Practice Realized Within the Methodology of Slovak Republic

1. Calculation of tax liability from employee's monthly salary
Gross salary
13.4% Social and health insurance contributions paid by an employee
316.94 € Monthly non-taxable portion of tax base
= *Tax base of income tax from dependent activity*
Advance tax = 19% rate x tax base
2. Calculation of employee's net monthly salary
Gross salary
13.4% Social and health insurance
19% The advance tax, from dependent activity income, reduced by tax bonus
= *Total net salary* (Bartošová, Paliderová, 2014)

Pension insurance It is one of five types of the social insurance that have been established by Act No 461/2003 Coll. on Social Insurance effective as of January 2004. These are the following two subsystems within pension insurance:

- *Old-age insurance* – the insurance to secure an income in old age and in case of death. It supplies old-age, early old-age, widow's, widower's and orphan's pensions.
- *Invalidity pension* – the insurance in case of the reduction of ability to perform the gainful activity due to a long-term unfavourable health condition of the insuree and in the case of death. It supplies invalidity, widow's, widower's and orphan's pensions.

Sickness insurance It is the insurance in case of the loss or reduction of income from gainful activity and to secure an income due to a temporal unfavourable health condition and pregnancy or maternity. The benefit types include the following: sickness, maternity, nursing and equalization benefits.

Unemployment insurance It is the insurance in case of income loss due to unemployment and to secure the income due to unemployment. The insuree is entitled to the unemployment allowance.

Guarantee Insurance It is the insurance in case of the employer's insolvency to satisfy employees' entitlements. It also serves for provision of the old-age pension insurance contributions that have not been paid by the employer to the old-age pension insurance fund.

Accident insurance It is the insurance of an employer that serves to guarantee him against economical load in the case of his responsibility against working injury and occupational disease of his employee. Such employer's responsibility emerges from the Labour Code (www.socpoist.sk).

19.1.2 Implementation of Tax Bonus in Net Salary Computation in SR

We present implementation of monthly tax bonus in SR in the following examples.

Example no 1
A taxpayer had gross salary of 1800 € in January 2017. He/she has four children, whom monthly tax bonus is claimed for.
1. Calculation of tax liability from employee's monthly salary in € (January 2017)

Gross salary		1800,00 €
13.4%	Social and health insurance	– 241,20 €
316.94 €	Monthly non-taxable portion of tax base	– 316,94 €
= Tax base of income tax from dependent activity		*1241,86 €*
Advance tax = 19% rate x tax base		*235,95 €*
Tax bonus		*85,64 €*

2. Calculation of employee's net monthly salary

Gross salary		*1800,00 €*
13.4%	Social and health insurance	– 241,20 €
19%	Advance tax reduced by tax bonus	– 150,31 €
= Total net salary		*1408,49 €*

Net salary of the taxpayer is 1408,49 € in January 2017

Example no 2
A taxpayer had gross salary of 850 € in January 2017. He/she has four children, whom monthly tax bonus is claimed for.
1. Calculation of tax liability from employee's monthly salary in € (January 2017)

Gross salary		850,00 €
13.4%	Social and health insurance contributions paid by an employee	– 113,90 €
316.94 €	Monthly non-taxable amount of tax base	– 316,94 €
= Tax base of income tax from dependent activity		*419,16 €*
Advance tax = 19% rate x tax base		*79,64 €*
Tax bonus		*85,64 €*

2. Calculation of employee's net monthly salary

Gross salary		*850,00 €*
13.4%	Social and health insurance	– 113,90 €
19%	The advance tax reduced by tax bonus	+ 6,00 €
= Total net salary		*742,10 €*

Net salary of the taxpayer is 742,10 € in January 2017

19.2 Tax Allowance in Czech Republic

Tax allowance It means childcare tax relief on the child that shares common living together with the taxpayer.

Criteria for Tax Allowance Eligibility for Child in Czech Republic
According to § 35c subsection 1 of the Income Tax Act 586/1992 Coll. in 2007, a taxpayer is eligible to tax allowance on maintained child depending upon a number of children sharing common household together with the taxpayer, as follows:

- 13,404 CZK per year for the first child
- 17,004 CZK for the second child
- 20,604 CZK for the third and every subsequent child

If more dependent children are living in a common household, they are judged jointly for tax allowance. If a taxpayer maintains his/her child only during one or more calendar months in the taxable period, the taxpayer may apply tax deduction of 1/12 per month. A taxpayer may claim tax bonus in the calendar month in which the child was born, systematic studies of the child for the future profession began, or the child was adopted or accepted for a foster care under decision of the competent authority (Pšenková 2016).

Tax allowance for a dependent child with disability ZTP/P is doubled. A taxpayer may apply for yearly tax allowance, if he/she declares income equalling to at least sixfold of the minimum wage, i.e. 66,000 CZK, and if tax bonus is at least 100 CZK per year (but maximally up to 60,300 CZK). A taxpayer may apply for the monthly tax allowance if lump sum of his/her monthly incomes from dependent activity reaches at least a half of the minimum wage, i.e. 5500 CZK, and if the monthly tax allowance is minimally 50 CZK per month (but maximally 5025 CZK). If a taxpayer claims tax allowance of a greater amount than the calculated tax liability for given taxation period, the resulting difference is named the *tax bonus*.

Dependent children can be judged jointly for tax allowance whereby the dependent child is denoted as own child, adopted child, child in foster care or grandchild of a spouse if his/her parents do not have the incomes, for which tax allowance can be applied (Široký 2013). Evolution of yearly and monthly tax allowance per dependent child in Czech Republic in the period 2008–2012 is shown in Table 19.1.

Table 19.1 Trend in child tax allowance in Czech Republic in the period 2008–2012

	Tax allowance per child (in CZK)	
Year	Per year	Per month
2012	13,404	1117
2011	11,604	967
2010	11,604	967
2009	11,604	967
2008	10,680	890

Source: After the Income Tax Act No. 586/1992 Coll

Table 19.2 Trend in tax allowance according to number of children in Czech Republic

	Child allowance per year (in CZK)				
No. of children	2013	2014	2015	2016	2017
Deduction for the first child	13,404	13,404	13,404	13,404	13,404
Deduction for the second child	13,404	13,404	15,804	17,004	19,404
Deduction for the third child	13,404	13,404	17,004	20,604	24,204
First child – holder of ZŤP/P	26,808	26,808	26,808	26,808	26,808
Second child – holder of ZŤP/P	26,808	26,808	31,608	34,008	34,008
Third child – holder of ZŤP/P	26,808	26,808	34,008	41,208	41,208

Source: After the Income Tax Act No. 586/1992 Coll

Table 19.3 Tax allowance per dependent child in CR, entered into force on April 1, 2017

No. of children	CZK per year	CZK per month
Deduction for the first child	13,404	1117
Deduction for the second child	17,004	1417
Deduction for the second child	20,604	1717
First child – holder of ZŤP/P	26,808	2234
Second child – holder of ZŤP/P	34,008	2834
Third child – holder of ZŤP/P	41,208	3434

Source: After amendments of Income Tax Act No. 586/1992 Coll

During years 2008–2012, tax allowance was independent to the number of dependent children in a common household, and the tax deduction was the same for every child. Growth of tax allowance in this period was 2724 CZK. Since 2013 onwards, a child with disability ZTP/P has been also entitled to tax allowance. In addition, since 2015 tax allowance has been depended to the number of maintained children as shown in Table 19.2.

During 2012–2017, tax allowance in Czech Republic (in terms of deduction for the first child) was not changing, but tax allowance for the second and next children has been increasing since 2015. Growth of 2400 CZK and 3600 CZK has been recorded for the second child and third and next child allowance, respectively.

Tax allowance per dependent child in Czech Republic, entered into force on April 1, 2017, is shown in Table 19.3.

19.2.1 Implementation of Tax Allowance in Net Salary Computation in Czech Republic

1. Calculation of employee's advance tax

Gross salary

+ 25% Social insurance contributions paid by an employer

+ 9% Health insurance contributions paid by an employer

Super gross salary = tax base

Rounded tax base to 100 CZK up

Advance tax = tax base * 15% tax rate

Tax allowance (non-taxable portion of tax base)

Tax relief for a maintained child ("tax bonus")

= Advance tax on personal income or tax bonus

2. Calculation of tax liability from employee's monthly salary

Gross salary (including basic salary, incentive pay, bonuses, remunerations, extra pay)

6.5% Social insurance contributions paid by an employee

4.5% Health insurance contributions paid by an employee

Advance tax on personal income (+ tax bonus for a maintained child)

=Monthly net salary of employee (*Pšenková*2016)

Super gross salary represents tax base increased by social and health insurance contributions paid by an employee and employer. The principle of super gross salary means that the tax base for income tax from dependent activity is calculated as a sum of gross salary and the contributions an employer is obliged to pay for social and health insurance of an employee (Pšenková 2016).

19.2.2 Practical Examples on Tax Allowance Implementation to Net Salary Computation in Czech Republic

Example no 3
Gross salary of a taxpayer was 48,638 CZK (i.e. 1800 €) in January 2017. The taxpayer has four children, for whom he/she applies child tax allowance.

1. Calculation of employee's advance tax

Gross salary		48,638 CZK
25%	Social insurance contributions	+12,160 CZK
9%	Health insurance contributions	+4377 CZK
Tax base (super gross salary)		*65,175 CZK*
Rounded tax base to 100 CZK up		*65,200 CZK*
Advance tax = tax base x 15% tax rate		9780 CZK (15% of tax base)
Basic personal allowance		– 2070 CZK (1/12 of 24,840 CZK)
Child allowance (for four children)		– 5968 CZK [1/12 of (13,404 + 17,004 + 2x20604)]
= Advance tax on personal income		*1742 CZK*
Entitlement to tax bonus for a maintained child		*0 CZK*

2. Calculation of tax liability from an employee's monthly salary

Gross salary		*48,638 CZK*
6.5%	Social insurance contributions	– 3162 CZK
4.5%	Health insurance contributions	– 2189 CZK
– Advance tax		– 1742 CZK
= Monthly net salary of employee		*41,545 CZK*

We compare the taxation in Slovakia and Czech Republic on the same scenario. As it is shown in the examples above, monthly net salary of a taxpayer is 1408,49 € within the methodology of Slovak Republic, while the monthly net salary of a taxpayer with the same gross salary and the same number of children is 41,545 CZK, that is, 1537,50 €, according to the methodology valid in Czech Republic. It means net salary increment of 129,01 € in Czech Republic, due to the amount of child allowance as well as due to lower taxation and insurance contributions.

Example no 4
Gross salary of a taxpayer was 22,968 CZK (i.e. 850 €) in January 2017. The taxpayer has four children, for whom he/she applies child tax allowance.
1. Calculation of an employee's advance tax

Gross salary		22,968 CZK
25%	Social insurance contributions	+5742 CZK
9%	Health insurance contributions	+2068 CZK
Tax base (super gross salary)		*30,778 CZK*
Rounded tax base to 100 CZK up		*30,800 CZK*
Advance tax = tax base x 15% tax rate		4620 CZK (15% of tax base)
Basic personal allowance		– 2070 CZK (1/12 z 24,840 CZK)
Child allowance (for four children)		– 5968 CZK [1/12 of (13,404 + 17,004 + 2x20604)]
= *Advance tax on personal income*		*0 CZK*
Tax bonus		*3418 CZK*

2. Calculation of a tax liability from an employee's monthly salary

Gross salary		*22,968 CZK*
6.5%	Social insurance contributions	– 1493 CZK
4.5%	Health insurance contributions	– 1034 CZK
Tax bonus		+ 3418 CZK
= *Monthly net salary employee*		*23,859 CZK*

In examples 2 and 4, we apply other scenarios to compare the taxation in Slovakia and Czech Republic. As it is shown in examples 2 and 4, monthly net salary of a taxpayer is 742,10 € within the methodology of Slovak Republic, while the monthly net salary of the taxpayer with the same gross salary and the same number of children is 23,859 CZK, that is, 882,97 €, according to the methodology valid in Czech Republic. It means net salary increment of 140,87 € in Czech Republic.

19.3 Conclusion

Tax bonus in Slovakia is relevant to tax allowance in Czech Republic. On the other side, the term "tax bonus" in Czech Republic is equal to the term "tax overpaid" in Slovakia. As it is seen from the illustrative examples, Czech income tax law is obviously more socially oriented, and it makes more effort to support families with a greater number of children and eventually to support families with handicapped children, while Slovak income tax law does not give stress upon these matters. The idea of optimal taxation is still actual in states with highly developed economy. Thus, the process of optimal taxation of incomes has to adapt to changing conditions within the country as well as demography trends. However the Czech taxation system should better react to these objectives. A good and well-established taxation system should fulfil demands on fair and reasonable allocation of tax load as well as on effective utilization of resources for given macroeconomic goals and undemanding administration.

References

Bartošová, V., & Paliderová, M. (2014). *Účtovníctvo podnikateľov I, Podvojné účtovníctvo*. Žilina: EDIS – Žilina University Publishers.

Bieliková, A., & Štofková, K. (2010). *Dane v teórii a praxi*. Žilina: EDIS – Žilina University Publishers.

Harumová, A. & Kubátová, K. (2014). *Dane podnikateľských subjektov*. In: Žilina, Poradca podnikateľa 2006.

Paliderová, M. (2015). *Účtovníctvo podnikateľov II, Jednoduché účtovníctvo*. Žilina: EDIS – Žilina University Publishers.

Pšenková, Y. (2016). *Comparison of tax burden of incomes from the dependent activity of employees in the Czech Republic and Slovak Republic in the context of globalization trends*. In: 16th International Scientific Conference "Globalization and its socio-economic consequences", Slovak Republic.

Schultzová, A. (2011). In: *Daňovníctvo*. Bratislava, Iura Edition.

Široký, J. (2013). In: *Dane v Evropské unii*. Prague 2013.

Chapter 20
The Application of Nonparametric Methods in Nonprofit Sector

Jaroslav Mazanec and Alzbeta Bielikova

Abstract This article deals with the funding of nonprofit organizations with emphasis on so-called tax assignation in the Slovak Republic. The aim of this paper is to identify the correlation between corporate tax of selected companies and contributions from tax assignation for corporate nonprofit organizations that were established by these enterprises. The sample includes 67 corporate nonprofit organizations. Information for quantification is gathered from various sources, i.e. financial administration of the Slovak Republic, Ministry of Finance of the Slovak Republic and Ministry of Interior of the Slovak Republic. For the quantification of correlation, we applied nonparametric methods (tests), i.e. Spearman test and Kendall test, within the Statistical Analysis Software (SAS). Based on the results, we claim that the correlation between corporate tax and tax assignation for corporate nonprofit organizations achieved a relatively high level. It means that corporate tax of selected companies has influence on contribution volume of tax assignation for corporate nonprofit organizations. Based on the results, we can claim that private companies establish nonprofit organizations due to the tax assignation. Via these sources, nonprofit organizations support a variety of charitable activities in the marketing area.

Keywords Nonprofit Sector · Non-Governmental Organization · Corporate Nonprofit Organization · Assignation Mechanism · Nonparametric Method · Nonparametric Test · Spearman Test · Kendall Test

---

J. Mazanec (✉) · A. Bielikova
University of Zilina, Faculty of Operation and Economics of Transport and Communications, Department of Economics, Zilina, Slovak Republic
e-mail: jaroslav.mazanec@fpedas.uniza.sk; alzbeta.bielikova@fpedas.uniza.sk

N. Tsounis, A. Vlachvei (eds.), *Advances in Panel Data Analysis in Applied Economic Research*, Springer Proceedings in Business and Economics,
https://doi.org/10.1007/978-3-319-70055-7_20

20.1 Introduction

In recent decades, we have recorded dramatic increase of the importance of nonprofit sector. It is associated with the process of democratization, liberalization and technological process. After 1989 in the Slovak Republic, the major source of funding for nonprofit organizations consisted mainly of grants from foreign foundations. In 2002, the Slovak government ratified tax law about assignation mechanism to support underfunded nonprofit sector. Interestingly, the Slovak Republic is the first country to introduce assignation mechanism in the tax system.

The purpose of tax assignation is to allow enterprises and individuals to give part of the tax paid for nonprofit organizations. Moreover, significant companies have established their foundations that focus on the promotion of culture, education, health, social care, etc. The main goal is to ensure the development of society. We can consider corporate nonprofit organizations as tool of corporate social responsibility (CSR). It is beneficial for the enterprises because it enables to improve corporate reputation in public (Moravcikova and Krizanova 2016). CSR is part of holistic marketing concept that emphasizes social, legal and environmental aspects of marketing activities (Musova 2016). For instance, Fair Trade is probably the best-known brand that is associated with CSR. Customers can help to people in need by buying product with brand of Fair Trade (Moravcikova and Gregova 2016). The principle of CSR is based on respect for all stakeholders, for instance, employees, etc. Based on survey about CSR, Krizanova et al. (2015) argued that employees are important success factor in enterprises. Next, Placier (2011) dealt with influence of recession on CSR based on cross-case analysis of three companies in the Czech Republic. Results show that recession had negative impact on CSR, mainly social sphere. On the other hand, it had positive influence mainly in cost management.

Nonprofit organizations participate in regional development and eliminate regional disparities in a significant way. Furthermore, in many cases, nonprofit organizations are more efficient in comparison with the public and private sector. It is connected to support of activities in the field of innovation and creativity (Corejova and Rostasova 2015). On the other hand, the sense of corporate nonprofit organizations is to build relationships with the society and to receive a part of tax paid in the form of assignation mechanism.

20.2 Literature Review

The nonprofit sector differs from the private sector. The main aim of the enterprise is to make a profit by providing goods and services in comparison with NGOs that focus on meeting the needs of specific population groups, for example, health care, education, etc. Moreover, the managers of NGOs cannot participate in the profit of nonprofit organizations. On the other hand, the primary advantage of the nonprofit sector is mainly transparency (Anheier and Seibel 1990). In 2006, Edelman Trust

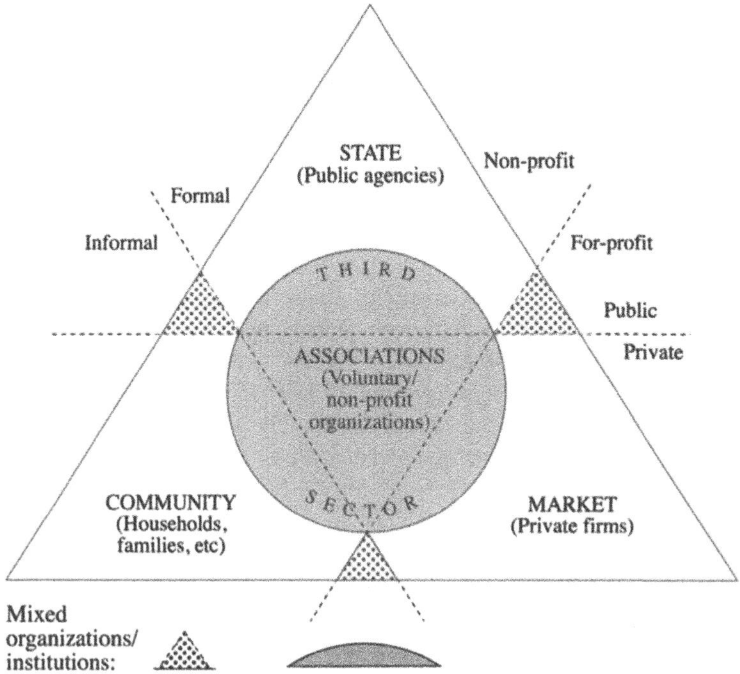

Fig. 20.1 Pestoff model (Evers and Laville 2004)

Barometer conducted a survey "Trust in Non-Governmental Organizations" on sample of nearly 2000 from 11 countries. Based on the survey, we can claim that NGOs are the most trustworthy institutions in Europe.

In recent, the nonprofit sector has been an indispensable part of the national economy. The activities of non-governmental organizations (NGOs) are focused on improving living standards, for instance, in the social sphere. The substantial part of theories about the nonprofit sector deals with the boundaries among private and nonprofit organizations. For instance, Pestoff (1991) created a model that defines the relationship among relevant sectors (private sector, public sector and nonprofit sector) especially in post-communist and Scandinavian countries (Anheier 2004; Nelson 2007) (Fig. 20.1).

In many publications about NGOs, they are not only using the term of nonprofit sector but also third sector. The notion of nonprofit sector is used in Anglo-Saxon countries, unlike the term of third sector that is used in European countries. The nonprofit sector includes organizations that cooperate with public and private sector. The notion of third sector indicates an alternative to public and private sector, for example, because of profit maximization and bureaucracy. The third sector is the basic unit of society. The third sector can be divided into local, national and international level. At the local level, nonprofit organizations build community life towards local development. At national level, NGOs are active in the field of health care and public-private partnerships. At the international level, NGOs are an important part of the development projects of the World Bank and other international institutions, for example, the European Union (EU). The international nonprofit organizations include, for example, Amnesty International (focused on human rights organizations), Greenpeace (focused on environmental protection), etc. Weisbrod (1988) claims that the reason for establishing nonprofit organizations is associated with inadequate provision of services in private and public sector, respectively. Expansion of the third sector relates to the expansion of civil intervention. On the other hand, third sector faces the challenge especially in transition countries after the collapse of the socialist system, for example, in the V4 countries (Zacharova 2015; Anheier and Kendall 2001).

The main problem of nonprofit sector is lack of money for funding various activities. The Slovakia legislation allows funding of NGOs through a specific instrument in the form of assignation mechanism. For interest, the Slovak Republic is the first country that ratified assignation mechanism in tax system in the world. Therefore, the idea of assignation mechanism is that individuals and legal entities can decide on the part of the tax paid. The advantage of assignation mechanism is that it combines the attributes of public and of private funding. The disadvantage of assignation is that nonprofit organizations must compete about tax assignation through marketing activities in contrast with the quality of a project. It means that a part of the assignation is used to pay marketing costs of the nonprofit organization (Stejskal 2012). It represents an indirect instrument in the form of 2% of the tax paid by individuals and legal entities. Individuals can give 3% of tax paid for some NGO. The necessary condition is that the individual must work at least 40 h as volunteer for NGO. The legal entities can give 1.5% (respectively, 2% of tax paid if legal entities provide donation in the amount of 0.5% of the tax paid for the nonprofit organization). The main condition for receiving funds in the form of assignation is the duty to pay a registration fee in the amount of 66 euros (Gregorova et al. 2009).

In the following part of this paper, we describe nonparametric methods that we use to quantify the correlation between the analysed variables, i.e. corporate tax of selected companies and contribution volume from tax assignation. Nonparametric methods are statistical methods of induction, which do not have specific characteristics of distribution of the quantitative variables, i.e. characteristics are independent on shape of distribution. Among nonparametric methods belong the value at risk, too (Frajtová-Michalikova et al. 2015). The reasons for the application of nonparametric tests are, for instance, ordinal character of the sample data and small sample size that does not enable to receive reliable conclusions based on parametric methods. In case of compliance with assumptions of parametric methods, we prefer parametric methods before nonparametric methods. The reason is that nonparametric methods use less information about the characteristics of statistical units. These methods have less ability to detect validity of hypothesis H0. The most common assumption of nonparametric methods is not having an awareness about the shape of the distribution. In the case of a small sample size, the use of parametric methods to estimate parameters is not correct. Therefore, a small sample size does not verify the shape of probability distribution, i.e. we prefer nonparametric methods (Pacakova et al. 2009).

In the case of failure in fundamental assumptions of parametric methods, we should apply nonparametric methods because these methods offer reliable results regardless of the shape of the distribution (Kliestik et al. 2015). Nonparametric methods guarantee that the likelihood of "type 1" is not greater than significance level. In the case of parametric methods, we know theoretical probability distribution of losses, but parameters are not known. Among parametric methods belong normal, Student's and Laplace's distribution (Kral and Kliestik 2015). In the case of nonparametric test with less "strength" of test – it is more important to correctly interpret the conclusion of the test, for instance, calculated value of the test is not in the critical field – accept H0, i.e. adoption of the underlying assumptions of equal significance level (α). Nonparametric tests that are commonly used include the test of randomness, the symmetry test and the test of independence.

Among the best-known nonparametric rank tests (within independence tests) are Spearman test and Kendall test that measure "strength" of ordinal dependence, i.e. rank of variable of X and of Y. The calculations are based on the two ranks of statistical units (so-called n) according to their characteristics or according to the same qualities in two situations, respectively, rating these two subjects.

Spearman test verifies the rank correlation between random variables. The main assumption of this test is information on the rank of analysed variables. Spearman test is calculated as:

$$R_s = 1 - \frac{6 \times \sum_{n=1}^{n} \left(R_{xi} - R_{yi}\right)^2}{n \times (n^2 - 1) - c} \tag{20.1}$$

where

c correlation coefficient in case of occurrence of match order
$(R_{xi} - R_{yi})$ the difference between the ranks of corresponding values X_i and Y_i
n number of values in each data set

The correction coefficient is deducted in the denominator in the case of numerous conformities in relation with sample size, because it causes to decrease variance. Correlation factor for average rank is calculated by the formula:

$$c = \frac{1}{2} \times \left\{ \sum_{k=1}^{px} \left(b_{x,k}^3 - b_{x,\ k}\right) + \sum_{k=1}^{py} \left(b_{y,k}^3 - b_{y,k}\right) \right\} \tag{20.2}$$

Spearman correlation coefficient R_s has interval < −1, 1>. If Spearman test has values of −1 or 1 – the test indicates a monotonous (positive or negative) correlation between variables "X" and "Y". If the Spearman test is equal to 0 – the test indicates validity of the hypothesis H0. Then we verify H0 according to critical value (α) that depends on the shape of alternative hypothesis. If the value of test statistic is in critical field at the significance level (α) – we claim that Spearman test is statistically significant, i.e. alternative hypothesis is statistically significant. "*T*" distribution is calculated by the formula:

$$t = \frac{r_s}{\sqrt{\frac{1-r_s^2}{n-2}}} \tag{20.3}$$

which has an approximative Student distribution with $(n-2)$, i.e. sample size $n \geq 10$ applies $T - t\ (n-2)$. For large sample size $n \geq 30$, we can apply:

$$Z = R_S \sqrt{n-1} \tag{20.4}$$

which has an approximative standard normal distribution with $Z - N\,(0, 1)$. Kendall test is a nonparametric test of rank correlation. It is used in the same cases as Spearman test. Kendall test was defined by M.G. Kendall in 1955. The process of Kendall test is similar to Spearman test. Kendall τ is calculated by the formula:

$$\tau = \frac{n_c - n_d}{\frac{n\times(n-1)}{2}} = \frac{S_T}{\frac{n\times(n-1)}{2}} \tag{20.5}$$

or

$$\tau = 1 - \left(\frac{2\,n_{i\,n\,v}}{\frac{n\times(n-1)}{2}}\right) \tag{20.6}$$

$$S_T = n_c - n_d = \binom{n}{2} - 2n_{i\,n\,v} \tag{20.7}$$

where

n_c number of concordants (ordered in the same way)
n_d number of discordants (ordered differently)
S_T difference between concordant and discordant rank
$n\ (n-1)/2$ total number of pair combinations

In the case of sample size is $n \geq 10$, we apply approximation by normal distribution. Distribution of Kendall τ converges faster to normal distribution as Spearman coefficient. It is calculated by the formula:

$$z = \frac{\text{tau}}{\sqrt{\frac{2(2n+5)}{9n(n-1)}}} = \frac{|S_T| \pm 1}{\sqrt{\frac{n(n-1)(2n+5)}{18}}} \tag{20.8}$$

Correction for discontinuities should be used:

$$z = \frac{|\text{tau}| \pm \frac{1}{\binom{n}{2}}}{\sqrt{\frac{2(2n+5)}{9n(n-1)}}} = \frac{|S_T| \pm 1}{\sqrt{\frac{n(n-1)(2n+5)}{18}}} \tag{20.9}$$

Kendall τ has interval < 0, 1>. If Kendall test is equal to 0, that is independence. If Kendall test is equal to 1, that is dependence. Kendall τ has different scale as Spearman test. It means that test results are not comparable. Kendall τ has lower values than Spearman test R_s. Between Kendall τ and Spearman R_S, apply the following relationship:

$$-1 \leq 3\tau - 2R_S \leq 1 \tag{20.10}$$

Kendall coefficient is better than Spearman coefficient that is sufficient for nonparametric test about correlation between variables. In case of rejection of H0, i.e. statistical significance, it is impossible to interpret. Kendall test is improved because it is sensitive to some types of dependency. It is not associated with any abilities of Spearman coefficient. Kendall coefficient measures "strength" of dependency between analysed variables. Sometimes Kendall test uses linear function of coefficient "T" with acronym "W" for which we apply available tables of critical values (Pacakova et al. 2015):

$$W = \frac{12 \sum_J T_J^2}{m^2 \, n \, (n^2 - 1)} - \frac{3 \, (n+1)}{n-1} \in \langle 0, 1 \rangle \tag{20.11}$$

In the case that $m \geq 8$, test statistics is of the form:

$$X_w^2 = m \, (n-1) \, W \tag{20.12}$$

which has an asymptotic chi-quadrant distribution with $(n - 1)$. The test is not exact for very different values of "m" and "n".

20.3 Methodology

The aim of this paper is to quantify the correlation between the corporate tax of selected companies and contributions from tax assignation for corporate nonprofit organizations and then find out the character of correlation, i.e. positive or negative character. The primary reason for calculation is the assumption that companies have established corporate nonprofit organizations based on current legislation of the Slovak Republic because enterprises want to obtain part of tax paid in the form of tax assignation for their corporate nonprofit organizations from the financial administration of the Slovak Republic. We set the following hypothesis about correlation between variables and character of correlation (positive or negative).

H0: Between corporate tax of selected companies and tax assignation of corporate nonprofit organization is not correlation.
H1: Between corporate tax of selected companies and tax assignation of corporate nonprofit organization is correlation.
H0: Between corporate tax of selected companies and tax assignation of corporate nonprofit organizations is a positive correlation.
H1: Between corporate tax of selected companies and tax assignation of corporate nonprofit organizations is a negative correlation.

The quantification requires necessary information from various sources. Information on contributions from tax assignation for nonprofit organizations are available on the official website of financial administrations of the Slovak Republic. Information on corporate tax is gathered based on financial statements that are published on the website of the Ministry of Finance of the Slovak Republic. Information on founders of corporate nonprofit organizations are gathered from the Ministry of Interior of the Slovak Republic. Information on contributions from tax assignation, corporate tax obligation and founders of corporate nonprofit organizations are gathered for 2016. The correlation is quantified based on Statistical Analysis Software (SAS).

The sample includes 67 corporate nonprofit organizations that are established by private entities, i.e. limited liability company or joint stock company, and obtained tax assignation.

20.4 Results

Based on information on corporate tax of selected companies and tax assignation of nonprofit organizations that are established by enterprises (Table 20.1) for year 2016, we quantified Spearman test and Kendall test.

Based on the results of Spearman test and Kendall test, we claim that among the variables, i.e. corporate tax and tax assignation, it is quite a strong correlation. Spearman coefficient reached the level of 0.65910. It is higher than Kendall coefficient that reached the level of 0.50781. Accuracy of tests is confirmed by significant level ($p < 0.001$) (Tables 20.2 and 20.3).

Figure 20.2 shows that between analysed variables (corporate tax and tax assignation) is a direct positive correlation. It means that we accept hypothesis H0 about correlation and hypothesis H1 about positive character of correlation. Based on these results, we can claim that the contributions of assignation mechanism depend on the corporate tax of private company that established corporate nonprofit organizations. Moreover, we can assume that major enterprises use nonprofit organizations to build the company's reputation. The correlation reaches more than 0.9173 (very strong) with 95% prediction ellipse.

Table 20.1 Input database for quantification of nonparametric methods – Spearman test and Kendall test

Acronym of NGO	Tax assignation [EUR]	Acronym of NGO founder	Corporate tax [EUR]
NGO 1	1,553,134,25	Company 1	60,100,000
NGO 2	1,337,707,65	Company 2	60,041,000
NGO 3	1,241,520,27	Company 3	85,420,000
NGO 4	971,212,25	Company 4	40,076,000
NGO 5	918,223,51	Company 5	17,786,000
NGO 6	855,980,06	Company 6	37,482,000
NGO 7	576,073,17	Company 7	31,116,000
NGO 8	565,249,96	Company 8	18,667,000
NGO 9	439,019,65	Company 9	17,657,000
NGO 10	403,604,88	Company 10	2,026,000
NGO 11	396,855,56	Company 11	19,636,776
NGO 12	313,867,74	Company 12	12,107,000
NGO 13	190,429,07	Company 13	4,069,077
NGO 14	176,439,47	Company 14	−15,364,000
NGO 15	113,415,19	Company 15	14,241,000
NGO 16	103,916,53	Company 16	4083
NGO 17	65,974,33	Company 17	19,589,000
NGO 18	65,917,70	Company 18	440,783
NGO 19	57,129,68	Company 19	667,142
NGO 20	52,608,98	Company 20	16,955,000
NGO 21	41,258,92	Company 21	966
NGO 22	40,537,79	Company 22	8811
NGO 23	39,501,68	Company 23	1,426,749
NGO 24	32,208,27	Company 24	5266
NGO 25	29,692,80	Company 25	239,291
NGO 26	29,151,91	Company 26	646,000
NGO 27	26,560,74	Company 27	68,440
NGO 28	20,419,20	Company 28	287,584
NGO 29	17,449,10	Company 29	26,491
NGO 30	15,265,32	Company 30	40,458
NGO 31	12,557,60	Company 31	326,008
NGO 32	11,485,70	Company 32	1,037,137
NGO 33	11,344,44	Company 33	772,763
NGO 34	11,331,68	Company 34	168,955
NGO 35	9579,63	Company 35	4513
NGO 36	9507,82	Company 36	40,503
NGO 37	9301,35	Company 37	323,717
NGO 38	8769,99	Company 38	282,022
NGO 39	8470,70	Company 39	285,706

(continued)

Table 20.1 (continued)

Acronym of NGO	Tax assignation [EUR]	Acronym of NGO founder	Corporate tax [EUR]
NGO 40	7582,69	Company 40	631
NGO 41	7029,54	Company 41	252,744
NGO 42	6932,22	Company 42	2890
NGO 43	6846,11	Company 43	23,529
NGO 44	5302,51	Company 44	72,792
NGO 45	4128,83	Company 45	67,193
NGO 46	3640,97	Company 46	2458
NGO 47	3391,54	Company 47	124,534
NGO 48	3262,64	Company 48	84,401
NGO 49	3208,38	Company 49	231,266
NGO 50	2817,53	Company 50	374,319
NGO 51	2641,87	Company 51	960
NGO 52	2473,86	Company 52	38,029
NGO 53	2446,89	Company 53	163,716
NGO 54	2435,21	Company 54	44
NGO 55	2386,48	Company 55	91,017
NGO 56	2153,45	Company 56	69,035
NGO 57	1763,78	Company 57	3012
NGO 58	1558,78	Company 58	59,070
NGO 59	1258,78	Company 59	2,725,301
NGO 60	1120,04	Company 60	960
NGO 61	734,14	Company 61	12,173
NGO 62	572,03	Company 62	10,101
NGO 63	335,91	Company 63	5037
NGO 64	321,88	Company 64	130,025
NGO 65	217,12	Company 65	5175
NGO 66	172,06	Company 66	960
NGO 67	14,40	Company 67	1171

(Authors based on Financial Administrations of the Slovak Republic, Register of Financial Statements, Register of Nonprofit Organizations – Foundations)

Table 20.2 The result of Spearman correlation coefficients and Kendall correlation coefficients

Spearman correlation coefficients $N = 67$ Prob > $\|r\|$ under H0, Rho = 0	
Corporate tax	Tax assignation
	0.65910
	<0.0001

(Authors based on SAS)

Table 20.3 The result of Kendall correlation coefficients

Kendall tau b correlation coefficients $N = 67$	
Prob > |tau| under H0, Tau = 0	
Corporate tax	Tax assignation
	0.50781
	<0.0001

(Authors based on SAS)

20.5 Discussion

In recently years, issue about tax assignation is popular among authors in the Czech Republic. For instance, Svidrova (2014) was interested in tax laws associated with NGOs based on Delphi method. Svidrova (2014) described possibility of private sector how to help NGOs via assignation mechanism in funding area. Svidrova (2014) demonstrated the importance of assignation mechanism due to sustainability of NGOs. Otavova et al. (2014) dealt with the significance of tax assignation connected to NGOs in the Czech Republic. Otavova (2014) analysed and quantified impact on taxpayer, nonprofit organizations and state budget. The primary aim of the paper was to determine advantages and disadvantages of assignation mechanism based on analysed models. Hladka and Hyanek (2016) researched the necessity of tax assignation for NGOs in the Czech Republic. Based on these papers, we can claim that tax assignation is important for nonprofit organizations. However, we should focus on ways of using finance in nonprofit organizations and then the efficiency of these organizations compared with private and public organizations.

20.6 Conclusion

We can claim that correlation among contributions from tax assignation for corporate nonprofit organizations and their founders in the form of enterprises is relatively strong based on Spearman test and Kendall test. Based on results of nonparametric methods (tests), we confirmed the assumption about the correlation between analysed variables. Results of the tests explain the strong relationship, i.e. volume of tax assignation of corporate nonprofit organizations depends on corporate tax of companies (founders of NGOs). It means that corporate nonprofit organizations are established by companies not only by building relationship with the public but also through tax assignation, because these "marketing activities" are funded by tax assignation.

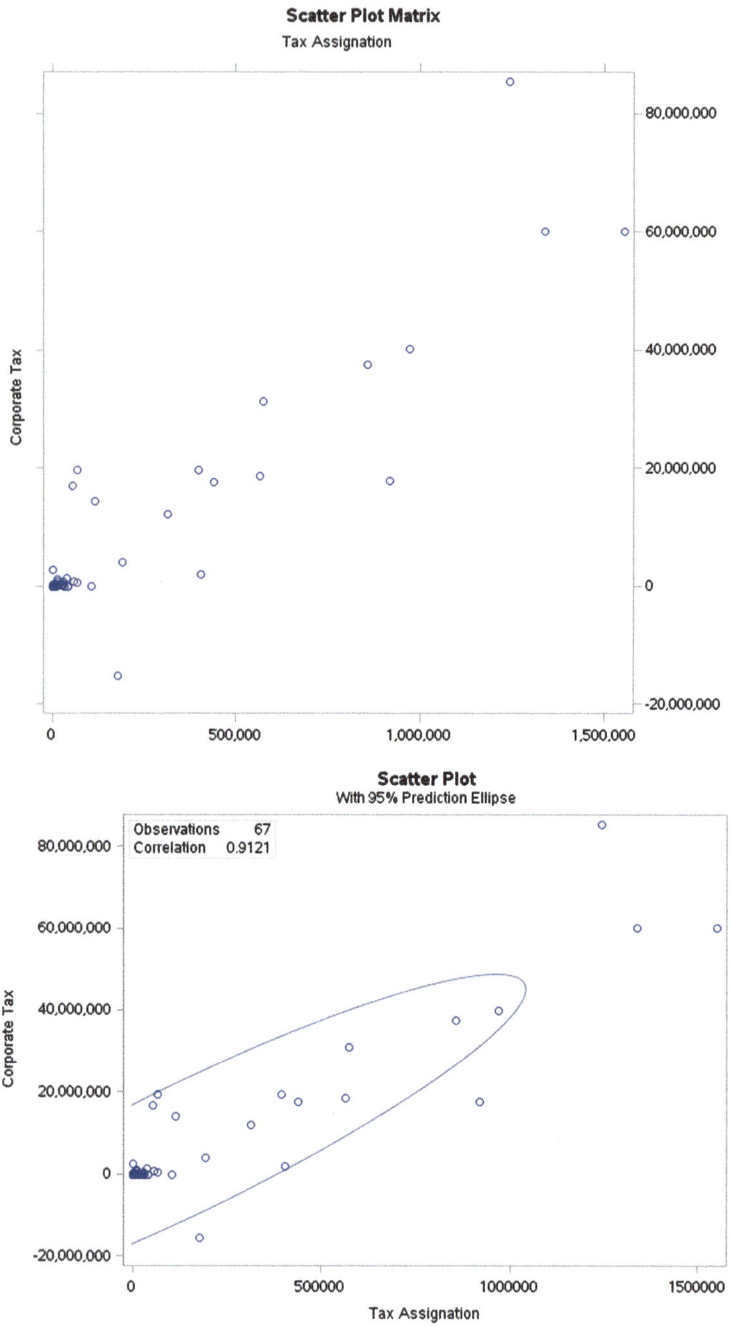

Fig. 20.2 The correlation between corporate tax and tax assignation (Authors based on SAS)

Acknowledgements This contribution was undertaken as part of the research project VEGA 1/0696/16 and project VEGA 1/0244/16: Personnel marketing as a new approach of ensuring and maintaining the skilled workforce in Slovak companies.

References

Anheier, H. K. (2004). *Nonprofit organizations: An introduction: Theory, management, policy*. New York: Routledge.

Anheier, H. K., & Kendall, J. (2001). *Third sector policy at the crossroads: An International nonprofit analysis*. London: Routledge.

Anheier, H. K., & Seibel, W. (1990). *The third sector: Comparative studies of nonprofit organizations*. Berlin: Walter de Gruyer.

Corejova, T., & Rostasova, M. (2015). Regional development, innovation and creativity. In *9th international conference on applied business research (ICABR), Talca, October 2014. Proceedings from IX international conference on applied business research ICABR 2014* (pp. 114–127). Brno: Mendel Univ Brno.

Evers, A., & Laville, J. L. (2004). *The third sector in Europe*. Great Britain: Edward Elgar Publishing Limited.

Frajtova-Michalikova, K., Kliestik, T., & Musa, H. (2015). Comparison of nonparametric methods for estimating the level of risk in finance. In N. Tsounis & A. Vlahvei (Eds.), *International conference on applied economics (ICOAE) July 2015, Procedia economics and finance* (Vol. 24, pp. 228–236). Kazan: Elsevier.

Gregorova, A.B., Marcek, E., & Mrackova, A. (2009). Analyza dobrovolnictva na Slovensku. *PANET*. http://dobrovolnictvo.sk/_subory/PDCS_Analyza_dobrovolnictva_SK.pdf. Accessed 23 Mar 2017.

Hladka, M., & Hyanek, V. (2016). Usefulness of tax assignation for the Czech tax system: The direction of debates on introducing. In D. Spalkova & L. Matejova (Eds.), *Proceedings of the 20th international conference on current trends in public sector research, Slapanice, January 2016. Current trends in public sector research* (Vol. 20, pp. 122–130). Slapanice: Masaryk University.

Kliestik, T., Musa, H., Musa, H., & Frajtova-Michalikova, K. (2015). Parametric methods for estimating the level of risk in finance. In N. Tsounis & A. Vlahvei (Eds.), *International conference on applied economics (ICOAE), Kazan, July 2015. Procedia economics and finance* (Vol. 24, pp. 322–330). Russia: Elsevier.

Kral, P., & Kliestik, T. (2015). Estimation of the level of risk based on the selected theoretical probability distributions. In M. Culik (Ed.), *Financial management of firms and financial institutions: 10th international scientific conference, PTS I-IV, Ostrava, September 2015. Financial management of firms and financial institutions-Ostrava* (pp. 603–610). Ostrava: VSB-TECH UNIV.

Krizanova, A., Moravcikova, K., & Rypakova, M. (2015). The social area of corporate social responsibility focusing on social policy. In G. Lee (Ed.), *5th international conference on applied social science (ICASS 2015), PT 1 October 2016. Advances in education research* (Vol. 80, pp. 339–344). Limassol: Information Engineering Research Inst.

Moravcikova, K., & Gregova, E. (2016). Fair trade as a tool of corporate social responsibility. In P. Hajek, T. Sahota, & M. A. Jones (Eds.), *CBU international conference proceedings 2016: Innovations in science and education, Prague, March 2016. CBU international conference proceedings* (pp. 340–345). Prague: Central Bohemia Univ.

Moravcikova, K. & Krizanova, A. (2016). Impact of corporate social responsibility on the company's reputation. In: Zhang, H. *ICMIBI international conference on applied social science and business (ICMIBI-ASSB 2016), Windsor, September 2016. Lecture notes in management science, 65*, Singapore Management & Sports Science INST PTE LTD, Singapore 20–25.

Musova, Z. (2016). Spolocenska zodpovednost v marketingovych aktivitach podnikov. *Ekonomicko-manazerske spektrum, 10*, 2–11.

Nelson, J. (2007). The operation of nongovernmental organizations (NGOs) in a world of corporate and other codes of conduct. Corporate social responsibility initiative. John F. Kennedy School of Government. https://www.hks.harvard.edu/m-rcbg/CSRI/publications/workingpaper_34_nelson.pdf. Accessed 23 Mar 2017.

Otavova, M., Solilova, V., & Grasgruber, M. (2014). Would be appropriate to introduce a tax assignation in the Czech Republic? In D. Nerudova (Ed.), *17th international conference enterprise and competitive environment 2014, Brno, March 2014. Procedia economics and finance* (Vol. 12, pp. 498–507). Amsterdam: Elsevier.

Pacakova, V., et al. (2009). *Statisticke metody pre ekonomov*. Bratislava: Iura Edition.

Pacakova, V., et al. (2015). *Statisticka indukcia pre ekonomov a manazerov*. Bratislava: Wolters Kluwer.

Placier, K. (2011). The impact of recession on the implementation of corporate social responsibility in companies. *Journal of Competitiveness, 2*, 83–98.

Stejskal, J., Kuvikova, H., & Matakova, K. (2012). *Neziskove organizacie vybrane problemy ekonomiky se zamerenim na nestatni neziskove organizace*. Prague: Wolters Kluwer ČR.

Svidronova, M. (2014). Tax Laws affecting the sustainability of NGOs in Slovakia. In D. Spalkova & L. Matejova (Eds.), *Proceedings of the 18th international conference current trends in public sector research, January 2014. Current trends in public sector research* (pp. 344–353). Slapanice: Masaryk University.

Weisbrod, B. (1988). *The nonprofit economy*. Boston: Harvard University Press.

Zacharova, A. (2015). *Ekonomicke a pravne aspekty neziskovych organizacii*. Bratislava: Wolters Kluwer.

Chapter 21
Why You Should Use High-Frequency Data to Test the Impact of Exchange Rate on Trade

Karam Shaar and Mohammed Khaled

Abstract This study suggests that testing the impact of exchange rate on trade should be done using high-frequency data. Using different data frequencies for identical periods and specifications between the USA and Canada, we show that low-frequency data might suppress and distort the evidence of the impact of exchange rate on trade in the short run and the long run.

Keywords Data frequency · Exchange rate and trade · J-curve theory · ARDL cointegration · US-Canada trade

21.1 Introduction

Among a variety of theories attempting to explain the impact of exchange rate movements on trade balance, J-curve theory gained most of the attention. The theory suggests that, as a result of currency depreciation, a country's trade balance follows a J-shaped pattern as it deteriorates in the short run and recovers to a higher level in the long run. The initial deterioration is due to the presumed stickiness of the traded quantities for reasons such as previously signed contracts on the supply side and habit formation on the demand side. Although this paper tests only the J-curve theory, its rationale is still applicable to other theories attempting to test the impact of exchange rate on trade.

Among the hundreds of studies which tested the J-curve theory, the most common empirical methodology is a combination of the autoregressive distributed lag (ARDL) approach to cointegration and the error correction model (ECM) (Pesaran et al. 2001). The desirability of this methodology in the literature is largely because it does not require a prior determination of which regression variables are

---

K. Shaar · M. Khaled (✉)
School of Economics and Finance, Victoria University of Wellington, Wellington, New Zealand
e-mail: mohammed.khaled@vuw.ac.nz

N. Tsounis, A. Vlachvei (eds.), *Advances in Panel Data Analysis in Applied Economic Research*, Springer Proceedings in Business and Economics,
https://doi.org/10.1007/978-3-319-70055-7_21

I(0) and which are I(1), as well as the direct and easy inference of short- and long-run impacts of exchange rate on trade balance.

However, the literature suffers from a key problem, the assumption that data frequency has no role in empirically investigating the relationship between exchange rate and trade. In this paper, we advocate the use of high-frequency data when testing the J-curve theory – or other theories of similar nature – for four different reasons.

First, while it is true that cointegration is a long-run notion, the short-run impact of exchange rate and error correction on trade is a vital component of the ECM. Low-frequency data, such as annual or quarterly, might obscure much of the evidence needed for understanding the short-run dynamics of the relationship as high and low values might average out over the course of one period in low-frequency data.

Second, regarding cointegration itself, it is thought by many researchers in the field that using low-frequency data is as good as using high-frequency data for testing long-run association. As stated by Bahmani-Oskooee (1996), "... using annual data over the 1960-90 period in this paper is as good as using quarterly or monthly data over the same period." However, cointegration tests with low-frequency data have lower power. As shown in a Monte Carlo experiment by Zhou (2001), the loss of power applies especially for small samples of less than 50 years (as is the case in most macroeconometric applications) and for models which involve autoregressive terms. In other words, low-frequency data might suppress the evidence of true cointegration.

Third, quantities and prices might change after exchange rate movements in a period as short as instantly. Using quarterly or annual data implicitly assumes that short-run changes in trade values and quantities take at least 3 months or a year to take place. Fourth, using annual data for ARDL cointegration increases the likelihood of including I(2) variables owing to the smoothing imposed on the data by the aggregation over time. This may lead to spurious cointegration conclusions in the ARDL approach where the test bounds assume the regressors to be purely I(0) or purely I(1) (Pesaran et al. 2001).

To address these issues, our paper tests the J-curve theory between the USA and Canada using the ARDL-ECM approach for two identical periods using monthly, quarterly, and annual data.

The findings confirm that (a) low-frequency data might suppress the evidence of cointegration, (b) higher frequency allows better understanding for the short-run dynamics of the relationship, and (c) lower frequency might cause some series to become I(2), which invalidates the ARDL cointegration approach.

The rest of the paper is organized as follows. Section 21.2 explains the research methodology, Sect. 21.3 presents the findings, and Sect. 21.4 concludes.

21.2 Methodology

We choose US-Canada bilateral trade relation as an example to investigate the research questions since it continues to be the most significant global trade relation in terms of total merchandise. Additionally, the data quality is perceived to be high (low discrepancy in the data reported by the trading partners) and is available for a long period.

Since the J-curve theory is being tested using real exchange rate (REX), we use the whole available sample of data starting from 1962, rather than since the breakdown of the gold standard in the early 1970s. As shown in Fig. 21.1, especially during a financial crisis like that around 2008, annual exchange rate obscures some of the information available in monthly data. Seasonality alone cannot explain the deviations of monthly data from annual averaged data. This problem remains even if the annual data are obtained at the end of month or mid-month observations at annual intervals.

The model used for investigating the J-curve theory is identical to that used in many studies in the field, which is a combination of ARDL cointegration as developed by Pesaran et al. (2001) and the ECM. We select two time periods for the empirical analysis. The first extends along the whole available period of 1962–2015. The second follows Bahmani-Oskooee and Wang (2008) on the same two countries and spans from 1962 to 2004. We use monthly, quarterly, and annual data for the same variables. That is, we investigate six variations of a model with two time periods, using three different data frequencies for each.

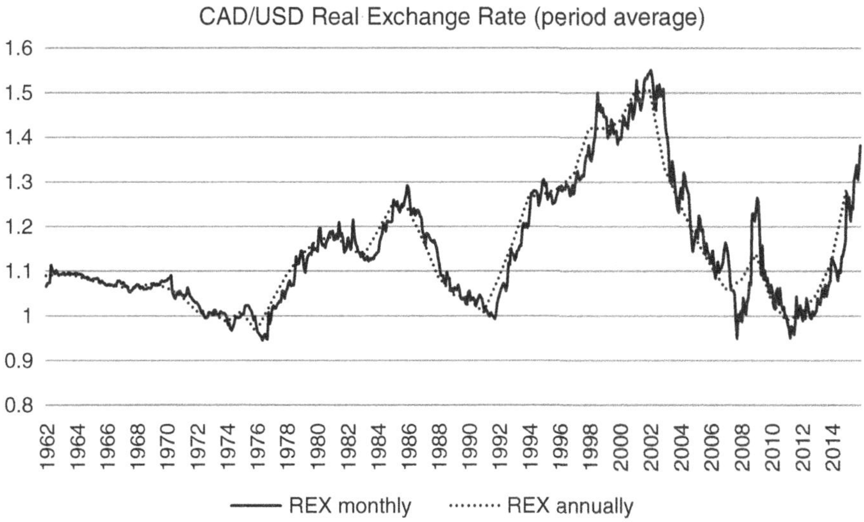

Fig. 21.1 Annual versus monthly exchange rate (1962–2015)

$$\Delta Ln\text{TB}_t = \alpha + \sum_{k=1}^{n_1} \varnothing_k \Delta \text{lnTB}_{t-k} + \sum_{k=0}^{n_2} \beta_k \Delta \text{lnUSGDP}_{t-k} + \sum_{k=0}^{n_3} \gamma_k \Delta \text{lnCGDP}_{t-k}$$
$$+ \sum_{k=0}^{n_4} \varphi_k \Delta \text{lnREX}_{t-k} + \delta_1 \text{lnTB}_{t-1} + \delta_2 \text{lnUSGDP}_{t-1} + \delta_3 lnCGDP_{t-1}$$
$$+ \delta_4 \text{lnREX}_{t-1} + u_t \tag{21.1}$$

where TB is trade balance defined as US exports to Canada divided by US imports from Canada. REX is real exchange rate defined as the number of Canadian Dollars per USD adjusted by the price levels in each country as measured by consumer price index. CGDP and USGDP are the GDPs of Canada and the USA. These two variables are not available on monthly frequency, so we apply repeated quarterly data on these in the monthly regressions since these are used only as controls. All the data are retrieved from IMF-IFS database. The data are available here.

Besides the first differences, lagged level variables appear in Eq. [21.1] to allow test for cointegration. To justify retention of these variables in the model, Pesaran et al. (2001) propose the use of F-test to determine the joint significance of lagged level variables with a new set of critical values. They tabulate the critical values for lower and upper bounds depending on the order of integration of the included variables. If the computed F statistic is larger than the upper-bound tabulated value, the null hypothesis of no cointegration can be rejected. After establishing cointegration, the short-run impacts can be inferred from the coefficients of the differenced variables. Long-run impacts are retrieved using FM-OLS estimation of the cointegration.

21.3 Findings

Before running our six regressions, we first ensure that all our variables are either I(1) or I(0) using the augmented Dickey-Fuller (ADF) and Phillips-Perron (PP) tests. The variables are all found to be I(1) using either test, regardless of the data frequency. The optimal lag structure for each regression is chosen by the Schwarz information criterion. Table 21.1 summarizes the estimates provided by each regression. For brevity, we report only the short-run estimates of the variable of interest, LnREX.

The results indicate the presence of the J-curve phenomenon for all four cointegrated regressions as REX appears to have a positive effect in the short run and negative effect in the long run. That is, a depreciation of USD is expected to worsen the US trade balance with Canada in the short run and improve it in the long run.

The findings confirm that aggregation over time suppresses the evidence of the long-run effect of exchange rate on trade. This is because the absence of cointegration can be established only using annual or quarterly data for the period

Table 21.1 Regression outputs of dependent variable $\Delta LnTB_t$

Period	1962–2015			1962–2004		
Frequency	Monthly	Quarterly	Annually	Monthly	Quarterly	Annually
ARDL (F)	3.95	4.61	4.19	4.2	2.07	3.58
Cointegrated?	Yes	Yes	Yes	Yes	No	No
$\Delta LnRex_t$			0.31(1.49)		−0.19 (−1.03)	
$\Delta LnRex_{t-1}$		0.29 (2.37)**				0.24(0.96)
$\Delta LnRex_{t-2}$	0.29 (2.31)**			0.36(1.86)*		
$\Delta Ln\ REX_{t-3}$		0.28(2.22)**				
LnREXt	−0.44 (−6.12)***	−0.27 (−2.72)***	−0.42 (−3.07)***	−0.55 (−4.78)***	−0.54 (−3.44)***	−0.27 (−1.14)
LnUSGDP	0.99 (3.84)***	0.18(0.42)	1.17 (4.70)***	0.43 (0.99)***	0.59 (0.91)	−1.27 (−4.6)***
LnCGDP	−1.03 (−3.9)***	−0.98 (−3)***	−1.19 (−4.68)***	−1.26 (−5.25)***	−1.3 (−3.79)***	1.19 (4.11)***
Intercept	−0.01 (−0.31)	1.06 (3.54)***	−0.01 (−0.17)	1.07 (2.54)***	0.98 (1.75)*	0.08 (0.66)
Adj. R^2	41%	33%	21%	41%	34%	35%
LM test	1.8	0.69	1.49	2.79*	1.85	2.32

*,**,*** indicate significance at 10%, 5%, and 1%, respectively. *Numbers inside parenthesis* are t-ratios. Critical ARDL F values are 3.77 and 4.35 at 10% and 5% levels of significance, respectively. LM serial correlation test reported values are F stats of Breusch-Godfrey test. HAC robust standard errors are applied for hypothesis testing when autocorrelation is present

1962–2004. In line with Zhou (2001), the results suggest that lower-frequency data might capture the long-run impact of exchange rate on trade only when the period is long enough. The annual sample of 1962–2004 was also used by Bahmani-Oskooee and Wang (2008) for the same trade relation but using sectoral trade data. Thus, it is also likely for them to have not found enough support for cointegration due to aggregation over time. They found support of cointegration for 80 sectors out of 152.

Additionally, for the regressions of 1962–2015, we see that monthly data can better explain the dynamicity of the relationship. It shows that the impact of REX on TB appears after 2 months, while quarterly and annual results are less accurate and show that the impact kicks in any time within the first quarter, or year, respectively. As reflected in adjusted R^2, we also note that monthly data – by using more information – provides a better fit of the same variables over the same period.

Finally, using low-frequency data might also cause a rarely discussed problem, which impacts the application of ARDL cointegration. That is, the inclusion of I(2) series. This is particularly problematic for studies in this field as there has been a tendency not to test for unit root at all since ARDL allows for the inclusion of I(0) and I(1) series without prespecifying the order for the test. For instance, Bahmani-Oskooee and Ratha (2004) state that: "The new critical values tabulated by Pesaran

Table 21.2 Unit root test for the variables from 1984–2009 (26 years)

	Order of integration		
Series\frequency	Monthly	Quarterly	Annually
LnRex	I(1)	I(1)	I(2)
LnTB	I(1)	I(1)	I(1)
LnUSGDP	NA	I(1)	I(2)
LnCGDP	NA	I(1)	I(2)

The results are confirmed by ADF as well as PP

et al. (2001) do take into consideration the stationarity properties of the series. For this reason, there is no need for pre-testing of unit roots."

Table 21.2 selects a particular sample from our study as an example of how aggregation over time might make some series I(2).

It should be noted that many studies test the impact of exchange rate on trade using annual data for 26 years or shorter.

21.4 Conclusion

This paper argues that the impact of exchange rate on trade should be investigated using monthly data and shows that using low-frequency data might suppress the evidence of a true relationship. It is further shown that using high-frequency data allows better understanding of the dynamics of the relationship and reduces the likelihood of using I(2) series.

References

Bahmani-Oskooee, M. (1996). Decline of the Iranian Rial during the postrevolutionary period: A productivity approach. *The Journal of Developing Areas, 30*(4), 477–492.

Bahmani-Oskooee, M., & Ratha, A. (2004). The J-curve dynamics of US bilateral trade. *Journal of Economics and Finance, 28*(1), 32–38.

Bahmani-Oskooee, M., & Wang, Y. (2008). The J-curve: Evidence from commodity trade between US and China. *Applied Economics, 40*(21), 2735–2747.

Pesaran, M. H., Shin, Y., & Smith, R. J. (2001). Bounds testing approaches to the analysis of level relationships. *Journal of Applied Econometrics, 16*(3), 289–326.

Zhou, S. (2001). The power of cointegration tests versus data frequency and time spans. *Southern Economic Journal, 67*, 906–921.

Chapter 22
On the Radio Spectrum Value for Telecommunication Market Participants

Tatiana Corejova, Mario Al Kassiri, Marek Valica, and Ivana Andrisková

Abstract Increasing demand for telecommunication services and increased competition for scarce spectrum has led to the introduction of spectrum pricing. Spectrum pricing is the term given to funding and licensing mechanisms that bring economic factors into spectrum management. Spectrum is one of the factors of production, and there is significant need to be able to assess spectrum value properly. It is a scarce but renewable public resource. The current assignment and allocation of spectrum is unlikely to be at market equilibrium, for the simple reason that economic factors have only had a very indirect impact (if any) on past allocation and assignment decisions. The aim of this paper is to discuss the access to the radio spectrum from the point of view of operators, regulator, and customers as well as the possibility of excludability and rivalry.

22.1 Introduction

With the development of market with mobile communications, increasing penetration of smartphone ownership, and use of mobile applications and data transmission, radio spectrum is becoming increasingly scarce because its capacity is limited. Frequency spectrum or radio spectrum is a part of electromagnetic spectrum, and it is a basic prerequisite for functioning of all wireless communication services (Laflin and Dajka 2007; Bozsoki 2012; Spectrum Management Fundamentals 2013).

Radio spectrum is, by reason of its immaterial, almost abstract nature, very difficult to quantify, but its importance is undeniable. Demand for radio spectrum

T. Corejova (✉) · M. Al Kassiri · I. Andrisková
University of Zilina, Faculty of Operation and Economics of Transport and Communications, Department of Communications, Zilina, Slovak Republic
e-mail: tatiana.corejova@uniza.sk; mario.alkassiri@fpedas.uniza.sk

M. Valica
University of Zilina, Zilina, Slovak Republic

N. Tsounis, A. Vlachvei (eds.), *Advances in Panel Data Analysis in Applied Economic Research*, Springer Proceedings in Business and Economics,
https://doi.org/10.1007/978-3-319-70055-7_22

is constantly growing, but the offer as well as capacity of this spectrum is limited and also regulated. Radio spectrum as a production factor in the process of market production, when certain combination of inputs produces outputs for customers (households or businesses), leads to the need of setting price of spectrum (Bazelon and Mchenry 2012; Bruwaene 2003; Cramton 2001; Doyle 2007; Sharif 2014).

What can this value be derived from? Several participants of telecommunication market divide the view on radio spectrum and its value. Is there an objective expression of the value of frequency spectrum? Within the solved issue, we focus on seeking answers for these questions, and we try to map the specifics that arise from telecommunication market. As a fundamental problem, we can identify the issue of determining the value of radio spectrum that would reflect the market balance and the fact that the value is identified by a regulator that is not sufficiently involved in the market mechanism (the amount of spectrum that is offered does not correspond to required amount, and it does not adapt to it in any way). That is because it has to maintain its independence and cope with an asymmetry of information, and on the basis of incomplete information, it should conclude to setting the price of spectrum – so that it would not be too high or too low – price that will ensure the maximization of produced outputs with the use of available spectrum (Struzak 2006a, b; Vitek 2014; Wang et al. 2010; Yan and Lc 2011; Song and Wang 2009).

The issue of a clear and comprehensive determination of radio spectrum within the framework of legislation and subsequent absence of evaluation methodology is after summarizing information reasonable from different points of view. Several participants of telecommunication network market with different perceptions and interests derive the view on radio spectrum according to their position in market. This is subsequently transferred into heterogeneous way of search for the value of radio spectrum. The main obstacle for regulator when trying to evaluate radio spectrum is a significant information asymmetry (Nachira and Mazzini 2011; Marks 2009; Malisuwan 2014).

22.2 Theoretical Basis

The perception of radio spectrum has varied in history, and it is also different nowadays depending on market participant who looks at it, as well as the choice of services for which the radio spectrum is used. Is thus radio spectrum as a natural resource public or private good? (Bozsoki 2012; Kejun 2005; Sharif 2014).

Radio spectrum (or more precisely its part used for provision of terrestrial television broadcasting) is perceived from a consumer's perspective as a public good (clean) – but this is no longer valid if we concentrate on the frequency allocations used for services of mobile operators. In this case we incline to the view that consumers perceive radio spectrum as a private good.

		Level of excludability	
		100% excludable	0% non-excludable
Level of rivalness	100% rival	Private goods	Common-pool resources
	0% non-rival	„Club“ goods	Public goods

Fig. 22.1 Matrix combination of rivalness and excludability of goods (Source: Connolly (1999))

Customer view (perception through services)		Level of excludability	
		100% Paid service	0% Free service
Level of rivalness	100% Duplex connection	Private goods (e.g. services of mobile operator)	Mixed goods (e.g. some RFID tags)
	0% Simplex connection	Club goods (e.g. satellite TV)	Public goods (e.g. TV, radio)

Fig. 22.2 Radio spectrum as a good – customer view

We follow the elementary division of economic goods (Fig. 22.1) which were defined and divided by P. A. Samuelson in 1954 (Lisý 2003), and this theory was later elaborated by further authors.

If we look at radio spectrum through the eyes of consumers, we perceive it through a service that is provided by radio spectrum. It is because consumers demand services – derived demand. Level of excludability is in this case determined by a price system or more precisely by the fact whether a service is paid or not. Level of rivalry can be perceived through a connection required by service. All wireless communication services used with a help of radio spectrum have a common feature – they transmit data. They just differ in the way in which data are transmitted: in one direction, simplex connection or, in both directions, duplex connections (eventually half-duplex connection) (Andriskova 2014; Arthur 2009; ICT 2013).

In case of duplex connection when a circuit is created, every other consumer connected to the network using a service reduces the amount of spectrum that can be used by other consumer. Therefore, radio spectrum used for services such as terrestrial television broadcasting is perceived by consumers as a public good unlike the parts of radio spectrum that are used for services of mobile operators (Fig. 22.2). Services of mobile operators can be used only by purchasing a SIM card of mobile operator, whereby the use of these services is further charged, and this ensures an exclusion from consumption. A clear evidence of rivalry can be illustrated in the case of "network congestion." In the case of large number of consumers connected to a network at the same time, a network capacity (or more precisely the amount of radio spectrum) is not sufficient, and connection is not established (Azcoitia et al. 2010; Prat and Valetti 2000).

Network operator/service provider view		Level of excludability	
		100% Individual authorization	0% General authorization
Level of rivalness	100% Limited number of rights	Private goods (FS used for services of mobile operators; radio)	Mixed goods X
	0% Unlimited number of rights	Club goods (FS used for e.g. satellite TV)	Public goods (FS used for e.g. RFID; WiFi)

Fig. 22.3 Radio spectrum as a good – service provider view

Regulator view		Level of excludability	
		100%	0%
Level of rivalness	100%	Limited natural resource which should be effectively redistributed	
	0%		

Fig. 22.4 Radio spectrum as a good – regulator view

If we look at the spectrum through the eyes of service providers/network operators who compete with each other concerning the use of spectrum, then the level of excludability is determined by conditions under which it is possible to gain access to radio spectrum (individual license/general license) and rivalry is determined by a number of existing rights. Radio spectrum used for services of mobile operators in terms of service provider/network operator is considered to be a private good (Fig. 22.3). Excludability and rivalry of spectrum as a good from the perspective of provider/operator do not result from the basic properties of spectrum, but they are determined administratively. In international cooperation to harmonize the use of the spectrum, it is a regulator who determines the conditions under which it is possible to gain access to radio spectrum. So regulator makes decisions about the excludability and rivalry of good.

Despite the fact that radio spectrum as a whole is a limited natural resource, when looking closely aiming at individual market participants, we can see that limitation is relative.

In economic theory, it is not possible to classify the radio spectrum as a public good or private good because of its diversity. It always needs to be seen in relation to selected service, and the views of individual market participants should be considered (Fig. 22.4).

Table 22.1 Attributes of goods for derivation of the value of radio spectrum

Attributes of goods for the derivation of the value	*Definition*	*Market participant* Customer	Service provider/network operator	Regulator
Usefulness	Ability to provide benefits	✓	✓	✓
Is it possible to derive the utility value of spectrum from the attribute?				
Utility	Rate of ability to bring benefits	✗[a] ✓[b]	✗✓	?
Scarcity *Usefulness* *Limitation*	Economic goods. The willingness to pay for them	✗	✗	✗
Production costs	In connection with building of telecommunication network	✗	✓	?

Source: Author
[a]Ordinal theory
[b]Cardinal theory

22.3 Utility Value of Radio Spectrum

The value of any good can be derived from utility value, scarcity, or production costs (Table 22.1).

Utility of good as a subset of usefulness is indicated by a rate of ability to bring benefit. Each of the market participants is aware of the fact that radio spectrum is able to provide benefits. The rate of ability to provide benefits is questionable. If we are able to quantify the rate of ability to provide benefits, then we are able to quantify the value of radio spectrum (Lisý 2003). Considering the ordinal theory, we are not able to quantify the value of radio spectrum; we can just compare it. Within the cardinal theory, consumer and service providers/network operators are able to derive the value of spectrum. Consumers perceive the radio spectrum through services. The value of spectrum is therefore derived from the benefits of the services consumed or more precisely from the price that consumers are willing to give for the use of service, i.e., a demand price. Concerning the service provider/network operator, the demand price is most often expressed by means of ARPU (average revenue per user) indicator. Regulator does not have direct access to information about average revenue per customer, and so there is an information asymmetry.

Scarcity of good is given by its utility value and limitation. If a good is useful and limited at the same time, we say that it is scarce. Radio spectrum as a natural resource is practically useful and limited over its whole width, but in some parts its limitation increases, i.e., it is relatively limited (Connolly 1999; Hirschleier 2005; Plum Consulting 2011; Song and Wang 2009).

Costs of good production we perceive in relation to radio spectrum, especially in relation to building of a telecommunication network which is a direct prerequisite for the provision of mobile communication service. Only the service provider/network operator is able to consider and derive the value of radio spectrum from the costs of production. Radio spectrum and its amount influence the rate of the costs related to network building. It is a determining factor.

22.4 Market Process and Creation of Radio Spectrum Utility Value

Utility value of radio spectrum is created in relation to individual market participants. All participants perceive radio spectrum from their own perspectives while pursuing their own interests. Summarization of market process and creation of radio spectrum utility value which is used for services of public mobile electronic communication networks is described in Table 22.2.

In the comparison we include the market as a place where market participants meet, and we describe market mechanism which arises at this point. We also include transnational institutions that are a part of telecommunication market in the broader sense.

22.5 Conclusion

In deriving the value of radio spectrum, we follow the neoclassical approach and Austrian school which considers a principle of usefulness and scarcity as the most important factor (Lisý 2003). From the comparison we can see that the value of radio spectrum arises from benefits of used service that is provided through radio spectrum.

The value of radio spectrum arises as a difference between revenues and expenses related to the use of a particular part of spectrum (Table 22.3).

Since the value of spectrum for regulator is theoretically zero, when trying to evaluate radio spectrum, it has to be aimed at the views of market participants. They are able to determine the value of radio spectrum and that is service provider/network operator or more precisely mobile operator. We incline to the following view. When regulators try to determine the value of radio spectrum, they become a part of market process, and to some extent they act as business persons within the meaning of public choice theory. Traditional economics assumes that the aim of government is to maximize some of the functions of social welfare. Public choice theory has a different view on this. Its followers take the view that government officials and politicians behave the same way as other members of society and their aim is to maximize their own usefulness (Lisý 2003). In order

Table 22.2 Attitudes of market participants in connection to radio spectrum used for public mobile communications

User		*How does he/she perceive radio spectrum?*	*On which side of the market does he/she stand?*	*What does he/she do with radio spectrum?*	*What are his/her interests?*	*What does he/she derive the utility value of radio spectrum from?*	*What is the value of radio spectrum?*
1	*Customer*	Private good	Demand (derived)	Consumes	Consume as much as possible at the lowest price	*Benefit from consumed service*	*Derived from benefits from the consumed services*
2	*Mobile operator*	Private good Input to the transformation process as a production factor	Demand	Buys (or more precisely leases)	Profit	*Benefit from the provision of service Production costs*	*Derived from benefits from the provision of services and production costs Revenues – expenses*
3	*Market (Collision 1,2,4,5)*	Subject of sale and purchase	Collision of demand and offer	Mediates the sale and purchase	Create an environment to maximize profit and economic growth	*Exchange value*	*MovableDepending on the value creation of other market participants*
4	*Authority (govern-ment, regulator)*	Limited natural resource	Offer (natural owner)	Offers available frequencies	Compromise (economic growth vs. revenues to the state budget)	✗	*Theoretically zero*
5	*ITU* et al.	Limited natural resource	✗	Ensures international harmonization	Economic growth	✗	*Theoretically zero*

Table 22.3 Revenues and expenses from the use of radio spectrum

Revenues	
ARPU	Market growth within a segment
	Competition among others: Operators Services
	The range of provided services
	Coverage: National coverage Roaming options
	Quality of service: Delay The number of dropped calls
	Investment in brand building
Users	Population growth
	Penetration of the market as a whole
	Market share of operator
Expenses	
Number of BTS	Frequency band
	Amount of spectrum
	Type of provided services
	Level of operation
	Quality of service
	Coverage
Backbone network – expenses	Number of BTS
	Price of backbone network
Expenses on BTS equipment	Harmonized band Nonharmonized band

Source: own processing according to source (Marks 2009; DotEcon 2015; ERC Report 1998; PWC 2014; Joint Berec WG 2012; PA 2010)

to simplify it, we can say that mobile operator then acts as a customer and regulator as a businessman. Despite this the public choice theory admits that all individuals have a will to sacrifice themselves for the public good. The national regulator and pricing authority in the area of electronic communications must follow the duties that support effective competition and effective investment and innovations. Determining the value of radio spectrum and subsequent price setting must therefore comply with these rules.

Acknowledgments This contribution was undertaken, as parts of the research project No VEGA 1/0515/15 Endogenous factors of the IPR intensive industries in the regional enterprise environment in Slovak Republic.

References

Andrisková, I. (2014). Pareto efficiency as a conjunction of spectrum and transport policy management. TRANS-MECH-ART-CHEM : X meždunarodnaja naučno-praktičeskaja konferencija : 26.-27.5.2014, Moskva. ISBN 978-5-7876-0219-7.

Arthur, D. (2009). *Little: Mobile Broadband, Competition and Spectrum Caps*. 5 s. http://www.gsma.com/spectrum/wp-content/uploads/2012/07/Spectrum-Mobile-[online] [cit. 2014–14-08] - broadband-competition-and-caps-report-2009.pdf

Azcoitia, S. A., Fernandez, M. A. M., & Verdura, L. M. G. (2010). Using bottom-up LRIC models to calculate radio spectrum value for mobile operators. *9th Conference on Telecommunications Internet and Media Techno Economics (CTTE)*, 7–9 June, 2010, s.1–7.

Bazelon, C., & Mchenry, G. (2012). *Spectrum value. Social Science Research Network*. TRPC. [online] [cit. 2014–18-08], http://ssrn.com/abstract=2032213

Bozsoki, I. (2012). *Spectrum management fundamentals. ICT regulation toolkit*. International Telecommunication Union. Geneva, Switzerland.

Bruwaene, K. B. (2003). *Estimating the value of spectrum*. [online] [cit. 2014–03-08], https://tech.ebu.ch/docs/techreview/trev_294-van_bruwaene.pdf

Connolly, S. (1999). *MUNRO, A.: Economics of the Public Sector* (536 p). Upper Saddle River: Fiunancial Times Press. ISBN 9780130966414.

Cramton, P. (2001). *Spectrum auctions*. [online] [cit. 2014–15-08] http://www.cramton.umd.edu/papers2000-2004/01hte-spectrum-auctions.pdf

DotEcon. (2015). *Spectrum awards database*. [online] [cit. 2016–04-03] http://www.dotecon.com/expertise/spectrum-awards-database/

Doyle, C. H. (2007). *The pricing of radio spectrum: using incentives mechanisms to achieve efficiency*. [online] [cit. 2014–17-08] https://www.itu.int/osg/spu/stn/spectrum/workshop_proceedings/Background_Papers_Final/Chris%20Doyle%20-%20Incentive%20based%20spectrum%20prices.pdf

ERC Report 53. (1998). *Report on the introduction of economic criteria in spectrum management and the principles of fees and charging in the CEPT* [online] [cit. 2014–07-08] http://www.erodocdb.dk/docs/doc98/official/pdf/Rep053.pdf

Hirschleier, J., a kol. (2005) *Price theory and applications, Seventh edition*. New York: Cambridge University Press. 340 s. ISBN 978-0-521-81864-3.

ICT Regulation Toolking. (2013). *Radio spectrum management*. [online] [cit. 2014–03-08], http://www.ictregulationtoolkit.org/5

Joint Berec/Rspg Working Group On Competition Issues. (2012). Report on exploring the economic and social value of radio spectrum for certain electronic communications services with respect to the frequency assignment procedures.

Kejun, Y. (2005). The process of the Study of Radio Spectrum Economic Value. *Chinese Radio, 8*, 11–14.

Laflin, N., & Dajka, B. (January 2007). A simple guide to radio spectrum management. *EBU Technical Journal*. [online] [cit. 2014–27-07] http://www.ebu.ch/fr/technical/trev/trev_309-spectrum.pdf

Lisý, J., a kol. (2003). Dejiny ekonomických teórií. Bratislava. Wolters Kluwer. ISBN 80-89047-60-2.

Malisuwan, S., a kol. (2014). Estimation of commercial value of spectrum: The approach adopted in Thailand. *Journal of Economics, Business and Management*, *2*(2), May 2014. [online] [cit. 2014–18-08], http://www.joebm.com/papers/104-N00005.pdf

Marks, P., a kol. (2009). *Estimating the commercial trading value of spectrum*. Plum Consulting.

Nachira, A., & Mazzini, G. (2011). The value of the radio spectrum: a comparison between theory and auctions. *2011 IEEE International Conference on Ultra-Wideband (ICUWB)*. 978-1-4577-1763-5.

Plum Consulting. (2011). *Methodologies for valuing spectrum: Review of the experts' report*. [online], http://www.plumconsulting.co.uk/pdfs/PLUM_March2011_Methodologies_for_Valuing_Spectrum_-_Review_of_the_Experts_Report.pdf

Prat, A., & Valleti, T. (2000). *Spectrum auctions versus beauty contests: costs and benefits*. 5 s. [online] [cit. 2014–014–08], http://istituti.unicatt.it/economia_impresa_lavoro_OECD-draft.pdf

PWC. (2014). *GNCC Spectrum Pricing Model project*. [online] [cit. 2016–30-03] http://www.gncc.ge/uploads/other/0/841.pdf

PA Consulting Group. (2010). *Study on comparability of frequency bands in different business models*. Conducted for Ministerie van Economische Zaken.

Sharif, H. (2014). *Spectrum economics*. [online] [cit. 2014–03-08] http://www.itu.int/net/itu_search/index.aspx?cx=001276825495132238663%3Anqzm45z846q&cof=FORID%3A9&ie=UTF-8&q=radio+spectrum+demand

Song, Q., & Wang, W. (2009). Research on economic evaluation methodology for radio spectrum resource management. *Management and Service Science, 2009. MASS '09. International Conference*. 1–6.

Spectrum management fundamentals. The need for spectrum management. (2013) [online] [cit. 2014–01-08] http://www.itu.int/en/ITU-R/seminars/rrs/Documents/Tutorial/SM_Fundamentals_Part1.pdf.

Struzak, R. (2006a). *Spectrum management & regulatory issues*. [online] [cit. 2014–25-07] http://ryszard.struzak.com/docs/4Spctrm_Mngmnt+RR.pdf

Struzak, R. (2006b). *Access to spectrum/orbit resources and principles of spectrum management*. [online] [cit. 2014–25-07], http://www.ictregulationtoolkit.org/en/toolkit/docs/Document/3268

Vítek, M. (2014). *Ocenění kmitočtového pásma jako omezeného přírodního zdroje*. [online] [cit. 2014–27-07] Dostupné na internete: <https://ekonom.feld.cvut.cz/web/images/stories/predmety/x16eet/eet02-oceneni_kmitoctu.pdf>

Wang, H., Wang, Q., & Jing, S. (2010). Spectrum pricing based on the method of modification to the benchmark price. *Information Science and Engineering (ICISE), 2010 2nd International Conference*. 2379–2382.

Yan, J. J., & Lc, T. J. (2011). Evaluation system of economic value of radio spectrum. *Journal of Beijing University of Posts and Telecommunications, 13*(4), 51–56.

Chapter 23
Real Options Games Between Asymmetric Firms on a Competitive Market

Elżbieta Rychłowska-Musiał

Abstract The main goal and the original contribution of this paper are to find and describe optimal investment strategies for asymmetric firms acting on a competitive market. Investment decision-making process is described as a game between two players, and the real options approach is used to find a value of an investment project; therefore, the paper falls in the area of the real options games (ROG). We also study the effect of a project risk level (measured by volatility) on a firm's investment strategy and examine a case of symmetric firms as well. It is no surprise that the advantage is mostly on the side of a dominant company, but under some circumstances, a weaker party has a very strong bargaining chip. Firms may cooperate, and their negotiations could be supported by a payoff transfer computed as the *coco value*. It also turned out that the cooperation between competitors gains in significance when a project risk is high regardless of whether firms are asymmetric or symmetric.

23.1 Introduction

It is by no means a simple matter to develop a firm in a competitive environment, especially if there are disparities in firms' market power. A firm has to strictly monitor changes occurring in the market and try to adapt its strategy to evolving circumstances. These changes and adaptation possibilities should be taken into account in evaluations that support decision-making processes. Real options are a tool which enables this (e.g., Dixit and Pindyck 1994; Luehrman 1998; Mun 2002).

The next key factor for firm's success on the market is its ability to cope with competitors. The firm should closely follow competitor's behaviors, try to understand them, and anticipate competitor's moves. Of course the effect of

E. Rychłowska-Musiał (✉)
Poznań University of Economics and Business, Poznań, Poland
e-mail: elzbieta.musial@ue.poznan.pl

N. Tsounis, A. Vlachvei (eds.), *Advances in Panel Data Analysis in Applied Economic Research*, Springer Proceedings in Business and Economics,
https://doi.org/10.1007/978-3-319-70055-7_23

competition should be incorporated into firm's decision-making process, as well. The game theory provides tools to do that (Smit and Ankum 1993; Grenadier 2000; Smit and Trigeorgis 2004; Chevalier-Roignant and Trigeoris 2011; Trigeogris and Baldi 2013).

The main goal and the original contribution of this paper are to find and describe optimal investment strategies for asymmetric firms acting on a competitive market. Investment decision-making process is described as a game between two players, and the real options approach is used to find a value of an investment project; therefore, the paper falls in the area of the real options games (ROG). We also study the effect of a project risk level (measured by volatility) on the firm's investment strategy and examine a case of symmetric firms as well.

The rest of the paper is structured as follows: Sect. 23.2 presents basic assumptions of a model of interaction between asymmetric firms and relations between model's parameters. Section 23.3 contains the real options games analysis. Main results are summarized in the Sect. 23.4. The next two sections present key findings of sensitivity analysis devoted to the impact of the project risk (Sect. 23.5) and the market share (Sect. 23.6) on firm optimal policies resulting from real options games between them. Section 23.7 concludes.

23.2 The Model of Interaction Between Firms

We consider two risk-neutral firms (A and B) operating on a competitive market. Each of them can make a new investment. Both competitors share the same investment opportunity – it is a shared option (Smit and Trigeorgis 2004, 35). Each of the firms may exercise the option by paying investment expenditure I, $I > 0$. We assume that the lifetime of the investment project is infinite.

The investment project generates cash flows (Y_t), which evolve in accordance with the geometric Brownian motion, with drift α, $\alpha > 0$ and volatility σ, $\sigma > 0$ under the risk-neutral measure. A risk-free asset yields a constant rate of return r; δ is a convenience yield ($\delta > 0$), and it reflects an opportunity cost of delaying construction of the project and instead keeping the option to invest alive (Dixit and Pindyck 1994, p.149). The present value of the project is determined by the discounting and accumulating of its future cash flows. It is equal to $V(Y_0) = \frac{Y_0}{\delta}$ (Dixit and Pindyck 1994, 181).

Further, let μ be the total expected rate of return from owning the completed project. It is a sum of the expected percentage rate of growth of Y_t (α) and the convenience yield (δ):

$$\mu = \alpha + \delta.$$

Then again, according to CAPM, let μ be the expected rate of return from holding a financial asset (non-dividend paying) perfectly correlated with Y_t; it complies with the following formula:

$$\mu = r + (r_{\mathrm{m}} - r) \cdot \frac{\sigma \cdot \rho_{\mathrm{m}}}{\sigma_{\mathrm{m}}},$$

where r_{m} is the expected return on the market, σ_{m} is the standard deviation of r_{m}, and ρ_{m} is the correlation of the asset with the market portfolio.

Under the assumption of constant risk-free rate (r) and constant expected return on the market (r_{m}), the significant links are between the project risk (σ), the opportunity cost of delaying investment (δ), and the expected percentage rate of change of cash flows (α) (Dixit and Pindyck 1994). We will assume that α is a fundamental fact about Y_t and there exist links only between σ and δ according to:

$$r + (r_{\mathrm{m}} - r) \cdot \frac{\sigma \cdot \rho_m}{\sigma_{\mathrm{m}}} = \alpha + \delta.$$

Considering the implementation of the project, a firm chooses between three basic strategies: *Wait*, *Invest*, or *Abandon*. The primary criterion for investment decisions is the comparison between the investment option value, the benefits of instantaneous investment, and zero. However, for the shared option, a firm has to include its rivals' decision into its decision-making process. A firm has to take into account both how its investment decision affects its competitor and how it itself may be impacted by rival reactions. Therefore, firms' strategic choices could be described as non-zero sum games.

When firms are both active on a market, there is a market power asymmetry between them. Without loss of generality, we will assume that firm A has u market share dominance ($0.5 < u < 1$); firm B is left with ($1 - u$) share. While only the one firm decides to invest, it obtains the whole market, and the firm which is deferring investment losses its market share toward the investing firm.

There are four possible cases of firms' decisions. The decision to invest or to defer is made at time $t = 0$, and functions of payments are as follows:

1. Firms A and B invest immediately and simultaneously. They share the project's benefits in accordance with their market shares; the payment for each firm is the net present value of the project:

$$NPV_0^A := NPV(u \cdot Y_t)\big|_{t=0} = V(u \cdot Y_0) - I;$$

$$NPV_0^B := NPV((1-u) \cdot Y_t)\big|_{t=0} = V((1-u) \cdot Y_0) - I,$$

where

u – the market share of firm A

2. Firms A and B defer and keep their investment options. The payment for each of them is the call option value from the Black-Scholes-Merton model (the

underlying asset is the present value of the project determined with an appropriate part of project's benefits ($u \cdot Y_t$ for firm A or $(1-u) \cdot Y_t$ for firm B), and the exercise price is the investment expenditure I):

$$F_0^A := F(u \cdot Y_t)\big|_{t=0};$$

$$F_0^B := F((1-u) \cdot Y_t)\big|_{t=0}.$$

3. Firm A invests immediately and gains the whole market. Its payment is the net present value of the whole project:

$$NPV_0 := NPV(Y_t)|_{t=0} = V(Y_0) - I,$$

firm B defers and its payment is zero. It is forced to abandon the investment project.

4. Firm A defers and firm B invests immediately. Then their payments are opposite to these of the case 3.

To visualize values of these payments and to analyze games, let us assume a basic set of parameters: investment expenditure $I = 6$ (in monetary unit); expiration date $T = 2$ (years); risk-free rate $r = 1.96\%$ (*YTM* of treasury bonds with maturity date equal to expiration date of investment option); the expected percentage rate of change of project cash flows $\alpha = 1\%$ (expert prediction); volatility of the project's benefits $\sigma = 60\%$; the expected return on the market $r_{\mathrm{m}} = 6.03\%$ (rate of return on market index WIG 2012–2016); the standard deviation of r_{m}, $\sigma_{\mathrm{m}} = 14.65\%$; and the correlation of the asset with the market portfolio $\rho_{\mathrm{m}} = 0.5$ (expert calculations). Assumptions about the parameters reflect a situation of a real company (a similar approach is used by authors of cited papers). Additionally we assume the firm A's market share is $u = 0.75$ (so 0.25 of the market pie is left for firm B).

We are going to consider different initial values of the cash flows generated by the project $Y_0 > 0$, which enables us to formulate games and find most advantageous strategies for each firm under different present values of the project $V_0 > 0$.

Figure 23.1 presents the option values (F_0^{A}, F_0^{B}), the benefits of instantaneous investment for the only investor (NPV_0), and the benefits when the firms invest immediately and simultaneously ($\mathrm{NPV}_0^{\mathrm{A}}$, $\mathrm{NPV}_0^{\mathrm{B}}$).

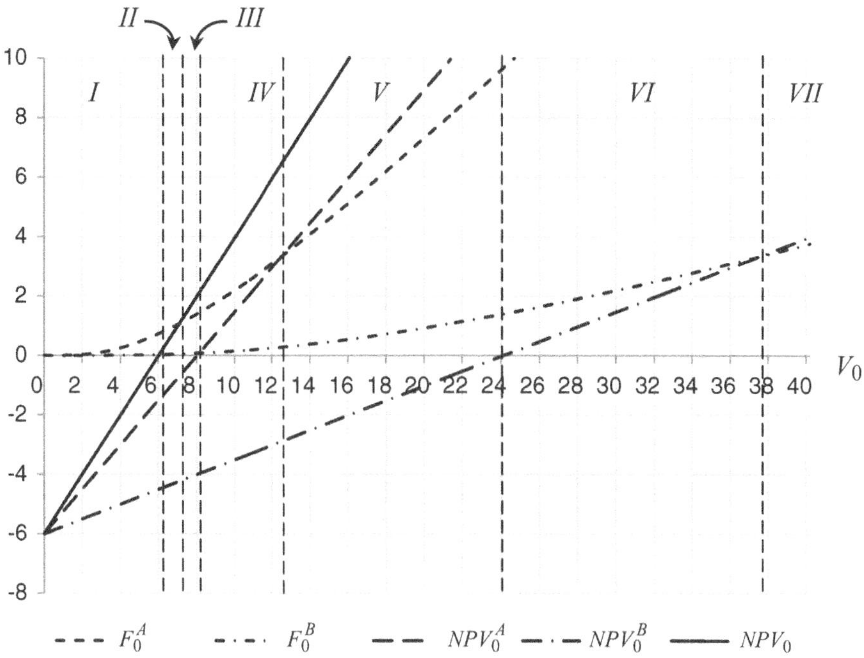

Fig. 23.1 The investment option values (F_0^A, F_0^B), the net present value for the only investor (NPV_0), and the net present values when both firms invest immediately and simultaneously (NPV_0^A, NPV_0^B) for different present values of the project (V_0) and regions of firms' interactions. Base case parameters (Source: own study)

23.3 Real Options Games Analysis

The type of the game, the way it is played, and the payments depend on the relationship between the values (payments): NPV_0, NPV_0^A,NPV_0^B, F_0^A, F_0^B, and 0. For each firm we can identify four types of these relationships, which lead to seven ranges of the present value of the project's benefits (V_0) (Fig. 23.1). In every region firms are playing different games, but these games have one general normal form, which is presented in Table 23.1.

We are going to determine a dominant strategy for each player in every game (if it exists) and indicate Nash equilibria. In the NE no player has anything to gain by changing only its own strategy. If the other player is rational, it is reasonable for each of them to expect its opponent to follow the recommendation of NE as well (Watson 2013, p.82). So the Nash equilibrium is a kind of prediction of how the game will be played for rational players. However, it is well known that the NE may, but not need to, give players the highest possible payoffs. In these cases, firms could consider negotiations as a way to achieve better results.

Table 23.1 Payoff matrix

		Firm B	
		Wait (W)	*Invest (I)*
Firm A	*Wait (W)*	$(F_0^A; F_0^B)$	$(0; \mathrm{NPV}_0)$
	Invest (I)	$(\mathrm{NPV}_0; 0)$	$(\mathrm{NPV}_0^A; \mathrm{NPV}_0^B)$

Source: own study

Table 23.2 Example of payoff matrix for region *I* ($V_0 = 5$)

	Wait (W)	*Invest (I)*
Wait (W)	(0.26; 0.01)	(0; −1)
Invest (I)	(−1; 0)	(−3; −5)

Table 23.3 Example of payoff matrix for region *II* ($V_0 = 6.24$)

	Wait (W)	*Invest (I)*
Wait (W)	(0.46; 0.02)	(0; 0.24)
Invest (I)	(0.24; 0)	(−2.26; −4.75)

In *region I* the net present value of the project is very low; it is lower than investment option values for both competitors and lower than zero ($\mathrm{NPV}_0^A < \mathrm{NPV}_0 < 0 < F_0^A$ and $\mathrm{NPV}_0^B < \mathrm{NPV}_0 < 0 < F_0^B$). Table 23.2 presents sample payoffs in the game for this region.

Keeping the investment option (waiting) is a dominant strategy for each firm. Since the strictly dominant strategy exists for each player, the game has the only one unique Nash equilibrium $(W; W)$. Both players achieve the highest possible payments $(F_0^A; F_0^B)$. In this region of project benefits V_0, when they are really low, waiting is the optimal decision for both competitors.

The situation completely changes when the net present value of the project for the only investor exceeds the value of the investment option for firm B (only), but when both firms invest at the same time, the net present values of the project remain negative ($\mathrm{NPV}_0^A < 0 < \mathrm{NPV}_0 < F_0^A$ and $\mathrm{NPV}_0^B < 0 < F_0^B < \mathrm{NPV}_0$, *region II*). It is a very attractive situation for firm B and an awkward one for firm A.

Sample payoffs in the game for this region are presented in Table 23.3.

Firm A has a dominant strategy – *Wait*, so if it is a rational player it delays investment decision. There is no dominant strategy for firm B, but, under the assumption of common knowledge, the B' best response to the A' strategy *Wait* is the strategy *Invest*, and the strategy profile $(W; I)$ is the Nash equilibrium. Therefore, firm B should invest and take the whole market.

The firm A could obviously anticipate it, and there arises a problem to find a way of arbitrating game which does take into account strategic inequalities but has a claim to fairness. There is also a circumstance which can strengthen A's bargaining position – it can threaten to invest immediately as well and cause a loss for firm B. Actually, firm A also loses in this case, but its loss is smaller than B' one.

So the firm A ought to negotiate with firm B an investment delaying. But implementation of negotiation's outcome may be quite difficult, and moreover there occurs another problem concerning payoff transfers. A first idea of how to solve this problem – the Nash arbitration scheme – was proposed by Nash (1950). But the Nash arbitration scheme is neither superior nor the only possible one. Another

Table 23.4 The *coco* decomposition of game in region *II* ($V_0 = 6.24$)

Cooperative component			Competitive component	
(0.24; 0.24)	(0.12; 0.12)	+	(0.22; −0.22)	(−0.12; 0.12)
(0.12; 0.12)	(−3.51; −3.51)		(0.12; −0.12)	(1.25; −1.25)

interesting solution of the payoff transfer problem has been described by Kalai and Kalai (2009) and Kalai and Kalai (2013) as a *cooperative-competitive value* (*coco value* for short). The calculation of the *coco value* relies on a natural decomposition of game into cooperative and competitive components. The *coco value* is a sum of the *maxmax* payoff for cooperative team game (equal for both players) and the *minmax* one for the competitive game (the value of the zero-sum game) which is an adjustment compensating transfer from the strategically weaker player to the stronger one (Kalai and Kalai 2009, p.2).

Table 23.4 presents a decomposition of the game from Table 23.3 into two components. The cooperative payoffs are obtained as *maxmax* solution of the first decomposition component. But these equal payments should be adjusted in order to take into account the strategic position of both parties. The value of this compensation is the value of the competitive zero-sum game. So, the *coco value* is computed as:

$$\text{Coco value} = (0.24; 0.24) + (0.2; -0.2) = (0.44; 0.04)\,.$$

So, an interesting possibility of the game solution is a strategy profile $(W; W)$ which is accompanied by payoff transfer of 0.02 from the firm A to the firm B.

At the first sight, it could appear unreasonable that B would be willing to obtain the *cocopayoff* of 0.04 instead of the payoff of 0.24 that it get by playing its best response to the A's dominant strategy. But we should notice that it contains also a price of protection against losses which would be faced by both in the case of simultaneous investment.

In *the region III* firms' positions remain also unsatisfactory ($\text{NPV}_0^A < 0 < F_0^A < \text{NPV}_0$ and $\text{NPV}_0^B < 0 < F_0^B < \text{NPV}_0$). For initial values of the project benefits falling under the region *III*, the game has two pure nonequivalent and noninterchangeable equilibria, $(W; I)$ and $(I; W)$, and a mixed strategy equilibrium where each player *Waits* with probability p $(p \bullet W, (1-p) \bullet I; p \bullet W, (1-p) \bullet I)$. This game has no dominant strategy for any player, so each of them may seek different equilibrium. Without coordination their decisions may lead to the strategy profile $(I; I)$. Obviously $(I; I)$ is not a good solution, since both A and B could be better off at strategy $(W; W)$ getting positive payoffs instead of negative ones.

Sample payoffs in the game for this region are presented in Table 23.5.

It is interesting that the *coco value* in this game is (1;1) + (1;−1) = (2;0).

It means that firm A has the stronger strategic position than firm B, and if negotiations about deferring investment project are opened, firm B will have nothing

Table 23.5 Example of payoff matrix for region *III* ($V_0 = 8$)

	Wait (*W*)	*Invest* (*I*)
Wait (*W*)	(0.85; 0.04)	(0; 2)
Invest (*I*)	(2; 0)	(−1.2; −4.4)

Table 23.6 Example of payoff matrix for region *V* ($V_0 = 14$)

	Wait (*W*)	*Invest* (*I*)
Wait (*W*)	(2.75; 0.21)	(0; 8)
Invest (*I*)	(8; 0)	(2.4; −3.2)

Table 23.7 Example of payoff matrix for region *VI* ($V_0 = 32$)

	Wait (*W*)	*Invest* (*I*)
Wait (*W*)	(10.61; 1.6)	(0; 26)
Invest (*I*)	(26; 0)	(13.2; 0.4)

to offer. So it seems that in this case, firm A should invest, and firm B is left to abandon the project.

We can observe a similar, or even better for A, situation in *the regions IV* and *V* ($0 < \mathrm{NPV}_0^A < F_0^A < \mathrm{NPV}_0$ or $0 < F_0^A < \mathrm{NPV}_0^A < \mathrm{NPV}_0$ and $\mathrm{NPV}_0^B < 0 < F_0^B < \mathrm{NPV}_0$). Firm A obtains benefits whenever it is an only investor, or both firms invest simultaneously on the market. Firm B experiences losses or has to abandon the project. The dominant strategy for firm A is *Invest*, and the B′ best response is *Wait* which means *Abandon* in these cases.

Sample payoffs in the game for the region *V* are presented in Table 23.6.

For firm B situation changes only when benefits from immediate investment (for both competitors) become positive simultaneously ($0 < F_0^{\mathrm{A}} < \mathrm{NPV}_0^{\mathrm{A}} < \mathrm{NPV}_0$ and $0 < \mathrm{NPV}_0^{\mathrm{B}} < F_0^{\mathrm{B}} < \mathrm{NPV}_0$ or $0 < F_0^{\mathrm{B}} < \mathrm{NPV}_0^{\mathrm{B}} < \mathrm{NPV}_0$, *regions VI* and *VII*). It occurs for very large present values of project benefits V_0.

For both players the strategy profile $(I; I)$ is the optimal one. *Invest* is the dominant strategy for both parties leading to the Nash equilibrium. The payoffs in this strategy profile are the best for both players. For high values of the project, *Invest* is the best natural decision. Sample payoffs in the game for the region *VI* are presented in Table 23.7.

23.4 Conclusions

The subject of the last section was interactions between asymmetric firms on a competitive market connected with investment project execution. We have shown that for different present values of project benefits firms are playing different games. We have tried to identify the solution of every game and propose the best strategy for each firm. Our findings may be summarized as follows:

1. Decision: invest, wait, or cooperate is always on the part of the dominant company on a competitive market, but under some circumstances, the weaker party may have a very strong bargaining chip.

2. The precise recognition of the competitor situation is particularly important when an economic analysis of an investment project made by a dominant market party suggests deferring the investment project execution and keeping an investment option. Where it is found that the weaker competitor could benefit being the only investor on the market the stronger competitor should propose cooperation to the weaker one (delaying investment project execution) in order to avoid losses. An attractive incentive to engage in this cooperation may prove to be payoff transfer computed as the coco value.
3. When the economic analysis of an investment project made by the dominant firm recommends an immediate investment, the dominant firm has no reason to cooperate with the weaker firm which should abandon the project.
4. *Invest* is a profitable strategy for both firms only for really large present values of the investment project.

23.5 The Impact of the Project Risk

A project risk is one of the more important factors having a direct effect on an optimal policy of a firm. To study this issue, we relax the assumption about a fixed project risk level. The sensitivity analysis was performed for $\sigma \epsilon [10\%; 120\%]$, and its results provide a basis for following conclusions:

1. When a project risk is low, the dominant firm has no motivation to cooperate with the weaker one because in this case, the situation when the investment execution is profitable only for the weaker competitor (region *II* of the present values of the project benefits) does not appear. The dominant firm ought to conduct a project value analysis and follow its recommendation: *Wait* or *Invest*.
2. When a project risk is high, cooperation between competitors gains in significance. The region *II* of the present values of the project benefits becomes larger, and for the wider range of these values, the dominant party should be willing to offer cooperation to the weaker partner in order to delay investment project and keep investment option. In the case of high risk, the compensation to the weaker firm for delaying investment execution (calculated as the *coco value*) should be greater than in the case of low risk.

23.6 The Impact of Sharing of a Market

The degree of the asymmetry between firms' market shares is the next significant factor which influences the type of games between firms and their optimal strategies. The sensitivity analysis was made for $u \epsilon [0.5; 1)$, and its findings are as follows:

1. The more significant the firms' market power differences are, the narrower the range of present value of the project benefits which could be an incentive to

Table 23.8 Example of payoff matrix for region *III*, $u = 0.5$ ($V_0 = 8$)

	Wait (*W*)	*Invest* (*I*)
Wait (*W*)	(0.55; 0.55)	(0; 2)
Invest (*I*)	(2; 0)	(−2; −2)

Table 23.9 Example of payoff matrix for a new region, the intersection of *IV* and *VI*, $u = 0.5$ ($V_0 = 15$)

	Wait (*W*)	*Invest* (*I*)
Wait (*W*)	(2.21; 2.21)	(0; 9)
Invest (*I*)	(9; 0)	(1.5; 1.5)

cooperation between firms. Under strong asymmetry conditions, the dominant firm is not forced to cooperation with the weaker one. The dominant firm strategy takes on a monopoly character.

2. When the disparity between firms market shares is low and they are more or less the same, another kind of problematic interactions between firms becomes increasingly important.

For quite a wide range of present value of the project benefits, there are no dominant strategies in games between firms, and neither of them has a strategic advantage (region *III*, $\mathrm{NPV}_0^i < 0 < F_0^i < \mathrm{NPV}_0$ for $i = A, B$). Sample payoffs in the game for this region in the case of symmetric firms are presented in Table 23.8.

This game has two pure nonequivalent and noninterchangeable Nash equilibria: (W;I) and (I; W) and a mixed one. Both players may seek different equilibria deciding *Invest* and obtaining, as a result, the worst possible payments.

Furthermore, there arises a new kind of interactions between firms: a game of a prisoner's dilemma nature. This kind of game we can observe for project values from a new region which is the intersection of regions *IV* and *VI* ($0 < \mathrm{NPV}_0^i < F_0^i < \mathrm{NPV}_0$ for i=A, B). Sample payoffs in the game for this region in the case of symmetric firms are presented in Table 23.9.

The game has a dominant strategy and one unique Nash equilibrium for each firm in this case (strategy profile (I; I)), but it does not seem to be a very happy choice, since both players would provide much higher payoffs choosing strategy: *Wait*.

In both cases coco values suggest cooperation but without any compensation. They are adequately equal, for the game from the Table 23.8:

$$\text{Coco value} = (1; 1) + (0; 0) = (1; 1)\,.$$

For the game from the Table 23.9:

$$\text{Coco value} = (4.5; 4.5) + (0; 0) = (4.5; 4.5)\,.$$

There is no dominant party in these relationships; thus, the teamwork could take the form of co-opetition, for example. The co-opetition is one of the types of interaction between firms on a market. It brings benefits from both the cooperation and competition, and it could mean investment expenditure sharing and then competing on the product market (e.g., Dagnino and Padula 2002; Rychłowska-Musiał 2017). This is particularly important because the range of present project values that determines prisoner' dilemma interactions between firms extends when risk increases.

23.7 Final Remarks

The basis of firm's strategic decisions should be not only attentive monitoring of changes occurring on the market and adaptation to evolving circumstances but also keeping track of competitor behaviors and incorporating them into firms' decision-making processes.

The effect of competition should be reflected in investment project valuation methods. If they fail to take account of the competition impact, the investment project will be overvalued.

But even if we can compute the proper value of the project (as the net present value or the real option value) taking into account the externalities, it may not be the only basis for investment decision-making under competitive market conditions, as it was shown in the paper. To make the optimal strategic decision, a firm has to try to predict its rival's decision and then to find the best response to it. Appropriate tools for solving these problems seem to be the real options games' approach and the *coco value* concept as a complement to the analysis.

References

Chevalier-Roignant, B., & Trigeoris, L. (2011). *Competitive strategy: Options and games*. Cambridge: The MIT Press.

Dagnino, G. B., Padula, G. (2002). Coopetition strategy. *A new kind of interfirm dynamics for value creation, second annual conference - innovative research in management*, Stockholm, 9–11 May 2002

Dixit, A. K., & Pindyck, R. S. (1994). *Investment under uncertainty*. Princeton: Princeton University Press.

Grenadier, S. R. (2000). *Game choices: The intersection of real options and game theory*. London: Risk Books.

Kalai, A., & Kalai, E. (2009). *Engineering cooperation in two-player games*, working paper. Evanston, IL.

Kalai, A., & Kalai, E. (2013). Cooperation in strategic games revisited. *The Quarterly Journal of Economics, 169*, 917–966.

Luehrman, T. A. (1998). Strategy as a portfolio of real options. *Harvard Business Review, 76*(5), 89–99.

Mun, J. (2002). *Real options analysis*. New York: J. Wiley.

Nash, J. F. (1950). The Bargaining Problem. *Econometrica, 18*, 155–162.

Rychłowska-Musiał, E. (2017). Value creation in a firm through coopetition: Real options games approach. Contemporary trends and changes in finance. *Proceedings from the 2nd Wroclaw international conference in finance*, Jajuga K, Orlowski LT, Staehr K (Eds.), Springer proceedings in Business and Economics, Springer

Smit, H. T. J., & Ankum, L. A. (1993). A real options and game-theoretic approach to corporate investment strategy under competition. *Financial Management, 22*(3), 241–250.

Smit, H. T. J., & Trigeorgis, L. (2004). *Strategic investment. Real options and games*. Princeton and Oxford: Princeton University Press.

Trigeogris, L., & Baldi, F. (2013). Patent strategies: Fight or cooperate?, *Real options annual conference*, Tokyo, 25–26 June 2013.

Watson, J. (2013). *An introduction to game theory*. New York: Norton W.W. & Company Inc..

Chapter 24
The Dynamic Effect of Bank Size on Earnings Volatility in Iranian Banking System

Mahshid Shahchera and Fatemeh Noorbakhsh

Abstract The importance of earnings volatility in banking system has long been accepted in the accounting and finance literature. Earnings volatility has an effect either through its relation to the discount rate or expected cash flows (earnings) in assessment models. Most of the studies have been focused on the relationship between cost of capital and earnings volatility. One established result is a positive relationship between earnings volatility and different measures in cost of capital. (J Money Credit Banking 29:300–313, 1997) state that large banks have more risky revenues than small banks; therefore, the degree of risky revenues is linked to bank size and type of bank. For this reason, we use Herfindahl-Hirshman index (HHI) and dummy variables for different types of banks in order to examine the relationship between earnings volatility and bank size in Iran.

We find that bank size is negatively related to earnings volatility; therefore, larger banks have lower earnings volatility compared to smaller banks. We use dummy variables in order to consider the relationship between bank type and earnings volatility. We identify different results according to different types of banks because state banks and specialized banks have positive impact on earnings volatility, while private and privatized banks have negative effects on earnings volatility. Therefore, state banks and specialized banks have more risky revenues, while private and privatized banks have less risky revenues.

Keywords Bank earnings volatility · Bank size · Market concentration

---

M. Shahchera (✉) · F. Noorbakhsh
Monetary and Banking Research Institute, Tehran, Iran
e-mail: mahshidshahchera@yahoo.com; sfnoorbakhsh@gmail.com

N. Tsounis, A. Vlachvei (eds.), *Advances in Panel Data Analysis in Applied Economic Research*, Springer Proceedings in Business and Economics,
https://doi.org/10.1007/978-3-319-70055-7_24

24.1 Introduction

The global financial crisis has showed an important debate related to bank size. The main issue in this regard is the relationship between bank size and earnings volatility, which is one of the important topics in banking system, since earnings volatility may cause uncertainty throughout the equity capital level and the failure of banks' soundness. Our approach is to consider whether size affects earnings volatility. To investigate the impact of bank size on earnings volatility, we need to consider different factors which are effective on bank size and earnings volatility. One of the important factors in earnings volatility is banking sector profitability. There is evidence, which shows the link between business cycle fluctuations and banking sector profitability. Considering the connection between business cycle fluctuations and banking sector profitability, we can examine the financial stability throughout Iranian banking system.

Different papers have considered the correlation between bank size variables and economic factors. De Haan and Poghosyan (2011) investigated differences in bank efficiency which might be related to bank size. They considered that efficiency and profitability can be used as instruments which are related to bank size. Also, according to Kunt and Huizinga (2011), total asset of bank could be a proxy for bank size. The volatility of bank revenue growth has indeed declined in the 1990s, and this reflects lower volatility within net interest income growth rather than diversification benefits from increased non-interest income. Non-interest income growth is much more volatile than net interest income growth, which is largely due to the volatile trading revenue.

In this paper, we attempt to consider the relationship between earnings volatility and bank size in Iranian banking system. Several studies, such as De Haan and Poghosyan (2011), emphasized on the correlation between earnings volatility and market conditions and business strategy and income. The global financial crisis has showed different viewpoints from several economists. Some of the economists and policymakers considered too big to fail as one of the main issues related to financial crisis. De Haan and Poghosyan (2011) argue that splitting banks and constructing small banks do not necessarily assure crisis prevention. For their evidence, they pointed out to the savings and loans crisis in the USA. Also, they consider that many small banks might operate similarly, which can lead to financial instability at the same time; therefore, they may become too important to fail. Many people have presumed that small and large banks act in a different manner; however, it may not be accepted while there is small evidence related to distinctions between small and large banks.

This paper is structured as follows. In Sect. 24.2 we consider the importance of bank size and earnings volatility. In Sect. 24.3 we review the recent studies regarding bank size and earnings volatility. In Sect. 24.4 we describe our dataset and the empirical model. In Sect. 24.5, we present the empirical results concerning the relationship between earnings volatility and bank size according to dynamic panel data (GMM model). Also, in the empirical model, we emphasize on different types of banks in Iranian banking system. In Sect. 24.6, we analyze our conclusion.

24.2 Bank Size and Earnings Volatility

There are plenty of explanations related to bank size in banking system. First, it is important to point out the issue considering the advantage of large banks in economies of scale, which affect the business model of banks. Larger banks would have better diversification, and therefore, facing fewer risks, which would allow them to operate with lower capital and less-stable funding. Also, larger banks can operate in different markets, and they might have an advantage in market-based activities. Market-based activities may use more leverage and unstable funding. Smaller banks are likely to have their comparative advantage in more traditional manner, and they would lend based on their relationships. Bank size has an effect on cost of debt, which makes banks more willing to use leverage and unstable funding and also engage in risky market-based activities. Large banks would affect by unreliable corporate governance. Bank managers are likely to increase their size in order to receive more bailouts (Murphy 1985; Gabaix and Landier 2008) or because they enjoy private benefits from the prestige of running a large firm (Jensen 1986). Managers can reach larger size by attracting additional funding and increasing bank leverage, or they can merge with other banks. Larger banks are able to use economies of scale for their own interests; also they can benefit from too-big-to-fail subsidies, despite of uncertainty of their value across countries and over different times. Although it is difficult to analyze the importance of larger banks, there is evidence that larger banks are likely to face specific corporate governance challenges. Early studies have emphasized that the economies of scale are limited for small banks, in which there is no evidence of economies of scale beyond US$10–US$50 billion in banks' assets (Benston et al. 1982; Berger and Mester 1997; Pcristiani 1997).

Bank size and optimal bank size are important issues in banking literature. Most of the studies related to economies of scale mainly focused on cost of economies which is the ability of banks to have efficient spending and performance. Kovner et al. (2014) estimated the total value in the US banking system for banks. The appropriate approach is to take into account the diversification abilities of larger banks. Studies, which considered possible changes in the input and product mix of banks, found economies of scale significantly effective. Wheelock and Wilson (2011) and Hughes and Mester (2013) emphasized that 1% increase in bank size would increase costs only 0.95% for both small and large banks. However, these results should be treated cautiously. Larger banks could diversify by moving from traditional deposit taking and lending to more cost-effective but riskier wholesale funding and market-based activities.

In the wake of global financial crisis in 2007–2010, as many banks were specified too big to fail, a number of economists and policymakers consider the structure of banking sector. According to Buiter (2009), bank size is one of the main issues related to financial crisis because the failure of larger banks could affect several parts of banking and financial sector in economy. It is already known that in different situations, larger banks behave differently from smaller banks. Hagendorff et al.

(2012) measured systemic bank size by the ratio of bank assets to GDP and argued that systemically large banks engaged in more risky activities than small banks. Due to the diversification, which has more benefits, large banks could be more efficient than small banks. Furthermore, according to economies of scale, larger banks are able to have more revenues and more money in order to invest. As can be seen through different studies, efficiency is linked to bank size. Also, Kunt and Huizinga (2011) estimated the bank size by two indices. The first index is systemic size which is estimated by ratio of liabilities to GDP, and second index is the bank size measured by total asset of banks. They state that although bank managers prefer to increase their bank size, in a small country, it is not necessarily beneficial to have larger banks. Along with comparison between large and small banks, Demetz and Strahan (1995) showed the strong relationship between bank size and diversification. It is well known that large banks have more opportunity to diversify than smaller banks. However, Demetz and Strahan (1995) pointed out that large banks are more associated to systematic risk. Therefore, the positive correlation between bank size and systematic risk might provoke difficulties in economic system.

According to Kunt and Huizinga (2000), bank profitability and bank interest margins could be considered as the elements of banking efficiency. They find out that greater financial development would positively correlate to the efficiency of banking sector that leads to increase growth. Dichev and Tang (2008) argue that there are two effective elements for earnings volatility. First is economic shocks, and second is due to problems in the accounting determination of income. Amel et al. (2003) find out that many banks and financial institutions have merged with each other in order to gain more profit and to grow in size. However, it is empirically improved that profitability of consolidation in banking sector is limited to a relatively small size. Albertazzi and Gambacorta (2009) point out that considering the link between business cycle fluctuations and banking profitability is one of the important macroprudential analyses. Considering the connection between business cycle fluctuations and bank profitability could be helpful in analyzing whether financial and banking sector are stable. Also, Albertazzi and Gambacorta (2009) stated that banking sector profitability is one of the main elements which predict the financial crisis.

The importance of earnings volatility for banks' asset value has long been accepted in accounting and finance literature. Such volatility has an effect either through its relation to the discount rate or expected cash flows (earnings) in assessment models. Most existing study has focused on the cost of capital. One established result is a positive relationship between earnings volatility and different measures of cost of capital. Beaver et al. (1970) provide evidence that the variance of the earnings-to-price ratio is the accounting variable that is most correlated with a firm's beta coefficient. Minton and Schrand (1999) find that historical earnings volatility is strongly associated with the beta coefficient, dividend payout ratio, and share price volatility. Gebhardt et al. (2001) show that earnings volatility – measured as the standard deviation of earnings per share – is strongly associated with the ex ante cost of capital implied from the residual income model.

Few recent studies directly test the link between the value of a firm and earnings volatility for US markets. Barnes (2001) shows that earnings volatility is negatively related to firms' asset value measured by the market-to-book ratio. Allayannis et al. (2005) cite that the same relation holds but only before controlling for cash flow volatility. There is virtually no study on the relation between current earnings volatility and future performance. Therefore, the effect of increased risk of such volatility could be affected through its influence on the level of future earnings.

Risk management theories provide several explanations related to reduction in earnings volatility that can increase the value of the bank through higher expected earnings. First, the probability of financial failure and its expected direct and indirect costs increase with earnings volatility. Second, higher earnings volatility is likely to reduce the supply of internal funds to finance investment opportunities and therefore increases the probability of facing more external funds (Smith and Stulz 1985; Graham and Rogers 2002).

The compensation of risk-averse and undiversified managers, whose expected utility is concave in compensation, increases with earnings volatility as a reward for bearing non-diversifiable risk (Smith and Stulz 1985). Motivated by the under-investment effect on expected cash flows, Minton et al. (2002) (hereinafter MSW) were first, who explore the impact of volatility on future earnings. They showed that current cash flow (earnings) volatility is negatively related to future cash flow (earnings) in terms of lower forecast error and less biased predictions. They illustrate that investors are not able to fully recognize the suggestions of performance volatility for future performance.

24.3 Literature Review

A number of studies have addressed the differences between small and large banks. There are many possible sources which have pointed out advantages and disadvantages of large banks. It is necessary to consider differences between small and large banks in order to estimate whether bank size affects earnings volatility or not. According to Carter and McNulty (2005), consolidations of small banks brought up questions regarding credit and profitability of small banks. In their methodology, they provide a model which distinguished bank size from loan size effects. They find out that larger banks have the advantage of credit card lending. Also, if small banks are able to process credit information, therefore, they could survive despite the prevailing presence of larger banks in the economic system. According to Couto (2002), the sustainability of a bank mostly depends on its ability to provide sufficient earnings to protect and increase its capital and payments to its shareholders. Lack of banking earnings might represent the failure of the bank. Also, banking earnings are an important indicator of financial health and soundness of banks which can be considered as an early indicator of weakness.

Studies related to economies of scope point out that there would be negative returns to scope when banks move into market-based activities. Interestingly, the source of these negative returns is not technological. Indeed, many studies point out to the benefits of the efficient use of information from lending in the market-based activities of banks (Kroszner and Rajan 1994; Puri 1996; Drucker and Puri 2005). The main source of negative returns to scope is the cost of factors in banks, which are engaged in market-based activities (Boot and Ratnovski 2012). Negative returns to scope for banks are more apparent in different situations such as lower market valuations (Laeven and Levine 2007; Schmid and Walter 2009), higher risk (De Jonghe 2010; Demirgüç-Kunt and Huizinga 2011; Brunnermeier et al. 2012; DeYoung and Torna 2013), and lower risk-adjusted returns (Stiroh 2004; Stiroh and Rumble 2006; Baele et al. 2007). This evidence point out not only to the destruction of shareholder value but also to potential costs for other stakeholders in the bank. However, it is likely that banks' involvement in market-based activities creates surplus for banks' customers. In this regard, according to social welfare perspective, returns to scope in banking system might still be positive.

Fayman (2009) considers that there are many differences in factors, which operate in profitability of small and large banks. For example, non-interest income as a ratio of total income is a significant predictor of profitability for larger banks, but for smaller banks, this variable is insignificant. Berger et al. (2001) consider that the bank size could influence its profitability. Further, Cornett et al. (2008) point out that the bank size has an effect on performance of bank stocks, while Zimmerman (1996) examines the performance of banks in California and finds out that the bank size is an influential factor representing bank performance. Berger et al. (2001) consider that structures of small and large banks are different from each other; therefore, small banks in comparison with large banks can make loans better. According to Nakamura (1993), Petersen and Rajan (1994), and Berger and Mester (2003), small banks compared with large banks are able to access to better credit information through the firm's deposit accounts. If the firm has only one deposit banking relation, the information might be only useful for making credit decisions. For instance, small firms dealing with small banks can fit this profile. In contrast, a large bank dealing with a large firm would have multiple banking relations, which would tend large bank to unable to monitor business deposit accounts.

Hirtle and Stiroh (2007) show that during 1997–2004, US banks increasingly focused on retail banking, which was associated with lower equity and lower accounting returns for all banks; however, volatility was significantly lower in large banks.

Also Stiroh (2006a, b) emphasizes that there would be diversification benefits between US financial holding companies. However, these benefits are more important to non-interest activities in investment, which made the profitability more volatile. In the financial holding companies, increased diversification does not improve profitability. There are different studies through the countries other than the USA. Smith et al. (2003) consider a sample of banks from 15 European Union countries which show that non-interest income is less stable than interest income.

In addition to channels between banking concentration and financial stability, the literature brings up other channels, such as diversification channel. Diversification can create multiple activities and internationalized banks, which can promote financial stability, since banks become less sensitive to national economic conditions. In addition, mergers and acquisitions are likely to raise market concentration; therefore, economies of scale can be reached which can increase banking diversification (Williamson 1986). Number of studies highlights the important role of diversification in risk reduction, particularly loan portfolio diversification. Stever (2007), for example, argues that small banks are riskier than large banks because they have fewer opportunities for diversification, which may cause higher profit volatility. Beck et al. (2007) point out that concentration improves the financial stability through diversification.

Berger et al. (2009) show the negative impact of higher market concentration on banks' portfolios and confirm the destabilizing concentration thesis. Raising power of banks in market will increase interest rates on loans, which will in turn eliminate the least risky customers of banks. Bank's default risk will surge, which will induce more bankruptcies. Thus, more concentration in banking system would create more risky loan portfolio. A study by Boyd and De Nicolo (2005) using data from 134 countries over the period 1993–2004 shows that riskier portfolios are more effective despite the survival of high revenues related to banking concentration. This situation is even more risky given that big banks generally try to minimize costs of monitoring. This would make them to concentrate their lending in a single industry in order to achieve economies of scale in data collection. Loan portfolio diversification will decrease, and banks will become much more sensitive to shocks with a negative impact on financial system stability.

24.4 Variables and Empirical Model

The dataset includes information on bank balance sheet that are obtained from banking and macroeconomic reports of Central Bank of Iran for the period 2000–2015. We estimated the model with an unbalanced panel data for 25 banks in Iranian banking system.

This section represents panel model estimation and econometric analysis. We employ a dynamic system GMM estimator, which is provided by Arellano and Bond to identify the relation between earnings volatility and bank size. In this estimation technique, autocorrelation and heterogeneous sectional effects would occur because of interrupted dependent variables. According to random effects for dynamic pooling data, the GLS estimator will be biased. Arellano and Bond proposed their process by generalized method of moments in 1991, which was more efficient than previous estimators. Generalized method of moments for dynamic panel models has been developed by Arellano and Bond. Matrix' tools were applied in the model in order to eliminate correlation between interrupted variables and explanatory variables.

The dependent variable is earnings volatility in Iranian banking system. The estimation framework is as follows:

$$\begin{aligned} ROASD\ \ i,t =& \alpha 1.ROASD\ i,t-1 + \mu 1.HHI\ i,t + \beta 1\ Depositratio\ i,t + \ldots \\ & + \gamma 1.Inflation + \delta 1.COSTRATIO\ i,t + \theta 1.NONinterestincome\ ij,t \\ & + \eta 1.BANK\ TYPE^{*}SIZE\ i,t + \varepsilon i,t \end{aligned} \tag{24.1}$$

$$\begin{aligned} ROASD\ \ i,t =& \alpha 1.ROASD\ i,t-1 + \mu 1.HHI^{*}SIZE\ i,t + \beta 1\ Depositratio\ i,t + \ldots \\ & + \gamma 1.Inflation + \delta 1.COSTRATIO\ i,t + \theta 1.NONinterestincome\ ij,t \\ & + \varepsilon i,t \end{aligned} \tag{24.2}$$

Demsetz and Strahan (1997) found out that large banks would have more risky revenues than small banks; therefore, the degree of risky revenues is correlated to bank size and bank type. For this reason, we use Herfindahl-Hirshman index (HHI) and indices, which indicate different types of banks in order to consider the relationship between earnings volatility and bank size in Iran.

Non-interest income ratio can be achieved from the proportion of non-interest income to the operating income. With non-interest-income ratio, we can understand the diversification and structure of income in Iranian banking system. We use Herfindahl-Hirshman index (HHI) in order to calculate market concentration at the state level in period *t*, which is square measure of market share of each bank in banking system. $Deposit\ Ratio_{i,t}$ indicates the ratio of deposits to total liabilities of bank *i* in year *t*.

Bank size can be calculated by relative measure of bank size, which is logarithm of total assets. Studies related to bank size, such as Schwerter (2011), suggest that "too big to fail" encourages larger banks to engage in excessive risky activities. Also, Poghosyan and DeHaan (2010) used *cost-to-income ratio*, which can be seen in the econometric model estimations 1 and 2. Cost-to-income ratio is total non-interest cost to total non-interest revenue ratio, and we use this ratio to proxy the efficiency of bank, when higher cost-to-income ratio implies less efficiency in bank.

Deposit ratio is calculated by deposits to total liabilities ratio for bank I at time *t*. We use dummy variables in order to indicate four types of banks, which are in our sample, including private banks, state banks, privatized banks, and specialized banks. Each dummy variable would be equal to 1, if the bank belongs to one of the four types mentioned in our sample, and D1, D2, D3, and D4 illustrate each dummy variable. We estimate the effect of bank type on earnings volatility, which is done by multiplying dummy variables with bank size indicator. In this estimation approach, earnings volatility for banks used as a dependent variable, and we consider standard deviation of return on assets (ROA) to proxy the earnings volatility.

In one country the economic outlook can greatly impact the financial. Borio and Lowe (2002) find that low and stable inflation promotes financial stability; therefore, we use inflation in order to consider macroeconomic effects on banking system.

However, Borio and Lowe (2002) consider that when inflation is low and stable, excess demand pressures on credit and banks' asset price are likely to increase.

24.5 Results and Estimations

Prior to the estimation of model, we run the unit root test for each variable in order to avoid quasi-regression problem for both time series and panel data. Therefore, Levin, Lin, and Chu test; Im, Pesaran, and Shin W-stat test; Fisher test; and Hadri test are used to consider common unit root of variables. The estimation results are reported in Table (24.1).

Dynamic relations contained interrupted variables, and because of such variables and heterogeneous sectional effects, autocorrelation problem would occur. Also, the GLS estimator would be biased in the random effects for dynamic pooling data. Therefore, Arellano and Bond proposed a new approach, which processed from generalized method of moments in 1991. In this method Arellano and Bond represented two-step GMM estimator, and the validity of matrix tools will be examined by Sargan test. In Sargan test the null hypothesis indicates that matrix tools are not correlated with interrupted variables. As can be seen, the null hypothesis is not rejected. Therefore, matrix tools are not correlated with interrupted variables, and the applied tools have necessary validity for estimation.

Tables 24.2 and 24.3 represent the results of estimations. The results show the significant lagged earnings volatility coefficient for all banks in our sample. Positive non-interest income ratio can reduce shareholder value. Banks with riskier investment activities have higher non-interest income ratio (Siggelkow 2003). According to results, non-interest income ratio has a negative impact on earnings

Table 24.1 Results of common unit root test

Variable	Levin, Lin, Chu t.	Im, Pesaran, Shin W-stat	ADF – Fisher Chi-square	PP – Fisher chi-square	Hadri stat
ROASD	−13.73 (0.000)	−3.401 (0.0003)	83.74 (0.0003)	149.284 (0.0004)	5.22 (0.000)
Cost ratio	−6.1557 (0.000)	−1.7527 (0.0003)	62.35 (0.0004)	133.72 (0.000)	3.97 (0.000)
Deposit ratio	−8.19 (0.000)	−1.33 (0.092)	66.057 (0.0636)	154.69 (0.000)	6.59 (0.000)
Non-interest income ratio	−15.698 (0.0002)	−3.7022 (0.0001)	79.552 (0.0001)	127.014 (0.0000)	6.07 (0.000)
HHI	−9.8574 (0.0002)	−3.576 (0.007)	100.583 (0.000)	289.688 (0.000)	8.28 (0.000)
Size	−29.88 (0.000)	−6.53 (0.0057)	121.43 (0.0007)	132.68 (0.000)	6.97 (0.000)
Inflation	−12.27 (0.000)	−1.61 (0.053)	68.42 (0.0427)	84.84 (0.0015)	11.18 (0.000)

Table 24.2 The effect of bank size on earnings volatility (Eq. 24.1)

Variables	Estimation 1	Estimation 2	Estimation 3	Estimation 4
ROASD(−1)	0.5135 (10.05)	0.4718 (9.64)	0.5239 (15.14)	0.496 (10.81)
HHI	−0.074 (−2.398)	−0.039 (−2.35)	−0.057 (−2.42)	−0.1673 (−1.832)
Cost ratio	1.85 (1.96)	3.22 (1.48)	2.32 (3.288)	1.514 (1.706)
Non-interest income ratio	−0.951 (−2.5)	−1.295 (−1.75)	−1.612 (−2.91)	−1.337 (−2.67)
Size*D1	−0.0522 (−1.95)	–	–	–
Size*D2	–	1.16 (1.933)	–	–
Size*D3	–	–	−1.063 (−1.912)	–
Size*D4	–	–	–	0.608 (1.699)
Inflation	0.026 (2.025)	0.023 (3.5)	0.027 (2.47)	0.147 (1.59)
J-stat	19.45	18.23	19.57	17.59

Table 24.3 The effect of bank size on earnings volatility (Eq. 24.2)

Variables	Estimation 1	Estimation 2	Estimation 3	Estimation 4
ROASD(−1)	0.5289(17.7)	0.5944(8.629)	0.5357(4.63)	0.5784(9.86)
HHI	−0.1749 (−1.54)	−0.075 (−2.23)	–	−0.089 (−1.87)
Deposit ratio	−1.365(−1.81)	−2.68(−1.98)	−1.076(−3.61)	−1.35(−1.98)
Cost ratio	1.992(1.86)	1.49(1.798)	1.368(1.69)	1.307(1.92)
Size	−0.4416(−1.95)	−0.038(−1.907)	–	–
Non-interest income ratio	−1.2156(−1.66)	–	–	−1.589(−2.25)
Inflation	0.041(1.56)	0.0225(1.61)	0.03713(2.055)	–
HHI*size	–	–	0.01565(3.31)	0.0265(1.79)
J-stat	17.979	18.01	31.35	22.95

volatility. According to Deyoung and Rice (2004), less traditional financial activities are associated with higher volatile revenue. Most Iranian banks have traditional financial activities; therefore, non-interest income ratio has a negative relationship with volatile revenue in Iranian banking system.

Banks with a relatively higher ratio of deposits face lower earnings volatility; therefore, banks could have better performance and more return. Cost ratio, which illustrates the performance of bank management, has positive effects on earnings volatility. The above discussions suggest that less efficient banks are more vulnerable to risk and crisis.

In this model, we consider inflation as one of the important macroeconomic variables, and we find that inflation has positive effects on earnings volatility.

The coefficient of market concentration is generally significant in account of interactions, which means that higher level of concentration face lower level of risk in Iranian banking system. There is an appropriate analysis regarding market concentration and earnings volatility, which is the connection between bank size and level of market concentration. According to results, the interaction between market concentration and bank size is significantly positive, which means larger banks located in concentrated markets face higher earnings volatility in Iranian banking system.

In our analysis, we consider dummy variables for different types of banks. In Iranian banking system, there are four types of banks (private, state, privatized, specialized). Different structures of different types of banks have an important impact on earnings volatility. Dummy variable (D1) is equal to 1 if the bank is a private bank and 0 otherwise. Dummy variable (D2) is equal to 1 if the bank is state bank and 0 otherwise. Dummy variable (D3) is equal to 1 if the bank is privatized bank and 0 otherwise. Dummy variable (D4) is equal to 1 if the bank is specialized bank and 0 otherwise. By multiplying these variables with bank size, we can distinguish different bank types according to their effect on earnings volatility. According to results, private bank dummy variable multiplied by bank size has a negative effect on earnings volatility. Also, the coefficient of multiplied privatized bank Dummy variable (D3) and bank size is negative. Therefore, private and privatized banks have negative impact on earnings volatility. On the other hand, the coefficient of multiplied state bank dummy variable and specialized bank dummy variable is positive. So, the state and specialized banks have positive effect on earnings volatility. The state and specialized banks have more volatile return and profitability volatility than private and privatized banks in Iranian banking system.

The coefficient of market concentration (HHI) is negative and significant, so market concentration has negative effect on earnings volatility.

The coefficient of deposit ratio is negative and significant at 1% level for ROA SD, which indicates negative relation between deposit ratio and standard deviation of return on assets. Also, bank size coefficient is negative and significant, which means that relative bank size has a negative effect on return volatility. In estimations, we multiplied bank-type dummy variables with bank size, which indicates the effect of bank type on earnings volatility. The relation between multiplied dummy variables with bank size and earnings volatility is different depending on the type of banks. State banks and specialized banks have positive impact on earnings volatility, while private and privatized banks have negative effects on earnings volatility. Therefore, we can conclude that state banks and specialized banks have more risky revenues compared with private and privatized banks in Iranian banking system.

24.6 Conclusions

The global financial crisis has caused economists to consider the issue of bank size and brought back this issue between policymakers. Since earnings volatility is one of the important factors in equity capital level and bank soundness, we analyze the relationship between bank size and earnings volatility in Iranian banking system for the period 2000–2015. Our goal is to consider whether bank size has an impact on earnings volatility. Also, market concentration has an influence on profitability; therefore, we investigate whether market concentration could affect bank earnings volatility or not. We use non-interest income ratio in order to find out the diversification and structure income in Iranian banks. The analysis showed that non-interest income ratio has a negative impact on earnings volatility, since in Iranian banking system, non-interest income ratio reduce risky revenues. Also, there is a negative relationship between deposit ratio and earnings volatility, which shows the ratio of deposits to total liabilities in Iranian banking system, and considering the cost ratio which shows the bank performance, we can find that ratio of cost to income is positively related to earnings volatility. We use dummy variables in order to consider the relationship between bank type and earnings volatility, and we understood that the relationship between bank type and earnings volatility is different, since state banks and specialized banks have positive coefficient on earnings volatility while private and privatized banks have a negative impact on earnings volatility. Therefore, state banks and specialized banks have more risky revenues, and the private and privatized banks have less risky revenues.

References

Albertazzi, U., & Gambacorta, L. (2009). Bank profitability and the business cycle. *Journal of Financial Stability, 5*(4), 393–409.

Allayannis, G., Rountree, B., & Weston, J. P. (2005). Earnings volatility, cash flow volatility, and firm value.

Amel, D., Barnes, C., Panetta, F., & Salleo, C. (2003). Consolidation and efficiency in the financial sector: A review of the international evidence. *Journal of banking and finance, 28*, 24932519.

Baele, L. O., De Jonghe, R. V. Vennet. (2007). Does the stock market value bank diversification? *Journal of Banking and Finance 31*(7), 1999–2023.

Barnes, D. (2001). Research methods for the empirical investigation of the process of formation of operations strategy. *International Journal of Operations & Production Management, 21*(8), 1076–1095.

Beaver, W. H., Kettler, P., & Scholes, M. (1970). The Association Between Market-Determined and Accounting-Determined Risk Measures, The Accounting Review, October 1970.

Berger, A. N., Mester, L. J. (2003). Explaining the Dramatic Changes in the Performance of U.S.Banks: Technological Change, Deregulation, and Dynamic Changes in Competition. *Journal of Financial Intermediation 12*, 57–95.

Berger, A. N., & Mester, L. J. (1997). Inside the black box: What explains differences in the efficiencies of financial institutions? *Journal of Banking and Finance*. https://ideas.repec.org/p/wop/pennin/97-04.html.

Berger, A. N., Goldberg, L. G., & White, L. J. (2001). The effects of dynamic changes in bank competition on the supply of small business credit. *European Finance Review*, 115–139.

Beck, T., Kunt, A., & Levine, R., (2007). Finance, Inequality and the Poor, The World Bank, Brown University and the National Bureau of Economic Research

Berger, A., Klapper, L., & Turk, R. (2009). Bank competition and financial stability. *Journal of Financial Services Research, 35*(2), 99–118.

Benston, G., Hanweck, G., & Humphrey, D. (1982). Scale economies in banking. A re-structuring and reassessment. *Journal of Money, Credit and Banking, 14*(4), 435–455.

Boot, W.A., & Ratnovski, L. (2012). Banking and Trading. IMF Working Paper. WP/12/238.

Borio, C., & Lowe, P. (2002). Asset prices, financial and monetary stability: exploring the nexus.BIS Working Papers No 114.
Brunnermeier, M. K., Dong, G. N, & Palia, D. (2012). Banks' Non-Interest Income and Systemic Risk. AFA 2012 Chicago Meetings Paper. Available at SSRN: https://ssrn.com/abstract=1786738 or https://doi.org/10.2139/ssrn.1786738
Buiter W. H., 2009, Negative Nominal Interest Rates:Three Ways To Overcome The Zero Lower Bound. Working Paper 15118 .http://Www.Nber.Org/Papers/W15118.
Boyd, J. H., & De Nicolo, G. (2005). The theory of bank risk taking and competition revisited. *Journal of Finance, 60*(3), 1329–1343.
Carter, D. A., & McNulty, J. E. (2005). Deregulation, technological change, and the business-lending performance of large and small banks. *Journal of Banking and Finance, 29*, 1113–1130.
Cornett, M. M., Marcus, A., & Tehranian, H. (2008). Corporate governance and pay-for-performance: The impact of earnings management. *Journal of Financial Economics, 87*(2), 357–373.
Couto, R. (2002). *Framework for the assessment of bank earnings*. Basel: Financial Stability Institute, Bank for International Settlements.
De Jonghe, O. (2010). Back to the basics in banking? A micro-analysis of banking system stability. *Journal of Financial Intermediation, 19*(3), 387–417.
Demetz, R., & Strahan, P. E. (1997). Diversification, size, and risk at bank holding companies. *Journal of Money, Credit and Banking, 29*(3), 300–313.
De Haan, J., & Poghosyan, T. (March 2011). *Bank size, Market concentration, and bank earnings volatility in the US, DNB working paper no. 282.*
Demetz, R., & Strahan, P. E., (April 1995). *Diversification, size, and risk at bank holding companies, Federal reserve bank of New York research paper no.9506.*
Demirgüç-Kunt, A., Huizinga H. (2011). *Do we need big banks? Evidence on performance, strategy and market Discipline*.www.Bis.org.worling paper.
Dichev, I. D., & Tang, V. W. (2008). Matching and the changing properties of accounting earnings over the last 40 years. *The Accounting Review:, 83*(6), 1425–1460.
Drucker S., & Puri, M. (2005). On the benefits of concurrent lending and underwriting.the Journal of Finance .vol. Lx, No. 6.
DeYoung, R., & Rice, T. (2004). Noninterest income and financial performance at U.S. commercial banks. *Financial Review, 39*, 101–127.
DeYoung, R., & Torna, G. (2013). Nontraditional banking activities and bank failures during the financial crisis. *Journal of Financial Intermediation, 2013, 22*(3), 397–421.
Fayman, A. (2009). Large banks versus small banks: How different are they? *Journal of Economic and Social Policy, 13*(1), Article 6.
Gabaix, X., & Landier, A. (2008). Why has CEO pay increased so much? *The Quarterly Journal of Economics, MIT Press, 123*(1), 49–100. 02.
Gebhardt, W. R., Lee, M. C., & Swaminathan, B. (2001). Toward an implied cost of capital. *Journal of Accounting Research, 39*(1), 135–176.
Graham, J., & Rogers, D. (2002). Do firms hedge in response to tax incentives? *Journal of Finance, 57*, 815–839.
Hagendorff, J., Keaseya, K., & Vallascasb, F. (2012). Systemic size, bank risk and systemic crises. http://www.bris.ac.uk/efm/media/conference-papers/corporate-finance/systemic-size.pdf.
Hirtle, B., & Stiroh, K. (2007). The return to retail and the performance of US banks (stiroh84@optonline.net). *Journal of Banking & Finance, 31*(4), 1101–1133.
Hughes, J. P., & Mester, L. J. (2013). Measuring the performance of banks: Theory, practice, evidence, and some policy implications. Working Papers from Federal Reserve Bank of Philadelphia, No 13-31.
Jensen, M. C. (1986). Agency costs of free cash flow, corporate finance, and takeovers. *The American Economic Review, 76*(2), 323–329.
Kovner, A., Vickery, J., & Zhou, L. (2014). Do big banks have lower operating costs?. *Economic Policy Review, 20*(2).

Kroszner, R., & Rajan, R. (1994). Is the Glass-Steagall Act Justified? A study of the U.S. experience with Universal Banking before 1933. *American Economic Review, 1994, 84*(4), 810–832.

Kunt, D. A., & Huizinga, H. (2000). Financial structure and bank profitability. http://siteresources.worldbank.org/INTFR/Resources/475459I108132178926/Kunt_Huizinga.pdf

Kunt, D. A., & Huizinga, H. (2011). *Do we need big banks? Evidence on performance, strategy and market discipline*. www.Bis.org.worling paper.

Laeven, L., & Levine, R. (2007). Is there a diversification discount in financial conglomerates. *Journal of Financial Economics, 85*(2), 331–367.

Minton, B., & Schrand, C. (1999). The impact of cash flow volatility on discretionary investment and the costs of debt and equity financing. *Journal of Financial Economics, 54*, 423–460.

Minton, B. A., Schrand, C. M., & Walther, B. R. (2002). The role of volatility in forecasting. *Review of Accounting Studies, 7*, 217–227.

Murphy, K. (1985). Corporate performance and managerial remuneration: An empirical analysis. *Journal of Accounting and Economics, 7*(1-3), 11–42.

Nakamura, L. I. (1993). Recent research in commercial banking: information and lending, Working Papers 93-24, Federal Reserve Bank of Philadelphia.

Peristiani, S. (1997). Do Mergers improve the X-efficiency and scale efficiency of U.S. banks? Evidence from the 1980s. *Journal of Money, Credit and Banking, 29*(3), 326–337.

Petersen, M. A., Rajan, R. G. (1994) The Benefits of lending relationships: evidence from small business data. *The Journal of Finance 49*(1), 3–37.

Poghosyan, T., & De Haan, J. (2010). Determinants of cross-border bank acquisitions in transition economies. *The Economics of Transition, 18*(4), 671–696.

Puri, M. (1996). Commercial banks in investment banking conflict of interest or certification role? *Journal of Financial Economics, 40*(3), 373–401.

Schmid, M., & Walter, I. (2009). Do financial conglomerates create or destroy economic value. *Journal of Financial Intermediation, 18*(2), 193–216.

Schwerter, S. (2011). Basel III's ability to mitigate systemic risk. *Journal of Financial Regulation and Compliance, 19*(4), 337354.

Siggelkow, N. (2003). Why focus? A study of intra-industry focus effects. *The Journal of Industrial Economics 51*(2), 121–150.

Smith, C., & Stulz, R. (1985). The determinants of firms' hedging policies. *Journal of Financial and Quantitative Analysis, 20*, 391–405.

Smith, R., Staikouras, C., & Wood, G. (2003). *Non-interest income and total income stability. London: Bank of England. Working Paper No. 198.*

Stever, R. (2007). *Bank size, credit and the sources of bank market risk by Ryan Monetary and Economic Department. BIS Working Papers No 238*

Stiroh, K., & Rumble, A. (2006). The dark side of diversification: The case of US financial holding companies. *Journal of Banking & Finance, 30*(8), 2131–2161.

Williamson, S. D. (1986). Costly monitoring, financial intermediation, and equilibrium credit rationing. *Journal of Monetary Economics, Elsevier, vol., 18*(2), 159–179.

Stiroh, K. J. (2004). Diversification in banking: Is non-interest income the answer? *Journal of Money, Credit, and Banking, 36*, 853–882.

Stiroh, K. J. (2006a). New evidence on the determinants of bank risk. *Journal of Financial Services Research, 30*, 237–263.

Stiroh, K. J. (2006b). A portfolio view of banking with interest and noninterest activities. *Journal of Money, Credit, and Banking, 38*, 1351–1361.

Wheelock, D. C., Wilson, P. W. (May 2011). Do large banks have lower costs? new estimates of returns to scale for U.S. Banks, *Research division Federal Reserve Bank of St. Louis working paper series working paper 2009–054E*. http://research.stlouisfed.org/wp/2009/2009-054.pdf

Zimmerman, B. J. (1996). Enhancing student academic and health functioning: A self-regulatory perspective. *School Psychology Quarterly, 11*(1), 47–66.

Chapter 25
The Selection of Human Resources in Slovak Companies

Pavol Durana and Darina Chlebikova

Abstract The article describes the methods of human resources selection in Slovak companies. The aim of the article is to describe the change in the approach in management of human resources selection. The selection of the employees is an integral part of human resource management. The severity of choice is the fact that every employee has certain personal assumptions, qualifications, performance and personal capacity, which are individually specific and reflect the level and scope of his employment eligibility. At the same time, any activity, profession and position is clearly defined set of requirements and demands with respect to various aspects of employee profiles. It is therefore important to select not only the right employee but also to use the most appropriate method of selection. On the base of analysing and comparing of the surveys realized in the year 2012 and in the year 2016, the difference in human resources selection will be identified. The detected gaps will be analysed, the possible root causes that could make them will be generated, and the next possible ways of development of human resources selection in Slovak companies will be recommended.

Keywords Selection · Human resources · Personnel management

25.1 Introduction

The selection of human resources is an activity of personnel management that follows after recruitment of human resources. The aim of selection is to identify and choose among job applicants those who are not only efficient but also will work for the employer in an expected manner and not in an adverse manner that reduces productivity and quality. The company in process of publishing its interest to occupy

P. Durana (✉) · D. Chlebikova
University of Zilina, Faculty of Operation and Economics of Transport and Communications, Department of Economics, Zilina, Slovak Republic
e-mail: pavol.durana@fpedas.uniza.sk; darina.chlebikova@fpedas.uniza.sk

N. Tsounis, A. Vlachvei (eds.), *Advances in Panel Data Analysis in Applied Economic Research*, Springer Proceedings in Business and Economics,
https://doi.org/10.1007/978-3-319-70055-7_25

any job uses different methods. Its choice depends mainly on the importance of the job, sources of potential applicant and ultimately the financial possibilities of the company.

25.2 Theoretical Background

The following sections will be described: a process of selection of human resources, the most used methods of selection of human resources and the use of personnel marketing in process of selection of human resources.

25.2.1 Process of Selection of Human Resources

When the human resources are selected, the company should try to ensure that its goals and objectives of future employee are very similar (Antosova 2008). This requirement has to be respected when solving the issue whether to occupy the free post in preference to external staff or employee from own resources. Ceniga and Sukalova (2015), Rebetak and Farkasova (2015) and Ponisciakova and Gogolova (2015) dealt with the solution of this issue. Personal experience gives generally priority to filling of free position from internal resources. However, if you cannot meet the need for employees from own sources, company will turn to external sources. Sukalova and Ceniga (2016) discuss that company obviously has no interest in acquiring any human resources. If we want the process to be effective, sequence of logical steps should be observed. That is why the process of selecting of human resources can be divided into several interrelated steps that lead to decisions in which candidate will be offered a job. The selection process might look like this:

1. The creation of comprehensive and clear picture of the company about what kind of human resources and what kind of motivation of human resources needs (Jarina 2013). It is therefore a precise job description, inclusion of employee in the organizational structure and communication links with other sites.
2. Election of the selection criteria (determination of requirements and demands) that employees should possess. Professional focus of applicant, achieved qualification, practice and knowledge are the so-called general assumptions. Ponisciakova (2015) argues that it is sometimes useful and necessary to find out the so-called personal characteristics (conscientiousness, responsibility, hard work, work ethic, ability to communicate, etc.).
3. Election of methods for the assessment of candidates, conducting selection procedures.
4. The final selection of the candidate (decision by comparing the information obtained to the selection criteria). Vendolska and Kacerova (2016) describe in their article key factors of successful job interview.
5. Inform applicants of the decision.

25.2.2 *Methods of Selection of Human Resources*

We use a lot of methods when the candidates are selected. Some of them can be used always, but some to only for finding out and verification of assumptions. The used methods have to be appropriate to the filled position, the nature of work on it and the corresponding requirements (Stefanikova and Masarova 2013). Currently, in Mihalcova (2007)'s opinion, the most used methods of selection of human resources are:

(a) References
(b) Combined interview
(c) Structured interview
(d) Unstructured interview
(e) Solving the problem
(f) Questionnaires
(g) Proficiency tests
(h) Psychological tests
(i) The stress interview
(j) Assessment centre
(k) IQ tests
(l) Interview with psychologist
(m) Graphology tests
(n) Physical tests

25.2.3 *Personnel Marketing as a Part of the Process of Human Resources Selection*

The concept of selection of human resources includes procedures and activities that are part of purposeful creating, developing and using of human potential on the basis of strategic objectives in line with the culture of the company (Mateides 2006). These activities are referred to as personal marketing, which is based on research of the labour market, position of the company on the labour market and creating good employer reputation (Stefanikova et al. 2015). Personnel marketing in this form are used to search, recruitment and selection of quality people, their stabilization in the company and to strengthening their loyalty (Gogolova et al. 2015).

25.3 Paper Objective and Methodology

The target of the paper is to analyse current situation of human resources selection in Slovak companies and to compare to the situation in the past. There were four key issues of finding out:

1. Used methods of selection of management
2. Used methods of selection of specialist and technical workers
3. Used methods of selection of administrative employees
4. Used methods of selection of workers

There was a research question as well: find out the percentage of changes of used methods of selection in every category of employees in year 2016 comparing to year 2012.

The information used in the article was gained from the primary and secondary sources:

(a) *Primary sources* – survey made by authors. The survey was realized in the year 2016. There were 322 respondents, and the aim of the survey was to detect the level of human resources selection in Slovak companies. The questions had close form.
(b) *Secondary sources* – survey made by Kachaňáková, Stachová and Stacho in the years 2010–2012. The survey sample of companies was randomly addressed. We only used three stages of their survey in year 2012, and there were 340 respondents. The questions had a form of open, close and scale questions. The main objective of annual survey was to detect the way of human resources management in Slovak companies. The next sources were foreign and domestic literature and articles linked to presented issue. The key area of interest was selection of human resources.

Some methods were used too: the *analysis* of results and gained information from primary and secondary sources and *synthesis* and the method of *deduction*, the first as a tool for overall review of level of human resources selection in Slovak companies and the second in order to support the conclusions, and the method of *induction* when the theories of development of employee selection in companies in Slovak Republic were discussed.

25.4 Result and Discussion

Right selection is a good starting point in the use of potential of human resources. Firstly the surveys detected the percentage use of methods of selection of management in years 2012 and 2016. The most used methods were references and combined and structured interview, and the least used were interview with psychologist, graphology tests and physical tests. In every method has got bigger its use only the use of solving problem and physical tests were the same. It is possible to think that the biggest growth in the future will be in the use of the assessment centre and solving the problem (Fig. 25.1).

Secondly, the surveys found out the use of methods of selection of specialist and technical workers in years 2012 and 2016. The most used methods were references and combined and unstructured interview, and the least used were graphology tests

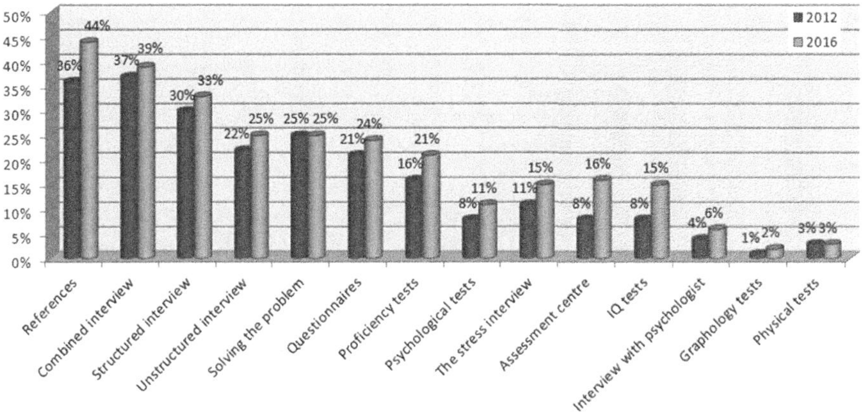

Fig. 25.1 Methods of management in the years 2012 and 2016 (*Source* Authors on the base of own finding out and on base of Kachanakova et al. (2013))

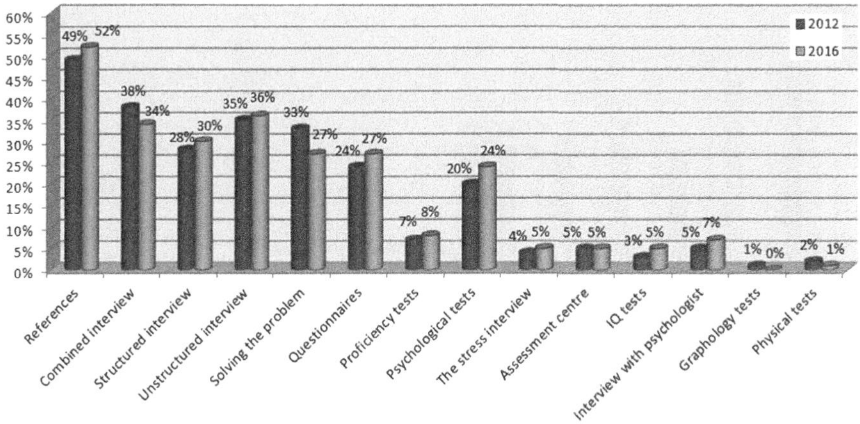

Fig. 25.2 Methods of specialist and technical workers in the years 2012 and 2016 (*Source* Authors on the base of own finding out and on base of Kachanakova et al. (2013))

and physical tests. The percentage use of method of selection of human resources is bigger or in the same way like in year 2010; only in structured interview, solving the problem, graphology tests and physical tests have the use descended. It is possible to premise that the certain growth in the future will be in the use of the stress interview and proficiency tests (Fig. 25.2).

Thirdly, the surveys showed the use of methods of selection of administrative employees in the years 2012 and 2016. The most used methods were references and combined and structured interview, and the least used were interview with psychologist, graphology tests and physical tests. The percentage use of method

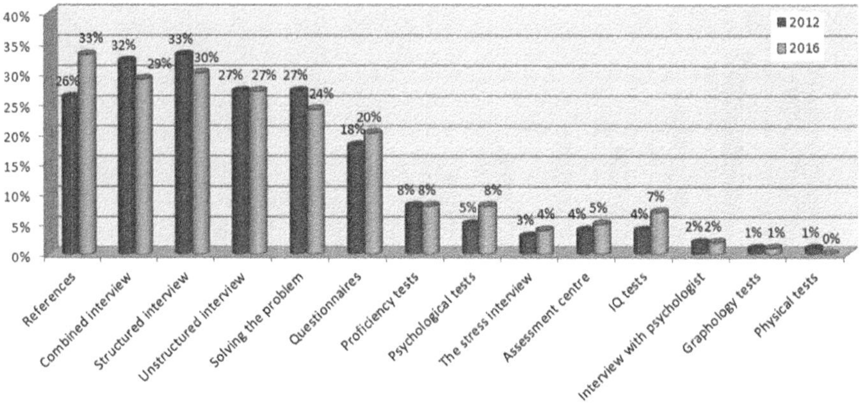

Fig. 25.3 Methods of administrative employees in the years 2012 and 2016 (*Source* Authors on the base of own finding out and on base of Kachanakova et al. (2013))

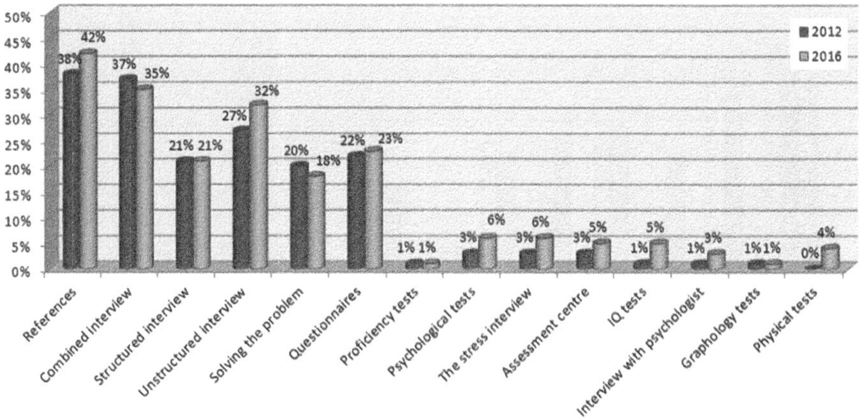

Fig. 25.4 Methods of workmen in the years 2012 and 2016 (*Source* Authors on the base of own finding out and on base of Kachanakova et al. (2013))

of selection of human resources is very similar to the year 2010. There were only little changes. It is possible to anticipate the growth of use in area proficiency tests and questionnaires (Figs. 25.3 and 25.4).

Finally the survey made by authors and the survey made by Kachanakova et al. described the use of methods of selection of workers in the years 2012 and 2016. The most used methods were references and combined and unstructured interview, and the group of no often preferred methods is very large. It included proficiency tests, psychological tests, the stress interview, assessment centre, IQ tests, interview with psychologist, graphology tests and physical tests. It is possible that little growth in the future will happen in the use of the proficiency tests, psychological tests and IQ tests.

25.5 Conclusion

The key issue in the selection of human resources is the assessment of work applicant; in this process the nature of the job with detected or declared candidate characteristics is compared. The condition of successful meeting is establishing criteria for the post to be filled, which are divided into company, departmental and criteria for the job, but also the determination of factors used to anticipate a successful work performance and finding quality information about the applicant.

The situation in human resources selection in Slovak companies in year 2016 has got better than in year 2012. Slovak companies pay bigger attention to human resources selection, because almost the use of every method in every category of employees is bigger than in past. It is a very big assumption that Slovak companies select the right applicant to the right job and it will be a win-win situation. There are still some gaps, so these systems stay in front of the way of development and improvement, especially in the area of the use of new methods of selection.

Acknowledgements This paper is an output of VEGA 1/0244/16 Personnel marketing as a new approach of the ensuring and maintaining the skilled workforce in Slovak companies, which authors gratefully acknowledge.

References

Antosova, J. (2008). *Manažment Ludskych Zdrojov v Praxi*. Kosice, SK: Berg.

Ceniga, P., & Sukalova, V. (2015). Prevention and protection of young people at work in new economy. *International Conference on Economics and Social Science (ICESS), advances in education research*, Vol. 86, pp. 94–99.

Gogolova, M., Ponisciakova, O., & Ivankova, K. (2015). The use of external personnel marketing in Slovakia. *Procedia Economics and Finance, 26*, 131–138.

Jarina, L. (2013). Influence of motivational factors and pay for performance improvement. *Ekonomicko-manazerske Spektrum, 7*(2), 21–26.

Kachanakova, A., Stachova, K., & Stacho, Z. (2013). *Riadenie Ludskych Zdrojov v Organizaciach Posobiacich na Slovensku*. Bratislava, SK: Iura Edition.

Mateides, A. (Ed.). (2006). *Manazerstvo Kvality*. Bratislava, SK: Ekonom.

Mihalcova, B. (2007). *Riadenie Ludskych Zdrojov*. Bratislava, SK: Ekonom.

Ponisciakova, O. (2015). New nature of globalization – new character of a manager in 21st century. *Procedia Economics and finance, 23*, 915–919.

Ponisciakova, O., & Gogolova, M. (2015). Exploiting the potential and possibilities of conscious human resource management in the process of globalization. *International scientific conference on globalization and its socio-economic consequences*, Rajecke Teplice, Slovakia, pp. 597–603.

Rebetak, M., & Farkasova, V. (2015). Potential employees. *Procedia Economics and Finance, 23*, 867–871.

Stefanikova, L., & Masarova, G. (2013). New skill requirements of financial managers. *International scientific conference on financial management of firms and financial institutions*, Ostrava, Czech Republic, pp. 928–933.

Stefanikova, L., Moravcikova, K., & Nadanyiova, M. (2015). Corporate social responsibility as a source of competitive advantage in enterprises of the Slovak Republic. *International conference on economics and social science, advances in education research*, Vol. 86, pp. 168–173.

Sukalova, V., & Ceniga, P. (2016). Current problems of employment juveniles in Slovakia. *International Conference on Information and Business Management (ISSGBM-IB), Book series: Lecture notes in management science*, Vol. 61, pp. 27–32.

Vendolska, I., & Kacerova, E. (2016). Flexible graduate is successful graduate. Key factors of successful job interview, results of a comparative analysis. *Journal of Competitiveness, 8*(2), 87–102.

Chapter 26
The Issue of Investment Decision-Making of Leveraged Projects

Lucia Michalkova and Erika Spuchlakova

Abstract Investment decision-making is based on many criteria and analysis. Currently, the projects imposed many requirements that are often in mutual contradiction or project is very risky. One example for increasing risk of the project is a financing by debt. The paper is focused on the issue of leveraged projects, because their valuation is different from the valuation of projects financed merely by equity, and an existence of some financial effects of leverage affects financial decision-making. Hence, a general method of quantification of net present value and adjusted net present value is described. Next, it is focused on sensitivity analysis as a one of the steps of risk analysis. The aim of the paper is to analyse the net present value of the certain leveraged project, make a sensitivity analysis of the project and identify significant factors that affect the project value. Finally, there are mentioned some weaknesses of sensitivity analysis and other methods used for risk analysis.

Keywords Adjusted net present value · Sensitivity analysis · Leverage · Tax shield

26.1 Introduction

Nowadays companies all over the world face the consequences caused by the financial crisis. Almost every one of them must be financed by debt, and one of the goals of the company is often to decrease risk (Corejova et al. 2014). Also it is difficult for any company to choose the variant of the offered investment opportunities that it will bring the most benefit, whether it is a short-term or long-term investment decision (Dengov and Gregova 2010). A second former is characterized by a high involvement of decision-makers on the outcome of the

L. Michalkova (✉) · E. Spuchlakova
University of Zilina, Faculty of Operation and Economics of Transport and Communications, Department of Economics, Univerzitna 8215/1, 01026 Zilina, Slovak Republic
e-mail: lucia.michalkova@fpedas.uniza.sk; erika.spuchlakova@fpedas.uniza.sk

N. Tsounis, A. Vlachvei (eds.), *Advances in Panel Data Analysis in Applied Economic Research*, Springer Proceedings in Business and Economics,
https://doi.org/10.1007/978-3-319-70055-7_26

decision. Therefore, the decision should include attitudes, opinions and judgments of the decision-maker, but it should be an outcome of an objective assessment of the decision situation (Grublova 2010).

In an environment of financial and investment decision-making, there are used formalized procedures for determining the most favourable option. As Bartošová et al. (2015) mentioned, internationally accepted methods are based on net present value calculation. These methods quantify the net benefit to an investor by determining the present value of cash flows arising from investing projects minus initial capital expenditures (Vochozka 2010). Determination of net present value is only the first step in the process of investment decision-making. It is also necessary to analyse riskiness of the project caused by changes in inputs. Sensitivity analysis is thus part of many financial analyses as well as first phase of risk analysis.

The aim of the paper is to analyse the net present value of the leveraged project, make a sensitivity analysis of this project and identify significant factors that affect the project value.

26.2 Net Present Value and Its Modification

Net present value (NPV) is defined as the difference between the net discounted cash flows from the investment and capital expenditure incurred for its realization. In other words, the net present value is the difference between the discounted cash inflows and investment outflows, as follows:

$$NPV = \sum_{i=1}^{n} \frac{\mathrm{CF}_i}{(1+R)^i} - \mathrm{INV} \tag{26.1}$$

where:

NPV – net present value

CF_i – cash flow in time i

i – discount rate

INV – investment, capital expenditure

n – expected project life

During the first years of the investment period, NPV is usually negative, then after a few years it should achieve a positive value. The project is accepted if NPV is positive, otherwise (negative NPV) of the project should not be accepted (Valaskova et al. 2015).

If a financial analyst quantifies unleveraged or leveraged project NPV, basic form of Eq. (26.1) should be modified. In the case of unleveraged project, cash flow is quantified on the basis of equity cash flow (ECF) discounted at the cost of capital of unleveraged project R_U. (Damodaran 2002) NPV of leveraged project can be quantified in three ways:

1. As *equity cash flow* discounted at *cost equity of leveraged project* R_E
2. As *free cash flow* (*FCF*) discounted at *weighted average cost of capital WACC*
3. As *NPV* modification called *adjusted net present value* (*ANPV*) (Lehutova et al. 2013)

Adjusted net present value is the most widely used method for leveraged project valuation created by Brealey et al. (2010). Term *"adjusted"* means sum of value of unlevered company adjusted for the side effects of financing to derive the value of leveraged company (Myers 1974). *ANPV* is based on value additivity method since it splits a project cash flow into pieces to value each piece separately and sums them.

$$APV = NPV + present\ value\ of\ financial\ side\ effects \qquad (26.2)$$

For valuing leveraged project, *ANPV* (in the case of company valuation also called *adjusted present value* – *APV*) is divided usually into two parts: *NPV* of unleveraged project and the value of *tax shield* (Luehrman 1997).

$$ANPV = NPV_U + PV(TS) \qquad (26.3)$$

$$ANPV = \sum_{i=1}^{T} \frac{ECF_{Ui}}{(1 + R_U)^i} - INV + \sum_{i=1}^{T} \frac{t.D_{i-1}.R_D}{(1 + R_D)^i} \qquad (26.4)$$

where:

ANPV – adjusted net present value
ECF_{Ui} – equity cash flow of unleveraged project
R_U– cost of equity of unleveraged project
t – tax rate
D_{i-1} – debt at time $i - 1$
R_D – cost of debt

Equity cash flow is expressed as follows:

$$ECF = EBIT\,(1 - t) + DEP - \Delta NWC - INV \qquad (26.5)$$

where:

EBIT – earnings before interest and tax
DEP – annual deprecation
ΔNWC – changes in net working capital

Tax shield increases net present value of project due to tax savings arising from tax deductibility of some expense. Therefore, it is preferable for the project to be financed both by equity and debt. Nevertheless the risk of bankruptcy is increasing simultaneously with the increase of debt. It is appropriate to optimize the debt in order to present value of the tax shield that would be greater than the present value of costs of financial distress and the net present value of the project would grow (Kliestik et al. 2014a, 2014b).

26.3 Sensitivity Analysis

Sensitivity analysis is one of the most commonly used but also the easiest methods of risk analysis of investment projects. The analysis is based on an assumption of the sensitivity (changes) of financial indicators to changes in input factors. Input factors, according to the changes which are triggered, are divided into low-risk and significant risk factors (Cisko and Kliestik 2013).

If financial indicator is aggregate and expressed as a function of n partial factors $A = f(F_1, F_2, \ldots, F_n)$, then the sensitivity of financial indicator on the first factor (and on other) can be quantified in two ways (Dluhosova 2010):

1. As a value at change of that factor $A^{F_1}_{1+\alpha} = f\left[(1+\alpha).F_1.F_2.\ldots F_n\right]$
2. As a value increase caused by the factor change $\Delta A^{F_1}_{\alpha} = A^{F_1}_{1+\alpha} - A = f\left[(1+\alpha).F_1.F_2.\ldots F_n\right] - A$, where α is the relative factor change, which can be positive or negative

In case, that function is linear, A can be expressed as follows:

$$\Delta A^{F_1}_{\alpha} = A^{F_1}_{1+\alpha} - A = \alpha.a_1.F_1 \tag{26.6}$$

Sensitivity analysis is presented on a model example of investment project. The task of financial manager is to decide whether the investment project shall be accepted or not. As a financial factor, we have chosen *adjusted net present value*, which reflects the most tax benefit caused by the tax deductibility of interest and the existence of *interest tax shield*. Therefore, it is assumed leveraged project with expected life of 4 years. The cost of unlevered capital R_U is assumed on 10.1%, the cost of debt R_D is assumed on 8.4% and tax rate is assumed on 21%. Other input factors are shown in Table 26.1.

The project is valued on the basis of *ANPV* criterion.

$$ANPV = NPV_U + PV(TS) \tag{26.7}$$

$$ANPV = \sum_{i=0}^{T} \frac{ECF_{Ui}}{(1+R_U)^i} - INV + \sum_{i=1}^{T} \frac{t.D_{i-1}.R_D}{(1+R_D)^i} \tag{26.8}$$

Table 26.1 Project input factors (€)

Time	0	1	2	3	4
EBIT		29	41	64	86
DEP		20	20	20	20
Δ NWC		3,6	17.8	20	17.5
D	60	45	30	15	0
INV	80				

Single-factor sensitivity analysis of the *ANPV* on given risk (input) factors can be expressed as follows:

$$\Delta ANPV_{\alpha}^{\text{risk factor}} = ANPV_{1+\alpha}^{\text{risk factor}} - ANPV \tag{26.9}$$

In the case of *EBIT, DEP, ΔNWC* and *D* it holds

$$\begin{aligned}\Delta ANPV_{\alpha}^{EBIT} =& ANPV_{1+\alpha}^{EBIT} - ANPV\\ =& (1+\alpha)\left(\sum_{i=0}^{T}\frac{EBIT_i(1-t)}{(1+R_U)^i}+\sum_{i=0}^{T}\frac{DEP_i}{(1+R_U)^i}-\right.\\ &\left.-\sum_{i=0}^{T}\frac{\Delta NWC_i}{(1+R_U)^i}--INV+\sum_{i=1}^{T}\frac{t.D_{i-1}.R_D}{(1+R_D)^i}\right)-\\ &-\left(\sum_{i=0}^{T}\frac{EBIT_i(1-t)}{(1+R_U)^i}+\sum_{i=0}^{T}\frac{DEP_i}{(1+R_U)^i}-\sum_{i=0}^{T}\frac{\Delta NWC_i}{(1+R_U)^i}-\right.\\ &\left.-INV+\sum_{i=1}^{T}\frac{t.D_{i-1}.R_D}{(1+R_D)^i}\right)=\alpha\sum_{i=0}^{T}\frac{EBIT_i(1-t)}{(1+R_U)^i}\end{aligned} \tag{26.10}$$

$$\Delta ANPV_{\alpha}^{DEP} = ANPV_{1+\alpha}^{DEP} - ANPV = \alpha\sum_{i=0}^{T}\frac{DEP_i}{(1+R_U)^i} \tag{26.11}$$

$$\Delta ANPV_{\alpha}^{\Delta NWC} = ANPV_{1+\alpha}^{\Delta NWC} - ANPV = -\alpha\sum_{i=0}^{T}\frac{\Delta NWC_i}{(1+R_U)^i} \tag{26.12}$$

$$\Delta ANPV_{\alpha}^{D} = ANPV_{1+\alpha}^{D} - ANPV = \alpha.t.R_D\sum_{i=1}^{T}\frac{D_{i-1}}{(1+R_D)^i} \tag{26.13}$$

According to Table 26.1 investment is one-off; hence in this special case, *ANPV* increase caused by investment change is expressed as

$$\Delta ANPV_{\alpha}^{INV} = ANPV_{1+\alpha}^{INV} - ANPV = -\alpha(INV) \tag{26.14}$$

The tax rate affects *ANPV* in two ways: as taxation of *EBIT* and as tax deduction of interest. Therefore, one-factor sensitivity analysis formula for tax rate is equal led to

$$\Delta ANPV_{\alpha}^{t}=ANPV_{1+\alpha}^{t}-ANPV=\alpha.t\left(\sum_{i=1}^{T}\frac{D_{i-1}.R_D}{(1+R_D)^i}-\sum_{i=0}^{T}\frac{EBIT_i}{(1+R_U)^i}\right) \tag{26.15}$$

Cost of unleveraged capital and cost of debt are non-linear component of *ANPV* formula. Due to non-linearity of R_U and R_D, *ANPV* increment is expressed as

$$\begin{aligned}\Delta ANPV_{\alpha}^{R_U} =& ANPV_{1+\alpha}^{R_U} - ANPV \\ =& \sum_{i=0}^{T} \frac{EBIT_i(1-t)}{(1+R_U(1+\alpha))^i} + \sum_{i=0}^{T} \frac{DEP_i}{(1+R_U(1+\alpha))^i} - \\ & - \sum_{i=0}^{T} \frac{\Delta NWC_i}{(1+R_U(1+\alpha))^i} - -INV - \left(\sum_{i=0}^{T} \frac{EBIT_i(1-t)}{(1+R_U)^i} + \right. \\ & \left. + \sum_{i=0}^{T} \frac{DEP_i}{(1+R_U)^i} - \sum_{i=0}^{T} \frac{\Delta NWC_i}{(1+R_U)^i} - INV \right)\end{aligned} \tag{26.16}$$

$$\Delta ANPV_{\alpha}^{R_D} = ANPV_{1+\alpha}^{R_D} - ANPV = \sum_{i=1}^{T} \frac{t.D_{i-1}.R_D}{(1+R_D(1+\alpha))^i} - \sum_{i=1}^{T} \frac{t.D_{i-1}.R_D}{(1+R_D)^i} \tag{26.17}$$

In the model example, we assume that the given input factors may fall or rise in the range of 10%, $\alpha \in \langle -0,1; 0,1 \rangle$. In Table 26.2 is shown the adjusted net present values of project depending on alpha. If the alpha is equal to zero, i.e. the risk of changes in input factors is zero, *ANPV* is 72.37 €.

For given values of input factors, all values of *ANPV* are positive. Therefore, the investment project should be accepted regardless of the alpha factor. The impact of each factor and the change of the adjusted net present value are shown in Fig. 26.1.

Additionally, changes in *ANPV* are obvious from Table 26.3 and Fig. 26.2.

Figures 26.1 and 26.2 show the impact of risk factors on *ANPV*. It should be noted that the increasing impact of input factors is expressed as a positive or negative slope of the line. Therefore, *ANPV* is the most positive sensitive to *EBIT* and vice versa the most negative sensitive to changes in INV. However, leverage of the project does not have such a big impact on *ANPV* as we expected. Debt and cost of debt have caused only a little increase in dependent variable. It should also be mentioned that the tax shield is only one of financial side effects influencing net present value (see Brealey et al. 2010).

26.4 Conclusion

Sensitivity analysis is the first step of investment risk analysis. It gives relatively easy determination of significant risk factors, as well as it should help to identify marginal values of alpha for which the project is not acceptable. However, mis-

Table 26.2 Factor impact on *ANPV* value (€)

Alpha	EBIT	DEP	Δ NWC	*D*	*t*	INV	Ru	Rd
10%	85.48	78.64	67.83	72.54	69.04	64.32	68.73	72.51
9%	84.17	78.01	68.28	72.52	69.37	65.12	69.09	72.49
8%	82.85	77.38	68.73	72.50	69.70	65.92	69.44	72.47
7%	81.53	76.75	69.18	72.48	70.03	66.72	69.79	72.45
6%	80.22	76.11	69.63	72.45	70.35	67.52	70.15	72.43
5%	78.90	75.48	70.08	72.43	70.68	68.32	70.51	72.41
4%	77.58	74.85	70.52	72.41	71.01	69.12	70.87	72.39
3%	76.27	74.22	70.97	72.39	71.34	69.92	71.23	72.38
2%	74.95	73.58	71.42	72.36	71.66	70.72	71.59	72.36
1%	73.63	72.95	71.87	72.34	71.99	71.52	71.95	72.34
0%	72.32	72.32	72.32	72.32	72.32	72.32	72.32	72.32
−1%	71.00	71.69	72.77	72.30	72.65	73.12	72.68	72.30
−2%	69.68	71.05	73.21	72.27	72.97	73.92	73.05	72.28
−3%	68.37	70.42	73.66	72.25	73.30	74.72	73.42	72.26
−4%	67.05	69.79	74.11	72.23	73.63	75.52	73.79	72.24
−5%	65.74	69.15	74.56	72.20	73.95	76.32	74.16	72.22
−6%	64.42	68.52	75.01	72.18	74.28	77.12	74.53	72.20
−7%	63.10	67.89	75.46	72.16	74.61	77.92	74.91	72.18
−8%	61.79	67.26	75.91	72.14	74.94	78.72	75.29	72.16
−9%	60.47	66.62	76.35	72.11	75.26	79.52	75.66	72.14
−10%	59.15	65.99	76.80	72.09	75.59	80.32	76.04	72.12

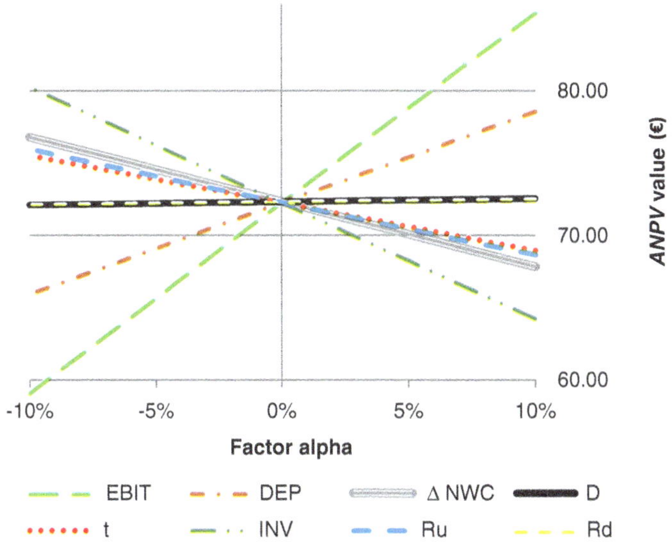

Fig. 26.1 *ANPV* depending on alpha

Table 26.3 Factor impact on *ANPV* increment

Alpha	EBIT	DEP	Δ NWC	*D*	*t*	INV	Ru	Rd
10%	13.16	6.33	−4.48	0.23	−3.27	−8.00	−3.58	0.19
9%	11.85	5.69	−4.04	0.20	−2.95	−7.20	−3.23	0.17
8%	10.53	5.06	−3.59	0.18	−2.62	−6.40	−2.88	0.15
7%	9.22	4.43	−3.14	0.16	−2.29	−5.60	−2.52	0.13
6%	7.90	3.80	−2.69	0.14	−1.96	−4.80	−2.17	0.11
5%	6.58	3.16	−2.24	0.11	−1.64	−4.00	−1.81	0.10
4%	5.27	2.53	−1.79	0.09	−1.31	−3.20	−1.45	0.08
3%	3.95	1.90	−1.35	0.07	−0.98	−2.40	−1.09	0.06
2%	2.63	1.27	−0.90	0.05	−0.65	−1.60	−0.73	0.04
1%	1.32	0.63	−0.45	0.02	−0.33	−0.80	−0.36	0.02
0%	0.00	0.00	0.00	0.00	0.00	0.00	0.00	0.00
−1%	−1.32	−0.63	0.45	−0.02	0.33	0.80	0.37	−0.02
−2%	−2.63	−1.27	0.90	−0.05	0.65	1.60	0.73	−0.04
−3%	−3.95	−1.90	1.35	−0.07	0.98	2.40	1.10	−0.06
−4%	−5.27	−2.53	1.79	−0.09	1.31	3.20	1.47	−0.08
−5%	−6.58	−3.16	2.24	−0.11	1.64	4.00	1.84	−0.10
−6%	−7.90	−3.80	2.69	−0.14	1.96	4.80	2.22	−0.12
−7%	−9.22	−4.43	3.14	−0.16	2.29	5.60	2.59	−0.14
−8%	−10.53	−5.06	3.59	−0.18	2.62	6.40	2.97	−0.16
−9%	−11.85	−5.69	4.04	−0.20	2.95	7.20	3.34	−0.18
−10%	−13.16	−6.33	4.48	−0.23	3.27	8.00	3.72	−0.20

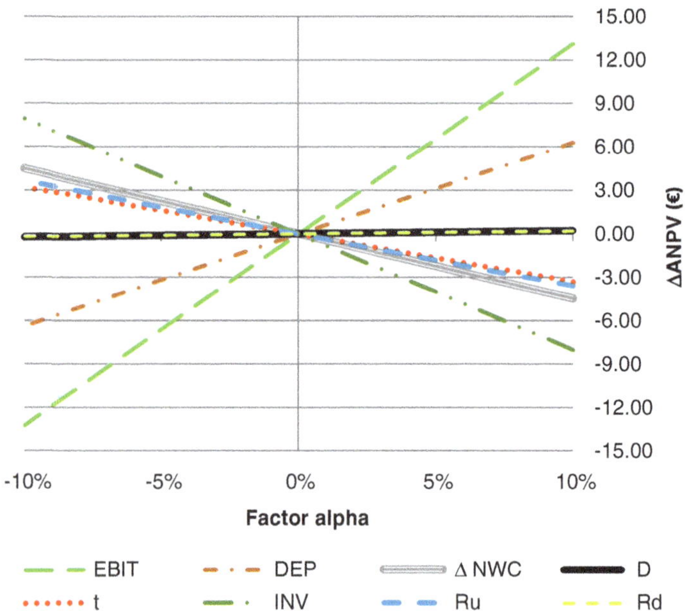

Fig. 26.2 *ANPV* increment depending on alpha

takenly chosen interval of alpha may distort investment decision-making. It should be determine as objectively as possible, such as probability distribution (Kral and Kliestik 2015).

On the other hand, single-factor sensitivity analysis examines the impact on just one factor to criterion variable and does not consider other risk factors. Hence, *multifactorial sensitivity analysis* (scenario analysis) or *Monte Carlo simulation* (Dinh 2016) are more appropriate because they analyse the impact of several factors on the financial (criterion) factor (Kliestik et al. 2014a, 2014b).

Buc and Kliestik (2013) and Gazdikova and Sustekova (2009) mentioned, project should be also analysed by cross-correlation between the input factors as the second step of risk analysis, since correlation may multiply the impact on the criterion value.

Acknowledgement The paper is an output of the science project VEGA 1/0428/17 Creation of New Paradigms of Financial Management at the Threshold of the 21st Century in Conditions of the Slovak Republic.

References

Bartošová, V., Majercak, P., & Hraskova, D. (2015). Taking risk into account in the evaluation of economic efficiency of investment projects: Traditional methods. *Procedia Economics and Finance, 24*, 68–75. Elsevier Publisher.

Brealey, R. A., Myers, S. C., & Allen, F. (2010). *Principles of corporate finance* (10th ed.). New York: McGraw-Hill/Irwin.

Buc, D., & Kliestik, T. (2013). Aspects of statistics in terms of financial modelling and risk. In: *7th International Days of Statistics and Economics, Prague, Czech Republic* (pp. 215–224).

Cisko, S., & Kliestik, T. (2013). *Financny manazment podniku II*. Zilina: EDIS Publishing.

Corejova, T., Bachanova, P. H., & Mockova, M. (2014). Industry and business study of architecture in terms of the Zilina Region. In: Nijkamp, P., Kourtit, K., Bucek, M., Hudec, O. (Eds.), *CERS 2014: 5th Central European Conference in Regional Science, Kosice, Slovakia, 05–08 October 2014* (pp. 125–135).

Damodaran, A. (2002). *Investment valuation: Tools and technique for determining the value of any asset* (2nd ed.). New York: Wiley.

Dengov, V. V., & Gregova, E. (2010). Economic decision-making under uncertainty and risk. Methodology and criteria for decision-making. *Ekonomicko-manazerske spektrum, 4*(2), 28–45.

Dinh, T. T. H. (2016). Evaluating the decision-making on a Public-Private Partnership to finance a road project in Vietnam. *Journal of International Studies, 9*(3), 124–137. 10.14254/2071-8330.2016/9-3/10.

Dluhosova, D. (2010). *Financni rizeni a rozhodovani podniku: analyza, investovani, ocenovani, riziko, flexibilita* (3rd ed.). Praha: Ekopress.

Gazdikova, J., & Sustekova, D. (2009). Selected statistical tools for financial analysis. *Ekonomicko-manazerske spectrum, 3*(2), 8–11.

Grublova, E. (2010). Attitudes to risk and ability to take risky decisions. *Ekonomicko-manazerske spectrum, 4*(2), 58–63.

Kliestik, T., Lyakin, A. N., & Valaskova, K. (2014a) Stochastic Calculus and Modelling in Economics and Finance. In: *2nd International Conference on Economics and Social Science (ICESS)*, Advances in Education Research, Shenzhen, China, Vol 61 (pp. 161–167).

Kliestik, T., Misankova, M., & Adamko, P. (2014b). Sensitivity analysis of credit risk models based on Greeks. In: *2nd International Conference on Management Innovation and Business Innovation (ICMIBI 2014)*, Lecture Notes in Management Science, Bangkok, Thailand, Vol. 44 (pp 99–104).

Kral, P., & Kliestik, T. (2015). Estimation of the level of risk based on the selected theoretical probability distributions. In: *10th International Scientific Conference Financial management of Firms and Financial Institutions, Ostrava, Czech Republic* (pp. 603–610).

Lehutova, K., Krizanova, A., & Kliestik, T. (2013). Quantification of equity and debt capital costs in the specific conditions of transport enterprises. In: *17th International Conference on Transport Means, Transport Means, Proceedings of the International Conference, Kaunas, Lithuania* (pp. 258–261).

Luehrman, T. A. (1997). Using APV: A better tool for valuing operations. *Harvard Business Review, 75*(3), 145–154.

Myers, S. C. (1974). Interactions of corporate financing and investment decisions implications for capital budgeting. *Journal of Finance, 29*(1), 1–25.

Valaskova, K., Kramarova, K., & Bartošová, V. (2015). Multi criteria models used in Slovak consumer market for business decision making. *Procedia Economics and Finance, 26*, 174–182, Elsevier Publisher.

Vochozka, M. (2010). Development of methods for comprehensive evaluation of business performance. *Politicka Ekonomie, 58*(5), 675–688.

Chapter 27
Volatility Modelling of Agricultural Commodities: Application of Selected GARCH Models

Corlise L. Le Roux

Abstract This paper does an empirical analysis of a selection of agricultural commodities, cocoa, coffee and sugar, as well as the currencies of the countries that produce the largest amount of the selected commodities, the Brazilian Real and the CFA Franc. In addition, the S&P GSCI Agriculture Index is included as an indication of overall agriculture prices as a comparison variable. The empirical analysis models the volatility of the variables included in the paper. The data will be evaluated by means of number of financial econometric models. The financial econometric models of the GARCH family models that will be used are the generalised autoregressive conditional heteroscedastic (GARCH) model, the Glosten-Jagannathan-Runkle generalised autoregressive conditional heteroscedastic (GJR-GARCH) model and the exponential GARCH (EGARCH) model. The models will be based on daily data from 1 January 2007 to 23 March 2017, split between the 2007–2009 financial crisis period and the period after the 2007–2009 financial crisis. The results suggest that volatility is present in the data, and therefore the models mentioned will be compared in order to identify which model is the best fitting model for the selected commodities, currencies and index. Overall, GARCH was the best fitting model for the S&P GSCI Agriculture Index during and after the financial crisis and EGARCH for the Brazilian Real. The remainder of the variables had different model results. Only the GJR-GARCH results for cocoa indicated that leverage effects exist which imply that negative shocks have a greater effect than positive shocks.

Keywords Cocoa · Coffee · Sugar · Brazilian Real · CFA Franc · GSCI Agriculture Index · GARCH · EGARCH · GJR-GARCH

C. L. Le Roux (✉)
University of Johannesburg, Johannesburg, South Africa
e-mail: corlisel@uj.ac.za

N. Tsounis, A. Vlachvei (eds.), *Advances in Panel Data Analysis in Applied Economic Research*, Springer Proceedings in Business and Economics,
https://doi.org/10.1007/978-3-319-70055-7_27

27.1 Introduction

The ever-changing nature of commodity prices in the world is an important concept to understand. The demand and supply of commodities are changing constantly as the world progresses and technology develops. From an agricultural perspective, weather, harvesting, storing, processing and transporting of commodities affect the quantity and quality of the commodity. Weather conditions and patterns around the world affect the production of agricultural commodities, and the related demand of commodities is also affected.

The volatility in the prices of commodities has a direct impact on final consumers as the price of food is impacted by production costs as well as by inflation. Understanding the volatility of commodity prices could assist producers and users in managing the risk of working with commodities. Commodities are used as financial assets in various forms, and understanding the volatility present in the price could be used to the advantage of the investor.

This paper evaluates the volatility behaviour present in six variables consisting of commodities, currencies and an index. The variables are cocoa, coffee and sugar, the Brazilian Real the CFA Franc and the S&P GSCI Agriculture Index. The empirical data analysis of the study will include correlation, Johansen cointegration test and three GARCH family models, the generalised autoregressive conditional heteroscedastic (GARCH) model (Bollerslev 1986), Threshold GARCH (TGARCH) model also known as the Glosten-Jagannathan-Runkle generalised autoregressive conditional heteroscedastic (GJR-GARCH) model (Glosten et al. 1993) and the exponential GARCH (EGARCH) model (Nelson 1991).

The remainder of the paper is structured as follows: part 2 provides a brief review of current literature. Part 3 discusses the methodology and explanation of the data. Part 4 illustrates the results and interprets the findings. The final part, part 5, discusses the conclusion and implication of the study.

27.2 Review of the Literature

Agricultural commodities are a vital source of life for the entire ecosystem in the world. Without agricultural commodities, living organisms would not be able to sustain themselves. Not all agricultural commodities are consumed by all living organisms, but nevertheless, they are an important resource. Many factors affect agricultural commodities, the largest being weather as well as conditions that the commodity is grown in.

Weather cannot be controlled, but the area in which the commodity is grown can be controlled and manipulated. Technology has advanced to such an extent that agricultural commodities can be grown in artificial conditions, where the "weather" is controlled. Prices of commodities are therefore not constant and as a result ever changing to the demand and supply around the world. Gaining an understanding how volatility in commodity prices behaves provides insight into the management of commodities.

GARCH modelling has been done in many forms and applied to a wide selection of datasets, other than agricultural commodities. This paper will however only focus on a selection of previous literature related to agricultural commodities.

Lama et al. (2015) investigated the performance of ARIMA, GARCH and EGARCH in the forecasting of prices of domestic oil prices from India, international oil prices as well as the international cotton price "Cotlook A" index. Monthly data from April 1982 to March 2012 was included in the dataset in order to determine which model provided the best forecasting accuracy. For the domestic and international oil prices, the AR(2)-GARCH(1,1) provided the most accurate forecasting performance, whereas EGARCH outperformed the other models for the international cotton price index.

Sendhil et al. (2014) applied the GARCH model to twenty agricultural commodities from 2009 to 2010 as well as from commencement of trading until 2014. The GARCH model was applied to evaluate spot prices against futures prices and found that low volatility was found in seven of the commodities. Four of the commodities showed constant volatility throughout the period analysed.

Certi et al. (2013) explored the relationships between the returns of 25 commodities which included agricultural commodities. The data period evaluated was from 2001 to 2011 and applied the dynamic conditional correlation (DCC) GARCH model in order to model volatility. The results indicated that correlations between commodity and stock markets change through time and are extremely volatile. The volatility increased since the 2007–2008 financial crisis.

27.3 Data and Methodology

The methodology adopted in this study is based on financial econometric models. The GARCH family models are applied to the included datasets in order to evaluate the volatility present in the datasets. The models that will be used are the generalised autoregressive conditional heteroscedastic (GARCH) model, the Threshold GARCH (TGARCH) model also known as the Glosten-Jagannathan-Runkle generalised autoregressive conditional heteroscedastic (GJR-GARCH) model and the exponential GARCH (EGARCH) model. The best fitting model will be determined by the Akaike information criterion (AIC) (Akaike 1974) and the Schwarz information criterion (SIC) (Schwartz 1978).

In addition, Johansen cointegration test between selected variables will be undertaken to identify if any long-run relationships exists between variables which will be utilised in order to run bivariate GARCH, GJR-GARCH and EGARCH models (Asteriou and Hall 2011; Johansen 1991; Luetkepohl 2011; Watson 1994).

The dataset included in this study is a selection of agricultural commodities, cocoa, coffee and sugar, as well as the currencies of the countries that produce the largest amount of these commodities. Cote d'Ivoire produces the largest amount of cocoa, whereas Brazil produces the largest amount of coffee and sugar. Therefore, the CFA Franc against the US Dollar represents Cote d'Ivoire, and the Brazilian Real against the US Dollar represents Brazil. A final variable, the S&P GSCI

Agriculture Index, was included as an indication of overall agriculture prices as a comparison variable.

Data from 1 January 2007 to 23 March 2017 was included in this study with a total of 2669 data points; however, it was divided into two sets in order to evaluate the difference between the volatility in the periods. The first period was from 1 January 2007 to 31 December 2009 which represents the 2007–2009 financial crisis. The second period, from 1 January 2010 to 23 March 2017, represents the period after the 2007–2009 financial crisis. The prices of the datasets are daily spot prices available for the included commodities, currencies and index from the Thomson Reuters Datastream database. EViews was utilised as the tool to run the financial econometric models.

The GARCH model as specified by Brooks (2014) is

$$\sigma^2 = \omega + \alpha\mu_{t-1}^2 + \beta\sigma_{t-1}^2$$

The GARCH model allows the conditional variance to be dependent on the included variables' own lags. σ in the above equation represents the estimated conditional variance for one period ahead of the selected variable.

The GJR-GARCH model includes leverage effects and is specified by Brooks (2014) as

$$\sigma^2 = \omega + \alpha\mu_{t-1}^2 + \beta\sigma_{t-1}^2 + \gamma\mu_{t-1}^2 I_{t-1}$$

where

$$I_{t-1} = \begin{cases} 1 \text{ if } \mu_{t-1} < 0 \\ \text{Otherwise} \end{cases}$$

where γ equals the asymmetry term representing the leverage effect. If the asymmetry term is positive and statistically significant, there is leverage present.

The EGARCH model also includes leverage effects and is specified by Brooks (2014) as

$$\ln\left(\sigma^2\right) = \omega + \beta \ln\left(\sigma_{t-1}^2\right) + \gamma \frac{\mu_{t-1}}{\sqrt{\sigma_{t-1}^2}} + \alpha \left[\frac{|\mu_{t-1}|}{\sqrt{\sigma_{t-1}^2}} - \sqrt{\frac{2}{\pi}} \right]$$

where γ equals the asymmetry term representing the leverage effect. If the asymmetry term is negative and statistically significant, there is leverage present.

27.4 Empirical Results

The graphical representation of the data is illustrated in Fig. 27.1. The graphical representations display the movements of the datasets during and after the 2007–2009 financial crisis. Two graphs are shown for each of the datasets included in the study, the daily level price on the line graph and on the log first differenced graphs. The log return graphs indicate that volatility clustering is present in the data.

The descriptive statistics of the variables are shown in Tables 27.1 and 27.2 during the crisis and after the 2007–2009 financial crisis, respectively. All the variables, except the Brazilian Real, are negatively skewed during the 2007–2009 financial crisis.

Table 27.2 shows that all the variables except coffee and the GSCI Agriculture Index were negatively skewed after the financial crisis. All the variables during and after the financial crisis are not normally distributed and exhibit leptokurtosis.

The augmented Dickey-Fuller (ADF) (Dickey and Fuller 1981) and Phillips-Perron (PP) (Perron 1989) tests are undertaken to determine if unit roots exist which is required to continue with the analysis. The results of the test ADF and PP tests are shown in Table 27.3. The results indicate that all variables are stationary at first difference at a 1% significance level.

The correlation results in Table 27.4 show that no strong positive or negative correlation relationships exist between the variables based on a log return basis.

VAR analysis and Johansen cointegration test was run between combinations of variables, which were:

- CFA Franc and cocoa
- Brazilian Real and coffee
- Brazilian Real and sugar
- S&P GSCI Agriculture Index and Brazilian Real
- S&P GSCI Agriculture Index and CFA Franc
- Cocoa and S&P GSCI Agriculture Index
- Coffee and S&P GSCI Agriculture Index
- Sugar and S&P GSCI Agriculture Index

The results indicated that only the Brazilian Real and coffee and coffee and the S&P GSCI Agriculture Index had one cointegrating relationship each during the crisis. The remainder of the results showed no cointegration.

Table 27.5 shows the ARCH LM tests results that indicate that during the crisis, only the Brazilian Real and coffee were statistically significant at a 1% level of significance using one lag. By increasing the lag periods, the remainder of the variables were statistically significant at either a 5% level of significance or at a 1% level of significance. After the crisis, however, all the variables were statistically significant at a 1% level of significance using one lag. Based on these results, the GARCH family models were estimated and included in the remaining part of this section.

The GARCH results for GARCH(1,1), GJR-GARCH(1,1) and EGARCH(1,1) are displayed in Tables 27.6 and 27.7. Table 27.6 provides the results related to

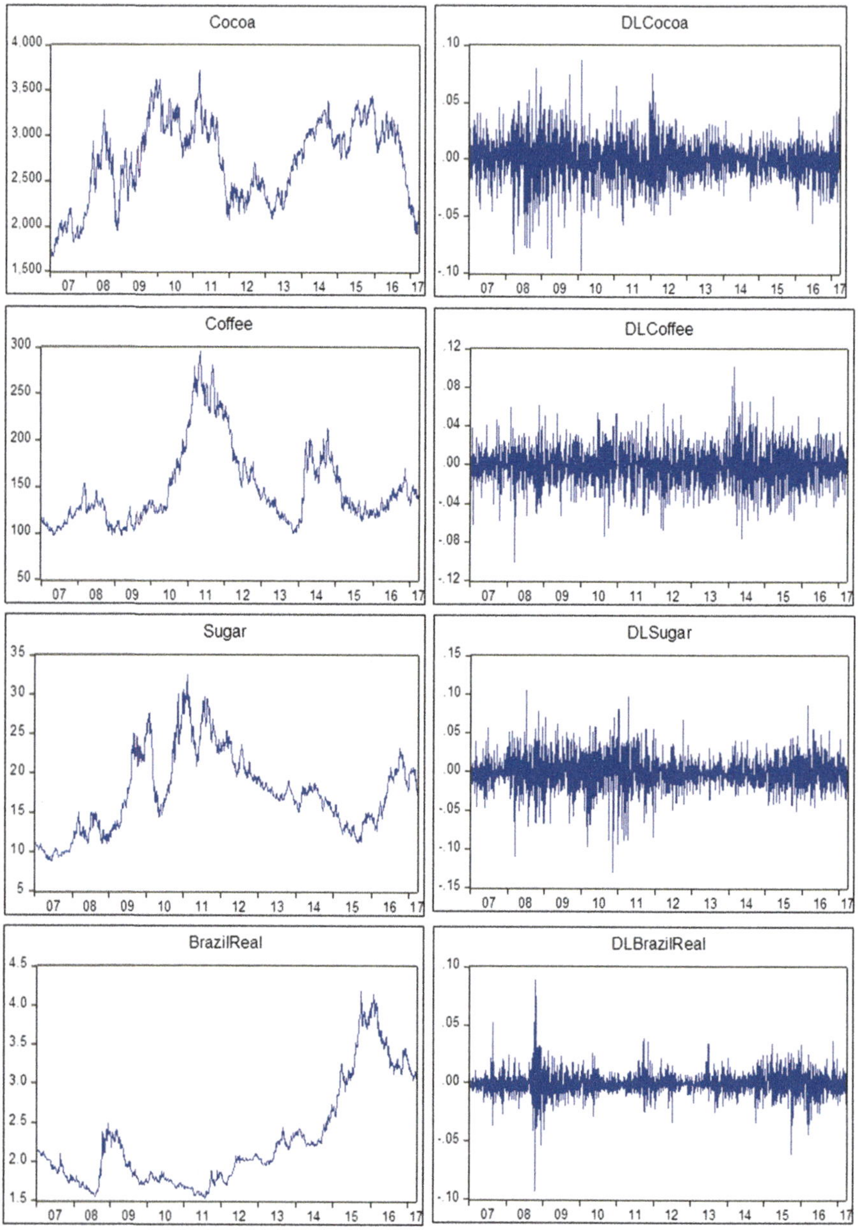

Fig. 27.1 Graphical representation of movement in the six variables (*Source*: Researcher's analysis)

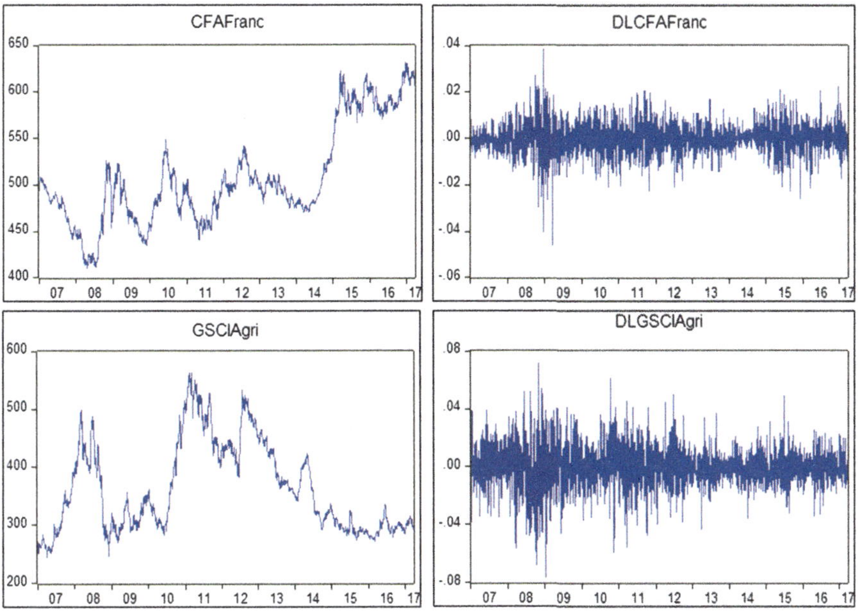

Fig. 27.1 (continued)

Table 27.1 Descriptive statistics (1 January 2007 to 31 December 2009)

	DLBRAZIL-REAL	DLCFAFRANC	DLCOCOA	DLCOFFEE	DLGSCIAGRI	DLSUGAR
Mean	0.000	0.000	0.001	0.000	0.000	0.001
Median	0.000	0.000	0.000	0.000	0.000	0.000
Maximum	0.089	0.038	0.080	0.063	0.072	0.106
Minimum	−0.092	−0.046	−0.087	−0.101	−0.076	−0.110
Std. dev.	0.012	0.007	0.020	0.015	0.018	0.021
Skewness	0.470	−0.251	−0.426	−0.467	−0.318	−0.030
Kurtosis	15.209	8.506	5.697	6.968	4.421	5.607
Jarque-Bera	4892.257	997.283	261.031	542.131	79.066	221.855
Probability	0.000	0.000	0.000	0.000	0.000	0.000
Sum	−0.205	−0.084	0.688	0.082	0.263	0.777
Sum sq. dev.	0.117	0.040	0.309	0.186	0.249	0.346
Observations	783	783	783	783	783	783

Source: Researcher's analysis

the financial crisis period and Table 27.7 provides the results after the financial crisis. The GARCH model that is deemed to be the best fitting model is the model with the smallest AIC and SIC result. For the period during the financial crisis, the GARCH(1,1) model is the best fitting model for CFA Franc, cocoa, coffee and the

Table 27.2 Descriptive statistics (1 January 2010 to 23 March 2017)

	DLBRAZIL-REAL	DLCFAFRANC	DLCOCOA	DLCOFFEE	DLGSCIAGRI	DLSUGAR
Mean	0.000	0.000	0.000	0.000	0.000	0.000
Median	0.000	0.000	0.000	0.000	0.000	0.000
Maximum	0.039	0.023	0.088	0.103	0.061	0.098
Minimum	−0.061	−0.026	−0.097	−0.076	−0.059	−0.130
Std. dev.	0.009	0.006	0.014	0.018	0.012	0.019
Skewness	−0.083	−0.045	−0.026	0.146	0.062	−0.430
Kurtosis	6.693	4.234	6.413	5.072	5.138	7.583
Jarque-Bera	1072.694	120.210	914.603	343.891	360.080	1706.854
Probability	0.000	0.000	0.000	0.000	0.000	0.000
Sum	0.585	0.285	−0.450	0.098	−0.191	−0.369
Sum sq. dev.	0.136	0.068	0.394	0.621	0.270	0.669
Observations	1884	1884	1884	1884	1884	1884

Source: Researcher's analysis

Table 27.3 Unit roots test using the augmented Dickey-Fuller and Phillips-Perron method

	Level		1st difference	
	Intercept	Trend and intercept	Intercept	Trend and intercept
ADF				
BRAZILREAL	−0.561	−1.984	−52.155***	−52.163***
CFAFRANC	−1.032	−2.721	−51.527***	−51.533***
COCOA	−2.767	−2.482	−54.948***	−54.969***
COFFEE	−1.792	−1.740	−49.254***	−49.249***
GSCIAGRI	−1.856	−2.003	−49.081***	−49.091***
SUGAR	−2.058	−1.975	−54.598***	−54.595***
PP				
BRAZILREAL	−0.503	−1.943	−52.200***	−52.211***
CFAFRANC	−1.044	−2.752	−51.527***	−51.533***
COCOA	−2.856	−2.601	−54.864***	−54.888***
COFFEE	−1.964	−1.919	−49.433***	−49.426***
GSCIAGRI	−1.946	−2.085	−49.059***	−49.068***
SUGAR	−2.076	−1.998	−54.564***	−54.562***

Source: Researcher's analysis
***Statistically significant at a 1% level of significance

S&P GSCI Agriculture Index. EGARCH is the best fit for the Brazilian Real and sugar according to the AIC and SIC results.

The existence of volatility clustering as tested by the GARCH models is evaluated based on the α- and β-coefficients. If the coefficients are positive and statistically significant, then it implies that volatility clustering is present in the dataset. If the sum of α- and β-coefficients is close to one, it means that shocks to the conditional variance will be extremely persistent (Brooks 2014).

Table 27.4 Correlation matrix

During crisis	*DLBRAZIL-REAL*	*DLCFAFRANC*	*DLCOCOA*	*DLCOFFEE*	*DLGSCIAGRI*	*DLSUGAR*
DLBRAZIL-REAL	1.000	0.376	−0.022	−0.014	−0.368	−0.264
DLCFAFRANC	0.376	1.000	−0.024	−0.035	−0.338	−0.192
DLCOCOA	−0.022	−0.024	1.000	0.289	−0.038	−0.071
DLCOFFEE	−0.014	−0.035	0.289	1.000	−0.020	0.015
DLGSCIAGRI	−0.368	−0.338	−0.038	−0.020	1.000	0.468
DLSUGAR	−0.264	−0.192	−0.071	0.015	0.468	1.000
After crisis	*DLBRAZIL-REAL*	*DLCFAFRANC*	*DLCOCOA*	*DLCOFFEE*	*DLGSCIAGRI*	*DLSUGAR*
DLBRAZIL-REAL	1.000	0.299	−0.151	−0.203	−0.195	−0.186
DLCFAFRANC	0.299	1.000	−0.172	−0.099	−0.173	−0.080
DLCOCOA	−0.151	−0.172	1.000	0.095	0.084	0.045
DLCOFFEE	−0.203	−0.099	0.095	1.000	0.183	0.184
DLGSCIAGRI	−0.195	−0.173	0.084	0.183	1.000	0.353
DLSUGAR	−0.186	−0.080	0.045	0.184	0.353	1.000

Source: Researcher's analysis

Table 27.5 ARCH LM test results

During crisis	*Lag*	*F-statistic*	*Obs*R-squared*	*Lag*	*F-statistic*	*Obs*R-squared*
DLBRAZILREAL	1	236.577***	181.986***	N/A	N/A	N/A
DLCFAFRANC	1	2.997	2.299	2	31.484***	58.478***
DLCOCOA	1	0.281	0.283	3	3.547**	10.552**
DLCOFFEE	1	8.548***	8.477***	N/A	N/A	N/A
DLGSCIAGRI	1	2.468	2.467	2	5.630***	11.140***
DLSUGAR	1	1.384	1.385	2	5.869***	11.607***
After crisis	*Lag*	*F-statistic*	*Obs*R-squared*	*Lag*	*F-statistic*	*Obs*R-squared*
DLBRAZILREAL	1	47.039***	45.940***	N/A	N/A	N/A
DLCFAFRANC	1	6.829***	6.811***	N/A	N/A	N/A
DLCOCOA	1	158.979***	146.745***	N/A	N/A	N/A
DLCOFFEE	1	19.668***	19.485***	N/A	N/A	N/A
DLGSCIAGRI	1	7.791***	7.767***	N/A	N/A	N/A
DLSUGAR	1	144.064***	133.958***	N/A	N/A	N/A

Source: Researcher's analysis
**Statistically significant at a 5% level of significance
***Statistically significant at a 1% level of significance

The asymmetry term present in the GJR-GARCH and EGARCH model indicates the effect of leverage present in the dataset. For the GJR-GARCH model, the asymmetry terms need to be positive and statistically significant to indicate leverage effects. For the EGARCH model, the opposite is true; the terms need to be negative and statistically significant in order to indicate leverage effects. If leverage effects are found in either of the models, it implies that negative effects will have a greater

Table 27.6 GARCH, GJR-GARCH and EGARCH results during the financial crisis

GARCH model	Variable	ω	α	β	γ	AIC	SIC
GARCH	DLBRAZILREAL	0.000	0.171***	0.825***	–	−6.640	−6.616
	DLCFAFRANC	0.000	0.046***	0.954***	–	**−7.363**	**−7.339**
	DLCOCOA	0.000	0.026***	0.970***	–	**−5.078**	**−5.054**
	DLCOFFEE	0.000	0.239***	0.319***	–	**−5.558**	**−5.534**
	DLGSCIAGRI	0.000	0.052***	0.934***	–	**−5.307**	**−5.283**
	DLSUGAR	0.000	0.051***	0.944***	–	−4.998	−4.974
GJR-GARCH	DLBRAZILREAL	0.000	0.242***	0.827***	−0.174***	−6.660	−6.630
	DLCFAFRANC	0.000	0.052***	0.957***	−0.017	−7.362	−7.332
	DLCOCOA	0.000	0.030***	0.970***	−0.007	−5.076	−5.046
	DLCOFFEE	0.000	0.164***	0.226**	0.159**	−5.558	−5.528
	DLGSCIAGRI	0.000	0.043**	0.930***	0.017	−5.305	−5.275
	DLSUGAR	0.000	0.061***	0.951***	−0.033**	−5.000	−4.970
EGARCH	DLBRAZILREAL	−0.411	0.193***	0.972***	0.108***	**−6.667**	**−6.637**
	DLCFAFRANC	−0.102	0.108***	0.998***	0.007	−7.362	−7.332
	DLCOCOA	−14.142	0.004	−0.802***	−0.058**	−4.994	−4.964
	DLCOFFEE	−5.053	0.404***	0.433***	−0.088***	−5.558	−5.528
	DLGSCIAGRI	−0.158	0.101***	0.990***	−0.007	−5.298	−5.268
	DLSUGAR	−0.199	0.114***	0.985***	0.035***	**−5.008**	**−4.979**

Source: Researcher's analysis
**Statistically significant at a 5% level of significance
***Statistically significant at a 1% level of significance

rise in volatility. The Brazilian Real and sugar do not have a negative asymmetry term which means that negative effects are the same as positive effects.

For the period after the financial crisis, the GARCH(1,1) model is the best fitting model for the S&P GSCI Agriculture Index and sugar. GJR-GARCH is the best fit for cocoa and coffee and EGARCH is the best fit for the Brazilian Real and the CFA Franc according to the AIC and SIC results. The results for the EGARCH asymmetry term is the same as during the crisis. The variables do not have a negative asymmetry term which means that negative effects are the same as positive effects. Coffee also does not have the correct asymmetry term to indicate leverage effects in the GJR-GARCH model, but cocoa does.

Considering the cointegrating equation, a simple bivariate model was applied to the variables showing cointegration. Cointegration was only present during the 2007–2009 financial crisis.

Diagnostics checking was applied to the models in order to check for serial correlation. In addition, the lack of long-term relationships between the commodities and currencies selected was of interest, and therefore the rolling correlations are shown in Fig. 27.2, separated during and after the 2007–2009 financial crisis. The rolling correlations lead to considering including more advanced GARCH models to evaluate these selected commodities. The correlations are changing constantly between the variables with distinct continuous upward and downward movements from the beginning of the financial crisis up until the present day.

Table 27.7 GARCH, GJR-GARCH and EGARCH results after the financial crisis

GARCH model	Variable	ω	α	β	γ	AIC	SIC
GARCH	DLBRAZILREAL	0.000	0.098***	0.900***	–	−6.922	−6.910
	DLCFAFRANC	0.000	0.029***	0.969***	–	−7.481	−7.469
	DLCOCOA	0.000	0.055***	0.934***	–	−5.735	−5.724
	DLCOFFEE	0.000	0.023***	0.967***	–	−5.229	−5.217
	DLGSCIAGRI	0.000	0.052***	0.939***	–	**−6.130**	**−6.119**
	DLSUGAR	0.000	0.030***	0.967***	–	**−5.301**	**−5.289**
GJR-GARCH	DLBRAZILREAL	0.000	0.117***	0.918***	−0.081***	−6.939	−6.924
	DLCFAFRANC	0.000	0.034***	0.980***	−0.027***	−7.486	−7.471
	DLCOCOA	0.000	0.031***	0.940***	0.039***	**−5.738**	**−5.724**
	DLCOFFEE	0.000	0.032***	0.970***	−0.026***	**−5.236**	**−5.221**
	DLGSCIAGRI	0.000	0.050***	0.938***	0.005	−6.130	−6.115
	DLSUGAR	0.000	0.027***	0.968***	0.006	−5.300	−5.286
EGARCH	DLBRAZILREAL	−0.289	0.154***	0.982***	0.070***	**−6.950**	**−6.935**
	DLCFAFRANC	−0.057	0.047***	0.998***	0.029***	**−7.490**	**−7.476**
	DLCOCOA	−0.226	0.113***	0.983***	−0.051***	−5.735	−5.720
	DLCOFFEE	−0.177	0.048***	0.982***	0.032***	−5.224	−5.209
	DLGSCIAGRI	−0.199	0.129***	0.989***	−0.005	−6.130	−6.115
	DLSUGAR	−0.061	0.061***	0.998***	0.002	−5.301	−5.286

Source: Researcher's analysis
***Statistically significant at a 1% level of significance

Table 27.8 Bivariate GARCH, GJR-GARCH and EGARCH results during financial crisis

GARCH model	Variable	ω	α	β	γ	AIC	SIC
GARCH	DLBRAZI-LREAL and DLCOFFEE	0	0.177***	0.820***		−6.640	−6.611
GJR-GARCH	0	0.254***	0.819***	−0.184	−6.661	−6.625	
EGARCH	−0.446	0.209***	0.970***	0.113	**−6.667**	**−6.631**	
GARCH	DLCOFFEE and DLGSCI-AGRI	0	0.052***	0.934***		**−5.305**	**−5.275**
GJR-GARCH	0	0.043**	0.930***	0.017	−5.303	−5.267	
EGARCH	−0.158	0.101***	0.990***	−0.007	−5.295	−5.259	

Source: Researcher's analysis
**Statistically significant at a 5% level of significance
***Statistically significant at a 1% level of significance

27.5 Conclusion and Implications

The objective of this paper was to model and evaluate the volatility present in the variables. The variables included were cocoa, coffee, sugar, the Brazilian Real, the CFA Franc and the S&P GSCI Agriculture Index. The variables were evaluated from

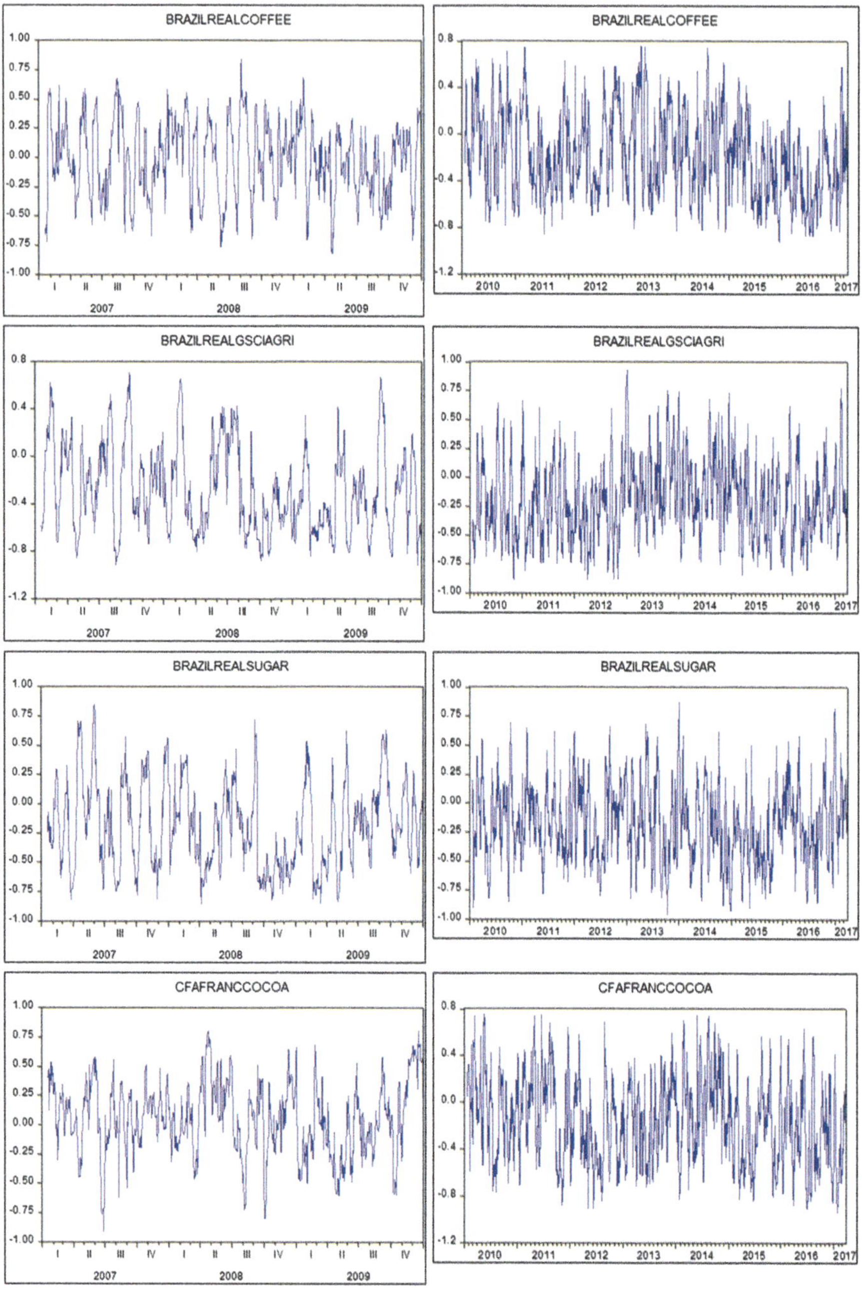

Fig. 27.2 Graphical representation of rolling correlations between variables (*Source*: Researcher's analysis)

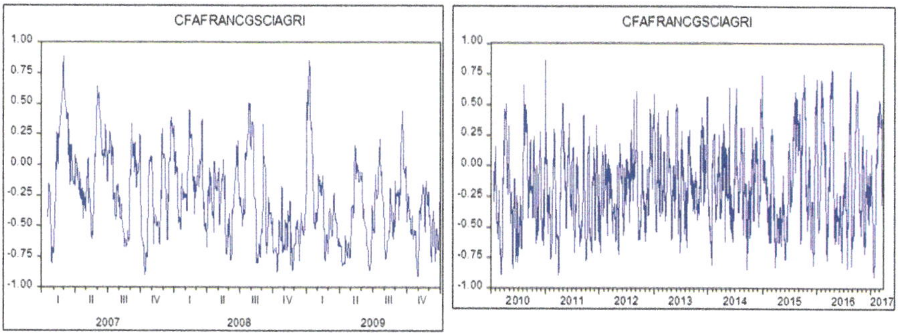

Fig. 27.2 (continued)

the start of the 2007–2009 financial crisis up until March 2017. The data period was split into two sets in order to evaluate the difference in the models during the 2007–2009 financial crisis and after the 2007–2009 financial crisis. During the financial crisis, the GARCH(1,1) model was the best fitting model for the CFA Franc, cocoa, coffee and the S&P GSCI Agriculture Index. EGARCH was the best fit for the Brazilian Real and sugar according to the AIC and SIC results. After the 2007–2009 financial crisis, the GARCH(1,1) model was the best fitting model for the S&P GSCI Agriculture Index and sugar. GJR-GARCH was the best fit for cocoa and coffee, and EGARCH was the best fit for the Brazilian Real and the CFA Franc according to the AIC and SIC results.

Overall, GARCH was the best fitting model for the S&P GSCI Agriculture Index during and after the financial crisis and EGARCH for the Brazilian Real. The remainder of the variables had different model results. Only the GJR-GARCH results for cocoa indicate that leverage effects exist which imply that negative shocks have a greater effect than positive shocks.

Further research can be done in order to further analyse this dataset based on the results of this study. Alternative volatility modelling models can be applied to the same dataset in order to further evaluate the volatility effects present in the variables. In addition, other commodities and countries can be analysed in order to determine if the volatility effects present in other variables are similar or not. Production and consumption trends can also be evaluated along with the prices of the commodities to identify and links that are present.

References

Akaike, H. (1974). A new look at the statistical model identification. IEEE Transactions on Automatic Control Ac-19:716-723.

Asteriou, D., & Hall, S. G. (2011). *Applied econometrics* (2nd ed.). New York: Palgrave Macmillan.

Bollerslev, T. (1986). Generalised autoregressive conditional heteroskedasticity. *Journal of Econometrics*, (3), 307–327.
Brooks, C. (2014). *Introductory econometrics for finance* (3rd ed.). Cambridge, UK: Cambridge University Press.
Creti, A., Joëts, M., & Mignon, V. (2013). On the links between stock and commodity markets' volatility. *Energy Economics, 37*, 16–28.
Dickey, D. A., & Fuller, W. A. (1981). Likelihood ratio statistics for autoregressive time series with a unit root. *Econometrica, 49*(4), 1057–1072.
Glosten, L. R., Jagannathan, R., & Runkle, D. (1993). On the relation between the expected value and the volatility of the nominal excess return on stocks. *Journal of Finance, 48*, 1779–1801.
Johansen, S. (1991). Estimation and hypothesis testing of cointegration vectors in Gaussian vector autoregressive models. *Econometrica, 59*(6), 1551–1580.
Lama, A., Jha, G. K., Paul, R. K., & Gurung, B. (2015). Modelling and forecasting of price volatility: An application of GARCH and EGARCH models. *Agricultural Economics Research Review, 28*(1), 73–82.
Luetkepohl, H. (2011). Vector autoregressive models. European University Institute Working Papers ECO 2011/30.
Nelson, D. B. (1991). Conditional heteroskedasticity in asset returns: A new approach. *Econometrica, 59*, 347–370.
Perron, P. (1989). The great crash, the oil price shock, and the unit root hypothesis. *Econometrica, 57*(6), 1361–1401.
Schwartz, G. (1978). Estimating the dimension of a model. *The Annals of Statistics, 6*, 461–464.
Senhil, R., Kar, A., Mathur, V. C., & Jha, G. K. (2014). Price volatility in agricultural commodity futures – An application of GARCH model. *Journal of the Indian Society of Agricultural Statistics, 68*(3), 365–375.
Watson, M. W. (1994). *Vector autoregressions and cointegration, Handbook of econometrics* (Vol. 4, pp. 2844–2910). Amsterdam: Federal Reserve Bank of Chicago.

Chapter 28
Increase the Standard of Living of Regions by Increasing the Quality of the Business Environment

Martin Buno, Silvia Zadnanova, and Zuzana Stofkova

Abstract The business environment reflects the quality of the economic conditions of the state. Its gradual improvement is the best way to support small- and medium-sized enterprises and how to improve quality of living standards of regions. One of the ways on how to determine the quality of the business environment can be accomplished by selecting foreign markets by selection analysis. We will compare countries of Visegrad groups. We will compare these countries on the basis of ten criteria which can be divided into four bigger groups: political criteria, economical criteria, technological criteria, and legislative criteria. In this data, we will use input data for large-scale analysis of selection of second level. Based on this research, we will be able to see which business environment is the most attractive for new investors, new capital, and new jobs. All those factors are very important for every region. With the improvement of the business environment, we will improve the standard of living of the region.

Keywords Region · Business environment · Selection analysis · Visegrad countries

28.1 Business Environment and Its Importance for Regions

It is not entirely clearly to define the business environment. In the process of continuous expansion of markets, globalization, and new technologies, business environment evolves dynamically.

Business environment is an enterprise and all that surround it and have influence on it (see Fig. 28.1). The business environment is a place of formation of enterprise

---

M. Buno (✉) · S. Zadnanova · Z. Stofkova
University of Zilina, Faculty of Operation and Economics of Transport and Communications, Department of Economics, Zilina, Slovak Republic
e-mail: martin.buno@fpedas.uniza.sk; silvia.zadnanova@fpedas.uniza.sk; zuzana.stofkova@fpedas.uniza.sk

N. Tsounis, A. Vlachvei (eds.), *Advances in Panel Data Analysis in Applied Economic Research*, Springer Proceedings in Business and Economics,
https://doi.org/10.1007/978-3-319-70055-7_28

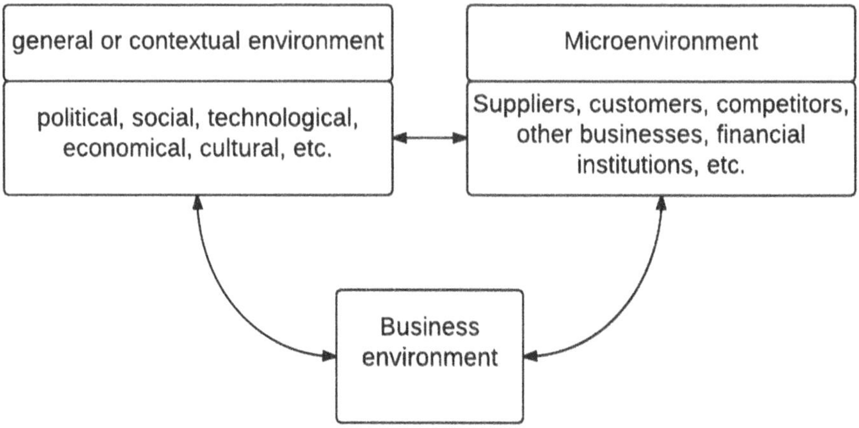

Fig. 28.1 The complexity of the business environment

and is the place where business processes are generated. Its quality is determined by economic, legal, political, technological, institutional, cultural, as well as ethical issues (Chlebikova 2015). The business environment in the broad sense reflects the quality of the economic conditions of the state. Its gradual improvement is the best way to support small- and medium-sized enterprises. It just creates one of the fundamental motivations for business. Quality business environment can be a direct impetus for poorer regions (Nevima 2014). This is the reason why we decided to compare the investing attractiveness of regions of Visegrad countries.

The biggest change of the business environment particularly the globalization of markets is caused by the development of technological environment. Already in the 1970s of the twentieth century came strong the change of the business environment from continuous to turbulent. Changes are caused by the development of technological environment. Changes in economic cycle, in product life cycles, in the structure and nature of competitions, and in customer behavior all changed the business environment (Stofkova and Stofko 2016).

Economic policy makers, as well as business entities, were forced more and more not only to respond to changes but also to anticipate new market situation. In the 1980s of the twentieth century, acceleration of dynamic changes in the business environment has deepened to the point of chaos (Hraskova et al. 2015).

From the beginning, society thought that for enterprises and state, it is a great deal of uncertainty and obstacles. As Kotler said, the only certainty for businesses and creators is uncertainty. Michael E. Porter in the 1990s of the twentieth century was the first who attempted to describe all the processes that affect the business environment. Porter responded mainly to changes caused by the globalization of markets (Paliderova and Hraskova 2016). He pointed out on the importance of technology and innovation of companies and countries that can significantly improve their quality of business environment.

In general, it states that the business environment is influenced by the impact of macroenvironment and microenvironment.

The microenvironment includes particular suppliers, customers, clients, intermediaries, and competitors.

The macroenvironment includes:

1. Political and legal environment: in particular, it is defined not only by the quality and stability of the political situation of country but also by the level of corruption, level of bureaucracy, and quality of justice.
2. Economic environment: defined as macroeconomic and microeconomic environments.
3. Demographic environment: demographic aspects touching one of the main pillars of the business environment – the human factor.
4. Ecological environment: possibilities for environmental protection in the process of production and product sales.
5. Sociocultural and technological environment: often referred to as an environment that determines the maturity and quality of a country.

As we mentioned above, we will compare Visegrad countries and their opportunities to obtain new investors in this article. New investors are very important for every region, because investors will bring new jobs, more money, and more opportunities for other companies (e.g., suppliers).

28.1.1 Short Description of the Weakest Regions of Visegrad Countries

The Czech Republic in terms of strengthening their economic competitiveness should focus its attention on several areas. The main areas are their energetic economic policy, reform of the education system (Slovakia has similar problems), and strengthening the innovation capacity of companies. Another important aspect is the infrastructure, especially the incomplete highway network and disaccented rail traffic.

Slovakia uses the euro as the only currency of the Visegrad countries. To improve competitiveness, Slovakia mainly needs to complete their infrastructure and increase flexibility of labor market. The big challenge for Slovakia is to increase their innovative capacity of businesses and reform their education system (Corejova and Al Kasiri 2016).

It is fundamental for Poland to transform its economy from manufacturing to services. Another challenge for Poland is to reduce the bureaucratic burden in business, in particular, to improve the conditions for small businesses. According to the results of PISA, this country has very good results (best from Visegrad countries), and there is assumption that they will be able to benefit from higher quality education in the future and use it as a competitive advantage (Jędruchniewicz 2015).

Hungary has infrastructure of good quality, especially highway network. Hungary also well draws on structural funds of the European Union. This country must make reform of public administration and strengthen their weaker regions with high unemployment rates.

There are too many ways on how to compare the quality of business environment. One of the ways on how to determine the quality of the business environment can be accomplished by selecting foreign markets by selection analysis. The criteria adopted are these set by the Entrepreneurs Association of Slovakia. The selection analysis is performed in several levels, with each level using a different group of evaluation criteria. The selection process can be divided in to large- and small-scale selection analysis. Small-scale analysis of selection of second level requires targeting – target selection segment (Kral and Bartošová 2016). That is the reason why we decided to use large-scale analysis of selection of second level.

It evaluates the business environment by criteria based on individual components of the international environment. In this analysis, scales are based on the basis of their importance and relevance (in this case we are talking about a certain degree of subjectivity). Consequential evaluation is formed on the relationship: $\sum$ (points of criterion * scale of criterion).

We decided to use the most important aspects according to investors and according to the Entrepreneurs Association of Slovakia. We can divide those criteria into four groups:

1. Political criteria:
   (a) Simplicity of starting a business (in days)
   (b) Level of corruption
2. Economical criteria:
   (a) Median gross hourly earnings (EUR)
   (b) Labor productivity per hour worked
   (c) Macroeconomic environment
3. Legislative criteria:
   (a) Enforcing contracts
   (b) Total tax rate (% of profit)
4. Technological criteria:
   (a) Getting electricity
   (b) Technological readiness
   (c) Infrastructure

28.1.1.1 Analysis of the Criteria

In this subchapter, we compare all the criteria mentioned in the previous chapter. We will draw on resources from several international studies such as Doing Business

2016 created by the World Bank, Paying Taxes 2016 created by the World Bank, The Global Competitiveness Report created by World Economic Forum, etc.

Data for simplicity of starting a business are from research Doing Business 2016.

As we can see from Table 28.1, the most positive conditions for starting business are in Hungary.

Data for second criterion level of corruption are from The Global Competitiveness Report 2016, where a value of 0 means there is no corruption and a value of 25 is the highest, which means there is serious problem with this issue (Table 28.2).

We included among the economical criteria the median gross hourly earnings (EUR), labor productivity per hour worked, and macroeconomic environment. The first two data are from Eurostat (Table 28.3).

Labor productivity per hour worked is calculated as real output (deflated GDP measured in chain-linked volumes, reference year 2010) per unit of labor input (measured by the total number of hours worked). Measuring labor productivity per hour worked provides a better picture of productivity developments in the economy than labor productivity per person employed, as it eliminates differences in the full-time/part-time composition of the workforce across countries and years (Table 28.4).

Data for macroeconomic environment are from The Global Competitiveness Report, where 1 is the lowest value and also the worst result and 7 is the highest value and also the best result (Table 28.5).

The next data are part of legislative criteria. We draw on the data from Doing Business 2016 and Paying Taxes 2016.

As we can see from Table 28.6, activity of the courts is most efficient in Hungary (Table 28.7).

The lowest tax burden is in Poland. Total tax rate creates 40.3 % of profit. The highest tax burden is in Slovakia (51.2 %).

We included among the technological criteria the technological readiness (The global Competitiveness Report 2016), infrastructure (The Global Competitiveness Report 2016), and getting electricity.

Value of getting electricity is from research Doing Business 2016. Value can range from 1 (the best value) to 189 (the worst value) (Table 28.8).

Hungary is significantly lagging in this criterion compared with the other Visegrad countries (Tables 28.9 and 28.10).

Table 28.1 Simplicity of starting a business (in days)

Criterion	Czech Republic	Hungary	Poland	Slovakia
Simplicity of starting a business (in days)	15	5	30	11.5

Source: The World Bank 2016

Table 28.2 Level of corruption

Criterion	Czech Republic	Hungary	Poland	Slovakia
Level of corruption (1–25)	11.3	20.5	1.5	19.2

Source: Schwab 2016

Table 28.3 Median gross hourly earnings (EUR)

Criterion	Czech Republic	Hungary	Poland	Slovakia
Median gross hourly earnings (EUR)	4.6	3.6	4.3	4.4

Source: Eurostat 2016a

Table 28.4 Labor productivity per hour worked

Criterion	Czech Republic	Hungary	Poland	Slovakia
Labor productivity per hour worked	108	101.8	114.2	113.2

Source: Eurostat 2016b

Table 28.5 Macroeconomic environment

Criterion	Czech Republic	Hungary	Poland	Slovakia
Macroeconomic environment	5.9	5.1	5.1	5.3

Source: Schwab 2016

Table 28.6 Enforcing contract (in days)

Criterion	Czech Republic	Hungary	Poland	Slovakia
Enforcing contract (in days)	611	395	685	708

Source: Pwc, World Bank Group 2016

Table 28.7 Total tax rate (% of profit)

Criterion	Czech Republic	Hungary	Poland	Slovakia
Total tax rate (% of profit)	50.4	48.4	40.3	51.2

Source: The World Bank 2016

Table 28.8 Getting electricity (1–189)

Criterion	Czech Republic	Hungary	Poland	Slovakia
Getting electricity (rank)	42	117	49	48

Source: The World Bank 2016

Table 28.9 Technological readiness (1 (worst result) – 7 (best result))

Criterion	Czech Republic	Hungary	Poland	Slovakia
Technological readiness (1–7)	5.5	4.5	4.8	4.8

Source: Schwab 2016

We draw on those data from The Global Competitiveness Report 2016. We can see that the Czech Republic has more improved technological readiness and also infrastructure.

Table 28.10 Infrastructure (1 (worst result) – 7 (best result))

Criterion	Czech Republic	Hungary	Poland	Slovakia
Infrastructure (1–7)	4.7	4.2	4.3	4.2

Source: Schwab 2016

Table 28.11 Large-scale analysis of selection of second level

Area of evaluation criteria	Political criteria	
Criteria	Simplicity of starting a business	Level of corruption
Scales	0.06	0.05
Czech Republic	5	5
Hungary	9	2
Poland	2	8.5
Slovakia	7	2

Table 28.12 Continuation of large-scale analysis of selection of second level

Area of evaluation criteria	Economical criteria		
Criteria	Median gross hourly earnings	Labor productivity per hour worked	Macroeconomic environment
Scales	0.07	0.06	0.05
Czech Republic	5.2	4.5	7.2
Hungary	4	5.2	7
Poland	5	5	7
Slovakia	5	5	7

Table 28.13 Continuation of large-scale analysis of selection of second level

Area of evaluation criteria	Legislative criteria	
Criteria	Enforcing contract	Total tax rate
Scales	0.08	0.08
Czech Republic	2.8	4
Hungary	4.5	4.3
Poland	2.2	5.5
Slovakia	2	4

28.2 Large-Scale Analysis of Selection of Second Level

In this subsection we will evaluate the quality of the business environment of the four V4 countries through large-scale analysis of selection of second level. Based on data from section 2.1.1, we can determine values for each criterion from 1 to 10, where 10 is the best score rating. Based on the expertise, we determine the amount of scales for each criterion. Scales are determined by information and knowledge we have. That is a disadvantage and we can consider it for limitation factor (Graham et al. 2015) (Tables 28.11, 28.12, 28.13, and 28.14).

Table 28.14 Continuation of large-scale analysis of selection of second level

Area of evaluation criteria	Technological criteria			Value
Criteria	Getting electricity	Technological readiness	Infrastructure	
Scales	0.02	0.07	0.07	
Czech Republic	7	6	5	2.91
Hungary	4	4	4	2.87
Poland	6.5	5	4	2.90
Slovakia	6.5	5	4	2.75

On the basis of the results, we can assess that for an investor, the best conditions for doing business are in the Czech Republic based on our criteria. The Czech Republic has the highest quality of infrastructure of the four countries of the Visegrad. The Czech Republic has also the best level of technological readiness. This aspect is one of the most important aspects for doing business. Macroeconomic environment in the Czech Republic has also the best results.

Slovakia reached the lowest value of result. The main problems of Slovakia are high levels of corruption, underdeveloped infrastructure, and in many sectors weaker technological readiness. All these aspects create a big challenge for Slovakia. As we can see, we can support regions by improving the business environment. Government should think of creating the most favorable conditions for business. New investors and new capital in regions can improve the way of living of inhabitants.

Acknowledgments This paper was undertaken as parts of the research projects VEGA 1/0733/15 and VEGA 1/0696/16.

A.1 Appendix

In the article we defined the complexity of the business environment. We explained that the interconnection between the growth of living standards and quality of the business environment is high. Then we chose ten criteria, which have the most significant impact on the investor and his decision of where will be his business. We chose these criteria based on research of Entrepreneurs Association of Slovakia. Output data from these criteria were used as input data for large-scale analysis of selection of second level. By using this analysis, we compared the quality of the business environment of Visegrad countries from the perspective of an investor. We found that the most prospective business environment is in the Czech Republic. Conversely, Slovakia reached the lowest value of result.

References

Chlebikova, D. (2015). Podnikateľské a konkurenčné prostredie v Slovenskej republike. In: *Ekonomicko-manažérske spektrum (EMS)*. – ISSN 1337–0839. – 9 editions, n. 1 (pp. 16–20).

Corejova, T., & Al Kasiri, M. (2016). Knowledge-intensive business services as important services for innovation and economic growth in Slovakia. In: *International Conference on Innovations in Science and Education (CBUIC), Prague, Czech rep.* (pp. 42–47).

Eurostat. (2016a). Median gross hourly earnings. http://ec.europa.eu/eurostat/statistics-explained/index.php/Earnings_statistics

Eurostat. (2016b). Labour productivty per hour worked. http://ec.europa.eu/eurostat/tgm/table.do?tab=table&init=1&language=en&pcode=tsdec310&plugin=1

Graham, J., Cateora, P., & Gilly, M. (2015). *International marketing* (pp. 122–126). New York: Mc-Graw-Hill Education. isbn:978-0077842161.

Hraskova, D., Nadanyiova, M., & Buno, M. (2015). The comparison of the quality of business environment in the countries of Visegrad group. In*: 4th World Conference on Business, Economics and Management (WCBEM)*, Ephesus, Turkey (pp. 423–430).

Jędruchniewicz, A. (2015). Monetary policy and investments in the polish economy. *Oeconomia Copernicana, 6(3)*, 7–22.

Kral, P., & Bartošová, V. (2016). Importance of company early warning system in globalizing market environment. In: *16th International Scientific Conference on Globalization and its Socio-Economic Consequences*, Rajecke teplice (pp. 1054–1060).

Nevima, J. (2014). *Competitiveness of regions of Visegrad four*. (pp. 16–18) isbn:978-8-7431-144-4.

Paliderova, M., & Hraskova, D. (2016). Dimension of innovation in enterpises. In: *16th International Scientific Conference on Globalization and its Socio-Economic Consequences*, Rajecke teplice (pp. 1613–1619).

Pwc, Wolrd Bank Group. (2016). *Paying taxes 2016*. Washington: The World Bank. https://www.pwc.com/gx/en/paying-taxes-2016/paying-taxes-2016.pdf.

Schwab, K. (2016). The Global Competitiveness report 2016–2017. World Economic Forum. isbn:978-1-944835-04-0.2016 http://www3.weforum.org/docs/GCR20162017/05FullReport/TheGlobalCompetitivenessReport2016-2017_FINAL.pdf

Stofkova, Z., & Stofko S. (2016). Some indicators of quality of life in a globalization world. In: *16th International Scientific Conference on Globalization and its Socio-Economic Consequences*, Rajecke teplice (pp. 2127–2134).

The World Bank. (2016). *Doing business 2016*. Washington: The World Bank. isbn:978-1-4648-0668-1. http://www.doingbusiness.org/~/media/WBG/DoingBusiness/Documents/Annual-Reports/English/DB16-Full-Report.pdf.

Chapter 29
Building a Sustainable Brand

Eva Kicová and Anna Križanová

Abstract It is extremely hard to succeed in business when brand is not considered between top three brands in the segment. Brand should be in people's minds in decision-making process of buying products or services. If it is not, the company is just fighting for market share mostly with price. Sustainability and responsible consumption are becoming an important part of our lives. This article presents a summary of expert opinions on the sustainable brand building and STP process. In addition, the aim of this paper is to declare why going sustainable is necessary. Furthermore, it enriches this knowledge by results of own research. Research is aimed to discover customers' readiness and preferences about sustainable lifestyle.

29.1 Introduction

The implementation of the sustainable marketing objectives to business plans should be a part of holistically conceived strategy. Once the managers dealt answers to two basic questions: "Is segment of sustainably minded consumers important for the company?" and "Is it possible to be different through sustainability?". Currently, we know that companies should be proactive. All of the actions leading to reduce the negative impact on the environment should be granted the same as educating customers and their support for responsible consumption.

The marketing process involves a variety of activities, and it deals with strategic and tactical actions. Sustainable marketing, same as conventional marketing, carries two major topics – marketing mix and marketing strategy. Marketing strategy is a continuous cycle in which individual sequences demand measuring, segmentation, targeting, and positioning that leads to form a *competitive advantage*. This process is shown in Picture 29.1. The scientists and marketers have put a lot of effort into

E. Kicová (✉) · A. Križanová
University of Zilina, Faculty of Operation and Economics of Transport and Communication, Department of Economics, Zilina, Slovak Republic
e-mail: eva.kicova@fpedas.uniza.sk

N. Tsounis, A. Vlachvei (eds.), *Advances in Panel Data Analysis in Applied Economic Research*, Springer Proceedings in Business and Economics,
https://doi.org/10.1007/978-3-319-70055-7_29

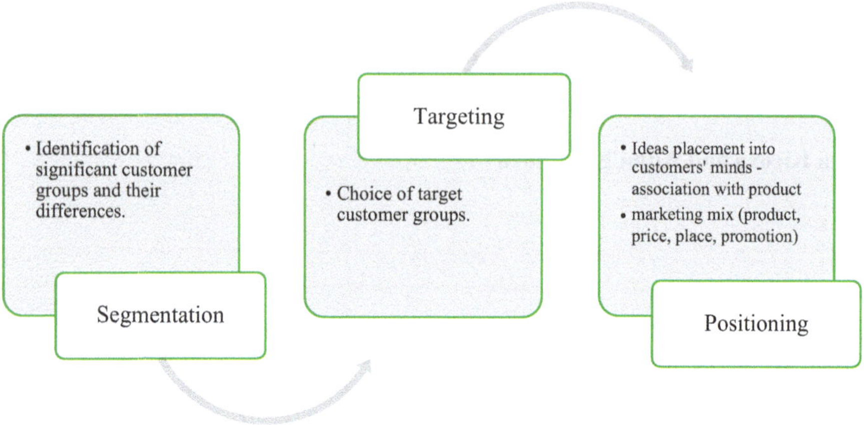

Picture 29.1 Process STP (Source: own process based on Birnerová and Križanová 2012)

defining and understanding what the relationship is between the level of sustainable awareness and customer buying behaviour.

There are hundreds of researches on sustainable customer behaviour. One thing is to carry out surveys about attitudes of customers but, on the other hand, categorize them into meaningful groups that describe and predict their buying behaviour. Then it is necessary to choose a group as an object to which a company creates a product and appropriate strategy for its placing on the market. It is obvious that a consumer who has ecological awareness, consciousness and behaviour will have a higher propensity to purchase sustainable products. There may be obstacles that limit such behaviour, such as lack of funds, unwillingness to change their lifestyle or sacrificing comfort, poor availability of organic products and so on. Companies use *marketing segmentation to define all characteristics*.

29.2 Literature Review

29.2.1 Sustainable Marketing Segmentation

Marketing segmentation was designed more than 40 years ago by sociologist Daniel Yankelovich (Majerova et al. 2015), one of the first analysts of public opinion. In 1964, he presented on pages of *Harvard Business Review* the idea of classifying customers based on criteria such as age, place of residence, income and other demographic factors that help businesses determine what products to develop and how they should be presented. Already at that time, Yankelovich claimed that non-demographic factors as values and lifestyle preferences influence the purchasing behaviour more than demographic factors.

In 1978, a group from Stanford Research Institute moved this knowledge to a higher level and presented the values and lifestyles (VALS) marketing tool classifying individuals based on nine psychological types to predict their behaviour (Sun et al. 2004). Factors such as the history of previous purchases and loyalty to the product tend to change a brand informed with the values and attitudes that lead the customer to see individual offer differently. Further proposals to divide customers have come later. Currently, a complex system of customer segmentation is offered by Nielsen. PRIZM® is customer segmentation based on the right combination of demographic factors, psychology, consumer behaviour and geographic data. It divides households into 66 demographically and behaviourally different types of segments.

Segmentation System P $ YCLE® (Nielsen 2016) is useful for marketers who need to understand the financial and investment behaviour of specific customers. It also considers the specific indicator IPA (income-producing assets), which represents the various sources of income. The result is 58 segments.

Customer segmentation is greatly affected by the current, highly innovative technical and technological environment that affects the use of marketing tools in the communications policy. The various smart devices such as smart phones, tablets and laptops offer many options of voice and non-voice services via an Internet connection.

Therefore, today it is more difficult to understand what type of communication the customer reacts and thus develop optimal marketing strategy and tactics. ConneXions® segmentation system integrates customer behaviour and lifestyle indicators and measures the use of technology by consumers for voice and data services to their providers and consumer electronics manufacturers to know about how cost-effective to produce and at the same time retain existing customers and acquire new ones. In this segmentation, there are 53 segments of customers enrolled in ten opportunity periods of human life.

Marketing segmentation concerning customer sustainable sensitivity was first performed in the United States by GfK Roper Organization. They interviewed 2000 consumers. The result was a different level of interest and motivation to buy sustainable products and lifestyle. Customers were classified in five groups according to the answers:

- True-blue greens
- Greenback greens
- Sprouts
- Grousers
- Basic browns

The survey was repeated several times, and the ratio between the individual segments remained unchanged until 2007. The organization has changed the methodology from personal questioning survey to the online questionnaire. It caused significant changes in the results. Segment truly green consumers have grown twice in 2 years. Several factors could cause the change: higher awareness about responsible consumption, increasing national government's interest and media interest. There is also a big difference to ask in personally or anonymously. Consumers see themselves in more sustainable light. We must also note that many surveys showed that there is a big difference between verbal demonstration, questionnaire replies and how customers act.

The conclusion of the study was to present recommendations about green products and meaningfully reduce the scepticism of consumers who are considered the environmental and sustainable efforts of businesses as a form of greenwashing.

The most comprehensive market research is considered LOHAS (Lifestyles of Health and Sustainability). Natural Marketing Institute (2016a, b), which is currently conducting surveys on LOHAS, divided the market in the following segments:

- LOHAS – very progressive segment focused on the environment and society. This segment requires undertakings to act more socially responsible and not be focused on price. Corporate reputation influences the choice of the brand they prefer, and they are also involved in disseminating information about companies and their activities.
- Naturalists – segment of consumers who are primarily concerned with their health and seek to avoid adverse health products. They also believe that companies should take responsibility for environmental and social solutions, and they are loyal to the brand which they consider carrying out good for society.
- Conventional – practical consumer group that tries to see the results of their conduct. They recycle, save energy and pay more for products that save energy and water in the long term.
- Drifters – a group of consumers who are not very conscious. They care about the environment only if they are not directly affected. They mostly buy sustainable products because it is a trend and want to be associated with environmental awareness.
- Unconcerned – this segment of consumers is not interested. Their buying behaviour is based on price, value, quality and convenience.

Overview of other segmentation proposals from other countries is shown in Table 29.1.

29.2.2 Targeting in Sustainable Marketing

Targeting selects target market segments that are most appropriate for the company. It is an integral part of marketing strategy, a second phase of the STP process.

The key criteria for the selection of the appropriate segment are the following:

- Segment size – the number of potential customers
- Potential segment growth – prognosis of number of customers in the future
- Segment attractiveness – the financial capacity of potential customers, the threat of entry of competitors, the possibility of substitutes and price of complements

Table 29.1 Review of segmentation based on different signs of sustainability

Survey name/author	Name of segments	Sign of segmentation
Joel Makower (2009)	Committed Conflicted Concerned Confused Cynical	Customers' action
Hartman Group (2007)	Radical involved (36%) Sustainable optimistic (27%) Believers in fate (20%) Cynically pessimists (9%) Pragmatic accepts (8%)	Consumers' activity
Landor and Associates (2006)	Not interested in sustainability (58%) With interest in sustainability (25%) Motivated (17%)	Interest in solving ecological problems
Bodur and Sarigollu (Turks' attitudes and solving sustainability issues 2005)	Active involved Passive involved (they support sustainable ideas, but they do not act) Indifferent	Behaviour towards the environment and engage in voluntary activities
Chan, K. (Marketing segmentation of green consumers in Hong Kong, 2000)	Light Half-light Dark	Perception of organic products, evaluation of the functionality of organic products, social norms and assessing information on sustainable products
J. Ottman (2011)	Animal lovers Outdoor enthusiasts Health fanatics Resource conservators	Customer's free-time interest

Source: Own process based on the literature search

Company must select its target segment based on its strategy and capabilities. It is not possible to serve all segments of the market to cover all the requirements and needs of customers.

Managers of enterprises initiate their strategic activities towards social responsibility with an emphasis on sustainable products to promote *sustainable responsible consumption* more than ever. The motivation for socially responsible behaviour comes from inner conviction, and it is a subjective opinion arising from the moral values. This is important for companies that want to gain a competitive *advantage by serving to customer which shares the same values.* This type of customers is what we call sustainable-conscious customers.

Based on segmentation divisions mentioned in the previous section, we know that each customer has other relationship towards environmental issues and addressing. Take it very simple; we can divide customers into two groups: involved in solving environmental problems or indifferent. Some purchase decisions of customers are based precisely on the degree of environmental responsibility. The result is that the sustainable market is growing. Estimates said that sustainable market has increased about 18% over the last 4 years, despite the recent economic crisis. Sustainable consumption is associated with *30:3 syndrome.*

Firstly, this phenomenon confirms the difference between what customers say and support and how they actually act. A third of consumers say it is very important for them to care for the environment, and ethical corporate behaviour is more than important, but the market share of these products does not exceed 3% (Kemper 2013). The second explanation is related to the prices of sustainable products. Customers feel the positive impact of such products on the environment, but they are not willing to pay a higher price. Polonsky says that sustainable marketing does not use its potential in terms of impact on the buying behaviour of customers nor in terms of efficiency of the environment improvement (Crispell 2014).

Nadanyiova (2016) adds that green marketing activities are not successful mainly for the following three reasons:

- Lack of trust from customers (greenwashing)
- Unwillingness to pay more for sustainable products
- Poor implementation and weak communication policy

Several surveys clearly have shown that consumers are willing to pay a higher price for the product if a higher price is also linked to additional benefits. For sure, it can be assumed that the sustainable market will grow significantly in the coming years. These estimates are mainly associated with the onset of generation "Z" (born after 2000), which is today considered the most sustainability oriented, technically and technologically most seem. Their vision of the world is strongly influenced by the nature of social equality, anti-discrimination laws and the use of renewable energy sources. They need to live in conditions where they are incorporated in the company value.

Surveys also clearly indicate that consumers expect the initiatives' transposition by companies and transnational corporations. Consumers expect higher standards, and they are convinced that businesses should be in solving process of environmental issues more effective than individuals. It includes safety and health issues as well. On the other hand, consumers do not consider manufacturers and traders as a trusted source of information. They have more trust in organizations generally perceived as independent and objective.

Therefore, it is company's decision what strategy and segment will be chosen for its target. For sure, it is possible to say that a company will determine their existence to extinction if it does not adjust to the current trends and conditions and does not begin to accept the appeal to the environmental responsibility of their activities.

29.2.3 Positioning

Positioning starts with product. It is a product, service, company, institution or person. Meanwhile, positioning is not about what you do with the product. Positioning is what you do with the mind of a potential customer. It is product placement in the customer's mind (Pavlik 2014).

Positioning is the third phase of the STP process. This is about creating perceptions, opinions and attitudes in the minds of customers associated with the brand or its products or services. We can therefore talk about placing information in the customer's mind and induce desired mental processes and content-related brand quality, price, commercial, design and style. Positioning means also estimation and creation of the future target groups, which means that it can affect the overall development of the *sustainable market.*

Representatives of many multinational corporations have said that they want to inspire their customers and enable them to reduce consumption of water and energy and the volume of waste generated through their products. Then customers can live a more sustainable life without making compromises in terms of price, design or functionality, which has a positive effect on society. Environmentally oriented marketing strategy and business philosophy create an intangible asset for the company in the form of building a positive brand image in the customers' minds.

Positioning of sustainable products must be a dynamic learning process and is not limited to the product. Company producing high-quality products, using truthful advertising and behaving in a socially and environmentally responsible manner with a history of meeting the demands of different groups of stakeholders creates a competitive advantage in the form of a positive reputation. Sustainable practices must be a part of corporate culture to ensure authenticity of sustainable business behaviour.

29.2.4 Hypothesis and Research Question, Methodology

Building a sustainable brand is linked to readiness of customer and their preferences. There is no segmentation of sustainable customers in Slovakia, so we decided to make a short survey. There are four main human activities during life: travelling (commuting to work), free-time activities, type of living and preferences about food lifestyle. We developed three quotes that are linked to those activities.

1. If I had a chance, I would select a place to live that is close to where I work, so I did not have to commute; therefore, I could reduce the impact of transport on the environment.
2. I prefer to repair the product before replacing with a new one, because I do not want to produce more waste.
3. It is worth to me to pay more for environmentally friendly products, because it saves money from the long-term period view and helps the environment.

In general, women are more sustainable-focused, because mostly they care about family, health, baby, etc. That is the reason why we have developed hypothesis about correlation between gender and answers to those three questions, because we expected that women are more sustainable-minded. The second group of hypotheses were linked to age of respondents. The reason was very clear; several surveys have said that generation Z is more sustainable.

29.2.4.1 First Group of Hypotheses

H1: There is a positive correlation between gender and willingness to live close to work if not commuting.
H2: There is a positive correlation between gender and willingness to repair a product instead of replacing with a new one.
H3: There is a positive correlation between gender and willingness to buy more environmentally friendly products.

29.2.4.2 Second Group of Hypotheses

This study applied the questionnaire survey to verify the hypotheses. The object of this research study was to develop readiness to accept sustainable products by customers. The questionnaires were randomly mailed to 600 people in different age, gender and economic status. There were 198 valid questionnaires from consumers (effective response rate 33.3% that included 87 males and 111 female). We used statistical methods as common percentage results and chi-square test to support hypotheses. The process of survey was conducted in January 2017.

For calculation correlation, we used chi-square formula:

$$x^2 = \sum \sum \frac{(O - E)^2}{E} \tag{29.1}$$

where x – chi-square obtained; $\sum$ – the sum of; O – observed score; E – expected score

29.2.5 *Empirical Results*

The following charts show results to our three questions. Seventy-two percent of respondents said yes or rather yes to first quote about commuting to work. That means there are majority of people who realize that travelling causes a big environmental impact and it is better to live close to work even for healthy lifestyle (Picture 29.2 and 29.3).

According to results of answers to second quote, respondents are responsible and they do not want to produce more waste. Almost 65% of respondents prefer to repair a product before replacing with a new one. Another big reason could be the factor of saving money as well (Picture 29.4).

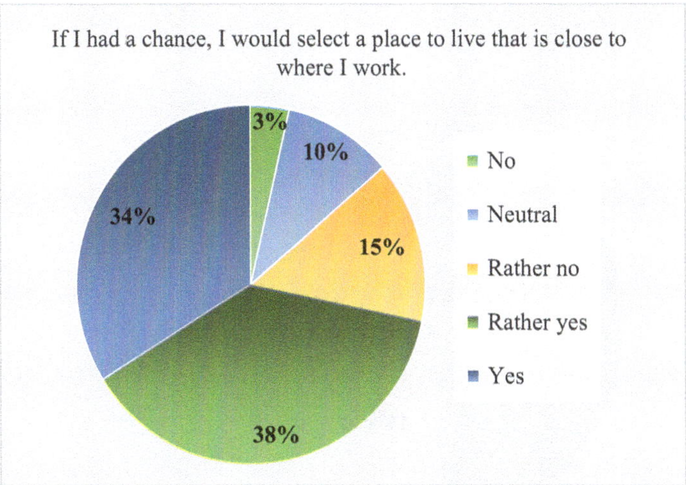

Picture 29.2 Results of first quote (Source: own process based on results of survey)

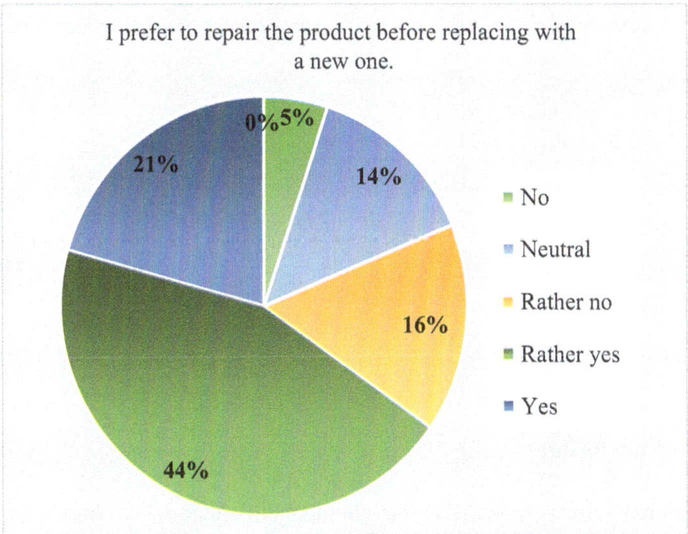

Picture 29.3 Results of second quote (Source: own process based on results of survey)

29.2.5.1 Hypothesis 1

H_{10}: There is no positive correlation between gender and willingness to live close to work if not commuting.

H_{11}: There is a positive correlation between gender and willingness to live close to work if not commuting.

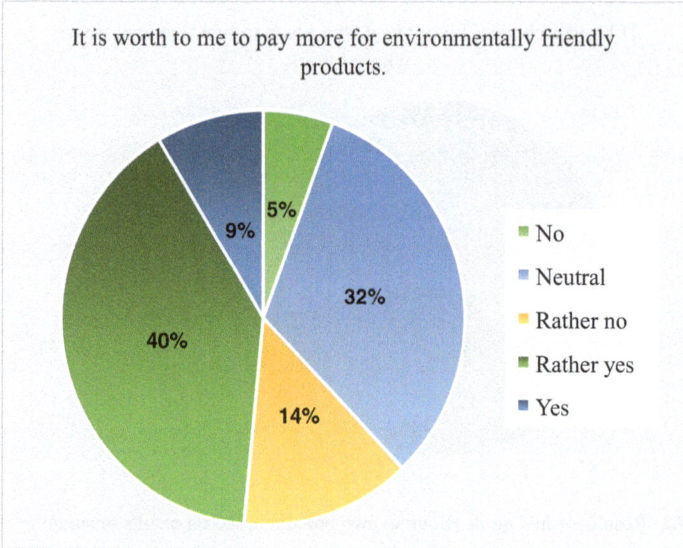

Picture 29.4 Results of third quote (Source: own process based on results of survey)

If I had a chance, I would select a place to live that is close to where I work						
Gender	No	Rather no	Neutral	Rather yes	Yes	Sum
Man	5	12	9	23	38	87
Woman	2	17	11	44	37	111
Sum	**7**	**29**	**20**	**67**	**75**	**198**

Chi-square: 6.124 – degrees of freedom (m-1(n-1) = 4 - *p*-value: 0.19)

29.2.5.2 Conclusion

Our calculated value is lower than the tabulated chi-square. The chart is located left by the border of the chart value in the field accept the null hypothesis. Thus, we assume that the null hypothesis is applied. We accept H_{10}, so there is a no positive correlation between gender and willingness to live close to work if not commuting.

29.2.5.3 Hypothesis 2

H_{20}: There is a no positive correlation between gender and willingness to repair a product instead of replacing with a new one.

H_{22}: There is a positive correlation between gender and willingness to repair a product instead of replacing with a new one.

I prefer to repair the product before replacing with a new one						
Gender	No	Rather no	Neutral	Rather yes	Yes	Sum
Man	6	12	10	41	18	87
Woman	4	20	17	47	23	111
Sum	**10**	**32**	**27**	**88**	**41**	**198**

Chi-square: 2.359 – degrees of freedom (m-1(n-1) = 4 - *p*-value: 0.67)

29.2.5.4 Conclusion

Our calculated value is lower than the tabulated chi-square. The chart is located left by the border of the chart value in the field accept the null hypothesis. Thus, we assume that the null hypothesis is applied. We accept H_{20}, so there is a no positive correlation between gender and willingness to repair a product instead of replacing with a new one.

29.2.5.5 Hypothesis 3

H_{30}: There is a no positive correlation between gender and willingness to buy more environmentally friendly products.
H_{31}: There is a positive correlation between gender and willingness to buy more environmentally friendly products.

It is worth to me to pay more for environmentally friendly products						
Gender	No	Rather no	Neutral	Rather yes	Yes	Sum
Man	4	18	28	34	3	87
Woman	7	9	36	45	14	111
Sum	**11**	**27**	**64**	**79**	**17**	**198**

Chi-square: 10.716 – degrees of freedom (m-1(n-1) = 4 - *p*-value: 0.029)

29.2.5.6 Conclusion

Our calculated value is higher than the tabulated chi-square. The chart is located right by the border of the chart value in the field reject the null hypothesis. Thus, we assume that the null hypothesis is rejected. We accept H_{31}, so there is a positive correlation between gender and willingness to buy more environmentally friendly products.

29.3 Summary

It is extremely hard to succeed in business when brand is not considered between top three brands in the segment. Brand should be in people's minds in decision-making process of buying products or services. If it is not, the company is just fighting for market share mostly with price. That means customers buy company's product or service because they consider it as same with other products, and they do not see any added value. If the company is in the top of mind of the consumer, company's brand is a leader and it produces added value to the product. Every strong brand has clear vision and execution effectively as it gets. The question is how to set up clear vision, mission and brand's values? The right way is sustainability today. This paper offers an overview of the expert opinions about sustainable brand issue, and it states the reasons why it is important to have a sustainable brand and behave responsibly. It presents a new STP process. Moreover, the study brings new facts related to customer's readiness to a sustainable lifestyle. We concluded that there is no positive correlation between gender and willingness to behave sustainably and responsibly in case of travelling to work and buying a new product to replace an old one. Surprisingly, women are willing to buy eco-friendly products even for a higher price, because they see long-term effects in this decision.

Acknowledgment This research was financially supported by the Slovak Research and Development Agency – Grant NO. APVV-15-0505: Integrated model of management support for building and managing the brand value in the specific conditions of the Slovak Republic.

References

Birnerová, A., & Križanová, M. (2012). *International Marketing*. Bratislava: Martinus.

Bodur, M., & Sarigollu, E. (2005). Environmental Sensitivity in a developing country: Consumer classification and implications. *Environment and Behaviour, 37*(4), 487–510.

Chan, K. (2000). Market segmentation of green consumers in Hong Kong. *Journal of International Consumer Marketing, 12*(2), 7–24.

Crispell, D. (2014). *Going green(ish)*. [online] [citované 2014–06-11]. Dostupné na internete http://www.ropercenter.uconn.edu/publicperspective/ppscan/125/1250928.pdf

Hartman Group. (2007). *Sustainability from Consumer's perspective*. Bellevue, WA: Tinder Box.

Kemper, J., et al. (2013). Competition-motivated corporate social responsibility. *Journal of Business, 66*, 1954–1963.

Landor and Associates. (2006). *Branding Reference*. London: Landor and Associates.

Majerová, J., Kliestik, T., & Misankova, M. (2015). Analysis of convergences and divergences of bankruptcy law institutes in the Slovak Republic and in the world. In *ICASS 2015 [elektronický zdroj]: 5th international conference on Applied social science: October 4–5, 2015, Limassol, Cyprus*. Bellflower: IERI & PRESS. ISBN 978-1-61275-072-9. CD-ROM, s. 34–39. (Advances in education research, Vol. 80. ISSN 2160-1070).

Makower, J., & Cara PIKE. (2009). *Strategies for the green economy: Opportunities and challenges in the new world of business*. New York: McGraw-Hill.

Nadanyiova, M. (2016). Global trends of the personnel marketing in service enterprises. In *Globalization and its socio-economic consequences [elektronický zdroj]: 16th international scientific conference: proceedings: 5th–6th October 2016 Rajecke Teplice, Slovak Republic*. Part III. Zilina: ZU University of Zilina. ISBN 978-80-8154-191-9. Online, s. 1474–1481.

Natural Marketing Institute. (2016a). LOHAS. [online] [citované 2014-06-13] Dostupné na internete <http://www.nmisolutions.com/index.php/research-reports/overview-and-summary-list >.

Natural Marketing Institute. (2016b). *Research report*. [online] [citované 2014–06-10] Dostupné na internete < http://www.nmisolutions.com/index.php/research-reports/overview-and-summary-list>.

Nielsen. (2016). *My best segments*:P$YCLE®. [online] [citované 2014-06-03] Dostupné na internete <http://www.nielsen.com/us/en/solutions/segmentation.html >.

Otmann, J. A. (2011). *The new rules of green marketing: Strategies, tools, and inspiration for sustainable branding*. San Francisco: Berrett-Koehler Pub.

Pavlík, L. (2014). HCA TV: *Čo je to Positioning*? Škola manažmentu Rona Hubbarda semináre a kurzy pre majiteľov firiem, manažérov a obchodníkov. [online] [citované 2014-05-10] Dostupné na internete http://www.skolamanazmentu.sk/blog/marketing-a-public-relations/co-je-to-positioning/.

Sun, T., Horn, M., & Merritt, D. (2004). Values and lifestyles of individualists and collectivists: A study on Chinese, Japanese, British and US consumers. *Journal of Consumer Marketing, 21*, 318–331. ISSN: 0736-3761.

Chapter 30
Facility Management as a Tool for Optimizing Business Costs

Ladislav Vagner and Viera Bartošová

Abstract According to the US Green Building Council, buildings consumed 36% of total energy consumption in the United States. As the importance of sustainability concept continues to grow, more researches have been focused on improving energy efficiency during building's operation phase.

Improving energy efficiency also helps to reduce business operating costs. That is the main reason why businesses are interested in saving energy. It is the facility management which takes care of business support activities. Facility management helps optimize the operational costs implicit in the infrastructure. In this paper, we looked at the experiment focused on improving energy efficiency. The measurement was carried out for 2 years, 2015 and 2016 (data was collected every day at 7 p.m.). Its main objective was to obtain the necessary data for experimental research. There were monitored and measured energy flows and information related to heating and hot water consumption in the building.

Keywords Facility management · Energy consumption · Thermal transmittance

30.1 Introduction

At the time when companies are waging price wars on customers, every help aimed on profitability increase is welcomed. Companies are forced to optimize their processes and procedures, so they could keep up with the competing businesses (Kicova and Kramarova 2013). Here the facility management has its place. Facility management helps companies to target their focus on the core business. It takes on many supporting activities. Therefore, it relieves the workers themselves, and as a result it increases their performance. Except of providing supporting activities,

L. Vagner (✉) · V. Bartošová
University of Zilina, Faculty of Operations and Economics of Transport and Communications, Department of Economics, Zilina, Slovak Republic
e-mail: ladislav.vagner@fpedas.uniza.sk; viera.Bartosova@fpedas.uniza.sk

N. Tsounis, A. Vlachvei (eds.), *Advances in Panel Data Analysis in Applied Economic Research*, Springer Proceedings in Business and Economics,
https://doi.org/10.1007/978-3-319-70055-7_30

facility management helps to decrease operation costs. By correct implementation of a facility management into the managing system, companies acquire the powerful tool in the business competition.

The aim of facility management is to streamline support processes in companies and to reduce their operating costs using the appropriate settings (Levitt 1997). It is a method of mutual harmonization of employees, work activities and working environment. It is a method of mutual harmonization of employees, work activities and working environment (Cotts et al. 2010).

In this article, we focus on the usage of facility management in association with the operational cost reduction. On this already performed experiment, we will show the weaknesses of the surveyed building. Based on the collected data, we have compiled a graphical overview, which indicates a better profitability of facility management application proposals.

30.2 Theoretical Background

Facility management is an interdisciplinary field primarily focused on operating, maintenance and care of objects (Rondeau et al. 2006). It should be performed not only during the phase of the operation but throughout building's life cycle, which usually lasts several decades. Apart from buildings such as hospitals, hotels, office "business" complexes, arenas and educational and congress centres, it also includes sport facilities, traffic centres and highways and parts of towns with the individual housing and multipurpose buildings.

Across the globe, there are two types of accepted definitions of facility management (FM). The first ones used in official national (BSI, UNI, DIN, etc.), continental (such as EN for Europe) and global (ISO) standards and norms. Second there are commercial standards and norms defining FM such as the ones from RICS, IFMA, etc. (Ameratunga and Baldry 2003). The definition of facility management according to EN 15221-1 says it is the integration of processes within an organization in order to ensure and develop the agreed services which support and enhance the efficiency of its illegal work (Falconer 2006).

Other sources describe facility management as an interdisciplinary field primarily focused on operation, maintenance and care of objects (Nawrocki 2015). It should be performed not only during the phase of the operation but throughout building's life cycle, which usually lasts several decades. Apart from buildings such as hospitals, hotels, office "business" complexes, arenas and educational and congress centres, it also includes sport facilities, traffic centres and highways and parts of towns with the individual housing and multipurpose buildings.

To explain the scope of facility management, we can use the definition of IFMA (International Facility Management Association, a respected representative of the majority of world facility managers) which defines facility management as "a profession that encompasses multiple disciplines to ensure functionality of the built environment by integrating people, place, processes and technology" (Pavlov 2014). Facility management (FM) is an effective form of outreach business management which aims to provide relevant, cost-effective services to support the main business activities (core business) and allow them to optimize (Slaichova and Marsikova 2013). The application of facility management is currently of interest, because it provides savings and optimization of operating costs, promotes increased employee performance and thus contributes to increase the profitability of the enterprise (Ponisciakova 2014). The most common forms of application of facility management in the enterprise are partial or complete outsourcing.

30.3 Process of Reducing Energy Consumption

The experimental research took place in the administration building. The building was built in 1988, and it was constructed with reinforced ferroconcrete skeleton. Side and braced upstairs walls are made of bricks CMD and MVC. The walls are covered with exterior cladding. The majority of the circuit building skin is made of facade porous concrete, which is gripped on the carrying skeleton system. The roof construction is flat with a decreased roof pitch.

The windows are originally made of aluminium and are double glazed. In consideration of its age, deterioration and the technical aspect, the windows do not comply with technical standards. The boundary conductance is $U = 2.78$ W/(m^2.K). Table 30.1 describes the current state of the specific heat loss of the reviewed building.

While planning the complex reconstruction, mandatory requirement for thermal properties of specific constructions cannot remain unnoticed. Those requirements, described in the technical standard STN 73 0540-2:2012 thermal protection of buildings, have to be respected at the design of building reconstruction. Whereas the sufficient minimal requirement for fulfilling the standard STN 75 0540-2: 2002 was just insulation of walls by expanded polystyrene thick from 6 to 8 cm, nowadays, it is from 10 to 12 cm, and after the year 2021, it can grow to 15 and more centimetres. Likewise it is in case of windows (Table 30.2).

Constructing literature defines heat transfer coefficient by the following formula (Garimella et al. 2016):

$$U = 1/\left(R_{\mathrm{N}} + R_{\mathrm{K}} + r_{\mathrm{N}}\right) \tag{30.1}$$

where

Table 30.1 Specific heat loss of the building – original state

Building facade	4078.9 [W/K]
Roof	1522.5 [W/K]
Ground floor	1287.2 [W/K]
Windows and doors	6403.3 [W/K]
Thermal bridges	1440.2 [W/K]
Heat loss	10261.1 [W/K]

Source: Produced by authors

Table 30.2 Total calculation of building insulation

Thermal transmittance of a construction				
Type of a building structure	*Maximal value* For buildings reconstructed in the past	*Normalized value* For renewed and new buildings	*Recommended value* From 1.1.2016	*Final recommended value* From 1.1.2021
	(W/(m^2.K))			
	U_{max}	U_N	U_{r1}	U_{r2}
Exterior wall and sloping wall above the living area with the angle >45°	0.46	0.32	0.22	0.15
<Flat wall and sloping roof above the living area with the angle <45°	0.3	0.2	0.1	0.1
The ceiling above external area	0.3	0.2	0.1	0.1
The ceiling under not heated area	0.35	0.25	0.15	0.1
	U_{max}	U_N	U_{r1}	U_{r2}
Windows, doors, glazed roof in circuit wall, internal dormer	1.7	1.4	1	0.8
Doors to other areas	4.3	3	2.5	<2

Source: Produced by authors

U is heat transfer coefficient in W/(m^2 K)
R_K is thermal resistance of a construction in m^2 K/W
$R_N = 0.13$ m^2 K/W is common and also normed resistance for heat transmission on the internal surface of the construction
$r_N = 0.04$ m^2 K/W is common and also normed resistance for heat transmission on the external surface of the construction

The measurement was carried out for 2 years, 2015 and 2016. Its main objective was to obtain the necessary data for experimental research. There were monitored and measured energy flows and information related to heating and hot water consumption on the building. The following graphs are showing sequentially measured values of the individual areas measured for the 2-year period. Studied areas have a similar pattern in both years. This indicates that the office building has stable energy requirements. The aim of graphical and tabular analysis is the partial evaluation of claims for the buildings' operation. By collecting the data, we get a better insight into consumption. The investor will have a better field for decision-making in which areas of reconstruction he will invest in priority. Also, it offers the opportunity to compare the change in consumption after reconstruction (Table 30.3).

Table 30.3 Monthly electricity consumption [kW/h]

	1	2	3	4	5	6	7	8	9	10	11	12
2015	37,979	36,112	38,599	26,759	30,128	26,382	23,843	31,862	31,148	34,613	38,976	36,778
2016	43,506	37,277	35,961	30,944	28,722	30,364	26,001	25,488	29,129	32,451	34,806	39,907
Estimate after reconstruction	26,164	22,419	21,627	21,110	19,594	20,714	17,738	17,388	19,872	19,516	20,932	24,000

Source: Produced by authors

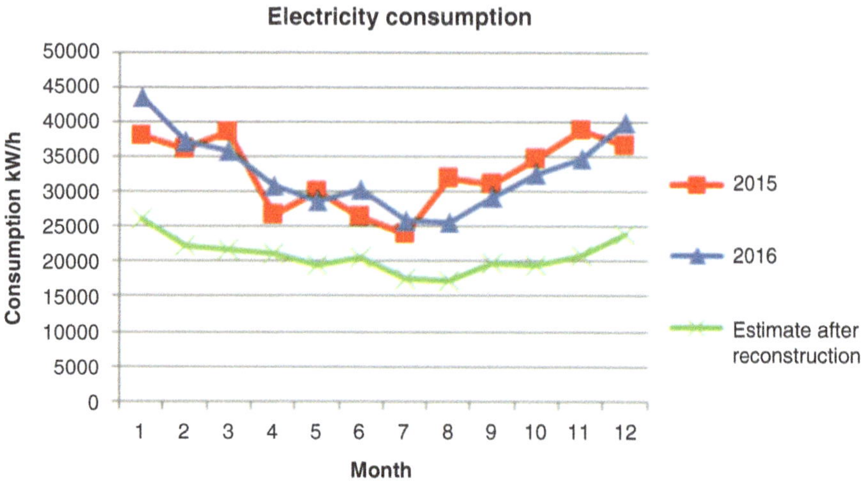

Fig. 30.1 Conduct electricity consumption

The electricity consumption behaviour was in both years alike. It has the shape of the curve as the letter U. The biggest factor affecting the shape of the curve is the weather and employees vacations. In winter the consumption is at the highest point. Employees often use in their office electric heaters and thereby increase the consumption of electricity. Then there is the lighting mostly used in higher rate in winter season. By insulation of buildings, we also expect a reduction of electricity consumption especially in winter months. The usage of LED technology can reduce energy consumption for lighting by up to approximately 70% annually (Fig. 30.1). In the picture, we can see that the curve estimate after reconstruction, is lower and its shape no longer resemble the letter U. The energy savings are visible here during the year (Fig. 30.2 and Table 30.4).

Monitoring of hot water consumption is particularly important for heating unit exchange decision. Based on the measured values, the enterprise may also decide to invest in solar panels as well. Likewise, the company may also make other decisions. The most common measure is usually lowering the temperature of the hot water circulation. Another measure, which usually is quite often effective, is the implementation of smart shower in the locker rooms that follow hot water consumption per employee. This measure has mainly a psychological impact on the behaviour of employees (Fig. 30.3 and Table 30.5).

Similarly to the electricity consumption curve and the heat consumption curve, we can see the shape of a letter U. In Fig. 30.3 we can see the whole continuance. The building is not heated at all in June–September. For this reason, the consumption equals to zero. The highest heat consumption is from November to February. The difference at the ends of the curve (January, February) is mainly caused by vacations. Between 12.23 and 1.1, the entire building is tempered to 12°, unlike in January, when it is heated the whole month. By replacing windows, building and roof

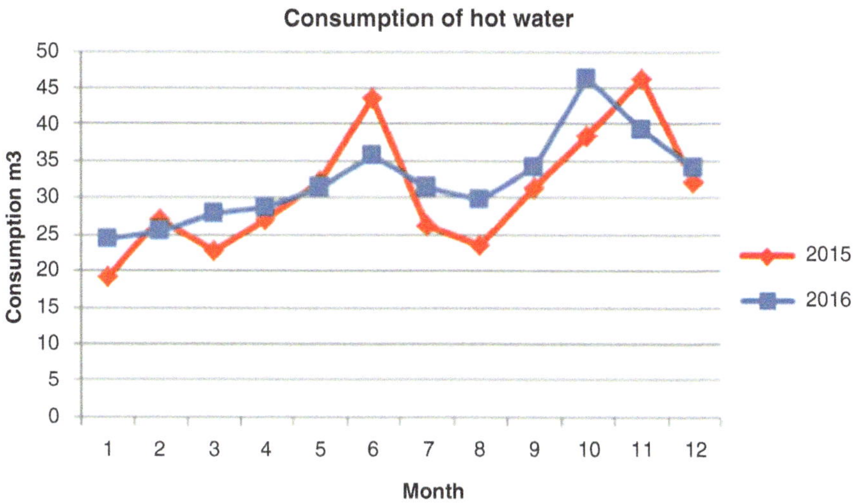

Fig. 30.2 Conduct consumption of hot water

Table 30.4 Monthly consumption of hot water [m^3]

	1	2	3	4	5	6	7	8	9	10	11	12
2015	19	27	23	27	32	44	26	24	31	38	46	32
2016	24	25	28	29	31	36	31	30	34	46	39	34

Source: Produced by authors

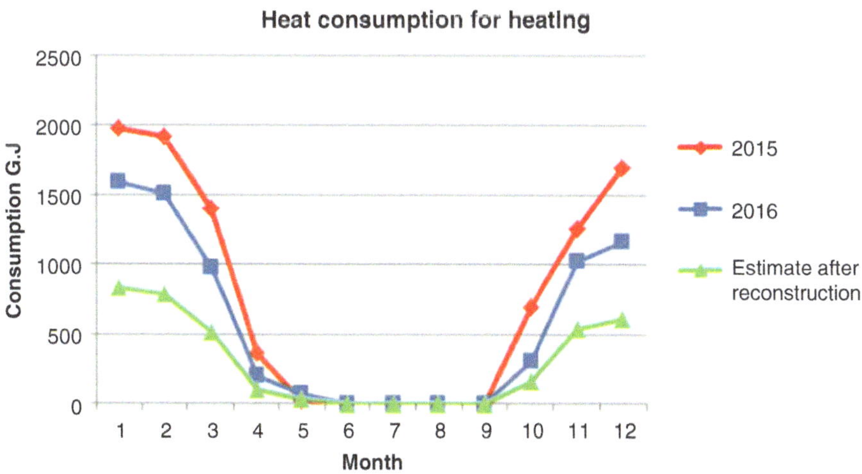

Fig. 30.3 Conduct of heat consumption for heating

insulation, we expect a significant reduction of heat consumption. Compared to 2015, in January it could be up to about 58% of savings.

Table 30.5 Monthly consumption for heating

	1	2	3	4	5	6	7	8	9	10	11	12
2015	1987	1921	1403	361	20	0	0	0	0	700	1258	1698
2016	1596	1506	979	201	75	0	0	0	0	307	1026	1172
Estimate after reconstruction	837	790	513	105	39	0	0	0	0	161	538	614

Source: Produced by authors

In the project, facility management is prepared by the use of thermal isolation material with a thickness of 120 mm on the outer wall is considered. That would provide a reduction in heat transfer coefficient (U) to a level 0.2 W/(m^2.K) from original levels 0.76 W/(m^2.K) which would represent 73.68% decrease. Reconstruction price of a building facade is around 55€/m^2 included VAT.

When replacing original windows, the replacement by six-chamber PVC windows with double isolation glass would be taken into consideration. The heat transfer coefficient (U), in this case, would drop after the windows' replacement from the original 2.78 W/(m^2.K) to 1.00 W/ (m^2.K). Price of replacement is around 500€/window included VAT.

Next step of the reconstruction would be the roof isolation. The roof at its original state does not meet the standards at $U = 0.63$ W/(m^2.K). After the reconstruction, we should get to the level of $U = 0.98$ W/(m^2.K). Reconstruction price of a roof construction is around 22€/m^2 including tax, and cost for insulation of a ground floor is around 35€/m^2 including VAT.

As followed from several studies, economic return on similar projects is around 10 years. Yet, this number may not be the final one; in case that the company would decide to continue the trend of so-called socially responsible enterprises, it could invest into other so-called green actions that would lead to a further energy cost reduction (Nadanyiova and Stefanikova 2015). Some of them could accelerate the return even more. However, if a company would like to use the best materials and technical elements of the market in the reconstruction, the estimated payback period would be on the contrary extended.

30.4 Conclusion

Every work-related activity includes actions, which do not necessarily cohere in achieving goals (Chlebikova and Bielikova 2015); however, without their contribution, we would hardly accomplish important results. No institution would be able to meet its business objectives without buildings, furniture, computer networks' security, technology equipment and other supporting subsistence activities. Here comes the facility management on stage.

Facility management helps optimize the operational costs implicit in the infrastructure, as we also managed to show in our experiment. The experiment revealed high operating costs of the administrative building. Its weaknesses were mainly heating and electricity consumption. This was particularly the winter months.

Higher electricity consumption was also recorded in this period. Building reconstruction and modernization of technical equipment, including lighting, can be greatly helpful for the enterprise. If the company opts for the reconstruction of the administrative building, it manages to significantly reduce operating costs. At the same time, the reconstruction extends the life cycle of the building and thus increases its value. It appears here how important it is for the company to deal also with supporting activities. In our opinion, that is why facility management has important position in any company.

Acknowledgements This paper has been prepared under financial support of VEGA No 1/0870/16 application of facility management in managing the transport companies in the Slovak Republic, which authors gratefully acknowledge.

References

Ameratunga, D., & Baldry, D. (2003). A conceptual framework to measure facilities management performance. *Property Management, 21*(2), 171–189.

Chlebikova D., & Bielikova A. (2015). Business environment and measurement of competitiveness of Slovak Republic. In: *10th International scientific conference financial management of firms and financial institutions* (pp. 422–428). Ostrava, ISBN 978-80-248-3865-6.

Cotts, D. G., Roper, K. O., & Payant, R. P. (2010). *The facility management handbook* (3rd ed.). New York: Amacom. xiv, 661 s., ISBN 978-0-8144-1380-7.

Falconer, H. (2006). The future of facilities management outsourcing. *Facility Management, 13*(5), 10–13.

Garimella, S., Fronk, B. M., & Thome, J. R. (2016). *Encyclopedia of two-phase heat transfer and: Condensation heat transfer method* (p. 342 s). New Jersey, NJ: World Scientific Pub. Pte. Ltd. ISBN 978-981-4623-24-7.

Kicova, E., & Kramarova, K. (2013). Innovations in outsourcing. In *7th international days of statistics and economics* (pp. 588–600). Praha: Melandrium. ISBN: 978-80-86175-87-4.

Levitt, A. M. (1997). *Disaster planning and recovery: A guide for facility professionals*. New York: Wiley. ISBN 0-471-14205-0.

Nadanyiova, M., & Stefanikova, L. (2015). The concept of green marketing and its impacts on Slovak consumers. In *3rd international conference on economics and social science (ICESS 2015), Advances in education research* (Vol. 86, pp. 24–30). Singapore: IERI & PRESS. ISSN 2160-1070.

Nawrocki, T. L. (2015). R&D activity and Core business efficiency on the example of technology companies. *Oeconomia Copernicana, 6*(4), 59–72. http://dx.doi.org/10. 12775/OeC.2015.029

Pavlov, V. K. (2014). Economic core region: Essence, the criteria for the formation and elemental composition. *Ekonomicko-manazerske spektrum, 8*(2), 26–35.

Ponisciakova, O. (2014). Controlling reporting in transport companies. In: *18th international conference on transport means, transport means – proceedings of the international conference* (pp. 206–210) Kaunas, Lithuania. ISSN: 1822-296X.

Rondeau, E. P., Brown, R. K., & Lapides, P. D. (2006). *Facility management* (2nd ed.p. 589 s). Hoboken, NJ: Wiley. ISBN 978-0-471-70059-3.

Slaichova, E., & Marsikova, K. (2013). The effect of implementing a maintenance information system on the efficiency of production facilities. *Journal of Competitiveness, 5*(3), 60–75.

Chapter 31
Brand Value and the Factors Affecting It

Margareta Nadanyiova and Jana Kliestikova

Abstract A brand is one way to distinguish products from each other, while simplifying consumers' decisions in choosing an appropriate product. However, sustaining and improving a brand's position in the market is not a simple process. This chapter discusses the essence of a brand, brand value, approaches to brand valuation, and the factors affecting brand value. As an example, the chapter includes a determination of the impact of advertising costs on brand value through linear dependence (correlation analysis). The results show that a company's advertising and brand value are linearly independent. Brand value is therefore not primarily dependent only on the level of advertising costs; rather, it depends on other factors as well.

31.1 Introduction

A brand has always been a way for companies to differentiate themselves and their products. Many authors have discussed the issue of brand and brand value (Gambetti and Ggraffigna 2015; Kurennaya 2017). The definition of a brand has been explored from a variety of perspectives. Keller (Tringh et al. 2016) highlighted the brand as a further dimension of a product that distinguishes it from other products. According to Kotler (Kotler 2001), the brand represents the declared product quality. Furthermore, the American Marketing Association and Marketing Accountability Standards Board agreed that a brand is a "name, term, design, symbol, or any other feature that identifies one seller's good or service as distinct from those of other sellers." (American Marketing Association 1995). Thus, the concept of a brand from a marketing point of view is similarly defined in many sources. More interesting are the subjective, descriptive expressions of marketing experts on what they mean by

M. Nadanyiova (✉) · J. Kliestikova
University of Zilina, Faculty of Operation and Economics of Transport and Communications, Department of Economics, Zilina, Slovak Republic
e-mail: margareta.nadanyiova@fpedas.uniza.sk

N. Tsounis, A. Vlachvei (eds.), *Advances in Panel Data Analysis in Applied Economic Research*, Springer Proceedings in Business and Economics,
https://doi.org/10.1007/978-3-319-70055-7_31

brand. Toman (Toman 2015) described a brand as follows: "A brand is still often seen as a symbol denoting a product or company. It is simplistically perceived as 'notice board over the entrance to the store. It then follows the effort to build the brand visible everywhere."

The entire process of building a brand—from brand design through its applications to effective communication with consumers—defines the term *branding*. Branding is not just about design but also strategy, which is even more important in the process (Krizanova 2015). The branding process should be carried out in a planned and responsible manner. The role of branding is therefore to give a name to a product, assign importance to brand, and thus place the brand in the customer's mind to distinguish it from competitors (Keller 2007).

31.2 Brand Value

The result of brand building is the potential to represent a certain value for the company. This value is often monetizable because companies invest substantial funding in the creation and management of a brand (Rodrigues and Martines 2016; Tringh et al. 2016). As a result, this effort leads to increased sales of branded production. Mostly, this element is referred to as the *added value* of products or services, which is based on how consumers perceive a brand in its price, market share, or the profit rate that the brand produces (Wang and Tzeng 2012).

During its lifecycle, each brand gains or loses value and/or the favor of consumers. The brand value is based precisely on the favor and loyalty of consumers together with brand image. This is an expression of what the brand represents to consumers, suppliers, competitors, dealers, or the company itself. Each of these groups looks at the brand value from different perspective. Brand value for the consumer is based on trust in the unchanging product quality, stable price, advantageous purchase, satisfaction from using the product, communication of the company with consumers, traditions, the consumer's associations with a particular brand, the prestige that accompanies the use of the product, among others. The latter two aspects are perhaps the most important.

The term *brand value* is often used interchangeably with the term *brand equity* (also known as market or consumer equity). Both terms are viewed as synonymous, whether in the academic field or within the practitioners. In our opinion, the definition of brand equity includes the perceived or behavioral value as well as the economic value and can be regarded as an indicator of the success of a brand (May et al. 2015; Van Der Meer 2016). Brand equity is a set of assets that are associated with a brand in customers' minds. Generally, brand equity indicates a brand's strength (i.e., brand worth). A brand's strength is linked with different brand associations, which allow a brand name to be more successful than non-branded names. The main aspects of brand equity are awareness, loyalty, and quality. According to Aaker (2003), brand equity is considered to be "the set or concept of brand associations, including the brand's incremental price premium, customers' satisfaction and loyalty, perceived quality and other brand's associations". However, in addition to these standard items, the value of the whole company is formed by extensive intellectual property, goodwill, and the price of the brands that the company has in its portfolio.

Without question, a strong brand provides a company with a great competitive advantage. A brand with a significant presence in the minds of consumers easily gains their trust and loyalty and can induce positive associations, leading to a reduction in marketing costs. Kotler and Keller (Keller 2007) summarized the benefits of a strong brand as follows:

- Perceptions of product performance and greater customer loyalty;
- Less vulnerability to competitive marketing campaigns;
- Higher margins and less flexibility in price increases by consumers;
- Improved business cooperation and support;
- Licensing opportunities and further expansion of the brand.

31.3 Approaches to a Brand Valuation

The process of branding provides a competitive advantage, especially in the long term. The value of a brand is a strategic asset for the company; in contrast is the brand image, which supports rather short-term results. In defining and exploring brand value, the scientific literature identifies two different perspectives: the customer and economic perspectives. The methods of brand valuation may thus be defined as follows:

1. *Behavioral*: Examines the response to the brand in terms of customer attitudes or in terms of purchase. Customers usually respond more positively to strong brands than to unbranded products or weaker brands.
2. *Financial*: Defines the financial brand value for companies and investors. Brand value is defined as the additional cash flow of branded products in comparison to cash flow arising under the sale of non-branded products, goodwill, and the price of brands that the company has in its portfolio.

Brand value is therefore considered to be one of the performance indicators contributing to a company's competitive advantage. The relationships between different concepts helps to create a brand. Brand value is an indicator that tries to represent the net present value of future revenue derived from the brand. The role of managers is therefore to maximize the long-term value of the future revenue derived from brands. (Wood 1999).

According to Kylianova and Lalikova (Kylianova et al. 2010), there are four approaches to a brand valuation in the Slovak Republic:

- Cost-based approach
- Income-based approach

- Market-based approach
- Indicative approach (applied only when it is not possible to use all of the above methods)

The *cost-based approach* takes into account all relevant historical costs that have been associated with a brand since its development or acquisition to the present market situation in the process of a brand valuation. However, this approach should be applied for the valuation of intangible assets other than brands (e.g. software, customer database). There are several reasons for this. First, the approach does not take into account attributes such as brand strength. Furthermore, it abstracts from a brand's market positon or brand's risk relative to other competitors, mostly historical or ex-post orientation. For long-existing brands, it can be difficult to identify all relevant incurred costs as well as a "starting point" of a brand's existence. However, the cost-based approach is a generally accepted method to quantify the fair value of assets, including intangible assets. The main advantage of this method is that it uses current market prices and equivalent utility to estimate a brand's value.

The *income-based approach* is based on the discounting or capitalizing of future anticipated revenues, profits, cash flow, or other financial indicators to the present value that a brand should generate during its remaining useful economic life. The application of this approach requires an analysis of a brand's historic and current profits and cash flows. Then, to properly forecast their future growth together with the risk that could be associated with it, an adequate discount rate and tax rate must be selected to estimate a remaining brand's useful economic life.

There are several income-based methods, including the following (International Organizational for Standardization 2010):

- Price/volume premium methods
- Profit-split method
- Multi-period excess earnings method
- Incremental cash flow method
- Royalty saving method

The *market-based approach* estimates a brand's value by the references to open market values of other brands. This approach is suitable only if the valuating assets are not unique and sufficient comparable transactions can be identified in the relevant market. With regard to a brand's value, identifying comparable brands or trademarks is a difficult task because the unique character of the brand must be clear as the principal aspects of its differentiation (Salinas 2009). It follows that brands are rarely comparable. However, this approach can provide some interesting insights in the estimation of a brand's value. Other methods are based on the market approach, such as the brand sale comparison method, royalty savings method, and brand equity valuation method. Market-based methods can be applied only if the market economy is sufficiently developed in trade with industrial rights. This kind of market is poorly developed in the Slovak Republic compared to other countries; therefore, the use of this method is difficult due to insufficient data on our conditions.

31.3.1 Composed Valuation Methods of Global Brands

Because brand value is a multidimensional concept, multiple measurements may increase the diagnostic power of research and the likelihood that a company's management will better understand the factors affecting branding. A combined financial and behavioral evaluation may eliminate the shortcomings of the previously described techniques. This evaluation is based on an analysis of the position of brands in the market and the purchasing behavior of customers. However, in this approach, some of the selected value factors contribute to its creation, whereas others are conversely consequences of the current value. The subjective selection and attribution of relative weights in individual evaluation criteria are also controversial. Therefore, despite its popularity, especially in media, this approach does not provide relevant insight into the effectiveness of a company's marketing activities to promote the brand.

The BrandZ Top 100 is a well-known approach for evaluating brand value with a combination of financial data analysis and the strength of brands in terms of customer relationships. This survey evaluates brands that come into direct contact with the consumer, as well as brands from business to business. The uniqueness of this project lies in the criteria used for evaluation and consideration of regional differences. The ranking of hundreds of the most valuable brands around the world is determined by a combination of two factors. First, the evaluation of brands are derived from interviews with more than a million respondents worldwide. Second, it includes a thorough rigorous analysis of financial and business impacts of the brand for the development of trade and growth in the company's market share (using data from Bloomberg and Datamonitor).

31.4 Capitalization of Income by Applying a Multiple to the Historical Returns, as the Interest Rate for Future Cash Flows

One of the composite methods is known as the *Interbrand method*, which involves two basic steps (Kylianova et al. 2010): the identification of the actual brand revenues and cash flow. The Interbrand valuation method takes into account the following factors:

- Leadership: The ability of the brand to be leader in the market sector by being dominant and able to influence the market
- Stability: A stable brand with loyal customers is more valuable
- Market: The evaluation of brands by the market environment
- Geography: The ability of a brand to transcend geographical and cultural boundaries

- Trend: The attractiveness of the brand direction to customers
- Support: Marketing and communication activities to promote the brand, which helps to improve brand value
- Security: The legal protection of the brand

The Interbrand company collects information from a large sample of respondents, such as consumers and managers, using a detailed questionnaire. Interbrand regularly conducts inspection visits to examine materials and the like. The Interbrand valuation methodology is globally recognized, and the company publishes an annual list of the 100 most valuable global brands.

31.4.1 The Impact of Factors Affecting the Brand Value

As part of the science project APVV - Slovak abbreviation of Slovak Research and Development Agency, our study "Integrated model of management support for building and managing the brand value in the specific conditions of the Slovak Republic" investigated the factors affecting brand value. We focused on the world's most valuable brands, based on rankings published by *Forbes* magazine, Interbrand, and BrandZ Top 100.

As mentioned, many different factors impact the brand value, such as costs, incomes, customer attitudes, and so on. As an example, we investigated the dependence between a company's advertising costs and the brand value.

31.4.2 Determination of the Impact of Advertising Costs on Brand Value through Linear Dependence

Advertising is a marketing communication tool for brand building and increasing brand value. In particularly, institutional advertising has a great impact on building brand value because it focuses on improving the brand's image, increasing its awareness, and promoting consumer loyalty. In contrast, product advertising highlights the characteristics and quality of products, which are its object.

Our survey focused on the rapidly developing technology field. Companies are constantly coming onto the market with new innovative products, to which competitors immediately react by offering substitute products with comparable characteristics. Therefore, it is necessary for a company to strengthen its brand value, which should result in a competitive advantage. Every year, many brands spend huge amounts of money just on advertising. However, advertising is useless if it does not bring the desired effect (i.e., it does not meet the target that was set at the start of the advertising process). The cause of failure may be an incorrect advertising strategy or ineffective communication. The impact of advertising and advertising costs incurred in brand value is very difficult to quantify because brand value is affected by many other factors in addition to advertising.

Table 31.1 The world's most valuable technology brands

Rank	Brand	Brand value ($B)	Change in brand value (%)	Brand revenue ($B)	Company advertising ($B)
1	Apple	154.1	6	233.7	1.8
2	Google	82.5	26	68.5	3.2
3	Microsoft	75.2	9	87.6	1.9
5	Facebook	52.6	44	17.4	0.281
7	IBM	41.4	−17	81.7	1.3
11	Samsung	36.1	−5	177.4	3.3
12	Amazon	35.2	25	104.5	3.8
15	Cisco	28.4	3	49.6	0.202
16	Oracle	28	4	37.2	0.055
17	Intel	27.7	7	55.4	1.8
27	SAP	21.6	10	23.1	–
38	HP	13.8	−6	102.1	0.859
52	Ebay	11.2	2	7.8	1
76	Sony	7.6	9	59.3	3.7
79	Netflix	7.4	31	6.8	0.714
82	Panasonic	7.1	13	63.4	–
84	Canon	7.1	−2	31.4	0.669

Our sample included 17 of the most valuable global technology brands based on the previously mentioned worldwide surveys (Interbrand, BrandZ Top 100, etc.) published in *Forbes* magazine. We assessed the impact of the advertising costs that were invested in 2015 on the brand value set for the year 2016. In our study, the consistency of input data played a key role in the methodical approach for quantifying brand value.

From the group of 17 ranked brands, we eliminated brands without information on the amount of advertising costs in 2015. This sample was thus reduced to 15 brands. Table 31.1 shows the world's most valuable brands in the technology industry with information about their rank, brand value, change in brand value, brand revenue, and company advertising costs (The World's Most Valuable Brands 2016).

Figure 31.1 shows a graphical representation (scatter plot) of the relationship between a company's advertising cost and brand value, which we tried to express by means of a linear function. We evaluated the relationship between brand value and the amount of advertising costs using the Pearson correlation coefficient (PCC), which is a measure of the linear dependence (correlation) between two variables, x and y:

$$R = \frac{\text{cov}\,(x, y)}{s_x * s_y} = \frac{\overline{xy} - \overline{x} * \overline{y}}{\sqrt{\overline{x^2} - \overline{x}^2} * \sqrt{\overline{y^2} - \overline{y}^2}} \quad (31.1)$$

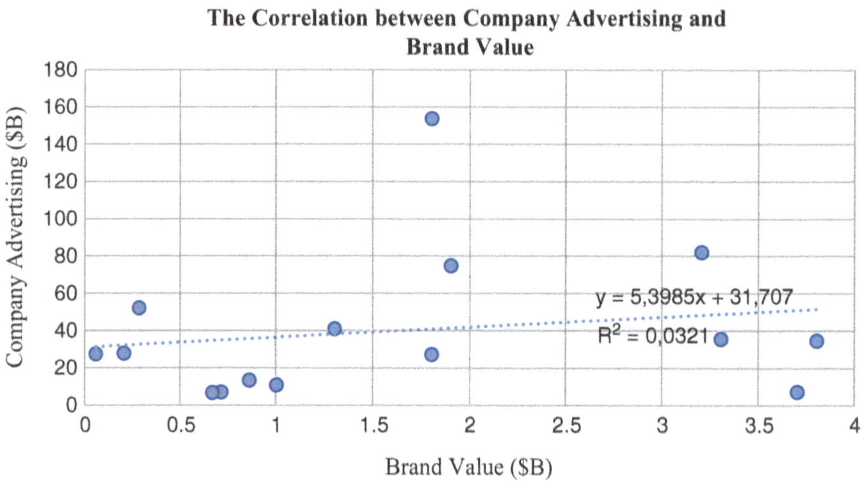

Fig. 31.1 The correlation between company advertising and brand value

Table 31.2 Summary output of regression statistics

Regression statistics	
Multiple R	0.179201706
R square	0.032113252
Adjusted R square	−0.042339575
Standard error	39.91523852
Observations	15

Analysis of variance	df	SS	MS	F	Significance F
Regression	1	687,1958791	687,1959	0.431323	0.522797009
Residual	13	20711,94145	1593,226		
Total	14	21399,13733			

	Coefficients	Standard Error	t Stat	P-value	Lower 95%	Upper 95%	Lower 95.0%	Upper 95.0%
Intercept	31.7070	16.9602	1.8694	0.0842	−4.9334	68.3474	−4.9334	68.3474
Company's advertising costs ($B)	5.3984	8.2199	0.65675	0.5227	−12.359	23.1566	−12.3596	23.1566

31.4.3 Results of the Correlation Analysis

Table 31.2 shows the results of our regression and correlation analysis, which we performed using Data Analysis in Excel.

The PCC value is close to zero (0.179201706), which means that the advertising costs and brand value are linearly independent. Therefore, it is necessary to verify whether this result is solely due to random examined parameters or whether they are indeed linear independent. For verification, we used the test of linear independence.

We evaluated the degree of causal dependence between the brand value and amount of advertising costs by applying a coefficient of determination, which is defined as the square of the correlation coefficient R. The value of the coefficient of determination in this case is $R^2 = 0.0321$, which means that only 3.21% of the variance brand value is explained by a linear relationship with advertising costs (regression line). Up to 96.79% of the variability values of brands can be explained by other causes, such as a linear relationship between the advertising costs and brand value.

The test of linear independence includes the following steps:

1. Determination of the null hypothesis:

$$H_0 : R = 0 \tag{31.2}$$

The correlation coefficient is considered to be null, so the variables are linearly independent.

2. Determination of the alternative hypothesis:

$$H_1 : R \neq 0 \tag{31.3}$$

The correlation coefficient is significantly different from zero. Thus, the variables are linearly dependent.

3. Selection of the significance level:

$$\alpha = 0.05 \tag{31.4}$$

4. Application of the test criteria:

$$T = R.\sqrt{\frac{n-2}{1-R^2}} \tag{31.5}$$

The test criteria is 0.656752212.

5. Critical field of the test:

$$|T| \geq t_{\alpha}\,(n-2) \tag{31.6}$$

where $t_{\alpha}(n-2)$ is the critical value of the t-distribution at the significance level α with n-2 degrees of freedom, to be 2,160,368,656.

6. Decision:

The inequality does not apply, so we do not reject the hypothesis H_0. Therefore, the correlation coefficient is zero and the variables are linearly independent.

31.5 Conclusion

Our results indicate that the brand values included in our analysis were not directly determined by the amount of advertising costs. Even highly rated brands had low advertising costs in comparison with brands of lower value. Brand value is therefore not primarily dependent on the level of advertising costs; rather, it additionally depends on the effectiveness of the advertising in marketing communications.

In the current competitive environment, it is necessary for companies to improve the value of their brands. Based on our analysis, brand building provides several competitive advantages, which can be summarized as follows:

- Improved customer loyalty
- Decreased vulnerability to competitive marketing events and crises
- Higher margins
- Greater cooperation and support from traders
- Increased effectiveness of marketing communications

Acknowledgements This chapter is based on the the science project APVV-15-0505, "Integrated model of management support for building and managing the brand value in the specific conditions of the Slovak Republic."

References

Aaker, D. A. (2003). *Brand building – budování značky* (p. 312). Brno: Computer Press.

American Marketing Association. (1995). Dictionary. .Available from: https://www.ama.org/resources/Pages/Dictionary.aspx?dLetter=B. Accessed 15 December 2016.

Gambetti, R. C., & Ggraffigna, G. (2015). Value co-creation between the "inside" and the "outside" of a company: Insights from a brandcommunity failure. *Marketing Theory, 15*(2), 155–178.

International Organizational for Standardization. (2010). *ISO 10668:2010 brand valuation – Requirements for monetary brand valuation* (p. 11). Geneva: ISO.

Keller, K. L. (2007). *Strategic brand management* (p. 796). Praha: Grada Publishing.

Kotler, P. (2001). *Marketing management* (10th ed.p. 719). Praha: Grada Publishing.

Krizanova, A. etc. (2015). Building a Brand in the Context of Sustainable Development. In *Proceedings of International Conference on Management Engineering and Management Innovation, PRC: Changsha, 2015* (pp. 79–84).

Kurennaya, A. (2017). Brand/story: Cases and explorations in fashion branding. *Fashion Style & Popular Culture, 4*(1), 124–126.

Kylianova, D., et al. (2010). *Hodnota značky a jej podiel na nehmotnom majetku podniku*. Banská Bystrica: Úrad priemyselného vlastníctva SR.

May, M., Monga, A. B., & Kalaignanam, K. (2015). Consumer responses to brand failures: The neglected role of honor values. *Brand Meaning Management, 12*, 257–291.

Rodrigues, P., & Martines, F. V. (2016). Perceptual and behavioural dimensions: Measuring brand equity consumer based. *Journal of Fashion Marketing and Management, 20*(4), 507–519.

Salinas, G. (2009). *The international brand valuation manual* (p. 420). Chicester: Wiley&Sons.

The World's Most Valuable Brands. (2016). Forbes Magazine. .Available from: https://www.forbes.com/powerful-brands/list/. Accessed 3 Feb 2017.

Toman, M. (2015). Co je to značka a proč ji budovat. Zubří: Intuitivni marketing .Available from: http://www.intuitivnimarketing.cz/marketing/co-je-znacka-proc-ji-budovat. Accessed 15 Jan 2017.

Tringh, G., Romaniuk, J., & Tanusondjaja, A. (2016). Benchmarking buyer behavior towards new brands. *Marketing Letters, 27*(4), 743–752.

Van Der Meer, T. G. L. A. (2016). Automated content analysis and crisis communication research. *Public Relations Review, 42*(5), 952–961.

Wang, Y. L., & Tzeng, G. H. (2012). Brand marketing for creating brand value based on a MCDM model combining DEMATEL with ANP and VIKTOR methods. *Expert systems with applicatios, 39*(5), 5600–5615.

Wood, L. (1999). Market power and its measurement. *European Journal of Marketing, 33*(5), 612–633. Available from: http://www.emeraldinsight.com/doi/abs/10.1108/03090569910262224.

Chapter 32
Does the Fall in Crude Oil Prices Really Affect the Malaysian Ringgit?

Muhammad Adli Amirullah and Zarinah Hamid

Abstract The sudden drop in Malaysian exchange rate triggers a big question mark and is of great concern to policy makers, investors, firms, and the Malaysian public at large. Theoretically, depreciation in any currency is not only caused by classical exchange rate determinant but various forces behind it. This study uses monetary approach to test the Malaysian exchange rate determinant. It also seeks to examine the correlation of Malaysian exchange rate with crude oil price. The sudden drop in the global crude oil price is one of the major factors of depreciation in the Malaysian Ringgit as claimed by some analysts. Using monthly data from January 2006 to March 2016 in the first regression, we adopted the monetary approach on exchange rate determinant without crude oil price variable and found that approximately 51% of the proposition of variation of the dependent variable is explained by the proposition of variation of the independent variables. When another explanatory variable, i.e., Brent crude oil prices, is added to the model, the results indicated that this variable is very significant and caused R^2 to increase tremendously to 91%. The model is further enhanced by remedying the multicollinearity problem and omitting one of the variables which has a high correlation with all other variables. In conclusion, the fall in crude oil prices does affect the Malaysian exchange rate heavily. The finding is useful to the policy makers to devise a policy in future which is less reliant on crude oil price.

Keywords Malaysia · Exchange rate · Malaysian Ringgit · Crude oil price

32.1 Introduction

In August 2015, Malaysia experienced a sharp decline in its exchange rate. It is stated that the ringgit depreciated approximately from RM3.80 against 1 USD to

M. A. Amirullah · Z. Hamid (✉)
International Islamic University Malaysia, Kuala Lumpur, Malaysia
e-mail: adliamirullah@gmail.com; inahumkc@iium.edu.my

N. Tsounis, A. Vlachvei (eds.), *Advances in Panel Data Analysis in Applied Economic Research*, Springer Proceedings in Business and Economics,
https://doi.org/10.1007/978-3-319-70055-7_32

approximately RM4.25 against 1 USD (Bank Negara Malaysia n.d.). It was the highest drop in Malaysian currency since the Asian financial crisis (Teh and Ling 2015). Many Malaysians especially those who do not understand the exchange rate market mechanism tend to blame everything on the federal government and central bank of Malaysia. Therefore, this study provides a basic understanding of the elements that actually determine the Malaysian exchange rate.

The aim of this study is to explicitly analyze the causes of fluctuations in the Malaysian exchange rate by using one of the theoretical approaches suggested in the literature review. By using econometric analysis, we will be able to clearly understand the real situation regarding the Malaysian Ringgit depreciation in August 2015. Thus, this study will help us to understand how several factors could contribute to the depreciation of the Malaysian exchange rate.

This model tests the determinant of Malaysian exchange rate using monetary approach. Two common approaches can be used to assess exchange rate changes. However, we decided to use the monetary approach as this approach includes trade flows in its assessment. Malaysia, being one of the countries where the economy heavily depends on trade (Rasiah 2011), is most suitable for applying this approach.

In addition, another objective of this study is to determine the significance level of crude oil prices toward the Malaysian exchange rate. According to Teh and Ling (2015), the Malaysian exchange rate does move consistent with Brent crude oil prices. Therefore, by performing the econometric analysis, we might be able to observe the level of significance of crude oil prices toward the Malaysian currency. Different studies on exchange rate determinant are based on developed countries such as the United States and the United Kingdom. However, there is a lack of current research on various themes of exchange rate determinant on developing countries, in general, and Malaysia, in particular. Our finding improves the understanding on the applicability of the monetary approach in the Malaysian case and the effect of crude oil prices on the Malaysian exchange rate.

The paper consists of five sections and begins with an introduction. Section 32.2 focuses on the related literature on the types of exchange rate system and its relation to oil prices. The third section explains the process and method adopted in this study. Section 32.4 presents empirical findings and analysis while the last section concludes.

32.2 Literature Review

32.2.1 Type of Exchange Rate System

In order to understand the theoretical model of exchange rate, one has to understand the basis of the exchange rate and the type of exchange rate system. Literally, exchange rate means the price of a nation's currency in terms of foreign country (Salvatore 2011). Technically, it is an indicator for both countries to trade their currency among each other. The exchange rate system is a system which a nation uses in order to determine its exchange rate. According to Yagci (2001), there are two extreme exchange rate systems, namely, the floating regime and hard peg regime.

The exchange rate has always been evaluated in terms of two variables which are domestic currency and foreign currency (Froyen 2013). Most of the time, exchange rate uses foreign currency as the base currency. Meaning, it measures the value of domestic currency to occur in one unit of foreign currency. For example, in 27 October 2015, the exchange rate on Malaysian Ringgit (MYR) against the US Dollar (USD) was 4.25 MYR/1 USD (Bank Negara Malaysia n.d.). It means that we need approximately 4.25 MYR in order to purchase 1 USD. Moreover, from this value itself, we can conclude that MYR is relatively "cheaper" against USD because it needs more than 1 MYR to purchase 1 USD. In contrast, we also can say that the USD is relatively "stronger" compared to MYR. Therefore, for simplicity, we will carry an exchange rate using the base currency per 1 unit foreign currency.

As stated before, there are two extreme exchange rate systems which are floating exchange rate system and hard peg exchange rate system. The floating exchange rate system highly depends on the foreign exchange market mechanism in order to determine the equilibrium of domestic exchange rate (Yagci 2001). Furthermore, Yagci (2001) argued that the national currency is regulated by the demand and supply in the foreign exchange market. These markets are believed to be highly vulnerable as it shifts and changes repetitively in a single day. However the theory also claims that the equilibrium will be ending up at the normal equilibrium range, although the demand for foreign currency and the supply of foreign currency fluctuate heavily. Thus, the floating exchange rate system applies to the most widely traded currencies such as USD and Eurodollar because it will enable them to steer the domestic economy freely.

On the other hand, the second extreme exchange rate system is the hard peg exchange rate. Yagci (2001) explained that it is a strict exchange rate regime which specified foreign currency at a fixed rate. There is clearly no independent monetary policy for the country. Besides that, Yagci (2001) further explained that dollarization is also considered as a hard peg regime where a country uses another country's currency as their legal tender. Example can be seen from a small country which is highly integrated in bigger neighbor countries. This type of exchange rate system is often used in order to control the behavior of domestic currency and to provide highest reliability for the economic policy regime. When domestic currency fluctuation magnitude is big enough, it may cause an indirect effect on the domestic economy as a whole, and this will be a big concern to the policy makers. Thus, this type of exchange rate system is used by a country to prevent from currency crisis since it has a low transaction cost and eliminate inflationary bias.

Moreover, there is an exchange rate system which falls between the two extremes. According to Yagci (2001), intermediate regime exchange rate and soft peg exchange rate are the middle path of two extremes. Intermediate regime is a managed floating system or a crawling broadband system in which the monetary authority actively intervene in the exchange rate market without specification of the rate. The authority may intervene directly or indirectly in order to make the exchange rate to be relatively stable and less volatile. This regime is mostly suitable for emerging economies which have relatively stronger financial market and capital market as well as a discipline macroeconomic policy (Yagci 2001). Whereas soft peg exchange rate regime is described as the exchange rate which pegged at fixed rate to a major currency or a basket of currencies (Yagci 2001), the peg is adjusted (devaluation or revaluation) when misalignment happens and the monetary authority will fix the preannounced rate of the currency or set the allowable band for the currency to fluctuate. This regime is mainly used by developing countries with limited link to financial and capital market as well as countries which are stabilizing from a significant high level of inflation.

As the world economy is growing, trading among countries also has increased. For that reason, the exchange rate market needs to be free but, at the same time, regulated to a certain degree to minimize fluctuations. Thus, this exchange rate regime has been widely used by most trading countries in the twenty-first century.

32.2.2 Theory on Exchange Rate Determinant: Monetary Approach

The theory in exchange rate determination has been widely explained by using several approaches. According to Salvatore (2011), these are the portfolio approach and monetary approach. In the portfolio approach, the wealth in the society is held in domestic securities and domestic currency. The factor that determines the fraction of these holdings is interest rate, exchange rate, and supply of foreign assets in the home country. However, the shortcoming of this model is it omitted the trade flows in its assessment. It is clear that the exchange rate is highly correlated with trade flows (Salvatore 2011). In other words, it is highly dependent on the price level of domestic and foreign countries. Thus, another approach has been introduced which is the monetary model.

Three fundamental concepts underscore the monetary model: the quantity theory of money, Cambridge cash-balance approach, and Keynesian monetary theory (Wilson 2009). Wilson (2009) explained that knowing these concepts will help us to understand why the monetary approach suggested that the determinants that have a potential effect on exchange rate are money supply, income level, and interest rate.

In addition, Noussair et al. (1997) supported the monetary approach by stating that trade flows and price level of an economy do explain exchange rate behavior. It means that exchange rate fluctuation does depend on trade flows and price level of an economy. Besides that, Kakkar and Yan (2014) and Fadli Fizari et al. (2011) also agreed on the monetary approach where they believed that interest rate has the potential to affect exchange rate. Therefore, factors that could affect exchange rate suggested by monetary approach include domestic money supply (Ms), domestic income level (Y), domestic interest rate (i), foreign money supply (Ms*), foreign income level (Y^*), and foreign interest rate (i^*) (Wilson 2009).

32.2.3 Exchange Rate and Oil Prices

In the light of our study, besides the original literature on exchange rate determinant, some analysts believe that some other factors cause exchange rate fluctuation. Although there is no literature review regarding the general relationship between crude oil price and exchange rate, some independent studies have examined the relationship between exchange rate and oil prices for specific countries. For instance, Teh and Ling (2015) believed that the plunge in international crude oil prices has a high correlation with the Malaysian exchange rate. They argued that Malaysia is a net exporter in the fossil fuel segment, and the decrease in fossil fuel prices will be a cause for concern. They roughly tested the relationship between Brent crude oil price (in terms of USD per barrel) and the Malaysian exchange rate (in terms of USD against MYR) and found that both variables have a similar movement from January 2013 to July 2015.

Besides that, Aliyu (2009) and Babatunde (2015) also argued that oil prices have the ability to affect Nigeria's exchange rate since Nigeria is an oil-producing country. In addition, Sajal (2011) also contended that India's exchange rate was heavily affected by oil price volatility. Hence, it can be concluded that exchange rate could be affected by the changes in crude oil prices.

In contrast, Yue et al. (2008) suggested that US exchange rate and oil prices are relatively independent of each other. Furthermore, an earlier study by Amano and Norden (1995) explained that theoretically oil prices will affect terms of trade of a country and therefore cause their exchange rate to fluctuate accordingly. Thus, some studies by economists since the late 1990s have explored the exchange rate-oil price relationship.

32.2.4 Malaysian Exchange Rate System

According to Umezaki (2006), Malaysia has been using its own national currency, which is the Malaysian Ringgit (MYR) since 1957 after independence. Before the dismantlement of the Sterling Area in 1972, Malaysian exchange rate policy was pegged to Pound Sterling. Then after 1973, the Ringgit was permitted to float until 1975. In the 1980s, the Malaysia Central Bank exchange rate policy focused on the stabilization of the exchange rate against the Singaporean dollar. The new policy leads the exchange rate into becoming a managed floating system in 1984. This exchange rate regime lasted until the 1997 Asian financial crisis. In 1998, the Malaysia Central Bank and the federal government unanimously agreed that the

Ringgit would be pegged to the US Dollar (USD) at 1 USD = 3.8 MYR (Ila et al. 2011; Mansor 2007; Naseem et al. 2008).

However, in July 2005, Malaysia switched back to the managed floating system to further stimulate its economic performance (Naseem et al. 2008). The major reason for policy alteration was to improve the position and gain structural changes in the global arena. Henceforth, Malaysia has been using the managed floating exchange rate system up until today.

32.3 Methodology

32.3.1 Choosing Functional Form, Variables, and Its A Priori Signs

Wilson (2009) explained the monetary model and derived an equation to get all the determinants. In building the monetary model of exchange rate determination, the first assumption is by assuming that at the equilibrium money supply should be equal to money demand (Froyen 2013).

According to the purchasing power parity theory, the equilibrium exchange rate between two currencies is equal to the ratio of the price levels in both nations (Salvatore 2011). Specifically

$$E = \frac{P}{P*} \tag{32.1}$$

where E is the exchange rate, P is the general price level of domestic country, and $P*$ is the general price level of foreign countries.

Thus, we can express (32.1) in terms of Keynesian monetary theory. Thus, it can be written as

$$E = \frac{iY^*\mathrm{Ms}}{i^*Y\mathrm{Ms}^*} \tag{32.2}$$

Furthermore, the next step is to take the log of (32.2) as suggested by Wilson (2009) and add a constant parameter on it. We can express it as

$$\log E = a\left(\log \mathrm{Ms}-\log \mathrm{Ms}^*\right) - b\left(\log Y-\log Y^*\right) + c\left(\log i-\log i^*\right) \tag{32.3}$$

where a, b, and c are the constant parameters. The monetary model for the foreign country is expressed with an asterisk. According to (32.3), we can conclude that monetary theory proposed that exchange rates are a monetary phenomenon affected by the money supply, income level, and interest rate (Cao and Ong 2000; Wilson 2009).

In addition, Wilson (2009) suggested that if we assume the coefficients of demand for money in domestic and foreign country are different, then from (32.3) we will get the following:

$$\log E = \gamma_0 - \alpha_0 + \log \mathrm{Ms} - \log \mathrm{Ms}^* - \alpha_1 \log Y + \gamma_1 \log Y^* + \alpha_2 \log i - \gamma_2 \log i^* \tag{32.4}$$

where αs and γs are constant coefficients.

Now we can get the monetary model of exchange rate determination in the following unrestricted form where β_0 is the constant coefficient and ε is the error term. Thus, the theoretical regression proposed by Wilson (2009) for the exchange rate is double-log, and it will be

$$\log E_t = \beta_0 + \beta_1 \log Y_t + \beta_2 \log Y_t^* + \beta_3 \log i_t + \beta_4 \log i_t^* + \beta_5 \log \mathrm{Ms}_t + \beta_6 \log \mathrm{Ms}_t^* + \varepsilon_t \tag{32.5}$$

Since our study here is testing the Malaysian exchange rate against the USD, our home country will be Malaysia and our foreign country will be the United States of America (USA). Furthermore, our dependent variable here would be Malaysian Ringgit per 1 USD. We denote it as E where if E increases, it means there is a depreciation in MYR and appreciation in USD. In contrast, if E decreases, there will be an appreciation in MYR and depreciation in USD.

As suggested by the monetary model, the first two variables are domestic money supply and foreign money supply. Mathematically according to (32.2), the a priori sign for domestic money supply is positive, whereas for foreign money supply, it is negative. The measurement data used in this study for money supply are currency in circulation. It is quantified in terms of its own national currency. Currency in circulation is used because it measures the liquidity of the money. Since the flexible exchange rate market is very volatile (Froyen 2013), it shows that the movement in the demand and supply of domestic and foreign money is very liquid. This proves that using currency in circulation is the most suitable in undertaking this regression.

Moreover, the third and fourth variables are the domestic unemployment rate and foreign unemployment rate. Although the monetary model suggested using national income level as the independent variable, we decided to substitute the national income level variable with the unemployment rate variable. This is because of unavailability of monthly data for national income level for both Malaysia and the United States. Hence, we used unemployment rate as an instrumental variable. The unemployment rate is a suitable instrumental variable for national income because according to McConnel et al. (2012), unemployment rate is highly correlated with gross domestic product which can be represented as national income level. Mathematically, Eq. (32.2) suggests that the a priori sign for the domestic income level is negative and foreign income level is positive toward the exchange rate. Since national income has negative correlation with the unemployment rate, thus we expect the domestic unemployment rate will have positive correlation with exchange rate, while the foreign unemployment rate is expected to have a negative correlation with exchange rate. The measurement data used in unemployment rate will be in percentage form.

In addition, the fifth and sixth independent variables are domestic interest rate and foreign interest rate, respectively. According to (32.2), mathematically domestic interest rate will have positive a priori sign, while the foreign interest rate will have a negative a priori sign. The data measurement for interest rate would be the government securities and the government bond interest rate in percentage form. The essential connection between interest rate and exchange rate is the capital inflow and capital outflow (Froyen 2013). The longer the investment, the higher interest earning an investor will gain. Therefore, we believe that the government bond interest rate can represent the interest rate for long-term investment which is the prominent factor that should be taken into this regression. Last but not least, the seventh variable is dated Brent crude oil prices as suggested by Teh and Ling (2015), and its a priori sign is negative. The unit of measurement for dated Brent crude oil price is USD per barrel.

In summary, the final theoretical equation will be as follows:

$$\log E_t = \beta_0 + \beta_1 \log \mathrm{Un}_t + \beta_2 \log \mathrm{Un}_t{}^* + \beta_3 \log i_t + \beta_4 \log i_t{}^* + \beta_5 \log \mathrm{Ms}_t + \beta_6 \log \mathrm{Ms}_t{}^* + \beta_7 \log \mathrm{Oil}_t + \varepsilon_t \tag{32.6}$$

where βs are the coefficients, Un_t is the domestic unemployment rate, $\mathrm{Un}_t{}^*$ is the foreign unemployment rate, i_t is the domestic interest rate, $i_t{}^*$ is the foreign interest rate, Ms_t is the domestic money supply, $\mathrm{Ms}_t{}^*$ is the foreign money supply, and oil_t is the crude oil price.

32.3.2 Choosing Sample Size

The time period for this regression is from January 2006 to March 2016. The data is on monthly basis, and in total, there are 123 observations from January 2006 to March 2016. January 2006 is chosen as the starting month because according to Umezaki (2006), the Malaysian exchange rate system has changed from the fixed exchange rate system to floating exchange rate system in late 2005. Thus, sample size observations from January 2006 to March 2016 are the most appropriate data set to be included in this regression.

The researcher named the variables in this paper as E, the exchange rate of MYR against 1 USD; Un is the domestic unemployment rate in percentage form, Un* is the foreign unemployment rate in percentage form, i is the domestic interest rate in percentage form, i^* is the foreign interest rate in percentage form, M is the domestic money supply in billions of USD, M^* is the foreign money supply in billions of

USD, and oil is dated Brent crude oil prices in USD per barrel. Note that all the data were extracted from the International Monetary Fund (IMF) database.

32.4 Empirical Findings and Analysis

The results of the estimation are obtained using ordinary least square method. We divided the regression into three models. All three models have a significant overall test statistic, and the adjusted R^2 has significantly improved from model 1 to model 2 by 179.85%. We encountered a multicollinearity problem in model 2 where the foreign money supply variable shows an absolutely high variance inflation factor value of 33.2232. In addition, we also observed that foreign money supply has a relatively high correlation coefficient with all other independent variables. Thus, we decided to omit foreign money supply variable and regressed model 3.

We decided not to omit foreign interest rate variable in model 3 although the variable is not significant. It is because there is no solid reason to omit the variable; besides, this variable is relatively important as argued in the literature review. In addition, we also tried to omit the variable, but the result seems insignificantly different from model 2. Therefore, we regarded model 3 as the final verdict.

Besides that, the estimation result as shown in Table 32.1 suggests that only two variables are very significant across three models which are domestic and foreign unemployment rate variables. According to model 3, a 1% increase in the domestic unemployment rate will result in an increase in exchange rate by 0.11%. A positive relationship exists between the unemployment rate and exchange rate. Note that unemployment rate is an instrumental variable in replacing national income variable. Since domestic national income has a negative relationship with the exchange rate (Wilson 2009) and also with the domestic unemployment rate (McConnel et al. 2012), then theoretically exchange rate and the domestic unemployment rate will have a positive relationship. The result shows that the variables are according to their a priori sign. Thus, it proved that as domestic unemployment rate increases, there is an increase in the exchange rate which indicates that the Malaysian Ringgit is depreciating.

Moreover, model 3 also shows that with a 1% increase in the foreign unemployment rate, there will be a decrease in the exchange rate by 0.08%. Since foreign income level has a positive relationship with the exchange rate (Wilson 2009) and negative relationship with its own unemployment rate (McConnel et al. 2012), then theoretically exchange rate will have a negative relationship with the foreign unemployment rate. Thus, the result is parallel with its expected sign, whereby if the foreign unemployment rate increases, the exchange rate will decrease, indicating that the Malaysian Ringgit is appreciating.

Furthermore, the domestic interest rate shows a significant relationship with exchange rate where a 1% increase in the domestic interest rate will lead to a 0.3% increase in exchange rate. This result seems in accordance with its expected sign where the increase in domestic interest rate will cause a domestic interest earning to

Table 32.1 Estimation results

	Model 1	Model 2	Model 3
Constant	−6.9887*** (−8.0095)	0.3794 (0.3938)	0.3437 (0.7544)
log Un_t	0.4587*** (5.9742)	0.1117*** (3.2249)	0.1122*** (3.4363)
log Un_t*	−0.1518*** (−5.7866)	−0.0778*** (−6.9511)	−0.0776*** (−7.5122)
log i_t	0.1319 (1.2479)	0.3032*** (6.9019)	0.3027*** (7.2182)
log i_t*	0.0454 (1.0614)	−0.0144 (−0.8126)	−0.0142 (−0.8447)
log Ms_t	−0.1088 (−0.9751)	0.0581 (1.2546)	0.0563*** (3.1474)
log Ms_t*	0.3780** (2.3344)	−0.0029 (−0.0421)	–
log Oil_t	–	−0.1995*** (−23.9832)	−0.1994*** (−24.7566)
R^2	0.5107	0.9185	0.9185
Adjusted R^2	0.4854	0.9135	0.9143
Durbin-Watson	0.2946	0.5671	0.5665
F-statistics	20.1811***	185.0935***	217.8165***

Notes: Un_t domestic unemployment rate, Un_t* foreign unemployment rate, i_t domestic interest rate, i_t* foreign interest rate, Ms_t domestic money supply, Ms_t* foreign money supply, Oil_t dated Brent crude oil prices

***, **, and * indicate significance at the 1%, 5%, and 10% levels, respectively Figures in round parentheses represent t-values

increase, subsequently leading to an increase in the demand of Malaysian Ringgit and finally making the exchange rate to rise indicating that the Malaysian Ringgit is depreciating.

Other than that, domestic money supply also is a very significant variable and the actual sign is according to its expected sign. There is a positive correlation between domestic money supply and exchange rate where a 1% increase in domestic money supply will lead to an increase in exchange rate by 0.06%. Theoretically, this is true since an increase in domestic money supply will lead to an increased inflation rate. Since inflation has a positive relationship with the exchange rate, then an increase in domestic money supply will cause the exchange rate to increase which indicates that the Malaysian Ringgit is depreciating.

Last but not least, Brent crude oil price variable is a highly significant variable. A 1% increase in Brent crude oil price will decrease the exchange rate by 0.2%. The negative value is in accordance with its expected sign and confirms a study by Teh and Ling (2015) who have argued that there will be a negative correlation between crude oil price and Malaysian exchange rate. It somehow explains why as the Brent crude oil prices dropped gradually in late 2014, the Malaysian Ringgit against USD also experienced a depreciation. Therefore, Brent crude oil prices do have the ability to affect the Malaysian exchange rate.

32.5 Conclusion

The foreign exchange rate market, especially those using the flexible exchange rate system, is considered as one of the most complex markets in economics because of the frequent fluctuations in the demand and supply (Froyen 2013). For simplicity, we chose a monetary approach as the method in regressing the Malaysian exchange rate. This study also examined the degree of Brent crude oil price effect on the Malaysian exchange rate as Teh and Ling (2015) claimed in their report. The result showed the final outcome indicates that more than 90% on adjusted R^2 and five out of six independent variables are significant toward the dependent variable. Those variables are domestic unemployment rate, foreign unemployment rate, domestic interest rate, domestic money supply, and Brent crude oil prices. Therefore, the results of this study help us to understand more about Malaysian Ringgit determinants.

The outcome of this study shows that crude oil price has the ability to affect the exchange rate especially for oil-producing countries such as Malaysia. Perhaps, it is because of the petrodollar system which dictates that oil must be globally traded in terms of USD. The study recommends future research to investigate the hypothesis, whereby if there is an alternative to the petrodollar system, then the oil-producing countries' currencies against USD will not be heavily affected as it is today. This finding is useful to the policy makers to devise a policy which is less reliant on crude oil because its price has the ability to affect Malaysian exchange rate. When Malaysian exchange rate is affected, Malaysian trade balance will be affected as well. Ultimately, it will affect Malaysian economy as a whole. Therefore, crude oil price may become the contemporary variable that could actually be the exchange rate determinant for modern times.

References

Aliyu, S. U. (2009). Impact of oil price shock and exchange rate volatility on economic growth in Nigeria: An empirical investigation. Bayero University Kano, Nigeria. Nigeria: Munich Personal RePEc Archive. Retrieved from http://mpra.ub.uni-muenchen.de/16319/

Amano, R. A., & Norden, S. V. (1995). Exchange rates and oil prices. International Department. Ontario: Bank of Canada. Retrieved from http://citeseerx.ist.psu.edu/viewdoc/download?doi=10.1.1.196.9390&rep=rep1&type=pdf

Babatunde, M. A. (2015). Oil price shocks and exchange rate in Nigeria. *International Journal of Energy Sector Management, 9*(1), 2–19. https://doi.org/10.1108/IJESM-12-2013-0001.

Bank Negara Malaysia. (n.d.). *Bank Negara Malaysia Central Bank of Malaysia*. Retrieved 5 1, 2016, from BNM Statistics: http://www.bnm.gov.my/index.php?ch=statistic&pg=stats_exchangerates&lang=en&StartMth=7&StartYr=2015&EndMth=8&EndYr=2015&sess_time=1200&pricetype=Mid&unit=rm

Cao, Y., & Ong, W. (2000). PPP and the monetary model of exchange-rate determination: The case of Singapore. 131-150. Retrieved from http://citeseerx.ist.psu.edu/viewdoc/download?doi=10.1.1.39.223&rep=rep1&type=pdf

Fadli Fizari, A., Nurul Syuhada, B., Nurmadihah, J., Zuraida, M., Norazidah, S., & Kamaruzaman, J. (2011). A vector error correction model (VECM) approach in explaining the relationship between interest rate and inflation towards exchange rate volatility in Malaysia. *World Applied Sciences Journal, 12*(3), 49–56.

Froyen, R. T. (2013). *Macroeconomics theories and policies*. England: Pearson.

Ila, P., Ajay, S., Anmol, S., & Vimal, B. (2011, July). The exchange rate regime in Asia: From crisis to crisis. *International Review of Economics and Finance, 20*(1), 32–43. https://doi.org/10.1016/j.iref.2010.07.004.

Kakkar, V., & Yan, I. (2014). Determinants of real exchange rates: An empirical investigation. Institute for Economies in Transition. Bank of Finland. Retrieved from https://helda.helsinki.fi/bof/bitstream/handle/123456789/8303/172944.pdf?sequence=1

Mansor, H. I. (2007, September). The yen-dollar exchange rate and Malaysian macroeconomic dynamics. *The Developing Economies, 45*(3), 315–338. https://doi.org/10.1111/j.1746-1049.2007.00045.x.

McConnel, C. R., Brue, S. L., Flynn, S. M., & Grant, R. (2012). *Economics: Principles, problems and policies*. New York: McGraw-Hill.

Naseem, N., Hui, B., & Law, S. (2008). Does ringgit misalign? An empirical investigation. *Proceedings of Applied International Business Conference*, (pp. 723–736). Kuala Lumpur. Retrieved from http://www.kantakji.com/media/9343/file807.pdf

Noussair, C. N., Plott, C. R., & Riezman, R. G. (1997). The principles of exchange rate determination in an international finance experiment. *Journal of Political Economy, 105*(4), 822–861.

Rasiah, R. (2011). *Malaysian economy: Unfolding growth and social change*. Kuala Lumpur: Oxford Fajar.

Sajal, G. (2011, May). Examining crude oil price: Exchange rate nexus for India during the period of extreme oil price volatility. *Applied Energy, 88*(5), 1886–1889. https://doi.org/10.1016/j.apenergy.2010.10.043.

Salvatore, D. (2011). *International economics trade and finance*. New York: Wiley.

Teh, K., & Ling, H. S. (2015). *Malaysian ringgit at multi-year low: What is the current state of the economy?* Kuala Lumpur: Bond Pricing Agency Malaysia.

Umezaki, S. (2006, December). *Monetary & exchange rate policy in Malaysia before the Asian crisis*. Chiba: Institute of Developing economies.

Wilson, I. (2009). The monetary approach to exchange rates: A brief review and empirical investigation of debt, deficit, and debt management. *The Journal of Business Inquiry*, 83–99.

Yagci, F. (2001, April). Choice of exchange rate regimes for developing countries. Africa region working paper series(16). The World Bank. Washington, D.C.

Yue, J., Ying, F., Hsien, T., & Yi, M. (2008, November). Spillover effect of US dollar exchange rate on oil prices. *Journal of Policy Modeling, 30*, 973–991. https://doi.org/10.1016/j.jpolmod.2008.02.002.

Chapter 33
The Impact of Exchange Rate Regimes on Economic Growth

Touitou Mohammed, M. Retia, K. Gaidi, and A. Boudeghdegh

Abstract The subject of this paper is articulate about the impact of exchange rate regimes on economic growth, through the identification of the various theoretical and empirical literature on exchange rate regimes and their performance in macro economy generally and economic growth particularly. In order to achieve this purpose, we used an econometrics' study to express the quantitative approach using time-series data (panel data), a sample consisting of about 25 countries during the period from 1980 to 2015, divided into three groups according to the classification of common realistic Reinhart and Rogoff et al. (2004) and Levy-Yeyati and Sturzenegger (European Economic Review, 49(6): 1603–1635, 2005). In order to know what kind of regimes, fixed or flexible or intermediate accompanied with higher economic growth. The economic results obtained indicate the existence of a positive relationship between exchange rate regimes and economic growth and give support to the hypothesis that if the developing countries adopt a fixed exchange rate regime, they will attain a higher growth rate than if they adopt a flexible or an intermediate regime, so the best economic growth rate has been linked to fixed exchange rate regime, followed by flexible regime and the intermediate regime ranked in the third position, and this supports the views of supporters of the "Bipolar View Theory" or "Corner Solution" in the selection of appropriate exchange rate regimes.

T. Mohammed (✉)
University of Algiers 3 "Faculty of Economics and Business", Dely Ibrahim, Algeria
e-mail: touitoutouitou@yahoo.fr

M. Retia
University of Media "Faculty of Economics and Business", Media, Algeria

K. Gaidi
University of Borj.B.A "Faculty of Economics and Business", Bordj Bou Arreridj, Algeria

A. Boudeghdegh
University of Jijel "Faculty of Economics and Business", Jijel, Algeria

N. Tsounis, A. Vlachvei (eds.), *Advances in Panel Data Analysis in Applied Economic Research*, Springer Proceedings in Business and Economics,
https://doi.org/10.1007/978-3-319-70055-7_33

Keywords Exchange rate regime · Classifications of exchange rate regime · Economic growth · Panel data

33.1 Introduction

Exchange rates and the choice of the exchange rate regime retain a centre stage in the post crisis environment especially for emerging economies (Klein and Shambaugh 2010a, b; Rose 2011; Ghosh et al. 2014). In particular, there is a significant divide between policymakers and economists regarding the impact of foreign exchange policies on growth. Whereas laymen and politicians are often intimately convinced that a lower exchange rate will spur growth, economists are generally sceptical that the relative price of two currencies may be a fundamental driver of growth over the long run. For most economists, the exchange rate is an endogenous variable, whose contribution to growth may be difficult to disentangle.

As a matter of fact, the question on whether engineering an exchange rate under valuation helps medium-term growth is still surprisingly unsettled in the literature. Finding an answer to this question would have far-reaching implications for the design of exchange rate regimes and the international monetary system more broadly. The key question of this paper is whether maintaining a relatively weak (nominal and real) exchange rate, such as through some form of sterilized intervention, or intervention coupled with capital controls, or any policy which has the same effect as a net subsidy to the tradable sector, impacts on economic growth in a lasting manner. Unlike Ghosh et al. (2014) and the previous literature therein quoted, we do not focus on crisis episodes in particular, nor on Önancial stability and economic risks. The focus is narrowly on headline per capita real GDP growth, because this is what ultimately national policymakers are mostly concerned about.

Our work is related to a body of literature trying to measure the link between exchange rate undervaluation and growth (see Eichengreen 2008 for a review). In particular, our benchmark is Rodrik (2008) who evaluates this nexus on a database of 188 countries and 11 5-year periods ranging from 1950 to 2004. Based on a measure of undervaluation where real exchange rates are adjusted for the Balassa-Samuelson effect, Rodrik finds that, at least for developing countries, an undervalued real exchange rate predicts stronger growth. The motivation for this finding is that tradable economic activities are special in developing countries as tradables suffer disproportionately from the institutional and market failures that keep countries poor. In Rodrik's view, a sustained real depreciation increases the relative profitability of investing in tradables and acts in a second-best fashion to alleviate the economic costs of these distortions.

33.2 Exchange Rate and Economic Growth

There is no fixed agreement on choosing the most suitable exchange rate to maintain macroeconomic stability. The choice of an appropriate exchange rate system must depend on the particular features of each country. Free-floating exchange rate regimes adopted by developed countries might not suit developing countries whose insurance markets are not so well developed and whose economy is not stable enough to absorb the risks from exchange rate volatility. Therefore, in theory, if the right regime is adopted, it could facilitate better business climate and potentially enhance economic growth in the long run.

Economic theory does not clearly articulate how exchange rate regimes can affect economic growth, and there are a limited number of studies which investigate this relationship. Most studies focus on how exchange rate impact international trade and investments. According to Levy-Yeyati and Sturzenegger (2002), exploration in the topic of exchange rates and growth has induced less research, "probably due to the fact that nominal variables are considered to be unrelated to longer-term growth performance" (p.2). Their research explored the implications for macroeconomic variables of choosing a particular exchange rate arrangement by assessing the impact of exchange rate regimes on inflation, money growth, real interest rates and real output growth. They found that the correlation between exchange rate and output growth existed, even though the influence might not be very clear.

Two interesting trends were found in a study conducted by Huang and Malhotra (2004) in 12 developing Asian countries and 18 advanced European countries over the period of 1976–2001. Firstly, they discovered that the choice of exchange rate regimes did not have significant impact on economic growth in European nations, although more flexible regimes were associated with higher growth. Secondly, developing countries in Asia which adopted managed float seemed to outperform other countries in the area which adopted different regimes. Therefore, their study concluded that exchange rates do impact economic growth but may depend on how developed the economy is. Moreover, Ghosh et al. (1996) found that there was a moderately weak connection between exchange rate regime and growth of output—one measure of economic growth. In his study, countries that maintained pegged exchange rate achieved higher investment yet attained lower productivity compared to countries with floating exchange rates (Ghosh et al. 1996). Overall, per capita growth was slightly lower in countries with fixed exchange rates. A different result presented by De Grauwe and Schnabl (2004) showed that higher output occurred under peg regimes in Central and Eastern Europe because of two main reasons. In addition to the eliminated exchange rate risk that stimulated international trade and international division of labour, fixed exchange rate promoted certainty which would lower interest rate and eventually spur investment and economic growth.

33.3 Methodology and Empirical Results

33.3.1 Methodology

The purpose of this section consists in an attempt of empirical validation on the pretended link between the exchange rate regime and economic growth; differently said, we will try to analyse empirically the impact of the exchange rate regime on economic growth.

On the basis on the assumptions of the neoclassical growth model, the growth rate of each country is supposed to be determined by the natural growth rate of its population on the one hand and by its rate of investment on the other hand. Regarding the level of development represented by a per capita income, it increases when the rate of investment gets up and reduces with the increase in the total population. The initial per capita income level in each country determines negatively the growth rate of both the product then the product per capita.

The structural factors of the initial period combined with the economic policy implemented are also influencing economic growth and other performance indicators.

Indeed, human capital is seen as an internal source of economic growth. According to Lucas (1988), technical progress can be made endogenous by investing in human capital.

Dissimilarities observed in the degrees of education of the labour force of countries in the initial period may procreate identical dissimilarities in the levels of their growth rates.

The most educated populations are alleged to generate the highest growth rates of the total product and even the per capita product. The total population, like its growth rate, will have a negative impact on the rate of growth of the per capita product, given that it will increase faster than the production outside the stable equilibrium footpath.

The econometric method employed in our work is distinguished by the use of panel data. Indeed, this tool allows us to take into account both the individual specificities of the different countries and a temporal dimension, which contributes to a very significant increase in the size of the sample.

Panel data econometrics appears to be a more appropriate research pathway in the empirical estimation of economic growth factors.

Our sample is based on a panel econometric analysis of a sample of 25 countries over the period 1980 to 2015.As a first step, we performed a block regression in OLS of our sample, but given the particular nature of the panel data, this technique is biased even though the estimates are consistent, as a result the estimation by OLS in an instant cross-sectional regression is compatible only insofar as to the extent that the individual effects are not correlated with the explanatory variables. In order to limit this bias, we performed a fixed effect regression, using the generalized quasi-least square method. A brief reminder on the panel data is necessary. Indeed, the panel data allow us to follow an individual i ($i = 1$ to N) over a period T ($t = 1$ to

T); the panel data econometrics thus appears the best way to take into account the phenomena economic growth because it provides a dynamic information for a large number of countries.

33.3.2 Model and Specification of Variables

The basic specification of our model is as follows:

$$\mathrm{GR}_t = \alpha_i + \eta_t + V_{i,t}\beta + X_{i,t}\delta + \xi_{i,t}$$

where:

GR_t is the growth rate of real GDP per capita in country *i* in period *t*.
α_i is the own effect to country *i*; this effect aims to capture the impact of the determinants of the country's growth rate other than the explanatory variables. It also represents unobservable factors and shows that these variables depend on the country and not the period.
Therefore, the own effect can be either fixed or random:

- Fixed own effect: That is to say a constant which varies depending on the country.
- Random own effect: That is to say a random variable drawn from a common distribution of mean α and variance σ.

η_t: It is the dummy variable of time; this variable takes into account the impact of shocks on economic growth.

Similarly, this variable is the variable that interests us the most.

In order to determine the impact of the exchange rate regime on economic growth, variables, fixed, flexible and intermediate, are dummy variables chosen as follows:

{Fixed = 1 If the country adopts a fixed exchange rate regime

=0 If not

{Flexible = 1 If the country adopts a flexible exchange rate regime

=0 If not

{Intermediate = 1 If the country adopts an intermediate exchange rate regime

=0 If not

$V_{i,t}$: It is a line vector of the determinants of economic growth defined at the beginning of period t.
$X_{i,t}$: It is a line vector of the determinants of economic growth defined by averages over the period.

$\xi_{i,t}$: It is a term of error, and it is assumed that these $\xi_{i,t}$are independent of one another. That is to say there is an absence of autocorrelation and there is a homoscedasticity and it is also assumed that the sum of these$\xi_{i,t}$ is zero.

The variables are defined by averages established over 5-year intervals, as it is commonly accepted that such a period is appropriately long to avoid the effects of economic cycles but is short enough to account for significant changes in a country given.

But, there are two variables that are defined at the beginning of each period and thus represent the starting conditions for a model of economic growth: the first is per capita income, and the second variable is a measure of the stock of human capital.

In this section, we seek to determine if the type of exchange rate regime effects on the economic growth.

The expected sign of coefficients associated with exchange rate regimes is, however, indeterminate because it is difficult to establish a priori whether economic growth is favoured by a fixed, flexible or intermediate exchange rate regime.

33.3.2.1 Dependent Variable

Growth rate of real GDP per capita, average established over 5 years (based on real GDP per capita data extracts from CD-ROM World Development Indicators WDI 2007 of the World Bank).

33.3.2.2 Explanatory Variables

- Real GDP per capita at the beginning of each period, average established over 5 years (calculated from real GDP data extracts from CD-ROM World Development Indicators WDI 2007 of the World Bank)
- Average number of years of secondary schooling of the population aged of at least 25 years at the beginning of each 5-year period (Barro and Lee (1996) data on educational attainment)
- Ratio of real government expenditure to GDP, average established over 5 years (based on actual public sector consumption and real GDP data extracts from CD-ROM World Development Indicators WDI 2007 of the World Bank)
- Ratio of the sum of real exports and imports to real GDP, average established over 5 years (based on export, imports data and real GDP extracts from CD-ROM World Development Indicators WDI 2007 of the World Bank)
- Ratio of gross private capital flows to GDP, average established over 5 years (data extracted from CD-ROM World Development Indicators WDI 2007 of the World Bank)
- Ratio of money and quasi money (M2) to GDP, average established over 5 years (data extracted from CD-ROM World Development Indicators WDI 2007 of the World Bank)

- Ratio of credit granted to the Private Sector/GDP, average established over 5 years (data extracted from CD-ROM World Development Indicators WDI 2007 of the World Bank)
- Ratio of real investment expenditure to real GDP, average established over 5 years (based on real investment expenditure data to real GDP extracted from CD-ROM World Development Indicators WDI 2007 of the World Bank)
- Dummy variable relating to the fixed exchange rate regime
- Dummy variable relating to the flexible exchange rate regime
- Dummy variable relating to the intermediate exchange rate regime

33.3.3 Result

Tables 33.1, 33.2 and 33.3 present the results of the regressions used to test the relationship between the exchange rate regime and economic growth. As indicated in these tables, most of the coefficients of the explanatory variables other than the relative variables to exchange regime (fixed, flexible, intermediate) are statistically significant and the sign predicted by the theory.

Indeed, the coefficient of the initial real GDP per capita is negative, while the coefficients relating to the average number of years of schooling, the openness to international trade, the gross flows of private capital, money and quasi money M2 and of investment in the private sector are positive.

In this table, it is found that the coefficient of the dummy variable relating to the fixed exchange rate regime is positive and statistically significant at the

Table 33.1 Results of estimates (total sample) (dependent variable: growth rate of real GDP per capita—estimates based on panel econometric data covering the period 1980–2015, average established over 5 years)

Classification of exchange rate regime	Regression
Real GDP per initial capita	−4.75290***
Initial average number of the years of schooling	0.1563***
Real government spending/GDP	−0.18951*
(Exports + real imports)/GDP	0.030963**
Gross private capital flows/GDP	0.71867**
Money and quasi money M2	0.059728**
Credit granted to the private sector/GDP	−0.50380
Investment to private sector/GDP	0.04163
Fixed exchange regime	0.018016***
Test of Sargan (*p*-value)	0.6936
Second-order correlation test	0.5491

Note: (***), (**), (*) indicate the statistical significance thresholds of the order of 1%, 5% and 10%, respectively

Table 33.2 Results of estimates (total sample) (dependent variable: growth rate of real GDP per capita—estimates based on panel data covering the period 1980–2015, average established over 5 years)

Classification of exchange rate regime	Regression
Real GDP per initial capita	−4.51284***
Initial average number of the years of schooling	0.1522***
Real government spending/GDP	−0.183912***
(Exports + real imports)/GDP	0.31534**
Gross private capital flows/GDP	0.71648**
Money and quasi money M2	0.582647
Credit granted to the private sector/GDP	0.21632
Investment to private sector/GDP	0.04625
Flexible exchange regime	0.0794351
Test of Sargan (p-value)	0.9701
Second-order correlation test	0.5302

Note: (***), (**) indicate the statistical significance thresholds of the order of 1%, 5% and 10%, respectively

Table 33.3 Results of estimates (total sample) (dependent variable: growth rate of real GDP per capita—estimates based on panel data covering the period 1980–2015, average established over 5 years)

Classification of exchange rate regime	Regression
Real GDP per initial capita	−5.3721 ***
Initial average number of the years of schooling	0.1532***
Real government spending/GDP	−0.20138***
(Exports + real imports)/GDP	0.25032*
Gross private capital flows/GDP	0.64921 **
Money and quasi money M2	0.624e10**
Credit granted to the private sector/GDP	0.26015
Investment to private sector/GDP	0.0398
Intermediate exchange regime	−0.013183**
Test of Sargan (p-value)	0.751385
Second-order correlation test	0.630217

Note: (***), (**), (*) indicate the statistical significance thresholds of the order of 1%, 5% and 10%, respectively

1% threshold. This result therefore supports our hypothesis that the exchange rate regime has a positive influence on economic growth.

The coefficient of the public expenditure variable is negative and statistically significant at the 10% threshold. The coefficients representing the gross flows of capital and the money and quasi money are positive and significant at the 5% threshold. On the other hand, the coefficients representing investment and financial development are not statistically significant. This may seem surprising if we take into account the results of the main empirical work on the issue. However, in a study of data defined by average established over 4 years covering 138 countries for the period 1965 to 1995, Easterly (2001) calls into questions the general perception according to which a greater accumulation dampens economic growth.

Whence and after the results of this table, it can be concluded that the fixed exchange rate regime is positively linked to economic growth. In this framework, Aloui and Sassi (2005) show in a study of 53 countries for the period from 1973 to 1998, and based on two classification methods, one is official and the other is based on the hybrid mechanical rule, that the fixed exchange rate regime is positively linked to economic growth, while all other exchange rate regimes have no clear effect on economic growth. Similarly, Ghosh et al. (1995) argue that a fixed exchange rate regime is associated with lower inflation and higher investment, and therefore with higher growth, due to the reduction in costs caused by the absence of uncertainty. Moreover, Frankel (1997) and Rose (2000) show that fixed exchange rates, precisely the monetary unions, favour the growth of international trade because they lead to a reduction in uncertainties and to the variability of exchange rates. On the contrary, Obstfeld and Rogoff (1995) show that fixed exchange rate regimes are likely to survive given the increasing integration of financial markets.

Table 33.2 shows that the coefficient of the dummy variable for the flexible exchange rate regime is not statistically significant.

The coefficient of the public expenditure variable is negative and statistically significant at the 1% threshold. The coefficient representing gross capital flows is positive and significant at the 5% threshold. Contrariwise, the coefficients representing investment, money and quasi- money and financial development are not statistically significant.

This result therefore supports that the flexible exchange rate regime has no clear effect on economic growth. In this framework, Calvo and Reinhart (2002) argue that in flexible exchange rate regimes, exchange rate shocks are more numerous, which can hamper economic growth. On the contrary, Bailliu et al. (2001a, b) consider that a flexible exchange rate regime can promote economic growth by allowing an economy characterized by nominal price and wage rigidity to cushion economic shocks and adjustments more easily, grace to fluctuations in the exchange rate.

Table 33.3 indicates that the coefficient of the dummy variable relating to the intermediate exchange rate regime is negative and statistically significant at the 5% threshold. The coefficient of the public expenditure variable is negative and statistically significant at the 1% threshold. The coefficients representing the gross flows of capital and the money and quasi money are positive and significant at the 5% threshold. On the other hand, the coefficients representing investment and financial development are not statistically significant. Hence, it can be concluded that there is a relationship between intermediate exchange rate regime and economic growth; in other words, the intermediate exchange regime reduces economic growth. The same result was found by Aloui and Sassi (2005) who showed that the intermediate exchange regime without nominal anchor reduces economic growth. Moreover, Obstfeld and Rogoff (1995) consider that intermediate exchange rate regimes are rather a source of instability and speculative attack. On the other hand,

Table 33.4 Results of estimates (total sample) (dependent variable: growth rate of real GDP per capita—estimates based on panel data covering the period 1980–2015, average established over 5 years)

Classification of exchange rate regime	1	2	3
Real GDP per initial capita	−5.20134***	−5.10945***	−5.19835***
Initial average number of the years of schooling	0.13185***	0.12062***	0.11758***
Real government spending/GDP	−0.21836 **	−0.21003***	−0.19738***
(Exports + real imports)/GDP	0.27938 *	0.26829*	0.26012*
Gross private capital flows/GDP	0.64710 **	0.63810**	0.63810**
Money and quasi money M2	0.65310**	0.063910**	0.063510**
Credit granted to the private sector/GDP	−0.05511	−0.056411	−0.03311
Investment to private sector/GDP	0.0225442	0.010009	−0.092910
Fixed exchange regime	0.01860 **	0.011508	
Flexible exchange regime	0.011908*		−0.097210
Intermediate exchange regime		−0.065709	−0.013408**
Test of Sargan (p-value)	0.7124	0.7173	0.7222
Second-order correlation test	0.5700	0.5449	0.5524

Note: (***), (**), (*) indicate the statistical significance thresholds of the order of 1%, 5% and 10%, respectively

Frankel (1999) has shown the importance and the capacity of intermediate exchange rate regimes to achieve the best performances, especially in terms of economic growth.

We estimate regressions in the following tables, combining fixed and flexible exchange rates, fixed and intermediate exchange rates and, finally, intermediate and flexible exchange rates.

Table 33.4 and according to regression 1 show that the coefficients of the dummy variables relating to fixed exchange rate regime and flexible exchange rate regime are both positive and statistically significant; the first is statistically significant at the 1% threshold, and the second is significant at the 10% threshold, which leads us to conclude that there is a positive relationship between the exchange rate regime and economic growth.

In regression 2, it is found that the fixed and intermediate exchange rate regimes are not significant; the first is positive, and the second is negative; that is to say, there is no significant relationship with these exchange rate regimes and economic growth, whereas in the third regression, it found that the intermediate exchange rate regime is significant at the 5% threshold and negative sign, while there is no clear link between flexible exchange rate regime and economic growth.

The regressions of Table 33.5 show that the coefficients of the dummy variables relating to the fixed exchange rate regime and the flexible exchange rate regime are positive and statistically significant; the first is significant at the 1% threshold, and the second is significant at the 5%. On the other hand, the coefficient of the dummy variable relating to the intermediate exchange rate regime is not statistically significant, from which we can conclude is according to all these regressions that

Table 33.5 Results of estimates (total sample) (dependent variable: growth rate of real GDP per capita—estimates based on panel econometric data covering the period 1980–2015, average established over 5 years)

Classification of exchange rate regime	Regression
Real GDP per initial capita	−4.8136***
Initial average number of the years of schooling	0.127482***
Real government spending/GDP	−0.21634***
(Exports + real imports)/GDP	0.33915**
Gross private capital flows/GDP	0.63975*
Money and quasi money M2	0.061948
Credit granted to the private sector/GDP	−0.068673
Investment to private sector/GDP	−0.142365
Fixed exchange regime	0.038963***
Flexible exchange regime	0.032037**
Intermediate exchange regime	0.022175
Test of Sargan (p-value)	0.7372
Second-order correlation test	0.6683

Note: (***), (**), (*) indicate the statistical significance thresholds of the order of 1%, 5% and 10%, respectively

fixed and flexible exchange rate regimes have a positive effect on economic growth while the intermediate exchange rate regime has no significant link with economic growth.

The results obtained throughout this work show the existence of a positive relationship between the exchange rate regime and economic growth. These results suggest that these countries will have an interest in questioning economically to circumvent the risks involved by a strong commercial opening, since this opening can generate spillovers due to unfavourable exogenous shocks, especially when the exchange rate is rather rigid. This is due to the low degree of flexibility of the regimes adapted by these countries. Similarly, this result that we have obtained confirms the results of Aloui and Sassi (2005) who found that the exchange rate regime with an anchor for the conduct of monetary policy, whether fixed or flexible exchange rate regimes or intermediate exchange rate regimes, exerts a positive influence on economic growth.

On the other hand, this result that we have obtained differs from the results of Mills and Woods (1993) and Levy-Yeyati and Sturzenegger (2002), since their results confirm the idea that there is no significant link between the exchange rate regime and economic growth. However, this idea is not justified by Calvo and Reinhart (2000a) who target their studies on a sample of developing countries.

However, Frankel (1999) has demonstrated the importance and capacity of intermediate exchange rate regimes for achieving the best performance especially for economic growth. Other authors such as Obstfeld and Rogoff (1995) and Eichengreen (1999) emphasize on the shortcomings and limitations of these intermediate exchange rate regimes. They have shown that these schemes have lower probabilities of survival in a world of integrated capital markets.

Finally, it can be deduced that this result which we have obtained differs in some of the studies based on the official typology, and the hybrid mechanical rule shows the importance of having an adequate system of classification of exchange rate regimes.

33.4 Conclusion

This paper aims to empirically validate the existence of an empirical link between exchange rate regimes and economic growth, using panel data econometrics, and a sample that consists of 25 countries over the period 1980–2015 and based on the classification method of Levy-Yeyati and Sturzenegger (2002).

Our own empirical research has certainly succeeded in establishing a positive and robust relationship between the exchange rate regime and economic growth, so it has been found that the fixed exchange rate regime has a positive influence on economic growth for the whole sample and for developing countries; on the other hand, the results found for the developed countries show that these countries have a greater interest in adopting a flexible exchange rate regime.

The answer remains mixed, as it is not yet clear that in the long term, the impact would not be negative. Finally, we can say that our empirical work does not answer all the questions raised by the theme of the interrelations between the exchange rate regime and economic growth, but nevertheless provides an interesting basis for reflection.

References

Aloui, C., & Sassi, H. (2005). Régime de change et croissance économique: Une investigation empirique. *Economie Internationale, 104*, 97–134.

Bailliu, J., Lafrance, R., & Perrault, J. F. (2001a). Régime de change et croissance économique dans les marchés émergents, Inc : Les Taux de Change Flottans: Une Nouvelle Analyse, *Acte d'un Colloque tenu à la Banque Centrale du Canada, Novembre 2000. Ottawa, Banque du Canada*. pp. 347–377.

Bailliu, J., Lafrance, R., Perrault, J. F. (2001b). Exchange rate regime and economic growth in emerging markets, In revising the case for Flexible Exchange Rates, *Proceedings of a conference held by the bank of Canada* (pp. 317–45).

Barro, R. J., & Lee, J. (1996). *International data on educational attainment: Updates and implications*. CID Working Paper 42.

Calvo, A. G., & Reinhart, C. (2000a). *Fixing for your life*. NBER Working Paper No. 8006.

Calvo, G., & Reinhart, C. (2000b). *Fear of floating*. www.puaf.umd.edu/papers/reinhart/fearrev.pdf.

Calvo, G. A., & Reinhart, C. M. (2002). Fear of floating. *Quarterly Journal of Economics, 117*(2), 379–408.

De Grauwe, P., & Schnabl, G. (2004). Exchange rates regimes and macroeconomic stability in central and Eastern Europe. *CESifo Working Paper, 1182*, 1–34.

Easterly, W. (2001). *The elusive quest for growth: Economists adventures and misadventures in the tropics*. Cambridge, MA: The MIT Press.

Eichengreen, B. (1999). Kicking from the habit: Moving from pegged ratesto greater exchange rate flexibility. *The Economic Journal, 109*, 1–14.

Eichengreen, B. (2008). *The real exchange rate and economic growth*. WorldBank PREM Network, Commission on Growth and Development Working Paper No.4.

Frankel, J. A. (1997). *Regional trading blocs in the world economic system*. Washington, D.C: Institute for International Economics.

Frankel, J. (1999). *No single exchange rate regime is right for all countries or at all times. Essays in international finance No. 215. Graham Lecture*. Princeton: Princeton University Press.

Ghosh, A. R., Gulde, A.-M., Ostry, J. D. & Wolf, H. C. (1995). *Does the nominal exchange rate regime matter*? IMF WP/95/121.

Ghosh, A. R., Gulde, A.-M., Ostry, J. D., & Wolf, H. (1996). *Does the exchange rate regime matter for inflation and growth?* Washington, DC: IMF.

Ghosh, A. R., Ostry, J. D., & Qureshi, M. S. (2014). Exchange rate management and crisis susceptibility: A reassessment. *IMF Working Paper Series, WP, 14*(11), 1.

Huang, H., & Malhotra, P. (2004). *Exchange rate regimes and economic growth*. Washington: International Monetary Fund.

Klein, M. W., & Shambaugh, J. C. (2010a). *Exchange rate regimes in the modern era*. Cambridge, MA: The MIT Press.

Klein, M. W., & Shambaugh, J. C. (2010b). *Exchange rate regimes in the modern era (with Michael Klein)*. Cambridge, MA: MIT Press.

Levy-Yeyati, E., & Sturzenegger, F. (2002). *Classifying exchange rate regimes: Deeds versus words*. Tella: Universidad Torcuato Di.

Levy-Yeyati, E., & Sturzenegger, F. (2005). Classifying exchange rate regimes : Deeds vs. words. *European Economic Review, 49*(6), 1603–1635.

Lucas, R. (1988). On the mechanics of economic development. *Journal of Monetary Economics, 22*, 30–42.

Mills, T., & Woods, G. E. (1993). Does the exchange rate regime affect the economy? Federally Reserve Bank of ST, Lounis review.

Obstfeld, M., & Rogoff, K. (1995). The mirage of fixed exchange rates. *Journal of Economic Perspectives, 9*(4), 73–96.

Rodrik, D. (2008). The real exchange rate and economic growth. In *Brookings papers on economic activity* (Vol. 2, pp. 365–412).

Rogoff, K., Hussain, M., Mody, A., Brooks, R., & Oomes, N. (2004). Evolution and performance of exchange regimes. In M. Feldstein (Ed.), *International capital flows* (pp. 441–453). Chicago, IL: University of Chicago Press.

Rose, A. K. (2000). One money, one market: The effect of common currencies on trade. *Economic Policy, 30*, 7–33.

Rose, A. K. (2011). Exchange rate regimes in the modern era: Fixed, floating and flaky. *Journal of Economic Literature, 49*(3), 652–672.

World Development Indicators WDI 2007 of the World Bank. (2007). February 1, 2007.

Chapter 34
Utilization the Process BIM – Building Information Modeling in Facility Management

Dominika Matusova and Viera Bartošová

Abstract Building Information Modeling (BIM) is increasingly getting the attention of organizations involved in architecture, engineering, and construction (AEC), as well as the owners and operators of buildings (facility managers and real estate managers). In this context, BIM is a digital model representing physical, technical, and functional characteristics of a building. BIM is a shared data and knowledge platform for all stakeholders involved and provides a basis for decision-making during the entire life cycle of a building: design, build, maintain, operate, and demolish. This article emphasizes that the big advantage is, in the virtual model of the building, all the necessary information centralized in one place, i.e., technical data sheets, assessments, and statements are simply elements of the profit model. This information is very important for facility management (FM) which must have all the information available for a quality and efficient operation of the building.

Keywords Facility management · Modeling · BIM

34.1 Introduction to Facility Management

Facility management focuses on the maintenance and restoration of the construction work, ensures maintenance of the physical condition of the facility, and aims to prolong the benefit from the property.

Benefit from the property is prolonged by targeted interventions in the form of restoration and reconstruction of structural components. In the facility, management plays the important role – the process BIM. Matsubayashi and Watanabe (2016) find on the development of a method of forecasting the time between problems of building components that integrates BIM data and building repair records.

D. Matusova (✉) · V. Bartošová
University of Zilina, Faculty of Operation and Economics of Transport and Communications, Department of Economics, Zilina, Slovak Republic
e-mail: dominika.matusova@fpedas.uniza.sk; viera.bartosova@fpedas.uniza.sk

N. Tsounis, A. Vlachvei (eds.), *Advances in Panel Data Analysis in Applied Economic Research*, Springer Proceedings in Business and Economics,
https://doi.org/10.1007/978-3-319-70055-7_34

34.2 Facility Management and Building Information Modeling

34.2.1 The Aspects of Facility Management

The role of facility management at a time of instability we can explain the background of the two categories of economic events. An unquestionable truth – business strategy, management function, and development trends.

Basic aspects of facility management are:

- FM is on the management of support processes (ancillary activities).
- FM is the merger process (secondary activities are centrally controlled FM).
- FM uniformly manages various supported activities (mainly services).
- FM is a measure of the quality of the contribution of the main process (and staff).
- The boundaries between the main and support processes set by management of the company and the time change.
- FM is not about revolution, but it is a continuous improving service.
- FM brings professionalism to supported processes.

According to Fig. 34.1, it is seen that facility management has various types of support services, and Building Information Modeling is included to property services.

Fig. 34.1 Facility management and support services

34.3 BIM

The term BIM – Building Information Modeling – comes from the United States. Every term and concept that is relatively new, like BIM, does not have any established definition, being still under evolution. Therefore, they are different variants of definitions in different professional sources. Consequently, what is BIM?

- According to Wikipedia is BIM: "Building Information Modeling is a process involving the generation and management of digital representations of physical and functional characteristics of a facility. The resulting building information models become shared knowledge resources to support decision-making about a facility from earliest conceptual stages, through design and construction, through its operational life and eventual demolition."

According to Berzakova and Bartošová (2016), all the businesses have managers who manage different activities or operations. These operations are usually divided into two basic groups, core activities and secondary activities that support the core ones. Figure 34.2 shows Building Information Management Framework (BIMF).

These institutions characterizes the term BIM this expressions:

- Royal Institution of Chartered Surveyors (RICS) – "BIM provides a common environment for all information defining a building, facility or asset, together with its common parts and activities. This includes building shape, design and construction time, costs, physical performance, logistics and more. More importantly, the information relates to the intended objects (components) and processes, rather than relating to the appearance and presentation of documents and drawings."
- Associated General Contractors (AGC) – as a resulting model, BIM is a system rich in data, object-oriented, intelligent, and parametric digital representation of an object, from which you can get and analyze the opinions and data appropriate to the needs of different users to obtain information that can be used for taking decisions and improve the equipment delivery process.

Authors Ponisciakova et al. (2015) inform that constant change is typical not only for social space but also for economic structure and business as well. Building Information Modeling can be used for the following main purposes:

- *Forensic analysis* – a building information model can be easily adapted to illustrate graphically potential failures, defects, and evacuation plans.
- *Facility management* – management can use BIM for spatial planning, reconstructions, and maintenance.
- *Visualization* – 3D representations are easy to generate.
- *Manufacturing/commercial drawings* – it is easy to create drawings for various building systems.

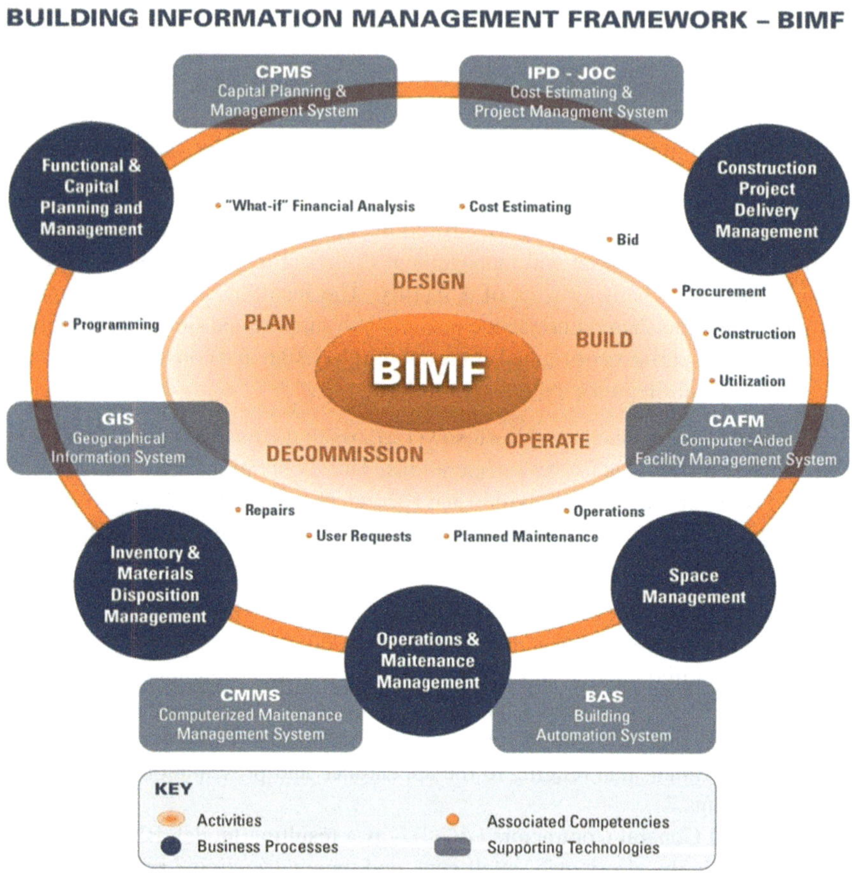

Fig. 34.2 Framework for Building Information Modeling

- *Estimated costs* – BIM software has integrated cost estimation functions. Significant quantities are automatically extracted and modified when there are changes in the model.
- *Construction schedule* – BIM can be effectively used to create material orders, production and supplies for a building, and its structural elements.
- *Conflicts and collision detection* – as models are created with a scale, in 3D space, BIM enables to visually check all major systems for collisions.

Advantages of BIM:

- *Capture reality* – the wealth of information that's easily accessible about project sites has expanded greatly with better mapping tools and images of Earth.
- *Waste not, want not* – with a shared model, there's less need for rework and duplication of drawings for the different requirements building disciplines.

- *Maintain control* – the digital model-based workflow involves such aids as autosave and connections to project history so that users can be certain they have captured their time spent working on the model.
- *Improve collaboration* – sharing and collaborating with models are easier than with drawing sets, as there are a lot of functions that are possible only through a digital workflow.
- *Simulate and visualize* – there are an increasing number of simulation tools that allow designers to visualize such things as the sunlight during different seasons or to quantify or the calculation of building energy performance.
- *Resolve conflict* – the BIM toolset helps automate clash detection of elements such as electrical conduit or ductwork that runs into a beam.
- *Sequence your steps* – with a model and an accurate set of sub-models for each phase during construction, the next step is a coordinated sequencing of steps, materials, and crews for a more efficient construction process.
- *Dive into detail* – the model is a great end point for a lot of knowledge transfer, but there's also a need to share a traditional plan, section, and elevation as well as other reports with your project team.
- *Present perfectly* – with all of the design completed on a capture and alteration of existing reality, the model is the ultimate communication tool to convey the project scope, steps, and outcome.
- *Take it with you* – with the added benefit of a model that's tied to a database, you have a great deal of intelligence at your fingertips.

According to Fig. 34.3, we can see different phases, such as documentation, fabrication, construction logistics, construction 4D/5D, operation and maintenance, renovation, conceptual design, detailed design, and analysis.

Authors Ponisciakova and Gogolova (2015) write that – in fact – both cognitive and conative skills affect the process of classifying people into job positions. As a result, senior managerial work is easier, and its self-understanding and development are ensured. Authors Janoskova and Kral (2016) emphasize that acceptance of risk of innovations is one of the key assumptions of innovative organization. Ivankova (2013) informs about different approaches to the strategic management, such as industry-based approach, resource-based approach, and relational approach. Gourlis and Kovacic (2015) inform that BIM (Building Information Modelling), as an emerging technology, bears promise to support processes integration thus enabling life cycle management of buildings. BIM model serves as a joint knowledge database where data transfer between various models is possible, thereby enabling follow-up studies, such as cost, thermal, and structural analysis. Specified benefits are proved by Stanford University Center's research, for instance, which has found out the following benefits on the bases of 32 large projects using BIM:

- A cost estimate with an accuracy of 3%
- Saving of up to 10% of the contract value through collision detection
- Forty percent elimination of not calculated changes
- A reduction of up to 80% in the time required for creating a cost estimate

Fig. 34.3 BIM and his stages

Acknowledgments This research was financially supported by the 1/0870/16 application of facility management in the management of transport companies in Slovakia, led by Assoc. Prof. Ing. Viera Bartošová, PhD., from the workplace, Faculty of Operation and Economics of Transport and Communications, University of Zilina.

Appendix

BIM models not only contain architectural data, but the full depth of the building information including data related to the different engineering disciplines such as the load-bearing structures, all the ducts and pipes of the different building systems, and even sustainability information as well with which all the characteristics of a building can easily be simulated well in advance. Data management – BIM contains information that is not visually represented at all. Scheduling information, for instance, clarifies the necessary manpower, coordination, and anything that might affect the outcome of the project schedule. Cost is also part of BIM that allows us to see what the budget or estimated cost of a project might be at any given point in the time during the project. Building operation is needless to say that all these data put in a BIM model is not only useful during the design and construction phase of a building project but can be used throughout the entire building life cycle helping to reduce the operation and management cost of buildings which is at least magnitude more than the entire cost of construction. Simply, BIM proves to be an innovative way how to manage projects. Kim et al. (2016) inform that – to rescue peoples in the disaster site in time – information acquisition of the current feature of collapsed buildings and terrain is quite important for disaster site rescue manager. Pasini et al. (2016) find that technologies for the acquisition, storage, and mining of big data are increasingly affecting the architecture, engineering, and construction (AEC) industry, modifying the way buildings are conceived and developed. Indeed, they will be no longer designed and managed only as financial products but also as service providers to support the needs of the occupants. Nical and Wodynski (2016) inform that BIM has been widely adopted by the construction sector, though facility management (FM) is still based on a variety of disparate FM systems. The operational phase requires comprehensive set of well-structured information regarding the building asset. Liao and Hsieh (2016) inform about labor safety and sanitation (LSS) management fees that have been troubling construction cost estimation for a long time. Due to the difficulties of estimating LSS facility costs, the present study aims to use a decision support system that's integrating BIM. Corejova and Al Kassiri (2016) write that all countries have to increase the outputs based on the knowledge, innovation, and creativity.

References

Berzakova, V., & Bartošová, V. (2016). The Basic Framework of Facility Management. In *ICMIBI International Conference on Applied Social Science and Business (ICMIBI-ASSB 2016)* (Vol. 65, pp. 3–8). Windsor.

Corejova, T., & Al Kassiri, M. (2016). Knowledge Triangle, Innovation Performance and Global Value Chain. In *16th International Scientific Conference on Globalization and its Socio-Economic Consequences* (pp. 329–336). Rajecke Teplice.

Gourlis, G., & Kovacic, I. (2015). Building information modelling for analysis of energy efficient industrial buildings – A case study. In *10th Conference on Sustainable Development of Energy, Water and Environment Systems* (Vol. 68, pp. 953–963). Dubrovnik.

Ivankova, K. (2013). Relačný prístup k strategickému manažmentu a jeho aplikácia. In *Ekonomicko-manažérske spektrum (EMS)*. – ISSN 1337–0839. – Roč. 2, č. 7 (2013), s (pp. 14–20).

Janoskova, K., & Kral, P. (2016). Acceptance of Risk of Innovations as an Important Assumption of Innovative Organization. In *International Conference on Information, Communication and Social Sciences (ISSGBM-ICS 2016)* (Vol. 66, pp. 3–7). Dubai.

Kim, C., Moon, H., & Lee, W. (2016). Data Management framework of Drone-Based 3D Model Reconstruction of Disaster Site. In *23rd Congress of the International-Society-for-Photogrammetry-and-Remote-Sensing* (Vol. 41, pp. 31–33). Prague.

Liao, Mu-Chun, & Hsieh, Ting-Ya. (2016). A Study on labor Safety and Sanitation Feasibility of BIM-Based Costing in Scaffolds. In *2nd International Conference on Humanity and Social Science* (pp. 177–181). Phuket.

Matsubayashi, M., & Watanabe, S. (2016). Forecasting Time between Problems of Building Components by Using BIM. In *International Conference on Computer Aided Architectural Design* (pp. 87–92). Budapest.

Nical, Aleksander K., & Wodynski, W. (2016). Enhancing Facility Management through BIM 6D. In *5th Creative Construction Conference* (Vol. 164, pp. 299–306). Budapest.

Pasini, D., et al. (2016). Exploiting Internet of Things and Building Information Modeling Framework for Management of Cognitive Buildings. In *2nd IEEE International Smart Cities Conference* (pp. 478–483). Trento.

Ponisciakova, O., & Gogolova, M. (2015). Exploiting the Potential and Possibilities of Conscious Human Resource Management in the Process of Globalization. In *15th International Scientific Conference on Globalization and its Socio-Economic Consequences* (pp. 597–603). Rajecke Teplice.

Ponisciakova, O., Gogolova, M., & Ivankova, K. (2015). The Use of Accounting Information System for the Management of Business Costs. In *4th World Conference on Business, Economics and Management* (Vol. 26, pp. 418–422). Ephesus.

Chapter 35
Modeling and Forecasting of British Pound/US Dollar Exchange Rate: An Empirical Analysis

Chaido Dritsaki

Abstract The aim of this paper is to develop and examine the characteristics of volatility of exchange rate on British pound/US dollar, using symmetric and asymmetric GARCH(p,q) models. Given that there are ARCH effects on exchange rate returns, we estimated ARCH(q), GARCH(p,q), and EGARCH(p,q) including these effects on mean equation. These models were estimated with maximum likelihood method using the following distributions: normal, t-Student, and generalized error distribution. The log-likelihood function was maximized using Marquardt's algorithm (1963) in order to search for optimal parameters. The results showed that ARIMA(0,0,1)-EGARCH(1,1) model with t-Student distribution is the best in order to describe exchange rate returns and also captures the leverage effect. Finally, for the forecasting of ARIMA(0,0,1)-EGARCH(1,1) model, both the dynamic and static procedures are used. The static procedure provides better results on the forecasting rather than the dynamic.

Keywords Exchange rate · Volatility · GARCH models · Forecasting

35.1 Introduction

Foreign exchange rate is regarded as the value of a currency in relation to another currency. It is one of the basic economic variables that foreign exchange investors, exporters, and governments consider for policymaking. It is well known that exchange rate is under the authority of central banks in a large extent as well as under other financial institutions.

C. Dritsaki (✉)
Department of Accounting and Finance, Western Macedonia University of Applied Sciences, Kozani, Greece
e-mail: dritsaki@teiwm.gr

N. Tsounis, A. Vlachvei (eds.), *Advances in Panel Data Analysis in Applied Economic Research*, Springer Proceedings in Business and Economics,
https://doi.org/10.1007/978-3-319-70055-7_35

During the last decades, the fluctuations of exchange rates have been an important issue on macroeconomic analysis and are of great interest in many scientists after the collapse of the Bretton Woods agreement on stable exchange rates between industrial countries of the twentieth century. The Bretton Woods system was an example of a negotiated monetary order defining monetary relations between the United States, Canada, Australia, Japan, and Western Europe. The obligation of each country was to adopt a monetary policy that maintained the exchange rate of $\pm 1\%$ by connecting its currency with gold. The Bretton Woods agreement created the International Monetary Fund (IMF) and the International Bank for Reconstruction and Development (IBRD).

In 1971, the United States unilaterally converted dollar to gold; thus, the Bretton Woods system came to an end. This activity made the dollar to be a reserve currency, and it was used from many countries. At the same time, other currencies such as British pound were considered as a currency of free fluctuations.

The fluctuations on exchange rates influence the competitiveness of exports and imports and debt payments of countries as well as international investment portfolios. Moreover, the fluctuations of exchange rates have impact on business economic cycles and capital flows, determining trade terms with other countries thus directing the economic life of each country.

During the last decades, there has been an extended discussion as far as the exchange rate volatility is concerned. As a consequence, several models have been developed in order to examine this volatility. The models that are often applied in measuring the instability of exchange rates are ARCH and GARCH models developed by Engle (1982) and Bollerslev (1986) and Taylor (1986), respectively.

This paper tries to develop and examine the characteristics of exchange rate volatility on British pound/US dollar using monthly data from August 1953 until January 2017. The remainder of the paper is organized as follows: Sect. 2 provides a brief literature review. Section 3 presents the analysis of methodology. Section 4 summarizes the data and the descriptive statistics. The empirical results are provided in Sect. 5, and Sect. 6 proposes the forecasting results. Finally, the last section offers the concluding remarks.

35.2 Literature Review

Many scientists on their paper examine the forecasting of exchange rates both on developed and developing countries using various approaches in a fundamental as well as technical level. The ARCH model for the exchange rate was first applied by Hsieh (1988) in order to examine daily data for five exchange rates. The results of his research support the view that if there is not a linear correlation on data but a nonlinear, then the model's form is multiplicative and not additive. So, he concludes that the generalized ARCH (GARCH) model can explain one part of the nonlinearity of exchange rates.

Most scientists paid more attention on bilateral exchange rates such as the paper of Mundaca (1991), Johnston and Scott (2000), Yoon and Lee (2008), Abdalla (2012), and others.

During the last years, many researchers deal with the forecasting of exchange rate volatility both on developed and emerging markets such as Sandoval (2006), Vee et al. (2011), Antonakakis and Darby (2012), Miletić (2015), Epaphra (2017), and others. Specifically, Sandoval (2006) examines the exchange rates of seven countries in Asia and Latin America regarding the US dollar. Using GARCH, GJR-GARCH, and EGARCH, he found that four out of seven exchange rates that follow asymmetric models are included on developed countries. Furthermore, forecasting on symmetric models showed better results than that of asymmetric models.

Vee et al. (2011) studied the forecast of exchange rate volatility of US dollar/Mauritian rupee. For the estimation they used daily data from the period 30 June 2003 until 31 March 2008 and the symmetric GARCH(1,1) model with generalized error distribution (GED) and the t-Student distribution. The results of their paper showed that generalized error distribution (GED) gives better results for exchange rate out-of-sample forecasts.

Antonakakis and Darby (2012) examine daily data from 8 November 1993 until 29 December 2000 for four exchange rates against the US dollar, such as the Botswana pula (BWP), Chilean peso (CLP), Cyprus pound (CYP), and Mauritius rupee (MUR). Applying ARCH, GARCH, EGARCH, IGARCH, FIGARCH, and the HYGARCH models, they conclude that the IGARCH model gives better results for out-of-sample forecast for all the examined exchange rates.

Miletić (2015) on his paper examines the hypothesis which refers that the exchange rate in emerging markets is more sensitive on negative crises than positive ones. In order to study the involved risk, he used daily data of exchange rate for the currencies of Hungary, Romania, Serbia, Great Britain, Japan, and European Union against US dollar as well as the symmetric and nonsymmetric GARCH models. The results of forecast showed that the symmetric models, both on developed and emerging markets (except the rate of Romania), have better return on the exchange rates of all examined currencies.

Finally, Epaphra (2017) on his paper uses nonlinear series for the forecasting of daily data on the exchange rate of Tanzania (TZS/USD) from 4 January 2009 until 27 July 2015. Using the symmetric GARCH model and the asymmetric EGARCH model, he concludes that the symmetric GARCH model gives better results on forecasting, but the asymmetric EGARCH presents leverage effect implying a higher next period conditional variance than negative shocks of the same sign.

35.3 Theoretical Background

Taking into account the papers of Mandelbrot (1963), Fama (1965), and Black (1976), many researchers found that the characteristics of exchange rate returns follow a nonlinear time dependence, while according to Friedman and Vandersteel (1982), the percentage of exchange rate follow a leptokurtic distribution. Moreover, in their papers Friedman and Vandersteel argue that small and big variances on exchange rate returns are clustered during that time and are distributed symmetrically with fat tails. The characteristics of these data follow the normal distribution and are included in an ARCH model, introduced by Engle (1982) or in a GARCH model developed by Bollerslev (1986).

While GARCH models can isolate the excessive kurtosis on returns, they cannot deal with the asymmetry of distribution. To cope with this problem, researchers made modifications on GARCH model, taking into account the distributions' asymmetry. Exponential GARCH (EGARCH) is considered a nonlinear model that deals with asymmetry and is developed by Nelson (1991).

35.3.1 ARCH(Q) Model

Engle (1982) developed the Autoregressive Conditional Heteroscedasticity (ARCH) model for testing the volatility of financial series. The basic ARCH model consists of two equations, a conditional mean equation and a conditional variance equation. Both equations should be estimated simultaneously given that variance is a mean equation. The mean equation estimates the conditional mean of the examined variable. It is important to test if there is an ARCH process on mean equation before estimating the models. In this case, the mean equation can be formed as an autoregressive AR process in combination with other explanatory variables. Thus, before estimating a GARCH models, we have to test for residuals' autocorrelation. The variance equation estimates this process as a typical autoregressive process. Both equations form a system that is estimated together with maximum likelihood method. So, ARCH model is an autoregressive process (AR) and is written as follows:

$$\varepsilon_t = z_t \sigma_t$$

$$\sigma_t^2 = \omega + \sum_{i=1}^{q} \alpha_i \varepsilon_{t-i}^2 \tag{35.1}$$

where z_t is an independently and identically distributed (i.i.d.) process with $E(z_t) = 0$ and $Var(z_t) = 1$. On the above model, we assume that ε_t is not serial correlated and has a zero mean and the conditional variance is σ_t^2. Also, since variance is positive for all t, then these relations must be valid, $\omega > 0$ and $\alpha_i \geq 0$.

ARCH model can describe volatility because the conditional variance of ε_t is an increasing function of ε_{t-1}^2. Furthermore, if ε_{t-1} is large in absolute value, then we expect σ_t^2 and ε_t to give large values too.

35.3.2 GARCH(p,q) Model

Bollerslev (1986) extended the ARCH model in a new one that allows the errors of variance to depend on its own lags as well as lags of the squared errors. In other words, it allows the extension of conditional variance to follow an autoregressive moving average (ARMA) process.

The GARCH model can be expressed as:

$$\sigma_t^2 = \omega + \sum_{i=1}^{q} \alpha_i \varepsilon_{t-i}^2 + \sum_{j=1}^{p} \beta_j \sigma_{t-j}^2. \tag{35.2}$$

We assume that for every $p \geq 0$ and $q > 0$, the parameters are unknown, and since the variance is positive, then the following relations must be positive too $\omega \geq 0$ and $\alpha_i \geq 0$ for every $i = 1, \ldots, q$ and $\beta_j \geq 0$ for $j = 1, \ldots, p$. If the parameters are constrained such that $\sum_{i=1}^{q} \alpha_i + \sum_{j=1}^{p} \beta_j < 1$, they imply a weak stationarity.

35.3.3 EGARCH(p,q) Model

For testing the asymmetry of volatility, various models have been developed. The EGARCH model is regarded as one of these models that captures asymmetric responses of varying variance to shocks and at the same time keeps the variance positive. The EGARCH model developed by Nelson (1991) can be expressed as:

$$\log \sigma_t^2 = \omega + \sum_{i=1}^{p} \alpha_i \left| \frac{\varepsilon_{t-i}}{\sigma_{t-i}} \right| + \sum_{j=1}^{q} \beta_j \log \sigma_{t-j}^2 + \sum_{k=1}^{r} \gamma_k \frac{\varepsilon_{t-k}}{\sigma_{t-k}} \tag{35.3}$$

where σ_t^2 is the conditional variance and ω, α_i, β_j, and γ_k are parameters to be estimated. On parameters ω, α_i, and γ_k, there are no restrictions. However, the parameter β_j should be positive and less than 1 in order to have stationarity. Moreover, γ_k parameter is an indicator of leverage effect meaning asymmetry and must be negative and statistically significant.

35.3.4 Estimation of GARCH Models

The GARCH models consist of two equations. The first one (mean equation) describes the data as a function of other variables adding an error term. The second equation (variance equation) determines the development of error conditional variance from mean equation as a function of the previous conditional variance of lagged error. Given that variance represents the second moment of this procedure, this implies that both equations form a system. In the case that there is an AR(q) or MA(p) process, then mean equation should consist these procedures. So, the mean will be an AR(q) or MA(p) process or an ARMA so the variance will of be the same procedure. In addition, we have to decide about the distribution of the error term according to the series data.

For the estimation of the family of GARCH models, the maximum likelihood method is used. This method enables the rates of return and variance to be jointly estimated. The logarithmic function of maximum likelihood is computed from the conditional densities of the prediction errors and is provided in the following form:

$$L = -\frac{1}{2}\sum_{t=1}^{n}\left[\ln(2\pi) + \ln\left(\sigma_t^2\right) + z_t^2\right] \tag{35.4}$$

where n is the number of observations, σ_t^2 is the conditional variance, $z_t^2 = \frac{\varepsilon_t^2}{\sigma_t^2}$, $\varepsilon_t = r_t - \mu$, and r_t is the rate of return. When there are no regressors (trend or constant), then the mean μ of residuals ε_t is symbolized as r_t. If on GARCH family models there is an AR(q) or MA(p) process, then the mean equation should consist these procedures. These procedures can be used as a filter on series' returns.

35.3.5 Diagnostic Checking of the Model ARCH-GARCH

The diagnostic tests of GARCH family models are based on residuals. We assume that residuals are independently and identically distributed following a normal or standardized t-distribution. Residuals' normality test is employed with Jarque and Bera (1980) test. Ljung and Box (1978) (Q-statistics) statistic for all time lags of autocorrelation is used for the serial correlation test. Also, for the conditional heteroscedasticity test, we use the squared residuals of autocorrelation function.

35.3.6 Forecast Evaluation

GARCH models are used for forecasting the variance of returns. The forecast on these models is computed in the sample as well as out of the sample. The best forecasting value is evaluated from mean square error. In addition, other indices we often use for forecasting returns are the mean absolute error (MAE), the root mean square error (RMSE), the mean absolute percentage error (MAPE), and Theil's inequality index (1967). These indices are computed as follows:

$$\mathrm{MSE} = \frac{1}{T}\sum_{t=1}^{T}\left(r_t^2 - \sigma_t^2\right)^2 \tag{35.5}$$

$$\mathrm{MAE} = \frac{1}{T}\sum_{t=1}^{T}\left|r_t^2 - \sigma_t^2\right| \tag{35.6}$$

$$\mathrm{RMSE} = \sqrt{\frac{1}{T}\sum_{t=1}^{T}\left(r_t^2 - \sigma_t^2\right)^2} \tag{35.7}$$

$$\mathrm{MAPE} = \frac{1}{T}\sum_{t=1}^{T}\left|\frac{r_t^2 - \sigma_t^2}{\sigma_t^2}\right| \tag{35.8}$$

Theil's inequality index is defined as:

$$U = \frac{\sqrt{\frac{1}{T}\sum_{t=1}^{T}\left(r_t^2 - \sigma_t^2\right)^2}}{\sqrt{\frac{1}{T}\sum_{t=1}^{T}\left(r_t^2\right)^2} + \sqrt{\frac{1}{T}\sum_{t=1}^{T}\left(\sigma_t^2\right)^2}} 0 \leq U \leq 1 \tag{35.9}$$

where r_t^2 is used as a substitute for the realized or actual variance, σ_t^2 is the forecasted variance, and T is the number of observations in the simulations (of the sample).

If Theil's inequality index is $U = 0$, then actual values of series are equal with the predicted $\sigma_t^2 = r_t^2$ for all t, so in this case, we can claim that there is a "perfect fit" between actual and predicted data. On the contrary, if $U = 1$, there is no proper forecasting for the examined model.

35.4 Data

The data used on this model of exchange rate return are monthly and refer to the British pound/US dollar exchange rate. The data span is from August 1953 until January 2017, a total of 763 observations. All data come from http://fxtop.com/en/historical-exchange-rates.php. Monthly percentage return of exchange rate is

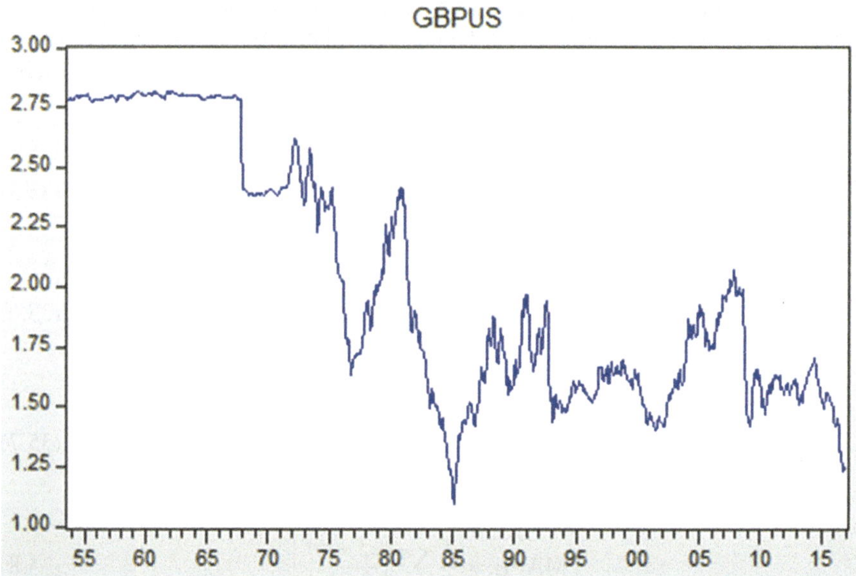

Fig. 35.1 Average monthly values of exchange rates of the British pound/US dollar

the first difference from natural logarithm of exchange rate and is given from the following equation:

$$R_t = 100^* \ln\left(\frac{X_t}{X_{t-1}}\right) = 100^* \left[\ln\left(X_t\right) - \ln\left(X_{t-1}\right)\right] \tag{35.10}$$

where R_t is the monthly percentage return to the exchange rate and X_t is the exchange rate at time t.

The average monthly values of exchange rates and their returns are presented in Figs. 35.1 and 35.2, respectively.

From Fig. 35.1, we can see that average monthly values of the exchange rate of British pound/US dollar present a random walk.

From Fig. 35.2 we can see that average monthly values of the British pound/US dollar exchange rate are steady. Also, the variance seems to be unstable; thus, we conclude that the exchange rate returns show volatility.

Following, Tables 35.1 and 35.2 present the correlograms, and we test if there is autocorrelation on average monthly returns of British pound/US dollar, as well as the ARCH effect, on the correlogram of average square monthly returns.

From the results of Table 35.1, we point out that the Ljung-Box statistic (Q-statistics) for all time lags of autocorrelation function are statistically significant meaning that there is serial correlation on the average monthly returns of the exchange rate British pound/US dollar. Furthermore, partial autocorrelation

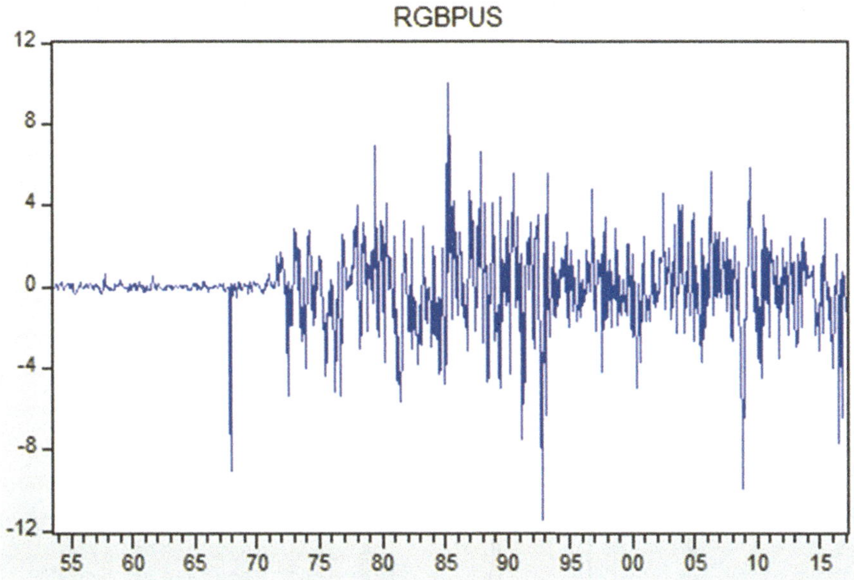

Fig. 35.2 Average monthly values of return of the exchange rate of the British pound/US dollar

coefficients show a long-run dependence among data (time lags of high order). This result, according to Bollerslev (1986), features GARCH models as the most suitable for the data of the British pound/US dollar exchange rate.

The results of Table 35.2 show that Ljung-Box (1978) statistic (Q-statistics) for all time lags of square residuals of autocorrelation function are statistically significant; thus, there is an ARCH effect on the return of British pound/US dollar exchange rate.

Continuing, the descriptive statistics of the return on British pound/US dollar exchange rate are presented.

The results of Table 35.3 show that average monthly returns of the British pound/US dollar exchange rate don't follow the normal distribution. Also, asymmetry's coefficient shows that the distribution of exchange rate returns is left asymmetric (−0.492), is leptokurtic ($k = 6.918$), and has heavy tails (see Fig. 35.3).

Continued, we test the stationarity of the average monthly returns of the British pound/US dollar exchange rate using Dickey-Fuller (1979, 1981) and Phillips-Perron (1998) tests.

The results in Table 35.4 show that the average monthly returns of the British pound/US dollar are stationary in their levels on both used test.

Table 35.1 Correlogram of average monthly returns of the exchange rate British pound/US dollar

Sample: 1953M08 2017M01
Included observations: 761

Autocorrelation	Partial Correlation		AC	PAC	Q-Stat	Prob
		1	0.336	0.336	86.251	0.000
		2	0.028	-0.096	86.832	0.000
		3	0.075	0.110	91.119	0.000
		4	0.034	-0.032	91.984	0.000
		5	-0.039	-0.039	93.168	0.000
		6	-0.039	-0.017	94.340	0.000
		7	-0.068	-0.063	97.919	0.000
		8	-0.014	0.042	98.063	0.000
		9	0.019	0.009	98.348	0.000
		10	-0.011	-0.015	98.444	0.000
		11	0.028	0.046	99.068	0.000
		12	0.051	0.015	101.05	0.000
		13	-0.011	-0.035	101.14	0.000
		14	-0.054	-0.046	103.41	0.000
		15	-0.046	-0.023	105.05	0.000
		16	0.007	0.038	105.08	0.000
		17	-0.006	-0.018	105.11	0.000
		18	0.103	0.144	113.34	0.000
		19	0.061	-0.032	116.26	0.000
		20	-0.007	-0.019	116.30	0.000
		21	0.050	0.050	118.25	0.000
		22	0.072	0.024	122.33	0.000
		23	0.016	0.002	122.55	0.000
		24	-0.053	-0.068	124.72	0.000
		25	-0.030	0.023	125.43	0.000
		26	-0.059	-0.061	128.18	0.000
		27	-0.078	-0.043	132.99	0.000
		28	-0.090	-0.049	139.42	0.000
		29	-0.048	-0.004	141.22	0.000
		30	-0.042	-0.044	142.64	0.000
		31	-0.022	0.011	143.03	0.000
		32	-0.015	-0.005	143.20	0.000
		33	0.008	0.020	143.25	0.000
		34	0.029	-0.002	143.92	0.000
		35	0.057	0.062	146.52	0.000
		36	-0.021	-0.072	146.86	0.000

After detecting stationarity, we determine the form of the ARMA(p,q) from the correlogram of Table 35.1. Parameters p and q can be defined from partial autocorrelation coefficients and autocorrelation coefficients, respectively, compared to the critical value $\pm\frac{2}{\sqrt{n}} = \pm\frac{2}{\sqrt{761}} = \pm 0.072$. Therefore, we can see that p value is between $0 \leq p \leq 3$ and q value is between $0 \leq q \leq 1$.

Table 35.2 Correlogram of average square monthly return of British pound/US dollar exchange rate

Sample: 1953M08 2017M01
Included observations: 761

Autocorrelation	Partial Correlation		AC	PAC	Q-Stat	Prob
		1	0.258	0.258	50.866	0.000
		2	0.091	0.026	57.242	0.000
		3	0.215	0.198	92.560	0.000
		4	0.103	0.002	100.74	0.000
		5	0.080	0.045	105.61	0.000
		6	0.135	0.072	119.54	0.000
		7	0.124	0.062	131.30	0.000
		8	0.083	0.020	136.62	0.000
		9	0.059	-0.006	139.30	0.000
		10	0.045	-0.009	140.84	0.000
		11	0.047	0.010	142.53	0.000
		12	0.044	0.007	144.03	0.000
		13	0.030	-0.005	144.74	0.000
		14	0.030	0.000	145.43	0.000
		15	0.031	0.005	146.17	0.000
		16	0.050	0.034	148.11	0.000
		17	0.029	-0.001	148.77	0.000
		18	0.103	0.095	157.13	0.000
		19	0.113	0.056	167.09	0.000
		20	0.107	0.068	176.02	0.000
		21	0.053	-0.027	178.20	0.000
		22	0.024	-0.026	178.67	0.000
		23	0.071	0.031	182.68	0.000
		24	0.047	-0.007	184.45	0.000
		25	0.046	0.009	186.14	0.000
		26	0.056	-0.005	188.60	0.000
		27	0.079	0.044	193.56	0.000
		28	0.084	0.044	199.19	0.000
		29	0.047	0.000	200.95	0.000
		30	0.044	0.002	202.49	0.000
		31	0.064	0.023	205.77	0.000
		32	0.061	0.024	208.73	0.000
		33	0.047	0.010	210.52	0.000
		34	0.029	-0.024	211.22	0.000
		35	0.047	0.015	212.98	0.000
		36	0.040	-0.004	214.26	0.000

So, Table 35.5 provides with the following values:

The results from the above Table indicate that according to Akaike (AIC), Schwartz (SIC), and Hannan-Quinn (HQ) criteria, ARIMA (0,0,1) model is the most suitable as far as the mean monthly returns for the British pound/US dollar are concerned (Table 35.6).

Table 35.3 Descriptive statistics of average monthly return on the British pound/US dollar exchange rate

	British pound/US dollar
Mean	−0.107116
Median	−0.004658
Maximum	10.05161
Minimum	−11.44903
Std. dev.	2.077774
Skewness	−0.492824
Kurtosis	6.918455
Jarque-Bera	517.6636
Probability	0.000000
Observations	761

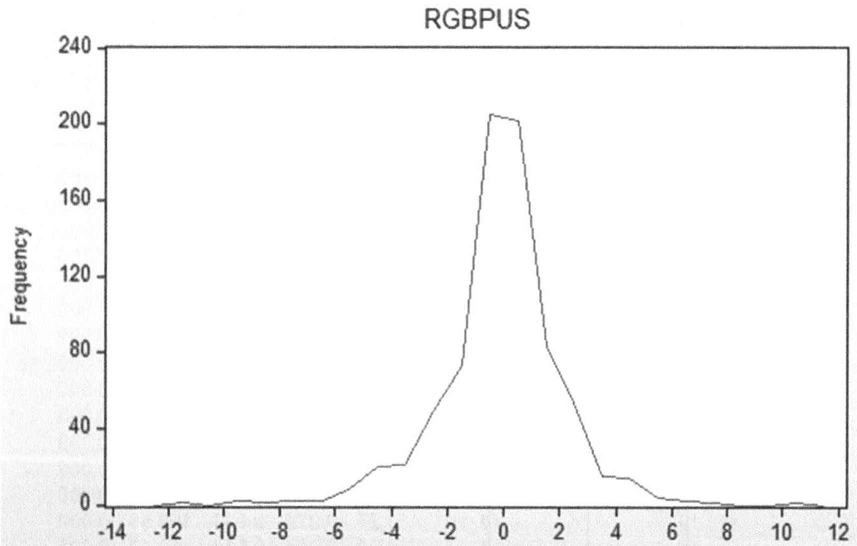

Fig. 35.3 Normal density graphs of the average monthly return of the British pound/US dollar exchange rate

After the estimation of the above model, we test for the existence of conditional heteroscedasticity (ARCH(q) test) from the squared residuals of the above model. Table 35.7 gives these results.

From the results of the above table, we conclude that autocorrelation and partial autocorrelation coefficients are statistically significant. Consequently, the null hypothesis for the absence of ARCH or GARCH procedure is rejected.

Table 35.4 Stationarity test of average monthly returns of the British pound/US dollar exchange rate

Variable	ADF		P-P	
	C	C, T	C	C, T
RGBPUS	−13.168(2)*	−13.162(2)*	−19.293[5]*	−19.282[5]*

Notes:
1. *, **, and *** show significant at 1%, 5%, and 10% levels, respectively
2. The numbers within parentheses followed by ADF statistics represent the lag length of the dependent variable used to obtain white noise residuals
3. The lag lengths for ADF equation were selected using Schwarz information criterion (SIC)
4. Mackinnon (1996) critical value for rejection of hypothesis of unit root applied
5. The numbers within brackets followed by PP statistics represent the bandwidth selected based on Newey-West (1994) method using the Bartlett kernel
6. *C*, constant; *T*, trend

Table 35.5 Model comparison between AIC, SIC, and HQ tests

ARIMA model	AIC	SC	HQ
RGBPUS			
(0,0,1)	**4.170**	**4.188**	**4.177**
(1,0,0)	4.187	4.205	4.194
(1,0,1)	4.173	4.197	4.182
(2,0,0)	4.180	4.205	4.190
(2,0,1)	4.175	4.205	4.186
(3,0,0)	4.171	4.201	4.182
(3,0,1)	4.173	4.209	4.187

Table 35.6 Estimation of ARIMA(0,0,1) model

Dependent Variable: RGBPUS
Method: ARMA Maximum Likelihood (Newton-Raphson)
Date: 02/16/17 Time: 13:38
Sample: 1953M09 2017M01
Included observations: 761
Convergence achieved after 2 iterations
Coefficient covariance computed using outer product of gradients

Variable	Coefficient	Std. Error	t-Statistic	Prob.
MA(1)	0.386569	0.025684	15.05084	0.0000
SIGMASQ	3.766458	0.129203	29.15146	0.0000

R-squared	0.126410	Mean dependent var	-0.107116
Adjusted R-squared	0.125259	S.D. dependent var	2.077774
S.E. of regression	1.943292	Akaike info criterion	4.169481
Sum squared resid	2866.275	Schwarz criterion	4.181661
Log likelihood	-1584.488	Hannan-Quinn criter.	4.174171
Durbin-Watson stat	2.003904		

Inverted MA Roots	-.39

Table 35.7 ARCH(q) test

Sample: 1953M08 2017M01
Included observations: 761

Autocorrelation	Partial Correlation		AC	PAC	Q-Stat	Prob
		1	0.210	0.210	33.682	0.000
		2	0.107	0.066	42.499	0.000
		3	0.224	0.199	80.901	0.000
		4	0.136	0.056	95.165	0.000
		5	0.116	0.060	105.45	0.000
		6	0.097	0.018	112.68	0.000
		7	0.129	0.073	125.58	0.000
		8	0.113	0.040	135.36	0.000
		9	0.056	-0.009	137.76	0.000
		10	0.064	0.005	140.98	0.000
		11	0.058	-0.001	143.55	0.000
		12	0.076	0.038	148.06	0.000
		13	0.046	-0.004	149.68	0.000
		14	0.015	-0.024	149.86	0.000
		15	0.053	0.018	152.03	0.000
		16	0.085	0.056	157.61	0.000
		17	0.036	-0.000	158.60	0.000
		18	0.108	0.086	167.64	0.000
		19	0.161	0.105	187.93	0.000
		20	0.119	0.057	199.11	0.000
		21	0.077	0.002	203.71	0.000
		22	0.028	-0.060	204.33	0.000
		23	0.077	0.012	208.96	0.000
		24	0.059	-0.007	211.68	0.000
		25	0.064	0.027	214.91	0.000
		26	0.061	-0.005	217.84	0.000
		27	0.078	0.031	222.68	0.000
		28	0.084	0.030	228.26	0.000
		29	0.079	0.043	233.20	0.000
		30	0.078	0.027	238.00	0.000
		31	0.099	0.041	245.82	0.000
		32	0.054	-0.011	248.11	0.000
		33	0.044	-0.001	249.66	0.000
		34	0.054	-0.003	252.02	0.000
		35	0.111	0.064	261.80	0.000
		36	0.067	-0.002	265.45	0.000

35.5 Empirical Results

Since there are ARCH effects on the returns of the British pound/US dollar exchange rate, we can proceed with the estimation of ARCH(q), GARCH(p,q), and EGARCH(p,q) models. The estimation of the parameters is accomplished using Marquardt's algorithm (1963). The parameters (coefficients) of estimated models

Table 35.8 Estimated ARIMA(0,0,1)-ARCH(1), ARIMA(0,0,1)-GARCH(1,1), and ARIMA (0,0,1)-EGARCH(1,1)

ARIMA(0,0,1)-ARCH(1)			
Parameter	Normal	t-Student	GED
ω	1.922(0.000)	1.059(0.000)	0.389(0.000)
α_1	0.670(0.000)	0.492(0.000)	1.461(0.000)
		DOF = 2.015(0.000)	PAR = 0.526(0.000)
LL	−1527.02	**−1330.33**	−1352.37
Jarque-Bera	283.085(0.000)	2401.15(0.000)	925(0.000)
Arch(1)	1.576(0.209)	0.078(0.779)	1.497(0.227)
$Q^2(1)$	1.584(0.208)	0.079(0.779)	1.504(0.220)
ARIMA(0,0,1)-GARCH(1,1)			
Parameter	Normal	t-Student	GED
ω	0.046(0.000)	0.001(0.151)	0.005(0.008)
α_1	0.300(0.000)	0.434(0.000)	0.481(0.000)
β_1	0.754(0.000)	0.731(0.000)	0.713(0.000)
		DOF = 3.584(0.000)	PAR = 0.862(0.000)
LL	−1366.284	−1192.552	**−1185.89**
Jarque-Bera	31749.92(0.000)	74012.98(0.000)	369713.06(0.000)
ARCH(1)	0.479(0.488)	0.0001(0.989)	0.00069(0.993)
$Q^2(1)$	0.482(0.487)	0.0002(0.989)	0.00007(0.997)
ARIMA(0,0,1)-EGARCH(1,1)			
Parameter	Normal	t-Student	GED
ω	−0.144(0.000)	−0.096(0.000)	−0.104(0.000)
α_1	0.304(0.000)	0.148(0.000)	0.178(0.000)
β_1	0.934(0.000)	0.967(0.000)	0.991(0.000)
γ_1	−0.028(0.235)	−0.071(0.015)	0.047(0.143)
		DOF = 3.572(0.000)	PAR = 0.849(0.000)
LL	−1357.22	**−1152.5**	−1197.00
Jarque-Bera	23082.45 (0.000)	74384.12(0.000)	32,936(0.000)
ARCH(1)	0.529(0.467)	0.595(0.440)	0.394(0.530)
$Q^2(1)$	0.528(0.467)	0.598(0.439)	0.396(0.529)

Notes:
1. Values in parentheses denote the p-values
2. LL is the value of the log-likelihood

and the test of normality, autocorrelation, and conditional heteroscedasticity of the residuals are provided in Table 35.8. A higher log-likelihood value (LL) yields a better fit.

Table 35.8 provides the estimations of all models and the standard errors of the parameters (coefficients) together with the value of log-likelihood function, as well as the normality test, autocorrelation test, and conditional heteroscedasticity test. From the above table, we can see that the ARIMA(0,0,1)-EGARCH(1,1) model with the t-Student distribution is the most suitable because all the coefficients are statistically significant in 5% level of significance, the log-likelihood value is the highest, and there is no problem in autocorrelation and the conditional heteroscedasticity. In addition, β_1 coefficient is positive and smaller than 1 showing the stationarity of the model. Also, γ_1 coefficient is negative and statistically significant indicating leverage result (asymmetry). Thus, this model can be used for forecasting.

35.6 Forecasting

For the forecasting of ARIMA(0,0,1)-EGARCH(1,1) model on the returns of British pound/US dollar exchange rate, we use both the dynamic and static procedures. The dynamic procedure computes forecasting for periods after the first sample period, using the former fitted values from the lags of dependent variable and ARMA terms. This procedure is called n-step ahead forecast. The static procedure uses actual values of the dependent variable. This procedure is called one-step ahead forecast. In the following figure, we present the criteria for the evaluation of forecasting the returns of British pound/US dollar exchange rate, using the dynamic and static forecast, respectively (Fig. 35.4).

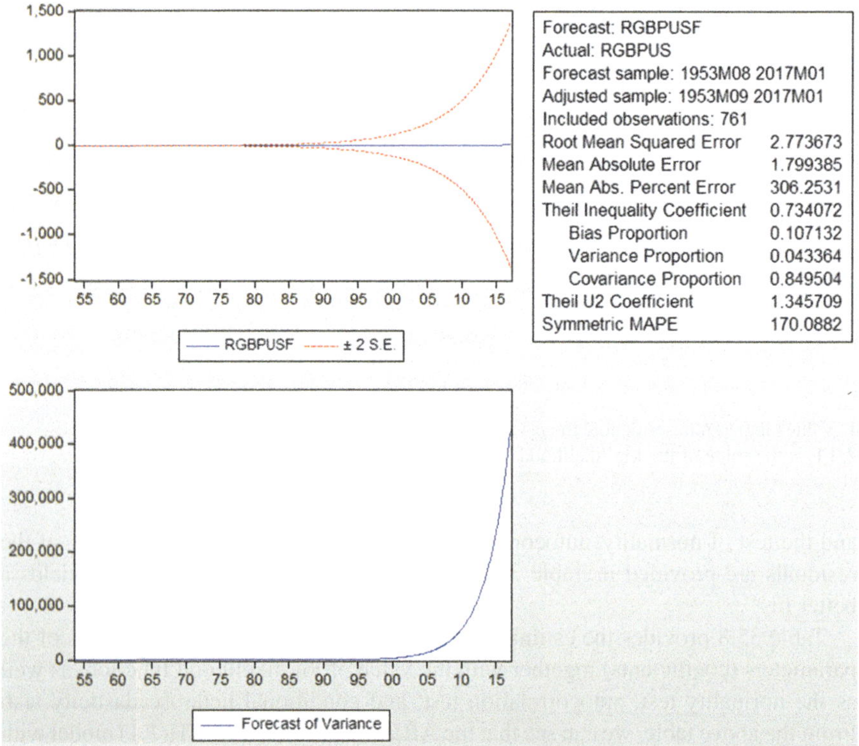

Fig. 35.4 Dynamic and static forecast of British pound/US dollar

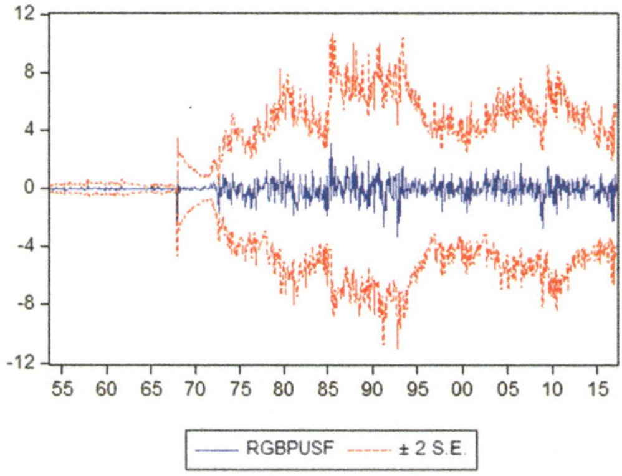

Forecast: RGBPUSF	
Actual: RGBPUS	
Forecast sample: 1953M08 2017M01	
Adjusted sample: 1953M09 2017M01	
Included observations: 761	
Root Mean Squared Error	1.944279
Mean Absolute Error	1.293437
Mean Abs. Percent Error	181.8269
Theil Inequality Coefficient	0.711621
Bias Proportion	0.002463
Variance Proportion	0.536025
Covariance Proportion	0.461512
Theil U2 Coefficient	0.996157
Symmetric MAPE	144.1550

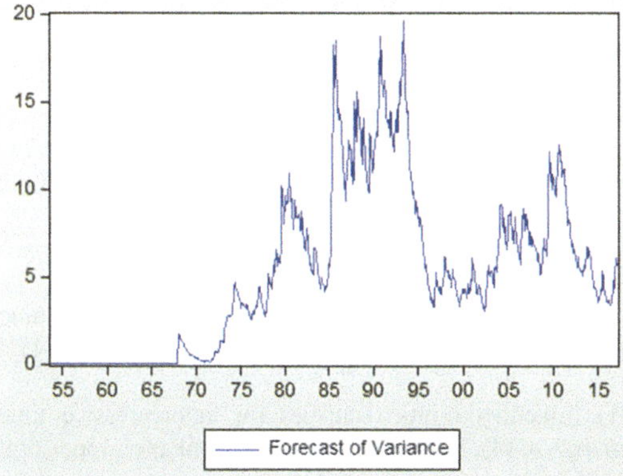

Fig. 35.4 (continued)

The above figure indicates that the static procedure gives better results rather than the dynamic (Theil's index is lower in the static procedure).

35.7 Discussion and Conclusion

This paper focuses on the formation of a model for the British pound/US dollar exchange rate. Due to the fact that exchange rate is regarded as a financial time series that may present volatility, it is more suitable to use models from GARCH family. More specific, the nonlinear ARIMA(0,0,1)-ARCH(1), ARIMA(0,0,1)-GARCH(1,1) και ARIMA(0,0,1)-EGARCH(1,1) models were used in order to register the volatility of symmetry effect as well as the asymmetry on exchange rate. Furthermore, the leverage effect is captured from the estimation of ARIMA(0,0,1)-EGARCH(1,1) model, showing that positive shocks cause lower volatility in relation to negative ones. Finally, the forecast of ARIMA(0,0,1)-EGARCH(1,1) model is evaluated, using both the dynamic and static procedure.

So, economic policymakers should forecast the future values of exchange rates using the equivalent models. The instability of exchange rate is an uncertainty measure on an economic environment for each country that should be forecasted. The main policy implication from the results of this paper is that since exchange rate instability may increase transaction costs and reduce the gains to international trade, the insight of exchange rate volatility estimation and forecasting is important for asset pricing and risk management.

References

Abdalla, S. Z. S. (2012). Modelling exchange rate volatility using GARCH models: Empirical evidence from Arab countries. *International Journal of Economics and Finance, 4*(3), 216–229. https://doi.org/10.5539/ijef.v4n3p216.

Antonakakis, N., & Darby, J. (2012). Forecasting volatility in developing countries' nominal exchange returns. MPRA Paper No.40875.

Black, F. (1976). Studies of stock price volatility changes. In *Proceedings of the 1976 Business Meeting of the Business and Economics Statistics Section*. American Statistical Association, Washington, DC (pp. 177–181).

Bollerslev, T. (1986). Generalized autoregressive conditional heteroskedasticity. *Journal of Econometrics, 31*(3), 307–327. https://doi.org/10.1016/0304-4076(86)90063-1.

Dickey, D. A., & Fuller, W. A. (1979). Distributions of the estimators for autoregressive time series with a unit root. *Journal of American Statistical Association, 74*(366), 427–431. https://doi.org/10.2307/2286348.

Dickey, D. A., & Fuller, W. A. (1981). Likelihood ratio statistics for autoregressive time series with a unit root. *Econometrica, 49*(4), 1057–1072. http://EconPapers.repec.org/RePEc:ecm:emetrp:v:49:y:1981:i:4:p:1057-72

Engle, R. F. (1982). Autoregressive conditional heteroskedasticity with estimates of the variance of U.K. inflation. *Econometrica, 50*(4), 987–1008. http://dx.doi.org/. https://doi.org/10.2307/1912773.

Epaphra, M. (2017). Modeling exchange rate volatility: Application of the GARCH and EGARCH models. *Journal of Mathematical Finance, 7*(1), 121–143. http://www.scirp.org/journal/jmf

Fama, E. F. (1965). The behavior of stock market prices. *Journal of Business, 38*(1), 34–105. https://doi.org/10.1086/29474.

Friedman, D., & Vandersteel, S. (1982). Short-run fluctuations in foreign exchange rates: Evidence from the data 1973-1979. *Journal of International Eonomics, 13*(1–2), 171–186.

Jarque, C., & Bera, A. (1980). Efficient tests for normality, homoscedasticity and serial independence of regression residuals. *Economics Letters, 6*, 255–259.

Johnston, K., & Scott, E. (2000). GARCH models and the stochastic process underlying exchange rate price changes. *Journal of Financial and Strategic Decisions, 13*(2), 13–24.

Hsieh, D. A. (1988). The statistical properties of daily foreign exchange rates: 1974–1983. *Journal of International Economics, 24*, 129–145.

Ljung, G. M., & Box.G.E.P. (1978). On a measure of a lack of fit in time series models. *Biometrika, 65*(2), 297–303. https://doi.org/10.1093/biomet/65.2.297.

MacKinnon, J. G. (1996). Numerical distribution functions for unit root and cointegration tests. *Journal of Applied Econometrics, 11*(6), 601–618. https://doi.org/10.1002/(SICI)1099-1255(199611)11:6<601::AID-JAE417>3.0.CO;2-T.

Mandelbrot, B. (1963). The variation of certain speculative prices. *Journal of Business, 36*(4), 394–414. http://www.jstor.org/stable/2350970.

Marquardt, D. W. (1963). An algorithm for least squares estimation of nonlinear parameters. *Journal of the Society for Industrial and Applied Mathematics, 11*, 431–441. http://www.jstor.org/stable/2098941

Miletić, S. (2015). Modeling and forecasting exchange rate volatility: Comparison between EEC and developed countries. *Industrija, 43*(1), 7–24. https://doi.org/10.5937/industrija43-6612.

Mundaca, G. G. (1991). The volatility of the Norwegian currency basket. *Scandinavian Journal of Economics, 93*(1), 53–73. https://doi.org/10.2307/3440421.

Nelson, D. B. (1991). Conditional heteroscedasticity in asset returns: A new approach. *Econometrica, 59*(2), 347–370. https://doi.org/10.2307/2938260.

Newey, W. K., & West, K. D. (1994). Automatic lag selection in covariance matrix estimation. *Review of Economic Studies, 61*(4), 631–654. http://hdl.handle.net/ 10.2307/2297912 (application/pdf).

Phillips, P. C. B., & Perron, P. (1998). Testing for a unit root in time series regression. *Biometrika, 75*(2), 335–346. https://doi.org/10.1093/biomet/75.2.335.

Sandoval, J. (2006). Do asymmetric GARCH models fit better exchange rate volatilities on emerging markets? Working Paper, Universidad Externado do Colombia, Odeon (pp. 99–116). Retrieved from http://foros.uexternado.edu.co/ecoinstitucional/index.php/odeon/article/viewFile/2654/2302

Taylor, S. J. (1986). *Modelling Financial Time Series*. New York: Wiley.

Theil, H. (1967). *Economics and information theory*. Chicago: Rand McNally and Company.

Vee, D. N. C., Gonpot, P. N., & Sookia, N. (2011). Forecasting volatility of USD/MUR exchange rate using a GARCH (1,1) model with GED and student's t-errors. *University of Mauritius Research Journal, 17*, 171–214.

Yoon, S., & Lee, K. S. (2008). The volatility and asymmetry of won/dollar exchange rate. *Journal of Social Sciences, 4*(7–9), 2008. http://dx.doi.org/. https://doi.org/10.3844/ jssp.2008.7.9.

Chapter 36
Modeling and Forecasting of US Health Expenditures Using ARIMA Models

Paraskevi Klazoglou and Nikolaos Dritsakis

Abstract This paper presents the practical steps to be analyzed in order to use autoregressive integrated moving average (ARIMA) time series models to forecast the total health expenditures, as a percentage of GDP, for the USA. The aim of this study is to identify the appropriate type of model based on the Box–Jenkins methodology. In particular, we apply the static one-step ahead forecasting method to the annual data over the period 1970–2015. The results from this study show that ARIMA (0,1,1) model is the appropriate model to forecast the US health expenditures in this period.

Keywords ARIMA model · Health expenditure · Box-Jenkins · Forecasting

36.1 Introduction

The meaning of health expenditure refers to any type of expenses made to improve or prevent health status worsening of a person or population. According to the literature, the three major health expenditure categories are the medical expenses and hospital and pharmaceutical spending. If we add the cost of medical schools, military health services, education, prevention, research, and operational expenses to the three categories mentioned above, we can obtain the total sum of health expenditure. The total health expenditure of a state is the sum of private and public consumption and private and public investment.

Over the last decade, there has been a health expenditure increase in developed countries. This is due to an increase in income, an epidemiologic transition, national insurance, demographic factors, an aging population, and biomedical technology.

P. Klazoglou · N. Dritsakis (✉)
Department of Applied Informatics, University of Macedonia, Economics and Social Sciences, Thessaloniki, Greece
e-mail: drits@uom.gr

N. Tsounis, A. Vlachvei (eds.), *Advances in Panel Data Analysis in Applied Economic Research*, Springer Proceedings in Business and Economics,
https://doi.org/10.1007/978-3-319-70055-7_36

Among the developed countries, an important rise in health expenditure, as a percentage of GDP, was observed in the USA that represents the highest total health expenditure (of GDP).

Health expenditure in the USA is financed by the public sector as well as private insurance carriers. The financial system in the USA is mainly based on employers, who through voluntary forms of insurance cover their employees insurance, while the state makes an effort to cover health services for vulnerable populations through government programs. In the USA, private companies offer health insurance policies and usually cover hospital care.

Health-care costs in the USA are continually rising. This increase causes a series of problems, all of which require the government to adopt policies in order to reduce expenditure. The need for more accurate projections of health expenditure in order to avoid the risk of uncertainty has led to the development and improvement of time series forecasting models over many years. Immense effort has been made by researchers for the development and improvement of time series forecasting models. One of the most important and widely used projecting models in time series analysis is the Box–Jenkins method (1976).

In Sect. 36.1, we present a brief description of health expenditure in the USA. The rest of this paper is as follows: Section 36.2 outlines a literature review, followed by a methodology analysis in Sect. 36.3. Section 36.4 describes the data, and the empirical results of the paper are analyzed in Sect. 36.5. Finally, conclusions of this study are presented in Sect. 36.6.

36.2 Literature Review

The number of researchers examining the influence of several determinants on health expenditure is growing. According to OECD data, countries with a higher GDP per capita tend to present higher health expenditure. It has been proved that in industrialized or developed countries, there exists a positive relationship between health expenditure levels and GDP (Newhouse 1977). According to other studies (Barros 1998), the GDP has been identified as the main factor which influenced the growth of health expenditure in all OECD countries, in the period 1960–1990.

Health systems around the world are often faced with common problems relating to health expenditure growth (Newhouse 1977; Leu 1986; Newhouse 1992; Getzen 2000). Future health expenditure projection is an important literary issue, which determines the growth rate. Box–Jenkins models, artificial neural network models (ANNs), and autoregressive distributed lag (ARDLs) models are the most popular for time series forecasting.

Lee and Miller (2002) used stochastic time series models to forecast the rise in health expenditure in the USA, using the health system for the US aging population (Medicare) with annual health spending as GDP percentage from 2002 to 2075. It was predicted that by 2075, Medicare expenditures will have increased to 8% of GDP from the current 2.2%. This rise is attributed to an equivalent rise in per capita health spending and the aging population.

For the projection of health spending in Canada, Di Matteo (2010) used data from 1965 to 2008. With the least-squares method (OLS) and the generalized least-squares method (GLS), he predicted the future values of health expenditure and pointed out that per capita spending during this period rose.

Chaabouni and Abednnadher (2013) used Tunisian annual health spending data from 1961 to 2008 to conduct forecasts using neural networks and an autoregressive distributed lag model and proved that such networks are more accurate in forecasting. They also concluded that the Tunisian health expenditure is rising in a non-analogous manner in relation to GDP.

Zhao (2015) employed annual health spending data of 34 member states of OECD and appraised the performance of forecasting methods based on three criteria – accuracy, precision, and certainty. Based on these criteria, he assessed the performance of univariate, multivariate, static, and dynamic panel data, ARIMA models, as well as VAR models and showed in contrast to Getzen and Poullier (1992) that simple statistical models (e.g., smoothing) and time series models provide better forecasts as against complex micro-panel data models.

36.3 Theoretical Background

The development and construction of ARIMA models as forecasting tools of economic variable values are known as the Box–Jenkins (1976) method. This approach in time series analysis is a method for investigating an ARIMA(p,d,q) model or $\varphi(L)\Delta^d Y_t = \delta + \theta(L)\varepsilon_t$ that adequately represents the stochastic process from which the sample was derived. This method includes the following steps:

- **Model identification**
  Firstly, the appropriate values of p, d, and q are determined in order to identify the exact ARIMA(p,d,q) model. The Box–Jenkins (1976) method uses the autocorrelation function, AC, and the partial autocorrelation function, PAC, to identify the ARIMA(p,d,q) model as well as unit root tests, such as ADF (Augmented Dickey–Fuller) (1979, 1981) test and PP Phillips–Perron (1998) test. The first step is to determine the value of d required to convert the nonstationary time series into stationary series. Once stationarity has been addressed, the next step is to identify the order of p for the autoregressive process and the order of q for the moving average process.
- **Model estimation**
  Model identification is followed by the estimation of orders p and q, from the parameters $\alpha_1, \ldots, \alpha_p$ for the autoregressive process (AR) and the parameters $\theta_1, \ldots, \theta_q$ for the moving average process (MA). The estimation methods which determine the number of parameters to estimate vary depending on the type and order of the model. If the series is an autoregressive process (AR), the coefficients can be estimated by the least-squares method. If the series also contains moving average process (MA) for the parameters estimation, nonlinear methods can be used, such as the maximum likelihood method.

- **Model checking**
  This step tests whether the type of ARIMA model estimated in the previous stage adequately explains the sample data. Model checking involves not only testing the significance of the coefficients but also estimating residual behavior and the order of the model. If the estimated model conforms adequately to the process from which the data was derived, the residuals should be independent of one another and constant in mean and variance over time (the white noise process). Residual checking is achieved by the Q statistic of Ljung–Box (1978), whereby the statistical significance of the autocorrelation coefficients is tested.
- **Model forecasting**
  Primarily, ARIMA model identification and estimation are used for forecasting. The appropriate model resulting from the steps mentioned above is used for the forecasting process of the time series' future values.

36.3.1 Autoregressive Process (AR)

A general average model of order p has the following form:

$$y_t = \alpha_1 y_{t-1} + \alpha_2 y_{t-2} + \cdots + \alpha_p y_{t-p} + \varepsilon_t \tag{36.1}$$

and with the lag operator L:

$$\left(1 - \alpha_1 L - \cdots - \alpha_p L^p\right) y_t = \varepsilon_t \tag{36.2}$$

36.3.2 Moving Average Process (MA)

A general moving average model of order q has the following form:

$$y_t = \mu + \varepsilon_t - \vartheta_1 \varepsilon_{t-1} - \vartheta_2 \varepsilon_{t-2} - \cdots - \vartheta_q \varepsilon_{t-q} \tag{36.3}$$

and with the lag operator L:

$$y_t = \mu + \left(1 - \theta_1 L - \theta_2 L^2 - \cdots - \theta_q L^q\right) \varepsilon_t \tag{36.4}$$

36.3.3 Autoregressive Moving Average (ARMA) Process

A general autoregressive moving average model of orders p and q, ARMA(p,q), has the following form:

$$y_t = \alpha_1 y_{t-1} + \alpha_2 y_{t-2} + \cdots + \alpha_p y_{t-p} + \mu + \varepsilon_t - \vartheta_1 \varepsilon_{t-1} - \vartheta_2 \varepsilon_{t-2} - \cdots - \vartheta_q \varepsilon_{t-q} \tag{36.5}$$

and with the lag operator L:

$$\left(1-\alpha_1 L-\cdots-\alpha_p L^p\right) y_t=\mu+\left(1-\theta_1 L-\theta_2 L^2-\cdots-\theta_q L^q\right) \varepsilon_t \tag{36.6}$$

or:

$$A(L)y_t=\mu+\Theta(L)\varepsilon_t \tag{36.7}$$

where:

$$A(L)=1-\alpha_1 L-\alpha_2 L^2-\cdots-\alpha_p L^p \tag{36.8}$$

$$\Theta(L)=1-\theta_1 L-\theta_2 L^2-\cdots-\theta_q L^q \tag{36.9}$$

36.3.4 Autoregressive Integrated Moving Average (ARIMA) Process

An ARMA(p,q) model following differences of the d order required to make the series stationary is known as autoregressive integrated moving average model of order (p,d,q) and symbolized as ARIMA(p,d,q).

The autoregressive integrated moving average ARIMA(p,d,q) model with the lag operator L is as follows:

$$\Phi(L)y_t=A(L)(1-L)^d y_t=\mu+\Theta(L)\varepsilon_t \tag{36.10}$$

where:

$$\Phi(L)=A(L)(1-L)^d \tag{36.11}$$

An ARIMA(p,d,q) process may have the following forms:

- Difference equation form, as a function of the past values and the past and current values of the disturbance term. Analyzing the polynomial:

$$\Phi(L)=A(L)(1-L)^d=1-\varphi_1 L-\varphi_2 L^2-\cdots-\varphi_{p+d} L^{p+d} \tag{36.12}$$

the model takes the form of:

$$y_t=\mu+\varphi_1 y_{t-1}+\cdots+\varphi_{p+d} y_{t-p-d}+\varepsilon_t-\theta_1\varepsilon_{t-1}-\cdots-\theta_q\varepsilon_{t-q} \tag{36.13}$$

- Inverted form, as a function of the past values and the current value of the disturbance term. Following inversion of the polynomial we obtain:

$$\Pi(L)y_t=\left(1-\sum_{j=1}^{\infty}\pi_j L^i\right) y_t=\varepsilon_t \tag{36.14}$$

therefore, the model becomes:

$$y_t = \pi_1 y_{t-1} + \pi_2 y_{t-2} + \cdots + \varepsilon_t \tag{36.15}$$

- Random shock form, as a function of the disturbance term and current and past values.

36.3.5 Forecast Error Statistics

The forecasting of ARIMA models is evaluated both in-sample and out-of-sample analysis. The optimum predicted value is assessed by the mean squared error (MSE). Other indicators usually used for measuring forecasting performance are the Mean Absolute Error (MAE), the Root Mean Square Error (RMSE), and the Theil (U-Theil) (1967) Inequality Coefficient. These indexes are given as follows:

$$\text{MSE} = \frac{1}{T}\sum_{t=1}^{T}\left(\widehat{Y}_t - Y_t\right)^2 \tag{36.16}$$

$$\text{MAE} = \frac{1}{T}\sum_{t=1}^{T}\left|\widehat{Y}_t - Y_t\right| \tag{36.17}$$

$$\text{RMSE} = \sqrt{\frac{1}{T}\sum_{t=1}^{T}\left(\widehat{Y}_t - Y_t\right)^2} \tag{36.18}$$

Theil Inequality Coefficient is as follows:

$$U = \frac{\sqrt{\frac{1}{T}\sum_{t=1}^{T}\left(\widehat{Y}_t - Y_t\right)^2}}{\sqrt{\frac{1}{T}\sum_{t=1}^{T}\left(\widehat{Y}_t\right)^2} + \sqrt{\frac{1}{T}\sum_{t=1}^{T}(Y_t)^2}} \quad 0 \le U \le 1 \tag{36.19}$$

where:

Y_t: Is the actual value of the endogenous variable Y in time t.

$\widehat{Y}_t$: Is the revised value of the endogenous variable Y in time t.

T: Is the number of observations in the simulation (of a sample).

If the Theil Inequality Coefficient $U = 0$, the actual values of the series are equal to the estimated values $Y_t = \widehat{Y}_t$ for all t. This case presents a perfect fit between the actual and predicted values. Alternatively, if $U = 1$, there is no such correct forecasting for the sample being investigated.

36.4 Data

In this study, annual time series data are used for total private and public health expenditures, as a percentage of GDP, for the USA over the period 1970–2015. The data are obtained from the OECD statistical database and used for forecasting.

36.5 Empirical Results

In Fig. 36.1, the rate of US health expenditure at levels is presented over the specific period.

Evidently, from Fig. 36.1, the US health expenditures, as a percentage of GDP, present a random walk. In the table below, the variable estimation, as a function of time, is presented to identify whether a trend exists or not.

The results in Table 36.1 and the accompanying graph indicate that there exists a trend in the model being estimated. Hence, this is an indicator that the time series is nonstationary. Onward, the autocorrelation plot is also used to assess the stationarity (Fig. 36.2).

It is obvious from the figure above that the autocorrelation coefficients decline slowly, which indicates that the series is nonstationary.

Therefore, the next step is to apply the above tests anew to ascertain if the series is stationary at first difference. Fig. 36.3 shows the percentage of health expenditure at first difference.

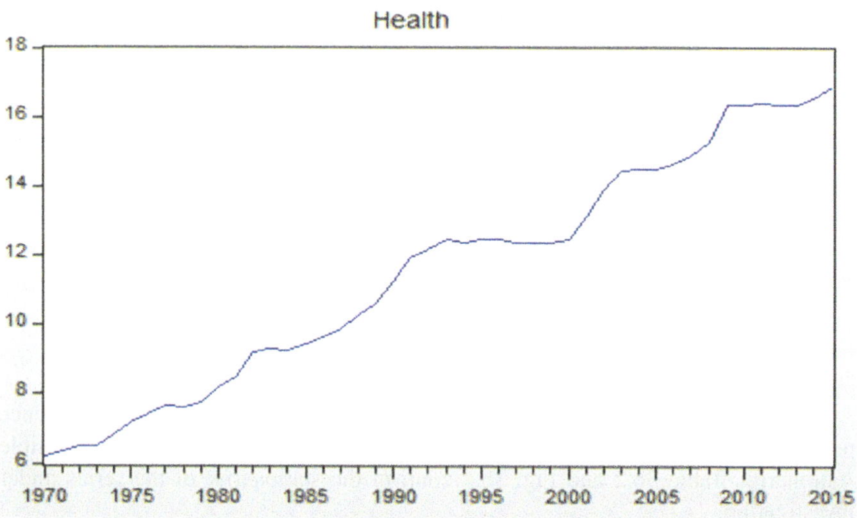

Fig. 36.1 The percentage of US health expenditure from 1970 to 2015

Table 36.1 Estimation of the percentage of health expenditure

Dependent Variable: HEALTH
Method: Least Squares
Date: 02/07/17 Time: 11:27
Sample: 1970 2015
Included observations: 46

Variable	Coefficient	Std. Error	t-Statistic	Prob.
C	5.952287	0.110694	53.77248	0.0000
@TREND	0.248090	0.004237	58.55133	0.0000

R-squared	0.987328	Mean dependent var	11.53431
Adjusted R-squared	0.987040	S.D. dependent var	3.351319
S.E. of regression	0.381519	Akaike info criterion	0.953192
Sum squared resid	6.404492	Schwarz criterion	1.032698
Log likelihood	-19.92341	Hannan-Quinn criter.	0.982975
F-statistic	3428.258	Durbin-Watson stat	0.447490
Prob(F-statistic)	0.000000		

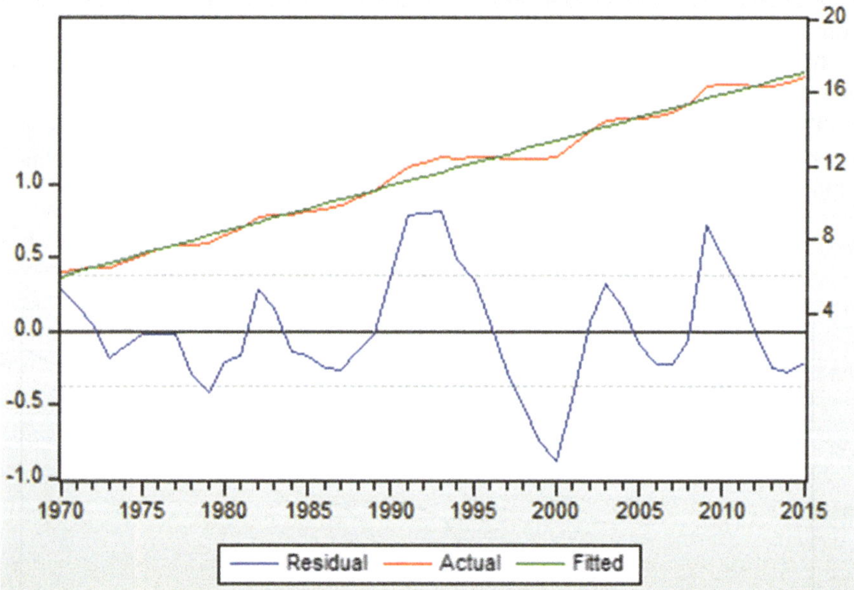

In Fig. 36.3, it is observed that the health expenditure rate at first difference presents strong fluctuations. It could be regarded as an indication of possible stationarity. Table 36.2 and Fig. 36.4 confirm the stationarity of the series under investigation.

As shown in Table 36.2 and Fig. 36.4, the series is stationary.

Date: 02/07/17 Time: 11:35
Sample: 1970 2015
Included observations: 46

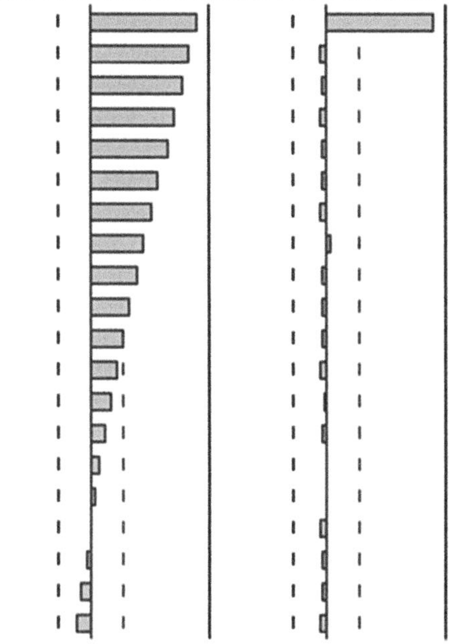

Autocorrelation / Partial Correlation (lag)	AC	PAC	Q-Stat	Prob
1	0.938	0.938	43.205	0.000
2	0.874	-0.052	81.570	0.000
3	0.809	-0.043	115.20	0.000
4	0.741	-0.063	144.05	0.000
5	0.673	-0.034	168.46	0.000
6	0.605	-0.041	188.67	0.000
7	0.535	-0.058	204.90	0.000
8	0.474	0.031	217.98	0.000
9	0.413	-0.048	228.17	0.000
10	0.352	-0.038	235.78	0.000
11	0.294	-0.029	241.24	0.000
12	0.234	-0.057	244.80	0.000
13	0.179	-0.011	246.95	0.000
14	0.126	-0.030	248.05	0.000
15	0.078	-0.005	248.48	0.000
16	0.036	0.006	248.58	0.000
17	-0.006	-0.050	248.58	0.000
18	-0.048	-0.049	248.76	0.000
19	-0.089	-0.045	249.41	0.000
20	-0.131	-0.052	250.87	0.000

Fig. 36.2 The autocorrelation and partial autocorrelation plots for health expenditure at levels

The stationarity of the series is confirmed by the unit root tests of Dickey–Fuller (1979, 1981) and Phillips and Perron (1998).

The results presented in Table 36.3 confirm that the series is stationary at first difference.

The form of ARMA(p,q) model is determined from the results of Fig. 36.4. The parameters p and q of the ARMA model can be defined by observing the partial autocorrelation and autocorrelation coefficients, respectively, comparing them with the critical value $\pm\left(2/\sqrt{n}\right) = \pm\left(2/\sqrt{46}\right) = \pm 0.294$.

From the values of partial autocorrelation coefficients and autocorrelation coefficients shown in Fig. 36.4, the value of p will be between $0 < p < 1$, and, respectively, the value of q will be between $0 < q < 1$. Using the above values, the optimum ARMA(p,q) model is selected from the lowest values of the AIC, SC, and HQ criteria. The values of p and q are given in the table below.

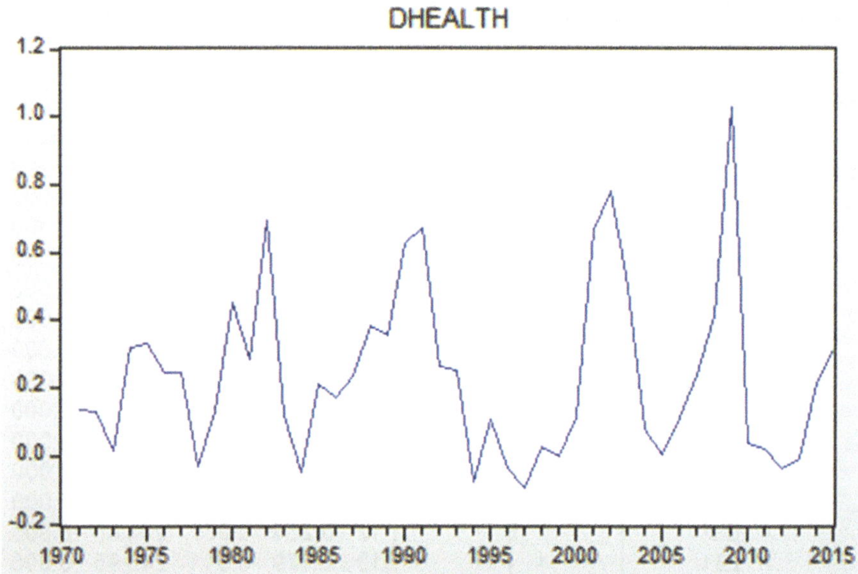

Fig. 36.3 The Percentage of US health expenditure at first difference

The results in Table 36.4 indicate that according to Akaike (AIC), Schwartz (SIC), and Hannan–Quinn (HQ) (1979) criteria, the most appropriate model is the ARIMA (0,1,1).

The results in Table 36.5 prove that there is no problem relating to the statistical significance of the coefficients. As it follows, the existence of autoregressive conditional heteroskedasticity (ARCH(q) process) is tested by the squared residuals of the model above. These results are given in Table 36.6.

The results from Table 36.6 show that all autocorrelation and partial autocorrelation coefficients are not statistically significant. Hence, the ARCH or GARCH process is rejected. Consequently, health expenditure is projected by using the ARIMA (0,1,1) model.

For health expenditure forecasting, the static one-step ahead forecasting method is used. Static forecasting extends the recursion forward from the end of the sample estimation, allowing one-step ahead projection both in structural samples and innovations.

Having chosen the form of the ARIMA (0,1,1) model, we present in Fig. 36.5 the graph of actual and predicted values of the model as well as of the innovations. However, some statistical indicators, such as Root-Mean-Square Error, Mean Absolute Error, and Theil Inequality Coefficient, are given in Table 36.7, in order to evaluate the model's forecasting performance.

As demonstrated by the figure above, the trend forecasting of the US health expenditure closely follows the actual values.

Table 36.2 Estimation of the percentage of health expenditure at first difference

Dependent Variable: DHEALTH
Method: Least Squares
Date: 02/07/17 Time: 11:38
Sample (adjusted): 1971 2015
Included observations: 45 after adjustments

Variable	Coefficient	Std. Error	t-Statistic	Prob.
C	0.232677	0.078193	2.975680	0.0048
@TREND	0.000191	0.002960	0.064564	0.9488

R-squared	0.000097	Mean dependent var	0.237073
Adjusted R-squared	-0.023157	S.D. dependent var	0.254973
S.E. of regression	0.257908	Akaike info criterion	0.170998
Sum squared resid	2.860208	Schwarz criterion	0.251294
Log likelihood	-1.847453	Hannan-Quinn criter.	0.200932
F-statistic	0.004169	Durbin-Watson stat	1.215890
Prob(F-statistic)	0.948820		

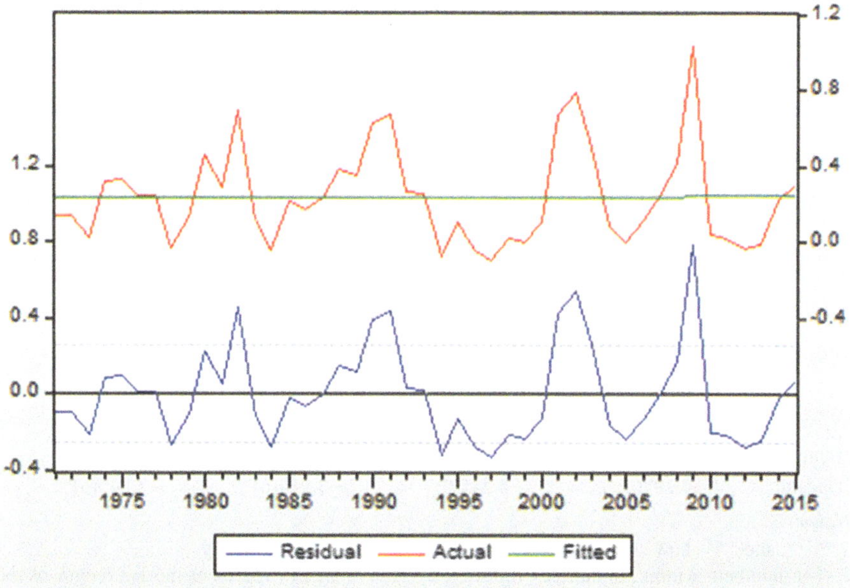

The results in Table 36.7 show that MAE (Mean Absolute Error) is 0.170, while RMSE (Root-Mean-Square Error) and Theil Inequality Coefficient are 0.231 and 0.385, respectively. In addition, in Table 36.7 the forecasting of the average value in a wide confidence interval ±2SE is represented by the above diagram.

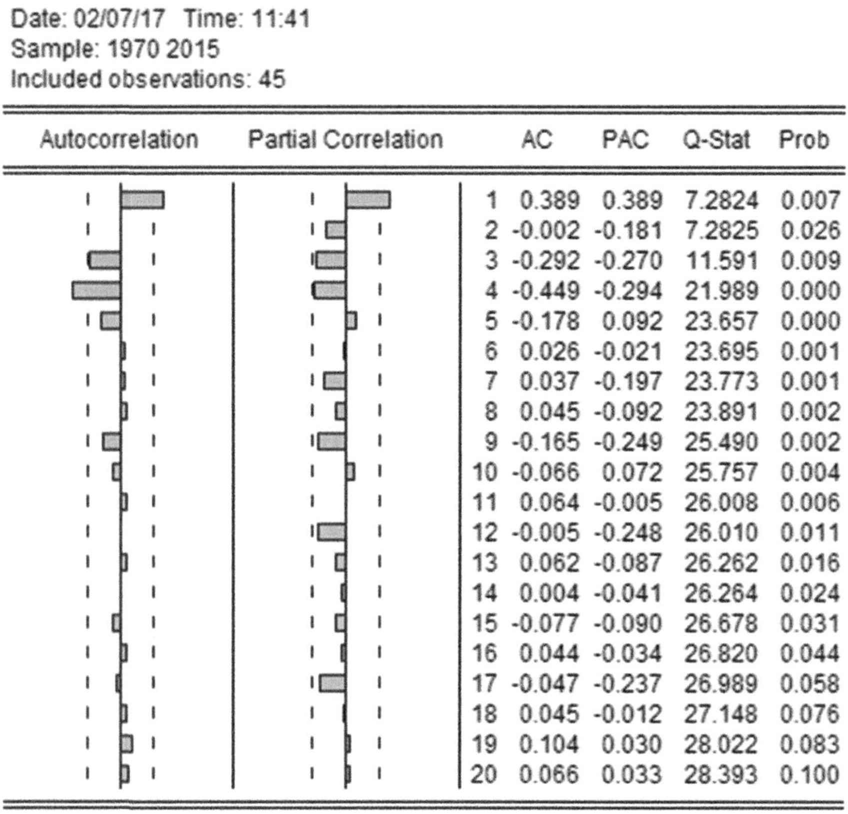

Fig. 36.4 The autocorrelation and partial autocorrelation plots for health expenditure at first difference

Table 36.3 Summary table of Augmented Dickey and Fuller and Phillips Perron unit root tests

	ADF		P-P	
Variable	C	C,T	C	C,T
Health	−0.422(1)	−1.052(1)	−0.255[3]	−1.725[2]
Dhealth	−4.297(0)*	−4.245(0)*	−3.914[6]*	−3.840[6]**

Notes:
1. *, **, and *** show significant at 1%, 5%, and 10% levels, respectively
2. The numbers within parentheses followed by ADF statistics represent the lag length of the dependent variable used to obtain white noise residuals
3. The lag lengths for ADF equation were selected using Schwarz Information Criterion (SIC)
4. Mackinnon (1996) critical value for rejection of hypothesis of unit root applied
5. The numbers within brackets followed by PP statistics represent the bandwidth selected based on Newey and West (1994) method using Bartlett Kernel
6. *C* constant, *T* trend
7. *D* first differences

Table 36.4 Comparison of the models via the AIC, SIC, and HQ criteria

ARIMA model	AIC	SC	HQ
Dhealth			
(1,1,0)	0.053	0.174	0.098
(0,1,1)	**0.045**	**0.165**	**0.089**
(1,1,1)	0.082	0.243	0.142

Table 36.5 Estimation of the ARIMA (0,1,1) model

Dependent Variable: DHEALTH
Method: ARMA Maximum Likelihood (OPG - BHHH)
Date: 02/28/17 Time: 12:31
Sample: 1971 2015
Included observations: 45
Convergence achieved after 11 iterations
Coefficient covariance computed using outer product of gradients

Variable	Coefficient	Std. Error	t-Statistic	Prob.
C	0.236743	0.067666	3.498697	0.0011
MA(1)	0.399330	0.145848	2.737985	0.0090
SIGMASQ	0.053396	0.010977	4.864240	0.0000

R-squared	0.159991	Mean dependent var	0.237073
Adjusted R-squared	0.119991	S.D. dependent var	0.254973
S.E. of regression	0.239187	Akaike info criterion	0.045057
Sum squared resid	2.402833	Schwarz criterion	0.165501
Log likelihood	1.986222	Hannan-Quinn criter.	0.089957
F-statistic	3.999736	Durbin-Watson stat	1.917502
Prob(F-statistic)	0.025702		

Inverted MA Roots	-.40

36.6 Conclusion

This paper aims to construct a model for US health expenditure forecasting covering the period 1970–2015. Using the Box–Jenkins method, the ARIMA (0,1,1) model was developed and proved to be the optimum for US health expenditure forecasting. This model is based on adjustment of observed values, and its objective is to reduce the difference between the model values produced and the observed ones as close as possible to zero. For health expenditure predicting, the static one-step ahead forecasting method is used. Static forecasting extends the recursion forward from the end of the sample estimation, allowing one-step ahead projection both in structural samples and innovations.

Table 36.6 ARCH(q) process test

Sample: 1970 2015
Included observations: 45

Autocorrelation	Partial Correlation		AC	PAC	Q-Stat	Prob
		1	0.216	0.216	2.2507	0.134
		2	-0.140	-0.196	3.2191	0.200
		3	-0.107	-0.031	3.7976	0.284
		4	-0.116	-0.119	4.4962	0.343
		5	-0.140	-0.119	5.5286	0.355
		6	-0.149	-0.146	6.7316	0.346
		7	0.096	0.115	7.2436	0.404
		8	0.306	0.210	12.600	0.126
		9	-0.009	-0.153	12.604	0.181
		10	-0.066	0.026	12.870	0.231
		11	-0.009	-0.002	12.874	0.302
		12	0.015	0.055	12.889	0.377
		13	-0.012	0.033	12.898	0.456
		14	-0.045	0.005	13.034	0.524
		15	0.028	-0.024	13.089	0.595
		16	-0.037	-0.129	13.188	0.659
		17	-0.108	-0.019	14.076	0.662
		18	0.041	0.084	14.210	0.715
		19	0.210	0.188	17.799	0.536
		20	0.012	-0.132	17.811	0.600

Table 36.7 Comparative statistics

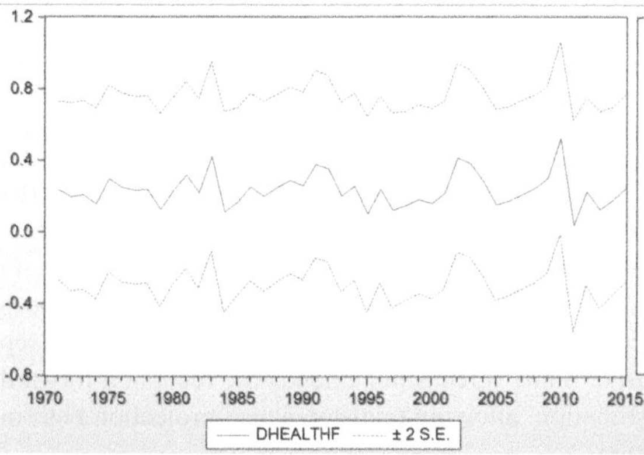

Forecast: DHEALTHF	
Actual: DHEALTH	
Forecast sample: 1970 2015	
Included observations: 46	
Root Mean Squared Error	0.231157
Mean Absolute Error	0.170552
Mean Abs. Percent Error	554.9330
Theil Inequality Coefficient	0.385294
Bias Proportion	0.000005
Variance Proportion	0.478797
Covariance Proportion	0.521198
Theil U2 Coefficient	0.478552
Symmetric MAPE	82.86957

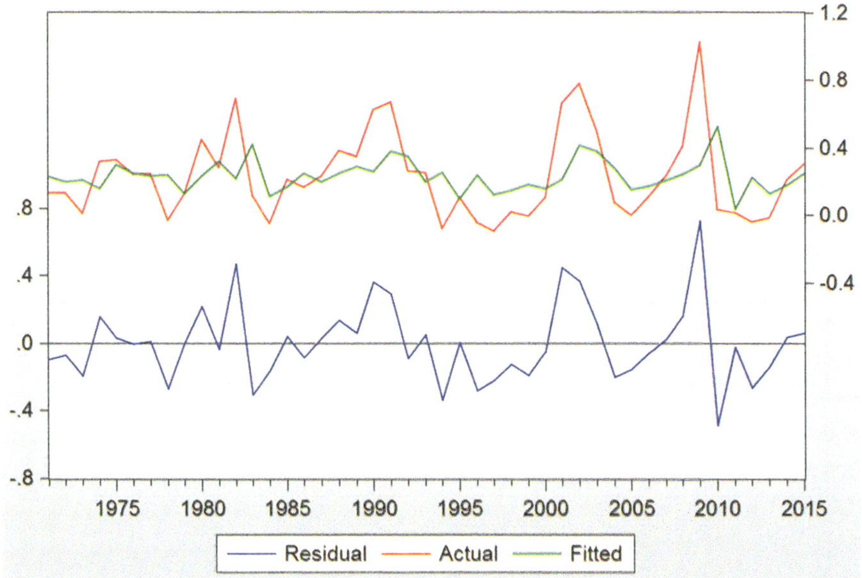

Fig. 36.5 The plot of actual values and forecast values by ARIMA (0,1,1)

References

Barros, P. P. (1998). The black box of health care expenditure growth determinants. *Health Economics, 7*, 533–544.

Box, G. E. P., & Jenkins, G. M. (1976). *Time series analysis. Forecasting and control*. San Francisco: Holden-Bay.

Chaabouni, S., & Abednnadher, C. (2013). Modelling and forecasting of Tunisia's health expenditures using artificial neural network and ARDL models. *International Journal of Medical Science of Public Health, 2*, 495–503.

Dickey, D. A., & Fuller, W. A. (1979). Distributions of the estimators for autoregressive time series with a unit root. *Journal of American Statistical Association, 74*(366), 427–431.

Dickey, D. A., & Fuller, W. A. (1981). Likelihood ratio statistics for autoregressive time series with a unit root. *Econometrica, 49*(4), 1057–1072.

Di Matteo, L. (2010). The sustainability of public health expenditures: Evidence from the Canadian federation. *European Journal of Health Economics, 11*(6), 569–584.

Getzen, T. (2000). Forecasting health expenditures: Short, medium, and long term. *Journal of Health Care Finance, 26*, 56–72.

Getzen, T., & Poullier, J.-P. (1992). International health spending forecasts: Concepts and evaluation. *Social Science and Medicine, 34*, 1057–1068.

Hannan, E. J., & Quinn, B. G. (1979). The determination of the order of an autoregression. *Journal of Royal Statistical Society, B14*, 190–195.

Lee, R., & Miller, T. (2002). An approach to forecasting health expenditures, with application to the U.S. medicare system. *Health Services Research, 37*(5), 1365–1386.

Leu, R. E. (1986). The public-private mix and international health care costs. In *Public and private health services: Complementarities and conflicts* (pp. 41–63). Oxford and New York: Blackwell.

Ljung, G. M., & Box, G. E. P. (1978). On a measure of a lack of fit in time series models. *Biometrika, 65*(2), 297–303.

MacKinnon, J. G. (1996). Numerical distribution functions for unit root and cointegration tests. *Journal of Applied Econometrics, 11*(6), 601–618.

Newey, W. K., & West, K. D. (1994). Automatic lag selection in covariance matrix estimation. *Review of Economic Studies, 61*(4), 631–653.

Newhouse, J. (1977). Medical care expenditures: A cross-national survey. *Journal of Human Resources, 12*, 115–152.

Newhouse, J. (1992). Medical care costs: How much welfare loss? *The Journal of Economic Perspectives, 6*, 3–21.

Phillips, P. C. B., & Perron, P. (1998). Testing for a unit root in time series regression. *Biometrika, 75*(2), 335–346.

Theil, H. (1967). *Economics and information theory*. Chicago: Rand McNally and Company.

Zhao, J. (2015). Forecasting health expenditure: Methods and applications to international databases. Working Paper, Centre for Health Economics and Policy Analysis.

Chapter 37
Industry Competitiveness Using Firm-Level Data: A Case Study of the Nigerian Insurance Sector

Godwin Enaholo Uddin, Kingsley M. Oserei, Olajumoke E. Oladipo, and Damilola Ajayi

Abstract With reforms to pioneer the Nigerian insurance sector toward a more competitive level, such had been envisaged to drive her participatory contribution to national development since over the years her huge economic potential has been relatively tapped minimally. Thus in view to ascertain empirically the height of competitiveness so far achieved, this work therefore seeks to analyze the Nigerian insurance sector market performance with the focus to perform market power studies. Thereby adopting the concentration measure as well as the Panzar-Rosse methodology using random effect panel estimation for the period 1999–2008, the study established the level of competitiveness in both the life and non-life (General Business) insurance sub-sectors. Having computed a ten insurance firms'

This work appreciates the mentorship of Associate Professor Olufemi Saibu, Department of Economics, University of Lagos, Nigeria. Also, Anthony Musonda Simpasa, Principal Research Economist, Office of the Chief Economist, African Development Bank Group, and Philippe Vassilopoulos of the CGEMP Crew, Universite Paris, Dauphine. All errors are strictly the authors'.

G. E. Uddin (✉)
School of Management and Social Sciences, Pan-Atlantic University, Lagos, Nigeria
e-mail: guddin@pau.edu.ng

K. M. Oserei
Nigerian Economic Summit Group (NESG), Lagos, Nigeria

Department of Economics University of Lagos, Lagos, Nigeria

Alpha Morgan Capital Managers Limited, Lagos, Nigeria
e-mail: osereikingsley@yahoo.com

O. E. Oladipo
Access Bank Plc, Lagos, Nigeria
e-mail: jumok17@yahoo.com

D. Ajayi
Department of Economics, University of Lagos, Lagos, Nigeria
e-mail: oludamiajayi@gmail.com

N. Tsounis, A. Vlachvei (eds.), *Advances in Panel Data Analysis in Applied Economic Research*, Springer Proceedings in Business and Economics,
https://doi.org/10.1007/978-3-319-70055-7_37

concentration ratios alongside deriving the value of the Panzar-Rosse H-statistic for both sectors, the non-life sub-sector was evident to be more competitive relative to the life sub-sector. Hence, it is envisaged that further attempts to engender competitiveness in either of the sub-sectors would include efforts to ensure all participating firms are enlisted on the Nigerian Stock Exchange in order to enhance their prowess of contributing to national development.

37.1 Introduction

A prime constituent of every country financial system notably is the insurance business, and many reforms pioneered in the Nigerian Insurance industry have been pointers for a reinvigorated and competitive industry. Pan African Capital (2013) had noted the insurance sector to evidently play an important role in the development of any nation, by transferring risks from businesses and individuals. That by playing an active role in the stability and efficient diversification of risks, it thus contributes immensely to economic development. The relevance of the insurance sector therefore cannot be overemphasized.

It is unfortunate however that the importance of this sector in the Nigerian economy has not being fully grasped; its participatory contribution to the national income has relatively been minimal despite the high economic potential which has been untapped (Meristem Securities 2014). More so, from an outlook of the Nigerian Insurance Industry with the National Insurance Commission (NAICOM) established through Decree No 1of 1997 and ever since pioneering the drive to enhance access to affordable insurance products, build confidence in the Nigerian Insurance market, promote public understanding of insurance mechanisms, eliminate fake insurance products, and develop and sustain insurance brokerage and agency that is poised for championing the course of the industry's contribution to the nation's Gross Domestic Product (GDP), the sector has remained receded in its impact on the Nigerian economy (NAICOM 2010).

The militating factors though posited to hamper the progress of the sector include low insurance coverage level, low penetration rate (or ratio), low level of acceptance, low insurance patronage, shallow perception among the populace, lack of awareness, neglect of retail end markets, non-remittance of insurance premium by insurance intermediaries such as insurance agents and brokers, nonpayment of premium as and when due especially by government and government agencies, unsettlement of claims on the part of the insurers, fake insurance intermediaries, unscrupulous claims by the insured, undercapitalization by insurers, lack of innovative products and services or customized products, poor financial reporting, lack of transparency, non-listing of some insurers on the floor of the Nigerian Stock Exchange (NSE), and undervaluation of the industry amidst others (Pan African Capital 2013; KPMG Africa 2015).

With various reform processes ongoing in the industry, huge potential abound consequently to exhibit the more *lucrativeness* of insurance business in Nigeria especially in her financial capacity to underwrite big insurance risks. The Market Development and Restructuring Initiatives (MDRI), the No-premium No-cover, the waves of mergers and acquisitions exercise, government supports and legislations, the local content initiatives in the oil and gas sector, the cabotage law in the maritime industry, the compulsory life insurance, etc. all account for measures to strengthen the working mechanism or framework of the sector (Pan African Capital 2013). The introduction of the Universal Banking mandate by the apex bank (i.e., the Central Bank of Nigeria – CBN) in 2001 alongside the already existing Bank and Other Financial Institutions Act (BOFIA) of 1991 however with the view to revitalize the Nigerian financial landscape as well as its adoptive practice by firms in the Nigerian financial system notably enabled the entrance of an almost unlimited number of participating firms in the insurance sub-sector (CBN 2012) and such partly promoted the competiveness in the Nigerian insurance industry. The later onward and compulsory recapitalization of insurance firms in 2005 enforced also by the CBN particularly seemed to have heightened the level of the industry's competiveness as it then delimited the number of participating firms in the sub-sector (see Table 37.4 in Appendix), thereby eliminating the prevalence of rent-seeking firms operating in the insurance market and then fostered the growth of core insurance firms to be the players in the Nigerian insurance sector (CBN 2012; Fashoto et al. 2012).

In fulfilling its role as insurers and risks takers, insurance companies pool large sums of money in order to perform their roles creditably. Thus, a strong and competitive insurance industry is a compelling imperative for Nigeria's economic growth and development (Ujunwa and Nwanneka 2011).

Against this background therefore, there are good reasons to assess the Nigerian insurance sector market performance with the view to perform market power studies on firms in the Nigerian insurance market. One of which is to contribute to the literature with focused and detailed research into the competiveness of firms in the Nigerian Insurance sector. The level of competitiveness thereof is evident by the extent of market power enjoyed by these firms. With the objective to assess the competitiveness in the Nigerian insurance sector, the study begins with a review of related literature (Sect. 37.2). Section 37.3 discusses the methodology and data issues, while Sect. 37.4 presents the estimated results and discussion. Section 37.5 concludes the work.

37.2 Literature Review

37.2.1 Definitions of Insurance and Risk

The place of insurance and risk in modern business practice has been acknowledged by various scholars in the literature. In this case, the understanding of insurance and risk in business is pivotal for proper place of insurance and risk in modern business practice. Isenmila (2002) defined insurance as a contract whereby a person called the insurer or assurer agrees in consideration of money paid to him, called the premium, by another person, called the insured or assured, to indemnify the latter against loss resulting to him on happening of certain events.

According to Ujunwa and Nwanneka (2011), insurance is generally defined as the pooling of funds from the insured (policy holders) in order to pay for relatively uncommon but severely devastating losses which can occur to insured. Insurance as a contract is between two parties where one party called the insurer undertakes to pay the other party called the insured a fixed amount of money on the occurrence of a certain event. To Obasi (2010) cited by Ujunwa and Nwanneka (2011), insurance is contract between the person who buys insurance and an insurance company who sold the policy.

Risk on the other hand is the chance of a loss, the possibility that a predicted result differs from the actual result. Identifiable risks could be categorized into pure risk and speculative risk. Pure risks are risks which can only lead to a loss. Usually pure risks are not associated with the pursuit of profit, for example, risk for private use of a car. Speculative risks, on the other hand, are chances of losses or gain, for gambling. They are avoidable risks (Isenmila 2002).

37.2.2 Overview of the Nigerian Insurance Sector

The insurance sector in Nigeria have being buttressed to be of a passive role in the economic development of the country, lagging behind with major policy reforms given the huge economic potential that remains largely untapped in the industry. Particularly with the much population and GDP growth rate averaging 7.4% over the last decade, the penetration ratio has continued to lag behind those of other formal financial services with a performance of 0.7% penetration rate and less than 1% contribution to GDP. Also over the years, the insurance business in the country has been focused mainly on the underwriting of risks for companies, so much so the reason for the low penetration ratio because it is skewed toward some sectors such as trade, transports, etc. and neglecting the retail end-markets (Pan African Capital 2013; KPMG Africa 2015).

Furthermore, it is imperative to note that the Nigerian insurance market is a broker market because brokers control about 90% of the premium income, while the remaining 10% is left for insurance agents and direct marketing by insurers with implications being that insurers tend to struggle to cover policy payment in case of any claim arising and also are left with limited funds to invest in the economy, of which consequently reduces its level of profitability and contribution to the economy as well as aggravating the waning public perception (Pan African Capital 2013).

Examining thereof the level of transparency among participating firms in the Nigerian Insurance sector, findings from NAICOM revealed that as at August 27, 2013, only 29 insurance firms were listed on the NSE with their insurance stocks poorly valued at the market as 20 out of the 29 insurance stocks were trading at nominal value of 50 Kobo (Pan African Capital 2013).

Despite however a seemingly poor industry outlook, the insurance sector boasts of a huge cash flow generating capacity with total gross premium presenting a possible opportunity and progressive trend for improvement. Available industry data shows that the total industry gross premium stood at N233.75 billion and N200.38 billion for the year 2011 and 2010, respectively, compared to N60.20 billion and N53.82 billion in total claims for the industry for the same period. This depicts an annual growth rate of 16.66% and 5.48% in 2011 and 2010 for total gross premium compared to 11.87% and −13.16% for industry's total claims (Pan African Capital 2013).

37.2.3 Development of Insurance Business Regulation in Nigeria

The first major step at regulating the activities of insurance business in Nigeria was the report of J.C. Obande Commission of 1961, which resulted in the establishment of Department of Insurance in the Federal Ministry of Trade and which later transferred to the Ministry of Finance. The report also led to the enactment of Insurance Companies Act 1961, which came into effect on 4 May 1967 (NAICOM 2015).

The 1961 Act focused mainly on the activities of direct insurers, made provisions for registration and record keeping. In 1968, Insurance Companies Regulations was put in place to facilitate the implementation of Act No 58 of 1961 which then classified insurance business into different classes for registration purpose and relevant forms for record keeping (NAICOM 2015).

Insurance Decree No 59 of 1976 was enacted putting together the provisions of the various laws. The 1976 Decree among others made the following provision: condition for authorization of insurers, mode of operation, amalgamation and transfer, administration and enforcement, and penalties. Thus, the Insurance Decree No 59 of 1976 constituted the first all-embracing law for the regulation and supervision of insurance business in Nigeria (NAICOM 2015).

In 1968, concern was given to life insurance business, and it led to the enactment of Decree 40 of 1988 which made provisions among others for assignment of life insurance policy, named beneficiary on life insurance policy document (NAICOM 2015).

The Federal Government of Nigeria promulgated the Insurance Special Supervisory Fund (ISSF) Decree 20 of 1989 to strengthen the manpower need of the Insurance Supervisory Board. That Decree mandated all insurance companies to contribute 1% of their gross earning to the fund (NAICOM 2015).

Decree No 58 of 1991 was enacted improving provisions of Decree No 58 of 1979 and No 40 of 1988. The major highlights of the 1991 Decree include increased paid-up share capital of insurers and reinsurers in respect of non-life business and life business, respectively, compulsory membership of trade associations, management of security fund by NIA, and practice of No-premium No-cover (NAICOM 2015).

In 1992, the ISSF Decree No 62 was enacted, establishing a body known as National Insurance Supervisory Board, bringing out insurance supervision outside core civil service, changing designation of Chief Executive from Director of Insurance to Commissioner of Insurance, and setting up the Board of Directors to oversee the affairs of the established body. All this provisions were made to attract high-level manpower. The provisions of Decree No 62 of 1992 and 58 of 1991 were reviewed for effective supervision and efficient insurance market, bringing into enactment Decree No 1 and 2 of 1997, National Insurance Commission, and Insurance Decree, respectively (NAICOM 2015).

The following provisions were made in reviewing Decree No 62 of 1992 and Decree No 1 of 1997: change of name from National Insurance Supervisory Board to National Insurance Commission, establishment of Governing Board, staffing, source and application of funds, control and management of failed and failing insurance companies, and supervisory functions and powers (NAICOM 2015).

Decree No 58 of 1991 was improved on with Decree No 2 of 1997 in the following areas: by raising the paid-up share capital for different categories of insurance companies, qualification of Chief Executive, and insurance of government properties amidst others (NAICOM 2015).

37.2.4 Evaluation of the Nigerian Insurance Sector Reforms

Financial reforms, according to Ebong (2006) cited in Iganiga (2010), are deliberate policy response to correct perceived or impending crisis and subsequent failure. Reforms in the financial industry are aimed at addressing issues such as governance, risk management, and operational inefficiency. Financial reforms are specifically driven by the need to achieve consolidation, competition, and convergence of financial architecture.

Insurance sector therefore as a sub-sector, is part of the broader financial system reforms in Nigeria. According to FSS (2010), the industry started in 1921, went through indigenization decree of 1972, and became open in the 1980s.

To further reposition the sector for competiveness and confidence, NAICOM was set up by Acts of 1997. Six years after, the Insurance Act was enacted, and the Insurance guidelines for consolidation and recapitalization were first issued. The results of the measures have led to the promotion of insurance sector depth and efficiency (FSS 2010).

Furthermore, as stated in FSS (2010) the vision statement of the sector read as follows: "To become insurance sector of first choice in Africa noted for high level of capacity, transparency, efficiency and safety and attain 15th position in world insurance premium generation by the year 2020," and the major reform efforts to achieve the above vision were highlighted as follows: to ensure that the sector is financially sound (capacity), creating an efficiency market structure (efficiency), creating consumers trust in the sector (safety), and engendering competitiveness. However, efforts to engender competitiveness have further promoted concentrated market structure in the industry.

IMF (2010) in a study notably examining the competitiveness in Nigerian insurance sector and using concentration ratio technique established findings that the non-life insurance market, relatively to the life insurance market, was highly concentrated. The study revealed that top 10 insurers account for over 50% of the market gross/written premium in non-life insurance business in Nigeria, while one insurer (AIICO) held 20% of market share in life insurance business.

37.2.5 Justification of the Study

Fashoto et al. (2012) examined the Nigerian Insurance landscape with the focus of assessing the pre-recapitalization and post-recapitalization of the operating insurance firms as of 2008 using performance surveys and applying AHP Model.

Pan African Capital (2013) also assessed the performance of insurance firms in Nigeria and although implicit in the work was an insight into the competiveness, such was largely descriptive.

Meristem Securities (2014) which also was a descriptive work adopted briefly the Herfindahl-Hirshman Index (HHI) to evaluate the level of competition in Nigerian Insurance sector.

KPMG Africa (2015) was also largely descriptive but with little emphasis on competitiveness and was regional-focused not Nigeria-centered.

The study will therefore go beyond the descriptive studies using econometric specification to determine the level of competitiveness with the inclusion of variables that are relevant in determining the outcome. Thus, we adopted the Panzar-Rosse (PR) H-statistic to ascertain the degree of competitiveness and used the concentration ratio technique also to show the degree of market power prevalent within the market and enjoyed by these firms over the period under review. The beauty of the paper therefore is the up-to-date analysis it provides, which is a variant from other studies.

37.3 Methodology

37.3.1 Theoretical Framework

The study adopts the concentration ratio analysis and the Panzar-Rosse (1987) methodology in measuring competitiveness in the Nigerian insurance sector. Criticisms however of the Panzar-Rosse (1987) model were emphasized by Simpasa (2013).

37.3.1.1 The Concentration Measures

Vassilopoulos (2003) noted that two schools of thought dominate academic research in examining market power, which defined by the US Department of Justice and Federal Trade Commission (2002) means the ability of single firm or a group of competing firms in a market to profitably raise prices above competitive levels and restrict output below competitive levels for a sustained period of time.

Thus, a competitive market is such that needs many sellers and in such market sellers are price takers and cannot affect the market price because if they charge a higher price, buyers will go elsewhere. While thanks to competition as whenever prices for a product become too high relative to costs, consumers switch their demand to other products, or other companies discover the profitable market, enter the market, and conquer market shares since the ability to substitute away from high-priced products, on the demand side or on the supply side, is the key disciplining force on a free market, putting pressure on companies and constraining their behavior such that they cannot arbitrarily raise prices without losing market shares and, as in the long run, the competitive pressure is essential for the economic efficiency of the market; a monopoly, in contrary, has the ability to drive prices up without the fear that other sellers will undercut his price since he can produce less and set his product at a higher price that will allow him to make extra profits, and by restricting output, the monopolist diverts resources from their highest value use (deadweight loss). At the high prices, transfers of money from consumers to monopolists occur (Vassilopoulous 2003).

However, all markets are somewhere in between perfect competition and monopoly. If a market has just a few large sellers they will act just like a monopoly and they will be able to set the market price to some extent. But of course, not all high prices are due to market power but rather a scarcity rent, provided there is a demand response, so that the price can only rise to what the last consumer is willing to pay. Antitrust literature identifies two types of market power: horizontal and vertical. Horizontal market power is exercised when a firm profitably drives up prices through its control of a single activity. Vertical market power arises when a firm involved in two related activities uses its power to raise prices and increase profits for the overall firm (Vassilopoulous 2003).

In a competitive market thereof, the most profitable strategy notably to be adopted by a price-taking producer is the bidding of output and such a firm also is said to have market power when it acts in a manner that is intended to change market prices but maintains them at a noncompetitive level for a sustained period of time (Vassilopoulous 2003). The concentration measures which are computed using varied concentration structural indexes like the market shares, the HHI and his many refinements, and the residual supply indexes thus serve as an aid to show empirically such market power, but this study will focus on the use of market shares.

While according to the Harvard school and their structure-conduct-performance (S-C-P) paradigm, there is a causal relationship running from industry structure through the behavior of existing firms to the performance of the market, measured by, e.g., pricing since as market concentration increases, the equilibrium price departs more and more from the perfectly competitive level and goes toward the monopoly level, the Cournot model according to which oligopolists set quantities provides a theoretical justification for this thinking: As market concentration increases, the equilibrium price departs more and more from the perfectly competitive level and goes toward the monopoly level, and so for the Harvard school, there is a one-to-one correspondence between market power and market concentration; the Chicago school on the other hand holds the opposite view as they believe that firms grow big and get a large market share because they are more efficient than other firms: Efficient firms grow; inefficient firms become smaller and disappear. That the causal relationship thereby runs from efficiency to market structure (and profitability). The Chicago school model as a result is consistent with the Bertrand model of competition according to which oligopolists set prices (Vassilopoulous 2003).

Using the concentration ratio analysis technique, we seek to detect market power by examining three components of the firms' balance sheet thereby providing us ascertained evidence to the level of market power exhibited by these firms. Thus, it shows the prevailing market structure operated by these firms. More so, it will envisage the level of dominance out-playing in the Nigerian insurance landscape.

37.3.1.2 The Panzar-Rosse Methodology

As cited by Simpasa (2013), the H-statistic proposed by Panzar and Rosse (1987) have been widely employed in empirical models of measuring market competitiveness and market power. The H-statistic, the sum of revenue elasticities with respect to varied inputs, measures the extent to which a change in input is reflected in the firms' equilibrium revenue. Market structure notably is determined by the magnitude and sign of the H-statistic. Briefly, its interpretation is summarized in Table 37.1 as follows:

The empirical PR methodology would employ the models as follows:

As the Nigerian insurance sector is categorized into life insurance sub-sector and non-life insurance sub-sector, models 1 and 2 would be adopted to capture these sub-sectors, respectively.

Hence, for life insurance sub-sector:

$$\mathrm{GRPM1}_{\mathrm{it}} = \beta_0 + \beta_1 \mathrm{WTPM1}_{\mathrm{it}} + \beta_2\ \mathrm{TAST1}_{\mathrm{it}} + \beta_3\ \mathrm{GRCM1}_{\mathrm{it}} + \beta_4 \mathrm{MEXP1}_{\mathrm{it}} \cdots \tag{37.1}$$

Table 37.1 Interpretation of the Panzar-Rosse H-statistic

Value of H-statistic	Market structure characterization
$H \leq 0$	Monopoly
$0 < H < 1$	Monopolistic competition
$H = 1$	Perfect competition
Market equilibrium test	
$\mathrm{E} = 0$	Equilibrium
$\mathrm{E} \leq 0$	Disequilibrium

Source: Simpasa (2013)

where

β_0 denotes constant term
β_1, β_2, β_3, and β_4 are the revenue elasticities
GRPM1 represents gross premium taken as the revenue of firms in the life insurance business
WTPM1 represents written premium of firms in the life insurance business
TAST1 represents total asset of firms in the life insurance business
GRCM1 represents gross claim of firms in the life insurance business
MEXP1 represents management expenses of firms in the life insurance business

While for non-life (or general business) insurance sub-sector:

$$\mathrm{GRPM2_{it}} = \beta_0 + \beta_1 \mathrm{WTPM2_{it}} + \beta_2\ \mathrm{TAST2_{it}} + \beta_3\ \mathrm{GRCM2_{it}} + \beta_4\ \mathrm{MEXP2_{it}} \cdots \tag{37.2}$$

where also

β_0 denotes constant term
β_1, β_2, β_3, and β_4 are the revenue elasticities
GRPM2 represents gross premium taken as the revenue of firms in the non-life insurance business
WTPM2 represents written premium of firms in the non-life insurance business
TAST2 represents total asset of firms in the non-life insurance business
GRCM2 represents gross claim of firms in the non-life insurance business
MEXP2 represents management expenses of firms in the non-life insurance business

From the models (Eqs. 37.1 and 37.2), $H = \beta_1 + \beta_2 + \beta_{3,} + \beta_{4,}$ the sum of the revenue elasticities with respect to varied inputs.

NB: The difference between gross premium and written premium is taken to be reinsurance cost.

37.3.2 Analytical Framework

The concentration ratio computation for both life and non-life (or general business) insurance firms' classification, respectively, will entail evaluation based on their gross premium, total assets, and gross claims as a ratio of the industry's gross premium, total assets, and gross claim for the period 1999–2008.

Annual panel observations from 1999 to 2008 for 27 insurance firms in the Nigerian insurance sector (20 out of 25 listed on NSE and 7 others not listed on NSE, respectively; see Table 37.5 in Appendix) and the panel estimation approach would be used to estimate the Panzar-Rosse H-statistic while also using the data so collated the degree of concentration for the Nigerian insurance market will be established using the concentration ratio analysis technique.

37.3.3 Data Issues

Following Fashoto et al. (2012) classification, the data to be adopted for the study include annual panel observations from 1999 to 2008 for 20 insurance companies that deal with general business only out of 27, 10 insurance companies that deal with life business only out of 12, and 10 insurance companies that deal with both life and general business only out of 14, making a total of 40 insurance firms out of 54 as at 2008 – a proportion of about 76% of the insurance firms operating as at the period, while one is an insurance company that insure other insurance companies, as well as industry statistics collated from Nigerian Insurers Association (NIA) 2005 and 2009 Statistical Journals and Central Bank of Nigeria (CBN) Statistical Bulletin 2012. It is notable that this study captures 25 out the 29 insurance firms listed on Nigerian Stock Exchange as at September 2013 (Pan African Capital 2013), the excluded firms being Continental Reinsurance, Staco Insurance Plc, Unity Kapital Assurance Plc, and Universal Insurance Company due to unavailability of data.

37.4 Results and Discussions

37.4.1 Concentration Ratio Analysis

From the concentration ratio analysis technique, the market power exhibited by the 22 and 26 insurance firms in both life and non-life insurance sub-sectors, respectively, using a ten-firm concentration ratio – CR_{10} (%) – is illustrated in Tables 37.2 and 37.3.

For an analysis of the degree of concentration in both sub-sectors, the market power of the ten largest insurance firms by asset size as at 2008 was examined out of 22 in the life insurance sub-sector, while on the other hand the ten largest

Table 37.2 Ten life insurance firm concentration ratios, CR_{10} (%)

	Gross premium	Total assets	Gross claims
1999	42.03	82.80	35.79
2000	82.84	67.15	81.24
2001	87.25	29.63	14.99
2002	70.25	80.35	22.17
2003	70.18	6.35	43.93
2004	48.64	37.52	70.28
2005	81.64	51.84	38.41
2006	66.02	76.36	60.94
2007	55.52	77.21	76.21
2008	67.48	53.35	56.06

Source: Computed by authors

Table 37.3 Ten non-life insurance firm concentration ratios, CR_{10} (%)

	Gross premium	Total assets	Gross claims
1999	26.29	44.19	26.84
2000	61.75	49.07	56.57
2001	60.47	21.39	13.59
2002	53.13	43.54	10.19
2003	44.58	3.23	16.60
2004	54.17	60.85	18.52
2005	22.57	50.76	22.00
2006	53.54	64.29	56.28
2007	69.04	64.14	57.55
2008	61.99	52.94	66.15

Source: Computed by authors

insurance firms by asset size as at 2008 were examined out of 26 in the non-life (or general business) insurance sub-sector.

It is prudent to state here that, of the 27 insurance firms examined in the study, 1 did life business only, 5 did general business only, and 21 did both life and general businesses.

Examining Table 37.2 above shows the life insurance companies' market structure as indicated by the ten-firm concentration ratios (CR_{10}) in three components of the insurance companies' balance sheet. The degree of concentration thereof in the life insurance sub-sector was evident across the years under review and relative to these three components.

With the inception of democratic system of governance in 1999, the life insurance business seemed to have flourished evidently as the ten large life insurance companies accounted for about 83% of the total industry assets, alongside a near average dominance of 42.03% and 35.79% in total industry gross premium and total industry gross claims, respectively.

Further on, enviable progress was vivid in 2000 with these companies accounting for a huge proportion of total industry receipt mobilization, i.e., gross premium as well as total industry payouts, i.e., gross claim of over 80% and total industry assets' share of about 70%.

In later years of 2001 and 2002, the tremendous height of business performance among these ten large life insurance companies was somewhat sustained with proportion of total industry gross claims tuned down below 25% (14.99 and 22.17 in respective years), while proportion of total industry gross premium was over 70%. The inadequacy of data for the worth of assets owned by some of these ten large life insurance companies in 2001 however impaired the effort to ascertain precisely their total industry assets' proportion.

Although maintaining still a strong business presence in 2003 with total industry gross premium at over 70%, the unavailability of data also for some of these companies in terms of their assets in order to aid know their proportion of total industry asset net worth and the increased total industry payouts to 43.93% could be likened to the electioneering process of the year. Whereas in 2004, the unprecedented fall in these ten large life insurance companies' proportion of total industry gross premium to 48.64%, a poor proportion of her total industry assets at 37.52% and a further increased proportion of total industry gross claims to 70.28% could be reiterated as due to uncertainties associated with the country's investment climate following an electioneering year.

However, the ten large life insurance companies accounted for more than 50% of total industry gross premium and assets in 2005. Their dominance also was seemingly pronounced over the years 2006 and 2008 with above-average concentration.

As regards the non-life insurance companies' market structure for the years under review and of which is depicted with Table 37.3, a fair and progressive business performance seemed also was recorded with the inception of democratic system of governance in 1999. In a similar manner, the ten large non-life insurance companies accounted for about 50% of the total industry assets between 1999 and 2002 except in 2001for which there was inadequacy of data for the worth of assets owned by some of these ten large non-life insurance companies. Though total industry gross premium and gross claim proportion were poor in 1999, i.e., only about 27%, respectively, they increased to more than average and decreased significantly, respectively, between 1999 and 2002.

The electioneering process and the unavailability of data also for some of these companies in terms of their assets in a way seemed to have engendered the below average total industry gross premium proportion of 44.58% in 2003, the increased total industry gross claim proportion from 10.19% in 2002 to 16.60% in 2003, and the inability to ascertain precisely their total industry assets' proportion.

The commencement of a new democratic regime in 2004 on the other hand could be implied as such that could have somewhat fostered the non-life insurance business performance – increasing total industry gross premium and assets proportion, respectively, to 54.17% and 60.85%, while the further increase in total industry gross claim proportion to 18.52% may be attributed to the uncertainties associated with the country's investment climate following an electioneering year.

A huge data deficit for non-life insurance businesses of most of these ten large non-life insurance companies in 2005, except in terms of their assets worth, largely constrained establishing findings for the non-life insurance sub-sector.

Other years however, i.e., 2006 and afterward, subsequently show a high degree of market power above-average concentration.

37.4.2 Panzar-Rosse H-Statistic

The Panzar-Rosse H-statistic established for both the life and non-life insurance sub-sectors, respectively, showed a higher degree of competitiveness in the non-life insurance sub-sector (see Tables 37.7 and 37.8 in Appendix).

The sum of the revenue elasticities for the life insurance sub-sector given as 1.004 shows that the life insurance market is deduced empirically to be competitive, following the H-statistic decision rule cited in Table 37.1. More so, with significant t-statistics and p-values except in terms of total assets and gross claims, a high weighted r-square and good Durbin-Watson statistic, the finding is envisaged as reliable.

For the non-life insurance sub-sector with the H-statistic given as 2.839, such shows that the non-life insurance market is seemingly more competitive relative to the life insurance market. This deduction is ascertained to be reliable also since with significant t-statistics except in terms of total assets, p-values, high weighted r-square, and good Durbin-Watson statistics.

37.5 Conclusion and Recommendations

The objective of the study being to assess the competitiveness in Nigerian Insurance Sector shows a high degree of market power or concentration by the ten insurance firms examined in both the life and non-life insurance sub-sectors, respectively.

The non-life insurance market however is evident to be more competitive relative to the life insurance market since with a higher H-statistic, and such is related to the study by IMF in 2010 attesting that the non-life insurance market relatively to the life insurance market is highly concentrated among other findings. More so, IMF (2010) stated that ten insurers account for over 50% of the market gross/written premium in non-life insurance business in Nigeria, while one insurer (AIICO) held 20% of market share in life insurance business.

The degree of competiveness however is envisaged to have been better ascertained in this study if two leading insurance firms – Industrial and General Insurance (IGI) and Leadway Assurance dominant in non-life and life insurance sub-sectors, respectively, were listed on the Nigerian Stock Exchange (NSE) since the study focused largely on insurance firms listed on the floor of the NSE.

37.5.1 Limitations of the Study

The scope of the study is limited by unavailability of data beyond 2008, and of which if provided could aid one carry out more robust analysis.

Appendix

Table 37.4 Number of reporting insurance companies

Years	1999	2000	2001	2002	2003	2004	2005	2006	2007	2008
	57	57	57	57	57	103	103	103	77	54

Source: Central Bank of Nigeria Statistical Bulletin, 2012

Table 37.5 List of insurance firms examined

1	African alliance insurance[a] – life business only
2	Consolidated hallmark insurance[a] – general business only
3	International energy insurance[a] – general business only
4	Investment and allied insurance Plc[b] – general business only
5	Prestige insurance Plc[b] – general business only
6	Wapic insurance Plc[b] – general business only
7	Alliance and general insurance[b] – life and general business
8	AIICO insurance[a] – life and general business
9	Cornerstone insurance[a] – life and general business
10	Crusader insurance[b] – life and general business
11	Custodian and allied insurance[a] – life and general business
12	Equity assurance[a] – life and general business
13	Goldlink insurance[b] – life and general business
14	Great Nigeria insurance[a] – life and general business
15	Guinea insurance[a] – life and general business
16	LASACO assurance[a] – life and general business
17	Law union and rock insurance[a] – life and general business
18	Linkage insurance[a] – life and general business
19	Guaranty trust insurance[a] – life and general business
20	Mutual benefit assurance[a] – life and general business
21	NEM insurance[a] – life and general business
22	Niger insurance[a] – life and general business
23	OASIS insurance[b] – life and general business
24	Regency alliance insurance[a] – life and general business
25	Sovereign trust insurance[a] – life and general business
26	Standard alliance insurance[a] – life and general business
27	UNIC insurance[a] – life and general business

Source: Nigerian Insurers Association (NIA) 2005 & 2009 Statistical Journals

NB: *a* Refers to firms listed on NSE and data available; *b* Refers to firms not listed on NSE but data available

Table 37.6 List of insurance firms unexamined

1	Universal insurance[a]
2	Unity Kapital assurance[a]
3	Staco insurance[a]
4	Royal exchange assurance[a]
5	Continental reinsurance[a]

Source: Prepared by authors
NB: *a* Refers to firms listed on NSE but data unavailable

Table 37.7 PR model panel estimation for life insurance sub-sector

Dependent variable: GRPM1				
Method: panel EGLS (cross-section random effects)				
Date: 03/16/16 time: 15:08				
Sample: 1999 2008				
Periods included: 10				
Cross-sections included: 22				
Total panel (unbalanced) observations: 150				
Swamy and Arora estimator of component variances				
Period weights (PCSE) standard errors and covariance (d.f. Corrected)				
Variable	**Coefficient**	**Std. error**	**t-statistic**	**Prob.**
C	411513.0	81633.21	5.041000	0.0000
WTPM1	0.567978	0.073366	7.741663	0.0000
TAST1	0.016491	0.020074	0.821526	0.4127
GRCM1	0.349094	0.247543	1.410239	0.1606
MEXP1	0.070305	0.030432	2.310217	0.0223
	Effects specification			
			S.D.	Rho
Cross-section random			296203.2	0.2936
Idiosyncratic random			459434.5	0.7064
	Weighted statistics			
R-squared	0.572109	Mean dependent var		470281.6
Adjusted R-squared	0.560305	S.D. dependent var		682059.0
S.E. Of regression	452073.6	Sum squared resid		2.96E + 13
F-statistic	48.46782	Durbin-Watson stat		0.976110
Prob(F-statistic)	0.000000			
	Unweighted statistics			

(continued)

Table 37.7 (continued)

R-squared	0.540583	Mean dependent var	929846.3
Sum squared resid	4.04E + 13	Durbin-Watson stat	0.716080

Correlated random effects – Hausman test				
Equation: Untitled				
Test cross-section random effects				
Test summary		Chi-Sq. statistic	Chi-Sq. d.f.	Prob.
Cross-section random		0.000000	4	1.0000
cross-section test variance is invalid. Hausman statistic set to zero				
WARNING: Robust standard errors may not be consistent with				
Assumptions of Hausman test variance calculation				
Cross-section random effects test comparisons:				
Variable	Fixed	Random	Var(diff.)	Prob.
WTPM1	0.554973	0.567978	−0.000220	NA
TAST1	0.019862	0.016491	0.000020	0.4526
GRCM1	0.401326	0.349094	0.002390	0.2853
MEXP1	0.076242	0.070305	0.000805	0.8342
Cross-section random effects test equation:				
Dependent variable: GRPM1				
Method: Panel least squares				
Date: 03/16/16 time: 15:11				
Sample: 1999 2008				
Periods included: 10				
Cross-sections included: 22				
Total panel (unbalanced) observations: 150				
Period weights (PCSE) standard errors and covariance (d.f. Corrected)				
Variable	**Coefficient**	**Std. error**	**t-statistic**	**Prob.**
C	395840.8	59647.87	6.636293	0.0000
WTPM1	0.554973	0.071849	7.724150	0.0000
TAST1	0.019862	0.020569	0.965601	0.3361
GRCM1	0.401326	0.252323	1.590521	0.1143
MEXP1	0.076242	0.041604	1.832541	0.0693
	Effects specification			
Cross-section fixed (dummy variables)				
R-squared	0.702318	Mean dependent var		929846.3
Adjusted R-squared	0.642301	S.D. dependent var		768183.0
S.E. Of regression	459434.5	Akaike info criterion		29.06969
Sum squared resid	2.62E + 13	Schwarz criterion		29.59154
Log likelihood	−2154.227	Hannan-Quinn criter		29.28170
F-statistic	11.70205	Durbin-Watson stat		1.086933
Prob(F-statistic)	0.000000			

Table 37.8 PR model panel estimation for non-life insurance sub-sector

Dependent Variable: GRPM2				
Method: panel EGLS (cross-section random effects)				
Date: 03/16/16 time: 15:30				
Sample: 1999 2008				
Periods included: 10				
Cross-sections included: 26				
Total panel (unbalanced) observations: 154				
Swamy and Arora estimator of component variances				
Cross-section weights (PCSE) standard errors and covariance (d.f. Corrected)				
Variable	**Coefficient**	**Std. error**	**t-statistic**	**Prob.**
C	341911.2	247968.8	1.378848	0.1700
WTPM2	0.292651	0.089862	3.256660	0.0014
TAST2	0.059926	0.034773	1.723377	0.0869
GRCM2	1.253232	0.530890	2.360625	0.0195
MEXP2	1.233235	0.512728	2.405242	0.0174
	Effects specification			
			S.D.	Rho
Cross-section random			0.000000	0.0000
Idiosyncratic random			2,221,724.	1.0000
	Weighted statistics			
R-squared	0.159491	Mean dependent var		1,190,760.
Adjusted R-squared	0.136927	S.D. dependent var		2,363,222.
S.E. of regression	2,195,474.	Sum squared resid		7.18E + 14
F-statistic	7.068381	Durbin-Watson stat		1.638484
Prob(F-statistic)	0.000031			
	Unweighted statistics			
R-squared	0.159491	Mean dependent var		1,190,760.
Sum squared resid	7.18E + 14	Durbin-Watson stat		1.638484

Correlated random effects - Hausman test				
Equation: Untitled				
Test cross-section random effects				
Test summary		Chi-Sq. statistic	Chi-Sq. d.f.	Prob.
Cross-section random		0.000000	4	1.0000
cross-section test variance is invalid. Hausman statistic set to zero				
WARNING: Robust standard errors may not be consistent with				
Assumptions of Hausman test variance calculation				
WARNING: Estimated cross-section random effects variance is zero				
Cross-section random effects test comparisons:				
Variable	Fixed	Random	Var(diff.)	Prob.
WTPM2	0.239392	0.292651	0.001463	0.1638
TAST2	0.067784	0.059926	0.000372	0.6837
GRCM2	1.563382	1.253232	−0.025265	NA
MEXP2	1.675316	1.233235	0.083101	0.1251

(continued)

Table 37.8 (continued)

Cross-section random effects test equation:				
Dependent variable: GRPM2				
Method: Panel least squares				
Date: 03/16/16 time: 15:32				
Sample: 1999 2008				
Periods included: 10				
Cross-sections included: 26				
Total panel (unbalanced) observations: 154				
Cross-section weights (PCSE) standard errors and covariance (d.f. Corrected)				
Variable	Coefficient	Std. error	t-statistic	Prob.
C	240378.7	243460.1	0.987343	0.3254
WTPM2	0.239392	0.097665	2.451151	0.0156
TAST2	0.067784	0.039764	1.704662	0.0908
GRCM2	1.563382	0.506536	3.086416	0.0025
MEXP2	1.675316	0.588210	2.848160	0.0051
	Effects specification			
Cross-section fixed (dummy variables)				
R-squared	0.283690	Mean dependent var		1,190,760.
Adjusted R-squared	0.116165	S.D. dependent var		2,363,222.
S.E. Of regression	2,221,724.	Akaike info criterion		32.23840
Sum squared resid	6.12E + 14	Schwarz criterion		32.83002
Log likelihood	−2452.357	Hannan-Quinn criter		32.47872
F-statistic	1.693425	Durbin-Watson stat		1.916617
Prob(F-statistic)	0.025323			

References

Central Bank of Nigeria. (2012). Statistical bulletin, Abuja, Nigeria.

Ebong, H. (2006). Banking Sector Reforms: Opportunities and Challenges. *Union Digest, 10*(1&2), 46–47.

Fashoto, S. G., Okokpo, G., Owolabi, O., & Gbadeyan, J. A. (2012). Application of AHP Model to Recapitalization in Insurance Companies of Nigeria. *Transnational Journal of Science and Technology, 2*(9), 16–30.

FSS. (2010). *Financial sector strategy*. Central bank of Nigeria, Abuja, Nigeria.

Iganiga, B. O. (2010). Evaluation of the nigerian financial sector reforms using behavioural models. *Journal of Economics, 1*(2), 65–75.

International Monetary Fund. (2010). *World economic outlook*, Washington, D. C., U.S.A.

Isenmila, P. A. (2002). *Insurance: Principles and practice*. Benin: Mindex Publishing Company Limited.

KPMG Africa. (2015). *Sector report: Insurance in Africa*, South Africa.

Meristem Securities. (2014). The Nigerian insurance sector- rich hunting ground for investment. *Proshare*.

NAICOM. (2010). *Annual report and statement of accounts*, Lagos, Nigeria.

NAICOM. (2015). *Our history*. http://www.naicom.gov.ng. Accessed 12 May 2015, Lagos, Nigeria.

Obasi, N. (2010). Policies, challenges, reforms and Nigerian disposition to insurance contracts. *The Fronteira Post,* March, *5*, 1–6.
Pan African Capital Plc. (2013). Insurance industry: A review.
Panzar, M., & Rosse, J. (1987). Testing for Monopoly Equilibrium. *The Journal of Industrial Economics, 35*, 445–456.
Simpasa, A. M. (2013). Competition and market structure in the Zambian banking sector. *African Development Bank Group*, Working Paper 168.
Ujunwa, A., & Nwanneka, J. (2011). Repositioning Insurance Industry for Operational Efficiency: The Nigeria Case. *Journal of Applied Finance and Banking, 1*(3), 15–32.
US Department of Justice and Federal Trade Commission. (2002). Horizontal merger guidelines.
Vassilopoulous, P. (2003). Models for the identification of market power in wholesale electricity markets. *Universite Paris–Dauphine*.

Chapter 38
Business Cycle Transmission from BRICS to Developing Countries, Some New Evidence

Argiro Moudatsou and Huseyin Kaya

Abstract Our motivation of running this research is the increasing importance of BRICS as a dynamic and emerging power with a growing role in global affairs. The topic of this research in recent years is extremely important given the progress of the international economy and the growing role of the BRICS into the world economical scene, particularly for the less developed countries. The BRICS members are all developing or newly industrialized countries but are distinguished (at least the original four) by their large, fast-growing economies and, more recently, by their significant influence on regional and global affairs.

This paper examines the role of emerging economies of Brazil, China, India, and Russia, as the new regional economic drivers for the less developed countries. To our knowledge, the case of the role of BRICS as dynamic emerging economies has not been entirely explored, so the target of our research is to contribute to this field.

We employ a Global Vector Autoregressive (GVAR) model to investigate the extent of business cycle transmission from BRICS to LDCs. Our research follows Samake and Yang (2011) work with a different sample of countries and different time span. Our sample includes Brazil, Russia, China, India, 10 EU countries, the USA, and 49 emerging and developing economies from Asia, Africa, Latin America, and Commonwealth of Independent States, covering the period 2000–2014.

Summarizing the results, we can notice that the BRICS doesn't seem to play any significant role as economic leaders for the less income countries of that region, neither do they seem to have strong links among them.

The low bilateral trade weights between the core economies and their counterparts in Asia and Africa, LA (Latin America), and CIS (Commonwealth of

A. Moudatsou (✉)
University of Applied Sciences (TEI) of Crete, Crete, Greece

Hellenic Open University, Patras, Greece
e-mail: moudatsou@staff.teicrete.gr

H. Kaya
Istanbul Medeniyet University, Istanbul, Turkey

N. Tsounis, A. Vlachvei (eds.), *Advances in Panel Data Analysis in Applied Economic Research*, Springer Proceedings in Business and Economics,
https://doi.org/10.1007/978-3-319-70055-7_38

Independent States) could be a possible explanation for the insignificant impact of a positive RGDP shock in the core economies. That is, the transmission via trade is trivial. The trade links are not strong enough to trigger transmission shock to the developing countries of Asia and Africa, Latin America, and CIS.

Keywords Global VAR (GVAR) · Impulse responses · Macroeconomic shocks · International business cycle · Economic growth

38.1 Introduction

In the aftermath of the recent global financial crisis, business cycle transmission has regained attention, to the extent that BRICS growth suffered much less from the crisis than that of advanced economies; they draw the attention of many economists in an attempt to assess their role in the global economic affairs.

Moreover, the emergence of BRICS provides another potential source of sustained external demand and source of financing for low-income countries, raising the prospects for faster growth and poverty reduction in the long term. The strong economic growth in BRICS resulting to a rise in global demand for commodities coupled with their rapid reserve accumulation could alter the terms of trade and the cost of financing for world trade (IMF 2011).

BRICS is the acronym for an association of five major emerging national economies: Brazil, Russia, India, China, and South Africa. The acronym BRIC was devised in 2001 by the then head of asset management at Goldman Sachs, Jim O'Neill, with a paper titled "Building Better Global Economic BRICS." Although the term "BRIC" was devised by O'Neill in 2001, Van Agtmael (2012) argues that the idea of rebranding emerging economies of the global south extends back to the 1980s. The BRICS countries collectively represent almost three billion people (43% of the world population), with a combined nominal GDP of $14.8 trillion (about a quarter of global income), 17% of world trade, and an estimated $4 trillion in combined foreign reserves. They occupy 20% of the world territory, and over the past 10 years, their aggregate income has been more than quadrupled. By 2018, overall economic output of the BRICS may overtake that of the USA. By 2020, 33% of world GDP may be accounted for by the BRICS. By 2027, China's GDP is expected to equal USA's, and by 2050, the BRICS economies may absorb 50% of global markets. Consumption in the BRICS countries has also grown steadily, and in the next decade, 70% of global car sales growth is projected to occur in these emerging economies (GovInn 2013).

A common criticism of the BRICS concept is that it is nothing more than an acronym for the four largest emerging market economies (and South Africa), but in economic and political terms, little else have in common. In economic terms, two are manufacturing-based economies and big importers of natural resources (China and India), and the other two are huge exporters of natural resources (Brazil and Russia). In political terms, Brazil and India are "noisy" but real democracies; China is authoritarian and Russia somewhat ambivalently in between (Beech 2011).

Despite their differences and the criticism that they are not more than a "GDP club," their initiative in 2013 to establish a new "development bank" aimed at mobilizing resources (worth $4.5 trillion over an initial 5-year period) for infrastructure projects in BRICS and other emerging economies and developing countries makes them a very serious player in the international economic scene. In theory, the idea was to supplant the World Bank as the main lending institution for the developing world. They also established a business council to facilitate private sector partnerships, a trade and development "risk pool," and a contingent reserve arrangement, with a pool of $100 billion to cushion member states against any future economic shocks. China is expected to contribute $41 billion to the reserve, followed by Brazil and Russia ($18 billion each) and South Africa ($5 billion). From the sociopolitical point of view, each one of them enhanced its international status from the first summit in 2009 in Yekaterinburg (Russia) which led to an establishment of a political platform under extremely turbulent economic and political circumstances. The BRICS relative economic stability and capacity to respond to the crisis lent credibility to their call for reform of the international system. Brazil, Russia, India, China, and, later on, South Africa have thus become the symbols of a global shift, from an old global economic system led by the so-called West (the USA and, to a lesser degree, European countries) to a new development course in which traditionally "underdeveloped" countries have come to play a leading role (Stuenkel 2014).

In this paper, we examine the leading role of this group of emerging economies Brazil, Russia, India, and China, as the new regional and global economic drivers for a number of selected less income countries via the transmission channel of international trade.

There are several channels of inter-market transmission. Some of them identified by the empirical work are international trade for exports and imports, investment, financial linkages, aid and R&D finances for productivity enhancement (Jha and McCawley 2011), etc.

Even though the spillover effect can be transmitted through many ways, we focus on the trade linkage channel, which in fact several empirical studies have been proven by Çakir and Kabundi (2011), Forbes and Chinn (2004), Baxter and Kouparitsas (2005), Frankel and Rose (1997 and 1998), and Inklaar et al. (2007) to be, among all other possible linkages, the most important source for explaining the international business cycle movement.

In our study, we believe that the trade channel is the most relevant to measure the spillover effects, in the context of BRICS since the trade links are much pronounced among them and between them and the less developed countries, under consideration. Besides since the most of developing countries in our sample have not developed yet an organized statistical system, there was a lack of data concerning financial markets (equity prices, stock prices, interest rates).

The rationale behind this trade linkage is in fact very simple: an increase in exports in one country automatically corresponds to a rise in imports of another country and vice versa, and since both export and import are one of the main components in output, a country's national income is thus inevitably affected. This positive transmission through trade is particularly vital for the low- and middle-income economies which are generally known to substantially rely on the export orientation to generate output growth for their economies. Given the importance of these countries as new players, in international economic political process, we have to note the following.

To our knowledge the empirical research for the whole group is limited. The most of research focus on the dominant role of China, not only for the developing countries but among the BRIC group itself. About India's role as growth leader for the developing country, there is not much empirical evidence, while for the role of Brazil and Russia, there is no empirical evidence, at all.

The common feature of these surveys is that all of them include in their sample only the more robust developing economies. A reasonable explanation is the lack of notable statistical data for the developing countries that do not permit the use of complicated econometric models necessary to estimate the spillover effects.

While the literature has focused on the individual BRICS as well as the coherence of the BRICS as a group, the interaction of BRICS economies with their developing partners has so far not received an equal degree of attention. The present paper aims to fill the particular gap.

The contribution of our research in addition to increasing the geographical coverage is that it extends the estimation period. Moreover using a big sample of many less developed and different economic countries selected from Africa, Asia, Latin America, and the Commonwealth of Independent States regions, we try to look at the prospect of the leading role of BRICS as new growth engines, for developing the world possibly giving a different direction compared to existing leaders as the USA and EU, an issue that is under question.

The rest of the paper is organized as follows: In Sect. 38.2 we review some of the relevant research results. In Sect. 38.3, we describe the GVAR methodology that we use. In Sect. 38.4, we discuss the data, model specification, and bilateral trade linkages among partners. In Sect. 38.5 we present the estimation and testing of the GVAR model. In Sect. 38.6 we present the dynamic analysis results. In Sect. 38.7 we summarize and conclude.

Appendices contain description of data and variables used in the model, the tables of countries and regions, bilateral trade weight matrices, the results from GVARX* estimations, the GIRFs graphs, and the GFEVD results.

38.2 Previous Research

In the globalized world, the implementation of effective macroeconomic policy requires both the consideration of domestic market conditions and interdependencies across countries.

Even though the spillover effect can be transmitted through many ways, the trade linkage channel has been proven by several empirical studies, i.e., Çakir and Kabundi (2011), Forbes and Chinn (2004), Baxter and Kouparitsas (2005), and Frankel and Rose (1997, 1998), to be, among all other possible linkages, the most important source for explaining the international business cycle movement.

The relationship between economic growth and international trade is extensively examined in the new endogenous growth theory. Among the important theories in endogenous school, Lucas (1988) elaborates a neoclassical theory of growth, and international trade suggested that the rate of economic growth in each country differs depending on its comparative advantage. Another pioneer work on this topic is that of Grossman and Helpman (1991) which demonstrates that international trade promotes economic growth as it induces the development of knowledge and technology. These factors in turn lead to a specialization in production, and coupling with economies of scale, cost of production is reduced. Innovation and new varieties are then introduced to the market at a faster rate, promoting growth and development.

In addition, the topic of economic growth and international trade is also widely discussed in terms of their relationship direction or causality effect.

There is an extensive literature supporting the idea of export-led growth; Balassa (1978) and Ram (1985), for example, suggest that exports play an important role in generating economic growth using regression of output growth on several export variables. The growth-led export is supported by Lancaster (1980), and Krugman (1984) propose that output growth enhances the level of labor skills and technology –factors responsible for the construction of a comparative advantage – and as a result promotes and facilitates higher exports. Meanwhile, the third strand of the literature concludes a two-way causality such as Helpman and Krugman (1985) and Bhagwati (1988). And lastly, the fourth strand of the literature found that there is no systematic relationship between growth and trade. With reference to the aspect of policy implication, the direction of the relationship can help the relevant authority designing appropriate policies which emphasize on export promotion in the case of export-led growth, whereas those promoting economic development and growth would be the proper answer for a setting where the growth-led export applies.

Regarding the relevant research about the BRICS as a new emerging growth engine, the researchers' opinions are diverged. Some of them claim the dynamic role of BRICS in creating positive growth spillovers with their trade partners, emphasizing the dominant role of China and India among them. The most of the researchers recognize the peculiarity of this group regarding the political, social, and economic heterogeneity of the countries that compose it.

However, all recognize the special geopolitical role they can play in the global economic and political life, since they are showing a readiness to assume responsibilities in proportion to their standing in the modern world.

Samake and Yang (2011) estimate with a GVAR model the growth spillovers from BRICS to less income countries (LICS) using a sample of 29 sub-Saharan, Asian, and Latin America LICs. The estimation results show that there are significant direct spillovers through trade, FDI, and real exchange rates, while indirect spillovers, through world oil prices, other commodity prices, global interest rates (proxied by the US Federal Fund Rate), and global demand also matter in many cases.

Morazan et al. (2012) using statistical data on trade, FDI, financial flows, and donation flows state that BRICS impact on LICs through these channels is significant, and these south-south efforts need to be reflected in EU development strategies.

Phuangsiri (2012) examines the role of three large emerging economies, China, India, and Brazil, as the new regional and global economic drivers. The results imply that both China and Brazil act as regional powers and seem to have a vital impact to their neighboring economies as well as extending their global growth driver role to the rest of the world. The results also imply the existence of the decoupling hypothesis of several developing countries from the USA and simultaneously an increasing integration with the large emerging economies.

Mlanchila and Takebe (2011), using descriptive statistics on FDI sectoral flows, FDI from BRICS and especially China, into many nonresource-rich countries as Angola, Liberia, Sudan, and Zambia, state that they play a significant role for growth in those countries.

Samargandi and Kutan (2016), by employing a Global Vector Autoregressive (GVAR) model, explore cross-country evidence of the effects of private credit shocks on economic growth, focusing on whether private credit shocks in one BRICS member state affect economic growth in the other BRICS. The empirical evidence shows only private credit shocks in India and China which have many spillover effects on the growth of the other countries. In other words, it is these two members of BRICS that matter at the global stage, whereas Brazil, Russia, and South Africa remain relatively unimportant.

De Castro (2013) examines changing geographical trade patterns of BRICS's exports in regard to significant changes in global trade shifts within the past decade. The assessment, by various trade indices, focuses on regional trade orientation among BRICS themselves and between BRICS and the Triad (the USA, EU, Japan). The export intensity assessment provided rather independent evidence of BRICS's current behavior than BRICS as a group.

Armijo (2007) approaches the issue from another perspective, if "BRICS countries is a viable analytical category" since the four do not share domestic political institutions, international goals, or economic structures and challenges. He considered the concept from political economy perspective and concludes that what makes the relative rise of BRICS compelling for the international and world politics is the future balance between democratic and authoritarian major powers.

Kregel (2009), analyzing the global crisis and the implication for developing countries especially the BRICS, states that the positive impact of export-led growth will be offset by the opposite impact of financial markets, so an alternative strategy will be required. One possibility is to build on domestic sources of demand. Focused on Brazil, the author states that it is well-placed to engage in such a strategy and already has a number of policies to support this alternative.

Stuenkel (2014) analyzing the process of summits, starting from 2009 onward, through which BRICS enhanced their international status as dynamic twenty-one-century emerging powers, claims that, even though their coherence as a group is questionable, they could be turning into representatives of dynamic economies. The author gives also the possibility that other emerging economies such as Indonesia, the Philippines, or Nigeria could be part of that group.

38.3 Methodology

The Econometric Model

Since the target of the research is to study how a macroeconomic shock can be transferred from the economies of the BRIC to the economies of less developed countries which are associated with them, it was decided to use a Global Vector Autoregressive (GVAR) model pioneered by Pesaran et al. (2004) and developed by Dees et al. (2007a, b).

Compared to other models, which allow studying interdependences and transmission of shocks across units (i.e., panel VAR, dynamic factor models, large-scale Bayesian VARs), GVAR model is more appropriate in that it allows modeling a global spillover of shocks in a large-scale macroeconomic system with a large set of countries. This technique gives a theory-consistent solution to the problem of dimensionality in international modeling.

The GVAR model is a multivariate and multi-country framework used to investigate cross-country interdependency. It is also capable of generating forecasts for a set of macroeconomic factors for a set of countries to which they have exposure risks. This model has been used in several studies of macroeconomic spillover effects and regional interdependence: Pesaran et al. (2006a) and Pesaran et al. (2006b), in a credit risk analysis; Chudik (2007), in an assessment of the role of the USA as a dominant economy; Dées et al. (2008) about the construction of a theoretically coherent measure of steady-state global economy; Pesaran et al. (2007), in a counterfactual experiment of the UK's and Sweden's decision not to join EMU; Samake Yang (2011), in analyzing the growth spillovers between BRIC and low-income countries; Dreger and Zhang (2013) in studying the interdependencies between the business cycles in China and the advanced economies; Cashin et al. (2012), in analyzing spillovers from macroeconomic shocks in systemic economies to the economies of MENA; Cesa-Bianchi et al. (2012) in studying the transmission of business cycles from China to Latin America via trade changes; Dees et al.

(2007a, b) exploring the international linkages of the euro area; Chudik and Smith (2013) in analyzing the dominance of the US economy; and Bussière et al. (2009) in modeling global trade flows.

Our GVAR model is composed of 63 countries (Brazil, Russia, India, China, and 59 developed and developing countries). The first step of estimating the GVAR model is to estimate the individual 63 country-specific vector error-correction models augmented by weakly exogenous country-specific foreign variables and two global variables. The general specification of a country-specific model (VARX*) can be described as follows:

$$X_{it} = a_{i0} + \sum_{j=1}^{pi} aij\, xi, t-j + \sum\nolimits_{j=0}^{qi*} \beta ijx^{*}i, t-j + \sum\nolimits_{j=0}^{gi} \gamma ijgt-j + u_{it} \quad (38.1)$$

where

t= 1,2…T is the time, i=0, 1, 2, …N is countries, 0 stands for the USA, X_{it} is a $k_{i\times 1}$ vector of country-specific or domestic variables, X_{it}^{*} is a $k^{*}_{i\times 1}$ vector of X^{*} weakly exogenous variables, g_t is a vector of global exogenous variables (here oil prices and nonenergy international commodity prices), a_{i0} is a constant, t is the linear trend, and u_{it} a $k_{i\times 1}$ is vector of idiosyncratic shocks serially uncorrelated country-specific shocks.

u_{it} is i.i.d with a zero mean, and a covariance matrix cov $(u_{it}, u_{jt)}{}')=\sum_{u,ij}$ for i≠j, p_{i} and q_{i}* are the lag orders of domestic and foreign variables, respectively.

The country-specific foreign variables result as domestic variables weighted by bilateral trade weights wij, which capture the importance of country j for country's i economy:

$$X^{*}{}_{it} = \sum\nolimits_{j=0}^{N} wijxij \quad (38.2)$$

where j =0,1,..N, w_{ii} =0, and $\sum_{j=0}^{N} wij$ =1. These weights are fixed and computed as countries' average on bilateral trade over 2000–2014 (see Appendix A for the formula).

Setting $Z_{it} = (X_{it}{}'\, , X^{*}{}_{it})'$, neglecting g_t for simplicity, and defining p_i= max(q_i, $q^{*}{}_{i}$), Eq. (38.1) of the individual models can be rewritten as

$$A_{i.0}\, z_{i,t} = a_{i.0} + a_{i,1}t + \sum\nolimits_{j=1}^{pi} AijZi, t-j + u_{i,t} \quad (38.3)$$

where $A_{i.0} = (I_{\text{k},i} - \beta_{\iota,0})$ and $A_{i,j} = (\alpha_{i,j} - \beta_{i.j})$.

The vector $z_{i,t}$ is then linked to $x_t = (x_{0,t}, x_{1,t} \ldots\ldots x_{\text{N},t})'$, a $K\times 1$ vector containing all the endogenous variables of the system, through the link bilateral trade matrix W_i, $(k_i + k^{*}{}_{i}) \times k$ dimension.

We can then write $z_{i,t} = W_i x_t$, i=0.1.2…N

Equation (38.1) can be rewritten as

$$A_{i.0}\ W_i x_t = \sum\nolimits_{j=1}^{pi} AijWiXt - j + u_{i,t} \tag{38.4}$$

After the estimated coefficients from the individual country-specific VARX models are stacked, we obtain the model for all the variables in the global system:

$$G_0 = \alpha_0 + \alpha_{1t} + \sum\nolimits_{j=1}^{pi} GjXt - j + u_t \tag{38.5}$$

where

G_0 is a vector of $(N\times 1)$ elements $(A_{i.0}\ W_i)$, i=01 . . . N.
Gj is a vector of $(N\times 1)$ elements $(A_{i,j}W_i)$ i=0.1 .2 ..N, j=1.2 . . . p
α_0 is a vector of $(N\times 1)$ elements $(\alpha_{0,0}\ \alpha_{1,0}\ ......\ \alpha_{N,0})$
α_1 is a vector of $(N\times 1)$ elements $(\alpha_{01},\ \alpha_{11},\ \alpha_{21}\ ....\ \alpha_{N1})$
u_t is a vector $(N\times 1)$ elements $(u_{0.t}\ u_{1,t}\ u_{2,t}\ .....\ u_{N,t})$

Variables included in each country-specific model (except the USA) include endogenous variables X_{it} =(y_{it}, rer$_{it,,}$ Dp$_{it}$, exp$_{it}$, imp$_{it}$) and exogenous variables X^*_{it} = (y^*_{it}, Dp$^*_{it}$, P_{oil}, P_{com}).

Variables included in the US model are as follows: endogenous variables X_{us}= (y_{us}, exp$_{\text{us}}$, imp$_{\text{us}}$, Dp, P_{oil}) and exogenous variables X^*_{us} = (y^*_{us}, rer*, Dp*, P_{com}).

The USA is included in the model as reference country because of its dominant role in the global economy. The US real exchange rate is included as a weakly exogenous foreign variable in the US model, since the value of US $ is determined by other economies. Oil prices (P_{oil}) is included as endogenous in the US model given the fact that since the USA is the largest economy in our sample, it is also likely to have the biggest influence.

The star (*) variables are the weakly exogenous and were constructed using bilateral trade weights.

(Variable definition, formula, and justification of the trade weights are reported in Appendix A.)

38.4 Data

Quarterly data for 65 countries (the BRICS, 10 EU members, the USA, and 49 emerging and developing economies from Asia, Africa, Latin America, and Commonwealth of Independent States) covering the period 2000–2014 is used. The USA and EU are included because of their dominant position in the global economy. For the classification of the countries in developing and emerging economies, we use the UN-DESA (United Nations-Development Policy and Analysis Division) tables.

The variables of interest are real gross domestic product (RGDP), inflation rate, real exchange rate, imports, and exports. In our model, imports and exports are modeled jointly because of the strong import content of exports that is because exporting firms typically import production components, inducing thus comovements between exports and imports. Oil prices and international nonenergy commodity prices are included as global variables.

The data, its sources, regions, weight matrices, and definition of variables used in the analysis are displayed in supplementary *Appendix A* Tables 38.1, 38.2, 38.3, and 38.4 *(see Appendix A)* (Graphs 38.1 and 38.2).

38.5 Overview of the Brics Economies and Their Trade Linkages

The BRICS are a 10% player in the global economy. Compared to the world economic aggregates, BRICS nominal GDP measures 9%, exports 10%, foreign direct investment 6%, and foreign reserves 24% of the world. In terms of per capita GDP, the BRICS economies are equivalent to the average developing nation. In terms of income levels, Brazil and Russia stand on par with Japan in the second half of the 1960s, China is on par with Japan around the 1960s, and India is on par with Japan in the first half of the 1950s.[1]

Regarding the BRICS growing presence in global trade and foreign direct investment, the percentage share of the BRICS in global export grew from 4.2% in 1992 to 10.1% in 2004, while the share of global trade among developed countries shrank from 52.6% to 42.1%. Approximately 10% of global exports is comprised of exports by the BRICS. However, among the BRICS countries, there is a large gap between China and the remaining three countries. China's exports are growing to 6.4% of global exports (2004), which contrasts with Russia (1.8%), Brazil (1.3%), and India (0.8%). The gap between China and the remaining three countries is also prevalent with respect to foreign direct investment (FDI). In comparison to 9.4% of global FDI inflows to China (2004, flow basis), there is a gap of approximately 3.4 11.8 times with Brazil (2.8%), Russia (1.8%), and India (0.8%). The value of FDI inflows to China is approximately 30% of FDI to developing countries.[2]

More recent World Trade Organization data on international trade reveal that BRIC's share continues to increase. BRIC's exports as percentage of total world increased from 15.6% in 2000 to 30.5% in 2014 with India possessing the greatest share (9,3% to 19.6%) followed by China (4.2% to 7.6%). On the other side, BRIC's imports as percentage of total world increased from 22.6% in 2004 to 41.5% in 2014 with China being the greatest player (from 13.8% to 20.2%) followed by India (from 6.5% to 19%).

[1]From the reports prepared by the Mizuho Research Institute Ltd. by the commission of the Economic and Social Research Institute in fiscal policy 2005

[2]The same report

In Appendix B Tables 38.5, 38.6, 38.7, 38.8, and 38.9, we can see that BRICS gain an increased share in international commodity trade, with China as a dominant unit among BRICS, followed by India and Brazil, while Russia possesses a smaller share. The USA and EU possess the biggest shares in international trade, a fact that give them the role of dominant regions in the global economy (Charts 38.1, 38.2, 38.3, 38.4, and 38.5).

38.5.1 Bilateral Trade Weights per Region

Before we proceed to the GVAR results, we present the bilateral trade weights among BRICS and the rest of the regions, just to have a first picture and some elements about the strength of trade links. This is helpful in the comparative performance analysis and the interpretation of the results of the dynamic analysis of the transmission of shocks.

The tables and the graphs give us the following information about the bilateral trade links between BRICS and the rest of the regions:

Africa: Among BRICS, China appears to have higher trade weights, followed by India. Both countries have tighter links with Botswana, Ghana, Kenya, and Tanzania, probably as competitors rather than partners.

Asia: India appears to have higher trade weights especially with Indonesia, Iran, Singapore, Thailand, and Turkey. China follows with lower trade weights. Regarding the rest of the BRIC, Russia has trade links with Iran and Turkey, while Brazil's weights are negligible.

CIS: Russia, as expected, seems to have higher trade weights, followed by India, while Brazil and China have the lowest weights in that region.

Latin America: Brazil and China have the highest trade weights followed by India. Brazil seems to have higher links with Mexico, Uruguay, and Venezuela, China with Honduras and Uruguay, and India with Uruguay. Russia's presence is not important.

Summarizing the results from the regional bilateral trade weights *(Appendix Part two*, Table 38.9*)*, we have to notice the following.

The bilateral trade between BRICS and their partners is of different degree of intensity.

Brazil's main partners are Latin America (35%), EU (37%), and the USA (20%). Russia's main partner is basically EU (74%). India's main partners are Latin America (20%), the USA (14%), and EU (44%). China's main partners are Latin America 33%, the USA (18%), and EU (35%).

Regarding the Rest of the Regions

In Africa, India has comparative higher trade weights than China, while the shares of Brazil and Russia are negligible. **In Asia,** India and then followed by China have higher trade weights. Brazil's and Russia's shares are not important. **In Latin**

America, Brazil and then followed by China and India have comparative higher trade weights. Russia's share is negligible**. In CIS,** Russia and then followed by India have comparative stronger weights. According the above analysis, it seems that Africa is a not so important trade partner for the BRICS, (instead accordingly to statistical data, it is a big FDI host region especially in source and infrastructure sectors form those two giants, but this is another issue for study). **In Asia,** China and India have stronger trade linkages, while in Latin America, Brazil and China have strong linkages followed by India in a lesser level.

Finally we should emphasize the fact the trade linkages among BRIC group are too weak (*Appendix Part two*, Table 38.10), while EU and the USA are the most important trade partners for each one of them. That is, BRICS are globalized more with EU and the USA than between them.

38.6 Individual GVARX* Estimation and Tests

38.6.1 Unit Root Tests

Although the GVAR methodology can be applied to stationary and/or integrated variables, the assumption that the variables included in the country-specific models are integrated of order one (or $I(1)$) – in Pesaran et al. (2004), Dees et al. (2007a, b), and Pesaran et al. (2009) – still plays an important role. The assumption allows us to distinguish short- and long-run relations and interpret those long run as cointegrating. Therefore, we begin our tests by examining the integration properties of the individual series under consideration. By applying the test on all 63 countries, we found that many of them were of different integration order. These happen because the sample consists of many different economies. In order to proceed and ensure the stability of our GVAR model, we constructed regions for each country group.

Then we identify the order of integration of endogenous and exogenous variables.

We applied unit root t-statistics based on weighted symmetric estimation of ADF (WS henceforth)-type regressions introduced by Park and Fuller (1995). Leybourne and Taylor (2004) and Pantula et al. (1994) provide evidence of superior performance of the *WS* test statistic compared to the standard ADF test or the GLS-ADF test proposed by Elliot and Timmermann (2004). The lag length employed in the *WS* unit root tests is selected by the Akaike Information Criterion (AIC) based on standard ADF regressions. The results of the *WS* statistics for the level, first differences, and the second differences of all the country-specific domestic and foreign variables in the GVAR model are reported in *Appendix B*, Tables 38.5 and 38.6. Asymptotic 5% critical values are used for both tests.

The I(1) assumption cannot be rejected for most of the endogenous and exogenous variables under consideration (*Appendix C*, Tables 38.11 and 38.12).

38.6.2 Long-Run Relationships-Cointegration Tests

It is important to stress that a possible misspecification of the cointegrating relationships can have a severe impact on the constructed GVAR model, with implications for the stability of the GVAR, the behavior of the impulse-response functions, and the shape of the persistence profiles. For all these reasons, in the following analysis, particular attention is given to testing for the number of cointegrating vectors and to their identification.

Assuming that the foreign variables are weakly exogenous, we estimate country-specific VARX* models, and then we test for the number of cointegrating vectors and for the weak exogeneity of foreign variables. Tests are conducted using the trace statistic at the 5% level of significance. The critical values for models including weakly exogenous variables are obtained from Mackinnon, Haug, and Michelis (1996).

The results are reported in *Appendix Part 2*, Table 38.7. It contains both the trace and maximum eigenvalue statistics used for determining the dimension of the cointegration space of the individual models, as well as the critical values for the trace statistic (*Appendix C*, Table 38.13).

The rank orders for each model are implied by the cointegration tests and selected according to the trace statistic. The results are quite heterogenous across countries suggesting that there is not only one cointegrating relationship in several economies (*Appendix C*, Table 38.14).

38.6.3 Weak Exogeneity Tests

The foreign variables X* are assumed to be weakly exogenous (long-run forcing for the domestic variables). That means that the foreign variables *do affect* the domestic variables in the long term, but the opposite is not true (i.e., there is no feedback from domestic to foreign variables in the long term). The testing result for weak exogeneity reports the results on joint significance test (F-statistics) for the error correction term in individual ECM which applied to each country separately (F-statistics).

The weak exogeneity hypothesis cannot be rejected for the most of country-regions in our sample, except the foreign inflation for Brazil, foreign exports for India and EU, and foreign GDP for India (*Appendix C*, Table 38.15).

38.6.4 *Other Features of the Country-Specific Models: Serial Correlation of the VECMX* Residuals*

Due to data limitations and the relatively large number of endogenous and exogenous variables involved, we were forced to set the lag order of exogenous variables for all country-specific models at 1. It is therefore important to check the adequacy of the country-specific models in dealing with the complex dynamic interrelationships that exist in the world economy.

Appendix 2, Table 38.10, provides F-statistics for Breusch-Godfrey LM tests of serial correlation of order 4 in the residuals of the error-correction regressions for variables in the GVAR model. The Ho of no serial correlation of the VECMX* Residuals is rejected for RGDP in cases of Brazil, India, and the USA, for China's inflation and for Brazil's, China's, and USA's exports (*Appendix C*, Table 38.16).

38.6.4.1 Contemporaneous Effects (Impact Elasticities) of Foreign Variables on Their Domestic Counterparts

The contemporaneous effects of foreign variables on their domestic counterparts can be interpreted as impact elasticities between domestic and foreign variables. They are particularly informative as it regards the international linkages between domestic and foreign variables. High elasticities imply strong comovements between them. The results are presented in Appendix C, Table 38.17. t-ratios were computed using White's heteroskedasticity consistent variance estimator. Note that the foreign variables are weighted averages of all foreign trade partners.

The impact elasticities for output are insignificant in all regions except Latin America where a 1% increase in foreign RGDP increases Latin America's RGDP by 0.10%.

The impact elasticity for inflation is significant and positive for Africa (0.47%), Brazil (0.11%), China (0.8%), India (0.42%), Russia (0.43%), and the USA (0.31%).

The results indicate that for GDP, there is no indication of business cycle comovements between the most regions. We should have it in mind when to interpret the dynamical analysis results.

38.6.4.2 Construction of GVAR and Persistence Profiles

There were 63 individual countries aggregated in 10 regions. The largest eigenvalue of the solved GVAR model was 1. Persistence profiles (PP) introduced by Pesaran and Shin (1996) were used to examine the effect of system-wide shocks on the dynamics of the long-run relations. PPs are based on a moving average representation of the GVAR, and they refer to the time profile of the effects of a shock on the cointegrating relations Dees et al. (2007a, b). PPs have a value of 1 at the time of impact and should converge to zero as the time horizon reaches infinity. Thus, PPs allow us to examine the speed at which the long-run relations converge to their equilibrium states.

In most cases, the convergence was quite rapid, often taking less than 2 years. In most cases, the value of PP was less than 10% after 8 quarters (2 years) from the first shock. Bootstrap means of PPs are plotted in Appendix C, Chart 38.6, and all regions and per pair of regions for a more detailed presentation.

38.7 Dynamic Analysis-Empirical Findings

We employ two measures of impact-influence.

1. Generalized impulse response function (GIRF). GIRF demonstrates a reaction of a variable over time in response to a one unit (one standard error) change in the shock variable (i.e., a positive shock to the real output of BRICS, what kind of effects does it have on the economies of DCs).
2. Generalized Forecast Error Variance Decomposition (GFEVD) shows the fraction of the variance explained by enabling the understanding of the true influence and dominant cause of change.

These two measurements help examine "the dynamic properties of the global model and to assess the time profile of the effects of shocks" (Dees et al. 2007a, b).

Generalized Impulse Respond Functions

We give a one standard error positive shock with 40 quarters time horizon to RGDP in each of the BRIC, EU and the USA (for comparison reasons), and measure the impact on the other regions' RGDP and exports. Since the positive shock on a country's GDP increases the demand for imports, that means that the exports of its trade counterparts will increase, which in turn results in positive impact on their RGDP. We want to capture the impact response on the trade partners' economy.

We run a bootstrap with 100 replications. The GIRF graphs show the bootstrap median estimates and the associated 90% bootstrap confidence bands aggregated according to the selected regions.

Before looking into the empirical findings, it should firstly be noted that in GIRF graphs, the thick line indicates the median point estimates as a consequence of one standard deviation shock, while the dotted line represents the bootstrapped mean values of GIRFs with the confidence interval of 90%. With respect to time horizon, short-term here refers to the impact of shock that occurred within 1 year, whereas long-run refers to the effect after 3 years from shock origination. Additionally, the paper reports the average impact of shock measured as the arithmetic average for the whole 40 quarters.

38.7.1 A Shock to Brazil's Output: Impact on Exports and RGDP of the Rest of the Regions

One positive standard error shock to Brazil's national income corresponds to approximately an increase of 2.6% in its GDP, in the first year. Looking at its imports (to check if this increase turns to be increased demand from abroad), the impact is positive (its imports increase by 9.5% in the first year but that does not translate to increase demand for exports for the rest of the regions). Looking at the GIRFs (*Appendix D*, Graph 38.3), the results are insignificant since the confidence interval contains zero. Looking at the impact on RGDP (Graph 38.4), we can see that it is insignificant too (except in the case of Russia where the impact is negative and significant). So our results on insignificant effects of the increase in Brazil RGDP on the other regions are confirmed.

38.7.2 A Shock to China's Output: Impact on Exports and RGDP of the Rest of the Regions

One positive standard error shock to China's output corresponds to 1.40% average increase in its GDP for the first year; it still remains positive, 13.92% for the whole time horizon and 0.34% at yearly average. The impact on China's imports is negative for the first year for the whole time horizon but insignificant.

The impact on the rest of the regions' exports is insignificant. The increase in China's output does not affect the demand for imports from the other regions (Appendix D, Graph 38.5).

The above results are confirmed by the response on RGDP. The impact on the other regions' RGDP (*Appendix D*, Graph 38.6) is insignificant except for the Latin America (LA) and BRIC regions. The impact for LA is positive, 0.9% average increase in the first year and 0.08% average yearly increase for the whole period. This could be an indication of the dominant role of China in LA region.

The impact on BRIC RGDP is also positive, but since the impact on individual BRICS is insignificant, the results seem to be influenced by an increase only in China's RGDP.

38.7.3 A Shock to India's Output: Impact on Exports and RGDP of the Rest of the Regions

One standard error positive shock to India's output corresponds to 3.8% increase in its RGDP in the first year. This increase in India's RGDP increases its demand for imports by 1.2% in the first year. This does not affect the exports of the rest of the region since the impact is insignificant (Appendix D, Graph 38.7). The impact on the rest of the regions' RGDP is also insignificant (Appendix D, Graph 38.8).

38.7.4 A Shock to Russia's Output: Impact on Exports and RGDP of the Rest of the Regions

One positive standard error shock to Russia's output corresponds to 4.03% increase to its RGDP in the first year. Russia's imports increase by 6.5% in the first year, but this increase is not translated to an increased demand for imports from other regions, so the impact on other regions' exports is not significant (*Appendix D,* Graph 38.9). The impact on other regions RGDP is also insignificant (Appendix D, Graph 38.10).

For comparative reasons, and since the USA still dominates the world economy, we proceed by analyzing the results on a positive shock to its output, on the economies of the regions.

38.7.5 A Shock to USA's Output: Impact on Exports and RGDP of the Rest of the Regions

One positive standard error shock to USA's output corresponds to 19.04% increase in its GDP in the first year. The impact on US imports is insignificant. The response on the exports of other regions is insignificant except on China's exports which are affected negatively (–13,07% for the first year). Also negative is the impact on EU exports (–4,6% for the first year) (*Appendix D*, Graph 38.11). The impact on RGDP of the other regions is insignificant (*Appendix D*, Graph 38.12).

Before we close the GIRFS analysis, we proceed regarding the regions of our sample on the "BRICS sight." That is, we give a one standard error positive shock to the BRIC region and check the impact on the other regions.

38.7.6 A Shock to BRICS Output: Impact on Exports and RGDP of the Rest of the Regions

One positive standard error shock to BRICS output corresponds to 1.58% increase in its GDP in the first year. The impact on BRICS imports is insignificant. The response on the exports on other regions is insignificant (*Appendix D*, Graph 38.13). However, the impact on China's and India's RGDP is positive (2.05% and 1.9%, respectively). The impact on RGDP of the other regions is insignificant (*Appendix D*, Graph 38.14).

38.8 Generalized Forecast Error Variance Decomposition

In order to compare the main findings from GIRF analysis, Generalized Forecast Error Variance Decomposition (GFEVDs) results are also presented. They give the fraction of endogenous variable variance that is explained by one shock to RGDP from the selected economies (BRIC, the USA). In fact, this offers a further explanation of the dominant influence deriving from the shock. The variance decompositions reported are the average value over the 40 quarter horizon.

Regarding African region, the estimated fraction of variance decomposition shows that a positive GDP shocks originating from China explain higher variation in RGDP imports and exports, while the impact from the RGDP shocks of the other region is negligible. It seems that there is a spillover effect, but compared to the GIRF outcomes, these results do not match. A possible explanation may be that the traded goods are of low value added that is why the impact on RGDP is insignificant.

For Asia we notice the higher fractions of variance explanation on exports and imports resulting from China's RGDP positive shock, even though the RGDP elasticity is very low. These results confirm our GIRF analysis results. Regarding the other regions, the impact elasticities are not important.

For Latin America's region, only China's fractions are too high in exports and imports. But the trade seems not to create any RGDP spillovers.

For CIS countries, a positive output only from China's explains a high proportion of RGDP variance, but this does not match to GIRF results.

Finally, regarding the BRICS as a region, a very impressive fraction of RGDP variation is explained by China's and India's RGDP positive shock. These results confirm the GRIF results about the impact of a positive output shock on BRICS' output. But since for the individual BRIC countries the impact is insignificant, this could be an indication of the dominant role of China among BRICS (*Appendix D*, Tables 38.18, 38.19, 38.20, 38.21, and 38.22).

38.9 Summary of Results

The bilateral trade weights matrix gives us important information about the trade linkages between the countries of our sample. We should emphasize that, among BRICS, the presence of India and China is evident almost in all developing country regions, while the presence of Brazil is evident only in Latin America, and the presence of Russia is evident only in CIS region. This is indicative of the dominant role of India and China as trade partners for the rest of the regions.

Africa's trade weights with BRICS are 0.69%, 0.06%, 0.8%, and 0.15% (with Brazil, Russia, India, and China, respectively). It is obvious that the shares are too low to create transmission effects through trade.

Asia's trade weights with BRICS are 2.67%, 5.60%, 12.84%, and 9.75%, respectively. It is obvious that Asia has stronger links with India, followed by China. It is obvious too that the trade shares are too low to create transmission effects.

CIS's trade weights with BRICS are 2.4%, 9.04%, 7.1%, and 2.9%, respectively. The trade links are stronger with Russia and India, while China is in the third position. Again, the shares are too low to create transmission effects from BRICS to CIS.

Latin America's weights with BRICS are 35.9%, 5.9%, 20%, and 33.1%, respectively. In this case, the shares are too high, and we expect to have transmission shocks from BRICS to Latin America.

Also, we should emphasize the fact the trade linkages among BRIC group are too weak, while EU and the USA are the most important trade partners for each one of the BRICS.

Summarizing the results of impact elasticities between domestic and foreign variables (contemporary effects table), we notice positive and significant impact elasticities of imports and exports, while for the RGDP, the elasticity coefficients are insignificant in most cases. These results indicate that for trade there are interregional comovements for most countries of our sample, while for GDP there is no indication of business cycle comovements between most regions. This could be an indication that the trade links and volume between the countries of the sample are not strong enough to create transmission effects.

Finally summarizing the results from dynamic analysis (generalized impact respond functions, GIRFs, and Generalized Forecast Error Variance Decomposition GFEVD), we should notice that in most cases, a positive shock on the output of the core economy (Brazil, Russia, India, China) does not affect the RGDP of their trade counterparts (developing countries of Africa, Asia, Latin America, and Commonwealth of Independent States).

38.10 Discussion

Summarizing the results, we notice that the BRICS don't seem to play any significant role as economic leaders for the Latin America regions, neither seem to have strong links among them.

The low bilateral trade weights between the core economies and their counterparts in Asia and Africa could be the explanation for the insignificant impact of a positive RGDP shock in the core economies. That is, the transmission impact via trade is trivial. The trade links are not strong enough to trigger transmission shock to the developing countries of Asia and Africa, Latin America, and CIS.

Regarding the Latin America region where the trade weights with Brazil, China, and India are relatively high, the insignificant impact from a positive shock can be explained by the composition of trade (the imports from BRICS are higher than the exports to the BRICS).

Our findings, up to this point, are on the contrary of the findings of other researchers (not many) in the same field. The most of them indicate the dominant role of China, not only for the developing countries, especially for Africa and Latin America, but among the BRIC group itself as well. About India's role as growth leader for the developing country, there is not much empirical evidence, while for the role of Brazil and Russia, there is no empirical evidence, at all. The common feature of these surveys is that all of them include in their sample only the more robust developing economies.

Our purpose was to examine if BRICS really can play a role as growth leaders for the developing world.

We use a large sample with economically different countries. Therefore, given the heterogeneity of members inside the BRIC group, we have to be skeptical about whether BRICS can operate as a group of growth engines, for developing countries. The above results should not lead to the conclusion that the growth of BRICS is irrelevant to the global economy since further examination taking into account other transmission channels and linkages (i.e., FDI, financial linkages, trade composition) should be examined. This is our next step, for further research.

Appendices

Appendix A: Data Description

The quarterly data set used for estimation in this paper cover the period 2000Q1–2014Q4.

The main data sources are CEIC, Direction of Trade-IMF, and the United Nations COMTRADE database. Whenever seasonally unadjusted data are collected from the source, the X-12-ARIMA seasonal adjustment in EViews package was used.

RGDP: Quarterly GDP volume series were taken from CEIC database. For seasonal adjustment, we used Census X12 method.

PPP-RGDP: Annual series were taken from IMF-WEO 2015.

Import-export: Quarterly series, in US$, were taken from IFS database.

Bilateral trade flows: Annual series were taken from COMTRADE database.

Consumer Price Index: Quarterly series, CEIC database, IMF data.

Exchange rate: Quarterly series were taken from BIS IMF database.

Table 38.1 Merchandise exports by region and selected economies, 2004–2014 (percentage of the world)

Exports (% of total world)	2004	2005	2006	2007	2008	2009	2010	2011	2012	2013	2014
Brazil	1.7	1.7	1.8	2.1	2.5	2.5	2.8	2.9	2.8	2.8	2.6
Russian Federation	0.4	0.4	0.5	0.6	0.7	0.5	0.5	0.6	0.7	0.7	0.7
India	9.3	11.1	11.8	12.7	14.1	16.8	13.8	14.8	18.8	21.3	19.6
China	4.2	4.6	5.2	5.5	5.4	6.6	7.2	7.0	7.1	7.7	7.6
European 28	21.1	20.6	20.7	21.3	21.1	20.9	18.7	18.2	17.2	16.6	17.0
USA	36.9	36.9	35.6	33.6	32.1	31.7	32.3	32.4	32.9	33.4	34.1
Other regions	26.4	24.6	24.4	24.2	24.0	21.1	24.7	24.1	20.4	17.4	18.3

Source: World Trade Organization database table: authors' calculations

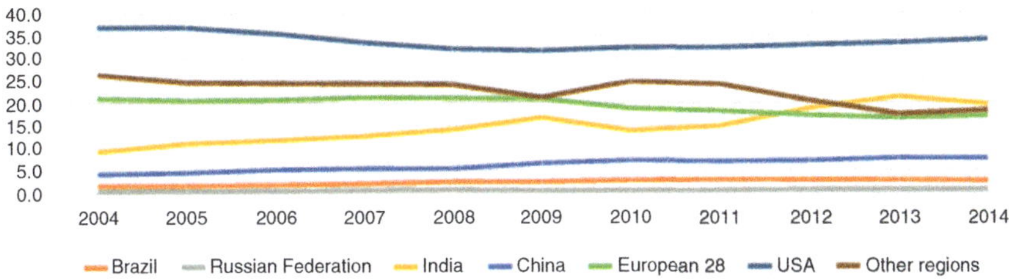

Graph 38.1 World exports per region

Definition of variables included in the GVAR model:

1. y_{it} = Real output: Log quarterly data seasonally adjusted, deflated by Consumer Price Index, CPI, in terms of US$ (y_{it}= ln(GDP_{it}/CPI_{it}). For deflating of GDP, we used CPI instead of GDP deflator, because GDP deflator series were not available for all countries and the sample had to be shrink which will cause estimation problems in our model.
2. Dp_{it}= Inflation Rate: DP_{it} = % change in CPI, {DP_{it}=ln (CPI_{it}) – ln (CPI_{it-1})}.
3. RER_{it} = Real Exchange Rate: log (ER/CPI_t), where ER is the nominal exchange rate against US$.
4. Imports: imp_{it} = Log quarterly series, US$.
5. Exports: exp_{it}= Log quarterly series, US$.
6. P_{oil} =Log of spot price for crude oil (Brent) in US$ per barrel.
7. P_{com} = Log of international nonenergy commodity prices.

Table 38.2 Merchandise imports by region and selected economies, 2004–2014 (percentage of the world)

Imports (% of total world)	2004	2005	2006	2007	2008	2009	2010	2011	2012	2013	2014
Brazil	1.5	1.5	1.5	1.3	1.5	1.3	1.3	1.4	1.4	1.2	1.3
Russian Federation	0.8	0.9	1.1	1.0	1.3	1.2	1.3	1.6	1.3	1.2	1.0
India	6.5	8.1	9.3	10.8	14.6	16.6	13.5	15.4	20.9	20.0	19.0
China	13.8	15.0	15.9	16.8	16.4	19.3	19.5	18.4	19.0	19.8	20.2
European 28	19.2	18.5	17.8	18.1	17.4	17.9	16.6	16.6	16.7	17.0	17.7
USA	27.4	26.8	26.5	26.3	25.8	25.4	26.0	25.8	26.0	26.6	26.9
Other regions	30.8	29.1	27.9	25.6	23.0	18.3	21.8	20.7	14.7	14.2	13.9

Source: World Trade Organization database table: authors' calculations

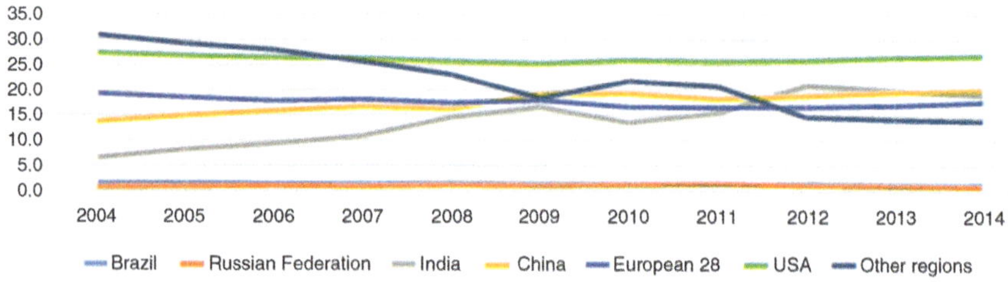

Graph 38.2 World imports per region

Weight Matrices

We use two types of weight matrices in our analysis:

1. *Trade weight matrix* captures the importance of country j for county i in terms of trade dependence (it is used for the structure of county-specific foreign variables). We use bilateral annual trade data between all countries of the sample (annual basis). Baxter and Kouparitsas (2004) in studying the determinants of business cycle comovements conclude that bilateral trade is the most important source of intercountry business cycle linkages. Imbs (2004) also provides further evidence on the effect of trade on business cycle synchronization. He concludes that while specialization patterns have a sizeable effect on business cycles, trade continues to play an important role in this process. He also notes that economic regions with strong financial links are significantly more synchronized. Focusing on global linkages in financial markets, Forbes and Chinn (2004) also show that direct trade appears to be one of the most important determinants of cross-country linkages. The trade shares capture the importance of country i for country j in terms of trade. So they show the degree of trade integration between countries. The country-specific models are connected then, because the foreign variables are entering the equations.

Table 38.3 List of countries and regions

Asia	Latin America	Commonwealth Independent States (CIS)	Africa[a]	EU	BRIC	USA
Bahrain	Argentina	Armenia	Botswana	Austria	Brazil	
Bangladesh	Bolivia	Azerbaijan	Ghana	Belgium	Russia	
Cambodia	Chile	Belarus	Kenya	Denmark	India	
Hong Kong	Colombia	Georgia	Malawi	France	China	
Indonesia	Costa Rica	Kazakhstan	Mozambique	Germany		
Iran	Dominican Republic	Kyrgyzstan	Sri Lanka	Italy		
Malaysia	El Salvador	Rep of Moldova	Tanzania	Netherlands		
Nepal	Guatemala	Tajikistan	Uganda	Spain		
Pakistan	Honduras	Ukraine	Zambia	Sweden		
Philippines	Mexico			UK		
Singapore	Nicaragua					
Thailand	Paraguay					
Turkey	Peru					
Vietnam	Trin Tobago					
	Uruguay					
	Venezuela					

[a]The African region shrunk due to the lack of statistical data over imports and exports for the period under investigation

The formula of bilateral trade weights is:

Wij= exports from country *i* to *j* + import from country *j* to county *i*/total trade of country *i*.

Note: Trade weights are computed as shares of exports and imports displayed in rows by region such that a row, but not a column, sums to one, the complete trade matrix used in the GVAR model. Because of the big size of the table, we couldn't present it here. The table is available upon request. Source of the data: UN COMTRADE annual data.

In the table below, we report the bilateral trade weights we used in the regional analysis.

PPP-GDP weight matrix captures a country's output share contribution to its own regional GDP (used for construction of regional variables). The original data come from IMF World of Economic Outlook 2015 PPP-GDP series measured in billions of current international dollar.

In our model, we also use regional variables since we evaluate the interdependence of the regions and the shock transmissions between them. The regional variables are constructed as weighted averages of the individual countries' endogenous variables. The weight here is the PPP-GDP shares, that is, the sum of average of each country's GDP to its regional GDP. These weights capture each country's contribution to its regional GDP.

Table 38.4 Bilateral trade weight matrix (based on fixed weights) (exports from i to j + imports from j to I/total trade of I) period 2000–2014. **BRICS rest of the regions**

Regions	Brazil	Russian	India	China
Africa	0.006974	0.000634	0.008488	0.001562
Asia	0.026729	0.056099	**0.12846**	0.097504
CIS	0.024063	0.090452	0.071035	0.029411
Latin America	**0.359292**	**0.059101**	**0.200924**	**0.331094**
USA	**0.205128**	**0.052552**	**0.148672**	**0.185661**
EU	**0.377814**	**0.741162**	**0.442421**	**0.354766**

(because of the big size of the table, we couldn't present it here. The table is available upon request)

Appendix B

Table 38.5 Bilateral trade weight matrix (based on fixed weights) (exports from i to j + imports from j to I/total trade of I) period 2000–2014. **Africa_BRICS**

Countries	Brazil	Russian	India	China
Botswana	0.0060	0.0000	0.0001	0.0000
Ghana	0.0006	0.0002	0.0014	0.0005
Kenya	0.0001	0.0002	0.0025	0.0004
Malawi	0.0000	0.0001	0.0004	0.0000
Mozambique	0.0001	0.0000	0.0007	0.0001
Tanzania	0.0000	0.0001	0.0023	0.0003
Uganda	0.0000	0.0000	0.0007	0.0001
Zambia	0.0000	0.0000	0.0005	0.0002

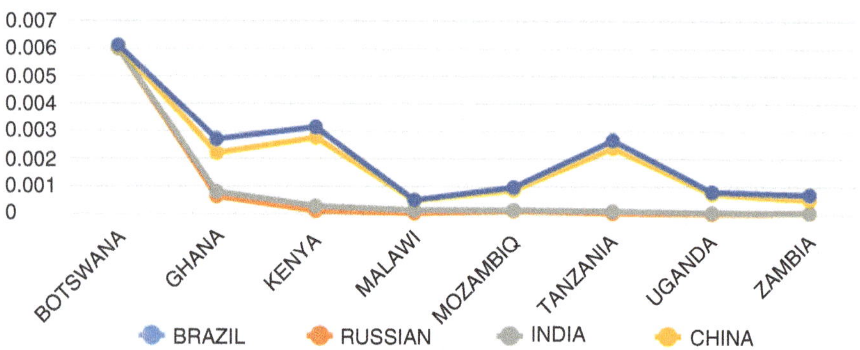

Chart 38.1 Africa_BRICS_bilateral trade weights, 2000–2014

Table 38.6 Bilateral trade weight matrix (based on fixed weights) (exports from *i* to *j* + imports from *j* to *I*/total trade of *I*) period 2000–2014. **Asia_BRICS**

Countries	Brazil	Russian	India	China
Bahrain	0.0005	0.0000	0.0023	0.0002
Bangladesh	0.0008	0.0004	**0.0131**	0.0021
Cambodia	0.0000	0.0000	0.0002	0.0005
HK	0.0004	0.0002	0.0002	0.0001
Indonesia	**0.0043**	0.0016	**0.0231**	**0.0155**
Iran	**0.0048**	**0.0079**	0.0099	0.0075
Malawi	0.0000	0.0001	0.0004	0.0000
Nepal	0.0000	0.0000	0.0070	0.0003
Pakistan	0.0005	0.0008	0.0031	0.0033
Philippines	**0.0023**	0.0010	0.0043	**0.0117**
Singapore	**0.0053**	0.0033	**0.0338**	**0.0277**
Sri Lanka	0.0002	0.0008	**0.0107**	0.0008
Thailand	**0.0047**	**0.0025**	**0.0119**	**0.0177**
Turkey	**0.0026**	**0.0347**	0.0049	0.0032
Vietnam	0.0003	0.0028	0.0036	0.0067

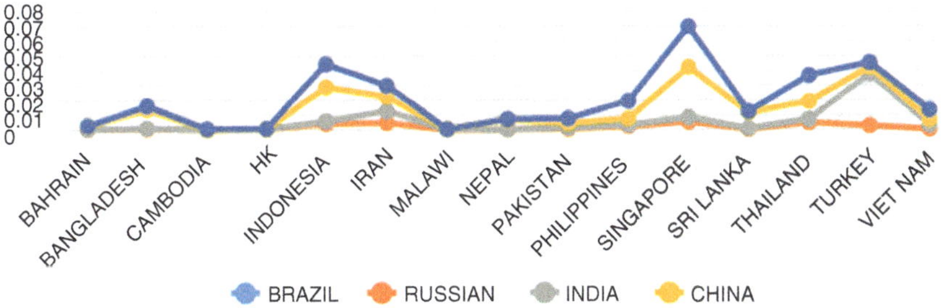

Chart 38.2 Asia_BRICS_bilateral_trade_weights, 2000–2014

Table 38.7 Bilateral trade weight matrix (based on fixed weights) (exports from *i* to *j* + imports from *j* to *I*/total trade of *I*) period 2000–2014. **CIS_BRICS**

CIS	Brazil	Russian	India	China
Armenia	0.0000	0.0010	0.0000	0.0000
Azerbaijan	0.0000	0.0029	0.0002	0.0002
Belarus	0.0008	0.0004	**0.0131**	0.0021
Georgia	0.0003	0.0013	0.0002	0.0000
Kazakhstan	0.0001	**0.0371**	0.0007	0.0043
Kyrgyzstan	0.0000	0.0016	0.0003	0.0005
Moldova	0.0000	0.0044	0.0000	0.0000
Tajikistan	0.0000	0.0015	0.0001	0.0001
Ukraine	**0.0228**	**0.0403**	**0.0564**	**0.0222**

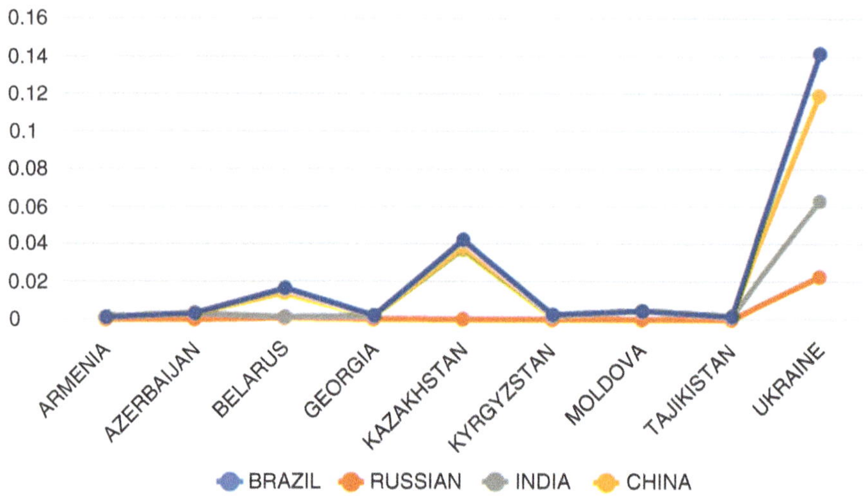

Chart 38.3 CIS_BRICS_bilateral_trade_weights, 2000–2014

Table 38.8 Bilateral trade weight matrix (based on fixed weights) (exports from *i* to *j* + imports from *j* to *I*/total trade of *I*) period 2000–2014. **Latin America_BRICS**

Countries	Brazil	Russian	India	China
Argentina	**0.0794**	0.0015	0.0053	0.0041
Bolivia	0.0060	0.0000	0.0001	0.0000
Chile	0.0000	0.0000	0.0002	0.0005
Colombia	0.0067	0.0005	0.0011	0.0007
Costa RICA	0.0017	0.0001	0.0002	0.0006
Dominican Rep.	0.0015	0.0001	0.0002	0.0002
EL Salvador	0.0006	0.0003	0.0001	0.0002
Guatemala	0.0010	0.0004	0.0002	0.0004
Honduras	0.0067	0.0016	**0.0401**	**0.1283**
Mexico	**0.0236**	0.0012	0.0033	0.0069
Nicaragua	0.0002	0.0002	0.0001	0.0001
Paraguay	0.0082	0.0001	0.0001	0.0002
Peru	0.0051	0.0004	0.0007	0.0018
Trin & Tob	0.0019	0.0000	0.0002	0.0001
Uruguay	**0.2051**	**0.0526**	**0.1487**	**0.1857**
Venezuela	**0.0117**	0.0003	0.0005	0.0012

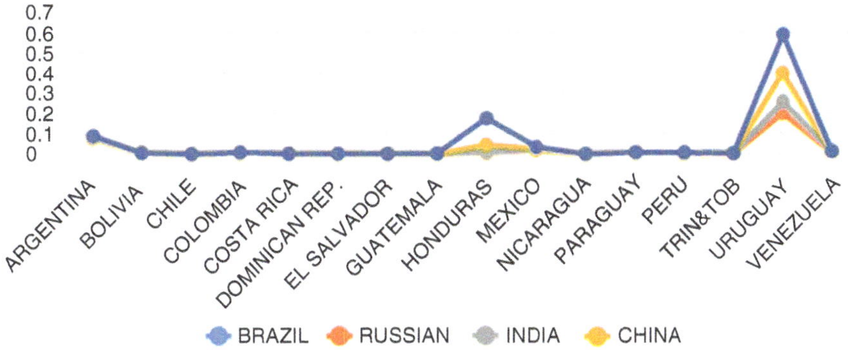

Chart 38.4 Latin America_BRICS_bilateral_trade_weights, 2000–2014

Table 38.9 Bilateral trade weight matrix (based on fixed weights) (exports from *i* to *j* + imports from *j* to I/total trade of *I*) period 2000–2014. **BRICS_rest of the regions**

Regions	Brazil	Russian	India	China
Africa	0.006974	0.000634	0.008488	0.001562
Asia	0.026729	0.056099	**0.12846**	0.097504
CIS	0.024063	0.090452	0.071035	0.029411
Latin America	**0.359292**	**0.059101**	**0.200924**	**0.331094**
USA	**0.205128**	**0.052552**	**0.148672**	**0.185661**
EU	**0.377814**	**0.741162**	**0.442421**	**0.354766**

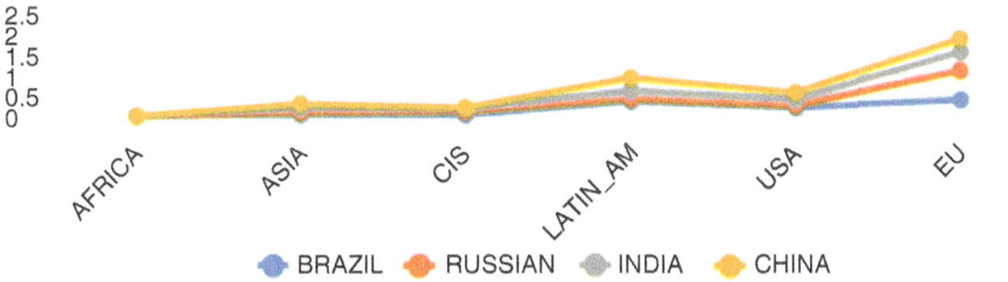

Chart 38.5 BRICS_Asia_Africa_CIS_Latin America_EU_US bilateral_ trade_weights, 2000–2014

Table 38.10 BRICS_bilateral_trade_weights

Country	Brazil	Russian	India	China
Brazil	0	0.009147	0.007054	0.010603
China	0.037691	0.066345	0.051598	0
India	0.007098	0.016088	0	0.011048
Russia	0.012979	0	0.014927	0.02286

Appendix C: GVARX Estimation Tests*

Table 38.11 WS unit root tests for the domestic variables at the 5% significance level (Based on AIC order selection criterion)

	Critical	Africa	Asia	Brazil	China	CIS	EU	India	Latina America	Russia	USA
y (with trend)	**−3.24**	−1.68	−1.38	−2.66	−2.30	−1.08	−2.37	−1.36	−3.01	−1.78	−1.85
y (no trend)	**−2.55**	−0.66	−0.34	0.57	1.08	−1.49	0.02	−0.11	0.04	0.24	−1.95
Dy	**−2.55**	−2.55	−2.42	−5.42	−4.71	−2.18	−3.47	−2.78	−2.79	−4.12	−2.38
DDy	**−2.55**	−6.03	−6.60	−7.20	−6.12	−3.70	−5.63	−8.73	−5.95	−5.52	−4.94
Dp (with trend)	**−3.24**	−3.51	−2.61	−1.18	−3.61	−3.80	−4.32	−1.31	−2.68	−0.87	−2.43
Dp (no trend)	**−2.55**	0.40	0.60	1.47	−0.38	1.16	0.29	−0.93	0.91	1.45	0.85
DDp	**−2.55**	−4.12	−3.62	−3.23	−3.11	−3.60	−4.54	−1.65	−4.54	−1.07	−4.43
DDDp	**−2.55**	−8.93	−6.43	−6.81	−25.91	−2.77	−5.41	−12.41	−8.41	−3.60	−6.58
er (with trend)	**−3.24**	−2.14	−2.71	−1.50	−1.01	−2.45	−1.28	−3.43	−1.73	0.13	
er (no trend)	**−2.55**	0.52	−2.21	−1.35	−0.04	0.49	−1.03	−3.44	−0.94	0.57	
Der	**−2.55**	−3.50	−5.07	−7.02	−5.98	−3.36	−4.08	−4.32	−3.69	−4.43	
DDer	**−2.55**	−4.80	−7.07	−7.96	−6.63	−5.93	−7.49	−5.97	−6.65	−7.42	
exp (with trend)	**−3.24**	−1.54	−2.17	−1.99	−2.45	−1.55	−2.10	−2.24	−3.32	−2.04	−2.89
exp (no trend)	**−2.55**	0.26	0.32	−0.69	−0.48	−0.89	−0.81	−0.08	−0.75	−0.54	−0.82
Dexp	**−2.55**	−7.74	−6.45	−3.25	−3.59	−5.52	−3.75	−3.73	−4.27	−4.73	−3.02
DDexp	**−2.55**	−6.37	−7.86	−16.97	−5.04	−6.00	−9.70	−9.50	−5.26	−6.48	−18.52
imp (with trend)	**−3.24**	−2.28	−2.97	−2.92	−2.06	−1.97	−1.70	−1.92	−3.93	−2.24	−2.68
imp (no trend)	**−2.55**	0.17	−0.02	−0.29	−0.01	−0.44	−0.81	0.04	−1.23	−0.59	−1.13
Dimp	**−2.55**	−2.91	−5.31	−4.25	−4.02	−2.63	−3.81	−5.61	−4.14	−3.87	−4.43
DDimp	**−2.55**	−5.29	−8.31	−9.65	−10.41	−13.70	−8.36	−6.24	−5.02	4.41	−7.15

Table 38.12 WS unit root tests unit root tests for the foreign variables at the 5% significance level (Based on AIC order selection criterion)

	Critical value	Africa	Asia	Brazil	China	Cominstates	EU	India	Latin America	Russian Federation	USA
ys (with trend)	−3.24	−1.97	−1.20	−1.32	−1.47	−2.38	−1.16	−1.57	−2.27	−2.11	−2.52
ys (no trend)	−2.55	−0.61	−0.86	−0.90	−0.84	0.02	−1.17	−0.76	1.05	−0.50	0.00
Dys	−2.55	−3.36	−2.11	−2.10	−2.11	−3.47	−3.32	−3.44	−4.57	−3.18	−3.68
DDys	−2.55	−3.82	−5.29	−5.29	−5.27	−5.63	−5.05	−4.96	−8.86	−4.99	−3.90
Dps (with trend)	−3.24	−3.24	−3.49	−2.91	−3.06	−4.32	−3.99	−2.95	−3.67	−4.71	−2.45
Dps (no trend)	−2.55	0.65	0.19	0.28	0.52	0.29	0.16	0.27	−0.37	0.12	1.03
DDps	−2.55	−4.60	−4.28	−3.90	−4.54	−4.54	−4.35	−4.34	−3.11	−4.58	−4.09
DDDps	−2.55	−5.18	−5.66	−5.94	−5.85	−5.41	−4.96	−5.22	−25.63	−4.87	−4.90
ers (with trend)	−3.24	−3.29	−1.87	−2.26	−2.88	−1.28	−1.33	−2.84	−1.03	−2.24	−2.60
ers (no trend)	−2.55	−0.43	−0.83	−0.51	−0.66	−1.03	−1.26	−0.25	−0.04	−0.68	−2.27
Ders	−2.55	−5.43	−4.69	−4.88	−4.85	−4.08	−3.81	−4.79	−6.01	−4.53	−6.01
DDers	−2.55	−7.02	−5.67	−6.21	−7.55	−7.50	−6.60	−6.12	−6.53	−6.64	−7.83
exps (with trend)	−3.24	−2.05	−2.61	−2.76	−2.73	−2.10	−2.97	−2.39	−2.46	−1.89	−2.44
exps (no trend)	−2.55	−0.73	−0.85	−0.85	−0.83	−0.81	−0.88	−0.77	−0.50	−0.66	−0.76
Dexps	−2.55	−4.14	−4.34	−4.31	−4.35	−3.75	−3.87	−4.31	−3.75	−3.82	−4.21
DDexps	−2.55	−5.82	−5.29	−5.22	−5.28	−9.70	−5.01	−5.50	−5.14	−6.08	−5.45
imps (with trend)	−3.24	−2.45	−2.76	−2.92	−2.94	−1.70	−3.27	−2.65	−2.02	−1.97	−3.02

Table 38.13 WS unit root tests for the global variables at the 5% significance level (Based on AIC order selection criterion)

	p_{oil} (with trend)	p_{oil} (no trend)	Dp_{oil}	Dp_{oil}	p_{com} (with trend)	p_{com} (no trend)	Dp_{com}	Dp_{com}
Critical value	−3.24	−2.55	−2.55	−2.55	−3.24	−2.55	−2.55	−2.55
Statistic	−2.94	−0.86	−6.42	−6.31	−2.78	−0.81	−5.86	−8.53

Table 38.14 VARX* orders and cointegrating relationship in the country-specific models for the major trading blocs

Country	Lag orders for domestic variables	Lag orders for foreign variables	Cointegrating relations
Africa			1
Asia	2	1	1
Brazil	2	1	1
China	2	1	1
Cominstates	2	1	1
EU	2	1	1
India	2	1	1
Latin America	2	1	1
Russian Federation	2	1	1
USA	2	1	1

Order of weak exogeneity regression equations

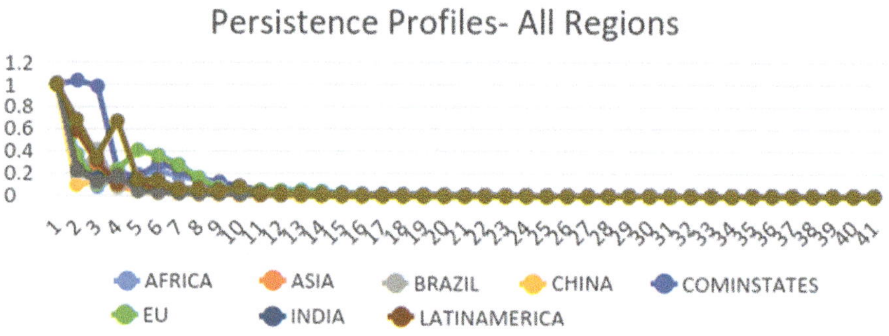

Chart 38.6 Persistence profiles

Table 38.15 Test for weak exogeneity at the 5% significance level

Order of weak exogeneity regression equations (p*, lag order of domestic variables; q*, lag order of foreign variables)			Test for weak exogeneity at the 5% significance level						
Country	p*	q*	F test	Fcrit_0.05	ys	Dps	ers	poil	pcom
Africa	1	1	F(1,45)	4.06	0.02	0.94	0.15	4.08	**5.01**
Asia	1	1	F(1,45)	4.06	1.17	3.63	0.08	0.38	2.08
Brazil	1	1	F(1,45)	4.06	0.00	5.18	1.42	0.01	0.32
China	1	1	F(1,45)	4.06	1.54	0.30	0.18	0.04	**5.97**
Cominstates	1	1	F(1,45)	4.06	0.11	0.04	0.73	0.03	5.27
EU	1	1	F(1,45)	4.06	0.97	4.00	1.46	4.14	**22.15**
India	1	1	F(1,45)	4.06	0.13	0.01	4.08	0.35	**6.61**
Latin America	2	1	F(1,39)	4.09	3.74	0.66	0.28	0.18	0.80
Russian Federation	1	1	F(1,45)	4.06	2.06	1.56	0.08	2.42	**9.74**
USA	1	1	F(1,46)	4.05	0.10	1.24			1.04

Table 38.16 F-statistics for the serial correlation test of the VECMX* Residuals

		Fcrit_0.05	y	Dp	er	exp	imp	p_{oil}	p_{com}
Africa	F(4,41)	2.599969	1.09417	1.435663	0.493942	2.142423	2.040696		
Asia	F(4,41)	2.599969	0.598026	2.596805	2.263184	0.377605	0.685763		
Brazil	F(4,41)	2.599969	**3.115863**	1.209454	0.788	**3.364657**	1.604979		
China	F(4,41)	2.599969	0.391995	**8.611401**	2.635062	**4.311973**	2.518791		
Cominstates	F(4,41)	2.599969	0.539356	2.27687	0.422917	1.071955	3.58106		
EU	F(4,41)	2.599969	2.555339	2.217095	1.638764	2.285436	1.988833		
India	F(4,41)	2.599969	**4.351062**	1.975551	1.585456	2.713659	0.85454		
Latin America	F(4,41)	2.599969	2.094912	1.273895	0.882643	2.127763	0.336716		
Russian Federation	F(4,41)	2.599969	1.313965	1.860524	0.151087	2.028683	1.699272		
USA	F(4,43)	2.588836	**7.054805**	1.153418		**4.71161**	0.086545	0.426572	

Table 38.17 Contemporaneous effects of foreign variables on domestic counterparts (t-ratios were computed using White's heteroskedasticity consistent variance estimator)

		y	Dp	er
Africa	White's adjusted SE	0.188331	0.472872	0.129269
Africa	t-ratio_White	0.563369	**6.330513**	**−3.81262**
Asia	White's adjusted SE	0.068495	0.214283	0.453361
Asia	t-ratio_White	0.232098	−0.57274	−1.0926
Brazil	White's adjusted SE	0.12065	0.118515	1.142522
Brazil	t-ratio_White	−0.92683	4.155271	−0.5118
China	White's adjusted SE	0.141349	0.806538	0.44081
China	t-ratio_White	−0.94417	**2.947542**	0.057891
Cominstates	White's adjusted SE	0.487447	0.826668	0.085912
Cominstates	t-ratio_White	1.450223	0.424677	−1.9693
EU	White's adjusted SE	0.026343	0.03825	0.05829
EU	t-ratio_White	−0.69559	1.556034	**−4.62902**
India	White's adjusted SE	0.174012	0.422831	0.594848
India	t-ratio_White	0.337455	**−3.412**	1.313594
Latin America	White's adjusted SE	0.10558	0.042833	0.189263
Latin America	t-ratio_White	**2.508492**	0.252113	1.088063
Russian Federation	White's adjusted SE	0.189527	0.43481	0.751805
Russian Federation	t-ratio_White	0.197713	5.365419	**−2.6615**
USA	White's adjusted SE	0.829615	0.311001	
USA	t-ratio_White	1.266412	**2.642508**	

Statistically significant coefficients are highlighted

Persistence Profiles per region

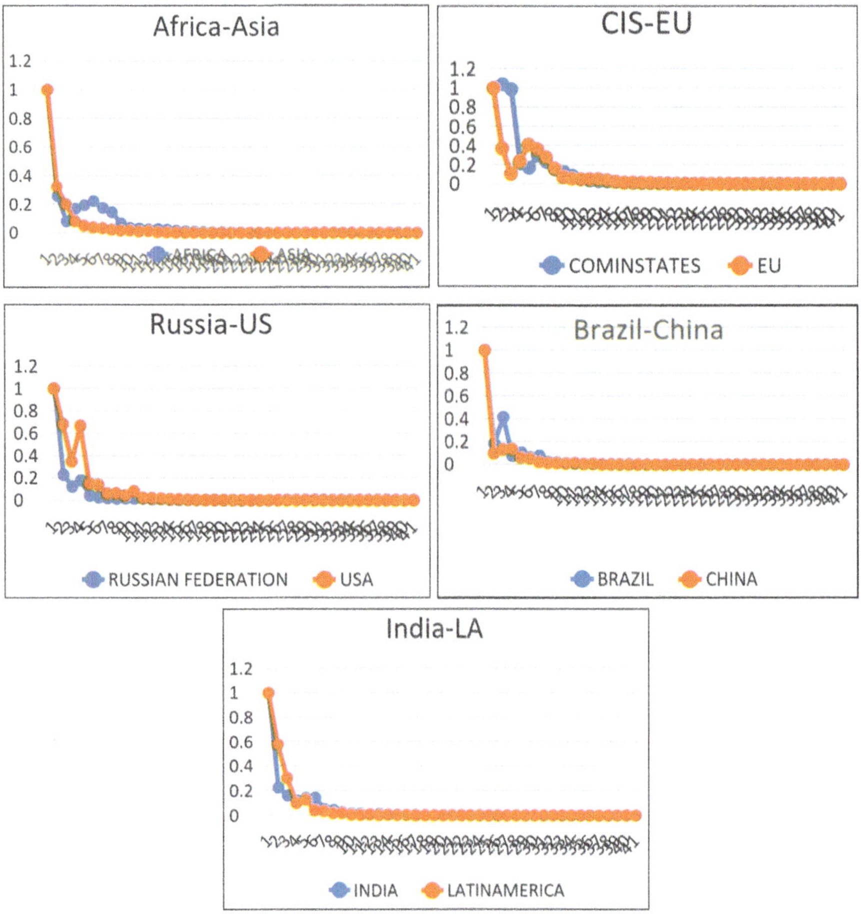

Appendix D: Dynamic Analysis Results-Generalized Variance Decomposition Results

Order of countries in graphs (Africa, Asia, Brazil, China, Cominstates, EU, India, Latin America, Russian Federation, the USA, BRICS)

The bars represent the bootstrapped mean values of the GIRF across the sample, while the 90% bootstrapped confidence intervals are represented by the thinner lines.

The bars represent the bootstrapped mean values of the GIRF across the sample, while the 90% bootstrapped confidence intervals are represented by the thinner lines.

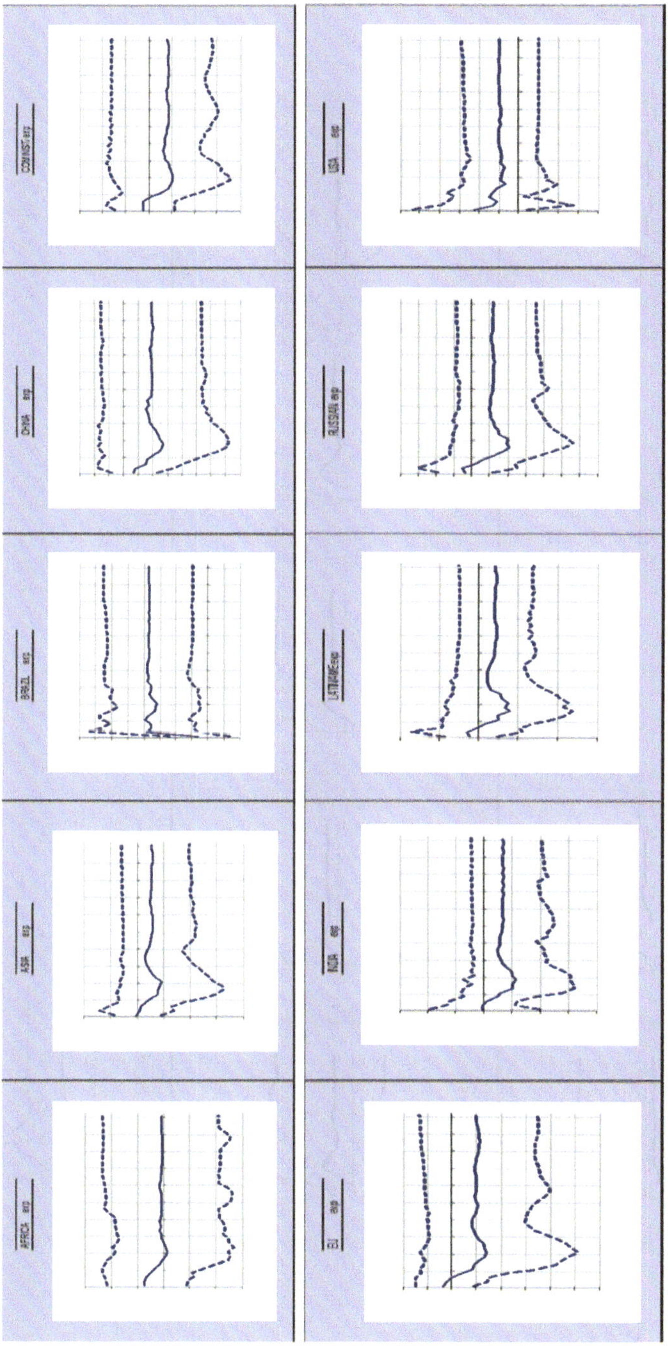

Graph 38.3 One s.e. positive shock to Brazil's RGDP – generalized impulse response functions for other regions' *exports*

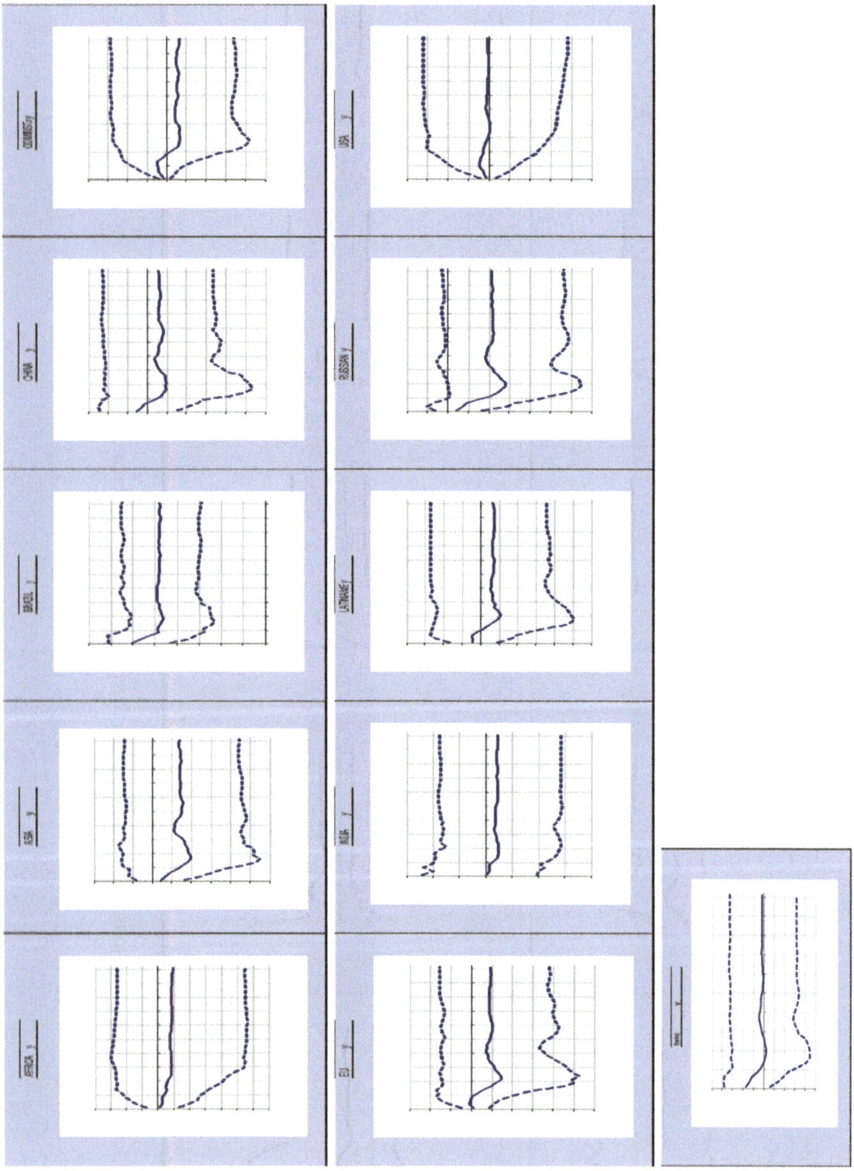

Graph 38.4 One s.e. positive shock to Brazil's RGDP – generalized impulse response functions for other regions' RGDP

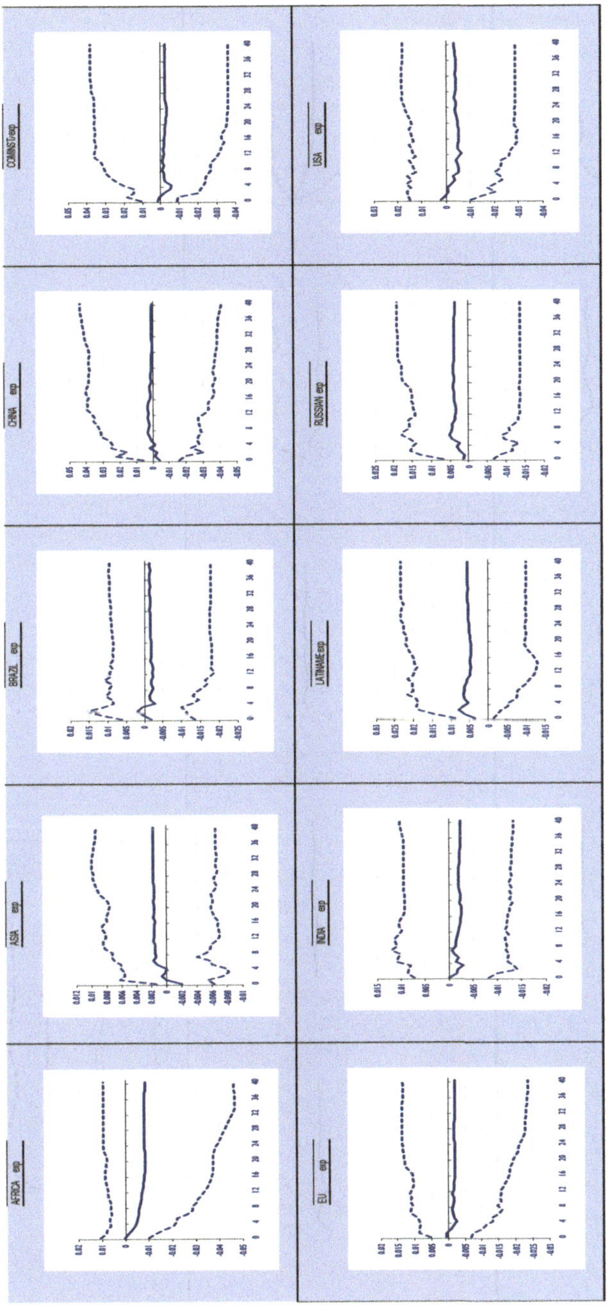

Graph 38.5 One s.e. positive shock to China's RGDP – generalized impulse response functions for other regions' *exports*

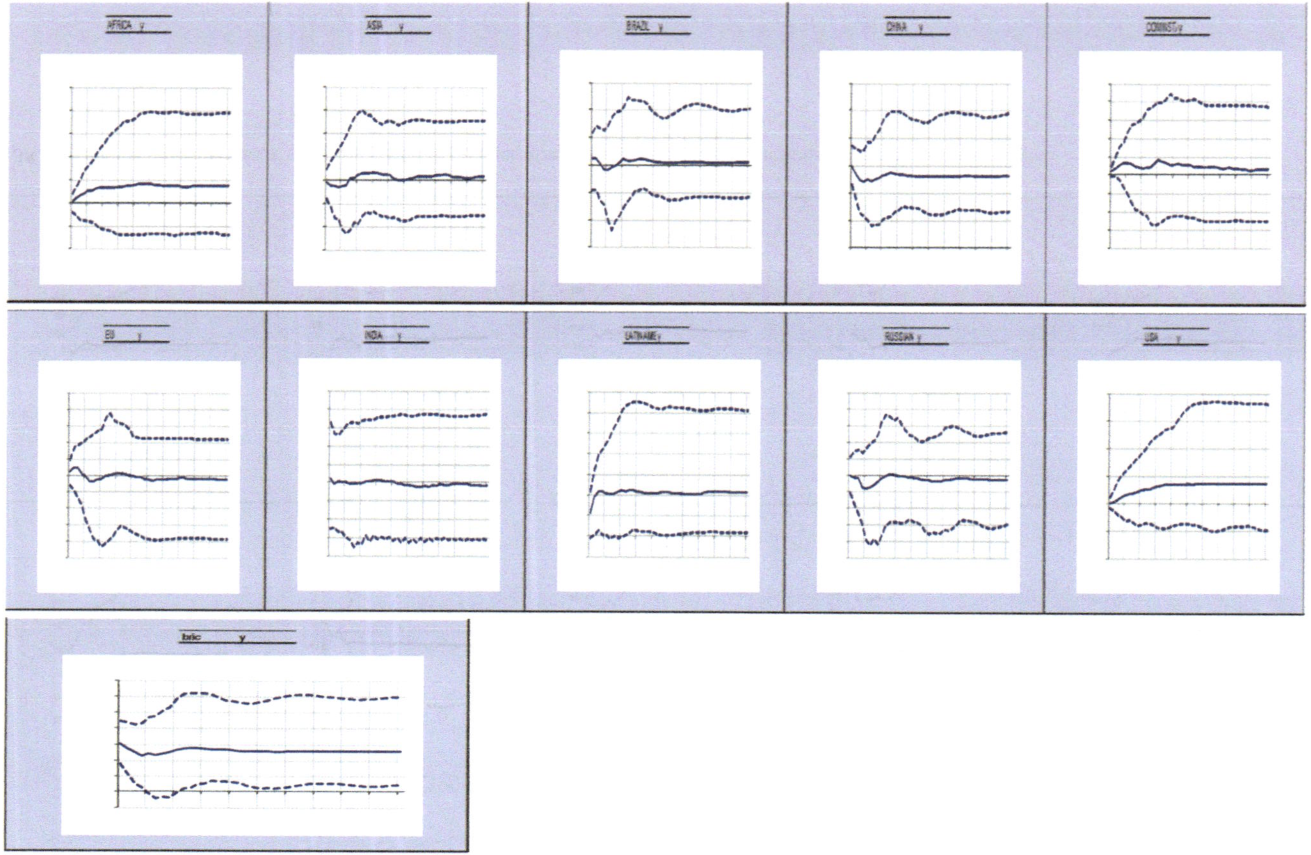

Graph 38.6 One s.e. positive shock to China's RGDP – generalized impulse response functions for other regions' RGDP

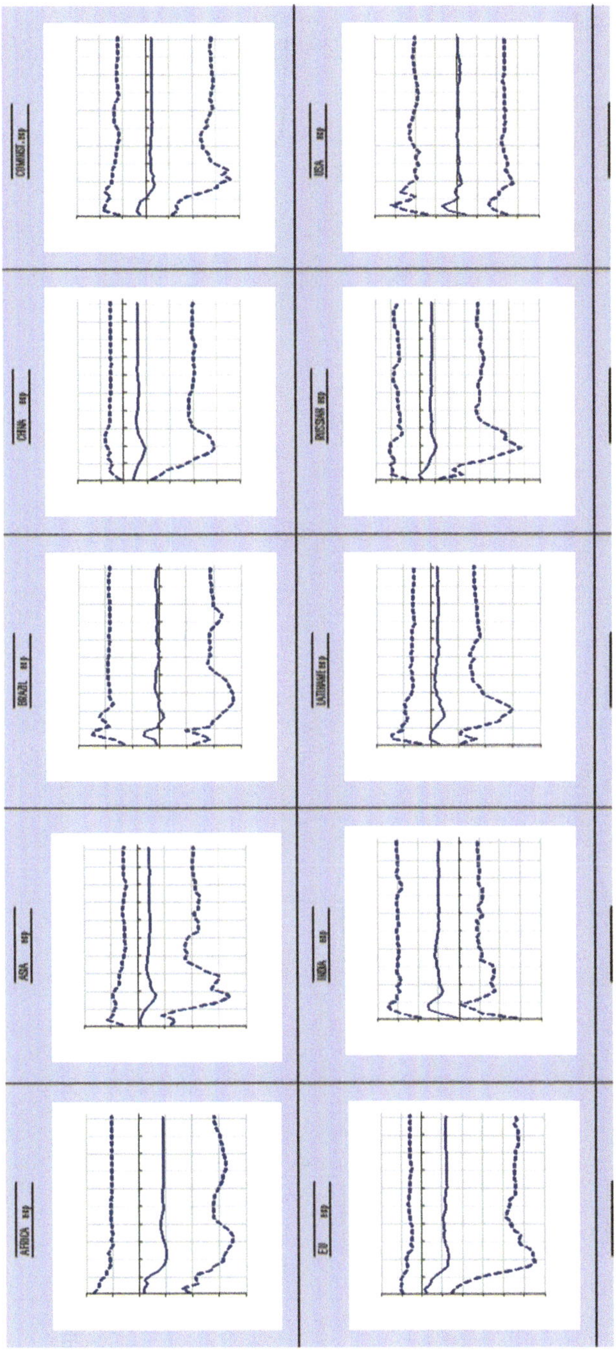

Graph 38.7 One s.e. positive shock to India's RGDP – generalized impulse response functions for other regions' *exports*

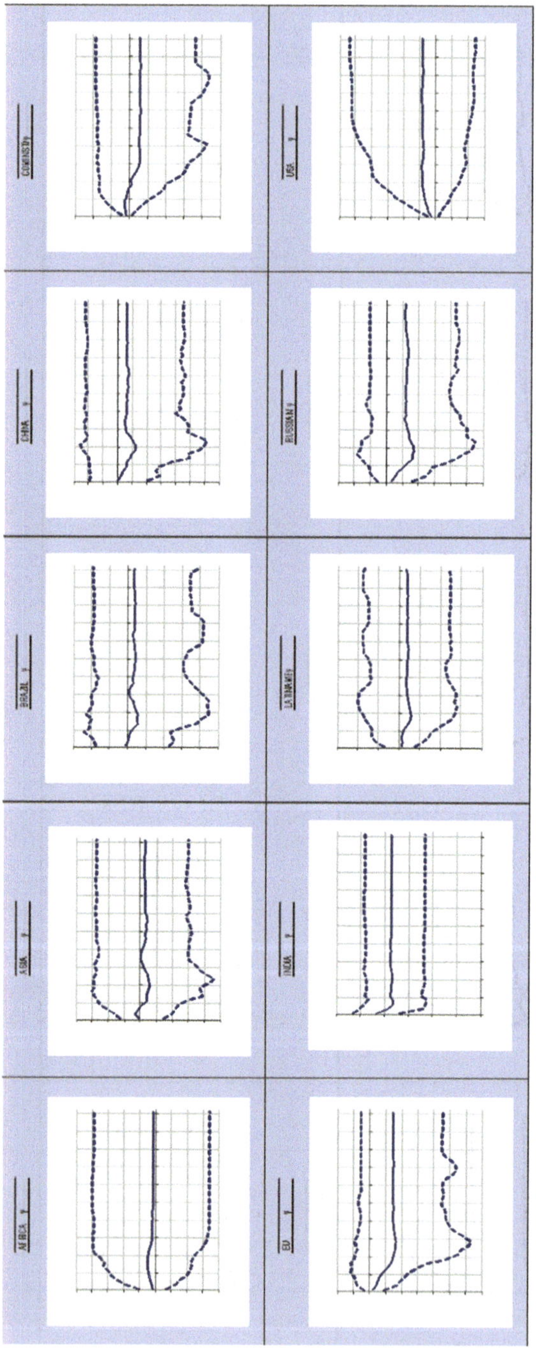

Graph 38.8 One s.e. positive shock to India's RGDP – generalized impulse response functions for other regions' RGDP

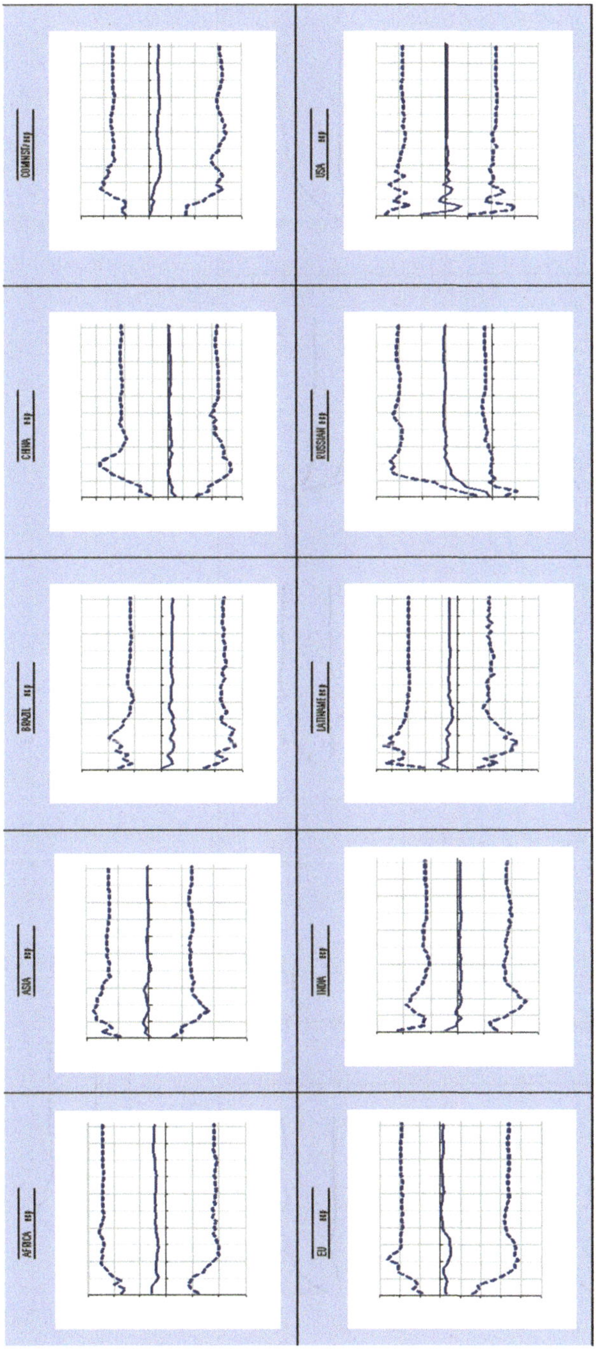

Graph 38.9 One s.e. positive shock to Russia's RGDP – generalized impulse response functions for other regions' *exports*

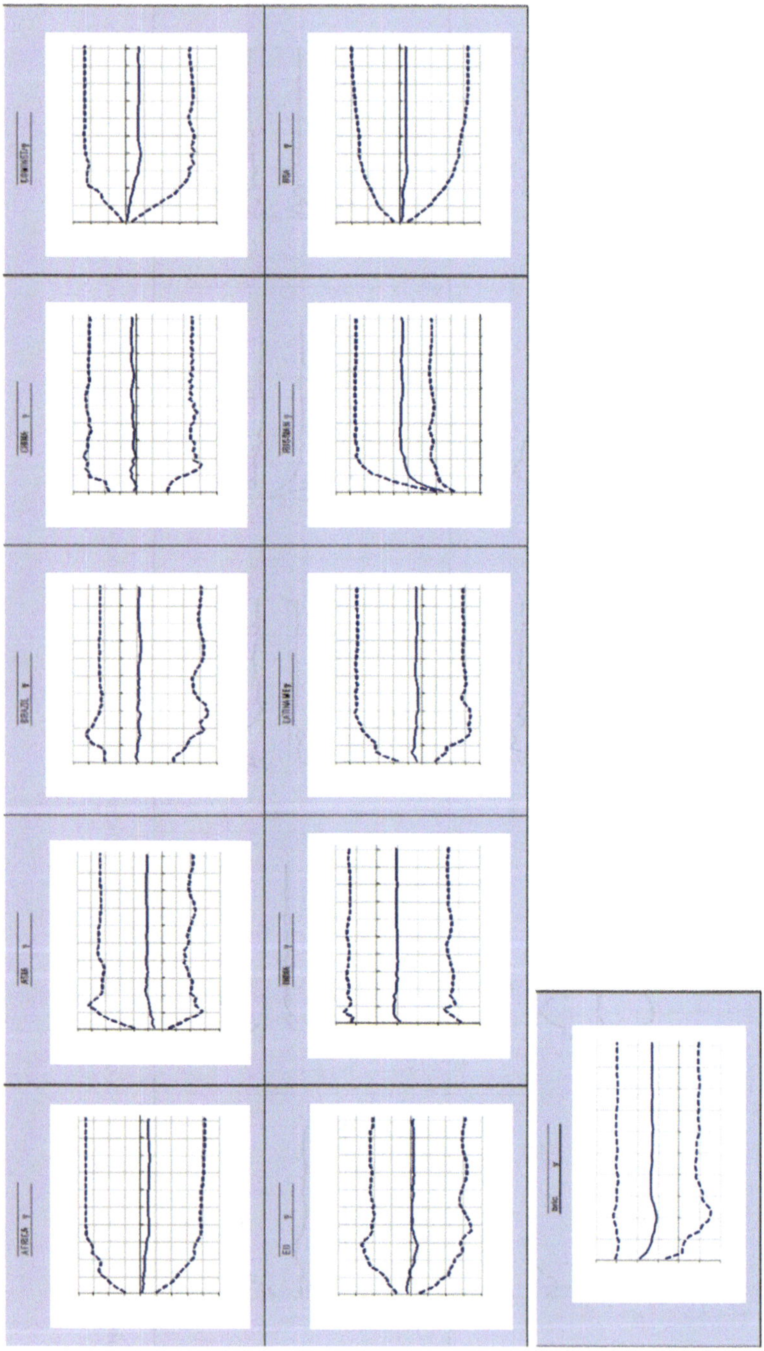

Graph 38.10 One s.e. positive shock to Russia's RGDP – generalized impulse response functions for other regions' RGDP

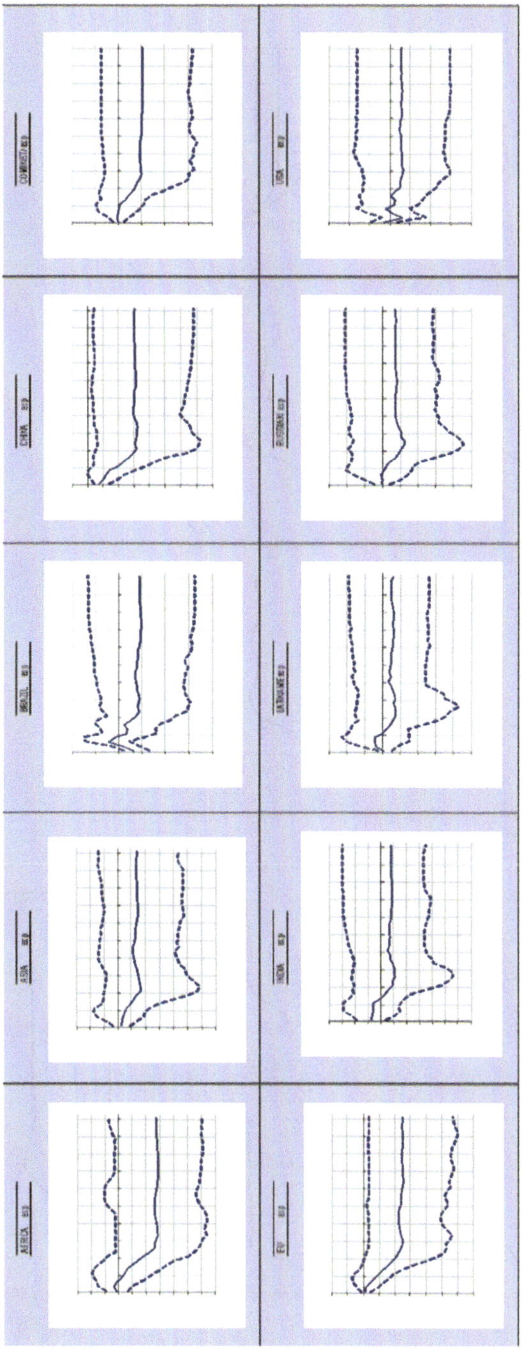

Graph 38.11 One s.e. positive shock to the USA's output – generalized impulse response functions for other regions' *exports*

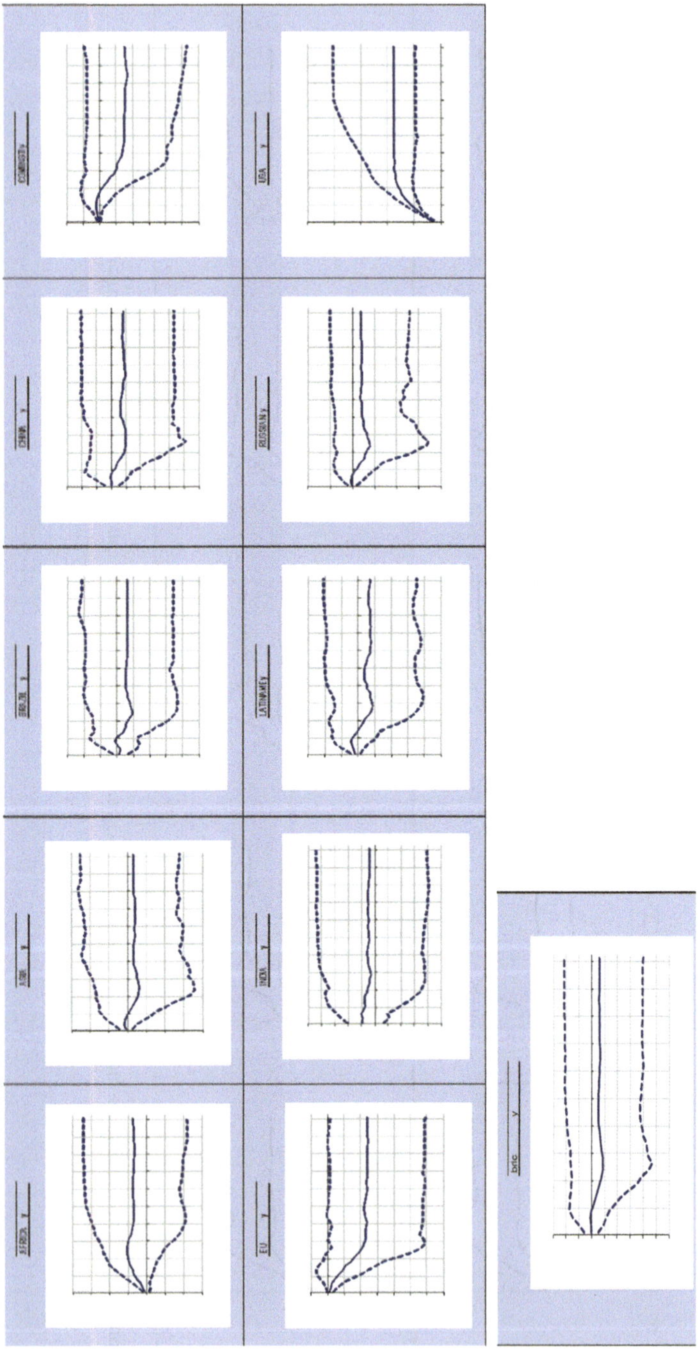

Graph 38.12 One s.e. positive shock to the USA's output – generalized impulse response functions for other regions' RGDP

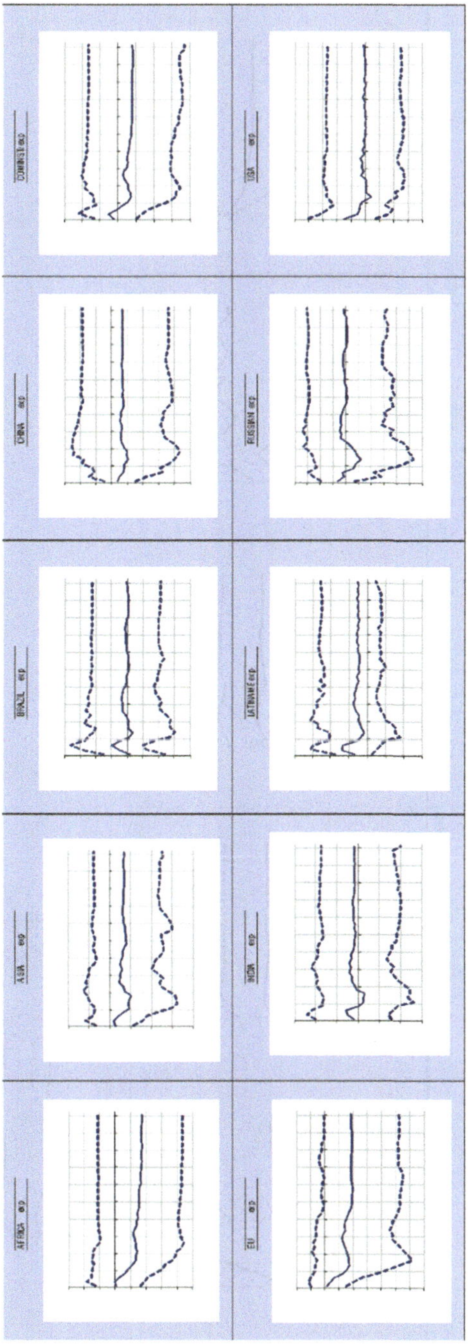

Graph 38.13 One s.e. positive shock to BRIC's RGDP – generalized impulse response functions for other regions' *exports*

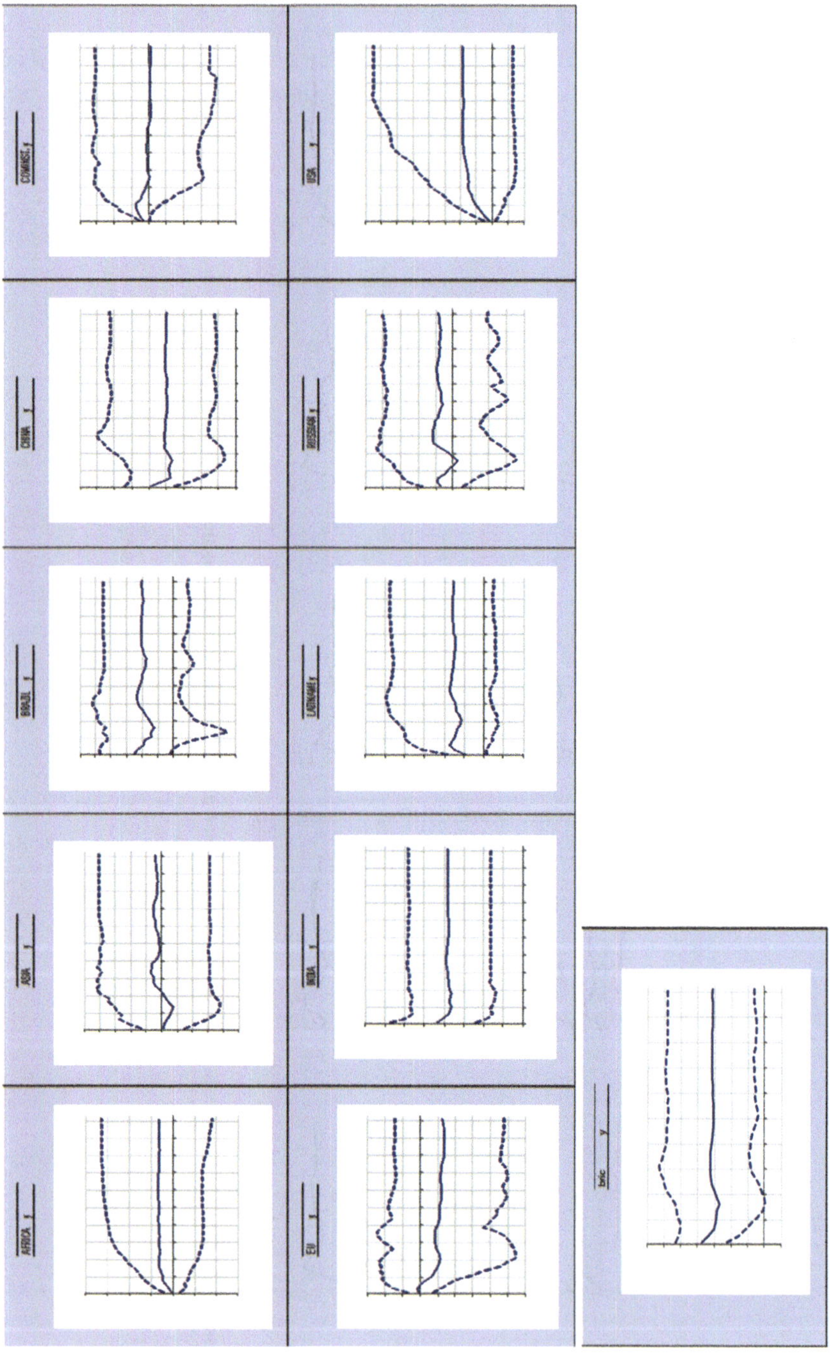

Graph 38.14 One s.e. positive shock to BRIC's RGDP – generalized impulse response functions for other regions' RGDP

Dynamic Analysis-Generalized Variance Decomposition Results

Table 38.18 GFEVDs of Africa, explained by the RGDP shocks from the selected economies

	y	Dp	er	exp	imp
Brazil	0.002	0.005	0.003	0.013	0.011
China	**0.101**	**0.331**	0.036	**0.151**	**0.134**
India	0.002	0.004	0.025	0.001	0.009
Russia	0.000	0.003	0.001	0.010	0.020
USA	0.000	0.003	0.000	0.003	0.000

Table 38.19 GFEVDs of Asia, explained by the RGDP shocks from the selected economies

	y	Dp	er	exp	imp
Brazil	0.001	0.051	0.028	0.003	0.004
China	0.045	**2.691**	**0.370**	**0.291**	**0.414**
India	0.013	0.018	0.017	0.000	0.000
Russia	0.005	0.039	0.009	0.004	0.002
USA	0.005	0.066	0.002	0.004	0.000

Table 38.20 GFEVDs of Latin America, explained by the RGDP shocks from the selected economies

	y	Dp	er	exp	imp
Brazil	0.001	0.060	0.035	0.003	0.012
China	**0.625**	**3.508**	**1.522**	**0.122**	**0.056**
India	0.001	0.046	**0.103**	0.019	0.000
Russia	0.000	0.029	0.011	0.006	0.000
USA	0.053	**0.154**	**0.189**	0.002	0.030

Table 38.21 GFEVDs of CIS, explained by the RGDP shocks from the selected economies

	y	Dp	er	exp	imp
Brazil	0.010	0.002	0.002	0.010	0.003
China	**0.466**	**0.419**	0.009	0.091	0.027
India	0.028	0.009	0.001	0.008	0.008
Russia	0.011	0.003	0.008	0.006	0.005
USA	0.021	0.014	0.001	0.001	0.011

Table 38.22 GFEVDs of BRICS explained by the RGDP shocks from the selected economies

	y	Dp	er	exp	imp
Brazil	0.042	0.003	0.021	0.005	0.005
China	**6.833**	**0.448**	**0.260**	**0.468**	**1.108**
India	**0.182**	0.007	0.003	0.008	0.008
Russia	0.066	0.003	0.017	0.011	0.008
USA	0.006	0.013	0.005	0.010	0.008

Literature Review

Armijo, L. E. (2007). The BRIC countries (Brazil, Russia, India, and China) as analytical category: Mirage or insight? *Asian Perspective, 31*(4), 7–42.

Balassa, B. (1978). Exports and economic growth: Further evidence. *Journal of Development Economics, 5*, 181–189.

Baxter, M., & Kouparitsas, M. (2004). Determinants of business cycle comovement: a robust analysis. *Journal of Monetary Economics, 52*(1), 113–157.

Baxter, M., & Kouparitsas, M. (2005). Determinants of business cycle co-movement: A robust analysis. *Journal of Monetary Economics, 52*, 113–157.

Beech, H. (2011, April 14). Why the BRICS Summit wont accomplish anything, *TIME Magazine*. http://world.time.com/2011/04/14/why-the-brics-summit-wont-accomplish-anything/. Accessed 19 Nov 2014.

Bhagwati, J. (1988). *Protectionism*. Cambridge, MA: MIT Press.

Bussiere, M., Chudik, A., & Sestieri, G. (2009). *Modelling global trade flows: Results from a GVAR model* (European Central Bank, Working Paper Series 1087).

Çakir, M., & Kabundi A. (2011). *Trade shocks from BRIC to South Africa: A Global VAR analysis* (Economic Research Southern Africa. Working Papers No. 250).

Cashin, I., Mohaddes, K., & Raissi, M. (2012). *"The global impact of the systemic economies and MENA business cycles", IMF Working Paper 12/255*. Washington: IMF.

Cesa-Bianchi, A., Pesaran, M. H., Rebucci, A., Xu, T., & Chang, R. (2012). China's emergence in the world economy and business cycles in Latin America. *Economia, 12*(2), 1–75.

Chudik, A. (2007). *In Search of Equilibrium: Estimating Equilibrium Real Exchange Rates in Sub-Saharan African Countries*. Washington: IMF.

Chudik A., & Smith V. (2013). *The GVAR approach and the dominance of the US economy*. Federal Reserve Bank of Dallas Globalization and Monetary Policy Institute.

De Castro T., (2013). Trade among BRICS countries: Changes towards closer cooperation? *Ekonomická revue – Central European Review of Economic Issues 16*.

Dees, S., Mauro, D., Pesaran, H., & Smith, V. (2007a). Exploring the international linkages of the Euro area: A global VAR analysis. *Journal of Applied Econometrics, 22*, 1–38.

Dees, S., Holly, S., Pesaran, H., & Smith, V. (2007b). Long run macroeconomic relations in the global economy. *Economics: The Open-Access, Open-Assessment E-Journal, 1*(2007–3), 1–58.

Dées, S., Gasteuil, A., Kaufmann, R., & Mann, M. (2008). *"Assessing the factors behind oil price changes", ECB Working Paper No. 855*. Francfurt: ECB.

Dreger, C. and Zhang, Y., (2013), "Does the economic integration of China affect growth and inflation in industrial Countries?" FIW Working Paper 116, Wien: Forschungsschwerpunkt Internationale Wirtschaft.

Elliot, G., & Timmermann, A. (2004). Optimal forecast combinations under general loss functions and forecast error distributions. *Journal of Econometrics, 122*(1), 47–79.

Forbes, K., & Chinn, M. (2004, August). A decomposition of global linkages in financial markets over time. *The Review of Economics and Statistics, 86*(3), 705–722.

Frankel, J., & Rose, A. (1997). Is EMU more justifiable ex post than ex ante? *European Economic Review, 41*, 753–760.

Frankel, J., & Rose, A. (1998). The endogeneity of the optimum currency area criteria. *Economic Journal, 108*, 1009–1025.

GonInn (Centre for the Study of Governance Innovation) (2013, December). *On the BRICS of collapse? Why emerging economies need a different development model*. University of Pretoria (South Africa), Demos/Rockefeler Fountation.

Grossman, G., & Helpman, E. (1991). *Innovation and growth in the global economy*. Cambridge: MIT Press.

Helpman, E., & Krugman, P. (1985). *Market structure and foreign trade*. Cambridge, MA: MIT Press.

Imbs, J. (2004). Trade, finance, specialization and synchronization. *Review of Economics and Statistics, 86*(3), 723–734.

Inklaar, R., Jong-A-Pin, R., & Haan, J. (2007). Trade and business cycles synchronization in OECD countries – a re-examination. *European Economic Review, 52*(4), 646–666.

Jha, S., & McCawley, P. (2011). *South–South Economic Linkages: An overview*. (ADB Economics Working Paper Series No. 270).

Kregel, J. (2009, October). The global crisis and the implications for developing countries and the BRICS: Is the 'B' really justified? Brazilian Journal of Political Economy, vol. 29, n 4(116), pp. 341–356

Krugman, P. (1984). Import protection as export promotion. In H. Kierzkowski (Ed.), *Monopolistic competition in international trade*. Oxford: Oxford University Press.

Lancaster, K. (1980). Intra-industry trade under perfect monopolistic competition. *Journal of International Economics, 10*, 151–175.

Leybourne, S., & Taylor, R. (2004). On tests for changes in persistence. *Economics Letters, 84*(1), 107–115.

Lucas, R. (1988). On the mechanics of economic development. *Journal of Monetary Economics, 22*(1), 3–42. 49.

Mackinnon, J. G., Haug, A. A., & Michelis, L. (1996). Numerical distribution functions of likelihood ratio tests for co-integration. *Journal of Applied Econometrics, 14*, 563–577.

Mlanchila, M., & Takebe, M. (2011). *FDI from BRICS to LICs: Emerging growth driver?* (IMF Working Papers Series).

Morazán, P., Knoke, I., Knoblauch, D., Schäfer, T. (2012). *The role of BRICS in the developing world* European Parliament: Directorate-General for external policies of the Union-policy Department

Pantula, S. G., Gonzalez-Farias, G., & Fuller, W. A. (1994). A comparison of unit root test criteria. *Journal of Business and Economic Statistics, 12*, 449–459.

Park, H. J., & Fuller, W. A. (1995). Alternative estimators and unit root tests for the autoregressive process. *Journal of Time Series Analysis, 16*(4), 415–429.

Pesaran, M. H., & Shin, Y. (1996). Cointegration and Speed of convergence to equilibrium. *Journal of Econometrics, 71*, 117–143.

Pesaran, M. H., Schuermann, T., & Weiner, S. M. (2004). Modeling regional interdependencies using a global error-correcting macroeconometric model. *Journal of Business and Economic Statistics, 22*, 129–162.

Pesaran, M., Schuermann, T., Treutler, B. J., & Weiner, S. (2006a). Macroeconomic dynamics and credit risk: A global perspective. *Journal of Money, Credit and Banking, 38*(5), 1211–1261.

Pesaran, M. H., Schuermann, T., & Treutler, B.-J. (2006b). Global business cycles and credit risk. In *The risks of financial institutions, National Bureau of Economic Research Publications* (pp. 419–474). Chicago: University of Chicago Press.

Pesaran, M. H., Smith, L. V., & Smith, R. P. (2007). What if the UK or Sweden had joined the Euro in 1999? An empirical evaluation using a global VAR. *International Journal of Finance and Economics, 12*, 55–87.

Pesaran, M. H., Schuermann, T., & Zafaronni, P. (2009). Model averaging in risk management with an application to future markets. *Journal of Empirical Finance, 16*, 280–350.

Phuangsiri, P. (2012). *Measuring the Southern growth engine: China, India, and Brazil as regional and world economic powers.* Master Thesis, Lund University Publications.

Ram, R. (1985). Exports and economic growth: Some additional evidence. *Economic Development and Cultural Change, 33*, 415–425.

Samake, I and Yang, Y., (2011), "Low Income Countries' BRIC Linkage: Are there Growth Spillovers?", IMF Working Paper 11/267, Washington:IMF.

Samargandi, N., & Kutan, M. (2016). Private credit spillovers and economic growth: Evidence from BRICS countries. *Journal of International Financial Markets Institutions and Money, 44*, 56–84.

Stuenkel, O. (2014). Emerging powers and status: The case of the first Brics summit. *Asian Perspective, 38*(1), 89–110, Janeiro 2014.

Van Agtmael, A. (2012). Think again: The BRICS. *Foreign Policy, 196*, 76–79.

Chapter 39
Assessment of Financial Risks in the Insurance Sector Using the Sensitivity Analysis

Vladimir Bakes and Katarina Valaskova

Abstract Companies in the modern dynamic market environment must undergo various types of risks. The importance of each type of risk is different for each specific company depending on the nature of its business, the regional scope, markets of operation, corporate organizational structure, etc. The risk management function within the company is carried out in respect of financial risks, operational risks and legal risks. Financial risk comprises market risk (including currency risk, interest rate risk and other price risk), credit risk and liquidity risk. The primary objectives of the financial risk management function are to establish risk limits and then ensure that exposure to risks stays within these limits. In the insurance sector, the risk management programme is focused on the unpredictability of situations in the financial markets and seeks to minimize any potential adverse effect on the financial results of insurance companies. The contribution illustrates and explains one of the most common and simplest methods of the risk assessment, the sensitivity analysis, in a practical example using the Slovak insurance company.

39.1 Introduction

Financial risks are associated with financial markets, and to simplify it, we can say that they are related to the structure of the corporate financial assets and liabilities. In the literature, there are various definitions of financial risks. A financial risk is a potential financial loss of a subject; it is not an existing realized or unrealized financial loss, but the loss in the future resulting from the financial or commodity instrument or portfolio (Jilek 1999). A financial risk is a likelihood of financial loss or loss of profits as results of an opposite development compared to the expectations (Markovic 2007).

V. Bakes · K. Valaskova (✉)
University of Zilina, Faculty of Operation and Economics of Transport and Communications, Zilina, Slovak Republic
e-mail: katarina.valaskova@fpedas.uniza.sk

N. Tsounis, A. Vlachvei (eds.), *Advances in Panel Data Analysis in Applied Economic Research*, Springer Proceedings in Business and Economics,
https://doi.org/10.1007/978-3-319-70055-7_39

Financial risks can be divided according to the different classification criteria. Most often, however, the financial risks are classified on the basis of the criterion – instrument and market segment – which distinguishes credit, market, liquidity, operational and business risks (Cisko and Kliestik 2013).

Credit risk is the risk of loss due to a debtor default as they do not pay their obligations under the terms of the contract and thereby cause certain losses to the creditor. The risk of loss due to the change of market variables is typical for market risks. Market risks include risk interest rate which measures the loss as a consequence of changes in prices of instruments sensitive to the interest rate (e.g. volatility of interest rates, shape of yield curves) but also equity, commodity, currency, correlation and credit spread risks (Misankova et al. 2014). Liquidity risk monitors shares and operations on the financial market and distinguishes the risk of loss in the case of current insolvency and the risk of loss as a result of the low liquidity of the market with financial instruments which do not allow to close position and thus reduce an access of the financial sources. Operational risk is a risk of default of in-company processes or of people (Spuchlakova et al. 2014). This risk category includes transaction risk, operation control risk (defects in management of the corporate activities) and system risks (imperfections in computer systems and equations quantification). Business risks inform about the environment in which the risk occurs. We have to consider legal, reputation, taxation, credit rating, currency convertibility, disaster and regulatory risks.

39.2 Risk Management in the Sector of Insurance

The risk of insurance contracts relates to the fact that it is not clear whether or when an insurance event will occur or how big the related claim will be. It is evident from the nature of an insurance contract that such risk is incidental and cannot be predicted. In the case of insurance contracts that were valued using the probability theory, the main risk the company is facing is that the amount of insurance claims may be higher than the related insurance provisions (Bartošová 2007). This may occur if the amount or significance of actually occurred insured events is higher than originally assumed. Insured events are random, and the actual number and amount of claims and benefits may vary from year to year from the level calculated using statistical techniques. Experience shows that the larger the portfolio of similar insurance contracts, the smaller the relative variability of the expected outcome. In addition, a more diversified portfolio is less likely to be affected by a change in any subset of the portfolio (Szabo et al. 2005). Companies try to develop their own insurance underwriting strategy to diversify the type of insurance risks. Factors affecting the insurance risk include insufficient diversification of risk in view of its type and size, geographical location and the type of the industrial sector.

The underwriting strategy is part of the risk underwriting process which considers the insurance company planned underwriting performance mainly in other non-life insurance and actuarial risks (Crouhy et al. 2000). The plan specifies types of insurance that can be offered during the period and is focused on target customer groups. The strategy is further developed to include individual types of underwriting and limits for individual underwriters, as well as the level and type of insurance, the territory and the industry. The purpose is to ensure that underwritten risks are well diversified in the insurance portfolio. Insurance contracts with wrong claim development are reviewed annually (business property insurance and liability insurance) by underwriting officials who are authorized to refuse renewal of a contract or change its terms on renewal or refuse its extension (Kliestik et al. 2015).

Natural disasters to which insurance companies are exposed are the most significant risks in this area. In recent years, damages to property have been more and more often caused by floods or inundations. To reduce the risk of claims due to floods, insurance companies implement maximum claim limits for one and for all insured events, during the insurance term which is applied to property contracts above a certain insured amount according to the product policies (Svabova and Durica 2015). Insurance companies also use the system for mapping risky areas and regions for over-the-limit property risk.

Actuarial risk management is regulated by individual insurance product methodologies that include underwriting competencies and powers. For business property insurance, particularly for those businesses involved in industrial production, insurance company uses a risk management methodology and techniques applied in determining risks and analysing losses or potential losses prior to the risk underwriting through modelling loss scenarios; it also cooperates with reinsurers and other coinsurance companies regarding risk diversification.

39.3 Financial Risks in the Insurance Sector

An insurance company is exposed to financial risk through its financial assets, financial liabilities, insurance liabilities, reinsurance assets and liabilities. In particular, the key financial risk is that the proceeds from its financial assets are not sufficient to fund the obligations arising from its insurance and investment contracts. The most important components of this financial risk are market, credit and liquidity risks (Jorion 2003). The most important components of market risk are interest rate risk, currency risk and price risk.

In general, the risk management programme is focused on the unpredictability of situations in the financial markets and seeks to minimize any potential adverse effect on the financial results of insurance companies

Liquidity Risk The underlying principle of assets and liabilities management is to invest in such securities that, by their nature, correspond to the insurance contracts covered by them. The insurance company approaches insurance contracts in life and non-life insurance differently.

For non-life insurance, which is mostly use in the business environment, the insurance company purchases debt securities with short-term and midterm maturity, mainly with variable interest rates, taking into account that insurance contracts in non-life insurance are considered short term, with a maturity within 1 year (Annual report of Komunálna poisťovňa 2015). Therefore, they manage the securities portfolio in such a way as to make the respective cash inflows cover claims arising from liabilities from insurance contracts at each moment.

Insurance companies are exposed to daily calls on their available funds, mainly due to insurance operations (insurance claims). Liquidity risk is the risk that sufficient funds will not be available at a reasonable cost to cover due liabilities from insurance contracts. Companies set limits to maintain a sufficient amount of cash equivalents to cover all due liabilities.

Market Risk The most important components of market risk are interest rate risk, currency risk and price risk. The interest rate risk is the risk that future cash flows from a financial asset fluctuate due to changes in the market interest rate. Insurance and investment contracts with fixed and guaranteed conditions give rise to claims and benefits that are fixed and guaranteed at the inception of the contract. Therefore, the guaranteed interest rate is the main risk for insurance companies because the income from financial assets may not cover claims and benefits as they fall due (Bartošová et al. 2015). Companies manage this risk through cash flow matching. Market risk is managed through monitoring of market values of financial assets, calculations of value at risk, sensitivity analysis and stress tests. Market Risk Analyser, which is part of SimCorp system, is utilized for the mentioned calculations.

The currency risk arises mainly from securities and liabilities denominated in other currencies. In general, many companies prefer investing in assets denominated in currencies in which the corporate liabilities are denominated, thus mitigate the currency risk arising from the nature of its business activities.

The price risk is the risk of a change in the fair value of financial instruments from movements in market variables other than changes in interest rates and currency exchange rates. Insurance companies are exposed to price risk due to its investment in equity securities; the risk is mainly exposure to movements in prices of securities affected by developments in equity markets. Companies manage the risk by monitoring the sensitivity of profits to that risk.

Credit Risk Insurance companies have exposure to credit risk, which is the risk that a counterparty will be unable to pay amounts in full when due. Key areas where the companies are exposed to credit risk are amounts due from insurance contracts, amounts due from reinsurance, amounts due from intermediaries, securities issuers, cash and other receivables (Crouhy et al. 2000).

The company uses several tools to manage insurance receivables from the insured – one of them being the reminder process for overdue receivables that is carried out in regular intervals.

If unsuccessful, the company takes other measures, using a several-stage collection process (intervention activities, court settlement and seizure). In addition, the company monitors receivables on a monthly basis, by checking their payments and ageing structure (Fabozzi and Peterson 2003). Based on this, the default risk is assessed, and the value of impaired receivables is reduced by setting up an impairment provision.

Credit risk of issuer of securities is managed through the investment strategy and rules, which are regularly reassessed in cooperation with the main shareholder of the company.

39.4 Sensitivity Analysis of a Chosen Insurance Company

Sensitivity analysis is one of the most common and simplest methods of the financial risk assessment. Sensitivity analysis examines the sensitivity of the criterial parameter (e.g. net present value, ROE, profit, etc.) to changes in input factors (selling price, amount of realized production, input prices, interest rates, capital costs, wages, capacity utilization, etc.). Factors which cause only a little change of the criterial parameter are considered low risk because the sensitivity of this indicator to changes in these factors is small. And vice versa, factors causing significant changes in the criterial parameter are high-risk parameters. It is important to focus only on those input factors which have significant impact on the criterial parameter and are associated with the highest degree of uncertainty.

The sensitivity analysis provides, despite its simplicity, very important and reliable information about possible threats by identifying the most significant risk factors and quantifying the level of threat to the economic value of the investment project. The sensitivity analysis may result in the determination of limits of the rejection of the input variables, i.e. values of input variables in which the variable indicated inefficiency of the criterial parameter.

To do the assessment of the financial risks in the insurance company, we choose the Slovak company Komunálna poisťovňa a.s. Vienna Insurance Group which is a commercial insurance company with a universal licence, operating on the Slovak insurance market since 1994. Its mission is to provide high-quality insurance products and services in the areas of life insurance, motor and citizens property insurance, liability insurance as well as industrial risks insurance (Annual report of Komunálna poisťovňa 2015).

In this contribution, we evaluate the risk factors having the significant impact on the profit of the insurance company (Annual report of Komunálna poisťovňa 2015). We consider the following risk factors: net insurance premium earned (NIPE), financial investments income (FII), commissions from reinsurers (CfR), net realized gains from financial assets (GFA), net income from revaluation at the fair value of the financial investment (NIR), other income (e.g. income from sale of fixed assets; abb. OI), insurance benefits (from long-term contracts; abb. IB), insurance claims (on short-term contracts; abb. IC), acquisition costs of insurance contracts (CIC), marketing and administration costs (MAC) and other operating costs (OOC).

The values of these risk parameters from the year 2015 were used to calculate the profit of the insurance company (a line with 0% change of risk factors) and also to provide the sensitivity analyses and measure the changes of the profit if the input parameters change by 3, 5, 6, 7, 8, 9 and 10% in optimistic and pessimistic way.

To determine the profit of the insurance company, we use the following equation:

Table 39.1 Impact of changes of net insurance premium earned on the total profit (thousand €)

Δ %	NIPE	FII	CfR	FGA	NIR	OI	IB	IC	CIC	MAC	OOC	Profit
10%	162,795	8018	13,347	1207	742	605	96,091	20,445	18,874	6204	1386	24,152
9%	161,315	7945	13,226	1196	750	600	97,159	20,672	19,084	6273	1401	22,672
8%	159,835	7872	13,105	1185	758	594	98,227	20,900	19,293	6342	1417	21,192
7%	158,355	7799	12,983	1174	766	589	99,294	21,127	19,503	6410	1432	19,712
6%	156,875	7726	12,862	1163	775	583	100,362	21,354	19,713	6479	1448	18,232
5%	155,395	7653	12,741	1152	783	578	101,430	21,581	19,922	6548	1463	16,752
3%	152,435	7508	12,498	1130	799	567	103,565	22,035	20,342	6686	1494	13,792
0%	**147,995**	**7289**	**12,134**	**1097**	**824**	**550**	**106,768**	**22,717**	**20,971**	**6893**	**1540**	**9352**
−3%	143,555	7070	11,770	1064	849	534	109,971	23,399	21,600	7100	1586	4912
−5%	140,595	6925	11,527	1042	865	523	112,106	23,853	22,020	7238	1617	1952
−6%	139,115	6852	11,406	1031	873	517	113,174	24,080	22,229	7307	1632	472
−7%	137,635	6779	11,285	1020	882	512	114,242	24,307	22,439	7376	1648	−1008
−8%	136,155	6706	11,163	1009	890	506	115,309	24,534	22,649	7444	1663	−2488
−9%	134,675	6633	11,042	998	898	501	116,377	24,762	22,858	7513	1679	−3968
−10%	133,196	6560	10,921	987	906	495	117,445	24,989	23,068	7582	1694	−5448

$$\begin{aligned} \text{PROFIT} = {} & (\text{NIPE} + \text{FII} + \text{CfR} + \text{FGA} - \text{NIR} + \text{OI}) \\ & - (\text{IB} + \text{IC} + \text{CIC} + \text{MAC} + \text{OOC}) \end{aligned} \tag{39.1}$$

Table 39.1 quantifies the impact of changes of risk factors on the total profit of the insurance company. It is obvious that factors which belong to the revenues increase in the optimistic development, while those of costs decrease and such conditions influence the total profit increase, too. It can be said that there is a positive correlation between the profit and net insurance premium earned, financial investments income, commissions from reinsurers, net realized gains from financial assets and other income. The profit calculated in the table reflects the changes of the net insurance premium earned; to conclude the higher the level of the risk factor, the higher the level of the profit of the company.

As it may be seen in the table, some factors decrease in the optimistic way and, vice versa, increase in the pessimistic development. And so there is a negative correlation between the profit and net income from revaluation at the fair value of the financial investment, insurance benefits, insurance claims, costs of insurance contracts, marketing and administration costs and other operating costs. Table 39.2 depicts the quantified development of the total profit of the insurance company considering the gradual changes of all risk factors.

The determined data may be interpreted as follows:

- The increase of net insurance premium earned by 10%, i.e. from 147,995 € to 162,795 €, causes the increase of the total profit of 158%, from 9352 € to 24,152 €.

Table 39.2 Development of the corporate profit determined by changes in risk factors

Profit (thousands €)											
Δ %	NIPE	FII	CfR	FGA	NIR	OI	IB	IC	CIC	MAC	OOC
10%	24,152	10,081	10,565	9462	9434	9407	20,029	11,624	11,449	10,041	9506
9%	22,672	10,008	10,444	9451	9426	9402	18,961	11,397	11,239	9972	9491
8%	21,192	9935	10,323	9440	9418	9396	17,893	11,169	11,030	9903	9475
7%	19,712	9862	10,201	9429	9410	9391	16,826	10,942	10,820	9835	9460
6%	18,232	9789	10,080	9418	9401	9385	15,758	10,715	10,610	9766	9444
5%	16,752	9716	9959	9407	9393	9380	14,690	10,488	10,401	9697	9429
3%	13,792	9571	9716	9385	9377	9369	12,555	10,034	9981	9559	9398
0%	**9352**	**9352**	**9352**	**9352**	**9352**	**9352**	**9352**	**9352**	**9352**	**9352**	**9352**
−3%	4912	9133	8988	9319	9327	9336	6149	8670	8723	9145	9306
−5%	1952	8988	8745	9297	9311	9325	4014	8216	8303	9007	9275
−6%	472	8915	8624	9286	9303	9319	2946	7989	8094	8938	9260
−7%	−1008	8842	8503	9275	9294	9314	1878	7762	7884	8869	9244
−8%	−2488	8769	8381	9264	9286	9308	811	7535	7674	8801	9229
−9%	−3968	8696	8260	9253	9278	9303	−257	7307	7465	8732	9213
−10%	−5448	8623	8139	9242	9270	9297	−1325	7080	7255	8663	9198

- The decrease of the insurance benefits by 10%, i.e. from 106,768 € to 96,091 €, also causes the increase of the total benefits of 114%, from 9352 € to 20,029 €.
- The maximal loss is reached in the pessimistic development of the risk factor net insurance premium earned by 10%.

The following figure depicts the impact of the most significant risk factors on the total profit of the insurance company.

The more significant the impact of a single risk factor, either in a positive or in a negative direction, the steeper the line (curve) showing the impact of this change. And vice versa, the less significant the impact of changes of risk factors, the closer the lines (curves) to the horizontal axis. Figure 39.1 shows that, for example, the impact of the factor net insurance premium earned is greater than the impact of the factor insurance claims in a positive direction.

To sum up, if the insurance company wants to receive positive profit, maintain its position on the market and eliminate financial risks in all forms, it should focus on the increase of the net insurance premium earned which forms the revenues part and, on the other hand, minimize insurance benefits and insurance claims which are the main components of costs. Sensitivity analysis may be used as an estimation method for future prediction of significant risk factors to avoid insolvency and unhealthy development and reduce possible financial risks.

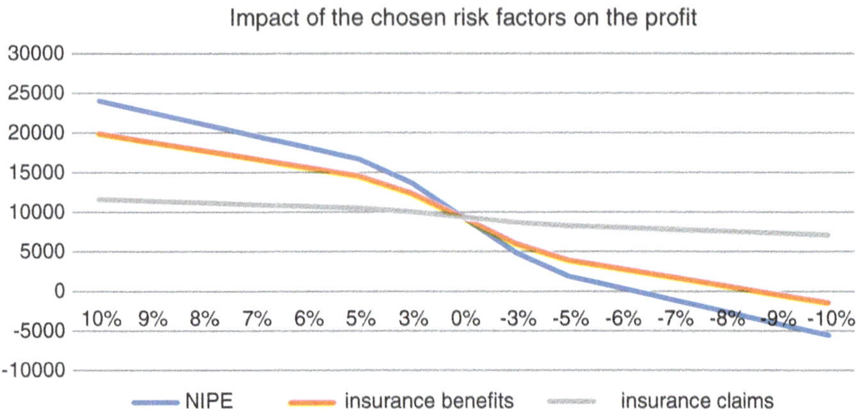

Fig. 39.1 Impact of the chosen risk factors on the profit

39.5 Conclusions

An insurance company is exposed to financial risk through its financial assets, financial liabilities, insurance liabilities, reinsurance assets and liabilities. In particular, the key financial risk is that the proceeds from its financial assets are not sufficient to fund the obligations arising from its insurance and investment contracts.

Insurance companies belong to the entities that very intensively perceive risk in any forms. This fact makes the crucial role of the risk management in the management of these organizations. Insurance companies must handle temporal uncertainty of the repayment of earned insurance premiums and also the uncertainty about their extent, particularly in non-life insurance. Risk management in the insurance companies must solve many diverse problems as they intensively work with risks.

In this paper we depicted the basic definitions and classification of the financial risks, and we presented the basic aspects of the risk management in the insurance sector as well as the real forms of financial risks in the insurance companies. The illustrative example helps to understand the sensitivity analysis, which is one of the most common and simplest methods of the financial risk assessment and reveals the most significant risk factors that influence the level of profit of the chosen Slovak insurance company.

Acknowledgements The contribution is an output of the scientific project VEGA 1/0428/17 Creation of new paradigms of financial management at the threshold of the twenty-first century in the conditions of the Slovak Republic.

References

Annual report of Komunálna poisťovňa. (2015). Vienna Insurance Group, Slovakia.

Bartošová, V. (2007). Determinants of firm's capital structure and their identification in practice. *Ekonomiczne problemy usług, 8*, 9–14.

Bartošová, V., Majercak, P., & Hraskova, D. (2015). Taking risk into account in the evaluation of economic efficiency of investment projects: traditional methods. *Procedia – Economics and Finance, 24*, 68–75.

Cisko, S., & Kliestik, T. (2013). Finančný manažment podniku II. EDIS, Žilina.

Crouhy, M., Mark, R., & Galai, D. (2000). *Risk management*. New York: McGraw- Hill.

Fabozzi, J. F., & Peterson, P. (2003). *Financial management and analysis*. Hoboken: Wiley.

Jilek, J. (1999). Finanční rizika. Praha: Grada Publishing.

Jorion, P. (2003). *Financial risk manager*. Hoboken: Wiley.

Kliestik, T., Musa, H., & Frajtova-Michalikova, K. (2015). Parametric methods for estimating the level of risk in finance. *Procedia – Economics and Finance, 24*, 322–330.

Markovic, P. (2007). Manažment finančných rizík podniku. Iura Edition, Bratislava.

Misankova, M., Valaskova, K., Cug, J., & Zvarikova, K. (2014). Comparison of selected measures of financial risk. In *Management innovation and business innovation:2nd international conference on management innovation and business*. Singapore Management and Sports Science Institute, 8–9 Dec 2014.

Spuchlakova, E., Frajtova-Michalikova, K., & Mirtus, M. (2014). Credit risk measurement. In *Economics and social science: 2nd international conference on economics and social science*. Information Engineering Research Institute, 29–30 July 2014.

Svabova, L., & Durica, M. (2015). Základy poistnej matematiky. Dolis, Bratislava.

Szabo, L., Vrcholova, T., & Dubovicka, L. (2005). Manažment rizika. Ekonóm, Bratislava.

Chapter 40
Calculation of Tax Shields Using the Method of Adjusted Present Value

Katarina Valaskova and Vladimir Bakes

Abstract A tax shield is a reduction in taxable income for an individual or corporation achieved through claiming allowable deductions such as mortgage interests, medical expenses, charity donations, amortization, and depreciation. These deductions reduce a taxpayer's taxable income for a given year or defer income taxes into future years. Interest expense is, as opposed to dividends and capital gains, tax deductible; therefore the tax shield (being a benefit of debt financing over equity financing) is an important factor influencing the company's capital structure choice. The contribution presents basic methods of the tax shield calculations with a practical application of a chosen method in conditions of the Slovak construction company to illustrate and explain the tax shields determination.

40.1 Introduction

A tax shield is an effect of an increase of the return on equity in a capital structure of a company. Interests of the debt as a part of the costs decrease profit, which is used to pay a tax, and so the tax burden of the company is reduced. The total return of the equity increases. While academic research, in general, agrees on the importance of taxes for capital structure decisions, there is still a wide range of estimates of the magnitude of the tax shield. Worldwide researches have identified not only the level of debt, the tax rate, credit risk, bankruptcy probability, and the future financing policy of the company as important variables influencing the value of the tax shield.

Some governments are concerned about the excessive use of the corporate debt by certain investors, especially private equity investors. One potential strategy to influence corporate capital structure choices is to cut the tax deductibility of interest.

K. Valaskova (✉) · V. Bakes
University of Zilina, Faculty of Operation and Economics of Transport and Communications, Zilina, Slovak Republic
e-mail: katarina.valaskova@fpedas.uniza.sk

N. Tsounis, A. Vlachvei (eds.), *Advances in Panel Data Analysis in Applied Economic Research*, Springer Proceedings in Business and Economics,
https://doi.org/10.1007/978-3-319-70055-7_40

By doing so tax authorities reduce the tax shield and remove a significant benefit of the debt financing over the equity financing.

The main aim of the paper is to define the theoretical fundamentals of tax shields and the presentation of the methods used to calculate tax shields. The paper is divided into three sections. Firstly, a brief literature review is presented and then the basic methods of tax shields evaluation, and the last section depicts the calculation of the tax shield in the conditions of the Slovak Republic.

40.2 Literature Review

The tax shield may be defined as a contribution for the company as the costs of debt are not a subject of taxation, but they decrease the tax base (Buus et al. 2007). The value of tax shields defines the increase of the company value as a result of tax savings given by the interests paid (Fernandez 2007). According to Hrvoľová, the value of the tax shield is defined as an increase of the company value as a result on tax burden decrease due to the payment of interests (Hrvolova 2006).

There is not any consensus in the literature about the appropriate way of the tax shield calculation. Many authors – Modigliani and Miller (1963), Myers (1974), Miles and Ezzell (1980), Harris and Pringle (1985), Damodaran (2004), Copeland et al. (2000), Arzac and Glosten (2005), and Fernandez (2007) – indicate many ways and methods of the tax shield calculation; they often reflect the present value of tax savings as a consequence of payments of the debt interests.

Table 40.1 indicates the results of the mentioned authors and of their algorithms for the tax shield calculation.

Miller and Modigliani (1963, p. 436) suggest a deduction of tax savings with a risk-free rate. Harris and Pringle (1985) and Ruback (2002) advise to discount the tax savings to capital costs for an unlevered company. Miles and Ezzell recommend to discount the tax savings only in the first year for the debt price and in the following years for the costs of capital of the unlevered company (Miles and Ezzell 1980). But on the other hand, the financial literature does not bring a clear determination of a discount rate which is theoretically appropriate for the tax benefits of interests (Copeland et al. 2000).

Table 40.1 Algorithms for the tax shield calculation

Theory	Tax shield calculation
Modigliani–Miller	$E+D=V_u+PV[R_f;DTR_f]=V_u+DT$
Myers	$\mathrm{VTS}=PV[K_d;DTD_d]$
Miles–Ezzell	$\mathrm{VTS}=PV[K_U+TDK_d](1+K_U)/(1+K_D)$
Harris–Pringle	$\mathrm{VTS}=PV[K_U+DK_dT]$
Damodaran	$\mathrm{VTS}=PV[K_U;DTK_U-D(K_D-R_f)(1-T)]$
Fernandez	$\mathrm{VTS}=PV[K_U+DTK_U]$
Miller	$\mathrm{VTS}=0$
With costs of leverage	$\mathrm{VTS}=PV[K_U;DK_UT-D(K_D-R_f)]$
Method of practitioners	$\mathrm{VTS}=PV[K_U;DTK_D-D(K_D-R_f)]$

The value of the tax shield is dependent on the character of the stochastic process of the debt increase. The value of tax shields in the markets without leverage costs equals to the tax rate as a multiple of a present debt plus a multiple of the value of the tax rate of the future net increase of the debt (Bartošová and Kral 2016). An alternative of the claims of Modigliani and Miller and Miller and Ezzell is an evaluation of the algorithm for the companies that have stable accounting value of the leverage ratio. Miller and Modigliani method is used only when the company debt value is determined; Miles and Ezzell formula is typical for the calculation of the debt as a multiple of the value of the security market ($D_t = L.\ S_t$). The theory of Modigliani and Miller assumes a constant discount rate for the debt increase; Miles and Ezzell theory presumes a rate for $t = 1$ and costs of equity for $t > 1$. The appropriate discount rate to increase the debt in the time $t = 1$ is negative, according to Miles and Ezzell, if the expected growth (g) is lower than $(K_U - R_f)/(1 + R_f)$. This explanation is very simple and easy to use but also unrealistic, as there is hardly any company using this kind of financial politics (Stanton and Seasholes 2005).

40.3 General Determination of the Tax Shield Value

A present value of the debt (D_0) is a difference between the value of the future interests and future debt increase (ΔD_t):

$$D_0 = \sum_1^{\infty} E\ [M_t\ \text{.interests}] - \sum_1^{\infty} E\ [M_t.\Delta D_t] \tag{40.1}$$

$\sum_1^{\infty} E\ [M_t\ \text{.interests}]$ is a value of future interests, and $\sum_1^{\infty} E\ [M_t.\Delta D_t]$is a value of a future debt increase. The value of the tax shield is the product of the interest value and the tax rate:

$$\text{VTS}_0 = T.\sum_1^{\infty} E\ [M_t\ \text{.interests}] = T.D_0 + T.\sum_1^{\infty} E\ [M_t\ .\Delta D_t] \tag{40.2}$$

where

T tax rate
D_0 present value of a debt

The last equation is usable for companies with any type of the growth. It shows that the value of tax shields is dependent only on the stochastic character of the process with the debt increase. The value of the present debt increase is given by the financial strategy of the company (Kramarova et al. 2014).

The present value of the leverage company equals to the sum of the debt value and equity or to the sum of the value of the unlevered company and the value of the tax shields:

$$V_{L0} = S_0 + D_0 = V_{u0} + \text{VTS}_0 \tag{40.3}$$

where

V_{L0} value of a levered company
S_0 equity value
D_0 debt value
V_{u0} value of an unlevered company
VTS_0 value of tax shields

If the company has a stable accounting value of the leverage, α is considered an appropriate discount rate for the expected debt increase and the discount rate for the tax shield, where $t = 2$, is given by the equation

$$1 + K_{\tau S2} = \frac{(1 + R_f) . (1 + \alpha) . (1 + g)}{1 + \alpha + g . (1 + R_f)} \tag{40.4}$$

where

$K_{\tau S2}$ discount rate for the tax shield in $t = 2$
R_f risk-free rate
α expected return on the increase of assets
g expected growth

It is necessary to derive the appropriate discount rate for the value of expected taxes. If it is assumed that the discount rate for the increase of assets is K, then the discount rate for the expected value of taxes of the unlevered company is also K. But in case of the discount rate for the expected values of the levered company, it is distinguished considering the individual theories (Modigliani & Miller 1963). According to Miles and Ezzell, the correct discount rate to calculate expected tax shields is the risk-free rate, in the horizon $t = 1$, or the required return (K) on assets ($t > 1$). Modigliani and Miller claim that the average discount rate of the expected tax shields is the risk-free rate in any time horizon and also that taxes of the levered company are riskier than the taxes of the unlevered one. But, Miles and Ezzell present the same risk for both taxes in the period $t > 1$.

If the nonexistent costs are used, it means that the expected free cash flows are not dependent on the leverage effect and the value of the tax shield is expressed as follows:

$$\mathrm{VTS} = G_U - G_L \tag{40.5}$$

where

VTS value of the tax shield
G_U present value of taxes paid by an unlevered company
G_L present value of taxes paid by a levered company

The value of tax shields is the difference between the present value of two flows with different risk levels, i.e., the present value of taxes paid by the unlevered company and the present value of taxes paid by the levered company (Paliderova et al. 2015). The costs of tax shields may be divided into two main parts: a risk-free rate of return and a risk premium.

The risk of tax shields is given by the volatility of its rate of return which is influenced by the volatility of the tax rate and of the paid interests which is an item decreasing the tax base up to the level to which EBIT covers interests (Cernikova and Malikova 2013). Factors that influence the volatility of the paid interests are the volatility of EBIT, volatility of the debt value, and volatility of the tax rate. The tax rate is easy to plan if there are not any unpredictable changes in a fiscal policy. Considering the income tax, the deterministic element is very significant, and vice versa, the stochastic element is weak (Michalkova 2016). That is the reason why the problem of volatility of the yield of tax shields may be restricted to the volatility of EBIT, volatility of costs of debt, and volatility of a debt value.

We reason that the volatility of EBIT can be excluded as a risk determinant. The identification of the tax shield value may be assumed if there is a probability of the foreseeable duration of the company (Miller 1977). This assumption may be considered if EBIT can cover the interests; in the future time horizon, it has to cover also the costs of equity. EBIT has to cover the costs of equity as well as the costs of debt. Benefits of the interest tax shield are threatened if EBIT is lower than the interests of the debt. In the long-term horizon, this situation may be excluded, as company would not be able to continue in its operation.

Risk of the tax shield approximately equals to the risk of the debt, and costs of tax shields are almost the same as the costs of debt; $r_T \approx r_D$. Then the benefit of the tax shield is given by the formula

$$D_\tau . r_{D,\tau} . t = \varepsilon_{T,\tau} \tag{40.6}$$

where

D_τ debt value
$r_{D,\tau}$ costs of debt in the period τ
t income tax rate
$\varepsilon_{T,\tau}$ value of a tax shield in the period τ

If the yield methods based on the discount of the profit are used, the benefit for investors to the debt is

$$D_\tau . r_{D,\tau} = \varepsilon_{D,\tau} + (D_{\tau+1} - D_\tau) \tag{40.7}$$

where

D_τ debt value
$D_{\tau+1}$ debt value in the period $\tau + 1$
$\varepsilon_{D,\tau}$ yield of tax shield in the period τ

The difference between the Eqs. (40.6) and (40.7) is in the use of an accrual base which is preferred in the international standards. As a consequence, the tax shield is calculated from the total accounting interests and not only from the part paid by creditors. Thus, it can be said that using the yield method means that the value of the tax shield is not a product of the debt value and the tax rate of the corporation income tax $D_\tau . t \neq T_\tau$.

Equation (40.8), using the substitution for all X; $X \in \{D, E, U\}$, determines the equation between the sum of the costs of equity and debt on the one side and the sum of the tax shield costs and costs of the unlevered capital on the other side.

$$U_r\; r_{U,r} + T_r.r_{T,r} = D_r.r_{D,r} + E_r.r_{E,r} \quad (40.8)$$

where

$r_{E,r}$ costs of equity
$r_{D,r}$ costs of debt
$r_{T,r}$ costs of the tax shield
$r_{U,r}$ costs of the unlevered capital

The equation of the weighted average costs ($r_{F,t}$) may be derived from the previous equation:

$$F_\tau.r_{F,\tau} = U_\tau\; r_{U,\tau} + T_r.r_{T,\tau} \quad \text{and} \quad F_\tau.r_{F,\tau} = D_\tau.r_{D,\tau} + E_\tau.r_{E,\tau} \quad (40.9)$$

where

$r_{D,\tau}$ costs of debt in the period τ
$r_{E,\tau}$ costs of equity in the period τ

Next modification of the equation forms the equation which is used to calculate the weighted average costs of capital (WACC):

$$\text{WACC}_r = \frac{E_\tau}{E_\tau + D_\tau}.r_{E,\tau} + \frac{D_\tau}{E_\tau + D_\tau}.r_{D,\tau} \quad (40.10)$$

where

E_τ value of equity
D_τ market value of debt
$r_{D,\tau}$ costs of debt in the period τ
$r_{E,\tau}$ costs of equity

Method of the Adjusted Present Value (APV) There are many theories describing the calculation of the tax shields value. One of them is the adjusted present value which was presented by Myers in 1974 and which indicates to calculate the value of tax shields by the discount of the tax savings to the prejudice of the debt (Myers 1974). The argument is that the risk of the tax savings resulting from the debt is the same as the risk of the debt.

The sum of the debt and the value of equity of the company equal to the net present value of the tax saving and of the tax shield value:

$$E_0 + D_0 = Vu_0 + \text{VTS}_0 \quad (40.11)$$

where

E_0 equity of the company
D_0 debt value
Vu_0 value of the unlevered company without taxes
VTS_0 value of the tax shield

The market value of the company is then

$$Vu_0 = PV_0\,[Ku_0; \mathrm{FCF}_0] \quad (40.12)$$

where

PV_0 present value of a company
Ku_0 required rate of return of assets
FCF_0 free cash flow

A combination of the Eqs. (40.11) and (40.12) gives the equation to calculate the value of tax shield:

$$\mathrm{VTS}_0 = E_0 + D_0 - Vu_0 = PV_0\,[\mathrm{WACC}_t; \mathrm{FCF}_t] - PV_0\,[Ku_t; \mathrm{FCF}_t] \quad (40.13)$$

Various procedures of the tax shield calculation should bring the same results (Fernandez 2007), if all types of prognoses are used properly (one or more time periods, variable or constant debt, etc.). The value of the tax shield influences the value of the corporate equity, the relation between required rate of return and return on assets, and finally also the relation between WACC and the required rate of return of assets.

40.4 Determination of the Tax Shield Value in a Slovak Company

Let's consider a company of the construction industry which has the following economic results: EBIT 650000 €, growth of EBIT 4,5% p.a., tax rate 19%, and expected return of equity 12%.

If it is needed, company changes its capital structure once a year. Using the equation to calculate the value of the unlevered company we get

$$V_U = \frac{(1 - 0.19) \times 650\,000}{0.12 - 0.045} = 7\,020\,000\ € \quad (40.14)$$

We also assume that the company has 60,000 € in a risk-free debt ($r_p = 5{,}5\%$) and a constant ratio of the unpaid debt is expected in the future.

The value of the tax shield is calculated using the APV method, and we add the value of the unlevered company (7,020,000 €). It is important to remind that each tax shield is recorded a year back in the expected yield of the debt (r_p) and the other years in the expected yield of equity (r_a). It is because the tax shield of the first year is known in the present, but other tax shields are dependent on the future value of the company. We assume that the company will have a constant ratio of the unpaid debt in the future; the weight of the debt will increase. The growth of the company is related to the value of r_a. So, the tax shield in that year is

$$\mathrm{ITS}_{t=1} = r_D.D_L \quad , \quad t = 1^T \quad \Rightarrow \quad 627 = 0.055 \times 60\,000 \times 0.19 \tag{40.15}$$

The present value of all tax shields is

$$S = PV\,(\mathrm{ITS}) = \frac{627}{1.055} + \frac{627 \times 1.045}{1.055 \times 1.12} + \frac{627 \times \;\; 1.045^2}{1.055 \times 1.12^2} + \cdots = \frac{627}{0.12 - 0.045} \times \frac{1.12}{1.055} = 8\,875\,€ \tag{40.16}$$

The value of the equity equals to the value of the levered company minus the debt value and the present value of interest tax shields is

$$E_L = V_U - D_L + S = 7\;020\;000 - 60\;000 + 8\;875 = 6\;968\;875\;€ \tag{40.17}$$

Using the previous equation shows that the value of the levered company (V_L) is not higher than the value of the unlevered company (V_U) adjusted of the interest tax shield value:

$$\begin{aligned} V_L &= E_L + D_L = V_U + S \\ 6\;968\;875 &+ 60\;000 = 8\;875 + 7\;020\;000 \\ 7\;028\;875\;€ &= \;7\;028\;875\;€ \end{aligned} \tag{40.18}$$

The costs of equity, if $k = 1$, can be calculated as

$$\begin{aligned} r_E &= \left[1 + \frac{D_L}{E_L}\left(1 - \frac{r_D t}{1 + r_D}\right)\right] \times r_A - \left[\frac{D_L}{E_L}\left(1 - \frac{r_D t}{1 + r_D}\right)\right] \times r_D \\ &= \left[1 + \frac{60\;000}{6\;968\;875}\left(1 - \frac{0.055 \times 0.19}{1.055}\right)\right] \times 0.12 \\ &\quad - \left[\frac{60\;000}{6\;968\;875}\left(1 - \frac{0.055 \times 0.19}{1.055}\right)\right] \times 0.055 = 12.15\;\% \end{aligned} \tag{40.19}$$

The application of the APV method in this case is simple because all parameters grow in a constant pace. APV is easy to use also when the debt value is constant or when it changes deterministically in the time period. Although, in cases, when cash flows in the company change during the time period, the calculation of the future tax shield is more complicated.

40.5 Conclusions

The tax shield is one of the reasons why the use of external resources in the company is cheaper than the use of equity. Its effect is generated by the interest of the loan which is usually tax deductible. The capital cash flow assumes that the risk of the tax shield is equal to the risk of the operating free cash flow. The value of the debt and interests will be proportionate to the future value of the company, and future tax savings depend on the level of the future operating profit. However, if the company does not have enough operating profit to pay tax, the interest of the borrowed capital cannot be used to lower taxes. The risk of tax savings will therefore be higher than the interest rate risk.

There are three basic methods used to determine tax shields. The first one is the method of the adjusted present value which discounts free operating cash flow in unlevered costs of capital, and the result is the value of the unlevered company. Then we add the present value of the tax shield to calculate the value of the levered company. The second is the method of WACC which discounts free operating cash flow in a form of weighted costs of capital to get the value of the levered company. Finally, the third is the method of the capital cash flow which discounts capital cash flows in unlevered costs of capital to determine the value of the levered company. The most general of these is the method of the adjusted present value, which can be adopted in any assumptions of the corporate debt policy and of the tax shield risks. However, if we use this approach, the presumption of the unlevered discount rate includes an appropriate debt policy as well as using the formula for the tax shield value determination.

In this paper we depicted the basic definition and algorithms of the tax shields, and we presented the basic methods of its calculation. The illustrative example helps to understand the determination of tax shield in the conditions of the Slovak Republic.

Acknowledgments The contribution is an output of the scientific project VEGA 1/0428/17 and creation of new paradigms of financial management at the threshold of the twenty-first century in the conditions of the Slovak Republic.

References

Arzac, E. R., & Glosten, L. R. (2005). A Reconsideration of Tax Shield Valuation. *European Financial Management, 11*, 453–461.

Bartošová, V., & Kral, P. (2016). A methodological framework of financial analysis results objectification in the Slovak Republic. In *3rd international conference on business and economics, European proceedings of social and behavioural,* Future ACAD, Nicosia, 21–23 Sept 2016.

Buus, T., Strouhal, J., & Brabanec, T. (2007). Aplikace moderních metod oceňování v případe nekotovaných společností. Oeconomica, Praha.
Cernikova, M., & Malikova, O. (2013). Capital structure of an enterprise – Open questions regarding its displaying under the Czech Legislative conditions. In *11th international conference on Liberec Economic Forum*, Sychrov, Czech Republic, 16–17 Sept 2013.
Copeland, T. E., Koller, T., & Murrin, J. (2000). *Valuation: Measuring and managing the value of companies*. New York: Wiley.
Damodaran, A. (2004). *Damodaran on valuation*. New York: Wiley.
Fernandez, P. (2007). Valuing companies by cash flow discounting: 10 methods and 9 theories. *Managerial Finance, 33*, 853–876.
Harris, R. S., & Pringle, J. J. (1985). Risk-adjusted discount rates extensions form the average-risk case. *Journal of Financial Research, 8*, 237–244.
Hrvolova, B. (2006). *Analýza finannčých trhov*. Bratislava: Sprint.
Kramarova, K., Gregova, E., & Cisko, S. (2014). Changes in the corporate tax in Slovakia - tax licence. In *Business and management 2014 : The 8th international scientific conference: Selected papers*. Vilnius, Lithuania, 15–16 May 2014.
Michalkova, L. (2016). Tax shield validation method under the global conditions. In *16th international scientific conference on globalization and its socio-economic consequences*. Rajecke Teplice, Slovakia, 5–6 Oct 2016.
Miles, J. A., & Ezzell, J. R. (1980). The weighted average cost of capital, perfect capital markets and project life: A clarification. *Journal of Financial and Quantitative Analysis, 15*, 719–730.
Miller, M. H. (1977). Debt and taxes. *Journal of Finance, 32*, 261–276.
Modigliani, F., & Miller, M. (1963). Corporate income taxes and the cost of capital: A correction. *American Economic Review, 53*, 433–443.
Myers, S. C. (1974). Interactions of corporate financing and investment decisions –implications for capital budgeting. *Journal of Finance, 29*, 1–25.
Paliderova, M., Bielikova, A., & Spuchlakova, E. (2015). Application of tax bonus under the Slovak and Czech republic. *Procedia – Economics and finance, 26*, 404–410.
Ruback, R. (2002). Capital cash flows: A simple approach to valuing risky cash flows. *Financial Management, 31*, 85–103.
Stanton, R., & Seasholes, M. (2005). The assumptions and maths behind WACC and APV calculations. U.C. Berkley, Canada.

Chapter 41
Some Remarks on the Quantification of the Company Financial Health

Erika Spuchlakova, Katarina Zvarikova, and Tomas Kliestik

Abstract In the field of company management arose several models which task is the prediction of company bankruptcy. According to a study of Aziz and Dar (Corp Govern 6(1): 18–33, 2006), the aim of bankruptcy prediction models is primarily the early detection of financial difficulties and then adoption and application of the most appropriate corrective actions. Detection of financial difficulties is very difficult; its cause is becoming more diverse. The aim of this paper is to analyse company financial health, the causes of company bankruptcies, and the characteristics of those companies and to clarify the forecasting tools (or bankruptcy prediction models). For these purposes, qualitative analysis was used which is mainly focused on the compilation of the results from the present studies. In addition to analysing the causes of company bankruptcies, we focused on the summary of the models that are used for predicting company bankruptcies and proved in advance to anticipate the impending financial difficulties of the company.

41.1 Introduction

In a rapidly changing world, it is necessary to adapt to new conditions. From day to day, approaches can vary. For proper company management, it is essential to have knowledge of their own financial situation. Assessment of the company's financial health is carried out by financial analysis which provides a number of methods on how to evaluate the company's financial health. Analysis indicators are often included in the company assessment, in obtaining bank loans and other financial resources to ensure the company functioning.

As the company focuses on the future and its planning, it is essential to forecast the financial situation. According to the results of the company's financial heath

E. Spuchlakova (✉) · K. Zvarikova · T. Kliestik
University of Zilina in Zilina, Faculty of Operation and Economics of Transport and Communications, Department of Economics, Žilina, Slovak Republic
e-mail: erika.spuchlakova@fpedas.uniza.sk

N. Tsounis, A. Vlachvei (eds.), *Advances in Panel Data Analysis in Applied Economic Research*, Springer Proceedings in Business and Economics,
https://doi.org/10.1007/978-3-319-70055-7_41

prediction, the company decides on the extension or limitation of their business. The use of information from financial analysis, in practice, depends on the management capability of the company.

There are many definitions of the company's financial health. Bartošová (2016) defines the financial health as "company with financial health could be considered the company which is at a given moment capable the meaning of its existence. In a market economy it means the achievement such a rate of recovery of invested capital which is required by investors relative to the height of the risk". Financial health is a characteristic of the financial condition of those companies that exhibit favourable proportions between the different aspects of their finances (Bellovary et al. 2007).

Financial health is defined as the condition where in the foreseeable future the company will not have any prolongation or prepayment inability. Achim et al. (2012). Such company exhibits sufficient profitability and adequate cover risks arising from indebtedness.

41.2 Methodology

In the first phase, the company's financial health analysis is searching for the answer to these questions: (i) Are there financial assumptions sufficiently generated for reproducing the company's operating capacity? (ii) How great is the risk for the company when incomes are declining due to the fixed costs of operating loss (negative profit before interest and taxes) or when there is a decline of operating profit due to interest burden that created the resulting loss (negative profit after tax)? (iii) Is liquidity that arises from operating activities sufficient that the company can continuously pay short-term commitments? (iv) Is the internal company cash flow able to cover any reduction in external resources? (Kliestik and Kliestikova 2015)

In the second phase, the financial analysis attempts to uncover the causes of the financially detected state by the balance sheet creation for the previous period. The basis of the financial health is given by the liability items, i.e. the volume of individual financial resources, equity, long-term liabilities, bank loans and short-term liabilities. The company's financial health is primarily tested by comparing the liabilities (i) to certain items in the income statement and (ii) to assets items in accordance with the funding rules (balance rules).

There are other variants of measurement. The profitability creates the pre-requisites for simple and extended reproduction, for continued existence of the company. Financial risks can threaten the company's existence by paying inability of extension which are grounds for declaring the competition or bankruptcy. The financial risks are associated with potential problems in operating or financing activities. In the operating activities, it is necessary to provide timely payment of short-term liabilities, and in the financial activities, it is necessary to provide timely payment of the outstanding amount and related interest.

Regarding the operating activities, insolvency risk is obtaining from the possible slowdown in the creation of debts due to the decreasing demand for finished products and after goods (realized operating risk) and also from the potential formation slowing of funds as a consequence of "bad" receivables (collection operating risk). Regarding the operating activities is obtaining the operating risk of loss, since the operating profit margin is reduced by decline in revenues due to fixed costs. In connection with the financial activities, the potential risk is obtaining by the lack of cash flow to cover maturing debt (financial risk of insolvency) and the risk of possible decline in earnings in relation to pay interest (financial risk of loss). In sum, operating activities (production and sales) are associated with the risk of decline of sales and collections, and financial activities (procurement of capital) are associated with the risk of decline of earnings and cash flows.

Financial strength and financial health are the characteristics of the financial company's credibility in terms of its current options to satisfy the legitimate demands of company partners. Financial strength and financial health depend also on management skills and efforts to convert such deeds, that on the financial behaviour. When the company's financial health is not "good", the company must focus on bankruptcy and on how to successfully handle this company crisis.

Most of the research related to company bankruptcies aims to generate predictive bankruptcy model, and as reported by Lukason and Hoffman (2014), research for the reasons, causes and processes that precede the decline remains in prior research neglected. When looking at the causes of company bankruptcies, we must realize that bankruptcy is the last phase of a company crisis. So first we need to focus on the definition and causes of corporate crisis. The crisis is a normal part of almost any company, and as noted by Spillane and Hough (2003), the ability of the company to successfully handle the crisis can mean the difference between survival and bankruptcy of a company. Regarding the definition of the concept of crisis and bankruptcy in the available literature, there is no clear consensus on the common definition. In previous studies, various definitions of bankruptcy were noted and different definitions were used. Despite the fact that there is no uniform definition of bankruptcy, we will follow the definition of Dimitras et al. (1996) which states that bankruptcy is a situation where the company fails to repay obligations to their creditors, preferred stock shareholders and suppliers, or the company went bankrupt under applicable law. Law legislation of a particular country often becomes a decisive role in the definition of bankruptcy in empirical work. Charitou et al. (2013) describe two benefits of legal definition of bankruptcy: (i) bankruptcy can be objectively dated, and (ii) it provides an objective criterion which allows researchers to easily classify a set of surveyed companies.

The role of bankruptcy prediction models is to reduce the risk of bankruptcy. According to Achim et al. (2012), the risk of bankruptcy is closely linked to the economic and financial risks. While the financial risk depends on the level of indebtedness, economic risk depends on the ratio between fixed and variable costs. In general, it can be said that the knowledge of these parameters allows us to quantify the risk of bankruptcy. Crisis management plays an important role in the quantification of bankruptcy risk whose activities are significantly different from the classical strategic management. According to Dubrovski et al. (2007), crisis management is short-term in nature and therefore becomes a part of the strategic management, especially in times of crisis. Hart et al. (2001) state that the activity of crisis management has significantly changed, which was caused mainly by the following passage from an industrial to a global company which enabled faster and easier movement of goods, service, technology, people and information. The level of risk increases with the effects of globalization.

The causes of bankruptcy can be analysed from two perspectives. The first is to compare the characteristics of healthy companies with the signs of company bankruptcy. The second is to focus only on bankruptcy companies. According to Mellahi and Wilkinson (2004), there are four factors that can distinguish whether there is a higher probability that a company gets into crisis: (i) the concentration of companies in the sector, (ii) the life cycle of the industry, (iii) the age of the company and (iv) the size of the company. On the other hand, Jackson and Wood (2013) concluded that the factors which determine the health of the enterprise can be grouped into three main groups: (i) the quality of company owner or company management, (ii) the characteristics of the sector and (iii) economic environment in which the company operates. If we look at the causes of the company bankruptcy from the second point of view, the company with financial difficulties may be (Achim et al. 2012) characterized by the following features: (i) inability to adapt to the environment in which it operates, (ii) reduction in turnover and profitability, (iii) the use of non-functioning instruments and procedures in management, (iv) the precarious financial situation and (v) low level of utilization of the means of production.

In disclosing corporate crises and examining the real causes of the crisis, it is important to clarify if the decline of the company is the result of a sudden cause, or an overall decline occurs gradually and is considered as the last phase of corporate crises. There are two different approaches that focus on gradual or sudden decline. According to Lukason and Hoffman (2014), under normal circumstances, the company did not fail immediately, but in a process of decline, which in individual companies varies by the length of the process.

Empirical research shows that bankruptcies of large companies are often the result of a long process of decline, while small and medium companies are characterized by a rapid onset of decline. Whether it makes sense to use predictive bankruptcy models or not depends on whether the decline of the company makes one cause or many causes at once. Some studies capture only the most important cause of bankruptcy. Such an approach is contrary to the assumption that bankruptcy is always contributed by several reasons. Other empirical studies (Mellahi and Wilkinson 2004) agreed with the theoretical assumption that the decline of the company rarely makes one cause or source too. However, there are arguments, e.g. Lukason and Hoffman (2014); in some extreme cases, bankruptcy can also cause one cause, such as management fault or an external shock.

Result from these conclusions if the decline of the company makes only one cause (usually a sudden or unexpected reason), bankruptcy cannot be predicted by any predictive bankruptcy model based on the use of corporate financial statements. On the other hand, if the decline of the company has a long-term process and does not arise suddenly, this decline can be predicted by a combination of financial indicators of corporate financial statements. In revealing the causes of company bankruptcies, it is therefore appropriate to use the right approach and methodology that can detect company declaim or bankruptcy in time.

The origin of the literature on the prediction of decline dates from the 1930s of the twentieth century when there first appeared studies on the analysis of the indicators in predicting future decline. The history is captured in the literature (Bellovary et al. 2007). In the first comprehensive approach to forecasting company decline, we can be guided by the study of Beaver (1966), who used the one-dimensional approach. This study created a theoretical and practical basis for the development of other methods.

Efforts to unify theory prediction of bankruptcies are still not successful, and therefore there are more structured bankruptcy model predictions. For clearest classification, a meta-analysis from Aziz and Dar (2006) can be considered, whose bankruptcy prediction models are divided into three groups: (i) statistical prediction models, (ii) models using artificial intelligence (AIES) and (iii) theoretical models.

In addition to this meta-analysis, we analysed many other extensive studies in order to ultimately create a uniform classification of bankruptcy prediction models, which are included in Table 41.1.

41.3 Discussion

Due to criticism of univariate analysis in 1968, Altman published the first multi-dimensional discriminant analysis. The main objective of this method is to obtain a linear combination of independent variables that would maximize the variation between groups of companies. Over time, this method also became a target of criticism because it violates the assumptions of multivariate normal distribution of variables and uses a linear instead of quadratic discriminant function. The main disadvantage of this method, however, is it is able to identify companies that are likely to go bankrupt, and it is unable to estimate the probability that bankruptcy might occur. Based on these disadvantages, the next step was to develop methods that would be able to provide such information.

Finding ways to limit discriminant analysis, models were established models with conditional probability. These models have been proposed as an alternative to the discriminant analysis. These models, however, are not widely prevalent in the prediction model, which explains the fact that the discriminant analysis does not require the same conditions, but the results are almost identical. The main models in this group can include logistic regression (LOGIT) and PROBIT. Logistic regression method is based on the function of cumulative probability. It was first used to predict bankruptcy of banks and companies. A multilogic model was developed which classifies companies according to the time they are expected to go on bankruptcy. PROBIT is essentially the same as LOGIT; just change the calculation. PROBIT is used least because it is more difficult to calculate.

Table 41.1 An overview of bankruptcy models

Model	Main features
Statistical models	
Univariate analysis	Traditionally focused on financial ratio analysis. Underlying rationale: If financial ratios exhibit significant differences across the failing and non-failing companies, then they can be used as predictive variables
Multiple discriminant analysis (MDA)	MDA model is a linear combination (a bankruptcy score) of certain discriminatory variables. Bankruptcy score is used to classify companies into bankrupt and non-bankrupt groups according to their individual characteristics
Linear probability model (LPM)	LPM expresses the probability of failure or success of a company as a dichotomous-dependent variable that is a linear function of a vector of explanatory variables. Boundary values are obtained to distinguish between failing and non-failing companies
Logistic regression (LOGIT)	Like LPM, LOGIT also expresses the probability of failure of a company as a dichotomous-dependent variable that is a function of a vector of explanatory variables. The dichotomous-dependent variable of LOGIT, however, is the logarithm of the odds that an event will occur. Such a transformation of LPM is accomplished by replacing the LPM distribution with a logistic cumulative distribution function. In application to bankruptcy, a probability of 0.5 implies an equal chance of company failure or non-failure. Therefore, where 0 indicates bankruptcy, the closer the estimate is to 1, the less the chance of the firm becoming bankrupt
PROBIT	It is possible to substitute the normal cumulative distribution function, rather than logistic, to obtain the PROBIT model. The rest of the interpretations remain the same as for the LOGIT model
Cumulative sums (CUSUM)	CUSUM procedures are among the most powerful tools for detecting a shift in a distribution from one state to another. In the case of bankruptcy prediction, the time series behaviour of the attribute variables for each of the failed and non-failed firms is estimated by a finite order VAR model. The procedure, then, optimally determines the starting point of the shift and provides a signal about the company's deteriorating state as soon as possible. The overall performance of the company at any given point in time is assessed by a cumulative (dynamic) time-series performance score (a CUSUM score). As long as a company's time-series performance scores are positive and greater than a specific sensitivity parameter, the CUSUM score is set to zero, indicating no change in the company's financial condition. A negative score signals a change in the company's condition

Partial adjustment processes	Partial adjustment models are a theoretic rationale of the famous Koyck approach to estimate distributed lag models; application of these models in bankruptcy prediction can best be explained by using cash management behaviour of the firms as an example, which refers to the management of cash by the firm from inflow to outflow, with failure being defined as the inability of the firm to pay financial obligations as they mature. Elasticities of cash balances with respect to the motive factors will be smaller in absolute magnitude for a failing firm than for a similar healthy company
Models using artificial intelligence: artificially intelligent expert system (AIES)	
Neural networks (NN)	Neural networks perform classification tasks in a way intended to emulate brain processes. The "neurons" are nodes with weighted interconnections that are organized in layers. Each node in the input layer is a processing element that receives a variety of input signals from source objects (information about firms, in the case of bankruptcy prediction) and converts them into a single output signal. The latter is either accepted as a classifying decision or retransmitted as an input signal to other nodes (possibly including itself). Signal processing continues until a classifying decision is reached (with some probability, the firm will fail) that satisfies prespecified criteria
Decision trees	It is a form of supervised learning in which a programme learns by generalising from examples (thereby mimicking the behaviour of many human experts). This kind of learning is exploited by decision tree procedures that use recursive partitioning decision rules to transform a "training" sample of data. In bankruptcy classification, the training sample is recursively partitioned into a decision tree in which the final nodes contain companies of only one type, bankrupt or healthy
Case-based reasoning (CBR) and recursive partitioning	CBR solves a new classification problem with the help of similar previously solved cases. CBR programmes can be applied directly to bankruptcy prediction by application of its typical four-stage procedure of (i) identification of a new problem, (ii) retrieval of solved cases from a "case library", (iii) adaptation of solved cases to provide a solution to the new problem and (iv) evaluation of the suggested solution and storage in the case library for future use
Genetic algorithm (GA)	Based on the idea of genetic inheritance and Darwinian theory of natural evolution (survival of the fittest), GAs work as a stochastic search technique to find an optimal solution to a given problem from a large number of solutions. GAs execute this search process in three phases: genetic representation and initialisation, selection and genetic operation (crossover and mutation). The process continues until the actual population converges towards increasingly homogeneous strings. In order to solve a classification problem like bankruptcy, researchers extract a set of rules or conditions using GAs. These conditions are associated with certain cut-off points. Based on these conditions, the model would predict whether or not a firm is likely to go bankrupt

(continued)

Table 41.1 (continued)

Model	Main features
Rough sets models	The aim of rough set theory is to classify objects using imprecise information. In a rough sets model, knowledge about the objects is presented in an information table that, in effect, works like a decision table containing sets of condition and decision attributes that is used to derive the decision rules of the model by inductive learning principles. Every new object (e.g. a company) can then be classified (healthy or in financial distress) by matching their characteristics with the set of derived rules
Theoretical models	
Entropy theory	One way of identifying financial distress is to examine changes in the structure of balance sheets, under the argument that companies try to maintain equilibrium in their financial structure. If a company's financial statements reflect significant changes in the composition of assets and liabilities on its balance sheet, it is more likely that it is incapable of maintaining the equilibrium state. If these changes are likely to become uncontrollable in the future, one can foresee financial distress in these companies
Gambler´ ruin theory	In this approach, the company can be thought of as a gambler playing repeatedly with some probability of loss, continuing to operate until its net worth goes to bankruptcy. With an assumed initial amount of cash, in any given period, there is a net positive probability that company's cash flows will be consistently negative over a run of periods, ultimately leading to bankruptcy
Cash management theory	Short-term management of corporate cash balances is a major concern of every company. An imbalance between cash inflows and outflows would mean failure of cash management function of the company, persistence of which may cause financial distress to the company
Credit risk theories (CreditMetrics, Moody's KMV model)	Credit risk theories are linked to the Basel I and Basel II accords and mostly refer to financial companies. Credit risk is the risk that any borrower/counterparty will default, for whatever reason. Following the Basel II guidelines, a number of recent attempts have been made to develop internal assessment models of credit risk These models and their risk predictions thereof are based on economic theories of corporate finance and are collectively referred to as credit risk theories. For example, JP Morgan's CreditMetrics and Moody's KMV models rely on option pricing theory, whereby default is endogenously related to capital structure and the company may default on its obligations if the value of its assets falls below a critical level (determined by the credit risk model)

Own processing based on Aziz and Dar (2006)

Although, these methods these methods and models can provide valuable information about the company's financial situation, in the future artificial intelligence will be applied to these models. In the recent past, more than 30 different methods were created, mostly using programming and artificial intelligence to forecast the financial situation.

The best known and most commonly used method is neural network. This method has several variations. The most common is a multilayer perceptron (MLP). Other variations include Cascor, probabilistic neural networks, self-organizing maps (SOM), learning vectors and many others (Odom and Sharda 1990). Very often decision trees are used in the company classifying *if-then* rules.

There is a noticeable trend at present penetration level programming techniques and various expert and intelligent systems. Currently superior in this regard are scientists, particularly from China and India. These scientists in predicting the financial situation of enterprises use methods such as case reasoning. Other methods used include algorithm support vector, genetic algorithm, fuzzy set theory, rough set theory (rough set), analysis of data packages (data envelopment analysis) or integer programming (integer programming).

41.4 Conclusion

The aim of this paper was to clarify the bankruptcy models. The main problem in preventing these bankruptcies are unpreparedness risk management companies and the lack of tools for precautionary measures. One of these measures is the bankruptcy prediction models, which with a certain probability can do early detection of impending financial problems of the company.

Decline of the company can be a long process of crisis in the company or it may be a sudden decline. In the event of bankruptcy, which is the last stage of a long-term crisis in the company, the decline is due to several causes; while on the other hand, sudden decline in the company is due to the unexpected cause to which management failed to respond adequately. If the decline is caused by several reasons, it is possible to use bankruptcy prediction models with an appropriate combination of financial indicators that can predict potential problems in the future.

The classification of bankruptcy causes is very difficult from a methodological point of view if not impossible to work only with quality indicators. If we imagine that we are worth 3000 companies, a score based on quality causes of bankruptcy is not an option. Moreover, it is almost impossible to measure some quality causes, since there is no methodology that would be able to capture these causes. We also believe that in predicting the company's financial situation, it is more appropriate to analyse medium and large companies as small companies since, as already mentioned, the decline of small companies is sudden and caused by a single cause. Therefore, it is not possible with sufficient accuracy and timeliness to predict financial situation in small companies. In identifying and researching the causes of company decline, our proposal takes into account factors such as size of company, age of company and life cycle stage of companies or sectors.

Acknowledgements The contribution is an output of the scientific project VEGA 1/0428/17 and creation of new paradigms of financial management at the threshold of the twenty-first century in conditions of the Slovak Republic.

References

Achim, M. V., Mare, C., & Borlea, S. N. (2012). A statistical model of financial risk bankruptcy applied for Romanian manufacturing industry. *Procedia Economics and Finance, 3*, 132–137.

Altman, E. I. (1968). Financial ratios, discriminant analysis and the prediction of corporate bankruptcy. *The Journal of Finance, 1968*, 589–609. https://doi.org/10.1111/j.1540-6261.1968.tb00843.x.

Aziz, M. A., & Dar, H. A. (2006). Predicting corporate bankruptcy: Where we stand? *Corporate Governance, 6*(1), 18–33. https://doi.org/10.1108/14720700610649436.

Bartošová, V. (2016). Optimal debt level as part of enterprise health prediction. *International Journal of Applied Business and Economic Research, 14*, 3799–3806.

Beaver, W. H. (1966). Financial ratios as predictors of failure. *Journal of Accounting Research, 4*, 71–111.

Bellovary, J. L., Giacomino, D. E., & Akers, M. D. (2007). A review of bankruptcy prediction studies: 1930 to present. *Journal of Financial Education, 33*(4), 3–41.

Charitou, A., Dionysiou, D., Lambertides, N., & Trigeorgis, L. (2013). Alternative bankruptcy prediction models using option-pricing theory. *Journal of Banking & Finance, 37*(7), 2329–2341.

Dimitras, A. I., Zanakis, S. H., & Zopounidis, C. (1996). A survey of business failures with an emphasis on prediction methods and industrial applications. *European Journal of Operational Research, 90*, 487–513. https://doi.org/10.1016/0377-2217(95)00070-4.

Dubrovski, D., et al. (2007). Management mistakes as causes of corporate crises: countries in transition. *Managing Global Transitions, 5*, 333–354.

Hart, P., Heyse, L., & Boin, A. (2001). Guest editorial introduction new trends in crisis management practice and crisis management research: Setting the agenda. *Journal of Contingencies and Crisis Management, 9*, 181–188.

Jackson, R. H., & Wood, A. (2013). The performance of insolvency prediction and credit risk models in the UK: A comparative study. *The British Accounting Review, 45*, 183–202. https://doi.org/10.1016/j.bar.2013.06.009.

Kliestik, T., & Kliestikova, J. (2015). Selected issues of selection of significant variables in the prediction models. *Financial Management of Firms and Financial Intuitions, 9*, 537–543.

Lukason, O., & Hoffman, R. C. (2014). Firm Bankruptcy Probability and Causes: An Integrated Study. *International Journal of Business and Management, 9*, 80. https://doi.org/10.5539/ijbm.v9n11p80.

Mellahi, K., & Wilkinson, A. (2004). Organizational failure: a critique of recent research and a proposed integrative framework. *International Journal of Management Reviews, 5–6*, 21–41.

Odom, M. D., & Sharda, R. (1990). A neural network model for bankruptcy prediction. In *1990 IJCNN international joint conference on neural networks. 1990* (pp. 163–168).

Spillane, J., & Hough, M. (2003). Crisis planning in small businesses: Importance, Impetus and Indifference. *European Management Journal, 21*, 398–407.

Chapter 42
Measuring the Globalization Degree of Foreign Direct Investments from 2001 to 2012: First Interpretations

Bruno G. Rüttimann and Pavlos Stamatiou

Abstract This paper measures the globalization degree of financial capital investments based mainly on elaborated UNCTAD data from 2001 to 2012. The paper is a joint research project and sets the base for an annual update to gain insight into the rational logic of foreign direct investments (FDI). The globalization degree is measured with a new statistical entropy risk metric which computes the interweaving of capital flows. The FDI Capital Globalization type 2a is part of a more comprehensive globalization types model. The entropy-based metrics used to compute the interweavement of capital flows is based on a Boltzmann-derived concept of entropy, i.e., the higher the order (high inequality), the lower the entropy, leading to a new defined statistical entropy. Translated to economy, the higher the inequality (high concentration of flows), the lower the entropy, i.e., the lower the globalization degree resulting in a higher risk of the economic system. The first results show that FDI during the analyzed period are globalizing. Different than the trade globalization of type 1, where Asia has emerged to become the most globalized region, for the FDI, Europe shows to be the most globalized region. The questions to be answered in this long-term study will deal whether the weakening global trade volume will be substituted by increasing capital investment in new emerging regions or what drives the investment logic.

42.1 Introduction

Globalization is a natural phenomenon of an open economic system. Liberalization and deregulation of trade barriers as well as for capital investments in real economy

B. G. Rüttimann (✉)
Inspire AG/ETH Zürich, Zurich, Switzerland
e-mail: brunoruettimann@bluewin.ch; bruno.ruettimann@inspire.ethz.ch

P. Stamatiou
University of Macedonia, Thessaloniki, Greece
e-mail: stamatiou@uom.edu.gr

N. Tsounis, A. Vlachvei (eds.), *Advances in Panel Data Analysis in Applied Economic Research*, Springer Proceedings in Business and Economics,
https://doi.org/10.1007/978-3-319-70055-7_42

for production and service facilities have been leading to an increase in trade and FDI (foreign direct investments) creating new jobs and therefore new potential for wealth generation. Inequalities in business opportunities have been the driving force of globalization during the last decades. This inequality has also been leading to global migration to economic centers of major business opportunities. Indeed, the development of economic globalization is a mix of increase in physical trade, sustained foreign direct investments, financial market repercussions, and an augmented human mobility, all supported by telecommunication and increase in transparency of efficient market places via the World Wide Web. The lack of a comprehensive scholastic omnipotent "globalization law" to model the growing number of transactions and to understand the evolving industry logic of globalization has been leading to formulate a comprehensive globalization types model (Rüttimann 2007; Rüttimann 2009, 2011a; Grinin et al. 2014). This, at the same time, cognitive and normative model has already been successfully applied within integrated MNE (multinational enterprises) of the aluminum industry during strategy sessions to form and to discuss with business managers' strategic globalization initiatives (see studies of Rüttimann 2008a, b, 2010a, 2011). This comprehensive model describes trade globalization type 1, financial type 2, as well as human globalization type 3 and subtypes leading to the seven economic globalization types. Due to its cognitive and normative character, this model may also be applied at business schools to teach students. Whereas the type 1 trade globalization has been analyzed in recent years leading to the Trade Globalization Postulates (Rüttimann 2013, 2014a, 2015), showing first signs for the inverse Kuznets evolution, as well as integrating Heckscher-Ohlin, Stolper-Samuelson, and Linder's trade models, or the financial globalization type 2b (Rüttimann 2014, b, 2016) modeling the pivotal influence of financial markets on real economy, the capital globalization FDI type 2a of this globalization model has been left apart. The aim of this paper, and the possible following ones, is now to model FDI, gaining insights into the dimension of the globalization degree of FDI and the investor's logic to set up new business sites expanding the business scope to new geographic regions. This topic might become even more important due to the weakening global trade volume and increasing sentiment of nationalism and protectionism.

There is a widespread belief among policy makers that FDI and trade are the most important factors in the process of economic development of an economy. Particularly, FDI has been considered as one of the best alternatives to fuel economic growth, mainly for developing countries (Stamatiou and Dritsakis 2015).

In recent years, many countries have been interested in implementing policies aiming at attracting more and better (greenfield investments) FDI in order to enhance their economic performance and stimulate domestic employment. The revival of this interest is due to the recent financial crisis. In 2015, the world FDI inflows increased to 1.76 billion US dollars (almost 40% compared to 2014) reaching its highest level, since the outbreak of the crisis of 2008 (UNCTAD 2016).

Global economic crisis of 2008 had as a result a large number of studies in the broader area of FDI. In current literature, most of the published studies examine the relationship between foreign direct investments and other macroeconomic variables (such as exports, unemployment, and economic growth), either for one country or for a group of countries. On the other hand, there are very few studies that examine the link between FDI and globalization.

Luas (1988) argued that foreign direct investment can create positive effects on the production process of the host country. The main mechanisms for these externalities are the adoption of foreign technology and know-how, as well as the creation of linkages between foreign and domestic firms. These benefits, combined with the direct capital financing, show that foreign direct investments can play a vital role in the modernization of the national economy and promotion of economic growth (Luas 1988).

Vintila (2010) argued that FDI affects the economic growth of a country, both directly and indirectly through exports (Vintila 2010). In an open economy, technology and knowledge can also be transferred through exports and imports, and consequently economic growth can be promoted (Grossman and Helpman 1997). However, economic theory does not identify a clear relationship between FDI and trade.

Markusen and Venables (1988) supported that the relationship between foreign direct investments and trade is positively related (complementary) between asymmetric countries and negative (substitutes) between symmetric countries (Markusen 1984). In addition, Helpman et al. (2004) argued that the relationship between exports and FDI can be complementary or substitute, depending on the type of FDI (Markusen and Venables 1988). There are two different types of FDI: horizontal foreign direct investment (multinational companies have a subsidiary in each interest country in order to reduce transport costs) and vertical FDI (multinational companies place every stage of the production process in different countries, depending on the cost benefits). Markusen (1984) argued that horizontal FDI has a negative effect on exports (Helpman 1984). On the other hand, Helpman (1984) argued that vertical FDI and trade may be positively correlated (Helpman et al. 2004). Thus, the relationship between them can be either positive or negative.

The economic linkage between countries has been strengthened mainly by FDI flows (third wave of globalization). Donciu (2013) supported that the increasing interdependence of world economies has been driven mainly by developments in foreign direct investments. In recent years, the new trends in the field of FDI refer to the growing percentage of developing and emerging countries in the global flows of FDI (Donciu 2013). On the other hand, Gilpin (2000) argued that although the world has become increasingly economically and technologically integrated, the political fragmentation still remains among self-interested states. The forces of economic globalization have made the international economy to become more independent (Gilpin 2000). Further, a recent study has shown that globalization has a positive impact on financial flows and particularly on FDI. In addition, trade openness in combination with the market size, global communications, and urban population can also influence the FDI flows (Stamatiou 2017).

Different types of indicators have been developed to measure the multiple dimensions of globalization, for a non-exhaustive comparison (see studies of Caselli 2006; Dreher et al. 2010; Ghemawat and Altman 2013). The evolution of world economic development is monitored, e.g., by the WTO (World Trade Organization) as well as the yearly published KOF ETH Zurich globalization indicator (Swiss Economic Institute of Swiss Federal Institute of Technology). KOF uses a multidimensional index to capture economic, social, and political dimensions of globalization (Dreher 2006). All these types of indicators have a rather descriptive character measuring merely the evolution of globalization. Other research is rather focused on measuring the intrinsic nature of globalization, i.e., how globalization originates and its effects. Such research aiming to understand trade patterns, evolution of value chains, destination of investments, behavior of networks, as well as AB models (agent based) are described (see studies of Gallegati et al. 2008; Battiston et al. 2006; Gabrielli 2012; Karunaratne 2012; Pietronero et al. 2013; Stiglitz 2004). It is not intended here to perform a comparative analysis of existing research work but based on a new defined globalization metric (Rüttimann 2007, 2010b, 2011; Rüttimann 2012) to complement an ongoing study presented first in 2009 at the occasion of a globalization congress at the University of Ostrava and published by the University of Stettin in Europa Regionum (Rüttimann 2010b), and institutionalized finally from 2011 onwards Rüttimann (2011), based on the theory developed by Rüttimann (2007) for the globalization type 1 of trade. We will use the same inequality indicator to analyze FDI as already used to model the globalization of trade. The hereafter used indicator is a specific developed globalization indicator having normative character, i.e., bearing the intrinsic globalization law (Rüttimann 2007, 2010b, 2011; Rüttimann 2012).

The present paper is the first step in building the structure to measure the globalization degree of capital type 2b and to understand the evolution of FDI. The next papers will be yearly updates with new data, observing the further evolution of FDI globalization compared to the trade globalization, and added with the gained insights of FDI logics, the derived rational model will be continuously monitored and tested for consistency.

42.2 Theoretical Background

In the following, we will apply the globalization measure according to Rüttimann (2007, 2010b, 2011b) and Rüttimann (2012) not to foreign trade flows but to the capital FDI flows. From the paradigmatic interpretation of thermodynamic entropy, we can define risk as a dualistic view of order in an economic system; therefore the more order (i.e., inequality) that exists in an economic system, the more risky the economic system (or vice versa, the more equality a system shows, the less risk it presents). The greater the inequality compared to the riskless state with equality $\psi_{XY} = 1$, the larger the risk of an atomic element. Whereas in the here presented context inequality refers rather to a single element of a system, the concept of risk can be aggregated to the entire system.

42.2.1 *Measuring Globalization: Entropy-Based Inequality Risk Metric*

According to the Pigou-Dalton transfer principle and the interpretation of entropy law, we will apply the minimum risk principle (Rüttimann 2007, 2010b, 2011; Rüttimann 2012) to analyze the FDI flows, i.e., the capital globalization type 2a dealing with monetary flows, by applying it to which country X (origin, donator) invests in, i.e., transfers money to which countries Y, and which country Y receives money (destination, beneficiary) from which countries X represented by the capital FDI matrix $C = [c_{xy}]$ corresponding to the trade matrix $T^{\alpha}=[t^{\alpha}{}_{XY}]$ used for type 1 globalization. The interweavement of financial capital flows reflects the order (concentration of flows resulting in low entropy) or disorder (even distribution resulting in high entropy) of the FDI system, and therefore this new metric represents a paradigmatic approach of Boltzmann entropy of a thermodynamic system leading to statistical entropy. For an FDI system, we can build the investment share vector (portfolio) of an economy and calculate the inequality measure ψ_{XY} as the invested share of X in Y compared to the overall invested share of X. For economy X then, we can calculate the risk $r_X(\psi_{XY})$ of its portfolio of investment in the economies Y. The more the inequalities in each region Y tend to 1 the lower the risk value and therefore the higher the globalization degree of the region X. If the inequality is $\psi_{XY} = 1$ for all Y, then region X has the same investment share in all regions Y, and its portfolio of capital flows is proportional to the market composition according to its financial economic power (or wealth). Instead of talking about entropy in economics, in the following, we prefer to talk about the risk of an economic system, which is more appropriate, i.e., the higher the entropy, the lower the risk of the economic system, i.e., the higher the globalization degree. This risk metric is a genotypic measure, bearing the intrinsic law of economic globalization.

42.2.2 *Globalization Logic: Maximizing Value Net of Risk (MVNR)*

Entropy is not the sole governing physical law of thermodynamics. Indeed, if a transformation happens, it is determined by free enthalpy. The same is also applicable to economics (Rüttimann 2007). By adding the concept of thermodynamic enthalpy to the economic system, we can also explain the presence of an eventual de-globalization trend (i.e., an increased order of the economic system corresponding to an increased inherent economic risk of the system, i.e., a reduction of entropy). This matches the fundamental economic law that a higher risk corresponds generally to a higher return.

Minimizing the risk is only one cardinal law (this law models the globalization extension); maximizing profit is the other cardinal one (this law models the supposed rational acting). Globalization is extending the business scope to new geographic areas, and the aim is:

- To increase the profit generation (explicit strategy of profit maximization)
- To reduce the risk of the portfolio (implicit law of risk minimization)

The final governing principle of economic globalization is therefore risk-deducted value maximization (Rüttimann 2007), i.e., MVNR (maximizing value net of risk). With this principle, we can explain the rationale of any economic actor not only for physical trade but also for monetary investments.

The inequality risk metric is constructed in that way, that when $\psi_{XY} = 1$ for all Y, then region X has the same investment share in all regions Y, and its portfolio of capital flows is proportional to the market composition according to its financial economic power (or competitiveness). This is very similar to the CAPM (capital asset pricing model), the inequality-related risk metric corresponding generally to nonsystematic risk, and when $\psi_{XY} = 1$, the related risk metric is equal to the systematic risk, i.e., the market risk corresponding to a "risk-free" investment of non-diversifiable risk.

42.3 Methodological Approach

To measure the globalization degree of a set of geographical regions, we have at first to define the "from-to" geographic system. We have defined the following geographic regions, based on simplicity reasons similar to UNCTAD reports. The regions are developed Europe, other developed regions, North America, Africa, Asia, Latin America and Caribbean, and CIS. The single countries belonging to the geographic regions are listed in Table 42.1 of the appendix.

We will apply the new inequality indicator based on statistical entropy which incorporates also the intrinsic reason of minimizing risk by even distribution of portfolio, formalizing a built-in rational explanation of globalization.

Let us define the capital flow matrix $C = [c_{XY}]$ showing the monetary flows from economic region X to economic region Y. We can now build the market share array of an economic region and calculate the inequality measure $\psi_{XY} = p_{XY}/p_X$ as the market share of X in Y compared to the overall market share of X obtaining the inequality matrix for the whole economic system $\psi = [\psi_{XY}]_\infty$. For economy X, we can calculate the risk $r_X(\psi_{XY})$ of its portfolio of activities in the countries Y as the second momentum of the elements belonging to the inequality array ψ_X relative to the attractor 1:

$$r_X\left(\psi_{XY}^{\alpha}\right) = \frac{\sum\limits_{y=A}^{Z}\left(\psi_{Xy} - 1\right)^2}{\operatorname{card}(Z)} \tag{42.1}$$

The more the inequalities in each country Y of supplying country X approach equality ($\psi_{XY} = 1$), i.e., the more even is the repartition of trade portfolio and therefore the interweavement with other economies, the lower the aggregated risk value and therefore the higher the globalization degree of the country X; this concept leads to the Central Theorem of Globalization (CTG) and its corollary (Rüttimann 2007), which we will apply. If the inequality is $\psi_{XY} = 1$ for all Y, then country X has the same market share in all countries Y, its portfolio of monetary flows is proportional to the market investment composition, and marginal matrix distribution according to its competitiveness and the inequality risk $r_X(\psi_{XY})$ will become 0, i.e., attain maximum globalization, i.e., maximum extension. The array $r_X(\psi_{XY})$, containing the single risk of each economy (Eq. 42.1), can be aggregated to the risk of the entire system of economies $r(\psi_{XY})$ representing the world globalization degree in terms of financial capital interweavement. Inequality measure and risk can be applied to supply ($\psi = [\psi_{XY}]_\infty$) or demand ($\psi = [\psi_{XY}]_1$); we will analyze in the following the pattern analysis rather than the supply side, i.e., the investments' marginal distribution of the FDI matrix. The aggregated world risk value, of course, is the same for both marginal distributions. We will interpret empirically the resulting patterns based on theoretical considerations.

The upper part of Table 42.2 in the appendix shows the world FDI flow matrix of the year 2012 (basic source UNCTAD); in the middle part, the derived investment share measures of the geographic regions; and in the lower part, relative investment inequalities calculated according to Rüttimann (2007, 2010b, 2011) and Rüttimann (2012). The single inequalities are then aggregated to a risk measure of each economic region according to the two dimensions of supply portfolio (monetary "exports") and demand structure (monetary "imports"); the matrix contains also geographic domestic investment c_{XX}. These individual "geographic" risk figures $r_X(\psi_{XY})$ for investments and $r_Y(\psi_{XY})$ for the invested region Y are finally aggregated to the world risk index $r(\psi_{XY})$ measuring the economic globalization degree, i.e., the extension of the world economic FDI system.

42.4 Analyzing FDI Patterns Between 2001 and 2012

The comparative evolution of world physical trade flows and monetary capital flows (FDI) is shown in Fig. 42.1. It shows clearly the flattening of trade volumes from 2012 onwards and the significant throwback in 2015. For the analysis of this globalization type we refer to Rüttimann (2013, 2014a, 2015). The FDI evolved from 1049 b$ in 2001 to 2392 b$ in 2012 according to re-elaborated data of UNCTAD source. The exact data for the FDI can be retrieved in Table 43.3 of the appendix. The question will be what evolution for the FDI from 2013 onwards can we expect when the data will be available?

The very high correlation $r = 0.92$ between trade and FDI for the corresponding periods 2003–2012 is shown in Fig. 42.2 and is with $r = 0.92$ very high. The outlier with abnormal high FDI belongs to the year 2007. The world FDI flows increased

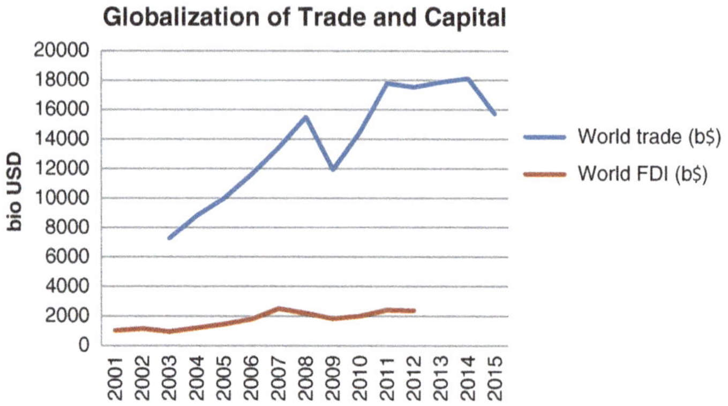

Fig. 42.1 Comparative evolution of world trade and FDI (period 2001–2015)

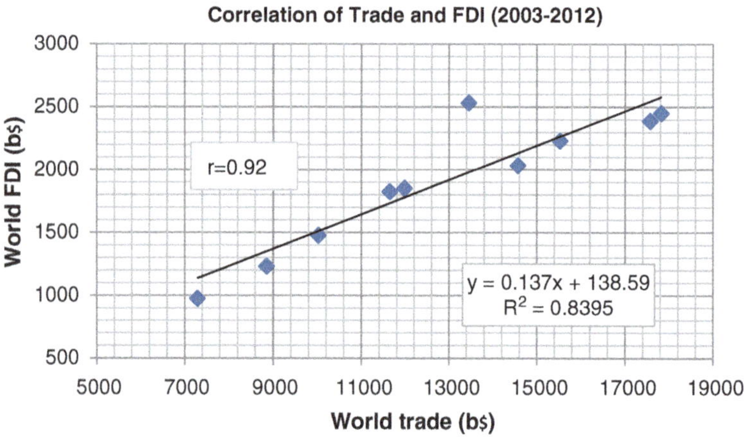

Fig. 42.2 High positive correlation between trade and FDI

significantly to 1.9 trillion US dollars in 2007 (and, according to UNCTAD, also beyond), reaching its highest point since 1970 (UNCTAD 2016) due to uncontrolled investment spending. After the beginning of the economic crisis of 2008, FDI flows show a significant decline resulting in the weakening of this linear correlation.

Nevertheless, according to that model, we may argue that FDI will follow world trade evolution. This, according to Markusen and Venables, would mean that in the observed period, investments were done with complementary countries. Also not considering domestic investments in the FDI matrix, this pattern of complementary economic regions does not seem to be realistic, or better appearing, at least not on macroeconomic level; the correlation on macroeconomic level seems rather to reflect economic growth or size of economic region (to be investigated). However, in this comparative context, the additional question arises, will the positive correlation becomes negative after 2015, i.e., not follow any more the present regression model?

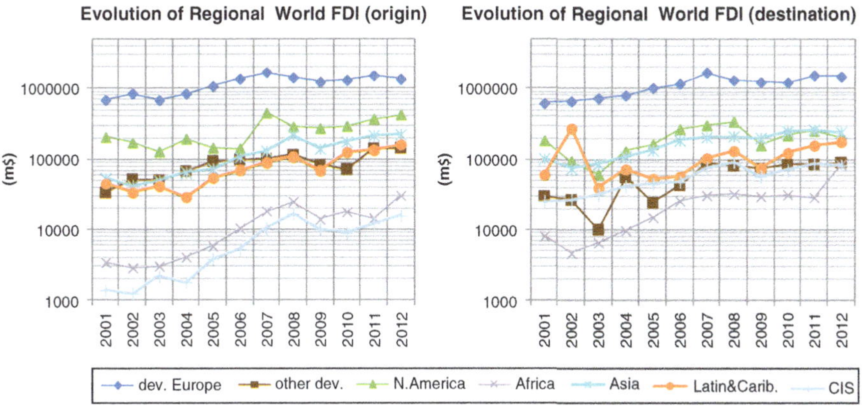

Fig. 42.3 Regional evolution of FDI flows. On the left side, the investing region X and on the right side the view of the receiving region Y (figures contain also domestic investments)

Indeed, the ongoing national protectionism and latent threat of rising import taxes could lead to a reduction of world trade and the forcedly reaction for MNE to increase FDI in strategic countries if imports are to be taxed. This would be the only possibility to participate at the business opportunities of foreign economies; we do not question here the competitiveness of boundary conditions such as labor cost. The low labor cost in combination with the level of taxation, the size of the host country market, the opening of the domestic economy, the political and economic stability, and the geographical position of the country are some of the most important factors for attracting FDI (Stamatiou 2017). It will be possible to answer this question only when FDI figures after 2015 will be available.

In Fig. 42.3 the evolution ofwhich geographic region invests how much (left side) as well as the evolution of the amount invested in the destination regions (right side) of FDI is shown. The regions of the origin of FDI can be segregated into three categories: the first is Europe investing by far the biggest amount of capital; the second category is composed of North America, Asia, other developed regions, and Latin America and Caribbean; and the last group is composed of Africa and CIS. The FDI are however directed to mainly two groups: Europe and the ROW, with Asia and North America being preferential target markets, noticing a converging of the countries of the second group (please note, the chart shows logarithmic scaling). Of course, as it is shown in Table 42.2 of the appendix for the year 2012, for the FDI figures comprising also of domestic investments, Europe and Asia are investing the lion's part of FDI in their own regions, especially Europe. Whereas during the observed period, all regions have increased their FDI engagement, Europe's investments from 2007 are stagnating on high level. The highest CAGR during the period 2001–2012 of FDI showed CIS with 25% and Africa with 22% both being the smallest FDI investors, reflecting the economic weakness of the regions. Asia having been the third largest FDI investor has a CAGR of 14%. Most investment interest is received by Africa with a CAGR of 24% (data not included). Indeed, in

2012 Africa received FDIs of 85 b$, a high increase from former levels; Europe and Asia were the largest investors in Africa (see Table 42.2); we have no information on what activities but most probably raw material and mining ore related, securing supply of strategic base materials (hypothesis not confirmed). Worthwhile to notice, in 2012, Latin America and Caribbean region invested more money than Europe or North America (some 42 b$) in Asia (Table 42.2). Nevertheless, the interest to invest in Asia is flattening (Fig. 42.3 right side).

If we look at the risk for each region calculated according to Eq. (42.1), risk intended as unequal interweavement, i.e., concentration of flows, we see the evolution of risk for the different regions as represented in Fig. 42.4, the left side displaying the risk, i.e., the globalization degree of investing regions, and on the right side, the attracted globalization interest of the invested regions. High origin risk means concentration of investments in preferred regions, high destination risk, meaning the receiving regions being invested by only few regions with unequal proportional distribution. It goes without saying; whereas the regional origin and destination risk of each economy may vary, the aggregated world risk is the same for origin and destination.

World FDI risk, i.e., the globalization intended as interweavement of monetary capital flows, in the period 2001–2012 has been reduced from 73.02 in 2002 to 2.76 in 2008, spreading investments more equally all over the world. However, from 2009 on, risk has been increasing again to reach 7.33 in 2012 showing a more selective investment policy. To talk already now to have evidence for an inverse Kuznets inequality, showing that globalization of FDI intended as interweavement has already come to an end, is by far too early. From Fig. 42.4, it clearly emerges that Europe has the lowest globalization risk spreading investments all over the world (reproducing best the world portfolio of investments), having attained in 2005 the lowest risk level with 0.11 and increasing the level to 0.22 in 2012. Europe is also a very sought-after investment region, attracting most of FDI, and in addition, it shows also the lowest risk signaling that all regions are interested to invest in Europe (with the exception of Africa). Despite the slowdown in economic growth worldwide, FDI inflows in Europe increased significantly from 350 billion US dollars in 2008 to 503 billion US dollars in 2017 (UNCTAD 2016). Europe continues to be one of the most attractive investment destinations. This is not only due to the rapid economic recovery of most European countries but it also relates to the uncertainty of emerging economies to sustain high growth rates. Also, the weakening of the euro in combination with the European Central Bank's (ECB) quantitative easing policies contributed to the increase of FDI inflows in Europe (Stamatiou 2017). Asia increased its FDI global engagement resulting finally with a risk of 3.51 in 2012 and a CAGR of −7% (Table 43.3 of the annex). The interest to invest in Asia has reduced the risk to 3.84 showing a CAGR of −8% in the observed period (evolution of destination figures not annexed), being increasingly attractive for all regions. Also North America's invested, i.e., destination, CAGR of −5% shows that North America is still an interesting investment from all over the world attaining in 2012 the risk level 0.33 only slightly above of Europe. Although CIS has the lowest FDI of only 16 b$, Africa with FDI of 31 b$ resulting in a risk of 42.22 shows a

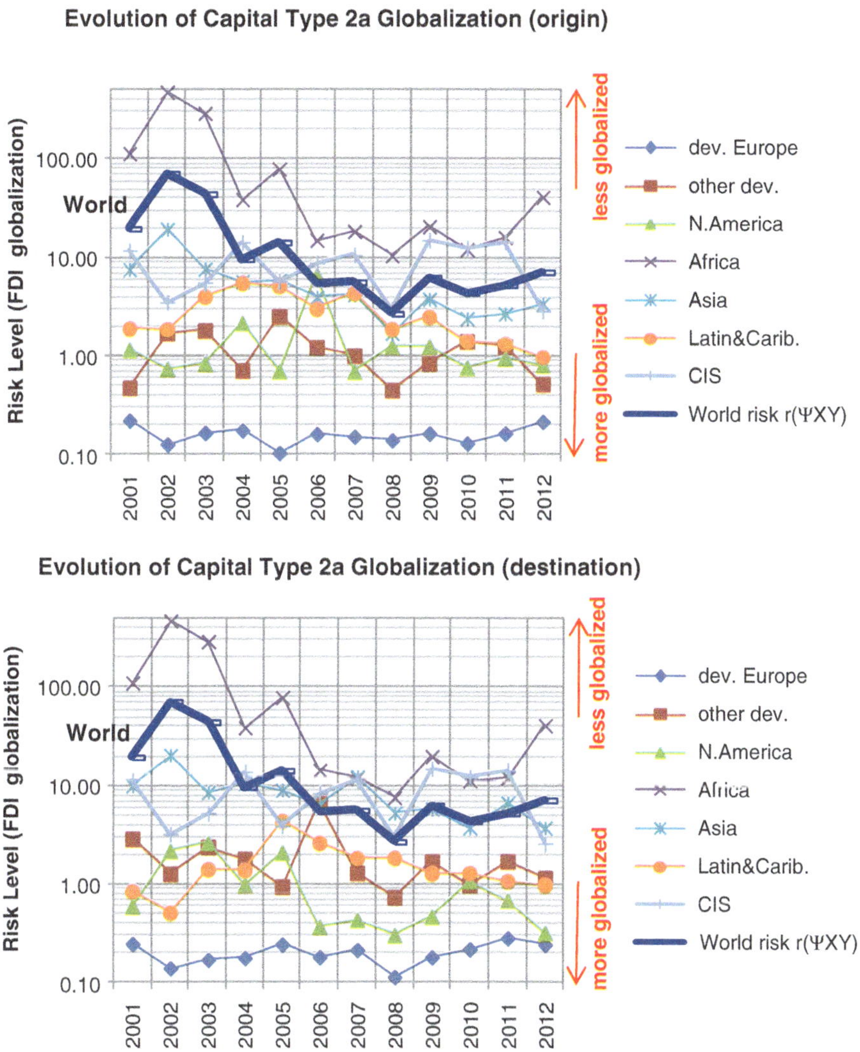

Fig. 42.4 Regional risk of different macroeconomic regions according to Table 43.3 (lower part for the origin) revealing heterogeneous evolution

less globalization extension than CIS with 2.96, despite being compared to CIS as a rather closed economy.

Building the correlation between FDI and related world risk (origin view), we obtain the regression model shown in Fig. 42.5. The applied model is the model calculated using all figures from 2001 to 2012. We left for the time being the unusual observations of the years 2002 and 2003, affecting the model. Generally, it shows that the risk level diminishes, i.e., the interweavement of globalization generally

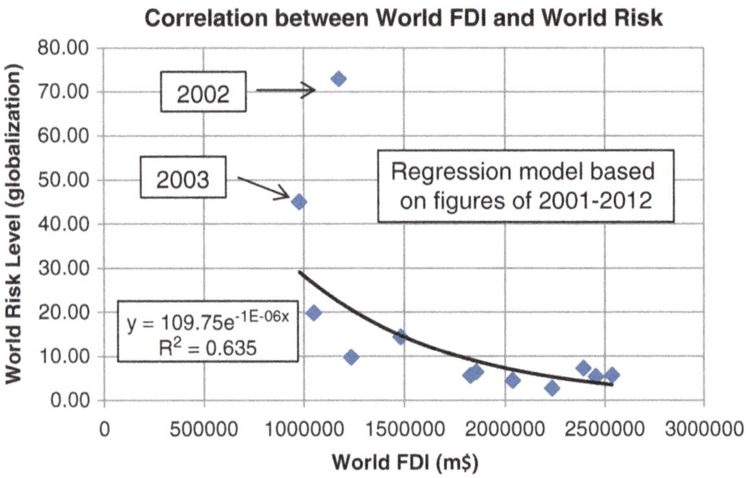

Fig. 42.5 Modeling FDI globalization on aggregate level with an L-model

increases with the growth of FDI volume. Different from trade exports, due to the fact that FDI are sometimes extended over two consecutive years for the same project, a deep dip as a consequence of the financial crisis of 2007 is not explicitly observable in Fig. 42.3, the effects rather being a flattening of FDI engagements. Nevertheless, we will use this model to be compared with additional data as soon as they will be available.

If we look at disaggregated data, i.e., at the evolution of regional risk shown in the lower part of Table 43.3 or Fig. 42.4 (left side), we get Fig. 42.6 showing a scatterplot of the regional FDI volume risk suitable to show an envelope curve. To model the explicit FDI volume risk, globalization on these disaggregated data might not be correct, each region experiencing for its own potentially an L-shaped curve according to its enterprise's economic possibilities. Nevertheless, also the enveloping curve shows an L-shaped curve.

Plotting the CAGR-derived data of FDI and relative risk as well as the average FDI volume in b$ in a three-dimensional scatterplot (data from Table 43.3) regarding the different macroeconomic geographical regions, we obtain Fig. 42.7 revealing the comparative evolution of globalization dynamics for the different geographic macroeconomic regions. From phenotypic analysis of Fig. 42.7, as might be logical, a high growth of FDI volume is rather feasible with smaller FDI volume, such as for CIS and Africa. On the other hand, also risk reduction is progressing faster for small FDI volumes. On the other hand, a high volume of FDI, such as Europe, is investing; having already attained a low risk (high globalization degree) according to Fig. 42.5 will show a further reduced CAGR of globalization. Being the absolute FDI volume in b$ the pivotal transitive element between the two Cartesian axes, a weak causal negative correlation of $R = -0.78$ between FDI CAGR and risk CAGR can be computed.

To analyze the origin and destination dimension of FDI globalization in volumes and relative risks, we use Fig. 42.8. The left side of Fig. 42.8 shows graphically how

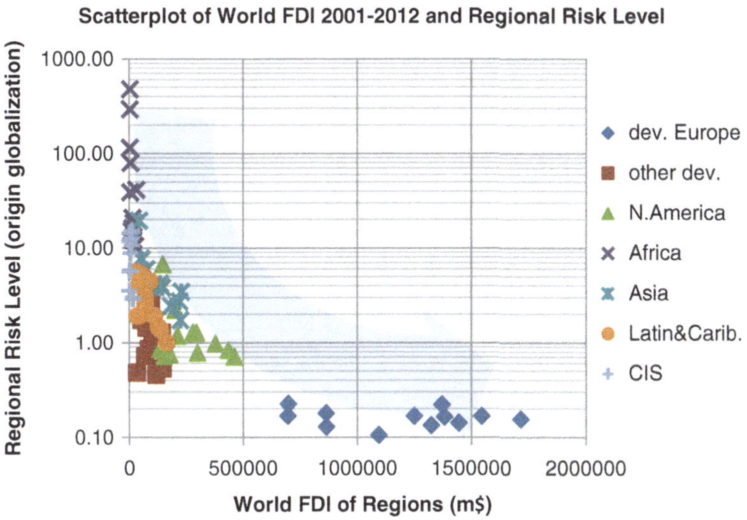

Fig. 42.6 Regional FDI volume risk pattern on disaggregated level

Fig. 42.7 Globalization dynamics for different macroeconomic regions

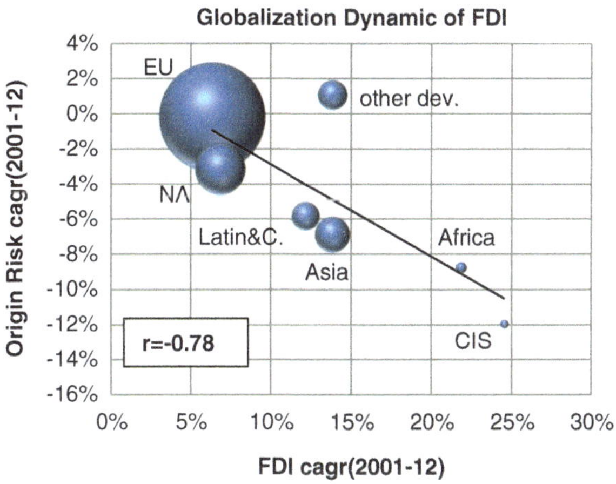

much an economic region invests and how much is invested in that region. North America and other developed regions are net donators, i.e., they invest more than others invest in their own region. CIS and Africa are more invested than they invest in other regions being net receiver of funds. Europe, Asia, and Latin America are nearly balanced. The right side of Fig. 42.8 shows the associated risk. The correct risk ranking should be ascertained by combining both dimensions resulting therefore to rank compared to ISO globalization lines. However, the origin view is a quite suitable approximation. From Fig. 42.8 (right side), we see that North America has a higher origin risk, i.e., investing FDI more unbalanced than it is invested in NA by other regions. The inverse is valid for "other developed" regions.

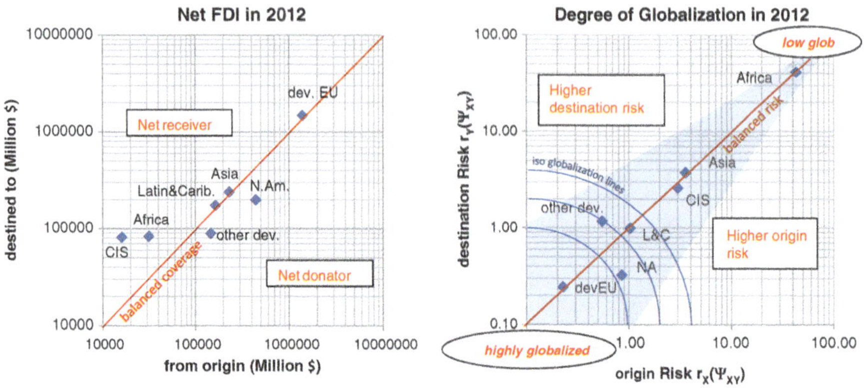

Fig. 42.8 Comparing the origin and destination view of FDI regions

For the globalization type 1 of trade, we have seen that high risk level, i.e., high inequality, usually originates from predominant autarchic economies such as CIS and South America. For the FDI, we cannot repeat this statement; it seems that high risk is rather given by economically weak regions (Africa). In this context, CIS is rather the exception, the high interest to conclude economic cooperation agreement induce to be more open for FDI transfers.

42.5 Conclusions

The present analysis gives the first insights into the globalization degree of FDI. From the observed period, it emerges that FDI are closely linked to trade evolution (positive correlation), i.e., to economic development, that would sustain Helpman's thesis of prevailing vertical FDI for the period 2003–2012. Also it emerged that globalization of FDI, i.e., the spreading of investments, has progressed, for all regions, independently of the economic power of an economic system. Further, it has emerged the dominating role of Europe in the globalization of FDI, from volume to spreading. However, what is surprising is that the European investment in the North American region has always been much bigger than the amount directed to the Asian region (data not annexed), despite the growing Chinese business opportunities. How FDI will evolve in the future may also depend of political economy for free trade (globalization type 1) and the evolution of unemployment, driving human migration to business-attractive regions (globalization type 3a). The FDI type 2a globalization will play a crucial role in the future.

42.6 Next Works

This paper will be the point of departure to analyze FDI from a globalization point of view. Further work will develop mainly in the following directions:

- Monitor the present globalization evolution of FDI and derive general FDI globalization postulates.
- Identify the driving logic for FDI.
- Will it become necessary and possible to split the rational of the FDI globalization type 2a in two subtypes: globalization type 2a–h (horizontal FDI) and globalization type 2a–v (vertical FDI)?

Appendix

Table 42.1 Which countries belong to which region

Regions	Countries
Europe	Norway, Iceland, Greece, Austria, Belgium, Bulgaria, Cyprus, Czech, Denmark, Estonia, Finland, France, Germany, Hungary, Ireland, Italy, Latvia, Lithuania, Luxemburg, Malta, Netherlands, Poland, Portugal, Romanian, Slovenia, Slovakia, Spain, Sweden, United Kingdom, Switzerland
N. America	Canada, United States of America
Africa	Algeria, Egypt, Libya, Morocco, Tunisia, Angola, Burkina Faso, Cameroon, Congo, Cote d'Ivoire, Equatorial Guinea, Ethiopia, Gabon, Ghana, Guinea, Kenya, Liberia, Madagascar, Mauritius, Mozambique, Nigeria, South Africa, Zambia, Zimbabwe
Asia	China, Hong Kong China, Macau China, Taiwan, Brunei, Cambodia, Indonesia, Malaysia, Philippines, Singapore, Thailand, Sri Lanka, Vietnam, Pakistan, Afghanistan, Bangladesh, Bahrain, Iraq, Jordan, Kuwait, Lebanon, Oman, Qatar, South Arabia, Turkey, Yemen, United Emirates, India
Latin America and Caribbean	Argentina, Bolivia, Brazil, Chile, Colombia, Ecuador, Paraguay, Peru, Suriname, Uruguay, Venezuela, Belize, Costa Rica, El Salvador, Guatemala, Honduras, Mexico, Nicaragua, Barbados, British Islands
CIS	Armenia, Azerbaijan, Belarus, Kazakhstan, Kyrgyzstan, Moldova, Russian Federation, Ukraine, Uzbekistan
Other developed regions	Andorra, Australia, Bermuda, Israel, Japan, New Zealand

Based on UNCTAD (2016)

Table 42.2 World FDI matrix (in b$) with inequalities and risk measures for the year 2012

2012	Dev Europe	Other Dev.	N. America	Africa	Asia	atin& Caribbean	CIS		
FDI_{XY}	A	B	C	D	E	F	G	origin FDI	px
A	1046006	18871	125236	25512	35088	57750	64418	1372881.00	0.57
B	68533	13109	21391	3696	25013	12866	730	145338.00	0.06
C	266451	46091	32957	9474	8428	69622	3047	436070.00	0.18
D	0	0	607	19874	9162	8	1397	31048.00	0.01
E	44879	12863	11294	24195	125651	3641	5253	227776.00	0.10
F	66128	0	12290	2388	42196	34122	5512	162636.00	0.07
G	12151	102	0	1	620	216	2832	15922.00	0.01
dest.FDI	1504148.00	91036.00	203775.00	85140.00	246158.00	178225.00	83189.00	2391671.00	1.00
P_Y	0.63	0.04	0.09	0.04	0.10	0.07	0.03	1.00	
P_{XY}-	A	B	C	D	E	F	G		px
A	0.70	0.21	0.61	0.30	0.14	0.32	0.77		0.57
B	0.05	0.14	0.10	0.04	0.10	0.07	0.01		0.06
C	0.18	0.51	0.16	0.11	0.03	0.39	0.04		0.18
D	0.00	0.00	0.00	0.23	0.04	0.00	0.02		0.01
E	0.03	0.14	0.06	0.28	0.51	0.02	0.06		0.10
F	0.04	0.00	0.06	0.03	0.17	0.19	0.07		0.07
G	0.01	0.00	0.00	0.00	0.00	0.00	0.03		0.01
	1.00	1.00	1.00	1.00	1.00	1.00	1.00		1.00
ψ_{XY}	A	B	C	D	E	F	G		$r_X(\psi_{XY})$
A	1.21	0.36	1.07	0.52	0.25	0.56	1.35		0.22
B	0.75	2.37	1.73	0.71	1.67	1.19	0.14		0.54
C	0.97	2.78	0.89	0.61	0.19	2.14	0.20		0.85
D	0.00	0.00	0.23	17.98	2.87	0.00	1.29		42.22
E	0.31	1.48	0.58	2.98	5.36	0.21	0.66		3.51
F	0.65	0.00	0.89	0.41	2.52	2.82	0.97		1.01
G	1.21	0.17	0.00	0.00	0.38	0.18	5.11		2.96
									7.33
$r_Y(\psi_{XY})$	0.25	1.20	0.33	42.01	3.84	1.02	2.66	*7.33*	$r(\psi_{XY})$

Network of FDI by region (source: UNCTAD/Stamatiou)

Table 42.3 Evolution of FDI and risks during 2001–2012 for different macroeconomic regions

Origin view													
FDI_{xy}	2001	2002	2003	2004	2005	2006	2007	2008	2009	2010	2011	2012	cagr(01–12)
dev. Europe	698806	864840	696297	863669	1095239	1384394	1716549	1447199	1251100	1326622	1546999	1372881	6%
other dev.	33989	52947	51289	68338	95317	99744	102847	116652	84512	73300	142540	145338	14%
N.America	210413	176166	132318	200493	150034	145500	462940	295518	279973	300794	380157	436070	7%
Africa	3529	2950	3109	4172	5972	10694	18580	25549	14184	18147	14721	31048	22%
Asia	54727	42712	50052	66047	74071	108474	133378	223671	143744	180600	220699	227776	14%
Latin&Carib.	45971	34610	42600	29885	55787	71300	90422	108849	69838	128041	136088	162636	12%
CIS	1424	1276	2229	1843	3951	5442	10743	16919	10471	9203	12561	15922	25%
World FDI (m$)	1048859	1175501	977894	1234447	1480371	1825548	2535459	2234357	1853822	2036707	2453765	2391671	8%
Source: UNCTAD/Stamatiou													
$r_x(\psi_{XY})$	2001	2002	2003	2004	2005	2006	2007	2008	2009	2010	2011	2012	cagr(01–12)
dev. Europe	0.23	0.13	0.17	0.18	0.11	0.17	0.16	0.14	0.17	0.13	0.17	0.22	0%
other dev.	0.49	1.76	1.87	0.73	2.59	1.25	1.03	0.46	0.87	1.46	1.30	0.54	1%
N.America	1.21	0.77	0.87	2.25	0.72	6.82	0.72	1.30	1.30	0.80	0.99	0.85	–3%
Africa	115.94	483.34	295.59	39.69	80.71	15.22	18.72	10.67	21.00	12.34	16.42	42.22	–9%
Asia	7.70	19.65	7.80	5.82	6.03	4.05	4.29	1.76	3.89	2.48	2.77	3.51	–7%
Latin&Carib.	1.96	1.93	4.13	5.67	5.29	3.11	4.48	1.95	2.59	1.48	1.38	1.01	–6%
CIS	12.00	3.59	5.69	14.55	5.93	8.99	10.84	3.07	15.35	12.92	14.84	2.96	–12%
World risk $r(\psi_{XY})$	19.93	73.02	45.16	9.84	14.48	5.66	5.75	2.76	6.45	4.52	5.41	7.33	–9%

Source: Rüttimann/Stamatiou

References

Battiston, S., Delli Gatti, D., Gallegati, M., Greenwalt, B. C., & Stiglitz, J. E. (2006). Effects of globalization in a model of production networks embedded in geographical space. *ETH working paper*.

Caselli, M. (2006). On the nature of globalization and its measurement, *UNU-CRIS occasional papers*, No 3.

Donciu, E. C. (2013). Globalization and foreign direct investments. *CES Working Papers, 5*(2), 177–186.

Dreher, A. (2006). Does globalization affect growth? Evidence from a new index of globalization. *Applied Economics, 38*(10), 1091–1110.

Dreher, A., Gaston, N., Martens, P., & Boxem, L. V. (2010). Measuring globalization - opening the black box. A critical analysis of globalization indices. *Journal of Globalization Studies, 1*(1), 166–185.

Gabrielli, A. (2012). Clustering and ranking countries and their products: A network analysis. *Proceedings of European Center for Theoretical studies in nuclear physics and related areas (ECT Conference)*, 23–27 July, Trento, Italy.

Gallegati, M., Greenwald, B. C., Richiardi, M. G., & Stiglitz, J. E. (2008). The asymmetric effect of diffusion processes: Risk sharing and contagion. *Global Economy Journal, 8*(3), 1–22.

Ghemawat, P., & Altman, S. (2013). Depth index of globalization – And the big shift to emerging economies. Pankaj Ghemawat/IESE Report, University of Navarra, Spain.

Gilpin, R. (2000). *The challenge of global capitalism: The world economy in the 21st century*. Princeton: Princeton University Press.

Grinin, L., Ilyin, I., & Korotayev, A. (2014). *Globalistics and globalization studies - Aspects & dimensions of global views*. Volgograd: Uchitel Publishing House. 978-5-7057-4028-4.

Grossman, G. M., & Helpman, E. (1997). *Innovation and growth in the global economy*. Cambridge, Massachusetts: MIT Press.

Helpman, E. (1984). A simple theory of international trade with multinational corporations. *Journal of Political Economy, 92*, 451–471.

Helpman, E., Melitz, M. J., & Yeaple, S. R. (2004). Export versus FDI with heterogeneous firms. *The American Economic Review, 94*, 300–316.

Karunaratne, N. (2012). The globalization-deglobalization policy conundrum. *Modern Economy, 3*, 373–383.

Luas, R. (1988). On the mechanics of economic development. *Journal of Monetary Economics, 22*, 3–42.

Markusen, J. R. (1984). Multinationals, multiplant economies and the gains from trade. *Journal of International Economics, 16*, 205–226.

Markusen, J. R., & Venables, A. J. (1988). Multinational firms and the new trade theory. *Journal of International Economics, 46*(2), 183–203.

Pietronero, L., Cristella, M., & Tacchella, A. (2013). New metrics for economic complexity: Measuring the intangible growth potential of countries. *Proceedings of conference at Institute for New Economic Thinking (INET)*, 4–7 April, Hong Kong, China.

Rüttimann, B. (2009). Modelling economic globalization – The basic globalization types. *Proceedings of Global Studies Association (GSA) conference*, 2–4 September, London, UK.

Rüttimann, B. (2011a). A comprehensive globalization model to analyze industry logics: The seven economic globalization types. *Proceedings of international conference on applied economics (ICOAE)*, 25–27 August, Perugia, Italy.

Rüttimann, B. (2011b). An entropy-based inequality risk metric to measure economic globalization. *Proceedings of 1st conference on spatial statistics*, published by Elsevier in the series Procedia Environmental Sciences, 3: 38–43.

Rüttimann, B. (2012). Measuring spatial extension of economic globalization. *Journal of European Economy, 11*(7), 509–517.

Rüttimann, B. (2007). *Modeling economic globalization – A post-neoclassic view on foreign trade and competition*. Münster: Wissenschaft. 978-3-86582-447-9.

Rüttimann, B. (2008a). Which globalization for the aluminium industry – A normative analysis exploring alternative business model. *ALUMINIUM*, 84 1/2–2008, 16–22, 3–2008, 14–21, Giesel Verlag.

Rüttimann, B. (2008b). Which globalization for the aluminium industry. *Proceedings of the aluminium congress*, 23–25 September, Essen, Germany.

Rüttimann, B. (2010a). Globalisierung verstehen heisst märkte beherrschen – Wie man durch analyse der geschäfts - und Industrielogik ein normatives modell der globalisierungsformen erhält. iO new Management 5, Springer Verlag.

Rüttimann, B. (2010b). Measuring economic globalization: Entropy - based inequality risk metric. Europa Regionum, XIII: 7–23, University of Stettin, Szczecin.

Rüttimann, B. (2011). Werden die chinesischen halbzeugexporte die märkte überfluten?. DOW JONES NE Metalle Monitor, No 1.

Rüttimann, B. (2013). World trade and associated systems risk of global inequality: Empiric study of globalization evolution between 2003–2011 and regional pattern analysis. *Proceedings of International Conference on Applied Economics (ICOAE)*, 27–29 June, Istanbul, Turkey published by Elsevier in the series Procedia Economics and Finance, 5: 647–656.

Rüttimann, B. (2014a). World trade logics and measure of global inequality: Regional pattern and globalization evolution between 2003–2012. *Open Journal of Applied Sciences, 4*(4), 184–196.

Rüttimann, B. (2014b). Modeling financial type 2b globalization and its repercussion on the real economy. *Proceedings of international conference on applied economics (ICOAE)*, 27–29 June, Chania, Greece published by Elsevier in the series Procedia Economics and Finance, 14: 534–543.

Rüttimann, B. (2015). Measuring the globalization degree of trade from 2003–2013: Is globalization of economy coming to an end?. *Presented at Athens Institute for Education and research (ATINER) Conference, No. FIN2015–1540.*

Rüttimann, B. (2016). Modeling financial type 2b globalization and its effects on trade, investments, and unemployment. *International Journal of Computational Economics and Econometrics, 6*(2), 176 191.

Stamatiou, P. (2017). *Foreign direct investments, exports, unemployment and economic growth: Evidence from panel cointegration and causality analysis in EU countries*. PhD Dissertation, University of Macedonia, Greece.

Stamatiou, P., & Dritsakis, N. (2015). Granger causality relationship between foreign direct investments, exports, unemployment and economic growth. A panel data approach for the new EU members. *Proceedings of the 14th Annual European Economics and Finance Society (EEFS) conference*, Brussels, Belgium, 11–14 June 2015.

Stiglitz, J. E. (2004). Capital-market liberalization, globalization, and the IMF. *Economic Policy, 20*(1), 57–71.

United Nations Conference on Trade and Development (UNCTAD). (2016). http://unctadstat.unctad.org/wds/ReportFolders/reportFolders.aspx?sCS_ChosenLang=en. Accessed 15 Apr 2017.

Vintila, D. (2010). Foreign direct investment theory: An overview of the main FDI theories. *European Journal of Interdisciplinary Studies, 2*(2), 104–110.

Chapter 43
Gender Barriers in Employment and Their Policy Implications in Transition Economies

Theranda Beqiri

Abstract Economies in transition are well known for the very low activity rates in the labour market compared with western economies; Kosovo is amongst the countries which are in the early stages of transition with very low rates of employment and very high inactivity rates in the labour market, especially amongst the female participants. Policies regarding labour issues and human resources are in the first phases of implementation. In this independent empirical study, we use regression analysis to compare the differences between the public institutions and private sector as well as NGOs on implementation of the equal opportunity chances between gender regarding employment, by using the recruitment and selecting procedures. We find that there is gender inequality in private sector in recruitment and selection process, as the first barrier in entering the labour market. Therefore, implementation of recruitment and selection procedures is needed and should be implemented to reduce the barriers of new female entrants in the labour market, in order to have equal supply of the labour forces from both genders as well as an increased level of participation rates among females in the labour market.

Keywords Recruitment and selection · Gender inequality · Employment

43.1 Introduction

Gender equality in labour market has long been recognized as a fundamental principle and a fundamental right, and reducing gender gaps in the level of active participation in labour market, in the level of unemployment, and wage gaps is an objective of the states that are members of the European Union, and it is one of the main requests of the states from the transition economies in Europe that are aspiring European integration and membership.

T. Beqiri (✉)
Faculty of Business, University "Haxhi Zeka", Pejë, Republic of Kosovo
e-mail: Theranda.Beqiri@unhz.eu

N. Tsounis, A. Vlachvei (eds.), *Advances in Panel Data Analysis in Applied Economic Research*, Springer Proceedings in Business and Economics,
https://doi.org/10.1007/978-3-319-70055-7_43

Since, most of the females before the transition period were employed in the secondary jobs; they had little on job trainings, which influenced the possibilities of the future employment. Alternatively the work that has to do with caring activities and family duties is disproportionally allocated to females.

From research developed in CEEU countries and transition economies (Market 2003), individuals with lower level of education have higher chances to become unemployed during transition period. In CEEU countries, educated individuals are more mobile through a lower probability over time of remaining in inactivity and employment, and the higher mobility of females gives lower probability over time of remaining in employment and unemployment (Ward-Warmedinger and Macchiarelli 2013). Similar findings that lower education is related to unemployment are also found from Jurajda and Terrell (2009), where they found that in countries in transition, individuals with higher skill level had less chance of becoming unemployed since opportunity costs are higher if they become unemployed and the level of unemployment was higher in the regions with a higher share of low-skilled individuals, since demand for labour those with lower skills have fewer opportunities for mobility.

In urban areas the unemployment rate is usually lower than in rural areas. Studies that have been done so far in transition countries show that the main causes of this phenomenon are the difficulties in mobility of the workforce from one region to another and the lack of affordable housing in urban areas and high transport costs, which usually affect more females than males in job searching.

Kosovo is still in the early stages of transition with a high level of unemployment and a very low level of active labour participation, predominantly for females. In Kosovo according to the Labour Fource Survey (2015), the level of activity rate in labour market is very low with only 37.6%, from which only 18.1% of females were active and 56.7% of males, and from those active in labour market unemployment is very high in the level of 36.6% for females and 31.8% for males (Kosovo Agency of Statistics 2015). Unemployment is primarily an economic problem. Unemployment is a constant and persistent issue that is repeated, which constitutes a concern for society in general. The possibility of keeping under constant review by the state unemployment rate is important as it provides stability and economic growth.

Females in Kosovo are overrepresented in the public sector. More than half of employed females are working in the public sector either in the public institutions or state-owned enterprises; females prefer to work in public sector since they have more job security and are paid maternity leave, which usually are not the same in the private sector, where implementation of legislation regarding gender is not always implemented (Making the Labour Market Work for Females and Youth, Kosovo Human Development Report 2016).[1] Therefore in this research, we try to find which other barriers are more related to females than males in employment and

[1]Human Development Report Kosovo 2016.

job searching, where we concentrate in all institutions that have higher levels of female employment such as in public sector, small trade and service firms as well as NGOs by investigating the level of implementation of labour laws, laws against discrimination and laws for equal opportunity in employment.

Also the female entrepreneurial participation is very low with only 8,4% in total ownership of small and medium enterprises, and their activity in entrepreneurship is only 3.7% emphasizing unfavourable position of female entrepreneurs. This is also related to the overall position of females in labour market and the society which continues to be characterized by engrained traditional behaviours (Hoxha and Krasniqi 2008). Female participation in business ownerships is just above 10%, while in comparison with Europe and Central Asia, females have total ownerships of more than 30% and participate in ownerships for 36% of entrepreneurial activities and firms; one other reason that in Kosovo there is a smaller percentage of female owner entrepreneurs might be because females have very limited asset ownership of land and other properties (Maria Eugenia et al.; Davalos et al. 2012).

A proportion of the population in Kosovo is divided almost evenly between genders, males 50, 3%, and females 49, 7%; therefore we can say that the level of gender gaps in education is proportional when referring to statistical data. The level of participation in education is higher for males than females, although the gaps are narrowing each year. Fewer females attend high school and vocational high schools, and there are more school dropouts in high schools among females compared to males (MEST 2009). However the level of females in all levels of education has increased in recent years, and tertiary education is the only level of education where females have the highest percentage of participation of 51.5% compared to 48.5% for males (MEST 2011).[2]

When it comes to education, it increases labour market productivity, increasing the levels of education for females, increases developmental economic growth, improves functioning of political issues and has its own impact in investment in children's human capital (Hill and King 1995). The occupational segregation is also present among those females that are employed, and it is is Duncan & Duncan Segregation Index shows that 49% of females should change their professions in order to have the equally distributed professions among males and females (Beqiri 2016). According to the data from the Labour Force Survey of 2012, the public sector, the government and public enterprises are the main employers in Kosovo, and the employed females are an integral part of this sector employing about 67% of total female employment. Also in the private sector, there is a significant percentage of about 23% and about 10% in international organizations that have their offices in Kosovo and NGOs, and part of them are self-employed (Kosovo Agency of Statistics 2012; Kosovo Agency of Statistics 2015). In this independent study, we included 150 institutions, including government institutions, independent agencies, public enterprises, private enterprises and non-governmental organizations, which operate in the entire territory of Kosovo. The reason that we included a variety of

[2]*Educational statistics, ESK 2013/2014.*

institutions is that they present a more realistic and more comprehensive labour market in Kosovo, especially considering female employment.

Since there is a very low level of employment and participation rate of females in the labour market in Kosovo, in this study we are particularly interested in finding results on whether there is discrimination in recruitment and selection of employees regarding gender, which may acquaint with barriers for employment of females in the labour market, and especially for new female entrants, as well as discourage the existing active female labour market participants and jobseekers. We try to find answers by raising research questions as do recruitment and selection procedures exist in Kosovo institutions; if they do exist, then are they used correctly regarding equal opportunity chances and in accordance to existing labour laws in Kosovo; and do the ways of finding jobs differ between males and females.

43.2 Literature Review on Gender Inequality in Labour Market

Human capital theory connects occupations and wages to the lifetime participation in the labour market and combines it with family obligations; therefore if we assume that the participation in labour market will be interrupted for family obligations, then the employees will choose professions in which the penalty and loss of skills will be lower, and as for employers, the benefits in investing in that human capital will be smaller (Anker 1997). Accordingly, the explanation of the gender inequality in earnings can be explained by interruptions in participating in the labour market for females and by the decisions on their human capital investment (Polachek and Siebert 1993). In addition, females spend twice as much time compared to men caring for children on a daily basis; on average they spend double hours than men.

For this reason, due to childcare and career disruptions, females have fewer incentives to invest in human capital. However, if the demand in the labour market is distributed between males and females equally, and they have equal skills and experience, sometimes the work will be offered to men because statistics show that many females leave the labour market when they reach late 20s to engage in child caring. Unpaid work includes present and future well-being of the family. In most countries females do more of the household work than males, but that also depends on the level of the development of the country and the issue that they do less work in the labour market to provide for families (Miranda 2011). For this reason, due to childcare and career disruptions, females have fewer incentives to invest in human capital. And from those which are chosen to be employed, the investment in their human capital will be lower since their skills will depreciate or be forgotten during the years that they will be engaged in household production or the time that they raise children. Since, some females expect to dedicate time to the household sector, shortening the payoff period and reducing the returns on the investment (Borjas and Van Ours 2000; Borjas 2016).

In developed economies the labour legislation and laws against discrimination are functional, and therefore there is a higher stability in reducing gender gaps, compared with developing countries and countries in transitions to which the asymmetry of information and informal labour market is higher. As well as the level of population in a country can have an impact on the labour market of that country and the issue of labour market dynamics in the country, institutional theories of the labour market are different. What they hold in common is the view that institutional structures, practices and restrictions – informative, cognitive, economic, social, organizational and political – influence labour market processes and outcomes in ways that are not usually conceived under conventional competition.

Institutional forces also represent the influence of a range of institutional bodies such as trade unions, governments and corporations on pay and workforce allocation. Institutional theories suggest that, even with deregulation, wage-setting process will be developed in a way that will modify the social costs or the cost efficiency of competition in the labour market transition.

Institutions unlike classic labour markets introduce market rules and regulations which define the dimensions of the labour market; these rules and regulations may be formal (formalized) and informal (customs, traditions, etc.)[3]: in form of individual policies that are followed by employment private firms and in form of collective contracts signed by unions and by government legislation.[4] Since private institutions are mostly the main ones which generate job creation in transition countries, they usually impose their own regulation in recruitment and selection procedures.

Becker's theory of discrimination in tastes and investments in human capital also gives explanation of underinvestment in female children human capital compared to males, which leads to lower skills for females, and the discrimination starts before entering the labour markets with less education for females and less incentives to invest in developing their skills. Although, underinvestment in female children human capital compared to males, have changed in the latest years with equal proportion of investments in both genders. With the trends of decline in family size, and increase of service sectors businesses where females have the higher level of employment. But also with the changes in higher level of participation of females in the labour market in most of the western economies, to the rational choices of the occupation for females (Gary Becker 1975, 1994; Gary Becker and Sowell 1981; Becker 1992).

Regarding statistical discrimination it starts with authors (Arrow 1972; Phelps 1972), and it exists when individuals attach different estimates of productivity based on the group to which the individual belongs. Thus, discrimination is not the result of prejudice or the pursuit of pecuniary gain but rather the imperfect information that confronts employers in the screening process (Bielby and Baron

[3] *Ekonomksi i Punës Pg 27 Stefan Qiriqi.*

[4] *Institutional labour economics, benefit levels and unemployment Moira Wilson Social Policy Agency.*

1986). The only information employers have at the time of hire is information on characteristics that are thought to be correlated with productivity, e.g. education, experience, age, test scores, etc. Since employers know these characteristics are imperfect predictors of actual productivity and because information costs are usually high, they incorporate a subjective element into their hiring decisions. According to employer discrimination model, because men and women are assumed to be equally productive, if men are paid the value of their productivity, then women will be paid less than the value of their productivity. In this case, the employer acts as if there is a nonfinancial cost associated with employing a woman equal in money terms to d_r (the discrimination coefficient). To the employer, the cost of employing a man is his wage, W_m, and the cost of employing a woman is her wage plus the discrimination coefficient ($W_f + d_r$). This means that the only way that this employer would hire a female is if he can pay her less than he pays his male employees ($W_f = W_m - d_r$). Neoclassical competitive models have the assumption that discrimination only can be temporary. If two groups share similar productivity profiles under competitive conditions where at least some employer prefers profits to prejudice, eventually all workers must be paid the same wage, as long as both groups will have the same average productivity (Darity 1998).

43.3 Regression Analysis and Results

43.3.1 Results 1

As we mentioned earlier from Becker and statistical theories, sometimes employers discriminate before entering the labour market, and this can be explained with equal treatment in the recruitment and selection process. For testing the explanatory hypothesis for the unequal treatment in recruitment and selection regarding gender, we have developed some research questions relevant to this issue:

Research question 1 – Which is the way that you have found this job: through open announcement, direct application, unemployment office or through recommendation, own networks or relatives.

Research question 2 – Does your institution have procedures and manual of recruitment and selection process under the existing labour law[5] (Labour Law 2017)?

Research question 3 – Do you think that recruitment and selection process is implemented correctly taking into consideration gender equality in your institution?

The questionnaire also considers the general variables such as age, gender and the type of institution that they work for, public or private sector or NGOs. From 586

[5]Labour law, Law No.03/L — 212. Republic of Kosovo.

respondents in our research sample, males make up 53% of employees surveyed while females 47% of those interviewed.

Age of respondents: the highest per cent is in younger age, 47% in age from 21 to 35 years, 35% at age 36–50 years and 18% at age 51–65 years.

According to our first research question for the way females and males found their jobs, we can say that for males, getting the job through application directly to the employer is made by 31% of them while from the announcements in the newspapers, web sites and other media by 39% of them, and through employment offices by 11% while from references and from their acquaintances, relatives or former employers from 19% of them. For females finding job with direct application to an employer consists 31% of them, from announcement in newspapers and other media 48%, by employment offices 10% of them, while from the references from acquaintances, relatives or from the former employers 11% of them. We can conclude that females are weaker in having contacts with informal networks to find jobs than males. Since, males in about 19% of cases have found jobs of these networks compared to females in 11% of cases. But in other ways through regular procedures, the percentages do not differ a lot, or we can say that they are equal in the ways of finding jobs between males and females in Kosovo.

The null hypothesis is:

H$_0$: $\bar{a}=0$ Unequal gender treatment exists in the recruitment and selection process which has their consequences in increasing the inactivity of the active labour force.

First we will verify that the variables that we have used in this model are correlated, we will test their significance and we will check for multicollinearity. In Table 43.1 we see that gender is related with recruitment and selection and is significant with 0.116 in the level of 0.01; it is also correlated with gender recruitment and selection procedures. Here we can see that the sign is negative

Table 43.1 Table of correlation coefficients

		Gender	Recruitment and selection	Procedures of R&S	The way of finding job
Gender	Correlation Pearson	1	.116[a]	0.073	−.083[b]
	Sig. (2-tailed)		0.005	0.079	0.045
Recruitment and selection	Correlation Pearson	.116[a]	1	.844[a]	0.023
	Sig. (2-tailed)	0.005		0.000	0.580
Procedures of R&S	Correlation Pearson	0.073	.844[a]	1	0.010
	Sig. (2-tailed)	0.079	0.000		0.805
The way of finding job	Correlation Pearson	−.083[b]	0.023	0.010	1
	Sig. (2-tailed)	0.045	0.580	0.805	
	N	586	586	586	586

[a]Correlation is significant 0.01 (2-tailed)
[b]Correlation is significant 0.05 (2-tailed)

−0.083* and significant at 0.05 level; this negative correlation with gender can be explained in that gender has a negative correlation with those organizations that do not apply recruitment and selection procedures correctly. Correlation is significant and highly correlated between implementing recruitment and selection properly and having procedures of recruitment and selection in 0.844 and is significant at 0.01 levels. While the correlation between ways of finding job and gender variable is not significant.

This study is developed in two general points of view, first with all the collective data for all the institutions and then divided by the institutions, public, private sector and NGOs, and their comparison in separate empirical analysis.

43.3.2 Results of Regression Analysis Model

The regression model that we use is formulated to form the independent or explanatory variables such as gender, age, institution, the existence of procedures for recruitment and selection and ways of finding job, while the dependent variable is gender equality in recruitment and selection.

Multiple regression formula[6] (Wooldridge 2002):

$$Y'' = \bar{a} + \beta\ \text{Gen} + \beta\text{Age} + \beta\text{Inst} + \beta\text{ProcR\&S} + \beta\text{WFJ} + \varepsilon$$

where $Y'' = \bar{a}$ is the predicted variable and Y the dependent variable

Independent variables are $X1$, gender; $X2$, age; $X3$, institution; $X4$, procedures of R&S; and $X5$, the way of finding job.

$R2$ can also be from −1 to 1 and measures the relationship between variations of a dependent variable that can be explained statistically by one or more independent variables, set in an econometric model. R square R is used to find out how appropriate the independent variables are to predict the dependent variable; R square value is less inflated when the number of independent variables is greater.

Table 43.2 shows that R square is 0.723, i.e. relatively high, and adjusted R square is 0.721 which means that the independent variables fit the model and are appropriate to explain the dependent variable, and we can say that about 72% of inequality in recruitment and selection is explained by the independent variables.

Table 43.2 Recruitment and selection: model summary

Model	*R*	*R* square	Adjusted *R* square	Std. error of the estimate
1	.850[a]	0.723	0.721	0.25543

[6] *Wooldridge, M. J Introductionary Econometrics – A Modern Aproach pg82, 2002 ISBN-13:9780324113648, South-Western.*

Table 43.3 Explanatory coefficients – dependent variable recruitment and selection

Model		Unstandardized coefficients		Standardized coefficients	t	Sig.
		B	Std. Error	Beta		
1	(Constant)	0.181	0.063		2.882	0.004
	Gender	0.065	0.022	0.067	3.033	0.003
	Age	0.035	0.014	0.054	2.426	0.016
	Institution	−0.046	0.016	−0.063	−2.870	0.004
	Procedures of R&S	0.778	0.020	0.842	38.364	0.000
	The way of finding job	0.007	0.011	0.014	0.639	0.523

While on the ANOVA table (Appendix 1), $F = 302{,}850$ is with the degrees of freedom 5 and is higher than that given in Table F (Appendix B), therefore the model is significant, or we can say that sig is 0.000 < 0:05 which is alpha, then sig <alpha which means that the model is statistically significant.

From Table 43.3 we can see which independent variables explain the dependent variable. We use standardized beta coefficients measured by standard deviation:

Gender has significant value $p = 0.03$ and <0.05, while its coefficient is 0.065, and this represents that for every unit increase in the differences in gender inequality in the recruitment process, inequality increases for 6% points rites, if we consider that all other variables remain constant.

Age has the value $p = 0.016$ and is significant and is <0.05, while its coefficient is 0.035, and this represents that for each additional unit of years, inequality in the recruitment process increases to 0.3 units if we consider that the other variables remain constant.

Institution has $p = 0.04$ which is significant and <0.05, while its coefficient is – 0.046, and this represents that for institution, depending on the type of the institution public, private, or NGO, the impact of equality in the recruitment process is reduced by 0.4 units.

Procedures of recruitment and selection have the value of $p = 0.00$, i.e. they are very significant and <0.05, while their coefficient is 0, 778 which represents a great explanatory effect, which means that for an additional unit in the regulation of recruitment and selection or proper implementation of procedure according to equal opportunity chances, inequality is reduced in the recruitment and selection process regarding gender for 77% points.

The way that females and males found their jobs is not significant since there is $p = 0.523$ which is greater than 0.05, while its coefficient does not explain the dependent variable, i.e. in our case inequality in recruitment and selection process. In this regression model of recruitment and selection, out of the five independent variable, four of them are significant, so we can say that the data are suitable and fit for this model and they do explain the model and the dependent variable which in this case is unequal gender treatment in the recruitment and selection.

Table 43.4 Recruitment and selection – model summary for public institutions, private sector and NGOs

Institution	R Model	R square	Adjusted R square	Std. error of the estimate
Public institution	.982[a]	0.965	0.964	0.08996
Private sector	.812[a]	0.659	0.654	0.29298
NGOs	.615[a]	0.379	0.339	0.31420

Therefore we can say that the null hypothesis **H$_0$:** ā=0 is proven, and unequal treatment divided by gender exists during the recruitment and selection process. Although gender does not have a high explanatory level, inequality still exists.

43.3.3 Results of the Regression Analysis Model: Comparison of Public and Private Sector and NGOs

Since in the first model we don't have separate regression analysis considering the respondents' working institutions, in the following calculation, we use the same model, but we divide it into three separate data samples taking into account the institution that they are working: public institutions, private sector and NGOs.

In Table 43.4 results of the regressions for separate institutions, public institutions, private sector and NGOs, are presented.

From the results of the separated regression for Public institutions outlined below show that R square is 0.965 and adjusted R square 0.964 which means that the independent variables explain variable dependent variable, and we can say that about 96% of inequality in recruitment and selection process of independent variable is explained for public institutions. In results for private sector R square is 0.659 and adjusted R square is 0.654 which means that the independent variables explain the dependent variable, and we can say that about 65% of inequality in recruitment and selection regarding gender is explained by the independent variables. For the results from separate regression for NGOs R square is 0.379 and adjusted R square is 0.339, which means that the independent variables explain the dependent variable, and we can say that about 33% of the model is explained by the independent variables.

Public institutions – From the results of Table 43.5, we can see the difference with the first model in public institutions. In this regression the statistically significant variable is recruitment and selection procedures which has a value of $p = 0.00$, i.e. they are very significant and are <0.05, while their coefficient is 0.97, which represents high level of explanatory factor, which means that if the procedures of recruitment and selection exist in the institution the process of recruitment and selection without gender discrimination increases for 0.97% points, if we keep the other variables constant. Other explanatory variables are not significant, meaning that there is not any unequal treatment in recruitment and selection process.

Table 43.5 Recruitment and selection – regression coefficients of public institutions, private sector and NGO

	Public institution	P	Private sector	p	NGO	P
Coefficients	B	Sig	B	Sig	B	Sig
(Constant)	0.029	0.352	0.060	0.532	0.514	0.013
Gender	0.012	0.298	0.104	0.004	0.146	0.068
Age	−0.006	0.403	0.072	0.003	0.005	0.928
Institution	0.978	0.000	0.727	0.000	0.378	0.000
Procedures of R&S	−0.006	0.214	0.015	0.432	−0.032	0.476

Private sector – Institutions have different results; gender is significant since $p = 0.004 < 0.005$ and its coefficient is 0.104, and this signifies that for every unit increase in the differences in gender inequality in the recruitment and selection process, there is an increase of 10% points, if we consider that all other variables remain constant.

Age is also significant since $p = 0.003$ and is <0.005 and its coefficient is 0.072, and this represents that for each additional year (cycle),[7] the disparity in the recruitment process increases for 7% points, if we consider that all other variables remain constant.

Process of recruitment and selection is very significant, and its coefficient is 0.727 indicating that the improvement for a unit in the recruitment and selection procedures and the equality in the recruitment and selection increases for 72% points.

Non-governmental organizations (NGOs) – Multiple regression results for NGOs are similar to those of public institutions: the only statistically significant explanatory variable is recruitment and selection procedures with a p value of $0.000 < 0.005$. Its coefficient has a value of 0.378, meaning that if procedures of recruitment and selection exist in the institution, i.e. the NGOs, the process of recruitment and selection without gender discrimination increases by 0.378%, *ceteris paribus*.

From the empirical results, we can emphasize that the independent variables are almost all explanatory and they all present a model, with an exemption of the dependent variable on how the respondents have found their job (43.3). Also the expected result is the one which improves the procedures of recruitment and selection that have the highest influence in reducing gender inequality in recruitment and selection process (43.5).

Also from the data presented, and their explanatory coefficients, we can say that it is proved that the null hypothesis holds that there is an unequal gender treatment

[7]In questionary the age cycle is 15 years.

during recruitment and selection process, but it is only proven that this hypothesis holds for the private sector; we did not find any proof that the same is also valid for public institutions and NGOs.

43.4 Discussion and Conclusions

Labour market in transition economies is very dynamic, and various information that are often needed for the labour market often do not arrive at the right time; therefore we can have asymmetrical information. Since the labour market does not depend only on supply and demand for labour but also from laws, employment policies, development policies, education system and development level of a country. This is particularly important in transitional economies where the unemployment level is very high and especially for females; therefore the role of the policies and regulations should incentivize education, and human capital investment for females is needed by proper legislative labour market regulations to encourage active labour market participation and new entrants in the labour market. In Kosovo this is very important since it is in the early stages of transition and has a very high level of unemployment and high level of inequality. Reduced activity in the labour market may be influenced by a variety of factors, such as higher participation of young people in education; this may be partly true for Kosovo since it has the youngest population in Europe; one other fact may be that a large number of unemployed and especially women are discouraged by the job search, as well as discouraged to enter employment in the informal economy where gender inequality is higher in the labour market. Overall low participation of females in the labour force in Kosovo may also be associated with stereotypes of gender roles and family traditions. In Kosovo, similar to other transition economies which are aspiring in becoming part of the European Union, the labour law and law against discrimination are in place and reflect the market-oriented economy and are against discrimination, but policymakers will have to find a way through the secondary legislation and work inspectorate to encourage and incentivize especially private sector in their implementation of rules and legislations, since from the research it is shown that employment procedures and recruitment and selection are gender biased.

It is mentioned in the literature review that gender discrimination can start prior to entering the labour market, but in this research, we concentrate on unequal treatment in recruitment and selection as the first barrier to enter the labour market. From the research gender shows that it is correlated with recruitment and selection and has a negative correlation with those organizations that do not have the procedures of recruitment and selection or do not use them properly. Correlation is significant between proper recruitment and selection and their procedures. From our research we found that, although the level of education of females in Kosovo is increasing and participation rate in tertiary education is higher than males, participation rates in labour market are very low and there are inequalities and barriers in recruitment and selection process which may impose lower participation rates in labour market for females; one important issue is also the traditional families and rural area population and their lack of mobility to urban areas.

The research indicates that state and public organizations are more responsive than private firms to changes in the normative environment. Important facts that we found is that depending on the institution where respondents work, gender and age affect the increase or reduction of inequality in recruitment and selection process; this is predominantly proven in the private sector since they have the highest level of explanatory coefficients. This can also prove that private sector in Kosovo is not implementing labour laws and anti-discrimination laws and other anti-discrimination legislations. From separate models we can see that this is not a matter of public institutions and NGOs, where variables such as age and gender are not significant and do not explain the model, and therefore we can say that alternative hypotheses hold that there is no unequal treatment divided by gender, which is in compliance with earlier research on institutional theories. Where according to institutional theories, the success of the state and public institutions lies in their ability to satisfy the criteria set by social requests of the population. State and public institutions will adopt practices and claims of the civil society's requests because they depend on public opinion about the legitimacy of resources and are more likely to be judged regarding policymaking and procedures and structures of their implementation; therefore institutional theory has finally begun to acknowledge that institutional environments can and do change institutions (McGuire et al. 2002).

One of the recent studies suggests quotas for females in the organizations in order to introduce cultural change and also recognizes potentials of females and their skills in the labour market (Tatli et al. 2013). The skills acquired in education and training before entering the labour market may be necessary in order to carry out the work efficiently or can be used as a screening device for entry into the labour market. In both cases, those who do not possess the skills that are needed in labour market present a barrier to entry into the labour market; therefore the policymakers in Kosovo should concentrate and encourage research on the skills that are needed in the labour market and develop vocational trainings for jobseekers. They should also incentivize and have friendly business environment for females in developing new entrepreneurial skills and have higher possibility to access grants and loans for business startups. Monitoring of the implementation of labour law and laws on gender discrimination in the implementation of paid leave, annual leave and sick leave. To build up awareness through NGOs and the media are crucial in increasing awareness about the importance of gender equality in the labour market and implementation of the labour law in Kosovo, Law Nr. 03 / L-212 and especially Article 5 concerning the prohibition of discrimination.

There is a need for more sustainable policies and institutional promotion regarding gender inequality in Kosovo. Also legislation and regulations for which will give incentives in equal opportunities in a variety of broader occupations for females. This will help in reducing horizontal segregation in education as well as that of employment; it will also help in reducing gender inequality and increase participation of females in the labour market.

From the experience of the European Union states, they have more females employed in part-time jobs; this could help in creating family-oriented policies in which females could have an opportunity to take care of family obligations as well as being employed in part-time jobs.

Appendix

Appendix A: Correlations: Recruitment and Selection

Correlations

		Gender	Recruitment and selection	proceR&S	Job finding
Gender	Pearson correlation	1	.116[a]	0.073	−.083[b]
	Sig. (2-tailed)		0.005	0.079	0.045
Recruitment and selection	Pearson correlation	.116[a]	1	.844[a]	0.023
	Sig. (2-tailed)	0.005		0.000	0.580
proceR&S	Pearson correlation	0.073	.844[a]	1	0.010
	Sig. (2-tailed)	0.079	0.000		0.805
Job finding	Pearson correlation	−.083[b]	0.023	0.010	1
	Sig. (2-tailed)	0.045	0.580	0.805	
	N	586	586	586	586

[a]Correlation is significant at the 0.01 level (2-tailed)
[b]Correlation is significant at the 0.05 level (2-tailed)

Appendix B: Recruitment and Selection: Regression

REGRESSION/MISSING LISTWISE/STATISTICS COEFF OUTS R ANOVA /CRITERIA = PIN(0.05) POUT(0.10) /NOORIGIN /DEPENDENT rekrselekt.
/METHOD = ENTER Gender InstprocR&SFindjob.

Variables entered/removed[a]

Model	Variables entered	Variables removed	Method
1	Job finding, proceR&S, age, institucioni, gender[b]	.	Enter

[a]Dependent variable: recruitment and selection
[b]All requested variables entered

Model summary

Model	R	R square	Adjusted R square	Std. error of the estimate
1	.850[a]	0.723	0.721	0.25543

[a]Predictors: (constant), job finding, proceR&S, age, institucioni, gender

ANOVA[a]

Model		Sum of squares	df	Mean square	F	Sig.
1	Regression	98.800	5	19.760	302.850	.000[b]
	Residual	37.843	580	0.065		
	Total	136.643	585			

[a]Dependent variable: recruitment and selection
[b]Predictors: (constant), job finding, proceR&S, age, institucioni, gender

Coefficients[a]

Model		Unstandardized coefficients		Standardized coefficients		
		B	Std. error	Beta	t	Sig.
1	(Constant)	0.181	0.063		2.882	0.004
	Gender	0.065	0.022	0.067	3.033	0.003
	Age	0.035	0.014	0.054	2.426	0.016
	Institucioni	−0.046	0.016	−0.063	−2.870	0.004
	proceR&S	0.778	0.020	0.842	38.364	0.000
	Job finding	0.007	0.011	0.014	0.639	0.523

[a]Dependent variable: recruitment and selection

Appendix C: Recruitment and Selection, Regresion Public Institution

Regression

Variables entered/removed[a,b]

Model	Variables entered	Variables removed	Method
1	Job finding, age, proceR&S, gender[c]	.	Enter

[a]Dependent variable: recruitment and selection
[b]Models are based only on cases for which institution, public institution
[c]All requested variables entered

Model summary

Model	R Institucioni, public institution (selected)	R square	Adjusted R square	Std. error of the estimate
1	.982[a]	0.965	0.964	0.08996

[a]Predictors: (constant), job finding, age, proceR&S, gender

ANOVA[a,b]

Model		Sum of squares	df	Mean square	F	Sig.
1	Regression	52.297	4	13.074	1615.720	.000[c]
	Residual	1.918	237	0.008		
	Total	54.215	241			

[a]Dependent variable: recruitment and selection
[b]Selecting only cases for which institution, public institution
[c]Predictors: (constant), job finding, age, proceR&S, gender

Coefficients[a,b]

Model		Unstandardized coefficients		Standardized coefficients	t	Sig.
		B	Std. error	Beta		
1	(Constant)	0.029	0.031		0.933	0.352
	Gender	0.012	0.012	0.013	1.043	0.298
	Age	−0.006	0.008	−0.010	−0.838	0.403
	proceR&S	0.978	0.012	0.984	79.552	0.000
	Job finding	−0.006	0.005	−0.015	−1.247	0.214

[a]Dependent variable: recruitment and selection
[b]Selecting only cases for which institution, public institution

Appendix D: Recruitment and Selection, Regression Private Institutions

Regression

Variables entered/removed[a,b]

Model	Variables entered	Variables removed	Method
1	Job finding, proceR&S, age, gender[c]	.	Enter

[a]Dependent variable: recruitment and selection
[b]Models are based only on cases for which institution = private institution
[c]All requested variables entered

Model summary

Model	R Institucioni, private institution (selected)	R square	Adjusted R square	Std. error of the estimate
1	.812[a]	0.659	0.654	0.29298

[a]Predictors: (constant), job finding, proceR&S, age, gender

ANOVA[a,b]

Model		Sum of squares	df	Mean square	F	Sig.
1	Regression	45.035	4	11.259	131.165	.000[c]
	Residual	23.348	272	0.086		
	Total	68.383	276			

[a]Dependent variable: recruitment and selection
[b]Selecting only cases for which institution, private institution
[c]Predictors: (constant), job finding, proceR&S, age, gender

Coefficients[a,b]

Model		Unstandardized coefficients		Standardized coefficients		
		B	Std. Error	Beta	t	Sig.
1	(Constant)	0.060	0.096		0.626	0.532
	Gender	0.104	0.036	0.104	2.889	0.004
	Age	0.072	0.024	0.107	2.966	0.003
	proceR&S	0.727	0.033	0.792	22.264	0.000
	Job finding	0.015	0.019	0.028	0.786	0.432

Appendix E: Recruitment and Selection, Regression NGO

Regression

Variables entered/removed[a,b]

Model	Variables entered	Variables removed	Method
1	Job finding, gender, age, proceR&S[c]	.	Enter

[a]Dependent variable: recruitment and selection
[b]Models are based only on cases for which institution, NGO
[c]All requested variables entered

Model summary

Model	R	R square	Adjusted R square	Std. error of the estimate
	Institucioni, NGO (selected)			
1	.615[a]	0.379	0.339	0.31420

[a]Predictors: (constant), job finding, gender, age, proceR&S

ANOVA[a,b]

Model		Sum of squares	df	Mean square	F	Sig.
1	Regression	3.730	4	0.933	9.446	.000[c]
	Residual	6.121	62	0.099		
	Total	9.851	66			

[a]Dependent variable: recruitment and selection
[b]Selecting only cases for which institution, NGO
[c]Predictors: (constant), job finding, gender, age, proceR&S

Coefficients[a,b]

Model		Unstandardized coefficients		Standardized coefficients	t	Sig.
		B	Std. error	Beta		
1	(Constant)	0.514	0.200		2.567	0.013
	Gender	0.146	0.078	0.189	1.858	0.068
	Age	0.005	0.061	0.009	0.091	0.928
	proceR&S	0.378	0.071	0.544	5.295	0.000
	Job finding	−0.032	0.044	−0.074	−0.717	0.476

[a]Dependent variable: recruitment and selection
[b]Selecting only cases for which institution, NGO

References

Anker, R. (1997). Theories of occupational segregation by sex: An Overview. *International Labour Review, 136*(3), 315–339.

Arrow, K. J. (1972). *Racial discrimination in economic life*. Lexington, Mass: Lexington Books.

Becker, G. (1975). 2 National bureau of economic research human capital: A theoretical and empirical analysis, with special reference to education. 1994. "Human capital revisited.", *Journal of Chemical Information and Modeling, 53*(9), 1689–1699.

Becker, G. S. (1992). The economic way of looking at life. *Revista Universidad EAFIT, 29*(89), 7–21.

Becker, G., & Sowell, T. (1981). Affirmative action and equal opportunity.

Becker, G., Sowell, T., & Vonnegut, K. Jr. (1982). *Discrimination, affirmative action, and equal opportunity*. The Fraser Institute. Canadian Cataloging in Publication Data Bibliography: p. Includes index. ISBN 0-88975-039-4.

Beqiri, T. (2016). Labour market trends in transition economies with emphasis on gender inequalities. *Acta Universitatis Danubius Oeconomica, 12*(4), 72–85.

Bielby, W. T., & Baron, J. N. (1986). Men and women at work: Sex segregation and statistical discrimination. *American Journal of Sociology, 91*(4), 759–799.

Borjas, G. J. (2016). *The labour supply of undocumented immigrants*. No. orrc15-02. National Bureau of Economic Research Working Paper 22102 1050 Massachusetts Avenue Cambridge, MA 02138 March 2016.

Borjas, G. J., & Van Ours, J. C. (2000). *Labour economics* (Vol. 2). Boston: McGraw-Hill.

Darity, W. A. (1998). Intergroup disparity: Economic theory and social science evidence. *Southern Economic Journal, 64*(4), 806–826.

Davalos, M. E., Sattar, S., Simler, K., Bidani, B., Reva, A., Tsirunyan, S., & Orlando, M. B. (2012). *Kosovo – Gender gaps in education, health, and economic opportunities*. The World Bank Group Europe and Central Asia region poverty reduction and economic management. Washington, DC: World Bank. http://documents.worldbank.org/curated/en/371251468030245833/Kosovo-Gender-gaps-in-education-health-and-economic-opportunities

Hill, M. A., & King, E. (1995). Women's education and economic well-being. *Feminist Economics, 1*(2), 21–46.

Hoxha, D., & Krasniqi, B. (2008). Female entrepreneurship in Kosova: Does gender difference hypothesis hold? *International Journal of Business and Management Science, 1*(1), 49–65.

Jurajda, Š., & Terrell, K. (2009). Regional unemployment and human Capital in Transition Economies. *Economics of Transition, 17*(2), 241–274.

McGuire, D., Garavan, T., O'Donnell, D., & Dineen, D. (2002). "Labour market flexibility: In S. W. Polachek & W. S. Siebert (1993). *The economics of earnings*. Cambridge: Cambridge University Press Institutional Theory Perspective." http://eresearch.qmu.ac.uk/382/

Miranda, V. (2011). Cooking, caring and volunteering: unpaid work around the world. *OECD Social, Employment, and Migration Working Papers* (116): 0_1,3–4,6–39. http://search.proquest.com/docview/857720244?accountid=17225

Phelps, E. (1972). The statistical theory of racism and sexism. *American Economic Review, 62*(4), 659–661.

Polachek, S. W., & Siebert, W. S. (1993). *The economics of earnings*. Cambridge: Cambridge University Press.

Tatli, A., Vassilopoulou, J., & Ozbilgin, M. (2013). An unrequited affinity between talent shortages and untapped female potential: The relevance of gender quotas for talent management in high growth potential economies of the Asia Pacific region. *International Business Review, 22*(3), 539–553.

Ward-Warmedinger, M., & Macchiarelli, C. (2013). *Transitions in labour market status in the EU transitions in labour market status in the EU*. (7814): 34.

Other References

Kosovo Agency of Statistics. "*Results of the labour force survey 2012*". Social Statistics Department Labour Market Sector.

Kosovo Agency of Statistics. "*Results of the labour force survey 2015*". Social Statistics Department Labour Market Sector.

Labour Law. (2010/03-L-212) ... of Kosovo: Last accessed.01.10.2017. http://www.kuvendikosoves.org/common/docs/ligjet/2010-212-eng.pdf

LFS (2015). http://documents.worldbank.org/curated/en/171731476272117466/pdf/108978-WP-P156426-Labour-Force-Survey-2015-PUBLIC.pdf

Making the Labour Market Work for Females and Youth, Kosovo Human Development Report. (2016). Last accessed 27/01/2017 http://www.ks.undp.org/content/kosovo/en/home/library/poverty/kosovo-human-development-report-2016.html

Market, Labour. "*Unemployment in Kosova*." Research paper, Riinvest (2003). Ministry of Education Science and Technology, MEST (2009). National Action Plan Against School Abandonment 2009–2014.

Ministry of Education Science and Technology, MEST. *Strategy for Development of Higher Education in Kosovo* (2009-2015), Qirici Stefan: Ekonomiksi i Punes, Tiranë 2005, University Lectures

Ministry of Education Science and Technology, MEST. "*Kosovo Education Strategic Plan* (2011-2016)" http://www.masht-gov.net/advCms/documents/KESP_2011_2016.pdf

Wooldridge, M. J. *Introductionary Econometrics – A Modern Approach pg82*, 2002 ISBN-13:9780324113648, South-Western.

Chapter 44
Intergenerational Persistence of Child Labor in Brazil

Temidayo James Aransiola and Marcelo Justus

Abstract Early theoretical studies pointed to the probability of child labor to perpetuate itself among generations of the same family through forgone education. Recent empirical studies do not reject this hypothesis, thus, affirming that children from parents who were child laborers are more likely to start working at early age. Despite significantly contributing to literature, no empirical evidence was provided concerning the *tipping point* at which the vicious cycle of child labor may turn virtual. In this study, we test the hypothesis that such cycle may be reverted if the minimum age for work is increased. To pursue this objective, we used a pooled sample from 2004 to 2014 PNAD data to estimate probit models. Aside from reaffirming the existence of intergenerational persistence of child labor, we found that the *tipping point* of the child labor cycle is observed if the minimum age for work is increased.

Keywords Child labor trap · *Tipping point* · Minimum age for work

44.1 Introduction

There is consensus in literature that poverty can perpetuate itself over family generations, especially, through education, igniting a poverty cycle. Having that poverty is a potential motivator of the supply of child labor, it is likely that the cycles of both are also correlated. In other words, parents who forwent education due to work during childhood are bound to earn lower income when adult (Justus et al. 2015) and, thus, remain poor. Moreover, poverty situation may drive such

We thank FAPESP (State of Sao Paulo Research Foundation) for financial support.

T. J. Aransiola (✉) · M. Justus
Institute of Economics, University of Campinas, Campinas, São Paulo, Brazil
e-mail: temidayo.aransiola@hotmail.com; mjustus@unicamp.br

N. Tsounis, A. Vlachvei (eds.), *Advances in Panel Data Analysis in Applied Economic Research*, Springer Proceedings in Business and Economics,
https://doi.org/10.1007/978-3-319-70055-7_44

parents to send their children to work in order to support family income to reach subsistence level (Basu and Van 1998). As a result, such children may reinstate the same cycle faced by their parent, igniting the child labor and poverty cycle. However, it is important to note that such relationship is most likely to hold, on the one hand, if work and education are mutually exclusive choices – which is not always true (Kassouf 2015) – and, on the other hand, if work reduces the quality of acquired human capital compared to that required in the labor market.

The existence of intergenerational persistence of child labor and poverty was suspected and emphasized by Alfred Marshall in the nineteenth century. Thereafter, Basu (1999) proposed a theoretical model which indicated how poverty cycle can trigger a vicious cycle of child labor through forgone education. This author connoted such relationship as the *child labor trap* and referred to the point at which such vicious cycle becomes virtuous as the *tipping point*. Subsequently, Emerson and Souza (2003) extended this model and, using cross-sectional analysis of Brazilian data, provided empirical evidence that parents who were child laborers are more likely to send their children to work compared to parents who were not child laborers. In line with these authors, (Aquino et al. 2010) empirically pursued similar objective, although exploiting differences of such trap between urban and rural areas of Brazil.

Comparing the findings of both empirical studies, one is led to infer that there is, indeed, the risk of *child labor trap* in Brazil. Unlike these previous studies which presented a static analysis, here in Fig. 44.1, we illustrate how this trap evolved over time. Moreover, this figure presents not only the trapped children, those who

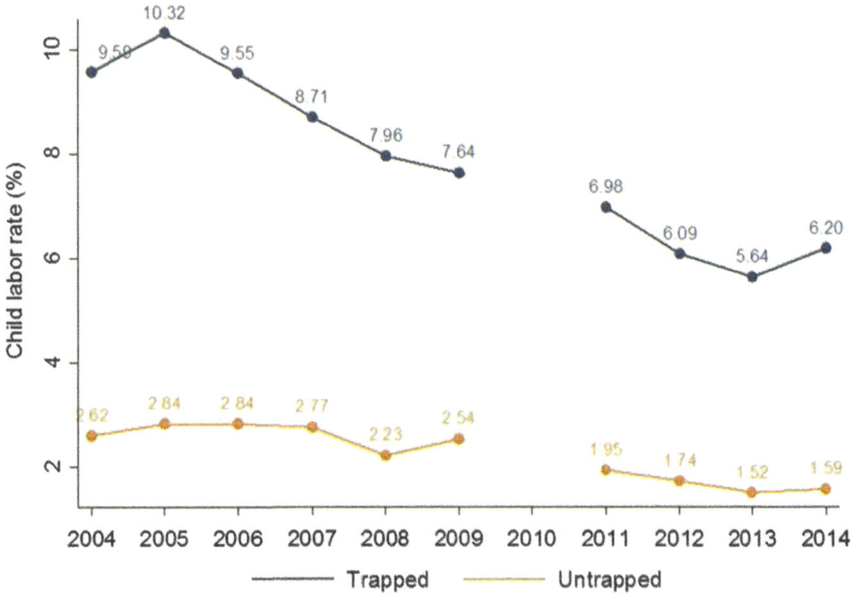

Fig. 44.1 Percentage of trapped and untrapped children in the vicious cycle of child labor (Source: Prepared using 2004–2009 and 2011–2011 PNAD data)

work and have parents who were child laborers – unlike previous studies, but also spotlights untrapped children, those who work but whose parents were not child laborers.

Firstly, we focus on the trapped children. Fortunately enough, the incidence of intergenerational perpetuated child labor reduced expressively during the period between 2004 and 2014. This indicates that parents who were child laborers are being able to break the vicious cycle of child labor due to the general reduction of poverty, increased access to education, easier access to credit facilities, and greater awareness of the negative impact of child labor. Aside from the continuous and systematic reduction of the proportion of trapped children, especially between year 2005 and 2013, abrupt increase was observed from year 2004 to 2005 and from year 2013 to 2014. Therefore, we consider that it is important to control for time shocks.

Surprisingly, the untrapped children, who should not be working in the first place according to conventional theories, seemed not to be highly affected by this socioeconomic betterment. Recalling Basu (1999) and Emerson and Souza (2003), forgone education for the sake of work during childhood as a result of poverty is what feeds the vicious cycle. If this argument holds, parents who were not child laborers should be better off during adulthood and should not send their children to work.

Unlike in trapped children, the evolution of the proportion of those untrapped seems to be less responsive to reductions over time. This proportion was clearly stagnant during the period of 2004 and 2007, and only slight fluctuations[1] were observed in subsequent years. Notwithstanding, reduction was observed in 2011 compared to previous years. However, as from the year 2011, this proportion becomes relatively stagnant once again. It is also worthwhile to note that not even the abrupt increase observed in 2014 was able to cause expressively increase in the proportion of untrapped children. These observations call for attention on these specific child laborers. However, our focus here is on trapped children.

Despite the contributions of Emerson and Souza (2003) and Aquino et al. (2010), we observe that no information was provided concerning the possibility of reverting the vicious cycle of child labor. Therefore, we seek to enrich this topic in the following ways: (a) analyze the existence of intergenerational persistence of child labor controlling time shocks between year 2004 and 2004; (b) indicate the intensity of the vicious cycle according to the age group at which parents entered the labor market; and (c) point the minimum age for work, which reverts the vicious cycle, thus, contributing to the debate concerning the best minimum age for employment in Brazil.

In a recent studies, Kassouf (2015) showed that the proportion of children and adolescents who conciliate work and study increased in Brazil over time. Therefore, we assume that work and study are not mutually exclusive choices and that child labor affects the quality of human capital acquired, mainly, due to shortage of time for rest, play, study, and assimilation of academic knowledge. The hypothesis alleged to support this study is that the vicious cycle may be reverted if the minimum

[1]Remember that PNAD was not carried out in 2010.

age for employment is increased to, at least, a level at which the human capital acquired through education is sufficient to secure a better-paying work to meet family's financial needs.

This study is divided in six sections, including this introductory one. In sections "Theoretical Background" and "Previous Studies," we provide the theoretical and empirical studies, respectively, that support the alleged hypothesis and give insights concerning results to be expected during empirical exercises. Section "Methodology" presents the empirical strategy used, and empirical results are provided in section "Results." Section "Concluding Remarks" is conclusive.

44.2 Theoretical Background

In terms of dynamics concerning child labor, few are those who consider its long-run consequences. One of the first remarkable and documented perceptions concerning the existence of intergenerational persistence of child labor is that of Alfred Marshall in 1985. In the author's words:

> But the point on which we have specially to insist now is that this evil is cumulative. The worse fed are the children of one generation, the less will they earn when they grow up, and the less will be their power of providing adequately for the material wants of their children; and so on to following generations. And again, the less fully their own faculties are developed, the less will they realize the importance of developing the best faculties of their children, and the less will be their power of doing so. And conversely any change that awards to the workers of one generation better earnings, together with better opportunities of developing their best qualities, will increase the material and moral advantages which they have the power to offer to their children. (Marshall 1895)

It is clear that Marshall (1895) was more concerned about the cycle of poverty driven by the faculty or human capital of children from a certain generation. However, one can easily deduce that given the high demand and deregulation of child labor in the nineteenth century during the industrial revolution, the cycle of poverty was followed by the cycle of child labor. Aside from pointing to the existence of this vicious cycle, Marshall (1895) also suggested its reversion through better labor market conditions, which permits parents to provide better living conditions and education to children. Admitting that work during childhood jeopardizes human capital accumulation of children which, in the future, tends to limit their future productivity and in turn perpetuate poverty, Basu (1999) developed the theoretical model of *child labor trap*.

The author considers an overlapping generation model with two periods. In the first period, the individual is a child and lives with his parents, and in the second period, the same individual is parent and has a child. In this model, work and study (*proxy* for source of human capital) were considered mutually exclusive choices. In a day, a child is considered to spend fraction e of his time at work and $1 - e \equiv h$ in school. Supposing that the level of adult human capital depends on the amount of time spent in school during childhood, the total labor unit of an adult, L_t, is given by

$$L_t = L(h_{t-1}), \quad L' > 0, \; L'' < 0 \tag{44.1}$$

Thus the wage of one unit of adult labor in a labor market with perfectly inelastic demand is given by

$$\bar{V}L(1 - e_{t-1}) \equiv W_t \tag{44.2}$$

It was also assumed that there is a certain level of wage, $\underline{W}$, below which parents send a child to full-time work ($e = 1$), and a level of income, $\bar{W}$, above which children are sent to school ($e = 0$). Assuming the *substitution axiom*, one can write e as a function of parent's wage, thusly

$$e_t \equiv e_t = e(W_t) \equiv e(\bar{V}L(1 - e_{t-1})) \equiv e_t = \Phi(e_{t-1}) \tag{44.3}$$

where Φ is upward sloping and bounded at $e(\bar{V}L(0)) = e(\bar{V})$. Similar to the model presented by Basu and Van (1998), this dynamic model points out two stable equilibria and one unstable equilibrium. At one stable equilibrium point, a parent sends his/her child to work full-time. Such child acquires no human capital (through education) and continues to be poor when adult and, therefore, has to send his/her child to work. In other words, this equilibrium point depicts the *child labor trap*. On the other way round, the child is sent to school at the other stable equilibrium point. In this case, such child, when adult, earns adequately and, thus, faces a virtuous cycle.

In the case of *child labor trap*, Basu (1999) suggested government intervention in order to reverse the cycle of either poverty or child labor. The author also claimed that if there is a large effort to educate a certain generation, the economy will reach a "tipping point" at which the vicious cycle turns virtuous. However, the sum of investment required for this effort may turn such intervention unrealistic, especially in developing countries. In this sense, the author points that the availability of credit to poor families or study loan may incentivize poor parents to enroll their children in school and not send them to work. Regarding the effect of credit availability to poor families, Ranjan (2001) and Das and Deb (2006), based on theoretical frameworks, concur that the incidence of child labor can be reduced by credit-related policies. However, Das and Deb (2006) emphasize that such policies only have effect in the long run.

Emerson and Souza (2003) contributed to the theoretical model presented by Basu (1999) providing a similar theoretical model and an example of how intergenerational persistence of child labor may emerge using the Cobb-Douglas utility function. Upholding the assumptions made in Basu (1999) regarding parent's altruism, family composition, luxury and substitution axiom, credit constraints, and human capital accumulation, Emerson and Souza (2003) were able to illustrate how the trap may be generated. Additional assumption was made that families with little education need children's contribution through work compared to richer families. With this, parents have to make the decision to send children to work or not in each period. The utility function of such family is given as

$$U_t = U(c_t, h_{t+1}) \tag{44.4}$$

where c_t and h_{t+1} denote family's total consumption and child's acquired human capital, respectively. Here, it is clear that the family cares about the future human capital of the child, which is accumulated in the present through education. Having the human capital assumption, parent's and child's income is given as $w_t^a = h_t$ and $w_t^c = 1 - e_t$, respectively, where e_t is the amount of time that a child spends in school. Thus, family income is given by $W_t = w_c^a + w_t^c$, which is subjected to meet the budget constraint of $c_t \leq W_t$.

Supposing that all individuals have the innate level of human capital of 1 which becomes greater due to education, children and uneducated adults have one unit of human capital and, therefore, earn the same in the labor market. This can be formally represented by

$$h_{t+1} = f(e_t) \qquad \text{where } f(0) = 1, f(1) = \bar{h} > 1, \text{ and } f'(e_t) \geq 0 \; \forall \, e_t \in [0, 1] \tag{44.5}$$

In this model, the challenge adults face is to

$$\max_{e_t} U(h_t + 1 - e_t, f(e_t)) \tag{44.6}$$

The solution to such problem is e_t^*, which is a function of h_t, and the law of motion is $h_{t+1} = f(g(h_t)) \equiv \Phi(h_t)$. Although the $\Phi()$ may assume any form, the case study here is that in which $f(\cdot)$ and $g(\cdot)$ are positively related. In this case, a *child labor trap* may occur giving rise to two stable equilibria (at point $h_t = 1$ and point $h_t = \bar{h}$) and one which is unstable (at point $h_t = h^*$). Specifically, point $h_t = h^*$ is critical in the sense that it marks the threshold which separates the case in which the child does nothing but work ($h_t = 1$) from that in which child only study ($h_t = \bar{h}$).

To this point, it is noticeable that both Basu (1999) and Emerson and Souza (2003) emphasized that child labor may be transmitted across generations, through the level of human capital acquired by parents. Therefore, theoretical studies indicate a positive relationship between past child labor and present child labor. Note that none of these studies explicitly pointed the effect of the specific age at which parents entered the labor market. However, logical deduction leads to expect that the earlier parents started working, the lesser human capital they were able to acquire through formal education and thus the higher the likelihood of their children to work.

44.3 Previous Studies

Numerous studies concur that child labor interferes with the education of children in the sense that it compels them to evade school prematurely or conciliate work and schooling, thus, reducing children's accumulation of human capital. However, it is important to note that aside from forgone education, *child labor trap* may be sustained through cultural and social norms such as filial obligations (Emerson and Souza 2003; López-Calva et al. 2002).

Concerning empirical evidence of the intergenerational persistence of child labor, only two studies were found for Brazil, which are those of Emerson and Souza (2003) and Aquino et al. (2010). Aside from the theoretical framework presented in section "Theoretical Background," Emerson and Souza (2003) provided empirical evidence which confirms the hypothesis that parents who were child laborers during childhood are more likely to send their children to work at early age. In specific, the authors used 1996 Brazilian Household Surveys data (henceforth, PNAD) to estimate probit and Cox proportional hazard models. Having that the PNAD data provides information regarding the occupational status of children and the age at which parents started work, one can easily verify the intergenerational persistence of child labor among generations of the same family. It is important to add that the major reason why these authors adopted the 1996 PNAD data was because it provides not only information concerning parents, but also that of grandparents in respect of level of education and income. Thus, these authors were able to decently model the persistence of child labor across three generations, which is undoubtedly one of the major strengths of their study.

In the probit model, the response variable, which assumes 1 if child works and 0 otherwise, was adjusted against regressors such as dummy variables for parents who were child laborers, parent's education, number of brothers, child's gender, and level of urbanization of family's residence. These authors further controlled for grandparent's level of education in order to enhance the *proxy* for family income. However, no statistical significance was found for direct relationship between grandparent's level of education and the probability of grandchild to work. This result indicated that, despite being a brilliant move, the control for grandparent's income or level of education is irrelevant. Consequently, there is no need to restrict studies to the 1996 PNAD data for the sake of controlling grandparent's variables.

Notwithstanding, statistically robust evidence was found for the positive relationship between early work of parents and the probability of children to work. Specifically results from all empirical exercises pointed that early labor of mothers has greater impact on the decision of children to work or not compared to that of fathers. These authors also confirmed that parent's education is one, but not the only, important factor which drives the *child labor trap*. The reason for this is that despite isolating the effect of family income and parent's level of education, the child labor cycle persisted. Therefore, conclusion was drawn that the effect of parental child labor may be more complex than the supposed human capital relationship. With this, Emerson and Souza (2003) pointed out the likelihood of such persistence to be attributed to cultural or social norms, buttressing the crucial points made by Marin et al. (2012) and CONAETI (2011) concerning the cultural roots of child labor in Brazil.

Aquino et al. (2010) contributed to the study of Emerson and Souza (2003) by also empirically investigating the existence of *child labor trap* in Brazil adopting probit models and using data from 1992 and 2004 PNAD. As upgrade, these authors performed separate analysis for rural and urban areas in order to verify if the intergenerational persistence of child labor can be attributed to peculiarities of the Brazilian rural and urban areas. Aside from reaffirming the existence of the trap, evidence was found that the effect of parental child labor is greater in the rural areas compared to urban areas and that the magnitude of the effect reduced substantially between 1992 and 2004.

In contribution to both empirical studies reviewed in this section, we provide information concerning how the specific age at which parents started working affects the intensity of this trap. Most importantly, we provide the first empirical evidence concerning the *tipping point* at which the vicious cycle of child labor turns virtuous.

44.4 Methodology

44.4.1 Data and Sample

The database used here was obtained from the PNAD conducted by the IBGE, covering the period of 2004–2009 and 2011–2014. Acknowledging from Emerson and Souza (2003) that it is unnecessary to control for grandparents' variables, we opt not to limit analysis to 1996 PNAD data and, thus, used a larger sample. Aside from providing current figures of the child labor cycle, this choice permitted to control time variations of the child labor cycle and to expressively increase sample size.

We opted to filter the overall data to best fit the objectives of this study. The first filter was to restrict the sample to individuals between age 5 and 15, retaining about 19% of the overall sample (see Sample I in Fig. 44.2). As the major interest is the intergenerational persistence of child labor, we further restricted the database

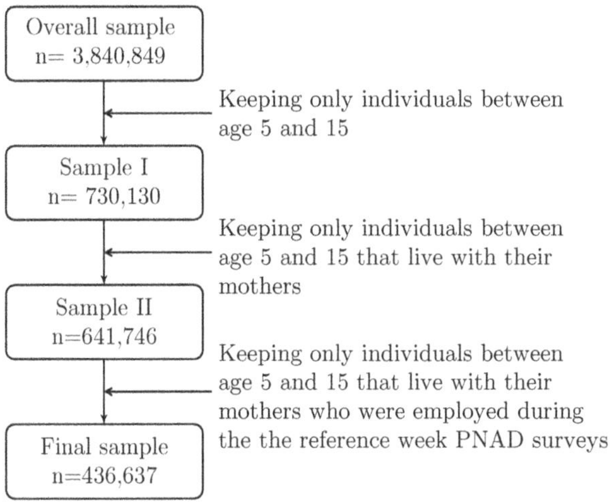

Fig. 44.2 Filtration of pooled sample of PNAD data (2004 to 2009 and 2011 to 2014) (Source: Prepared by author. Note: n denotes the number of observations)

to children and adolescents between age 5 and 15 who live with their mothers. The reason for this is that the PNAD only registers as family members those individuals who live in the same household and consider one another as family. The loss in Sample II due to this filter was modest (about 12% of Sample I) since we focus on young individuals who, in most cases, are still dependent on parents.

Furthermore, the PNAD question concerning the age at which individuals started working is only directed to those who were employed during the reference week of surveys. This engendered additional unavoidable and crucial filter which caused loss of about 32% from Sample II. Thus, the empirical analysis is limited to child laborers who live in the same household with their mothers who were employed during the reference week of the PNAD surveys.

We acknowledge that such filters may cause severe implication to analysis, especially since children with unemployed parents tend to be more vulnerable. For this, we compare statistics of the overall and final samples in Table 44.1. Note that despite the expressive reduction of sample size, the mean and standard deviation of variables from the overall and final samples converge.

The average rate of child labor in Brazil during the period in view was about 7%. During this same period, it was observed that about 51% of the mothers contained in the sample were child laborers. Specifically, about 12% of these mothers entered the labor market at or before the age of 9, and, approximately, 40% of them started working between the age of 10 and 14. Specifically, the average age at which mothers start working is 14.

Furthermore, all estimates were computed using the weights or sample expansion factors provided by the IBGE in the data files.

44.4.2 Empirical Model

Our response variable is a dummy, which is 1 if the child or adolescent is a child laborer and 0 if otherwise (`childlabor`). Therefore, the conventional OLS model is inadequate because such variables are Bernoulli distributed. Thus, probit models are resorted. Details regarding the construct and properties of probit models presented in this section are based on Cameron and Trivedi (2010).

The regressors considered are dummy variable which is 1 if the individual's mother was a child laborer and 0 otherwise (`CLmom`); seven dummy variables which control for the age bracket at which the individual's mother started working (`CLmombelow9`, `CLmom10-14`, `CLmom15-17`, `CLmom18-19`, `CLmom20-24`, `CLmom20-24`, and `CLmomabove30`), with individuals below age 17 being used as base group; age at which individual's mother started working (`CLmomage`) and its square; mother's age (`agemom`); mother's level of education measured in years of schooling (`mothereduc`); average per capita family income (`famincome`); family size (`familysize`); a dummy variable which is 1 if the individual is male and 0 otherwise (`male`); dummy variable which is 1 if the individual is enrolled in school and 0 otherwise (`childeduc`); dummy variable if the individual resides in

Table 44.1 Summary statistics

	Variable	Description	Filtered sample		Overall sample	
			Mean	Std. Dev	Mean	Std. Dev
Individual's variables	childlabor	1 for child laborer and 0 non-child laborer	0.0703	0.2557	0.0415	0.1994
	famincome	Average family per capita income (in reais – R$)	711.01	1183.82	617.19	1076.32
	male	1 for male and 0 for female	0.5064	0.5000	0.5106	0.4999
	childeduc	1 if enrolled in school and 0 if not	0.9610	0.1937	0.7603	0.4269
	urban	1 for residence in urban area and 0 for rural	0.8036	0.3972	0.8161	0.3874
	asians	1 if skin color is yellow and 0 if not	0.0029	0.0539	0.0028	0.0527
	mulatto	1 if skin color is brown and 0 if not	0.5004	0.5143	0.4998	0.4996
	black	1 if skin color is black and 0 if not	0.0032	0.0561	0.0572	0.2323
	white	1 if skin color is white and 0 if not	0.4187	0.4933	0.4154	0.4928
	familysize	Family size	4.51	1.57	4.45	1.59
Mother's variable	CLmom	1 if mother was child labor and 0 if not	0.5140	0.4998		
	CLmomage	Age at which mother started working	14.72	5.11		
	CLmomage2	Square of age at which mother started working	242.82	225.57		
	CLmom0-9	1 if mother started working at or before age 9 and 0 if otherwise	0.1174	0.3220		
	CLmom10-14	1 if mother started working between age 10 to 14 and 0 if otherwise	0.3965	0.4892		
	CLmom15-17	1 if mother started working between age 15 to 17 and 0 if otherwise	0.2387	0.4263		
	CLmom18-19	1 if mother started working between age 18 to 19 and 0 if otherwise	0.1211	0.3263		
	CLmom20-24	1 if mother started working between age 20 to 24 and 0 if otherwise	0.0831	0.2761		
	CLmom25-29	1 if mother started working between age 25 to 29 and 0 if otherwise	0.0257	0.1583		
	CLmom30-above	1 if mother started working at or after age 30 and 0 if otherwise	0.0172	0.1299		
	mothereduc	Mother's level of education (in years of studies)	7.56	4.39		
	agemom	Mother's age	36.03	7.15		

Note: Number of observations for filtered sample is 436,637 and for overall sample is 730,130 an urban area and 0 otherwise (`urban`); five dummy variables for skin color or race[2] (`white` as base group, `asians`, `black` and `mulatto`)[3]; group dummy variable for each year to control for time shocks in child labor (`dummy for years`); and control for long-run tendency of a time series effect of child labor (`linear trend`).

Regarding the main variable of interest, `CLmom`, it is important to highlight that as the PNAD data does not provide information concerning fathers, those of mothers will be used as *proxy* to control for parental background. Evidences from Emerson and Souza (2003) pointed that mother's level of education has relatively higher impact on child labor decisions. Thus, we assume that conclusions drawn from mother's variables can serve as *proxy* for both parents.

44.5 Results

The hypothesis which we analyze in contribution to previous studies is that the child labor cycle is reversible through the minimum age for work. The empirical strategy used to reach this objective is the probit model estimated by maximum likelihood.

The marginal effects observed from model I to V are presented in Table 44.2. These effects were calculated for discrete changes in dummy variables and at means for continuous variables. The modeling exercise adopted here is a cumulative incremental procedure of group regressors. Loosely speaking, category of regressors was gradually incremented in the model in order to verify the stability of other estimates.

As the modeling exercise transit from model I to III, which is the complete benchmark model with all regressors, we observe that the signs and statistical significance remained unaltered. Note that the `dummy for years` was included in all models to account for time shocks. However, the importance of such control was tested by carrying out the Wald tests of simple and composite linear hypotheses on the benchmark model. With a Wald test value of $\chi^2 = 681.96$, the null hypothesis that all dummies for years are equal to 0 is rejected at a level of 1%. Thus, the control of dummy variables for time is important. In model IV, we substituted `CLmom` for a group of dummy variables to control for the age bracket in which the individuals mother started working (`CLmombelow9`, `CLmom10-14`,..., `CLmomabove30`). Such control enables to verify the depth of the *child labor trap* given the age at with the individuals' mothers started working. Lastly, in model V, these age brackets were substituted for the specific age at which mother's started working and its square (`CLmomage` and `CLmomage squared`, respectively). The reason for this is to observe if there is a quadratic relationship between this variable and the probability

[2]The Brazilian Institute of Geography and Statistics (IBGE) classifies race/skin color according to physical appearance which is self-declared by individuals. These categories are white, black, yellow (Asian-Brazilians), brown (mulatto), and indigenous.

[3]Indigenous population was excluded due to the small number of observations.

Table 44.2 Marginal effects for discrete changes in dummy variables and at means for continuous variables

Response variable: `childlabor`

Category of regressors		I	II	III	IV	V
Individual's variables	`male`	0.0363***	0.0367***	0.0356***	0.0411***	0.0410***
		(0.001)	(0.001)	(0.001)	(0.001)	(0.001)
	`childeduc`	−0.0354***	−0.0359***	−0.0233***	−0.0248***	−0.0250***
		(0.001)	(0.001)	(0.001)	(0.002)	(0.002)
	`urban`	−0.0783***	−0.0756***	−0.0551***	−0.0701***	−0.0686***
		(0.001)	(0.001)	(0.001)	(0.001)	(0.001)
	`asians`	−0.0120**	−0.00872	−0.00459	−0.00249	−0.00210
		(0.006)	(0.006)	(0.006)	(0.008)	(0.008)
	`mulatto`	0.0102***	0.00858***	0.00466***	0.00454***	0.00434***
		(0.001)	(0.001)	(0.001)	(0.001)	(0.001)
	`black`	0.0118***	0.0102***	0.00326**	0.00347*	0.00397**
		(0.001)	(0.001)	(0.001)	(0.002)	(0.002)
Family's variables	`famincome`		0.000889***	0.00305***	0.00192***	0.00237***
			(0.000)	(0.000)	(0.001)	(0.001)
	`familysize`		0.00432***	0.00330***	0.00394***	0.00395***
			(0.000)	(0.000)	(0.000)	(0.000)

Mother's variables	agemom			0.00252***	0.00303***	0.00295***
				(0.000)	(0.000)	(0.000)
	mothereduc			−0.00274***	−0.00349***	−0.00340***
				(0.000)	(0.000)	(0.000)
	CLmom			0.0467***		
				(0.001)		
	CLmombelow9				0.0563***	
					(0.002)	
	CLmom10-14				0.0345***	
					(0.002)	
	CLmom15-17				0.0108***	
					(0.002)	
	CLmom18-19				−0.00590***	
					(0.002)	
	CLmomage					−0.0107***
						(0.000)
	CLmomage squared					0.000202***
						(0.000)
Time variables	dummy for years	yes	yes	yes	yes	yes
	linear trend	yes	yes	yes	yes	yes
Number of observations		436,637	432,586	432,586	432,586	432,586
Pseudo R^2		0.094	0.095	0.156	0.155	0.156
Log likelihood		−72473004.3	−69762172.9	−56189902.0	−45534918.3	−45447071.3
LR χ^2(degree of freedom)		23493.1(15)	22949.3(17)	29977.3(20)	25252.8(23)	25787.4(21)

Note: Standard errors calculated using the delta method is in parentheses; ***, **, and * denote significance at 1%, 5%, and 10%, respectively of children to work. If such relationship exists, the next step is to find the specific age at which this probability is minimum.

As per control variables, signs from `famincome`, `childeduc`, and `urban` corroborate those from previous studies. Specifically, poverty is affirmed to be negatively related to child labor; the enrollment of children and adolescents in schools reduces their likelihood to work; and the incidence of child labor is lesser in the urban areas.

Moreover, it was found that boys are more likely to be child laborers compared to girls. The debate herein is that the number of female child laborer is prone to be underestimated because a great number of girls work as housekeepers, babysitters, or domestic workers (Guarcello et al. 2007; Repórter Brasil 2013). However, numerous studies have shown that the incidence of child labor is more frequent among boys (Kassouf 2001; Emerson and Souza 2003; ILO 2007; Inaiá 2008; Repórter Brasil 2013; ILO 2013, to mention few). The set of dummy variables for skin color indicates that the incidence of child labor is higher among the mulatto and black population compared to the white population.

The coefficient of the primary interest variable, `CLmom`, indicates that children and adolescents, whose mothers were child laborers, are most likely to be child laborers compared to other children. This observation affirms the theoretical postulate of Basu (1999) and supports the evidence found in Emerson and Souza (2003) and Aquino et al. (2010) regarding the existence of intergenerational persistence of child labor. According to these authors, the trap is manifested through forgone education or low accumulation of human capital during childhood which, in turn, reduces future productivity and earnings. Individuals in such situation tend to remain poor and are induced to send their children to work at early age. However, we acknowledge that the *child labor trap* may also emerge as a result of unobservable factors such as social and cultural norms (López-Calva et al. 2002; Marin et al. 2012).

The group variable that controls for the age group at which individuals' mothers started working provides more detail concerning the trap. The estimate for `CLmom0-9` indicates that the probability of *child labor trap* is highest among children whose mothers started working at or before the age of 9 compared to those whose mothers entered the labor market at later ages. Curiously, the marginal risk of the trap drops from 5.63 to 3.45 percentage points (p.p.) as the mother's entrance in the labor market is postponed to the age group of 10–14 (indicating reduction of about 39%). Further deferral of mother's entrance in the labor market to the age bracket of 15–17 provoked greater reduction of this risk from 3.45 p.p. to 1.08 p.p. (reduction of almost 69%).

What can be deduced at this point, which is innovative to previous studies, is that the later an individual enters the labor market, the less likely he/she is induced to send children to work. The coefficient for `CLmom18-19` appears negative, indicating a nonlinear relationship between the probability of child labor and the age at which mothers started working. Thus, the model points that children from parents who enter the labor market at this age tend to be involved in other activities other than work.

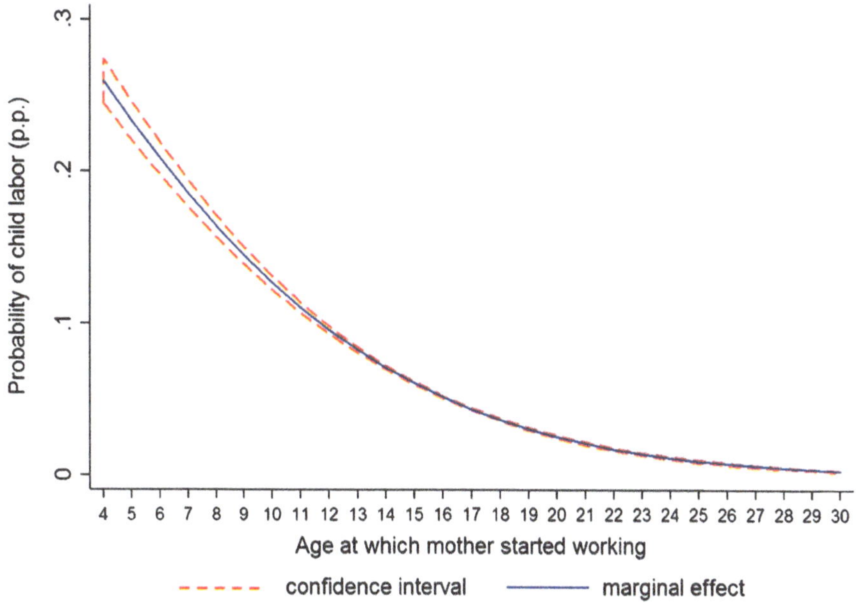

Fig. 44.3 Marginal effect of the age at which mothers started working (Source: Prepared using estimates from model I in Table 44.2. Note: The continuous line is the estimated marginal effect, and the broken lines represent confidence interval)

The suspicion of nonlinear relation in model IV incited the control of the `CLmomage` and `CLmomage squared` in model V so as to calculate the specific age in which this *tipping point* falls. Not surprisingly, the sign for these variables was negative and positive, respectively. Moreover, having an expressively low value for `CLmomage squared`, it is deducible that the function is more likely to be asymptotic and not quadratic. Nevertheless, we found that the minimum point of this function is reach at about the age of 26.5. Thus, this model shows that the probability of children to work is close to null if parents started working at the age of 26.5. Note that it is around this age at which a large number of Brazilian students complete their undergraduate studies.

For illustration of this result, Fig. 44.3 presents the marginal effect of the age at which mothers started working on the probability of their children to work. Clearly, the relationship is negative, asymptotic, and minimum at age 26.5. Thus, every additional year of postponement of entry into the labor market reduces the risk of child labor trap till its minimum. Aside from the calculated marginal effects represented by the continuous line, we also presented the confidence interval for the same, which is represented by the broken lines. Notably, the extremely straight intervals indicate that estimates are very precise.

Curiously, Justus et al. (2012) found a similar result for the best age to enter the labor market. Specifically, these authors found that the hourly earnings from work are maximum when males and females start working at age 27.3 and 22.6, respectively. Therefore, our result corroborates that found by these authors that the minimum age for work set at 14 is, still, low to eradicate the negative impact of child labor in adulthood.

In short, the result found in this study provides evidence which corroborates previous literature concerning child labor trap. Specifically, we found that the probability of a child to work is negatively related to the age at which his/her parents started working. Most importantly, our empirical result does not permit to reject the hypothesis that child labor cycles can be reverted if the minimum age for work is increased.

44.6 Concluding Remarks

In this study, we investigated the intergenerational persistence of child labor, focusing on its *tipping point*. The hypothesis alleged concerning this objective is that families with child laborers are likely to be trapped in the vicious cycle of child labor, which can eventually be reverted. This hypothesis is founded on the argument that individuals who were child laborers accumulated less human capital through education and are likely to be less competitive in the labor market and are, thus, subjected to lower earnings when adults. Consequently, such individuals are prone to remain in poverty and perpetuate child labor among subsequent generations of the same family. Therefore, on the contrary, if individuals defer their entry into the labor market and focus on accumulating minimum required human capital, they stand greater chances of getting better-paying jobs in the labor market and, therefore, break the child labor cycle.

We tested this hypothesis using pooled sample of 2004 to 2009 and 2011 to 2014 PNAD data to estimate probit models. Empirical results sustained the hypothesis of the existence of *child labor trap*, and a tipping point was observed. Similarly to previous studies, we found that the risk of child labor in a given generation is negatively related to the age at which parents started working. However, this risk becomes minimum if individuals enter the labor market after the age of 26.

In Brazil, there is an intense political debate as to the minimum age for work, especially through Proposals of Constitution Amendment (PEC, in Brazilian acronym). In 2011, Deputy Dilceu Sperafico presented PEC 18/2011 which suggested the reduction of this age from 16 to 14 based on the argument that such proposal will amplify the children's right in the sense that it formalizes the work of those who really need to work and guarantee them labor and security rights. In the same year, PEC 35/2011 was submitted by Deputy Onofre Agostini supporting that work is beneficial to children and their families, especially, in the financial, moral, and educational sense if these working children and adolescents are also enrolled in school and adequately followed up. In 2013, PEC 274/2013 was forwarded by Deputy Edinho Bez who, in line with the deputies mentioned earlier as per the minimum age for work, argued that work is educative for children and adolescents and also reminded that "an empty mind is a devil's workshop" Congresso em Foco (2015).[4] In February of 2016, these PECs were recovered during debates in the National Congress and continued in discussion till October 4, 2016, with the final review of Deputy Betinho Gomes which deemed the PECs as unacceptable.

In accordance with this decision, empirical result from this study firmly opposes these PECs and suggests that the minimum age for work should not be reduced from 16 to 14. In fact, we found that the risk of intergenerational persistence of child labor is lower if individuals enter the labor market at subsequent ages. Thus, the minimum age may be adjusted to coincide with the end of compulsory education (age of 17) and, thus, meet the specifications of the ILO Convention 138 concerning the compatibility of minimum age for work and compulsory education. Nevertheless, we acknowledge that increase in the minimum age may provoke adverse effects on families which solely depend on income from child labor. In such a case, we suggest a focal and generous assistance conditioned to child education.

Our results also corroborate literature concerning the capacity of large educational investment on a generation to revert poverty and child labor cycles in subsequent generations. However, in line with Basu (1999), we admit that such policy may be too fanciful, especially for developing countries.

References

Aquino, J. M., Fernandes, M. M., Pazello, E. T., Scorzafave, L. G., et al. (2010). Trabalho infantil: Persistência intergeracional e decomposição da incidência entre 1992 e 2004 no brasil rural e urbano. *Revista de Economia Contemporânea, 14*(1), 61–84.

Basu, K. (1999). Child labor: Cause, consequence, and cure, with remarks on international labor standards. *Journal of Economic Literature, 37*(3), 1083–1119.

Basu, K., & Van, P. H. (1998). The economics of child labor. *American Economic Review, 88*, 412–427.

Cameron, A. C., & Trivedi, P. K. (2010). *Microeconometrics using Stata* (Vol. 2). College Station: Stata Press.

CONAETI, C. (2011). *Plano nacional de prevenção e erradicação do trabalho infantil e proteção adolescente trabalhador*. Brasília: Ministério do Trabalho e Emprego.

Congresso em Foco. (2015). Deputados querem reduzir idade mñima para trabalho. http://congressoemfoco.uol.com.br/. Accessed 13 May 2015.

Das, S. P., & Deb, R. (2006). A dynamic analysis of child labor with a variable rate of discount: Some policy implications. *The B.E. Journal of Economic Analysis & Policy, 5*(1), 1–30.

Emerson, P. M., & Souza, A. P. (2003). Is there a child labor trap? Intergenerational persistence of child labor in Brazil. *Economic Development and Cultural Change, 51*(2), 375–398.

Guarcello, L., Lyon, S., Rosati, F. C., & Valdivia, C. (2007). *Children's non-market activities and child labour measurement: A discussion based on household survey data*. Understanding Children's Work (UCW Programme). Geneva: ILO.

ILO. (2007). Explaining the demand and supply of child labour: A review of the underlying theories. Technical report, ILO/IPEC-SIMPOC.

[4]The "Congresso em Foco"(Congress in focus, in English) is a journalistic site which covers facts and information, specifically, from the Brazilian National Congress.

ILO. (2013). Marking progress against child labour: Global estimates and trends 2000–2012. Technical report, International Labor Organization (ILO), IPEC (International Programme on the Elimination of Child Labor (IPEC)).

Inaiá, M. M. C. (2008). O trabalho infantil no Brasil contemporâneo. *Caderno CRH, 21*, 551–569.

Justus, M., Kawamura, H. C., & Kassouf, A. L. (2012). Socioeconomic conditions and risk of mental depression: An empirical analysis for Brazilian citizens. *Economics Research International, 2012*, 1–20.

Justus, M., Kawamura, H. & Kassouf, A. L. (2015). What is the best age to enter the labor market in Brazil today? *EconomiA, 16*(2), 235–249.

Kassouf, A. L. (2001). Trabalho infantil: Escolaridade x emprego. *Economia, 2*(2), 549–586.

Kassouf, A. L. (2015). Evolução do trabalho infantil no brasil. *Sinais Sociais, 9*(27), 9–45.

López-Calva, L. F., et al. (2002). *Social norms, coordination, and policy issues in the fight against child labor*. México: Colegio de México.

Marin, J. O. B., Schneider, S., Vendruscolo, R., & de Castilho e Silva, C. B. (2012). O problema do trabalho infantil na agricultura familiar: O caso da produção de tabaco em Agudo-RS. *Revista de Economia e Sociologia Rural, 50*(4), 763–786.

Marshall, A. (1895). *Principles of economics*. London: The English Language Book Society.

Ranjan, P. (2001). Credit constraints and the phenomenon of child labor. *Journal of Development Economics, 64*(1), 81–102.

Repórter Brasil. (2013). *Brasil livre de trabalho infantil: contribuições para o debate sobre a eliminação das piores formas do trabalho de crianças e adolescentes*. Repórter Brasil – Organização de comunicação e projetos sociais.

Chapter 45
Consequences of External Macroeconomic Shocks Transmission Through International Trade Channel: The Case of the Central and Eastern European Countries

Vilma Deltuvaitė

Abstract The Central and Eastern European countries (CEECs) have undergone different types of shocks and structural changes during the last two decades. Firstly, the CEECs had moved from a state-planned to a market-based economic system, with private ownership of assets and market-supporting institutions. These changes were exacerbated by the collapse of historic trading relationships and fiscal shocks to state budgets. Secondly, in European Union (EU) enlargement process, Czech Republic, Hungary, Poland, Slovenia, Slovakia, and the Baltic countries Estonia, Latvia, and Lithuania joined the European Union in 2004, Bulgaria and Romania in 2007, and Croatia in 2013. Thirdly, some of the CEECs (Slovenia, Slovakia, and the Baltic countries) have recently adopted the euro and joined to the euro zone. Fourthly, the global financial crisis (GFC) that started in 2007–2008 played a significant role in a downturn in economic activity leading to the 2008–2012 global (including the EU) economic recession. The main research questions are how these external shocks and structural changes affected foreign trading relationships of the CEECs and economic integration of this group of countries at the regional and global level and which type of external macroeconomic shocks causes the spillover effect transmission through international trade channel? The main findings of this study are as follows:

1. The shocks from the EU countries can be directly transmitted to the CEECs due to the intense international trade relations.
2. The shocks originated in the United States, China (except Hong Kong), Switzerland, Russia, and Turkey could be indirectly transmitted to the CEECs through international trade relations with the EU.

V. Deltuvaitė (✉)
Kaunas University of Technology, Kaunas, Lithuania
e-mail: vilma.deltuvaite@ktu.lt

N. Tsounis, A. Vlachvei (eds.), *Advances in Panel Data Analysis in Applied Economic Research*, Springer Proceedings in Business and Economics,
https://doi.org/10.1007/978-3-319-70055-7_45

3. The results of the Johansen cointegration test suggest that the long-run relationship among the CEECs and EU exists.

In addition, the empirical results suggest that the exchange rate shock positively affects the real GDP growth in the CEECs; however, depreciation of the currencies of the main export partners decreases the export flows to these countries. The economic growth in the main export countries positively affects the real GDP growth and real export flows in CEECs. An increase in consumption in the main export countries positively affects the real GDP growth in the CEECs; however, a negative impact of consumption on the real export flows to the main export countries is observed. In addition, the effect of macroeconomic shocks is more significant on real export flows.

45.1 Introduction

The Central and Eastern European countries (CEECs) (Bulgaria, Czech Republic, Estonia, Hungary, Latvia, Lithuania, Slovakia, and Slovenia) are one the most open economies worldwide (except Croatia, Poland, and Romania). Due to the high degree of economic openness, the CEECs are vulnerable to the external shocks that can be transmitted through international trade channel. Small economies like the CEECs have to specialize in producing few goods and services in order to attain optimal scale and be competitive. Due to the small size of their domestic markets, small countries must export those goods and services in exchange for the imports of the goods and services that are not produced in these countries. The CEECs have undergone different types of shocks and structural changes during the last two decades. The main research questions are: (1) how these external shocks and structural changes affected foreign trading relationships of the CEECs and economic integration of this group of countries at the regional and global level and (2) which type of external macroeconomic shocks causes the spillover effect transmission through international trade channel? The objective of this study is to assess the economic integration of the CEECs at the regional and global level focusing on the international trade flows and to assess the consequences of external macroeconomic shocks transmission through international trade channel. The following research methods were used in this paper: the systemic, logical, and comparative analysis of the scientific literature, analysis of the statistical data and Johansen cointegration test, and panel regression analysis.

45.2 Literature Review

Two related strands of the scientific literature investigate the economic integration of the European Union (EU) (including the CEECs). The first strand of the literature (Zoltán et al. 2001; Tajoli and De Benedictis 2006; Clemente et al. 2009; Martínez-

Zarzoso et al. 2011; Monfort et al. 2013; Rozmahel et al. 2013; Ezcurra and Rodríguez-Pose 2013; Van Ewijk and Arnold 2015; Fetahi-Vehapi et al. 2015, etc.) focuses on different aspects of economic integration of the EU and CEECs. While the second strand of the literature (Elliott and Fatás 1996; De Santis 2004; Albulescu 2011; Feldkircher 2015, etc.) focuses on the transmission of different types of shocks through international trade channel and the impact on economic integration of the EU and CEECs. However, recent empirical studies investigate only very specific issues related to the economic integration of the EU and CEECs, while a comprehensive analysis on the economic integration of the CEECs is still missing.

Zoltán et al. (2001) analyzed the potential and actual trade in the three CEECs (the Czech Republic, Hungary, and Poland) using the gravity model. The empirical results show that actual trade of analyzed CEECs converges to the estimated potential trade. The differences in the speed of convergence among the three countries, according to authors, are based on the product structure of exports and the effects of foreign direct investment. Tajoli and De Benedictis (2006) investigated the trade integration between the EU-15 and four CEECs (Poland, Hungary, Romania, and Bulgaria). The empirical results suggest that the CEECs' convergence toward the EU export structure has been long and profound and the process of convergence is still continuing. The authors argue that the effects of trade integration on trade patterns are very country-specific. According to Tajoli and De Benedictis (2006), the CEEC total exports toward the EU are related to other forms of integration, such as fragmentation of production. Clemente et al. (2009) analyzed the impact of the EU enlargements on the economic growth of EU members. The authors argue that the integration in the EU has a positive effect on the economic growth, especially for new EU members; however, this effect is short-lasting. Martínez-Zarzoso et al. (2011) investigated the role of the CEECs (Bulgaria, Czech Republic, Hungary, Poland, Romania, and Slovakia) in regional and global production networks. The authors state that the CEECs have become more integrated into regional production networks. The increased regional trade integration has had a positive impact on trade volumes and varieties between the Western Europe and Central-East Europe. Monfort et al. (2013) analyzed convergence in GDP per capita in the EU member states. The authors note that there are strong divergences in terms of income per capita within the EU. The empirical results suggest that there is neither clear subdivision between southern and northern EU countries nor between euro and non-euro countries. However, CEECs belonging to the euro zone are more converged with the Western economies. Rozmahel et al. (2013) assessed the homogeneity of an enlarged EU. They found significant convergence in terms of economic indicators in the EU but non-convergence in terms of institutional indicators. The recent financial crisis has strengthened the negative consequences of EU's heterogeneity. Ezcurra and Rodríguez-Pose (2013) analyzed the relationship between economic globalization and regional inequality. The authors found that there is a positive and statistically significant relationship between economic globalization and the magnitude of regional disparities. Countries with a higher degree of global economic integration tend to register higher levels of regional inequality.

Van Ewijk and Arnold (2015) analyzed the role of financial integration in the process of macroeconomic adjustment of countries belonging to the Economic and Monetary Union (EMU). The authors state that since the introduction of the euro, financial integration has negatively affected the macroeconomic adjustment process of countries within the EMU. Fetahi-Vehapi et al. (2015) analyzed the effects of trade openness on economic growth of Southeast European (SEE) countries. In the SEE countries with a high initial income per capita, the positive effect of trade openness on economic growth is identified; otherwise, there is no robust evidence between these two variables. The trade openness is more beneficial to countries with higher level of initial income per capita and foreign direct investment (FDI) and with higher gross fixed capital formation.

Elliott and Fatás (1996) analyzed the transmission of productivity shocks across countries (Japan, the United States, and Europe) and the responses of investment and the current account depending on the degree of propagation of shocks. They found that shocks to the United States propagate quickly to the other two economies, while European and Japanese shocks have little impact in other countries' productivity. They note that investment in other countries tends to react positively to productivity shocks, while productivity increases lead to current account deficits. The results also suggest that the response of the current account of the three countries is different and not related to the global or idiosyncratic nature of the shocks. De Santis (2004) investigated the transmission of currency shocks through international trade channel across the new EU members (Czech Republic, Estonia, Hungary, Lithuania, Latvia, Poland, Slovenia, and Slovakia). The results show that the transmission of currency shocks is very country-specific and depends on the direction of trade flows in a center-periphery framework (see also Corsetti et al. 1998). Albulescu (2011) analyzed the impact of financial instability on the degree of the CEECs' (Bulgaria, Czech Republic, Estonia, Hungary, Latvia, Lithuania, Poland, Romania, Slovenia, and Slovakia) economic and financial integration. The author states that financial instability negatively affects CEECs' economic and financial integration and hinders the process of the CEECs' integration into the EU. Feldkircher (2015) investigated the spatial propagation and the time profile of foreign shocks to the Central, Eastern, and Southeastern Europe (CESEE) and the Commonwealth of Independent States (CIS) applying a global VAR (GVAR) model. The results suggest that "the region's real economy reacts nearly equally strongly to a U.S. output shock as it does to a corresponding euro area shock." According to Feldkircher (2015), the role of the United States in shaping the global business cycle offsets the higher region's economic integration with the euro area. A strong negative effect of a shock in the euro area's as well as in US interest rate is observed in the CIS as well as in Southeastern Europe in the long run. A negative effect of an oil price hike in the region's economy, with the exception of Russia, is observed. Finally, the empirical results confirm the strong integration of advanced economies at the global level, while the responses in emerging European countries are more diverse and country-specific.

In summary, the analysis of the scientific literature reveals that the CEECs' convergence toward the EU export structure has been long and profound and the process of convergence is still continuing. The integration in the EU has a positive effect on the economic growth, especially for new EU members; however, this effect is short-lasting. The increased regional trade integration has had a positive impact on trade volumes of the CEECs. A positive effect of trade openness on economic growth was identified in most of the CEECs. The economic integration of the CEECs at regional level increased during the last decade; however, financial instability negatively influenced these countries' economic and financial integration.

45.3 Research Methodology and Data

The research on economic integration of the CEECs at the regional and global level will focus on the international trade flows among different countries and group of countries as well as on international trade structure of the CEECs. The following indicators of international trade structure from United Nations Conference on Trade and Development (UNCTAD) statistical databases will be used in this study: trade openness indicator, concentration index, diversification index, indicator of similarity in merchandise trade structures, trade complementarity index, and merchandise trade correlation index (see Table 45.1).

The economic integration of the CEECs within EU-28 as well as euro area will be assessed by using Johansen cointegration test. Engle and Granger (1987) argue that a linear combination of two or more nonstationary series may be stationary. According to Engle and Granger (1987), if such a stationary linear combination exists, the nonstationary time series are said to be cointegrated and may be interpreted as a long-run equilibrium relationship among the variables. This empirical study applied Johansen cointegration test (45.1) that was developed by Johansen (1991, 1995).

$$\Delta y_t = \Pi y_{t-1} + \sum_{i=1}^{p-1} \Gamma_i \Delta y_{t-i} + Bx_t + \varepsilon_t, \quad \text{Where}$$
$$\Pi = \sum_{i=1}^{p} A_i - I, \quad \Gamma_i = -\sum_{j=i+1}^{p} A_j \tag{45.1}$$

where Δy_t is a nonstationary I(1) variable (a quarterly real GDP growth of a single country) at time t, x_t is a deterministic variable (a quarterly real GDP growth of euro area or EU-28) at time t, and ε_t is an innovation.

Granger's representation theorem asserts that if the coefficient matrix Π has reduced rank $r<k$, then there exist $k \times r$ matrices α and β each with rank r such that $\Pi = \alpha\beta'$ and $\beta' y_t$ is $I(0)$. r is the number of cointegrating relations (the cointegrating rank), and each column of β is the cointegrating vector.

Data series may have nonzero means and deterministic trends as well as stochastic trends. Similarly, the cointegrating equations may have intercepts and deterministic trends. Therefore, in order to carry out the Johansen cointegration test,

Table 45.1 Indicators of international trade structure

Indicator	Description of indicator
Trade openness indicator	Sum of imports and exports of total trade in goods and services divided by GDP
Concentration index	The concentration index shows how exports and imports of individual countries are concentrated on several products or otherwise distributed in a more homogeneous manner among a series of products. Concentration index is a measure of the degree of market concentration that has been normalized to obtain values ranking from 0 to 1. An index value that is close to 1 indicates a very concentrated market (maximum concentration), and on the contrary, values closer to 0 reflect a more equal distribution of market shares among exporters or importers
Diversification index	The diversification index signals whether the structure of exports or imports by product of a given country differs from the structure of product of the world. Diversification index that ranges from 0 to 1 reveals the extent of the differences between the structure of trade of the country and the world average. The index value closer to 1 indicates a bigger difference from the world average. Diversification index is computed by measuring absolute deviation of the country share from world structure
Indicator of similarity in merchandise trade structures	The index of similarity by Grubel-Lloyd (1975) is an indicator that helps to determine whether the trade structures of a given country and the rest of the world are similar or not. The index of similarity signals whether the structure of exports or imports by product of a given country differs from the world. The index is calculated at the three-digit level of the SITC Revision 3 and ranges from 0 to 1. Value closer to 1 reveals the greater similarity of the trade structure between a given country and the rest of the world
Trade complementarity index	The merchandise trade complementarity index based on Michaely (1996) measures to what extent the export profile of country *j* matches the import profile of country *k*, the trade partner of country *j*. The index values range from 0 to 1 with 0 indicating that there is no correspondence between country *j's* export structure and country *k's* import structure and 1 indicating a perfect match in their export/import pattern
Merchandise trade correlation index	Merchandise trade correlation index is used to measure similarity of trade specialization index between economies. High similarity then can be considered that those economies compete in other in both exports and imports. Trade correlation index is a simple correlation coefficient between country's *k* and country's *j* trade specialization index. The resulting coefficient can take a value from −1 to 1. A positive value indicates that the economies are competitors in global market since both countries are net exporters of the same set of products. Consequently, a negative value suggests that the economies do not specialize in the production/consumption of the same goods and are therefore natural trading partners

Source: UNCTAD

an assumption regarding the trend underlying data should be made. This empirical study investigates the number of cointegrating relations under each of the five deterministic trend cases (2–6) considered by Johansen (1995) as:

1. The level data y_t have no deterministic trends, and the cointegrating equations do not have intercepts:

$$H_2(r): \quad \Pi y_{t-1} + Bx_t = \alpha\beta' y_{t-1} \tag{45.2}$$

2. The level data y_t have no deterministic trends, and the cointegrating equations have intercepts:

$$H_1^*(r): \quad \Pi y_{t-1} + Bx_t = \alpha\left(\beta' y_{t-1} + \rho_0\right) \tag{45.3}$$

3. The level data y_t have linear trends, but the cointegrating equations have only intercepts:

$$H_1(r): \quad \Pi y_{t-1} + Bx_t = \alpha\left(\beta' y_{t-1} + \rho_0\right) + \alpha_\perp \gamma_0 \tag{45.4}$$

4. The level data y_t and the cointegrating equations have linear trends:

$$H^*(r): \quad \Pi y_{t-1} + Bx_t = \alpha\left(\beta' y_{t-1} + \rho_0 + \rho_1 t\right) + \alpha_\perp \gamma_0 \tag{45.5}$$

5. The level data y_t have quadratic trends, and the cointegrating equations have linear trends:

$$H(r): \quad \Pi y_{t-1} + Bx_t = \alpha\left(\beta' y_{t-1} + \rho_0 + \rho_1 t\right) + \alpha_\perp\left(\gamma_0 + \gamma_1 t\right) \tag{45.6}$$

Johansen cointegration test has been performed using quarterly real GDP growth (seasonally adjusted and adjusted by working days) data for 11 CEECs: Bulgaria, Czech Republic, Croatia, Estonia, Hungary, Latvia, Lithuania, Poland, Romania, Slovakia, and Slovenia. Data for real GDP growth covers the period from 1995Q1 to 2015Q2.

This empirical study also focuses on macroeconomic shocks transmission through international trade channel in the CEECs and the vulnerability of this group of countries to the external macroeconomic shocks. The investigation of macroeconomic shocks transmission through international trade channel was examined by applying the cross-country fixed effects panel regression model (45.7).

$$Y_{i,t} = \alpha + \beta_{i,t} X'_{i,t} + \delta_i + \varepsilon_{i,t}, \quad \varepsilon_{i,t} \sim WN\left(0, \Sigma_\varepsilon\right) \tag{45.7}$$

where $Y_{i,t}$ is dependent variable characterizing economic situation in CEECs (real GDP change (RGDP) and real total export of goods change (REXPORT)), $X'_{i,t}$ is a k-vector of regressors (inflation shock (INFLATION_S), exchange rate shock

(EXCHANGE_S), GDP shock (GDP_S), export shock (EXPORT_S), final consumption expenditure shock (CONSUMPTION_S), investment shock (INVESTMENT_S), terms of trade index (TERMS_OF_TRADE), and trade openness (TRADE_OPENNESS)), and $\varepsilon_{i,t}$ are the error terms for $i = 1, 2, \ldots, M$ cross-sectional units (countries) observed for dated periods $t = 1, 2, \ldots, T$. The α parameter represents the overall constant in the model, while the δ_i represents cross-sectional fixed effects.

The dependent variables in the panel regression models are real GDP change and real total export of goods change in the CEECs, while different macroeconomic shocks (inflation, exchange rate, GDP, and its components (export, final consumption expenditure, and investment)) are calculated as weighted averages of these variables in main export partners of the CEECs representing more than 80–90 percent of total export to the world (33 countries).[1] The total list of dependent and independent variables in the panel regression models is presented in Table 45.2.

Panel regression analysis focuses on annual data for the same list of the CEECs. Annual data for the period of 2004–2014 have been obtained from different sources: bilateral export of goods data has been extracted from the IMF Direction of Trade Statistics (DOTS); bilateral exchange rates, data on concentration index of export, diversification index of export, terms of trade index, and trade openness indicator from the United Nations Conference on Trade and Development (UNCTAD); and all the others from the World DataBank (World Development Indicators).

45.4 Research Results

The trade openness indicators suggest that the CEECs (Bulgaria, Czech Republic, Estonia, Hungary, Latvia, Lithuania, Slovakia, and Slovenia) are the most open economies worldwide (except Croatia, Poland, and Romania). Small economies like the CEECs have to specialize in producing few goods and services in order to attain optimal scale and be competitive. Due to the small size of their domestic markets, small countries must export those goods and services in exchange for the imports of the goods and services that are not produced in these countries. Due to the high degree of economic openness, the CEECs are vulnerable to the external shocks that can be transmitted through international trade channel. However, some CEECs are more prone to the external shocks through real channel. The most diversified export and import portfolio in this group of countries has Poland, Croatia, and Romania. Poland also has the most similar international trade structure to the rest of the world.

[1]The total list of main export partners of the CEECs includes 33 countries (top 10 export countries of each CEEC have been included in this list): Austria, Belarus, Belgium, Bosnia and Herzegovina, Bulgaria, China, Croatia, Czech Republic, Denmark, Estonia, Finland, France, Germany, Greece, Hungary, Italy, Latvia, Lithuania, the Netherlands, Norway, Poland, Romania, Russia, Serbia, Singapore, Slovakia, Slovenia, Spain, Sweden, Turkey, Ukraine, the United Kingdom, and the United States.

Table 45.2 The list of dependent and independent variables in the panel regression models

Variable	Description of variable
Real GDP change (RGDP)	Real gross domestic product (GDP) change is an inflation-adjusted (GDP deflator) measure that reflects the change of the value of all goods and services produced by a domestic economy in a given year t compared to the previous year, expressed in base-year prices
Real total export of goods change (REXPORT)	Real total export of goods change is an inflation-adjusted (GDP deflator) measure that represents the change of value of all goods provided by a domestic economy to the rest of the world in a given year t compared to the previous year, expressed in base-year prices
Inflation shock (INFLATION_S)	Inflation shock is a weighted inflation (GDP deflator) change in the main export partners of a domestic economy that reflects the rate of price changes by applying annual bilateral export data of its export partners as weights
Exchange rate shock (EXCHANGE_S)	Exchange rate shock is a weighted exchange rate change between domestic country and its main export partners that reflects the bilateral exchange rate changes by applying annual bilateral export data of its export partners as weights
GDP shock (GDP_S)	GDP shock is a weighted real GDP change in the main export partners of a domestic economy that reflects the rate of real GDP changes by applying annual bilateral export data of its export partners as weights
Export shock (EXPORT_S)	Export shock is a weighted real export of goods and services change in the main export partners of a domestic economy that reflects the rate of real export changes by applying annual bilateral export data of its export partners as weights
Final consumption expenditure shock (CONSUMPTION_S)	Final consumption expenditure shock is a weighted real final consumption expenditure (the sum of private and general government consumption) change in the main export partners of a domestic economy that reflects the rate of real export changes by applying annual bilateral export data of its export partners as weights
Investment shock (INVESTMENT_S)	Investment shock is a weighted real gross domestic investment (gross capital formation) change in the main export partners of a domestic economy that reflects the rate of real gross domestic investment by applying annual bilateral export data of its export partners as weights
Terms of trade index (TERMS_OF_TRADE)	Terms of trade index is defined as the ratio of the export unit value index to the import unit value index
Trade openness indicator (TRADE_OPENNESS)	Trade openness indicator is the sum of exports and imports of goods and services measured as a share of gross domestic product

Diversification of export portfolio is important for developing countries because many developing countries are often highly dependent on relatively few products for their export earnings. Unstable prices for these products may subject a developing country exporter to serious terms of international trade shocks. Since the covariation in individual product prices is less than perfect, diversification into new primary export products is generally viewed as a positive development. The strongest positive effects are normally associated with diversification into manufactured goods, and its benefits include higher and more stable export earnings, job creation and learning effects, and the development of new skills and infrastructure that would facilitate the development of even newer export products. CEECs should extend the products in which they have a trade potential or extend potential trade prospects with new trade partners. CEECs can also focus attention on other nontraditional products that might be successfully exported.

Analyzing the regional and global economic integration of the CEECs, the flows of export and import have been divided into four main groups of countries: the Commonwealth of Independent States (CIS), EU-28, euro area, and the rest of the world. The analysis of export flows of the CEECs shows that some CEECs (Bulgaria, Croatia, and Slovenia) export a large share of products and services outside the EU (see Tables 45.3 and 45.4). The Baltic countries are highly dependent on export to the CIS (especially Lithuania). However, the largest share of export of CEECs goes to EU-28 and euro zone countries. The analysis of international trade flows of the CEECs shows that there are some structural changes in the export directions of this group of countries. For example, the Russian crisis in 1998 has changed the export directions of the Baltic countries. Surprising that the share of export to the EU has shrunk in most of the CEECs after these countries joined the EU and only in some cases (Bulgaria and Romania), this share remains stable.

The analysis of import structure of the CEECs reveals that Czech Republic, Poland, Slovakia, and Slovenia are highly dependent on the import from outside the EU while Lithuania on the import from the CIS (see Tables 45.5 and 45.6). In most of cases, the import structure of the CEECs depends on the import country (countries) of crude oil, natural gas, and oil products. However, the import portfolio of the CEECs is more diversified compared to the export portfolio.

The analysis of the import and export portfolio of the CEECs reveals that the main international trade partners of this group of countries are EU member states. Table 45.7 shows the member states' contribution to the intra-EU-28 trade of the EU. The main exporters within the EU are Germany, the Netherlands, France, Belgium, and Italy. The role of the CEECs in intra-EU trade is insignificant and ranging from 4.3 percent in Poland to 0.2 percent in Croatia.

Table 45.8 shows that the main importers within the EU are Germany, France, the United Kingdom, Belgium, Italy, and the Netherlands. These EU member states could have a direct impact on the economies of the CEECs as well as an indirect effect through direct international trade relations with other EU countries.

Despite the fact that EU member states are the main international trade partners of the CEECs, the analysis of the main international trade partners of the EU is also important and relevant. Table 45.9 shows the 20 main partners of the EU-

Table 45.3 Export matrix of the CEECs (Bulgaria, Croatia, Czech Republic, Estonia, Hungary, and Latvia) in 2004–2014

	Bulgaria				Croatia				Czech Republic				Estonia				Hungary				Latvia			
Year	The rest of the world	CIS	EU-28	Euro area	The rest of the world	CIS	EU-28	Euro area	The rest of the world	CIS	EU-28	Euro area	The rest of the world	CIS	EU-28	Euro area	The rest of the world	CIS	EU-28	Euro area	The rest of the world	CIS	EU-28	Euro area
2004	35	3	63	53	32	2	66	59	10	2	87	71	14	8	78	52	12	3	84	66	16	11	73	42
2005	36	3	62	51	35	2	63	56	11	3	86	69	16	8	76	53	14	4	82	63	13	13	74	45
2006	35	3	62	50	34	2	64	55	10	3	86	68	24	9	68	45	14	5	81	61	11	14	75	52
2007	35	5	61	48	38	2	60	51	11	4	86	67	20	10	70	49	14	6	81	60	10	14	76	53
2008	35	5	61	46	37	2	61	52	10	4	86	67	19	12	69	48	14	6	80	58	12	15	73	53
2009	31	4	65	49	37	2	61	53	11	3	85	67	18	13	69	49	14	6	80	59	15	14	72	53
2010	34	5	61	45	36	3	61	54	12	4	84	67	19	13	68	45	15	6	79	57	14	15	71	51
2011	32	5	63	46	37	3	60	52	12	5	83	66	22	12	66	42	17	6	78	55	14	15	72	52
2012	36	5	59	43	37	5	58	50	13	6	81	64	23	13	64	42	16	6	78	55	16	15	69	49
2013	35	5	60	45	35	4	62	52	13	5	81	63	18	13	69	45	17	6	77	56	14	16	70	49
2014	34	4	62	46	33	4	64	53	13	4	82	64	18	13	69	46	17	5	78	57	13	15	72	49

Source: UNCTAD

Table 45.4 Export matrix of the CEECs (Lithuania, Poland, Romania, Slovakia, and Slovenia) in 2004–2014

	Lithuania				Poland				Romania				Slovakia				Slovenia			
Year	The rest of the world	CIS	EU-28	Euro area	The rest of the world	CIS	EU-28	Euro area	The rest of the world	CIS	EU-28	Euro area	The rest of the world	CIS	EU-28	Euro area	The rest of the world	CIS	EU-28	Euro area
2004	16	16	67	46	12	8	81	61	22	2	76	60	10	3	87	56	18	5	77	56
2005	17	19	64	44	12	9	79	59	26	3	71	55	9	3	88	54	17	5	79	57
2006	15	21	64	43	11	9	79	58	25	4	71	54	9	3	87	52	16	5	79	56
2007	11	24	65	44	11	10	79	57	22	5	72	55	9	4	87	52	26	5	69	48
2008	14	26	60	40	11	10	78	57	23	6	71	54	9	6	86	50	29	5	66	45
2009	12	23	64	44	12	8	80	58	21	5	75	58	9	5	86	49	29	4	66	47
2010	12	27	61	41	13	8	79	57	22	5	72	55	10	5	85	48	31	4	65	46
2011	12	28	60	42	13	9	78	56	23	6	71	53	10	5	85	47	31	4	65	46
2012	10	30	61	41	14	10	75	54	24	6	70	52	11	5	84	46	31	5	63	45
2013	13	32	55	36	15	10	75	53	24	6	70	51	12	5	83	45	31	6	63	45
2014	13	32	55	35	15	8	77	55	23	6	71	52	12	4	84	46	30	5	65	45

Source: UNCTAD

Table 45.5 Import matrix of the CEECs (Bulgaria, Croatia, Czech Republic, Estonia, Hungary, and Latvia) in 2004–2014

	Bulgaria				Croatia				Czech Republic				Estonia				Hungary				Latvia			
Year	The rest of the world	CIS	EU-28	Euro area	The rest of the world	CIS	EU-28	Euro area	The rest of the world	CIS	EU-28	Euro area	The rest of the world	CIS	EU-28	Euro area	The rest of the world	CIS	EU-28	Euro area	The rest of the world	CIS	EU-28	Euro area
2004	25	18	57	45	21	8	71	58	22	6	72	60	15	18	67	50	19	7	74	61	10	18	72	53
2005	26	21	54	41	22	10	68	55	21	8	72	59	15	18	68	51	21	9	70	57	8	18	74	55
2006	28	21	51	39	22	11	67	54	21	8	71	57	14	18	68	49	20	10	71	56	9	14	77	57
2007	27	20	52	39	24	11	65	53	23	7	71	57	14	14	73	53	21	9	70	55	9	13	78	59
2008	26	23	51	37	25	11	64	52	24	9	67	54	14	12	74	54	20	11	69	55	8	16	76	57
2009	26	20	54	39	26	11	63	51	26	7	67	54	16	11	73	55	22	9	69	55	9	16	75	56
2010	21	21	59	42	28	12	60	49	29	8	63	50	16	12	72	51	23	9	68	53	10	15	75	56
2011	18	22	59	43	27	11	62	50	28	8	64	51	17	14	69	48	20	10	70	54	9	15	77	58
2012	18	24	59	43	27	10	63	51	27	8	65	51	16	16	69	49	19	11	71	55	8	15	77	59
2013	19	21	60	42	18	8	74	59	27	8	66	51	15	14	71	50	18	10	72	55	8	12	80	60
2014	21	18	61	43	17	7	76	61	27	7	66	51	15	12	73	51	16	9	75	57	8	12	80	58

Source: UNCTAD

Table 45.6 Import matrix of the CEECs (Lithuania, Poland, Romania, Slovakia, and Slovenia) in 2004–2014

	Lithuania				Poland				Romania				Slovakia				Slovenia			
Year	The rest of the world	CIS	EU-28	Euro area	The rest of the world	CIS	EU-28	Euro area	The rest of the world	CIS	EU-28	Euro area	The rest of the world	CIS	EU-28	Euro area	The rest of the world	CIS	EU-28	Euro area
2004	10	27	63	44	21	10	69	55	21	13	66	52	20	12	69	44	21	3	76	61
2005	11	31	58	39	22	12	66	53	23	14	64	50	24	13	63	39	23	3	75	60
2006	9	28	63	42	24	12	64	51	23	13	64	50	28	13	59	36	22	3	75	60
2007	10	22	68	46	25	11	64	51	18	10	71	54	32	10	58	35	24	3	73	58
2008	9	34	58	38	25	12	62	50	18	13	69	51	29	12	59	36	26	2	72	57
2009	8	33	59	39	28	10	62	49	18	9	74	53	36	10	54	31	27	2	71	56
2010	8	36	57	39	29	12	59	47	18	9	73	51	36	11	53	31	37	2	62	48
2011	10	36	55	37	26	15	59	47	17	10	73	51	34	13	53	31	36	2	62	48
2012	7	36	57	38	27	17	57	45	16	10	74	52	38	11	51	31	36	2	62	48
2013	7	33	60	41	28	14	58	46	15	9	76	54	35	11	54	30	36	2	62	48
2014	9	28	64	43	29	13	58	46	15	10	75	54	40	5	56	31	37	2	61	47

Source: UNCTAD

Table 45.7 Intra-EU-28 trade by member state in 2004–2014 (share of export by member state (%))

Country	2004	2005	2006	2007	2008	2009	2010	2011	2012	2013	2014
Germany	22.7	22.6	22.4	23.4	22.8	22.7	22.4	22.3	21.9	21.9	22.4
Netherlands	11.0	11.7	11.6	11.7	12.5	12.5	13.1	13.1	13.6	13.5	13.1
France	11.5	10.6	10.3	10.0	9.8	9.8	9.4	9.3	9.2	9.1	9.0
Belgium	9.1	9.2	8.9	8.9	9.0	9.1	8.8	8.7	8.6	8.7	8.5
Italy	8.5	8.3	8.2	8.4	8.0	7.7	7.6	7.5	7.5	7.4	7.4
United Kingdom	7.9	8.0	8.9	7.0	6.5	6.3	6.5	6.5	6.5	6.2	6.2
Spain	5.2	5.0	4.8	4.9	4.9	5.1	5.2	5.2	5.2	5.3	5.3
Poland	2.3	2.5	2.8	3.0	3.3	3.5	3.7	3.8	3.9	4.1	4.3
Czech Republic	2.3	2.4	2.6	2.9	3.1	3.1	3.3	3.5	3.5	3.5	3.7
Austria	3.4	3.3	3.2	3.3	3.3	3.2	3.3	3.2	3.2	3.3	3.2
Sweden	2.8	2.8	2.8	2.8	2.7	2.5	2.7	2.7	2.7	2.6	2.5
Hungary	1.8	1.9	1.9	2.1	2.1	2.2	2.2	2.2	2.2	2.2	2.3
Slovakia	0.9	1.0	1.2	1.4	1.5	1.6	1.6	1.7	1.9	1.9	1.9
Denmark	2.1	2.2	2.1	2.0	2.0	2.1	1.9	1.9	1.8	1.8	1.8
Ireland	2.5	2.5	2.2	2.1	2.0	2.3	2.0	1.8	1.9	1.7	1.6
Romania	0.7	0.7	0.7	0.8	0.9	1.0	1.1	1.1	1.1	1.2	1.3
Portugal	1.1	1.1	1.1	1.1	1.1	1.1	1.1	1.1	1.1	1.2	1.2
Finland	1.4	1.3	1.4	1.4	1.3	1.1	1.1	1.1	1.1	1.1	1.1
Slovenia	0.5	0.5	0.6	0.6	0.6	0.7	0.7	0.7	0.7	0.7	0.7
Bulgaria	0.2	0.3	0.3	0.3	0.3	0.3	0.4	0.4	0.4	0.5	0.5
Lithuania	0.2	0.3	0.3	0.3	0.4	0.3	0.4	0.4	0.5	0.5	0.5
Greece	0.4	0.4	0.5	0.5	0.5	0.5	0.5	0.4	0.4	0.5	0.4
Luxembourg	0.6	0.6	0.7	0.5	0.6	0.6	0.5	0.4	0.4	0.4	0.4
Estonia	0.2	0.2	0.2	0.2	0.2	0.2	0.2	0.3	0.3	0.3	0.3
Latvia	0.1	0.1	0.1	0.2	0.2	0.2	0.2	0.2	0.2	0.3	0.3
Croatia	0.2	0.2	0.2	0.2	0.2	0.2	0.2	0.2	0.2	0.2	0.2
Cyprus	0.0	0.0	0.0	0.0	0.0	0.0	0.0	0.0	0.0	0.0	0.0
Malta	0.0	0.0	0.0	0.0	0.0	0.0	0.0	0.0	0.0	0.0	0.0

Source: Eurostat

28 expressed in percent of the total export flow. The main export partners of the EU are the United States, China, Switzerland, Russia, and Turkey. The analysis of export structure of the EU reveals the growing role of China and Russia as export partners, whereas the role of the United States is slowly decreasing. The analysis of the export structure of the EU suggests that the shocks originated in the United States, China, Switzerland, Russia, and Turkey could be transmitted indirectly to the CEECs through international trade relations with the EU.

Table 45.10 shows the 20 main partners of the EU-28 expressed in percent of the total import flow. The main import partners of the EU are China, the United States, and Russia. During the last two decades, the increasing role of China and Russia as import partners of the EU is observed, whereas the role of the United States is

Table 45.8 Intra-EU-28 trade by member state in 2004–2014 (share of import by member state (%))

Country	2004	2005	2006	2007	2008	2009	2010	2011	2012	2013	2014
Germany	18.8	18.7	18.9	19.0	19.3	20.0	20.3	20.8	20.7	20.9	21.0
France	13.1	12.7	12.3	12.2	12.5	13.1	12.7	12.7	12.7	12.5	12.2
United Kingdom	10.6	10.8	11.3	9.6	8.6	8.6	8.8	8.6	9.3	9.3	9.6
Belgium	8.3	8.5	8.2	8.1	8.3	8.3	8.2	8.2	8.3	8.2	7.8
Italy	8.9	8.6	8.4	8.3	7.9	8.0	8.2	7.9	7.3	7.2	7.1
Netherlands	6.8	6.7	6.6	6.8	7.1	7.3	7.3	7.2	7.5	7.4	7.1
Spain	7.0	6.9	6.6	6.8	6.4	6.1	5.9	5.6	5.1	5.1	5.4
Poland	2.7	2.8	3.0	3.4	3.8	3.6	3.8	3.8	3.8	3.9	4.0
Austria	4.0	3.8	3.6	3.6	3.7	3.7	3.8	3.9	3.8	3.8	3.7
Czech Republic	2.2	2.3	2.5	2.6	2.8	2.7	2.9	3.0	3.0	3.0	3.1
Sweden	2.9	2.9	2.9	3.0	3.0	2.7	3.0	3.1	3.1	3.0	3.0
Hungary	1.7	1.7	1.8	1.9	1.9	1.8	1.8	1.9	1.9	2.0	2.1
Denmark	1.9	2.0	2.0	2.0	2.0	1.9	1.8	1.8	1.8	1.8	1.8
Slovakia	0.9	1.0	1.1	1.3	1.4	1.4	1.4	1.5	1.6	1.6	1.6
Portugal	1.7	1.8	1.8	1.8	1.8	1.9	1.8	1.6	1.5	1.5	1.5
Romania	0.9	1.0	1.1	1.4	1.5	1.3	1.4	1.5	1.5	1.5	1.5
Finland	1.4	1.5	1.5	1.5	1.5	1.3	1.3	1.4	1.3	1.4	1.4
Ireland	1.6	1.7	1.6	1.6	1.5	1.4	1.2	1.2	1.2	1.3	1.3
Greece	1.4	1.3	1.3	1.3	1.4	1.4	1.1	0.9	0.8	0.8	0.8
Bulgaria	0.3	0.4	0.4	0.5	0.5	0.5	0.5	0.5	0.5	0.6	0.6
Lithuania	0.3	0.3	0.4	0.5	0.5	0.4	0.4	0.5	0.5	0.6	0.6
Luxembourg	0.6	0.6	0.6	0.6	0.6	0.6	0.6	0.6	0.6	0.6	0.6
Slovenia	0.6	0.6	0.6	0.7	0.7	0.7	0.7	0.7	0.6	0.6	0.6
Estonia	0.2	0.3	0.3	0.3	0.3	0.3	0.3	0.3	0.4	0.4	0.4
Croatia	0.5	0.5	0.5	0.5	0.5	0.4	0.4	0.4	0.4	0.4	0.4
Latvia	0.2	0.2	0.3	0.3	0.3	0.2	0.3	0.3	0.4	0.4	0.4
Cyprus	0.2	0.2	0.2	0.2	0.2	0.2	0.2	0.2	0.1	0.1	0.1
Malta	0.1	0.1	0.1	0.1	0.1	0.1	0.1	0.1	0.1	0.1	0.1

Source: Eurostat

slowly decreasing. The role of Russia as import partner of the EU is increasing every year, while this country is the most important crude oil, natural gas, and oil product exporter. The analysis of the import structure of the EU shows that import portfolio of the EU is less diversified compared to the export portfolio.

The trade complementarity index can provide useful information on prospects for intraregional trade in that it shows how well the structures of a country's imports and exports match. The analysis results reveal that the best trade partners for the CEECs are their neighboring countries (see Table 45.11). Two countries with a high index may gain from trade expansion following a preferential trade agreement. However, a high complementarity index may not imply a gain from increased trade, if the two partners are at distant locations or with high transportation and transaction costs. A

Table 45.9 Extra-EU-28 trade by main partners in 2004–2014 (share of export by partner (%))

Partner	2004	2005	2006	2007	2008	2009	2010	2011	2012	2013	2014
United States	24.9	23.9	23.2	21.0	18.9	18.6	17.9	17.0	17.4	16.7	18.3
China	5.1	4.9	5.5	5.8	6.0	7.5	8.4	8.8	8.6	8.5	9.7
Switzerland	8.0	8.2	7.7	7.5	7.7	8.1	8.2	9.1	7.9	9.7	8.2
Russia	4.9	5.4	6.3	7.2	8.0	6.0	6.4	7.0	7.3	6.9	6.1
Turkey	4.3	4.3	4.3	4.3	4.2	4.1	4.6	4.7	4.5	4.5	4.4
Japan	4.6	4.2	3.9	3.5	3.2	3.3	3.3	3.2	3.3	3.1	3.1
Norway	3.3	3.2	3.3	3.5	3.3	3.4	3.1	3.0	3.0	2.9	2.9
South Korea	1.9	1.9	2.0	2.0	1.9	2.0	2.1	2.1	2.2	2.3	2.5
United Arab Emirates	2.0	2.5	2.2	2.2	2.5	2.3	2.1	2.1	2.2	2.6	2.5
Brazil	1.5	1.5	1.5	1.7	2.0	2.0	2.3	2.3	2.4	2.3	2.2
India	1.8	2.0	2.1	2.4	2.4	2.5	2.6	2.6	2.3	2.1	2.1
Saudi Arabia	1.3	1.5	1.5	1.6	1.6	1.7	1.7	1.7	1.8	1.9	2.1
Hong Kong	2.0	1.9	1.9	1.7	1.7	1.8	2.0	2.0	2.0	2.1	2.0
Canada	2.3	2.2	2.3	2.1	1.9	2.0	2.0	1.9	1.9	1.8	1.9
Singapore	1.7	1.6	1.7	1.7	1.7	1.9	1.8	1.8	1.8	1.7	1.7
Mexico	1.6	1.6	1.7	1.7	1.7	1.5	1.6	1.5	1.7	1.6	1.7
Australia	2.1	2.0	1.9	1.9	2.0	2.0	2.0	2.0	2.0	1.8	1.7
Algeria	1.0	1.0	0.9	0.9	1.2	1.4	1.2	1.1	1.3	1.3	1.4
South Africa	1.7	1.7	1.7	1.7	1.6	1.4	1.6	1.7	1.5	1.4	1.4
Nigeria	0.6	0.6	0.6	0.7	0.8	0.8	0.8	0.8	0.7	0.7	0.7

Source: Eurostat

high complementarity index may also be misleading if the size difference of two economies is large (i.e., a match in percentage terms does not imply a match in levels).

Merchandise trade correlation index is used to measure similarity of trade specialization index between economies. High similarity then can be considered that those economies compete in other in both exports and imports. Consequently, a negative value suggests that the economies do not specialize in the production/consumption of the same goods and are therefore natural trading partners. Analyzing merchandise trade correlation index of the CEECs, two groups of countries have been included in the analysis: CIS and EU-28 countries. The highest values among the CEECs indicate that the CEECs are competitors in global market since this group of countries are net exporters of the same set of products (see Table 45.12).

The long-run relationship among the CEECs' and EU (including euro area (EA)) member states' economies was explored by testing for cointegration among the quarterly real GDP growth (seasonally adjusted and adjusted by working days). Table 45.13 gives the summarized results of the CEECs' economic integration of all five trend assumption options. Slovakia is excluded due to the data availability. The results of the Johansen cointegration test suggest that the long-run relationship among the CEECs and EU exists.

Table 45.10 Extra-EU-28 trade by main partners in 2004–2014 (share of import by partner (%))

Partner	2004	2005	2006	2007	2008	2009	2010	2011	2012	2013	2014
China	12.6	13.6	14.3	16.2	15.7	17.4	18.5	17.1	16.3	16.6	18.0
United States	15.5	13.4	12.5	12.3	11.5	12.6	11.3	11.1	11.5	11.6	12.2
Russia	8.3	9.6	10.5	10.2	11.4	9.7	10.6	11.6	12.0	12.3	10.8
Switzerland	6.1	5.6	5.2	5.3	5.2	6.5	5.6	5.4	5.9	5.6	5.7
Norway	5.4	5.7	5.8	5.3	6.1	5.6	5.2	5.4	5.6	5.4	5.0
Turkey	3.2	3.1	3.1	3.3	2.9	2.9	2.8	2.8	2.7	3.0	3.2
Japan	7.3	6.3	5.7	5.5	4.8	4.7	4.4	4.1	3.6	3.4	3.2
South Korea	3.0	2.9	3.0	2.9	2.5	2.6	2.6	2.1	2.1	2.1	2.3
India	1.6	1.6	1.7	1.8	1.9	2.1	2.2	2.3	2.1	2.2	2.2
Brazil	2.1	2.0	2.0	2.3	2.3	2.1	2.2	2.3	2.1	2.0	1.9
Saudi Arabia	1.6	1.9	1.7	1.3	1.4	1.0	1.1	1.6	1.9	1.8	1.7
Algeria	1.5	1.8	1.8	1.4	1.8	1.4	1.4	1.6	1.8	1.9	1.7
Nigeria	0.5	0.7	0.8	0.7	1.0	0.8	0.9	1.4	1.8	1.7	1.7
Canada	1.6	1.5	1.5	1.7	1.6	1.6	1.6	1.8	1.7	1.6	1.6
Mexico	0.7	0.8	0.8	0.8	0.9	0.8	0.9	1.0	1.1	1.0	1.1
South Africa	1.5	1.5	1.5	1.5	1.6	1.6	1.3	1.3	1.1	0.9	1.1
Singapore	1.6	1.6	1.4	1.3	1.0	1.2	1.2	1.1	1.2	1.0	1.0
Hong Kong	1.0	1.0	1.0	0.8	0.8	1.1	0.9	0.6	0.6	0.6	0.6
United Arab Emirates	0.5	0.8	0.4	0.4	0.4	0.3	0.4	0.5	0.5	0.5	0.5
Australia	0.9	0.8	1.0	0.9	0.9	0.8	0.8	0.9	0.8	0.6	0.5

Source: Eurostat

The empirical results on external macroeconomic shocks transmission through real channel in the CEECs using fixed effects panel regression models are presented in Table 45.14. The empirical results suggest that the economic growth in the main export countries positively affects the real GDP growth in CEECs and real export flows. An increase in inflation in the main export countries suggests about increasing prices on products and services in these countries, thus, an increase of export flows from CEECs into these countries. Economic theory suggests that increasing prices foster an increase of export flows, while exporters are more interested in exporting their products and services to markets with higher price level.

The empirical results on macroeconomic shocks (different GDP components) transmission suggest that an increase of consumption in the main export countries positively affects the real GDP growth in the CEECs; however, a negative impact of consumption on the real export flows to the main export countries is observed. The statistically significant positive impact of investment growth on real GDP and real export flows growth of the CEECs is observed. In addition, the effect of macroeconomic shocks is more significant on real export flows.

However, some empirical results are quite diverse. The exchange rate shock (depreciation of the currencies of the main export partners) positively affects the real GDP growth of CEECs; however, these results are not consistent with the economic theory suggesting that depreciation of foreign currencies decrease the export flows

Table 45.11 Trade complementarity index (I) of CEECs in 2013

	Exporters							
	Bulgaria	I	Croatia	I	Czech Republic	I	Estonia	I
Importers	Estonia	0.6	Slovenia	0.6	Austria	0.6	Latvia	0.6
	Latvia	0.6	Republic of Moldova	0.6	Slovakia	0.6	Denmark	0.6
	Republic of Moldova	0.6	Latvia	0.6	Russian Federation	0.6	Luxembourg	0.6
	Slovenia	0.6	Estonia	0.6	Romania	0.6	Sweden	0.6
	Denmark	0.6	Denmark	0.6	Hungary	0.6	Slovenia	0.6
	Kyrgyzstan	0.5	Austria	0.5	Sweden	0.6	Finland	0.6
	Cyprus	0.5	Luxembourg	0.5	Poland	0.6	Republic of Moldova	0.6
	Armenia	0.5	Kyrgyzstan	0.5	Germany	0.6	Hungary	0.5
	Croatia	0.5	Ukraine	0.5	Kazakhstan	0.6	Austria	0.5
	Finland	0.5	Finland	0.5	Denmark	0.6	Turkmenistan	0.5
	Exporters							
	Hungary	I	Latvia	I	Lithuania		Poland	I
Importers	Romania	0.7	Estonia	0.6	Cyprus	0.7	Austria	0.7
	Sweden	0.6	Slovenia	0.6	Kyrgyzstan	0.6	Czech Republic	0.7
	Czech Republic	0.6	Denmark	0.6	Estonia	0.6	Denmark	0.6
	Slovakia	0.6	Sweden	0.6	Republic of Moldova	0.6	Russian Federation	0.6
	Russian Federation	0.6	Republic of Moldova	0.6	Latvia	0.6	Sweden	0.6
	Germany	0.6	Luxembourg	0.6	Denmark	0.6	Slovakia	0.6
	Poland	0.6	Finland	0.5	Luxembourg	0.6	Romania	0.6
	Austria	0.6	United Kingdom	0.5	Slovenia	0.6	Germany	0.6
	United Kingdom	0.6	Germany	0.5	Netherlands	0.6	Portugal	0.6
	Slovenia	0.6	Austria	0.5	Croatia	0.6	Croatia	0.6
	Exporters							
	Romania	I	Slovakia	I	Slovenia	I		
Importers	Sweden	0.6	Austria	0.6	Latvia	0.6		
	Uzbekistan	0.6	Sweden	0.6	Austria	0.6		
	Germany	0.6	Czech Republic	0.6	Sweden	0.6		
	Austria	0.6	Hungary	0.6	Russian Federation	0.6		
	Russian Federation	0.6	Romania	0.5	Hungary	0.6		
	Slovenia	0.6	Russian Federation	0.5	Romania	0.6		
	Denmark	0.6	France	0.5	Germany	0.6		
	Poland	0.5	Germany	0.5	Denmark	0.5		
	Estonia	0.5	Estonia	0.5	Estonia	0.5		
	United Kingdom	0.5	Poland	0.5	Luxembourg	0.5		

Source: UNCTAD

Table 45.12 Merchandise trade correlation index of CEECs in 2012

Country	Bulgaria	Croatia	Czech Republic	Estonia	Hungary	Latvia	Lithuania	Poland	Romania	Slovakia	Slovenia
Armenia	0.15	0.18	0.01	0.13	0.01	0.11	0.07	0.04	0.14	0.01	−0.05
Austria	−0.02	0.09	0.12	−0.01	0.03	0.00	−0.04	−0.01	0.03	0.14	0.18
Azerbaijan	−0.07	−0.04	−0.30	−0.13	−0.16	−0.10	−0.13	−0.14	−0.10	−0.10	−0.20
Belarus	0.02	0.11	0.08	0.14	0.05	0.20	0.34	0.20	0.17	0.13	0.02
Belgium	−0.09	−0.19	−0.18	−0.12	−0.02	−0.08	−0.02	0.05	−0.21	−0.07	−0.10
Bulgaria		0.25	0.22	0.29	0.33	0.11	0.37	0.25	0.45	0.21	0.06
Croatia	0.25		0.26	0.40	0.24	0.31	0.34	0.21	0.31	0.20	0.13
Cyprus	0.04	0.20	0.00	0.10	−0.01	0.05	0.02	−0.03	0.01	−0.05	−0.04
Czech Republic	0.22	0.26		0.32	0.37	0.18	0.22	0.31	0.34	0.35	0.24
Denmark	0.16	0.21	0.10	0.18	0.18	−0.04	0.16	0.08	0.05	−0.10	0.09
Estonia	0.29	0.40	0.32		0.26	0.43	0.33	0.28	0.29	0.24	0.16
Finland	0.06	0.17	0.07	0.16	0.05	0.10	0.01	0.04	−0.02	0.18	0.13
France	0.11	0.23	0.17	0.07	0.19	0.10	0.08	0.06	0.11	0.16	0.17
Germany	−0.05	0.10	0.26	0.01	0.03	−0.09	0.02	0.17	−0.04	0.09	0.20
Greece	0.09	0.09	0.02	0.05	−0.03	0.06	0.01	0.00	0.02	0.06	−0.10
Hungary	0.33	0.24	0.37	0.26		0.00	0.19	0.25	0.37	0.30	0.13
Ireland	0.03	0.11	0.08	0.16	0.09	0.15	0.14	−0.05	−0.09	−0.12	0.09
Italy	−0.01	0.08	0.02	−0.14	0.01	−0.11	0.04	0.08	−0.07	0.03	0.19
Kazakhstan	0.00	0.09	−0.12	0.12	−0.12	0.12	−0.03	−0.06	0.03	0.04	−0.20
Kyrgyzstan	0.13	0.11	0.00	0.14	0.05	0.06	0.02	0.06	0.03	−0.05	−0.05
Latvia	0.11	0.31	0.18	0.43	0.00		0.42	0.21	0.19	0.16	0.27
Lithuania	0.37	0.34	0.22	0.33	0.19	0.42		0.38	0.35	0.18	0.16
Luxembourg	−0.04	0.00	0.03	0.04	−0.08	0.15	0.01	−0.05	−0.09	0.03	0.18

Malta	−0.01	0.08	0.08	0.04	0.00	0.04	−0.05	−0.10	−0.02	0.03	0.15
Netherlands	−0.15	0.01	−0.06	−0.07	0.01	−0.13	0.01	0.02	−0.16	−0.04	−0.17
Poland	0.25	0.21	0.31	0.28	0.25	0.21	0.38		0.27	0.25	0.07
Portugal	0.13	0.26	0.21	0.17	0.19	0.05	0.06	0.19	0.17	0.16	0.15
Republic of Moldova	0.42	0.24	0.11	0.21	0.27	0.12	0.19	0.10	0.36	0.04	0.04
Romania	0.45	0.31	0.34	0.29	0.37	0.19	0.35	0.27		0.48	0.14
Russian Federation	0.11	0.13	0.06	0.14	−0.18	0.12	−0.06	−0.04	0.15	0.08	−0.20
Slovakia	0.21	0.20	0.35	0.24	0.30	0.16	0.18	0.25	0.48		0.12
Slovenia	0.06	0.13	0.24	0.16	0.13	0.27	0.16	0.07	0.14	0.12	
Spain	0.04	0.00	−0.02	−0.12	0.00	−0.04	−0.09	0.15	−0.11	−0.02	0.15
Sweden	0.12	0.18	0.11	0.13	0.00	0.06	0.07	0.04	0.05	0.07	0.18
Tajikistan	−0.01	0.14	−0.04	0.04	0.05	0.07	0.01	−0.02	0.08	−0.03	−0.10
Turkmenistan	0.07	−0.08	−0.20	0.02	−0.07	−0.06	−0.05	−0.12	−0.05	−0.12	−0.09
Ukraine	0.34	0.22	0.21	0.25	0.17	0.22	0.21	0.21	0.33	0.25	−0.06
United Kingdom	−0.07	0.17	0.13	0.01	−0.03	−0.01	−0.06	−0.16	−0.02	0.01	0.10
Uzbekistan	0.14	0.07	−0.14	−0.05	−0.07	0.04	0.03	−0.01	−0.07	−0.05	−0.24

Source: UNCTAD

Table 45.13 The summarized results of the CEECs' economic integration using Johansen cointegration test (a number of cointegrating relations (equations))

		None		None		Linear		Linear		Quadratic	
	Data trend	No intercept No trend		Intercept No trend		Intercept No trend		Intercept Trend		Intercept Trend	
Country	Test type	EU-28	EA	EU-28	EA	EU-28	EA	EU-28	EA	EU-28	EA
Bulgaria	Johansen trace statistic	2	1	2	1	2	2	2	1	2	2
	Max-Eigen statistic	2	1	2	1	2	2	0	1	0	2
Czech Republic	Johansen trace statistic	1	1	2	1	2	2	1	1	2	2
	Max-Eigen statistic	1	1	2	1	2	2	0	1	0	2
Estonia	Johansen trace statistic	2	2	1	1	2	2	0	0	2	2
	Max-Eigen statistic	2	0	0	0	2	2	0	0	0	0
Croatia	Johansen trace statistic	2	1	1	1	2	2	1	1	2	2
	Max-Eigen statistic	0	0	0	0	0	0	1	0	2	0
Latvia	Johansen trace statistic	2	1	1	1	2	2	1	1	2	2
	Max-Eigen statistic	0	1	1	1	2	2	0	0	2	2
Lithuania	Johansen trace statistic	2	1	2	2	2	2	2	1	2	2
	Max-Eigen statistic	2	1	2	0	2	0	2	0	2	2
Hungary	Johansen trace statistic	1	2	1	1	2	2	1	2	2	2
	Max-Eigen statistic	1	2	1	0	2	0	1	0	2	2
Poland	Johansen trace statistic	0	1	0	0	2	2	0	0	2	2
	Max-Eigen statistic	0	1	0	0	0	0	0	0	0	0
Romania	Johansen trace statistic	1	1	0	1	2	2	1	2	2	2
	Max-Eigen statistic	1	1	0	0	0	2	1	2	2	2
Slovenia	Johansen trace statistic	1	1	1	1	2	2	2	1	2	2
	Max-Eigen statistic	1	1	1	1	2	2	0	1	2	2

Source: author's calculation

Notes. There have been two statistics used (trace statistic and maximum eigenvalue statistic) in order to denote the rejection of the hypothesis at the 0.1 level

Table 45.14 The empirical results of fixed effects panel regression models

	Dependent variable – real GDP change (RGDP)		Dependent variable – real total export of goods change (REXPORT)	
Variable	Model 1	Model 2	Model 3	Model 4
C	−11.1176 (12.3299)	−21.7366 (14.4684)	−64.7453 (56.3376)	−47.6986 (52.3682)
GDP_S	1.59973***(0.12325)		5.83834***(0.5632)	
CONSUMPTION_S		1.2549***(0.2859)		−0.2774 (1.0349)
EXPORT_S		−0.2594**(0.0995)		0.3867 (0.3602)
INVESTMENT_S		0.4300***(0.09354)		1.5615***(0.3386)
EXCHANGE_S	0.21324***(0.06885)	0.1470*(0.0784)	−1.5670***(0.3146)	−1.7025***(0.2838)
INFLATION_S	0.43214*(0.22321)	0.2884 (0.2746)	2.1332**(1.0199)	2.4194**(0.9939)
TERMS_OF_TRADE	0.07233 (0.11195)	0.1199 (0.1295)	0.5500 (0.5115)	0.4329 (0.4686)
TRADE_OPENNESS	0.02205 (0.01971)	0.0840***(0.0241)	0.0169 (0.0900)	0.0163 (0.0871)
Country FE	Yes	Yes	Yes	Yes
Year FE	No	No	No	No
Observations	110	110	110	110
R^2	0.7980	0.7423	0.7451	0.7959
S.E. of regression	2.4289	2.7734	11.098	10.0382

Standard errors in parentheses. $^{***}p < 0.01$, $^{**}p < 0.05$, $^{*}p < 0.1$

to these countries and, thus, decrease the real GDP growth of exporting countries. However, the empirical results presented in Table 45.14 show that depreciation of foreign currencies decrease the export flows to these countries.

45.5 Conclusions

The CEECs (Bulgaria, Czech Republic, Estonia, Hungary, Latvia, Lithuania, Slovakia, and Slovenia) are one the most open economies worldwide (except Croatia, Poland, and Romania). Due to the high degree of economic openness, the CEECs are vulnerable to the external shocks that can be transmitted through international trade channel. Some of the CEECs, e.g., Lithuania, are more prone to the external shocks through real channel because it's import and export portfolio is less diversified compared to other CEECs. The largest share of export of the CEECs goes to EU-28 and euro zone countries suggesting that the shocks from the EU countries can be directly transmitted to the CEECs. The analysis of the import and export portfolio of the CEECs reveals that the main international trade partners of this group of countries are EU member states. Despite the fact that EU member states are the main international trade partners of the CEECs, the analysis of the export structure of the EU suggests that the shocks originated in the United States, China, Switzerland, Russia, and Turkey could be indirectly transmitted to the CEECs through international trade relations with the EU. The analysis of the trade complementarity index reveals that the best trade partners for the CEECs are their neighboring countries. The high values of the merchandise trade correlation among the CEEC indices indicate that the CEECs are competitors in global market since this group of countries are net exporters of the same set of products.

The results of the Johansen cointegration test suggest that the long-run relationship among the CEECs and EU exists. There are some recommendations for the CEECs in order to be less prone to the external shocks transmission through international trade channel. Firstly, CEECs should extend the products in which they have a trade potential or extend potential trade prospects with new trade partners. Secondly, CEECs can also focus attention on other nontraditional products that might be successfully exported. Thirdly, CEECs should extend their international trade relations with the foreign countries outside the EU which economic cycles differ from the EU and the largest world economies (United States, China, etc.).

The empirical results on macroeconomic shocks transmission through international trade channels in the CEECs suggest that the exchange rate shock positively affects the real GDP growth in the CEECs; however, depreciation of the currencies of the main export partners decrease the export flows to these countries. The economic growth in the main export countries positively affects the real GDP growth and real export flows in CEECs. An increase in consumption in the main export countries positively affects the real GDP growth in the CEECs; however, a negative impact of consumption on the real export flows to the main export countries is observed. In addition, the effect of macroeconomic shocks is more significant on real export flows.

Acknowledgment This research was funded by a grant (No. MIP-016/2015) from the Research Council of Lithuania.

References

Albulescu, C. T. (2011). Economic and financial integration of CEECs: The impact of financial instability. *AUCO Czech Economic Review, 5*, 27–45.

Clemente, J., Pueyo, F., & Sanz, F. (2009). Market potential, European union and growth. *Journal of Policy Modeling, 31*(5), 719–730. https://doi.org/10.1016/j.jpolmod.2009.04.002.

Corsetti, G., Pesenti, P., Roubini, N., & Tille, C. (1998). Competitive devaluation: A welfare based approach. NBER WP No 6889, 1998. doi: https://doi.org/10.3386/w6889.

De Santis, R. (2004). Trade as international transmission mechanism of shocks: The case of central Eastern European Countries. Doctoral dissertation. doi: https://doi.org/10.2139/ssrn.602341.

Elliott, G., & Fatás, A. (1996). International business cycles and the dynamics of the current account. *European Economic Review, 40*(2), 361–387. https://doi.org/10.1016/0014-2921(95)00123-9.

Engle, R. F., & Granger, C. W. J. (1987). Co-integration and error correction: Representation, estimation, and testing. *Econometrica, 55*, 251–276. https://doi.org/10.2307/1913236.

Ezcurra, R., & Rodríguez-Pose, A. (2013). Does economic globalization affect regional inequality? A cross-country analysis. *World Development, 52*, 92–103. https://doi.org/10.1016/j.worlddev.2013.07.002.

Feldkircher, M. (2015). A global macro model for emerging Europe. *Journal of Comparative Economics, 43*((3) (8)), 706–726. https://doi.org/10.1016/j.jce.2014.09.002.

Fetahi-Vehapi, M., Sadiku, L., & Petkovski, M. (2015). Empirical analysis of the effects of trade openness on economic growth: An evidence for South East European Countries. *Procedia Economics and Finance, 19*, 17–26. https://doi.org/10.1016/s2212-5671(15)00004-0.

Grubel, H. G., & Lloyd, P. J. (1975). *Intra-industry trade: the theory and measurement of international trade in differentiated products*. New York: Wiley. ISBN 0-470-33000-7.

Johansen, S. (1991). Estimation and hypothesis testing of cointegration vectors in Gaussian vector autoregressive models. *Econometrica, 59*, 1551–1580. https://doi.org/10.2307/2938278.

Johansen, S. (1995). *Likelihood-based inference in cointegrated vector autoregressive models*. Oxford: Oxford University Press. https://doi.org/10.1093/0198774508.001.0001.

Martínez-Zarzoso, I., Voicu, A. M., & Vidovic, M. (2011). CEECs integration into regional and global production networks. Discussion papers number 125. doi: https://doi.org/10.2139/ssrn.1850623.

Michaely, M. (1996). *Trade preferential agreements in Latin America: An ex-ante assessment*. World Bank Policy Research Working Paper.

Monfort, M., Cuestas, J. C., & Ordóñez, J. (2013). Real convergence in Europe: A cluster analysis. *Economic Modelling, 33*, 689–694. https://doi.org/10.1016/j.econmod.2013.05.015.

Rozmahel, P., Kouba, L., Grochová, L., & Najman, N. (2013). *Integration of central and Eastern European Countries: Increasing EU heterogeneity?* Working paper no. 9.

Tajoli, L., & De Benedictis, L. (2006). *Economic integration and similarity in trade structures*. Working paper 54. doi: https://doi.org/10.2139/ssrn.896669.

Van Ewijk, S. E., & Arnold, I. J. M. (2015). Financial integration in the Euro area: Pro-cyclical effects and economic convergence. *Economic Modelling, 44*, 335–342. https://doi.org/10.1016/j.econmod.2014.05.026.

Zoltán, J. M., Kovács, M. A., & Oszlay, A. (2001). How far has trade integration advanced? An analysis of the actual and potential trade of three central and Eastern European Countries. *Journal of Comparative Economics, 29*(2), 276–292. doi: https://doi.org/10.1006/jcec.2001.1709.

Chapter 46
Investment and Economic Growth

Carlos Encinas-Ferrer and Eddie Villegas-Zermeño

Abstract The variable gross investment or gross fixed capital formation is composed of two elements: the investment for replacement of the fixed capital consumed and new physical capital investment or net fixed capital formation. The latter is supposed to be the investment that allows the growth of productive capacity and, therefore, of economic growth in the medium and long term.

In this paper, we perform a statistical and econometric study of the variables mentioned to know their trends and determine if there is indeed a causal relationship between the net fixed capital formation and economic growth, the former being the independent variable.

We conducted our analysis on three countries: the USA, the Republic of Korea, and Brazil.

Keywords Gross national income · Adjusted net national income · Gross fixed capital formation · Fixed capital consumption · Net fixed capital formation · Economic growth

C. Encinas-Ferrer (✉)
Universidad del Valle de Atemajac Campus León, León, Gto, Mexico
e-mail: cencinasmx@yahoo.com.mx

E. Villegas-Zermeño
Departamento de Ciencias Económico Administrativas, Universidad Iberoamericana León, León, Gto, Mexico
e-mail: eddie.villegasz@gmail.com

N. Tsounis, A. Vlachvei (eds.), *Advances in Panel Data Analysis in Applied Economic Research*, Springer Proceedings in Business and Economics,
https://doi.org/10.1007/978-3-319-70055-7_46

46.1 Introduction

In an earlier research (Encinas-Ferrer and Villegas-Zermeño 2015),[1] concerning the causal relationship between foreign direct investment (FDI) and economic growth (EG), we confirm the results of previous researches carried out by several investigators. We used the Toda-Yamamoto (1995) test, and no causal relationship was found between FDI and EG.

This led us to verify if, using the same test, we would find results that showed the causality in the case of net fixed capital formation (NFCF), as an independent variable, and economic growth (EG) as the dependent one.

We wanted to check the validity of the model in a fully accepted relationship; the NFCF is the only dynamic variable in the macroeconomic equality GNI = C + I + G + (x-m), meaning GNI the gross national income and *I* the gross fixed capital formation (GFCF), formerly gross domestic fixed investment according to World Bank. To obtain the NFCF, we must subtract the consumption of fixed capital (FCC).

From the World Bank (WB) statistics, we obtained the FCC by subtracting the adjusted national net income (ANNI) from GNI. The result of this subtraction gives us not only the FCC but also the consumption or depletion of nonrenewable natural resources according to the studies updated in April of 2017 by the researchers of that international organization.

We subtract the above figures from the gross fixed capital formation (GFCF), and we obtain an approximate figure of the NFCF on which we have worked.

As we progressed in the construction of our tables, we observed behaviors and trends that led us to present a statistical analysis first and then to show the results of the econometric one.

46.2 Statistical Analysis

GNI,[2] as calculated by the World Bank, will serve as the initial variable of our analysis. At the same time, we will deduct the figures from the adjusted net national income (ANNI), recently updated by the researchers of that international organization and calculated from 1970. From the subtraction arises not only

[1]Carlos Encinas-Ferrer and Eddie Villegas Zermeño (2015), "*Foreign direct investment and gross domestic growth,*" International Conference on Applied Economics (ICOAE 2015) in Kazan, Russia, July 2–4, 2015. Elsevier, Procedia Economics and Finance, Science Direct Vol. 24, pp. 198–207.

[2]GNI (formerly GNP) is the sum of value added by all resident producers plus any product taxes (less subsidies) not included in the valuation of output plus net receipts of primary income (compensation of employees and property income) from abroad. Data are in constant 2010 US dollars (World Bank).

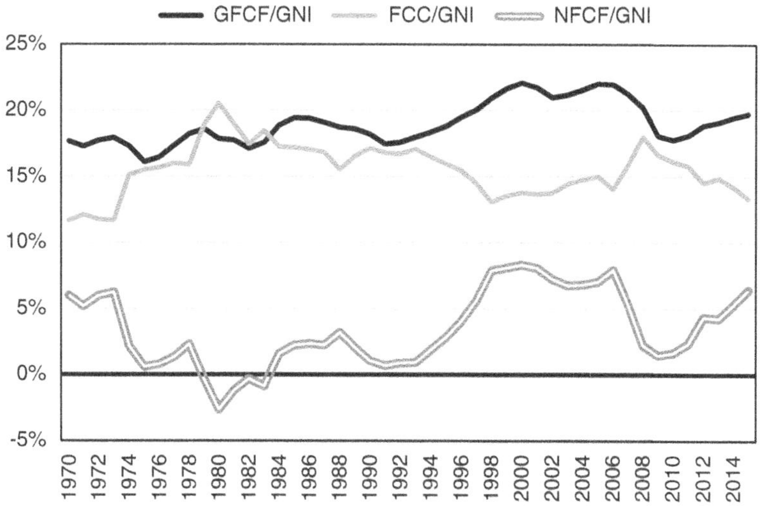

Fig. 46.1 USA: Coefficients GFCF/GNI, FCC/GNI, and NFCF/GNI (Source: Own elaboration with data from World Bank)

the consumption of fixed capital but also the depletion of nonrenewable natural resources.

That result is subtracted from GFCF, and we get NFCF which allows us to have a clearer view of long-term economic growth. The tables obtained are presented in the Appendix at the end of the article.

46.2.1 The USA

In Fig. 46.1 (derived from Table 46.1 in Appendix 1), we present the evolution of the GFCF/GN, FCC/GNI, and NFCF/GNI coefficients from 1970 to 2015.

GFCF has fluctuated around 20% of GNI but with a tendency to increase slightly. The average of the studied period is 19%. FCC has fluctuated around 15% of the GNI with a mean during the 46 studied years of 15.6%.

Regarding NFCF/GNI in relation to FCC/GNI, we observe a strong negative correlation between the two variables, which is −0.847.

Analyzing the absolute numbers in USS$ 2010 constant billions of dollars (trillions of dollars in the terminology USA), a very interesting phenomenon appears; throughout the studied period, the net investment in fixed capital has been inferior to the consumption of fixed capital and of natural resources (Fig. 46.2).

We have verified this phenomenon with various sources of information such as the tables of the Federal Reserve Economic Data (FRED) of St. Louis Fed, and it

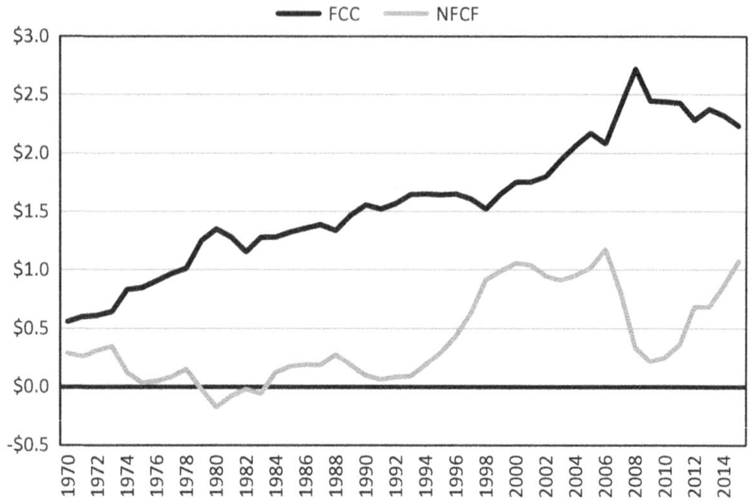

Fig. 46.2 USA: FCC and NFCF in US$ trillions of 2010 dollars (Source: Own elaboration with data from World Bank)

also appears this phenomenon has important environmental implications on the low rates of economic growth that we are observing worldwide.

In the case of the USA, as in other countries, we should note the strong correlation between the GNI and the consumption of fixed capital and natural resources that reaches 0.956. This figure tells us about the reality of actual unsustainable growth.

The Causal Link Between Gross National Income (GNI) and Net Fixed Capital Formation (NFCF) in the USA (1971–2015)

In the period between 1971 and 2015, the GNI in the USA grows continuously, while the NFCF increases and decreases sinusoidal.

Overall, there would appear to be a direct correlation between the GNI and the NFCF for the USA between 1971 and 2015 as noted in Fig. 46.3.

46.2.1.1 Estimation of Causality

For the specific cases of the GNI and the NFCF, the graphical test shows in both cases a growth during the period of study, although one the growth is constant and the second sinusoidal; that is, the series would appear to be nonstationary. Before verifying the VAR model, it is necessary to determine that these variables are stationary or in their absence if they are with some lags. To do this, we will perform the unit root tests for both variables. To do this, we will use the Dickey-Fuller (1979) test augmented with the Schwarz criterion.

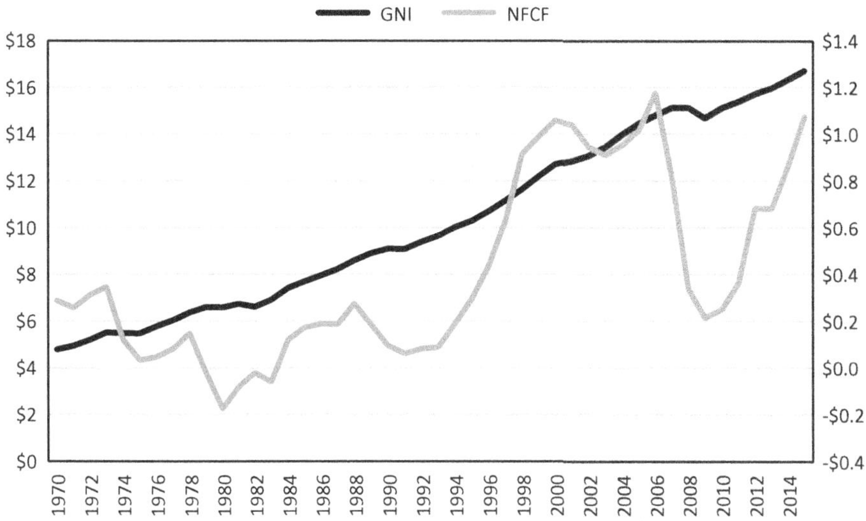

Fig. 46.3 USA GNI and NFCF in trillions of 2010 US$ dollars (Source: Own elaboration with data from World Bank)

In Tables 46.2 and 46.3 of the Appendix, we observe that the GNI and NFCF variables do not have unit roots in first differences, so we go in Table 46.4 to the stage of the self-regressive vectors (VAR) in which we find the result of a model of autoregressive vectors (VAR), missing to determine exactly the number of lags, for which we used the Akaike, Schwarz, and Hannan test (Table 46.5), and as we had anticipated the VAR model is established with two lags.

The VAR model (Table 46.6) shows that there is an integrated causal relationship since at the same time GNI causes NFCF and vice versa, calculating a correlation coefficient of 0.7379, so that the graphical test is confirmed.

46.2.2 The Republic of Korea

From Table 46.7 of the Appendix, we present the proportion to GNI that has had during the studied period the variables GFCF, FCC, and NFCF in Korea (Fig. 46.4).

From 1971, the first year of information for Korea in World Bank data, and until 1996, GFCF or gross fixed capital investment rose from 20% to 45%. During these years, the GNI grows annually at a rate of 9.16%. Starting in 1996, the GFCF decline began, reaching 29.2% of GNI in 2015. During this period, the GNI annual growth rate is reduced to 4.2%.

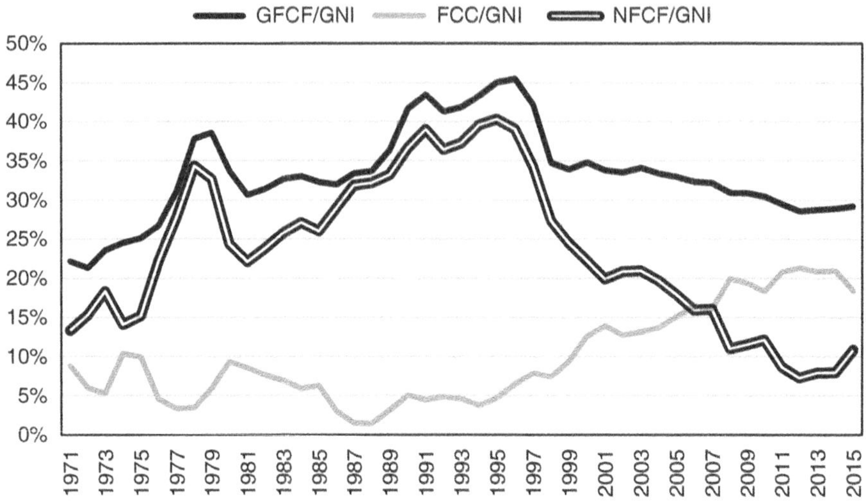

Fig. 46.4 Korea, own elaboration with data from World Bank

During this period, the FCC fluctuated around 5% of the GNI between 1971 and 1996, a period of high economic growth. From that last year, FCC began to grow rapidly from 5% to 20% of GNI in 2015.

Regarding NFCF, we observe an accelerated growth from 1971, going from 13.3% of GNI in that year to 40.3% in 1995. From 1995 to 2015, it started to decrease, stabilizing around 10% from 2008 and till the date.

In Fig. 46.4 we also see the negative correlation between FCC and NFCF which in the case of Korea is −0.833. A correlation coefficient − 1.00 would give us a perfect mirror graph.

In Fig. 46.5 we present the evolution of GNI and NFCF in absolute terms, trillions of US 2010 dollars.

We note that since 2007 the FCC variable is greater than NFCF which means that the net investment is not enough to cover consumption of fixed capital and natural resources.

The Causal Link Between Gross National Income (GNI) and Net Fixed Capital Formation (NFCF) in the Republic of Korea (1971–2015)

In the period between 1971 and 2015, the GNI in South Korea has a constant growth, while NFCF grows rapidly until 1996 and then decreases. At first glance, there is no apparent causality.

In general, we will verify whether there is a causal relationship or not (Fig. 46.6).

46.2.2.1 Estimation of Causality

For the specific cases of the GNI and the NFCF, the graphical test shows differences in the behavior during the period of study; at first glance, the series would seem to

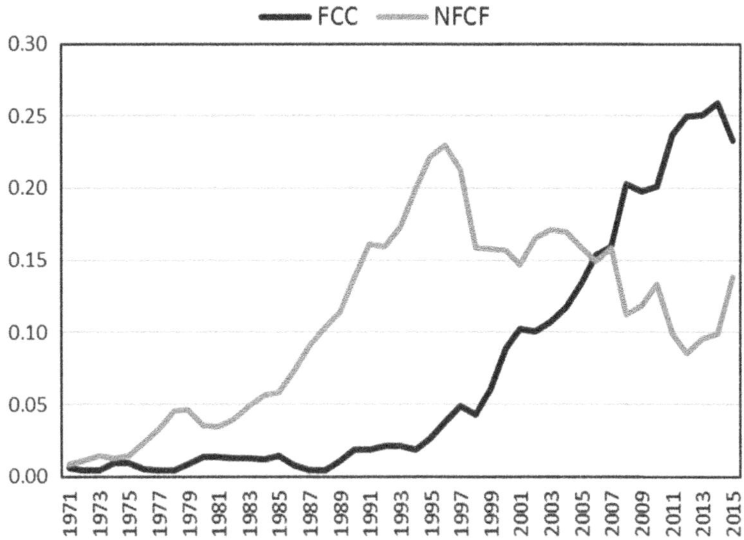

Fig. 46.5 Korea and US GNI and NFCF in trillions of 2010 US$ dollars (Source: Own elaboration with data from World Bank)

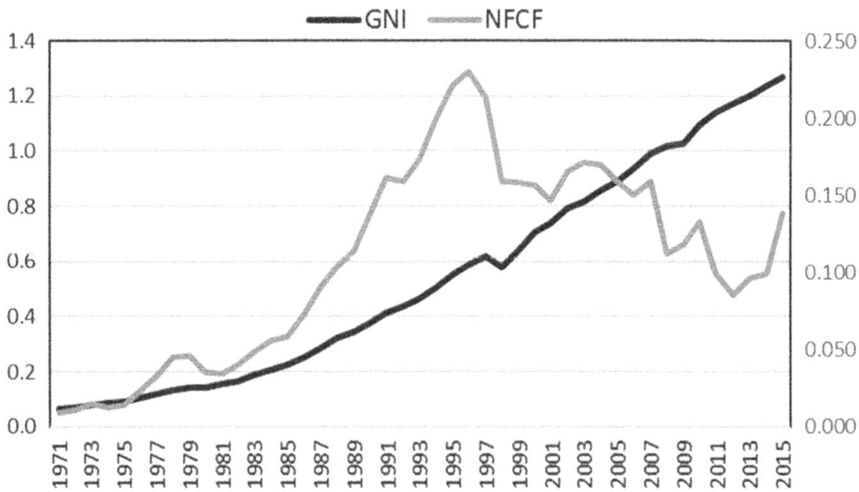

Fig. 46.6 Korea's GNI and NFCF in trillions of 2010 US$ dollars (Source: Own elaboration with data from World Bank)

be nonstationary. Before verifying the VAR model, it is necessary to determine that these variables are stationary or in their absence they are with some lags. To do this, we will perform the unit root tests for both variables. We used the Dickey-Fuller test augmented with the Schwarz criterion.

In Tables 46.8 and 46.9 of the Appendix, we observe that the GNI and NFCF variables do not have unit roots in first differences, so we go in Table 46.10 to the stage of the self-regressive vectors (VAR) in which we find the result of a model of autoregressive vectors (VAR), missing to determine exactly the number of lags, for which we used the Akaike, Schwarz, and Hannan test (Table 46.11), and as we had anticipated the VAR model is established with one lag.

The VAR model (Table 46.12) shows us that in the case of South Korea, we can say that the NFCF causes GNI, but not in a contrary way. The correlation coefficient is only 56.97%, which, while not bad, does not allow a relationship to be determined in both directions.

46.2.3 Brazil

In Fig. 46.7, derived from Table 46.13 of the Appendix, we observe the proportion that GFCF, FCC, and NFCF has had in Brazil with respect to GNI during the studied period.

From 1970 to 1975, the GFCF/GNI ratio increases from 21.35% to 26.49%. From that last year, it began to decrease and in 1984 is at 17.93%. Since then to date (2016), it has fluctuated around 19%. It is important to note that during the years that the relationship between GFCF and GNI is above 21%, the average annual real

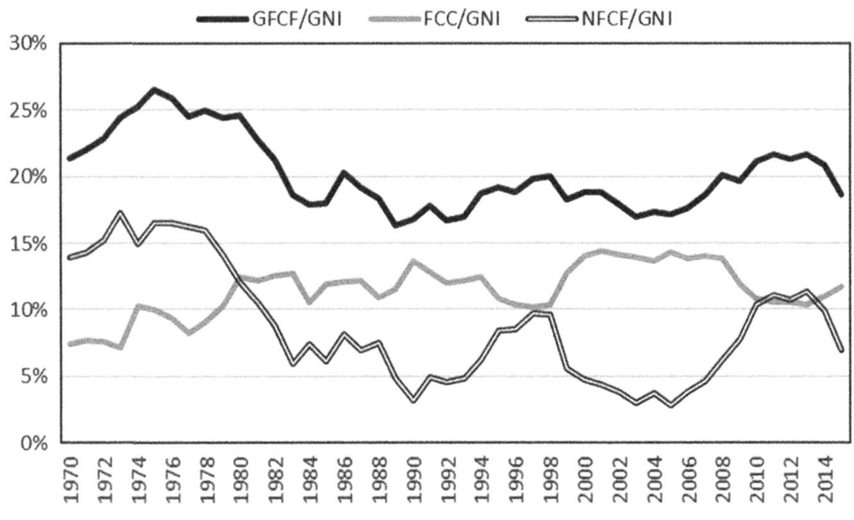

Fig. 46.7 Brazil (Source: Own elaboration with data from World Bank)

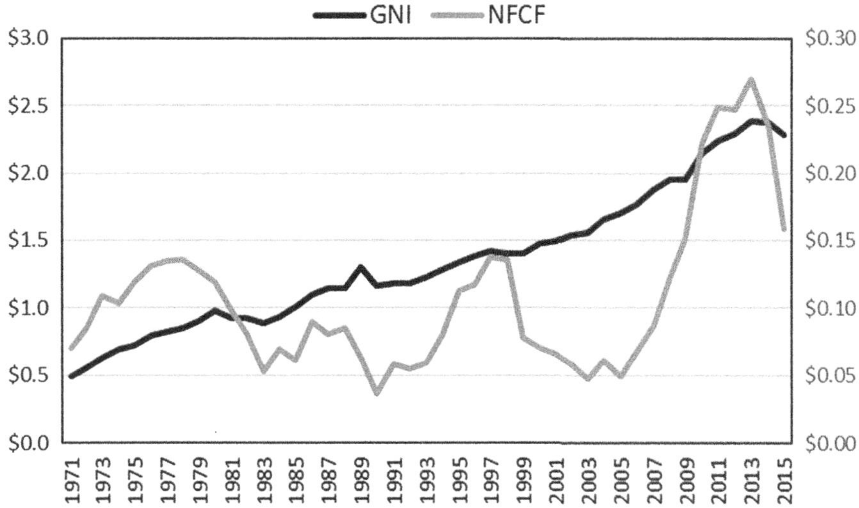

Fig. 46.8 Brazil's GNI and NFCF in trillions of 2010 US$ dollars (Source: Own elaboration with data from World Bank)

growth was 6.5%. From 1983 to 2015, with a percentage of 18.8%, the rate drops to 2.88% per year.

The ratio FCC/GNI increased from 7.37% in 1970 to 14.35% in 2001, remaining in that percentage until 2008 when it reduces, reaching 10.36% in 2013. From 2013 to 2015, it increases again to 11.71%.

NFCF/GNI shows a strong correlation with FGFCF/GNI during the period studied, 0.9384, and high negative correlation with FCC/GNI as in the other cases, −0.873.

The Causal Link Between Gross National Income (GNI) and Net Fixed Capital Formation (NFCF) in Brazil (1971–2015)
In the period between 1971 and 2015, the GNI in Brazil has a constant growth, not so the NFCF that has a sinusoidal behavior. At first glance, there is no apparent causality, but we must verify whether there is a causal relationship or not (Fig. 46.8).

46.2.3.1 Estimation of Causality

For the specific cases of the GNI and the NFCF, the graphical test shows differences in the behavior during the period of study; at first glance, the series would seem to be nonstationary. Before verifying the VAR model, it is necessary to determine that these variables are stationary or in their absence they are with some lags. To do this, we will perform the unit root tests for both variables. We used the Dickey-Fuller test augmented with the Schwarz criterion.

In Tables 46.14 and 46.15 of the Appendix we observe that the GNI and NFCF variables do not have unit roots in first differences, so we go in Table 46.16 to the stage of the Self-Regressive Vectors (VAR) in which we find the result of a model of autoregressive vectors (VAR), missing to determine exactly the number of lags, for which we used the Akaike, Schwarz, and Hannan test (Table 46.17) and as we had anticipated the VAR model is established with two lags.

In the case of Brazil (Table 46.18), we can say that NFCF causes GNI, but not that GNI causes NFCF. The correlation coefficient between the two variables is only 56.83%, that is, very low and does not allow a relationship to be determined in both directions.

46.3 Conclusions

Unlike the negative results found in previous studies about the causal relationship between foreign direct investment and economic growth, in the case of net fixed capital formation (NFCF) and economic growth (EG), we obtain positive results in the causal relationship between these variables in our actual investigation.

The correlation coefficient between gross fixed capital formation (GFCF) and gross national income (GNI) is much higher than between NFCF and GNI, which is explained by the high consumption of fixed capital and natural resources.

In the three countries studied, we find that the NFCF is less than the consumption of fixed capital and natural resources, which makes us think that the current model of development is not sustainable in the long term.

There is a clear relation between GFCF and EG. Korea achieved economic growth rates above 9% per annum when the GFCF reached 45% of GNI (1996). In recent years, this proportion has been reduced to 29%, and the EG decreased to 4.2% (2015). The behavior of these figures in the case of Brazil confirms this relationship.

Appendix

Table 46.1 USA

Year	GNI (constant 2010 US$)	Adjusted net national income (constant 2010 US$)	Fixed capital consumption (constant 2010 US$)	Gross fixed capital formation (constant 2010 US$)	Net fixed capital formation (constant 2010 US$)
1970	4,793,029,598,432	4,233,376,344,742	559,653,253,689	847,336,206,600	287,682,952,911
1971	4,953,748,432,574	4,354,111,756,395	599,636,676,179	856,106,547,300	256,469,871,121
1972	5,215,342,523,791	4,602,644,767,549	612,697,756,241	924,859,692,800	312,161,936,559
1973	5,521,664,252,676	4,876,805,906,230	644,858,346,446	989,983,041,700	345,124,695,254
1974	5,499,218,640,250	4,667,327,738,628	831,890,901,622	951,668,289,500	119,777,387,878
1975	5,475,797,201,744	4,626,788,673,074	849,008,528,670	881,692,665,300	32,684,136,630
1976	5,777,956,134,186	4,872,105,884,381	905,850,249,805	951,957,056,100	46,106,806,295
1977	6,048,477,927,493	5,080,563,293,320	967,914,634,174	1,050,122,178,900	82,207,544,726
1978	6,381,250,322,577	5,367,145,360,196	1,014,104,962,381	1,162,151,585,400	148,046,623,019
1979	6,603,201,048,500	5,352,736,536,129	1,250,464,512,371	1,228,311,108,700	−22,153,403,671
1980	6,585,350,214,734	5,234,971,838,932	1,350,378,375,802	1,175,690,359,400	−174,688,016,402
1981	6,745,106,944,796	5,465,193,449,357	1,279,913,495,439	1,197,899,700,100	−82,013,795,339
1982	6,620,636,717,075	5,465,766,465,085	1,154,870,251,990	1,133,473,374,100	−21,396,877,890
1983	6,922,414,521,476	5,644,987,993,140	1,277,426,528,335	1,216,392,913,000	−61,033,615,335
1984	7,415,934,653,098	6,136,551,191,528	1,279,383,461,570	1,399,374,273,600	119,990,812,030
1985	7,706,290,660,461	6,381,737,557,774	1,324,553,102,687	1,497,413,235,300	172,860,132,613
1986	7,959,921,714,005	6,603,613,793,738	1,356,307,920,267	1,543,968,192,400	187,660,272,133
1987	8,234,542,712,833	6,848,719,948,953	1,385,822,763,879	1,571,560,641,200	185,737,877,321
1988	8,586,939,784,011	7,252,016,408,268	1,334,923,375,743	1,608,619,856,000	273,696,480,257
1989	8,903,628,706,863	7,432,320,946,636	1,471,307,760,227	1,655,856,800,300	184,549,040,073
1990	9,087,275,521,608	7,528,718,667,996	1,558,556,853,612	1,654,199,478,900	95,642,625,288
1991	9,074,523,057,469	7,550,772,774,338	1,523,750,283,131	1,585,758,699,200	62,008,416,069
1992	9,393,737,854,318	7,824,203,738,293	1,569,534,116,025	1,651,461,075,100	81,926,959,075

(continued)

Table 46.1 (continued)

Year	GNI (constant 2010 US$)	Adjusted net national income (constant 2010 US$)	Fixed capital consumption (constant 2010 US$)	Gross fixed capital formation (constant 2010 US$)	Net fixed capital formation (constant 2010 US$)
1993	9,650,728,250,473	8,003,746,814,047	1,646,981,436,426	1,735,816,979,000	88,835,542,574
1994	10,026,529,524,356	8,373,600,530,652	1,652,928,993,705	1,841,870,608,900	188,941,615,195
1995	10,304,138,775,042	8,659,375,034,649	1,644,763,740,393	1,937,251,125,100	292,487,384,707
1996	10,697,130,924,938	9,044,830,978,445	1,652,299,946,493	2,086,082,943,300	433,782,996,807
1997	11,164,670,991,198	9,553,608,480,863	1,611,062,510,334	2,240,403,617,800	629,341,107,466
1998	11,652,324,592,057	10,128,056,430,420	1,524,268,161,637	2,439,747,193,000	915,479,031,363
1999	12,208,093,885,506	10,553,277,902,615	1,654,815,982,891	2,643,374,969,900	988,558,987,009
2000	12,717,625,684,239	10,964,664,924,229	1,752,960,760,010	2,810,276,509,700	1,057,315,749,690
2001	12,858,387,351,786	11,101,995,601,043	1,756,391,750,742	2,795,108,992,300	1,038,717,241,558
2002	13,082,244,508,484	11,280,773,912,568	1,801,470,595,916	2,745,810,055,100	944,339,459,184
2003	13,468,274,147,480	11,524,734,632,743	1,943,539,514,738	2,853,523,794,400	909,984,279,662
2004	13,998,045,799,718	11,931,516,577,374	2,066,529,222,344	3,019,108,956,600	952,579,734,256
2005	14,463,258,719,153	12,291,376,859,769	2,171,881,859,385	3,188,248,338,300	1,016,366,478,916
2006	14,816,442,788,208	12,733,474,804,431	2,082,967,983,777	3,257,700,697,400	1,174,732,713,623
2007	15,136,992,923,132	12,730,402,448,477	2,406,590,474,655	3,217,308,518,100	810,718,043,445
2008	15,136,324,484,900	12,412,252,933,491	2,724,071,551,408	3,061,487,053,700	337,415,502,292
2009	14,700,329,730,325	12,253,684,173,664	2,446,645,556,661	2,661,346,809,600	214,701,252,939
2010	15,121,133,000,000	12,680,120,470,590	2,441,012,529,410	2,691,106,900,000	250,094,370,590
2011	15,394,757,500,240	12,966,528,463,480	2,428,229,036,760	2,790,582,923,800	362,353,887,040
2012	15,718,982,998,353	13,435,867,078,063	2,283,115,920,290	2,965,669,504,100	682,553,583,810
2013	15,982,013,048,498	13,606,712,638,444	2,375,300,410,053	3,056,110,916,000	680,810,505,947
2014	16,355,114,119,358	14,034,058,301,993	2,321,055,817,365	3,185,605,824,800	864,550,007,435
2015	16,733,649,866,776	14,503,175,318,085	2,230,474,548,691	3,305,058,624,900	1,074,584,076,209

Source: Own elaboration with data from World Bank

Table 46.2 USA

Augmented Dickey-Fuller unit root on USA (NFCF)			
Null hypothesis: USA (GNI) has a unit root			
Exogenous: constant, linear trend			
Lag length: 0 (automatic – based on SIC, maxlag = 9)			
		t-statistic	Prob.[a]
Augmented Dickey-Fuller test statistic		−4.566719	0.0006
Test critical values:	1% level	−3.592462	
	5% level	−2.931404	
	10% level	−2.603944	

[a]MacKinnon (1996) one-sided *p*-values

Table 46.3 USA

Augmented Dickey-Fuller unit root on USA(NFCF)			
Null hypothesis: USA (NFCF) has a unit root			
Exogenous: constant, linear trend			
Lag length: 0 (automatic – based on SIC, maxlag = 9)			
		t-statistic	Prob.[a]
Augmented Dickey-Fuller test statistic		−3.870252	0.0047
Test critical values:	1% level	−3.592462	
	5% level	−2.931404	
	10% level	−2.603944	

[a]MacKinnon (1996) one-sided *p*-values

Table 46.4 USA

Vector autoregression estimates		
Date: 05/01/17 Time: 19:05		
Sample (adjusted): 1973–2015		
Included observations: 43 after adjustment		
Standard errors in () & t-statistics in ()		
	GNI	NFCF
GNI(−1)	0.91669	0.088523
	−0.16949	−0.13595
	[5.40844]	[0.65117]
GNI(−2)	0.083894	−0.067535
	−0.16722	−0.13412
	[−0.50171]	[−0.50354]
NFCF(−1)	0.887773	1.274883
	−0.21906	−0.1757
	[4.05265]	[7.25593]
NGCF(−2)	−0.791525	−0.519934
	−0.1946	−0.15608
	[−4.06742]	[−3.33110]
C	2.35E+10	−1.28E+11
	−9.60E+10	−7.70E+10
	[2.45632]	[−1.66807]

Table 46.5 USA

VAR lag order selection criteria						
Endogenous variables: GNI NFCF						
Exogenous variables: C						
Date: 05/01/17 Time: 19:06						
Sample: 1971–2015						
Included observations: 41						
Lag	LogL	LR	FPE	AIC	SC	HQ
0	−2378.255	NA	9.14e + 47	116.1100	116.1936	116.1405
1	−2223.223	287.37640	5.78e + 44	108.7426	108.9934	108.8339
2	−2212.021	19.67220[a]	4.07e + 44[a]	108.3913	108.8092[a]	108.5435[a]
3	−2208.568	5.727460	4.20e + 44	108.4179	109.0031	108.6310
4	−2203.973	7.172338	4.11e + 44	108.3889[a]	109.1412	108.6629

LR sequential modified LR test statistic (each test at 5% level), *FPE* final prediction error, *AIC* Akaike information criterion, *SC* Schwarz-Quinn information criterion, *HQ* Hannan-Quinn information criterion

[a]Indicates lag order selected by the criterion

Table 46.6 (USA)

VAR granger causality/block exogeneity Wald tests			
Date: 05/01/17 Time: 19:08			
Sample: 1971–2015			
Included observations: 43			
Dependent variable: GNI			
Excluded	Chi-sq	Df	Prob.
NFCF	17.59016	2	0.0002
All	17.59016	2	0.0002
Dependent variable: NFCF			
Excluded	Chi-sq	Df	Prob.
GNI	6.531802	2	0.0382
All	6.531802	2	0.0382

Table 46.7 Republic of Korea

Year	GNI (constant 2010 US$)	Adjusted net national income (constant 2010 US$)	Fixed capital consumption (constant 2010 US$)	Gross fixed capital formation (constant 2010 US$)	Net fixed capital formation (constant 2010 US$)
1971	66,362,452,883	60,512,307,828	5,850,145,055	14,714,908,071	8,864,763,016
1972	70,173,310,471	65,974,318,466	4,198,992,005	14,967,011,014	10,768,019,008
1973	80,067,690,983	75,846,105,767	4,221,585,216	18,895,865,032	14,674,279,816
1974	87,941,441,958	78,795,311,697	9,146,130,261	21,564,613,154	12,418,482,893
1975	93,448,025,585	84,163,001,817	9,285,023,767	23,493,813,887	14,208,790,120
1976	106,110,006,328	101,298,932,360	4,811,073,968	28,366,759,357	23,555,685,389
1977	118,500,174,519	114,532,331,455	3,967,843,064	36,923,814,583	32,955,971,519
1978	131,242,818,485	126,692,217,052	4,550,601,432	49,634,299,854	45,083,698,422
1979	141,566,471,850	133,232,271,340	8,334,200,509	54,614,355,007	46,280,154,497
1980	144,700,002,201	131,168,433,920	13,531,568,281	48,762,023,673	35,230,455,393
1981	154,174,314,824	140,970,064,156	13,204,250,668	47,254,584,349	34,050,333,681
1982	166,985,489,979	154,304,018,225	12,681,471,754	52,507,728,311	39,826,256,557
1983	188,681,936,349	175,664,970,102	13,016,966,247	61,669,421,783	48,652,455,536
1984	207,012,518,622	194,770,565,936	12,241,952,685	68,365,139,663	56,123,186,977
1985	222,787,722,010	208,828,317,055	13,959,404,955	71,969,802,924	58,010,397,969
1986	250,896,543,636	243,340,812,189	7,555,731,447	80,265,897,537	72,710,166,090
1987	283,908,095,627	279,626,908,423	4,281,187,204	94,786,618,207	90,505,431,003
1988	319,999,013,814	315,365,206,012	4,633,807,801	107,698,513,288	103,064,705,487
1989	343,673,220,802	332,969,861,806	10,703,358,995	124,920,005,967	114,216,646,972
1990	376,299,440,600	357,359,309,321	18,940,131,279	156,697,649,999	137,757,518,721
1991	412,892,408,040	394,573,842,386	18,318,565,654	179,319,051,434	161,000,485,780
1992	436,855,571,904	415,651,081,415	21,204,490,489	180,305,523,434	159,101,032,945
1993	464,307,607,650	443,068,771,266	21,238,836,385	194,237,822,209	172,998,985,824
1994	504,670,033,304	485,837,034,789	18,832,998,514	218,498,982,944	199,665,984,429

(continued)

Table 46.7 (continued)

Year	GNI (constant 2010 US$)	Adjusted net national income (constant 2010 US$)	Fixed capital consumption (constant 2010 US$)	Gross fixed capital formation (constant 2010 US$)	Net fixed capital formation (constant 2010 US$)
1995	548,988,433,742	523,215,502,234	25,772,931,508	247,122,614,758	221,349,683,250
1996	588,570,729,964	550,504,749,923	38,065,980,041	267,842,478,647	229,776,498,606
1997	621,190,647,232	572,234,241,348	48,956,405,884	261,688,032,598	212,731,626,714
1998	580,194,380,033	537,302,235,675	42,892,144,359	201,671,179,671	158,779,035,312
1999	644,458,770,561	583,663,079,331	60,795,691,230	218,493,259,526	157,697,568,295
2000	704,641,573,317	615,968,283,862	88,673,289,455	245,163,706,759	156,490,417,304
2001	736,857,231,914	634,450,561,262	102,406,670,652	248,916,709,412	146,510,038,761
2002	793,946,597,765	693,071,384,431	100,875,213,334	266,169,691,738	165,294,478,404
2003	817,385,065,829	709,830,277,309	107,554,788,519	278,943,325,655	171,388,537,136
2004	859,088,952,543	741,491,010,133	117,597,942,410	286,905,448,761	169,307,506,351
2005	887,518,679,003	753,716,866,739	133,801,812,264	292,631,790,191	158,829,977,927
2006	937,462,137,130	783,955,157,926	153,506,979,205	303,027,521,904	149,520,542,699
2007	989,383,749,716	829,848,641,818	159,535,107,898	318,142,641,262	158,607,533,364
2008	1,020,438,997,375	817,448,596,572	202,990,400,803	315,435,344,675	112,444,943,871
2009	1,025,297,841,977	827,181,550,493	198,116,291,483	316,372,751,957	118,256,460,473
2010	1,095,599,453,662	894,747,761,294	200,851,692,369	333,826,329,233	132,974,636,865
2011	1,141,316,444,322	903,988,124,072	237,328,320,250	336,595,041,265	99,266,721,016
2012	1,172,413,437,107	922,593,119,741	249,820,317,366	334,964,763,970	85,144,446,604
2013	1,202,799,721,732	952,449,462,878	250,350,258,854	346,024,993,491	95,674,734,637
2014	1,238,165,310,073	979,368,002,585	258,797,307,488	357,669,188,737	98,871,881,249
2015	1,272,539,650,337	1,039,439,024,883	233,100,625,455	371,412,581,170	138,311,955,715

Source: Own elaboration with data from World Bank

Table 46.8 Korea

Augmented Dickey-Fuller unit root test on D(GNI)			
Null hypothesis: KOR_GDP has a unit root			
Exogenous: constant			
Lag length: 0 (automatic – based on SIC, maxlag = 9)			
		t-statistic	Prob. [a]
Augmented Dickey-Fuller test statistic		−5.419937	0.0000
Test critical values:	1% level	−3.592462	
	5% level	−2.931404	
	10% level	−2.603944	

[a]MacKinnon (1996) one side p-values

Table 46.9 Korea

Augmented Dickey-Fuller unit root test on D(GNI)			
Null hypothesis: KOR_GDP has a unit root			
Exogenous: constant			
Lag length: 0 (automatic – based on SIC, maxlag = 9)			
		t-statistic	Prob. [a]
Augmented Dickey-Fuller test statistic		−4.726647	0.0004
Test critical values:	1% level	−3.592462	
	5% level	−2.931404	
	10% level	−2.603944	

[a]MacKinnon (1996) one side p-values

Table 46.10 Korea

Vector autoregression estimates		
Date: 05/01/17 Time: 19:21		
Sample (adjusted): 1973–2015		
Included observations: 43 after adjustments		
Standard errors in ( ) & t-statistics in []		
	GNI	NFCF
GNI(−1)	0.668853	−0.350140
	(0.18941)	(0.18377)
	[3.53133]	[−1.90527]
GNI(−2)	0.362604	0.361073
	(0.19474)	(0.18895)
	[1.86197]	[1.91092]
NFCF(−1)	0.471824	1.411376
	(0.20800)	(0.20182)
	[2.26835]	[6.99327]
NGCF(−2)	−0.389532	−0.454908
	(0.20334)	(0.19729)
	[−1.91568]	[−2.30573]
C	1.13E + 10	1.08E + 10
	(5.6E + 09)	(5.4E + 09)
	[2.03355]	[1.99599]

Table 46.11 Korea

VAR lag order selection criteria						
Endogenous variables: GNI NFCF						
Exogenous variables: C						
Date: 05/01/17 Time: 19:22						
Sample: 1971–2015						
Included observations: 41						
Lag	LogL	LR	FPE	AIC	SC	HQ
0	−2219.684	NA	4.00e + 44	108.3748	108.4584	108.4053
1	−2042.889	327.7189[a]	8.73e + 40[a]	99.94579[a]	100.1966[a]	100.0371[a]
2	−2039.210	6.460161	8.89e + 40	99.96146	100.3794	100.1137
3	−2034.926	7.105580	8.80e + 40	99.94759	100.5327	100.1607
4	−2031.210	5.799766	9.00e + 40	99.96147	100.7138	100.2354

LR sequential modified LR test statistic (each test at 5% level), *FPE* final prediction error, *AIC* Akaike information criterion, *SC* Schwarz-Quinn information criterion, *HQ* Hannan-Quinn information criterion

[a]Indicates lag order selected by the criterion

Table 46.12 Korea

VAR granger causality/block exogeneity Wald tests			
Date: 05/01/17 Time: 19:23			
Sample: 1971–2015			
Included observations: 43			
Dependent variable: GNI			
Excluded	Chi-sq	df	Prob.
NFCF	6.302479	2	0.0428
All	6.302479	2	0.0428
Dependent variable: NFCF			
Excluded	Chi-sq	df	Prob.
GNI	3.656662	2	0.1607
All	3.656662	2	0.1607

Table 46.13 Brazil

Año	GNI (constant 2010 US$)	Adjusted net national income (constant 2010 US$)	Fixed capital consumption (constant 2010 US$)	Gross fixed capital formation (constant 2010 US$)	Net fixed capital formation (constant 2010 US$)
1970	442,690,250,086	410,046,146,532	32,644,103,554	94,521,796,955	61,877,693,402
1971	494,553,339,787	456,338,493,460	38,214,846,327	109,029,440,229	70,814,593,902
1972	555,671,594,496	513,196,528,449	42,475,066,047	127,253,374,168	84,778,308,121
1973	631,047,891,414	585,706,577,482	45,341,313,932	153,964,711,743	108,623,397,811
1974	690,879,773,593	620,112,339,033	70,767,434,560	174,378,309,529	103,610,874,969
1975	722,378,956,551	650,133,652,919	72,245,303,632	191,352,894,576	119,107,590,944
1976	791,747,308,554	717,857,561,251	73,889,747,303	204,799,640,921	130,909,893,618
1977	826,904,094,515	758,840,390,608	68,063,703,907	202,402,181,942	134,338,478,035
1978	847,533,500,519	770,961,268,052	76,572,232,467	212,011,603,998	135,439,371,531
1979	901,972,190,896	809,469,062,093	92,503,128,803	220,249,704,974	127,746,576,170
1980	978,262,214,224	856,500,653,603	121,761,560,621	240,449,912,720	118,688,352,099
1981	926,891,567,832	814,048,716,201	112,842,851,631	210,657,311,340	97,814,459,709
1982	922,606,054,777	807,081,200,216	115,524,854,561	196,494,594,001	80,969,739,440
1983	883,693,962,422	771,397,539,399	112,296,423,023	164,862,175,377	52,565,752,353
1984	930,542,567,442	832,722,627,609	97,819,939,833	166,897,450,818	69,077,510,984
1985	1,008,911,172,933	888,941,530,711	119,969,642,222	181,568,809,823	61,599,167,601
1986	1,100,353,228,578	966,918,938,295	133,434,290,283	223,293,395,026	89,859,104,743
1987	1,148,389,737,486	1,007,953,712,438	140,436,025,048	220,749,019,192	80,312,994,144
1988	1,143,967,515,324	1,019,448,513,655	124,519,001,669	210,063,541,716	85,544,540,046
1989	1,300,277,797,039	1,150,666,560,513	149,611,236,527	212,607,695,081	62,996,458,555
1990	1,162,469,614,771	1,003,884,393,341	158,585,221,430	195,392,196,500	36,806,975,070
1991	1,185,154,823,134	1,032,489,923,931	152,664,899,203	211,187,333,051	58,522,433,847
1992	1,183,717,082,052	1,041,092,698,478	142,624,383,574	197,204,476,704	54,580,093,129
1993	1,231,980,141,469	1,081,687,279,832	150,292,861,638	209,679,117,669	59,386,256,032

(continued)

Table 46.13 (continued)

Año	GNI (constant 2010 US$)	Adjusted net national income (constant 2010 US$)	Fixed capital consumption (constant 2010 US$)	Gross fixed capital formation (constant 2010 US$)	Net fixed capital formation (constant 2010 US$)
1994	1,279,906,868,970	1,119,729,657,250	160,177,211,720	239,572,584,551	79,395,372,831
1995	1,339,072,426,036	1,194,421,829,628	144,650,596,408	257,037,435,827	112,386,839,419
1996	1,380,723,791,830	1,238,257,536,536	142,466,255,295	260,140,606,743	117,674,351,448
1997	1,419,983,410,658	1,275,714,815,382	144,268,595,276	282,045,134,483	137,776,539,207
1998	1,406,307,505,452	1,260,094,840,616	146,212,664,837	281,577,800,086	135,365,135,249
1999	1,402,306,392,560	1,223,316,521,160	178,989,871,400	256,593,114,172	77,603,242,772
2000	1,473,744,645,765	1,267,200,096,155	206,544,549,610	276,610,276,929	70,065,727,320
2001	1,492,366,675,141	1,278,085,814,535	214,280,860,606	280,217,627,082	65,936,766,477
2002	1,541,791,510,273	1,324,336,331,580	217,455,178,693	276,174,588,834	58,719,410,141
2003	1,558,780,587,582	1,340,955,410,466	217,825,177,116	265,167,924,878	47,342,747,762
2004	1,655,745,042,368	1,429,238,789,380	226,506,252,989	287,672,324,934	61,166,071,945
2005	1,707,338,482,470	1,462,945,531,367	244,392,951,103	293,301,194,211	48,908,243,108
2006	1,771,145,119,862	1,525,682,453,075	245,462,666,788	312,837,007,298	67,374,340,511
2007	1,876,630,264,162	1,613,072,069,741	263,558,194,421	350,228,649,559	86,670,455,138
2008	1,958,504,191,686	1,687,437,057,171	271,067,134,515	393,262,084,043	122,194,949,528
2009	1,957,708,645,417	1,724,544,015,817	233,164,629,600	384,871,395,156	151,706,765,557
2010	2,144,023,988,176	1,912,670,685,216	231,353,302,960	453,584,583,902	222,231,280,942
2011	2,236,503,912,444	2,000,666,666,366	235,837,246,078	484,583,056,646	248,745,810,567
2012	2,291,722,677,829	2,050,000,910,366	241,721,767,463	488,354,712,811	246,632,945,347
2013	2,382,304,246,451	2,135,370,301,413	246,933,945,038	516,812,902,141	269,878,957,103
2014	2,374,896,781,957	2,114,429,476,983	260,467,304,974	494,982,341,712	234,515,036,738
2015	2,281,991,209,952	2,014,679,634,312	267,311,575,641	426,147,307,937	158,835,732,296

Source: Own elaboration with data from World Bank

Table 46.14 Brazil

Augmented Dickey-Fuller unit root (NFCF)			
Null hypothesis: (NFCF) has a unit root			
Exogenous: constant, linear trend			
Lag length: 0 (automatic – based on SIC, maxlag = 9)			
		t-statistic	Prob.[a]
Augmented Dickey-Fuller test statistic		−6.264017	0.0000
Test critical values:	1% level	−3.592462	
	5% level	−2.931404	
	10% level	−2.603944	

[a]MacKinnon (1996) one-sided p-values

Table 46.15 Brazil

Augmented Dickey-Fuller Unit Root (NFCF)			
Null hypothesis: (NFCF) has a unit root			
Exogenous: Constant, linear trend			
Lag length: 0 (automatic – based on SIC, maxlag = 9)			
		t-statistic	Prob.[a]
Augmented Dickey-Fuller test statistic		−3.573292	0.0105
Test critical values:	1% level	−3.592462	
	5% level	−2.931404	
	10% level	−2.603944	

[a]MacKinnon (1996) one-sided p-values

Table 46.16 Brazil

Vector autoregression estimates		
Date: 05/01/17 Time: 19:45		
Sample (adjusted): 1973–2015		
Included observations: 43 after adjustments		
Standard errors in ( ) and t-statistics in [ ]		
	GNI	NFCF
GNI(−1)	0.659291	−0.049195
	(0.18523)	(0.07945)
	[3.55928]	[−0.61919]
GNI(−2)	0.352804	0.056886
	(0.18647)	(0.07998)
	[1.89198]	[0.71122]
NFCF(−1)	1.258808	1.425455
	(0.45027)	(0.19313)
	[2.79567]	[7.38075]
NGCF(−2)	−1.476772	−0.613442
	(0.45247)	(0.19407)
	[−3.26383]	[−3.16088]
C	5.71E + 10	1.17E + 10
	(2.5E + 10)	(1.1E + 10)
	[2.31022]	[1.10606]

Table 46.17 Brazil

VAR lag order selection criteria						
Endogenous variables: GNI NFCF						
Exogenous variables: C						
Date: 05/01/17 Time: 19:46						
Sample: 1971–2015						
Included observations: 41						
Lag	LogL	LR	FPE	AIC	SC	HQ
0	−2227.199	NA	5.77E + 44	108.7414	108.825	108.7719
1	−2103.375	229.5288	1.67E + 42	102.8963	103.1471 [a]	102.9876
2	−2096.18	12.63485[a]	1.43e + 42 [a]	102.7405	103.1584	102.8927 [a]
3	−2092.141	6.697985	1.43E + 42	102.7386 [a]	103.3237	102.9517
4	−2089.144	4.679279	1.52E + 42	102.7875	103.5398	103.0614

LR sequential modified LR test statistic (each test at 5% level), *FPE* final prediction error, *AIC* Akaike information criterion, *SC* Schwarz-Quinn information criterion, *HQ* Hannan-Quinn information criterion

[a]Indicates lag order selected by the criterion

Table 46.18 Brazil

VAR granger causality/block exogeneity Wald tests			
Date: 05/01/17 Time: 19:47			
Sample: 1971–2015			
Included observations: 43			
Dependent variable: GNI			
Excluded	Chi-sq	df	Prob.
NFCF	10.99093	2	0.0041
All	10.99093	2	0.0041
Dependent variable: NFCF			
Excluded	Chi-sq	df	Prob.
GNI	1.162873	2	0.5591
All	1.162873	2	0.5591

References

Encinas-Ferrer, C., & Villegas-Zermeño E. V. (2015). *Foreign direct investment and gross domestic growth*, International conference on applied economics (ICOAE 2015) in Kazan, Russia, July 2–4, 2015. Elsevier, procedia economics and finance, science direct (Vol. 24, pp. 198–207).

Dickey, D. A., & Fuller, W. A. (1979). Distribution of the estimators for autoregressive time series with a unit root. *Journal of the American Statistical Association., 74*(366), 427–431. https://doi.org/10.2307/2286348. JSTOR 2286348.

FRED Economic Data. Economic research. Federal reserve bank of St. Louis. https://fred.stlouisfed.org/. Consulted April 2017.

Toda, H. Y., & Yamamoto, T. (1995). Statistical inference in vector autoregressions with possibly integrated process. *Journal of Econometrics, 66*, 225–250.

World Bank, Data, Country. http://data.worldbank.org/country. Consulted for USA, Rep. of Korea and Brazil from April to May 2017.

Chapter 47
Does Financial Regulation Influence Bank Efficiency? A Study on UAE Banking Sector

Rachna Banerjee and Sudipa Majumdar

Abstract A well-functioning, stable, and efficient banking system contributes to the economic growth of a country. Financial regulation has been highlighted as an important factor which influences bank performance and safety as evidenced by some of the studies in the past. This study analyzes the relationship between financial regulation and bank efficiency in the UAE. First part of our study is modeled on DEA analysis and indicates an improvement in profit efficiency during the selected period. The second part of our study analyzed the impact of financial regulations on the banks' efficiency using Tobit regression. The regulatory variables included for this are loan to deposit ratio, advances to stable resources, total capital adequacy ratio, tier 1 capital to risk-weighted assets (RWA), provision coverage, and loan loss provision.

47.1 Introduction

A well-functioning, stable, and efficient banking system contributes to the economic growth of a country. Financial regulation has been highlighted as an important factor which influences bank performance and safety as evidenced by some of the studies in the past (Beltratti and Stulz 2009; Das and Ghosh 2009; Delis and Staikouras 2011; Lee and Chih 2013; Kale et al. 2015). However there have been conflicting views on the nature of influence that financial regulation and restrictions exert on bank efficiency and development. In a cross-country study, Barth et al. (2001) found an association between greater regulatory restrictions on bank activity and lower banking sector efficiency (see also Gaganis and Pasiouras 2013; Laeven and Levine

R. Banerjee (✉)
Department of Business, Higher Colleges of Technology, Dubai, United Arab Emirates
e-mail: rbanerjee@hct.ac.ae

S. Majumdar
Business School, Middlesex University, Dubai, United Arab Emirates
e-mail: S.Majumdar@mdx.ac.ae

N. Tsounis, A. Vlachvei (eds.), *Advances in Panel Data Analysis in Applied Economic Research*, Springer Proceedings in Business and Economics,
https://doi.org/10.1007/978-3-319-70055-7_47

2007). In yet another study, fewer regulatory restrictions have been found to aid exploitation of economies of scale (Claessens and Klingebiel 2000).

Contrary to the above view, Beck et al. (2006) argue that both bank efficiency and corporate governance of banks can be enhanced through a powerful supervisory agency that directly monitors and disciplines banks. A positive relation between capital ratios, loan ratios, and bank efficiency has been evidenced by similar studies (Das and Ghosh, 2009; Barth et al. 2013). Interestingly, there are studies which have either not found an association between various bank regulatory variables and efficiency or the association is not robust.

This study therefore contributes to the existing literature by analyzing the relationship between financial regulation and bank efficiency in the UAE. The findings will indicate whether the Central Bank of the UAE (CBUAE) regulations influence bank efficiency and which are the specific regulations which augur well, if at all, for promoting efficiency in the banking system. To the authors' understanding, this study has not yet been conducted on UAE banks and will therefore help to fill the research gap in exploring this relationship and its implications on banks' efficiency.

Accordingly this study will first analyze the efficiency of UAE banks during the period 2009–2015. This will allow us to explain the profitability of banks as measured by efficiency levels. This study is particularly relevant due to the selected time period. This period witnessed major regulatory reforms initiated by the CBUAE, viz., moving to CAR ratio as prescribed by BASEL III (2009), regulations for classification of loans and provisions (2010), and liquidity regulations (2012). This period also witnessed the aftermath of the 2008 financial crisis, the ripple effects of which was felt globally. Stagnating loans and advances together with rise in the nonperforming loans (NPLs) severely affected the profitability of UAE banks for the period 2009–2012. Although the UAE economy has rebounded in 2013 with increase in the GDP with robust earnings being declared by most of the local banks, few banks are ailing with high NPL levels. However, it is worth mentioning that most of the banks shored up their capital levels to an average of 20% by 2013 due to the support from the government and prudent supervision by the regulator. It would therefore be interesting to analyze whether there are manifestations of the above changes on the banks' efficiency.

Most of the existing literature on bank efficiency follows the input-oriented approach of cost and technical efficiency through estimations of economies of scale and scope. Output-oriented analysis on revenue is far less, and empirical evidence on profit efficiency of banks is even sparser. In our study, the objective was to look into the recovery of the banking sector after the crisis, whereby the objective of cost minimization had to be fulfilled along with maximization of revenues. Therefore, this paper looks into the important aspect of profit efficiency of banks which incorporates the important source of information for bank management during financial recovery.

The second part of our study will analyze the impact of financial regulations on the banks' efficiency. The variables included for this are loan to deposit ratio, advances to stable assets, total capital adequacy ratio, tier 1 capital to risk-weighted assets (RWA), provision coverage, and loan loss provision.

47.2 CBUAE Regulations and Bank Efficiency

CBUAE has rolled out a set of regulations over the years in line with BASEL norms and has actively monitored the banking sector. Some of these regulations included in this study are discussed in the following sections.

47.2.1 Liquidity Requirement

The regulatory requirements set up by the CBUAE reflect the regulator's continuous efforts for strengthening banking regulations and supervision of the banking industry. Financial regulations and its implementation in the UAE are continuously evolving. For controlling and monitoring liquidity risk, in May 2015, it issued regulations requiring banks to comply with liquidity ratios in line with BASEL III. These ratios include liquidity coverage ratio (LCR) and net stable funding ratio (NSFR). The approved banks will be required to begin the transition to LCR effective 2016 which will be fully implemented (LCR of 100%) by 2019, and these banks will also have to comply with NSFR effective 2018 (CBUAE circular, 2015). These liquidity regulations introduced in BASEL III are in response to the liquidity crisis which plagued most of the banking industries in the wake of the financial crisis in 2007–2008.

In preparation for the above requirements and ensuring better management of liquidity risk, CBUAE introduced two interim ratios in 2012 and liquidity assets ratio effective from 2013 until 2014, under which banks are required to hold 10% of their liabilities in highly liquid assets after which the LCR was planned to be implemented. Further, uses to stable resources ratio (USRR) of less than 100% were to be maintained by banks effective 2013 until 2017 after which NSFR would come into effect (CBUAE circular, 2012).

The other liquidity ratios monitored include liquid assets to total liabilities and loans to deposit ratio. Lee and Chih (2013) found that loan to deposit ratio affects big and small banks differently. While it has no significant impact on big banks, for smaller banks, a high loan to deposit was associated with less efficiency. A positive relation between profitability and liquidity was found in studies on bank profitability (Bourke 1989; Owolabi et al. 2011).

47.2.2 Capital Adequacy Requirement

CBUAE also regulates the capital requirements, loan loss provisions, and loans to deposit ratios of banks. In line with BASEL III capital rules, 2010, the regulator requires that banks hold a minimum total capital adequacy ratio (CAR) of 12% and tier 1 of 8%. Although BASEL III has rolled out revised capital rules in 2015 stipulating a minimum total CAR of 10.5% (including capital conservation buffer of 2.5%) and tier 1 of 8.5% of risk-weighted assets (RWA) putting pressure on banks to build up additional buffer, this is not likely to pose any challenges for the UAE banking sector which had an average total CAR of 18.3% and tier 1 of 16.6% (Financial stability report, 2015), comfortably above the BASEL III requirements, and therefore has high capitalization levels compared to its international peers.

Adequate capital levels serve as a cushion for absorbing the shocks to profitability and asset quality. High capital levels have been associated with greater profit efficiency in some studies (Kwan and Eisenbis 1997; Das and Ghosh 2009; Pessarossi and Weill 2009; Barth et al. 2013). High capital ratios help the large and medium banks to survive and consequently increase their profitability as argued by Berger and Bouwman (2013).

However, on another note, Berger et al. (1995) observes that although high capital ratio lowers the cost of insured debt thereby increasing profitability, the effect of capital ratio on banks' profitability is not sustained. Gorton and Winton (2000) showed that raising capital requirements forces banks to supply fewer deposits resulting in restricting the liquidity-providing role of banks. There have also been studies which found no evidence of influence of capital ratios and efficiency (Ayadi et al. 2015; Barth et al. 2012).

47.2.3 Loan Provisioning

With reference to loan loss provisions, CBUAE monitors two coverage ratios. Banks are expected to maintain specific provision of 150% and a general provision of 1.5% of RWA. (CBUAE circular, 2010). These regulations mirror the BASEL III guidelines. These ratios are typically higher for banks which have larger amount of expected bad loans and also indicate high risk despite being provisioned (Ayadi and Pujals 2005).

NPL levels of UAE banks have declined in 2015 as indicated by NPL ratio of 6.2% as against ratios of 7% which is a substantial drop from NPL of 8% recorded in 2013. This has contributed to increase in NPL coverage ratio of 110%.

47.3 Methodology

The models used in this study include DEA analysis and Tobit regression. The description and variables used for the analysis are discussed in the following sections.

47.3.1 Data Envelopment Analysis

The data was collected for the period 2009–2015, since the purpose of the study was to trace the recovery of the banks in the UAE during the post-crisis period and, moreover, to understand the role of financial regulations in the recovery process. The data has been collected from individual balance sheets and income statements from each bank for each year. All figures were adjusted for inflation rates using the World Bank Consumer Price Index (CPI) figures for the UAE. The study first uses a nonparametric linear programming model to calculate profit efficiency of each bank for each year, and these efficiency scores are then used in the regression model to determine the relationship between financial regulation and efficiency. In this study we adopt the intermediation approach to define the input-output matrix of the banks (Sealey and Lindley 1977) whereby banks are considered as intermediaries that collect deposits and purchase assets (inputs) to transform these into loans and investments (outputs). The data envelopment analysis (DEA) approach was adopted for estimating the profit efficiency of the banks, through linear programming techniques (Farrell 1957). DEA constructs the frontier of the most efficient decision-making units (DMUs) and then measures the relative distance function of all other DMUs for each year. The DPIN computer program (O'Donnell 2010) was used to compute the profit efficiency scores for the DMUs for the period 2009–2015 (Fig. 47.1).

An input-output bundle is defined by the set (x,y) where the output bundle "y" is produced from the input bundle "x" using the technology "T." The production possibility set can be defined as

$$T = \{x, y\} :: y \text{ is produced using } x\}$$

where the frontier of the production possibility set is given by $F(x,y) = 1$. The concept of frontier is especially important for the analysis of efficiency, because we measure efficiency as the relative distance to the frontier. Firms that are inefficient operate at points in the interior of the frontier, while those that are technically efficient operate along the frontier.

DEA is regarded superior to other efficiency approaches like the stochastic frontier or financial indicators since the nonparametric DEA uses linear programming which makes it possible to construct the production possibility set from an

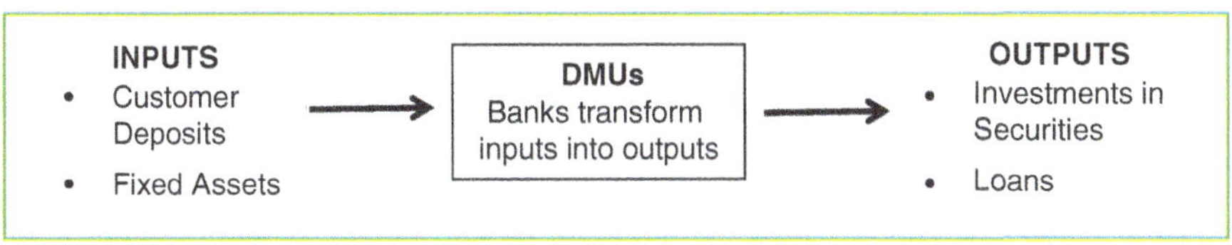

Fig. 47.1 Two inputs and two outputs used in the DEA model

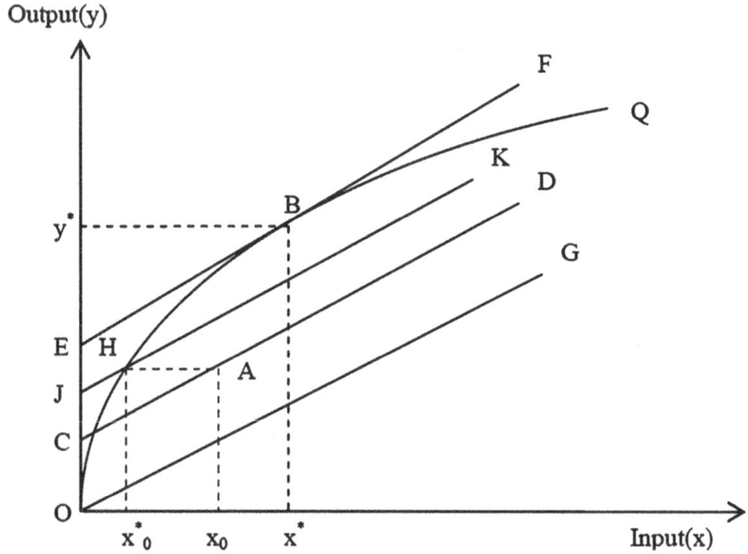

Fig. 47.2 Production function

observed data set of input-output bundles without assuming any functional form of the production technology. This methodology was introduced by Charnes et al. (1978) and later extended to variable returns to scale (VRS) by Banker et al. (1984). In this study, we are particularly interested in the profit maximization criterion of efficiency, given the bundles of inputs and outputs of the firms. If the input and output prices are given by "*w*" and "*p*," respectively, the profit function of the firm producing the output bundle y^0 from the input bundle x^0 is

$$\prod^{0} = py^0 - wx^0$$

In Fig. 47.2, *A* shows the actual input-output combination (x^0, y^0), *OQ* is the production function, and *CD* is the actual profit line. The objective of the firm is to reach the highest isoprofit line given its production function, which is given by *EF*. Let the optimal input-output combination at *B* be (x^*, y^*). However, given the inefficiency of the firm at the point *A*, the efficiency frontier that can be attained by this firm is at *H*, where it produced the same output y^0 using lesser inputs. Therefore, the firm maximizes profit by moving from point *A* to point *B* in two stages – in the first stage, the firm achieves technical efficiency from *A* to *H* and then improves allocative efficiency in the second stage from *H* to *B*. However, the profit efficiency score through the linear programming DEA calculates the distance function of the point *A* from the frontier *B*. For each DMU, DEA evaluates an efficiency score such that the most efficient DMUs are assigned an efficiency score of 1, representing the frontier. So each DMU would have a profit efficiency score that would strictly lie between 0 and 1.

47.3.2 *Tobit Multivariate Regression Analysis*

In the next section, we examine how the changes in the financial regulations by the Central Bank of the UAE have had an effect on the profit efficiency of the commercial banking system. The financial regulation variables required by CBUAE were classified into four categories: capital adequacy, asset quality, liquidity, and management efficiency. Accordingly, the ratios selected included total CAR, tier 1 to risk-weighted assets ratio, provision coverage, loan loss provision, loan to deposit ratio, advances to stable resources, and cost to income ratio as the explanatory variables.

The efficiency scores derived in the first stage DEA are regressed on the banking financial regulatory measures, as have been detailed earlier in Sect. 2. The important characteristic of the dependent variable is that the DEA values of the profit efficiency scores strictly lie between 0 and 1 and cannot be expected to have a normal distribution. So, for all firms who reach a score of "1," it is termed as being on the efficiency frontier and used as a benchmark. Therefore, we only know the true value for those firms that have scores between 0 and 1. Thus, we cannot expect the regression error to also meet the assumption of normal distribution, and the OLS regression method might lead to biased and inconsistent parameter estimates (Greene 1981). In the presence of the lower and upper limit of the dependent variable, we need to use the double-censored Tobit regression model (Coelli et al. 1998; Fried et al. 1999; Lin 2002; Wang et al. 2003). In our case there were no banks which had a profitability score of 0, and therefore the results of the empirical analysis will not be different if one specifies a one- or a two-sided Tobit model. Therefore, the DEA profit efficiency scores obtained in the first stage were used as dependent variables in the second-stage one-side censored Tobit model in order to allow for the restricted (0, 1] range of efficiency values. In our model, the efficiency scores are therefore right censored.

47.4 Results and Discussion

47.4.1 *Data and Variables*

Our initial DEA efficiency indices clearly indicate an improvement in profits of banks over the years, from 0.57 to 0.81 (Table 47.1), and the profits for the industry during this period were driven by Abu Dhabi Islamic Bank, Commercial Bank of Dubai, United Arab Bank, National Bank of Ras Al-Khaimah, and National Bank of Umm Al Qaiwain (Table 47.2). The banks which failed to recover from the crisis of 2008–2009 and have the lowest profit efficiency scores were Ajman Bank, Mashreq, and Bank of Sharjah. Profit efficiency score of the conventional banks (0.738) was higher than that of the Islamic banks (0.654), and the difference was weakly statistically significant at 90% confidence level, as can be seen from the results of the t-test for comparison of means (Table 47.3).

Table 47.1 Profit efficiency index: year wise

Year	Profit efficiency index
2010	0.5716
2011	0.6388
2012	0.6889
2013	0.7564
2014	0.8237
2015	0.8104

Table 47.2 Profit efficiency index: bank wise

Bank	Profit efficiency index
Abu Dhabi Islamic Bank	0.973
Commercial Bank of Dubai	0.937
United Arab Bank	0.918
National Bank of Ras Al-Khaimah	0.902
National Bank of Umm Al Qaiwain	0.894
Commercial Bank International	0.810
First Gulf Bank	0.724
Emirates NBD	0.721
Abu Dhabi Commercial Bank	0.713
Sharjah Islamic Bank	0.709
Dubai Islamic Bank	0.694
National Bank of Abu Dhabi	0.685
National Bank of Fujairah	0.644
Invest Bank	0.643
Emirates Islamic Bank	0.619
Mashreq Bank	0.514
Bank of Sharjah	0.451
Ajman Bank	0.439

Table 47.3 t-test for comparison of means: conventional versus Islamic banks

	Islamic banks	Conventional banks
Mean	0.653993	0.738414
Standard deviation	0.2081762	0.1843378
Observations	30	78
Degrees of freedom	47	
t stat	1.947	
$P(T <= t)$ two-tail	0.057	

Table 47.4 shows the results of the second-stage Tobit regression model. The final log likelihood is 72.7883 using all 108 observations in our data set. The likelihood ratio chi-square of 69.65 with 7 degrees of freedom with a p-value of 0.0000 indicates a satisfactory goodness of fit for the model that we have used. When analyzing data with censored regression, an equivalent statistic to R-squared does not exist since the model generates the maximum likelihood estimates through an iterative process and does not minimize variance as in an OLS procedure. Therefore, pseudo R-squared value is reported to evaluate the goodness of fit of these models.

Table 47.4 STATA output for Tobit regression model

Number of obs = 108			LR $chi^2(7)$ = 69.65	
			Prob > chi^2 = 0.0000	
Log likelihood = 72.788313			Pseudo R^2 = −0.9172	
dProf	Coef.	Std. err.	T	$P > \|t\|$
CAR	−0.0395[a]	0.0068085	−5.80	0.000
Tier1	0.0362[a]	0.006558	5.52	0.000
CIR	−0.0029[b]	0.0015481	−1.90	0.060
LDR	0.00878[a]	0.0013449	6.53	0.000
NPLCR	0.0005	0.000597	0.84	0.402
LLP	0.1094[a]	0.0327501	3.34	0.001
ASR	−0.0053[a]	0.0013105	−4.05	0.000
Cons	0.3061[c]	0.1456167	2.10	0.038

[a]Indicates significance at 99% level
[b]Indicates significance at 90% level
[c]Indicates significance at 95% level

STATA reports the natural logarithm of the likelihood, and in this case, the Tobit regression uses McFadden's R-squared. The ratio of the likelihoods of the models with and without intercepts is calculated, and the log of the ratio, therefore, will always be negative. The absolute value of the pseudo R-squared indicates a high goodness of fit for our model.

47.4.2 Discussion and Conclusion

Our initial DEA efficiency indices clearly indicate an improvement in profits of banks over the years and are efficient in generating profit. The results further indicate that the increase in profit efficiency was driven by the performance of conventional banks more than the Islamic banks. Bader et al. (2008) in their study on efficiency of conventional and Islamic banks of 21 countries including the Middle East find that conventional banks exhibit more stable revenue and profit performance than their Islamic counterparts.

On examining the impact of capital adequacy on bank efficiency, our findings produce mixed results. The total CAR has a significantly negative effect on the efficiency of UAE banks indicating that high CAR ratio results in lowering bank efficiency while Tier 1 to RWA has a significant positive impact on bank efficiency.

CAR is a ratio of capital to risk-weighted asset (RWA) values maintained by banks for credit, market, and operational risk, and it includes tier 1 and tier 2 capital. A negative sign indicates that high levels of capital maintained by UAE banks have resulted in decrease in its profit efficiency due to high cost of capital. Although Modigliani and Miller (1958) theory suggested that value of a firm is not affected by the quantity of debt and equity (irrelevance of capital structure), banks are concerned about the effect of new capital requirement on the lending rate and cost of capital.

They would prefer to have low proportion of equity not only because it is less costly compared to debt, but it also puts restriction on their ability to extend loan to firms and other actors in the economy (Aboura and Lepinette 2015). The average CAR of UAE banks is 20% during the period 2010–2015, which is very high compared to their international peers.

Altunbas et al. (2007) in their study on European banks found that banks with more capital tend to be less efficient and are also the ones to take excessive risk. Berger and Bonaccorsi di Patti (2006) find that low capital ratios are associated with higher bank efficiency. Capital requirements may increase risk-taking behavior as argued by Koehn and Santomero (1980), Kim and Santomero (1988), Besanko and Kanatas (1996), and Blum (1999). However a different perspective is presented by Dewatripont and Tirole (1994) which is a traditional approach to bank regulation and highlights the positive aspect of capital adequacy requirement. There are studies that have argued that capital adequacy requirement is one of the direct contributors to financial stability through its effects on bank failures, future problem loans, and risk-taking and consequently has a positive influence on efficiency (Berger and DeYoung 1997; Podpiera and Weill 2008; Podpiera and Podpiera 2008; Fiordelisi et al. 2011).

Loan loss provision has a significant positive impact on efficiency. Bank regulation relating to asset quality has helped in improving efficiency of the banking sector. DelisDietrich, and Wanzenried (2011) was the first study approximating credit risk or credit quality by the loan loss provisions over total loan ratio. Kosmidou et al. (2005) and Valverde and Fernandez (2007) provide evidence that credit risk positively affects bank profitability. However, contradictory findings also exist indicating that level of credit risk tends to be negatively associated with bank's profitability.

The findings on impact of liquidity on efficiency produced mixed results. Loan to deposit ratio (LDR) has significant positive impact on bank efficiency. Fries and Taci (2005) and Dietsch and Lozano-Vivas (2000) argued that a positive relationship between LDR and bank efficiency reflects developments in the regulatory and legal framework that supports both the financial intermediation process and lower cost to banks. Kosmidou et al. (2005) showed that a positive relationship may exist between the banks' liquidity and their performance. However Lee and Chih's (2013) study on bank efficiency confirms a negative relationship between small banks' efficiency and loan to deposit ratio. Molyneux and Thornton (1992) observe that an inverse relationship between efficiency and liquidity, particularly those imposed by authorities, is expected because these holdings represent cost to banks.

Advances to stable resources (ASR) show a significant negative effect and imply that the regulation for managing liquidity risk has not helped the banks in improving efficiency. The average advances to stable ratio of UAE banks in 2015 was 87% which is below the minimum level of 100%.

Cost to income ratio (CIR) showed a weak negative impact on bank efficiency. Increase in operating expenses of banks owing to increased loan loss reserves in the last 5 years has resulted in decrease in operating efficiency. Our result is consistent with most of the studies in the past (Athanasoglou et al. 2006; Goddard et al. 2004; Hess and Francis 2004).

47.5 Recommendations

Our study examines the effect of CBUAE regulations on bank efficiency and includes some recent regulatory requirements introduced in line with BASEL III recommendations. We find that the total capital adequacy level has a negative impact on bank efficiency, whereas the effect of tier 1 capital is positive. It is therefore recommended to impose regulations which put restrictions on level of risk and improve monitoring of the banks. High liquidity of the banks measured by ASR may be restricting the profit efficiency of banks as indicated by the negative sign. Increase in operating efficiency is required to improve profit efficiency and can be attained by lowering costs through digitalization of processes such as block chain technology which has been introduced recently only by Emirates NBD Bank in the UAE.

Bank regulations are imperative for better supervision and improving resilience of banks against potential crisis, but too much restrictions may not help in increasing efficiency of banks which is important for improving bank profitability and consequently overall economic growth.

References

Aboura, S., & Lépinette, E. (2015). Do banks satisfy the Modigliani-Miller theorem? *Economic Bulletin, 35*, 924–935.

Altunbas, Y., Carbo, S., Gardener, E. P. M., & Molineux, P. (2007). Examining the relationship between capita, risk and efficiency in European banking. *European Financial Management, 13*(1), 49–70.

Athanasoglou, P., Delis, M., & Staikouras, C. (2006). *Determinants of bank profitability in the Southern Eastern European Region*. Bank of Greece Working Paper, No. 47. Munich.

Ayadi, R., & Pujals, G. (2005). Banking mergers and acquisitions in the EU: Overview, assessment and prospects, chapters in SUERF studies. SUERF – The European Money and Finance Forum.

Ayadi, R., Naceur, S. B., Casu, B., & Quinn, B. (2015). Does basel compliance matter for bank performance? *Journal of Financial Stability*, 23, 15–32.

Bader, M. K., Mohamad, S., Ariff, M., & Hassan, T. (2008). Cost, revenue and profit efficiency of Islamic versus conventional banks: international analysis using data envelopment analysis. *Islamic Economic Studies, 15*(2), 23–76.

Banker, R., Charnes, A., & Cooper, W. W. (1984). Some models for estimating technical and scale inefficiencies in data envelopment analysis. *Management Science, 30*(9), 1078–1092.

Barth, J. R., Caprio, G., Jr., & Levine, R. (2001). Banking systems around the globe: Do regulations and ownership affect performance and stability. In F. S. Mishkin (Ed.), *Prudential supervision: What works and what doesn't* (pp. 31–88). Chicago: University of Chicago Press.

Barth, J-R., Caprio, G., & Levine, R. (2012). *The evolution and impact of bank regulations (Policy Research Working Papers)*. Washington, DC: The World Bank. dx.doi.org/10.1596/1813-9450-6288.

Barth, J.-R., Lin, C., Ma, Y., Seade, J., & Song, F.-M. (2013). Do bank regulation, supervision and monitoring enhance or impede bank efficiency? *Journal of Banking & Finance, 37*(8), 2879–2892.

Beck, T., Demirguc-Kunt, A., & Levine, R. (2006). Bank supervision and corruption in lending. *Journal of Monetary Economics, 53*, 2131–2163.

Beltratti, A., & Stulz, R. (2009). *Why did some banks perform better during the Credit Crisis: A Cross-Country study of the impact of Governance and Regulation (pp. 1–38)*. ECGI Working Paper Series in Finance, Working Paper 254/2009. https://doi.org/10.3386/w15180

Berger, A. N., Herring, R. J., & Szegö, G. P. (1995). The role of capital in financial institutions. *Journal of Banking and Finance, 19*, 257–276.

Berger, A., & E. Bonaccorsi D. P. (2006). Capital structure and firm performance: A new approach to testing agency theory and an application to the banking industry. *Journal of Banking and Finance, 30*, 1065–1102.

Berger, A. N., & Bouwman, C. H. S. (2013). How does capital effect bank performance during financial crisis? *Journal of Financial Economics, 109*(1), 146–176.

Berger, A., & DeYoung, R. (1997). Problem Loans and Cost Efficiency in Commercial Banks. *Journal of Banking and Finance, 21*, 849–870.

Besanko, D., & Kanatas, G. (1996). The regulation of bank capital: Do capital standards promote bank safety? *Journal of Financial Intermediation, 5*(4), 160–183.

Blum, J. (1999). Do capital adequacy requirements reduce risks in banking? *Journal of Banking Finance, 23*, 755–771.

Bourke, P. (1989). Concentration and other determinants of bank profitability in Europe, north American and Australia. *Journal of Banking and Finance, 3*(1), 65–79.

Charnes, A., Cooper, W. W., & Rhodes, E. (1978). Measuring the efficiency of decision making units. *European Journal of Operational Research, 2*(6), 429–444.

Claessens, S., & Klingebiel, D. (2000, April). *Competition and scope of activities in financial services*. Washington, DC: Mimeo, World Bank.

Coelli, T., Prasada Rao, D. S., & Battese, G. E. (1998). *An introduction to efficiency and productivity analysis*. Norwell, MA: Kluwer Academic Press.

Das, A., & Ghosh, S. (2009). Financial deregulation and profit efficiency: A nonparametric analysis of Indian banks. *Journal of Economics and Business, 61*(6), 509–528.

Delis, M., & Staikouras, P. (2011). Supervisory effectiveness and bank risk. *Review of Finance, 15*(3), 511–543.

Dewatripont, M., & Tirole, J. (1994). *The Prudential Regulation of Banks*. Cambridge: MIT Press.

Dietsch, M., & Lozano-Vivas, A. (2000). How the environment determines banking efficiency: A comparison between French and Spanish industries. *Journal of Banking and Finance, 24*, 985–1004.

Dietrich, A., & Wanzenried, G. (2011). Determinants of bank profitability before and during the crisis: Evidence from Switzerland. *Journal of International Financial Markets, Institutions and Money, 2*, 307–327.

Farrell, M. J. (1957). The measurement of productive efficiency. *Journal of Royal Statistical Society Association, Series, 120*(A), 253–281.

Fiordelisi, F., Marquez-Ibanez, D., & Molyneux, P. (2011). Effciency and risk in European banking. *Journal of Banking and Finance, Elsevier, 35*(5), 1315–1326.

Fries, S., & Taci, A. (2005). Cost efficiency of banks in transition: Evidence from 289 banks in 15 post-communist countries. *Journal of Banking and Finance, 29*, 55–81.

Fried, H. O., Schmidt, S. S., & Yaisawarng, S. (1999). Incorporating the operating environment into a nonparametric measure of technical efficiency. *Journal of Productivity Analysis, 12*, 249–267.

Gaganis, C., & Pasiouras, F. (2013). Financial supervision regimes and bank efficiency: International evidence. *Journal of Banking and Finance, 37*(12), 5463–5475.

Goddard, J., Molyneux, P., & Wilson, J. (2004). The profitability of European Banks: a cross-sectional and dynamic panel analysis. *Manchester School, 72*(3), 363–381.

Gorton, G., & Winton, A. (2000). Liquidity provision, bank capital and the macroeconomy. *SSRN Electronic Journal*. https://doi.org/10.2139/ssrn.253849.

Greene, W. H. (1981). On the asymptotic bias of the ordinary least squares estimator of the Tobit model. *Econometrica: Journal of the Econometric Society, 49*, 505–513.

Hess, K., & Francis, G. (2004). Cost income ratio benchmarking in banking. *Benchmarking: An International Journal, 3*, 303–319.

http://www.bis.org/bcbs/basel3.htm

http://www.centralbank.ae/en/index.php?view=article&catid=45%3Anoticesandcirculars&id=76%3Acirucularsndnoticesmaina&format=pdf&option=com_content&Itemid=295

Kale, S., Eken, M. H., & Selimler, H. (2015). The effects of regulations on the performance of banks: Evidence from the Turkish banking industry. *Journal of Centrum Cathedra: The Business and Economics Research Journal, 8*(2), 109–145.

Kim, D., & Santomero, A. M. (1988). Risk in banking and capital regulation. *Journal of Finance, 35*, 1219–1233.

Koehn, M., & Santomero, A. M. (1980). Regulation of bank capital and portfolio risk. *Journal of Finance, 35*, 1235–1250.

Kosmidou, K., Tanna, S., & Pasiouras, F. (2005). Determinants of profitability of domestic UK commercial banks: Panel evidence from the period 1995–2002. *Money Macro and Finance (MMF) Research Group Conference, 45*, 1–27.

Kwan, S., & Eisenbeir, R. (1997). Bank risk, capitalization and operating efficiency. *Journal of Banking and Finance, 12*(2 & 3), 117–131.

Lin, P. W. (2002). Cost efficiency analysis of commercial bank mergers in Taiwan. *International Journal of Management, 19*(3), 408.

Lee, T. H., & Chih, S. H. (2013). Does financial regulation affect the profit efficiency and risk of banks? Evidence from China's commercial banks. *The North American Journal of Economics and Finance, 26*(0), 705–724. dx.doi.org/%2010.1016/j.najef.2013.05.005.

Laeven, L., & Levine, R. (2007). Is there a diversification discount in financial conglomerates? *Journal of Financial Economics, 85*, 331–367.

Modigliani, F., & Miller, M. H. (1958). The cost of capital, corporate finance and the theory of investment. *American Economic Review, 48*, 261–297.

Molyneux, P., & Thornton, J. (1992). Determinants of European bank profitability: a note. *Journal of Banking and Finance, 16*, 1173–1178.

Owolabi, S., Obiakor, R., & Okwu, A. (2011). Investigating liquidity-profitability relationship in business organizations: a study of selected quoted companies in Nigeria. *British Journal of Economics, Finance and Management Science, 1*(2), 11–29.

O'Donnell, C. J. (2010). Measuring and decomposing agricultural productivity and profitability change. *Australian Journal of Agricultural and Resource Economics, 54*(4), 527–560.

Pessarossi, P., & Weill, L. (2009). *Do capital requirements affect bank efficiency? Evidence from China*. Bank of Finland, BOFT discussion papers, 2013. Helsinki. https://helda.helsinki.fi/bof/bitstream/handle/123456789/8311/172742.pdf?sequence=1

Podpiera, A., & Podpiera, J. (2008). The Czech transition banking sector instability: the role of operational cost management. *Economic Change and Restructuring, 41*(3), 209–219.

Podpiera, J., & Weill, L. (2008). Bad luck or bad management? Emerging banking market experience. *Journal of Financial Stability, 4*, 135–148.

Sealey, C. W., & Lindley, J. T. (1977). Inputs, outputs, and theory of production cost at depository financial institutions. *Journal of Finance, 32*, 1251–1266.

Valverde, S., & Fernandez, F. (2007). The determinants of bank margins in European banking. *Journal of Banking and Finance, 31*(7), 2043–2063.

Wang, K. L., Tseng, Y. T., & Weng, C. C. (2003). A study of production efficiencies of integrated securities firms in Taiwan. *Applied Financial Economics, 13*(3), 159–167.

Chapter 48
Competitiveness Index

Ourania Notta and Aspasia Vlachvei

Abstract In this work, an Industrial Competitiveness Index is used as a composite measure for multidimensional economic performance, covering profitability, productivity and output growth. The main advantage of this approach is the aggregation of the different dimensions of the competitiveness concept into one final index score on which an overall assessment can be based. This index approach enables relative competitiveness comparisons across industries, countries and over time. The competitiveness index of the food and beverage manufacturing sector in 17 countries is analysed empirically, using 2003–2007 Eurostat data. The results show that in 2003–2007 the competitiveness ranking is headed by beverage manufacture both in Europe and in each country separately. According to their geographical location, countries present some differences on competitiveness ranking. Cluster analysis based on the index scores for profitability, productivity and growth variables has been used to identify four different types of performance groups. The most competitive cluster includes the majority of the beverage industries.

48.1 Introduction

The existence of many different definitions of competitiveness indicates that the concept of competitiveness is, in fact, multidimensional in nature and that, as a consequence, it is difficult to deal with theoretically as well as empirically. At the firm level, the view of competitiveness can be given as: "A firm is competitive if it can

O. Notta (✉)
Alexander Technological Educational Institute of Thessaloniki, Department of Agricultural Technology, (Agricultural Economics Program), Thessaloniki, Greece
e-mail: ournotta@farm.teithe.gr

A. Vlachvei
Department of International Trade, Western Macedonia University of Applied Sciences, Kastoria, Greece
e-mail: vlahvei@kastoria.teiwm.gr

N. Tsounis, A. Vlachvei (eds.), *Advances in Panel Data Analysis in Applied Economic Research*, Springer Proceedings in Business and Economics,
https://doi.org/10.1007/978-3-319-70055-7_48

produce products and services of superior quality and lower costs than its domestic and international competitors (Buckley et al. 1988). Competitiveness is synonymous with a firm's long run profit performance and its ability to compensate its employees and provide superior returns to its owners." Hence, a firm's competitiveness can be measured by its relative price, market share and degree of profitability over a relevant period of time. If the firm is an exporter, market share can be measured at the global level. Product quality can also be assessed and compared.

Competitiveness is adopted as a management or economics idea that is superior to the traditional economic indicators such as profitability, productivity or market share, which are seen as being insufficient to enable continuous improvement of performance (Lu 2006). As declared by Buckley et al. (1988), the concept not only reflects past performance but also allows the perception of potential and the improvement of managerial processes. Traditional indicators can only reflect the historic quantitative facts. By embracing the aspects of performance, potential and process, competitiveness makes itself an inclusive concept that can be easily integrated into management, economics and operation research. This resonates with the suggestion that competitiveness can guide management on how to improve its competitiveness and in turn its long-term and sustainable performance (IMD 2004; Cattell et al. 2004). However, there is little empirical evidence of the co-relationship between competitiveness and sustainable performance. A possible reason for this is that the two concepts are highly controversial by nature, and so examining them empirically is not easy.

Following Canada's Agri-Food Competitiveness Task Force: *Competitiveness is the sustained ability to profitably gain or maintain market share*. The above definition has three measurable aspects – profits, market share and (sustained) time. So, competitiveness is attained if one is profitable with steady or increasing market share over time. The term focuses on results (profitability, market share), not on behaviour. So, the distinction between one who is competitive and one who has a high degree of competitiveness is that the first displays competitive behaviour, while the second shows results. The last distinction is important in that it implies that an analysis of competitiveness begins with the end – i.e. the industry has shown a high degree of profitability and an ability to gain market share.

In the literature, competitiveness is measured by a variety of indicators, like those reflecting competitive performance and those referring to competitive potential (Buckley et al. 1988). The first approach encompasses measures such as profits or market share which reflect the performance of firms in relation to their rivals, while the latter refers to a variety of factors and forces that enable firms to outperform their rivals. These range from features of environment over characteristics of industries and firms to elements of their behaviour such as cost or price behaviour, productivity or quality of their products. Competitiveness is also a relative concept, concerned with how competitive a firm is when compared to the rest of the industry. The last characteristic is concerned with its dynamic nature, which involves the dynamic transformation of competitive potentials through the competitive process into outcomes, corresponding to the framework suggested by Buckley et al. (1988).

The main objective of this work is the analysis of the current state of the EU food and beverage industry's competitiveness index. The analysis will focus on competitiveness indicators only (as opposed to competitiveness determinants!) The structure is as follows: After this Introduction section, competitiveness is discussed theoretically, and, using several measures, a composite indicator for sector competitiveness is derived using data for 17 EU countries, in the third section. The results from calculating the Industrial Competitiveness Index (ICI) for 17 EU countries, covering the period 2003–2007, are presented, while in the fourth section, the main conclusions are discussed.

48.2 Literature Review

Some authors view competitiveness with the competency approach. They emphasise the role of factors internal to the firms such as firm strategy, structures, competencies, capabilities to innovate and other tangible and intangible resources for their competitive success (Bartlett and Ghoshal 1989; Doz and Prahalad 1987; Hamel and Prahalad 1989, 1990). This view is particularly among the resource-based approach towards competitiveness (Prahalad and Hamel 1990; Grant 1991; Barney 1991; Peteraf 1983; Barney et al. 2001). Ability to develop and deploy capabilities and talents far more effectively than competitors can help in achieving world-class competitiveness.

For providing customers with greater value and satisfaction than their competitors, firms must be operationally efficient, cost-effective and quality conscious (Johnson 1992; Hammer and Champy 1993). Also related to this condition are a number of studies focusing on particular aspects like marketing (Corbett and Wassenhove 1983), information technology (Ross et al. 1996), quality of products (Swann and Taghave 1994) and innovative capability of firms (Grupp 1997). Some research (e.g. Ive et al. 2004) treats competitiveness as a modern word and uses productivity to stand for competitiveness without recognising the difference between the two concepts. Krugman (1994) mentioned that people who use the term "competitiveness" do so without a second thought. Some research, partly supported by Porter's (1980) argument that productivity is the true source of competitive advantage, defines competitiveness by using productivity. Porter defined competitiveness at the organisational level as productivity growth that is reflected in either lower costs or differentiated products that command premium prices. The generic strategies given by Porter also emphasises these criteria (Porter 1980). It has been said the company, industry or nation with the highest productivity could be seen as the most competitive (McKee and Sessions-Robinson 1989). While various productivity measurements, i.e. labour productivity, capital productivity or total factor productivity, have captured the cornerstone of research on achieving excellence in the industry (e.g. Arditi 1985; Chau and Walker 1988; Arditi and Mochtar 2000; Allmon et al. 2000), researchers (e.g. Cattell et al. 2004) have recommended a shift from looking just at productivity to the wider concept of competitiveness. The limitations of measuring productivity include lack of availability and reliability of data, failure to measure more important things (e.g. the effectiveness of project management, the quality level achieved and the innovations), the difficulty of productivity comparisons between industries, etc.(Cattell et al. 2004).

Other studies like Lipovatz et al. (2000) consider labour productivity, vertical integration, technological innovation and firm size to be critical factors for industrial competitiveness and apply multivariate analysis to assess these factors in the Greek food and beverage industries. Fischer and Schornberg (2007) argued that market share is a useful competitiveness indicator at the company level even when analysing aggregates; market shares may be problematic (Vlachvei and Notta 2011). According to Fischer and Schornberg (2007), profitability certainly is a key variable for assessing sector competitiveness (EU Commission 2005), and value added as a percentage of turnover is a kind of profit margin that one often has to rely. Fischer and Schornberg (2007) evaluate the competitiveness by calculating profitability, productivity and output growth and aggregating them into a single competitiveness index that is to say attributing scores depending on the maximum and minimum values among countries.

Wijnands et al. (2008) measured the competitiveness of eight subsectors, benchmarked them with four leading world economies, assessed the effect of differences in legal requirements and predicted future developments using scenario analysis. International economics indicators supplemented with data on legal issues from a survey conducted by leading experts were used to measure competitiveness. They calculated annual growth in a sector's share of real value added compared with growth in the total industry, annual growth in terms of the Balassa Index, growth in the export share on the world market, annual growth in labour productivity of the sector and annual growth in real value added of the sector. Then they standardise them so that all have the same mean (0) and the same variance (1) and use the (unweighted) mean value of these standardised scores to compute an overall measure of competitiveness.

On the other hand, Cetindamar and Kilitcioglu (2013) argue that firm competitiveness is based on three key pillars: competitive outcome/performance (growth, export, profit and customer and society), firm resources (human, financial and technology, innovation and design-based resources) and the managerial processes and capabilities (processes and systems in a company as well as leadership and sustainability of strategies). However, they have not tried to calculate the respective ten indicators. Laureti and Viviani (2010) obtain a synthetic measure of firm competitiveness using a Data Envelopment Analysis approach as a weighted average of Return on Sales, Return on Assets and Return on Equity. Then a Tobit model is considered to measure the influence of different factors on the measured competitiveness, like productivity. Bowen and Moesen (2011) test how the ranking of countries based on the World Economic Forum's (WEF) Global Competitiveness Index (GCI) is changed when the underlying primitive data dimensions of this composite index are aggregated using weights that are endogenously determined for each country, instead of aggregated using the WEF's fixed set of weights applied to all countries (Vlachvei and Notta 2016).

48.3 Empirical Analysis and Results

Following Fischer and Schornberg (2007) approach, we also define competitiveness as a function of profitability, efficiency, productivity and growth COMPS = *f*(PROS,EFFS,GROS). The index is calculating as a composite measure of profitability, productivity and output growth. The construction of the ICI (Industrial Competitiveness Index) builds on the methodology used for the calculation of the United Nations' Human Development Index (see United Nations Development Programme, UNDP 2002). First, we transform all measures into individual indices that are combined into three component indices (one each for profitability, productivity and growth):

$$I_k^{tij} = \frac{M_k^{tij} - M_k^{\min}}{M_k^{\max} - M_k^{\min}} \times 100$$

These component indices are then aggregated into the ICI.

We collected annual data from Eurostat databases covering structural business statistics for the period 2003–2007 (Eurostat 2011). Food processing sectors (DA15) and its 3-digit sectors (DA15x) are classified according to the statistical classification of economic activities in the European Community ("Nomenclature statistique des Activités économiques dans la Communauté Européenne," NACE). Profitability is measured by the ratio of 3-digit sector's annual gross operating surplus over the 3-digit sector's annual turnover. Productivity is measured as the ratio of 3-digit sector's (DA15x) gross value added over the annual subsector's annual employees. Output growth is measured as the ratio of 3-digit sector's annual production value of year t over production value of year t-1. In order to buffer the inherent year-to-year volatility in our data, we calculated a 4-year average (arithmetic means), for 2003–2007. All data were thoroughly checked for outliers, given the significance of the maxima and minima in the index calculation. Due to the calculation of 4-year averages, the impact of missing data was minimised.

Table 48.1 reports ICI scores in the component indices for the individual food industries, aggregated over 17 EU countries. The first column lists overall ICI scores (calculated as unweighted means of the industry ICI scores of all countries) for the period 2003–2007, while columns two to four list the values of the three component indices for the same period. Following Fischer and Schornberg (2007), the chosen calculation method for the ICI is suitable in order to compare absolute index scores across different industries.

The results reveal that beverage manufacturing (ICI score 36.17), the manufacture of miscellaneous food products (the manufacture of bread, fresh pasty goods and cakes, rusks and biscuits, cocoa, chocolate and sugar confectionery, macaroni, noodles, couscous and similar farinaceous products and the processing of tea and coffee) with ICI score 31.13 and the manufacture of grain mill products, starches and starch products (30.27) were the most competitive industrial activities in all 17

Table 48.1 Industrial competitiveness index scores and indices of profitability, productivity and growth for food and beverages subsectors in EU-17 for 2003–2007

	EUROPE (17 countries)			
Industry NACE category	ICI (2003–07)	Profitability index	Productivity index	Output-growth index
159	36,17	45,49	34,24	34,80
158	31,13	40,82	18,68	36,71
156	30,27	31,96	25,40	38,13
154	29,83	27,15	29,47	40,42
153	28,54	33,26	18,09	37,72
157	27,37	25,11	22,47	38,41
155	26,32	26,10	20,34	36,15
152	25,60	28,15	13,38	40,13
151	23,85	24,33	13,27	36,53

Source: Authors' calculations from Eurostat data
Note: Industries are ranked by ICI 2003–2007
The NACE categories describe the following food (sub-)industries:
151: Production, processing and preserving of meat and meat products
152: Processing and preserving of fish and fish products
153: Processing and preserving of fruit and vegetables
154: Manufacture of vegetable and animal oils and fats
155: Manufacture of dairy products
156: Manufacture of grain mill products, starches and starch products.
157: Manufacture of prepared animal feeds
158: Manufacture of other food products
159: Manufacture of beverages

European countries for the period 2003–2007. The manufacture of vegetable and animal oils and fats (29.83), the processing and preserving of fruit and vegetables (28.54) and the manufacture of prepared animal feed (27.37) were following in the list of the most competitive industrial activities. Finally, the manufacture of dairy products (26.32), the processing and preserving of fish and fish products (25.60) and the production, processing and preserving of meat and meat products (23.85) were least competitive. These results are consistent with Fisher and Schornberg's results (2007), for the previous period 1999–2002.

Table 48.2 reports overall aggregate ICI scores and the values of the three component indices for each of the 17 EU countries for the period 2003–2007. The results show that Ireland (36.32) was by far the most competitive EU food processing country in the period. The second most competitive EU food processing country is the UK (33.34) followed by Austria (31.74), Netherlands (31.09) and Greece (31.05). Portugal holds the last position with 23.71 ICI score.

Table 48.3 summarises the ICI scores for the individual EU country for each food industry. The results reveal that in a total of 17 countries, the beverage manufacturing sector is the most competitive sector in ten countries (Belgium, Czech Republic, Finland, France, Greece, Luxemburg, Netherlands, Portugal,

Table 48.2 Countries' industrial competitiveness index scores and indices of profitability, productivity and growth for food and beverages subsectors in EU-17 for 2003–2007

NACE_R1/INDIC_SB	DA15	Profitability index	Productivity index	ΔPROD index
Ireland	36,32	41,38	32,57	35,02
UK	33,34	39,48	22,87	37,67
Austria	31,74	37,90	18,86	39,28
Netherlands	31,09	28,21	86,46	40,28
Greece	31,05	39,41	11,43	42,29
Norway	30,01	29,24	23,04	38,40
Luxemburg	29,79	37,07	14,47	37,84
Belgium	28,81	26,98	21,87	37,60
Denmark	28,73	28,06	19,47	38,66
Spain	28,18	31,45	14,65	38,43
Italy	27,68	28,26	17,75	37,03
Finland	27,05	29,81	17,67	35,47
Germany	26,99	27,23	16,88	36,87
Sweden	26,16	27,43	18,70	32,36
France	25,77	25,79	17,15	35,29
Czech Republic	24,50	31,85	3,00	38,65
Portugal	23,71	30,07	6,65	36,97

Spain, Sweden), the second most competitive industry in two countries (Denmark and Ireland) and the third most competitive industry in two countries (Austria and UK). This sector comprises both alcoholic and non-alcoholic beverages. Furthermore, it includes geographically mobile industrial activities such as beer brewing and soft drink manufacturing but also location-tied subsectors such as wine making and mineral water bottling. This implicit heterogeneity of the beverage industry makes a meaningful cross-country comparison of the findings difficult (Fisher and Schornberg, 2006). Nevertheless, our results confirm that the beverage manufacturing industry has a well-established place in the European economy. The industry is usually defined in terms of a value chain centred on the actual production of the alcohol beverages. However, it is also includes a wide variety of important "backward" and "forward" linkages. The backward linkages include supply chain of agricultural and raw materials, capital equipment, transportation and energy, while the forward linkages relate to access to markets, transportation, distribution via retailers, wholesalers and hotels, restaurants and cafes (HORECA). The significant economic activities involved in the production and distribution of beer, wine and spirits generate considerable employment and provide an important source of tax revenue for many governments International Centre for Alcoholic Policies (2006).

Manufacture of grain mill products, starches and starch products represents the first position concerning competitiveness sector for Italy, the second position for six countries (Austria, France, Germany, Portugal, Sweden and UK) and the third position for two countries (Denmark and Norway). The manufacture of vegetable

Table 48.3 Industrial competitiveness index scores per country and per industry for 2003–2007 (Depending on the location)

Industry NACE category	151 ICI	152 ICI	153 ICI	154 ICI	155 ICI	156 ICI	157 ICI	158 ICI	159 ICI
Central Europe									
Austria	25,8*	31,9	37,8*[a]	29,1	28,6	36,8[b]	32,5	27,6	35,5[c]
Belgium	24,6	26,3	30,6[b]	28,1	27,5	29,4	25,9	29,4[c]	37,5[a]
Czech Republic	20,9	n/a	24,6[c]	21,4	20,73	23,2	23,7	26,0[b]	35,4[a]
Germany	25,1	23,7	25,2	30,5[a]	26,1	29,9[b]	28,6[c]	25,5	28,1
Luxemburg	24,4[c]	n/a	n/a	n/a	n/a	n/a	n/a	26,7[b]	38,2[a]
Netherlands	25,3	30,8	31,9[c]	34,1[b]	25,8	28,7	29,1	31,7	42,3[a]
Northern Europe									
Denmark	25,3	25,1	28,0	33,9[a]	n/a	30,4[c]	29,9	26,6	30,6[b]
Finland	25,1	27,7	29,6[b]	19,39	24,3	23,7	28,6	29,2[c]	35,9[a]
Ireland	22,2	19,5	31,8	31,8	32,3*[c]	32,7	27,0	68,7*[a]	60,9*[b]
Norway	24,2	26,5	31,4	36,1*[a]	26,2	32,5[c]	34,9*[b]	30,1	28,1
Sweden	22,0	24,2	21,8	30,1[c]	22,7	32,6[b]	18,6	27,6	35,6[a]
UK	24,7	27,7	34,0	40,0[a]	26,4	39,4*[b]	31,8	37,8	38,1[c]
Southern Europe									
France	20,4	21,5	24,2	27,1[c]	22,8	29,7[b]	24,2	26,4	35,6[a]
Greece	23,9	35,1*[b]	28,4	35,1[c]	29,6	28,6	28,1	30,5	40,0[a]
Italy	24,7	n/a	24,2	29,2[c]	25,8	32,2[a]	26,4	31,0[b]	28,0
Portugal	21,0	14,0	25,9	23,7	26,3[c]	26,4[b]	22,8	25,5	27,8[a]
Spain	25,4	24,1	26,9	27,6	29,8[b]	27,9	25,7	28,7[c]	37,4[a]

Source: Authors' calculations from Eurostat data
*The country with the highest competitiveness index for the sector
[a]First position concerning competitiveness sector for the country
[b]Second position concerning competitiveness sector for the country
[c]Third position concerning competitiveness sector for the country
[d]Fourth position concerning competitiveness sector for the country

and animal oils and fats is the most competitive sector for four countries (Denmark, Germany, Norway and UK), the second most competitive sector for Netherlands and the third most competitive sector for four countries (France, Greece, Italy and Sweden).

Depending on the geographical location, the countries of Southern Europe (France, Greece, Italy, Portugal and Spain) present as more competitive sectors, other than beverages, the manufacture of vegetable and animal oils and fats; the manufacture of grain mill products, starches and starch products, as expected; and the manufacture of dairy products. It is worth notice that processing and preserving of fish and fish products represent a high position concerning competitiveness for only one country among the countries of South Europe, Greece. Also, no country presents high competitiveness score for processing and preserving of fruit and vegetables sector although production of fruits and vegetables is coming from southern Europe.

The countries of Northern Europe (Denmark, Finland, Ireland, Norway, Sweden and UK) present as more competitive sectors, other than beverages, the manufacture of vegetable and animal oils and fats and the manufacture of grain mill products, starches and starch products. It is worth notice that manufacture of prepared animal feeds represents a high position concerning competitiveness for Norway. Finally, the manufacture of miscellaneous food products ranks high in Ireland and Finland concerning competitiveness. The competitiveness ranking for the countries of Central Europe (Austria, Belgium, Czech Republic, Germany, Luxemburg and Netherlands) is headed by manufacture of beverages. Beyond that, the countries divide high places competitiveness in all sectors, except dairy industry and fish products.

Although the above analysis by geographical location is expectedand generally useful, the generating performance rankings across countries and industries by using the index approach is not useful of identify and describe competitiveness groups of industries. In this case, cluster analysis can order countries and industries in groups of similar, three-dimensional performance variables (profitability, productivity and growth). Four competitiveness groups are obtained from the performed cluster analysis. Tables 48.4 and 48.5 report the respective cluster statistics, descriptions and names. Cluster 1 includes 19 industries with the majority of them being listed in the manufacture of beverages sector. The cluster 1 aggregates the most competitive industries with highest levels of profitability and productivity and contains more than 75% of all beverages industries (DA 159). Cluster 2 counts 36 industries and is characterised by high levels of profitability and growth but low levels of productivity. This cluster consists of 88% of the miscellaneous industries (DA 158, manufacture of other food products) and 41% of the processing and preserving of fruit and vegetables (DA 153). Cluster 3 constitutes 38 industries and is characterised by high levels of growth and productivity but lowest levels of profitability. In this cluster fall 64% of vegetable and animal oils and fats industries (DA 154), 47% of grain mill and starch products industries (DA 156) and 53%

Table 48.4 Cluster statistics

	Cluster 1	Cluster 2	Cluster 3	Cluster 4
Cluster description	Highly competitive	High profitability and growth but low productivity	High growth, high productivity but lowest profitability	Most common, lowest growth rates, lowest profitability
No of industries included	19	36	38	51
Mean index value: growth	35	40	39	36
Mean index value:VA/EMPL	28	12	25	12
Mean index value GOS/TURN	50	37	27	24

Source: Authors' calculations from Eurostat data

Table 48.5 Distribution of industries per cluster

Cluster 1
153 Austria, UK
156 Sweden, UK
158 Ireland, UK
159 Austria, Belgium, Czech Republic, Denmark, Finland, France, Greece, Ireland, Luxemburg, Netherlands, Spain, Sweden, UK
Cluster 2
152 Austria, Greece, Netherlands, UK
153 Czech Republic, Finland, Greece, Ireland, Norway, Portugal, Spain
154 Ireland Greece,
155 Greece, Portugal, Spain
156 Austria, Greece
157 Austria, Greece
158 Austria, Belgium, Czech Republic, Denmark, Finland, France, Germany, Greece, Italy, Luxemburg, Netherlands, Norway, Portugal, Spain, Sweden
159 Portugal
Cluster 3
153 Belgium, Netherlands
154 Austria, Belgium, Denmark, France, Germany, Italy, Netherlands, Norway, Spain, Sweden, UK
155 Austria, Belgium, Germany, Ireland, Netherlands
156 Belgium, Denmark, France, Germany, Ireland, Italy, Netherlands, Norway
157 Belgium, Denmark, Finland, Germany, Ireland, Italy, Netherlands, Norway, UK
159 Germany, Italy, Norway
Cluster 4
151 Austria, Belgium, Czech Republic, Denmark, Finland, France, Germany, Greece, Ireland, Italy, Luxemburg, Netherlands, Norway, Portugal, Spain, Sweden, UK
152 Belgium, Denmark, Finland, France, Germany, Ireland, Norway, Portugal, Spain, Sweden
153 Denmark, France, Germany, Italy, Sweden
154 Czech Republic, Finland, Portugal
155 Czech Republic, Finland, France, Italy, Norway, Sweden, UK
156 Czech Republic, Finland, Portugal, Spain
157 Czech Republic, France, Portugal, Spain, Sweden

of prepared animal feeds products manufacturing sector (DA 157). Finally, cluster 4 is the larger one with 51 industries and is overall least competitive, with the lowest growth, productivity and profitability. It is interesting to note that all meat processing industries in all countries are gathered into this cluster, while 71% of the processing and preserving of fish and fish products industries (DA 152) fall into this less competitive group.

48.4 Conclusions

This analysis has aimed at developing an Industrial Competitiveness Index as a composite measure for relative and multidimensional economic performance of EU F&D manufacturing industries, covering differences in levels and development of profitability, productivity and growth for 2003–2007. Following Fischer and Schornberg (2007), the main advantage of this approach is the aggregation of the different dimensions of the competitiveness concept into one final index score, on which an overall assessment can be based. In this way, industry ranking tables for EU and individual country can be obtained.

Our results show that in 2003–2007 the competitiveness ranking is headed by beverage manufacture both in Europe and in each country separately. Ireland was by far the most competitive EU food processing country in the period. According to their geographical location, countries present some differences on competitiveness ranking. Cluster analysis based on the index scores for profitability, productivity and growth variables has been used to identify four different types of performance groups. The most competitive cluster includes the majority of the beverage industries. Future research is needed for the measurement of the complex competitiveness index.

References

Allmon, E., Haas, C., Borcherding, J., & Goodrum, P. (2000). U.S. construction labour productivity trends, 1970–1998. *ASCE Journal of Construction Engineering and Management, 126*(2), 97–104.

Arditi, D. (1985). Construction productivity improvement. *ASCE Journal of Construction Engineering and Management, 111*(5), 1–14.

Arditi, D., & Mochtar, K. (2000). Trends in productivity improvement in the US construction industry. *Construction Management and Economics, 18*(1), 15–27.

Barney, J. (1991). Firm resources and sustained competitive advantage. *Journal of Management, 17*(1), 99–120.

Barney, J., Wright, M., & Ketchen, D. J. (2001). The resource-based view of the firm: Ten years after 1991. *Journal of Management, 27*, 625–641.

Bartlett, A., & Ghoshal, S. (1989). *Managing across borders*. Boston: Harvard Business School Press.

Bowen, H. P., & Moesen, W. (2011). Composite competitiveness indicators with endogenous versus predetermined weights An application to the World Economic Forum's global competitiveness index. *Competitiveness Review: An International Business Journal, 21*(2), 129–151. https://doi.org/10.1108/10595421111117434.

Buckley, P., Pass, C., & Prescott, K. (1988). Measures of international competitiveness: Critical survey. *Journal of Marketing Management, 4*, 175–200.

Cattell, K., Flanagan, R., & Jewell, C. A. (2004). Competitiveness and productivity in the construction industry: The importance of definitions. In Root et al. (Ed.), *Proceedings of the Construction Industry Development Board (CIDB) 2nd Conference* (pp. 25–35). Cape Town, South Africa, Construction Industry Development Board.

Cetindamar, D., & Kilitcioglu, H. (2013). Measuring the competitiveness of a firm for an award system. *Competitiveness Review: An International Business Journal, 23*(1), 7–22. https://doi.org/10.1108/10595421311296597.

Chau, K., & Walker, A. (1988). The measurement of total factor productivity of the Hong Kong construction industry. *Construction Management and Economics, 6*(3), 209–224.

Corbett, C., & Wassenhove, L. (1983). Trade offs? What trade-offs? competence and competitiveness in manufacturing. *California Management Review, 35*(4), 107–122.

Doz, Y. L., & Prahalad, C. K. (1987). *The multinational mission*. New York: The Free Press.

EU Commission. (2005). *EU sectoral competitiveness indicators*. http://europa.eu.int/comm./enterprise/enterprise_policy/competitiveness/doc/eu_sectoral_competitiveness_indicators.pdf. Accessed 24 May 2005.

Eurostat. (2011). *Coded—The European concepts and definitions database*. Retrieved January 3, 2005, from http://forum.europa.eu.int/irc/dsis/coded/info/data/coded/en.htm

Fisher, C., & Schornberg, S. (2006). *The competitiveness situation of the EU meat processing and beverage manufacturing sectors*. Paper prepared for presentation at the 98th EAAE Seminar 'Marketing Dynamics within the Global Trading System: New Perspectives', Chania, 29 June–2 July 2006. http://ageconsearch.umn.edu/bitstream/10028/1/sp06fi01.pdf

Fischer, C., & Schornberg, S. (2007). Assessing the competitiveness situation of EU food and drink manufacturing industries: An index – based approach. *Agribusiness, 23*(4), 473–495.

Grant, R. M. (1991). *Contemporary strategy analysis: Concepts, techniques and applications*. Ambridge, MA: Blackwell Ltd..

Grupp, H. (1997). The links between competitiveness, firm innovative activities and public R&D support in Germany: An empirical analysis. *Technology Analysis and Strategic Management, 9*(1), 19–33.

Hamel, G., & Prahalad, C. K. (1989). *Strategic intent*. HBR no.3, pp 63–76.

Hammer, M., & Champy, J. (1993). *Re-engineering the corporation*. New York: Harper Business.

IMD. (2004). *World competitiveness yearbook 2003*. Lausanne: IMD.

International Centre for Alcoholic Policies. (2006). *The structure of the beverage industry*. ICAP reports 17.

Ive, G., Gruneberg, S., Meikle, J., & Crosthwaite, D. (2004). *Measuring the competitiveness of the UK construction industry* (Vol. 1). London: Department of Trade and Industry (DTI).

Johnson, H. T. (1992). *Relevance regained*. New York, NY: The Free Press.

Krugman, P. (1994). Competitiveness: A dangerous obsession. *Foreign Affairs, 73*, 28–44.

Laureti, T., & Viviani, A. (2010). Competitiveness and productivity: A case study of Italian firms. *Applied Economics, 43*(20), 2615–2625.

Lipovatz, D., Mandaraka, M., & Mourelatos, A. (2000). Multivariate analysis for the assessment of factors affecting industrial competitiveness: The case of Greek food and beverage industries. *Applied Stochastic Models in Business and Industry, 16*(2), 85–98. https://doi.org/10.1002/1526-4025(200004/06)16:2<85::AID-ASMB384>3.0.CO;2-D.

Lu, W. S. (2006). *A system for assessing and communicating contractors' competitiveness*. Thesis submitted to the Degree of Doctor of Philosophy in the Department of Building and Real Estate, the Hong Kong Polytechnic University, Hong Kong.

McKee, K., & Sessions-Robinson, C. (1989). Manufacturing productivity and competitiveness. *Journal of Manufacturing, 3*, 35–39.

Notta, O., & Vlachvei, A. (2011). Competitiveness in Greek food and beverage industries. In *Proceedings of international conference on applied economics 2011*, TEI of Western Macedonia Press, ISBN 978-960-89054-5-0, ISSN 1791-9347.

Peteraf, M. A. (1983). The cornerstones of competitive advantage: A resource-based view. *Strategic Management Journal, 14*, 179–191.

Porter, M. (1980). *Competitive Strategy*. New York, NY: The Free Press.

Prahalad, C. K., & Hamel, G. (1990). *The core competence of the corporation* (pp. 79–91). Boston, MA: Harvard Business Review.

Ross, J. W., et al. (1996). Developing long-term competitiveness through IT assets. *Sloan Management Review, 38*(1), 31–42.

Swann, P., & Taghave, M. (1994). *Measuring price and quality competitiveness – a study of 18 British product markets*. Brookfield: Vermont, Ashgate Publishing Co.

United Nations Development Programme. (2002). *Deepening democracy in a fragmented world* (Human Development Report). Retrieved October 15, 2004, from http://hdr.undp.org/reports/view_reports.cfm?type_1

Vlachvei, A., & Notta, O. (2016). Firm competitiveness-theory, evidence and measurement. In A. Vlachvei, O. Notta, K. Karantininis, & N. Tsounis (Eds.), *Factors affecting firm competitiveness in the modern business world*. Hershey PA: IGI Global.

Wijnands, J. H. M., Bremmers, H., van der Meulen, B. M. J., & Poppe, K. J. (2008). An economic and legal assessment of the EU food industry's competitiveness. *Agribusiness, 24*(4), 417–439. https://doi.org/10.1002/agr.20167.

The manufacturer's authorised representative in the EU is Springer Nature Customer Service Centre GmbH, Europaplatz 3, 69115 Heidelberg, Germany. If you have any concerns regarding our products, please contact ProductSafety@springernature.com

Printed and bound by CPI Group (UK) Ltd, Croydon, CR0 4YY
30/09/2026
02225230-0019